More praise for *The Creation of Dr. B*

"[Pollak's] book fundamentally changes how we view Bruno Bettelheim. His brilliance, it is now clear, lay not in his professional accomplishments but in his extraordinary use of manipulation and control—of his patients, his intimates, his colleagues, his data and his credulous public."

—Carolyn Moore Newberger, Harvard Medical School psychologist, *The Boston Globe*

"Painstakingly reported, convincingly written. . . . [Pollak] adopts the sensible course—he presents massive amounts of information, then lets readers speculate on Bettelheim's motivations for themselves. . . . The book is much richer for Pollak's responsible handling of a difficult life." —Steve Weinberg, *Newsday*

"As one father put it: 'Bettelheim really sowed seeds of evil.' That is a harsh epitaph, but Pollak presents compelling evidence that Bettelheim may well have deserved it." —Mary Mackey, *San Francisco Chronicle*

"Pollak, who is likely to be furiously attacked by those invested in the Bettelheim legacy, powerfully demonstrates the flaccidity of the doctor's scholarship and the flimsy, if lofty-sounding, conclusions that the politics of fame allowed him to foist upon the world." —*Salon*

"This excellent book . . . calmly describes [Bettelheim's] transformation . . . [and] is not a heavy-breathing exercise in character assassination."
—Joseph Adelson, professor of psychology, University of Michigan, *Commentary*

"Pollak does a service by demonstrating how dangerous hero worship and psychoanalysis are in combination."
—Peter D. Kramer, author of *Listening to Prozac* and clinical professor of psychiatry at Brown University, *The Weekly Standard*

"As Pollak demonstrates, Bettelheim was a snake-oil salesman of the first magnitude." —Marie Winn, *Chicago Tribune*

"Pollak's biography makes a persuasive case that [Bettelheim] was a manipulative, domineering ego tripper who abused his charges and co-workers psychically if not physically. For all his public charisma and healing skills, he might have been the evil twin to the Wizard of Oz. —John Elson, *Time*

"It seems indisputable now that Bettelheim was a fraud and an inveterate liar. . . . [Pollak's] scholarship seems scrupulous, and his conclusions just—which makes him a writer very unlike his subject."

—Lev Raphael, *Detroit Free Press*

"Pollak has written a superb book, and one well worth reading not only for the subject itself but for what it reveals about the credulity of a nation in love with simple explanations." —Mark Shechner, *Buffalo News*

RICHARD POLLAK

THE CREATION OF DR. B

A Biography of Bruno Bettelheim

A TOUCHSTONE BOOK
Published by Simon & Schuster

TOUCHSTONE
Rockefeller Center
1230 Avenue of the Americas
New York, New York 10020

Copyright © 1997 by Richard Pollak
All rights reserved,
including the right of reproduction
in whole or in part in any form.
First Touchstone Edition 1998
TOUCHSTONE and colophon are registered trademarks
of Simon & Schuster Inc.
Designed by Edith Fowler
Manufactured in the United States of America

10 9 8 7 6 5 4 3 2 1

Library of Congress Cataloging-in-Publication Data

Pollak, Richard.
   The creation of Dr. B : a biography of Bruno
Bettelheim / Richard Pollak.
      p.   cm.
   Includes bibliographical references and index.
   1. Bettelheim, Bruno.   2. Psychoanalysts—
United States—Biography.   I. Title.
BF109.B48P65   1997
618.92'89'0092—dc20
[B]   96-30920   CIP
ISBN   0-684-80938-9
ISBN   0-684-84640-3 (Pbk.)

FOR DIANE

CONTENTS

PROLOGUE

IN THE FALL of 1943, my brother entered the Orthogenic School, the home for emotionally troubled children at the University of Chicago of which Bruno Bettelheim would become director the following year. Stephen was six years old and I was nine, my preadolescent insecurities compounded by the resentment I often felt because of the extra attention he received from our mother. She tried to mollify me, to explain that Stephen needed this cosseting because, well, he just did, he was "different." The Stephen of my memory is not different, he is a normal little brother with whom I roller-skated, ran our electric train, and, on Sunday mornings, while Bob and Janet Pollak tried to sleep, played orchestra, an exercise in which I stood on a chair and conducted our shellac recording of Mozart's *Jupiter* Symphony while Stephen sat and played imaginary instruments.

I eventually learned that he was, indeed, different, that he did poorly in school, was given to prolonged silences and frequent tantrums, and once lit a candle under our father's bed. The words I most often overheard applied to him were "autistic" or "retarded" or "backward," mysterious labels that sounded like an unbreakable code. Stephen began at the Orthogenic School as a day student, but Bettelheim soon insisted that he reside there. Over the months he made fewer and fewer visits home, becoming for me a kind of spectral sibling even before his death in 1948.

In the summer of that year, while he was on vacation from the school, we visited a farm in Cassopolis, Michigan, not far from our home in Chicago. Stephen and I were playing hide-and-seek in the loft of a barn when he slipped through an open chute camouflaged by hay and fell thirty-five feet, fracturing his skull on

the concrete floor of the milking room, where our parents found
him. In the days, months, and years to come, they dealt with their
devastation by burying Stephen—his death as well as his difficult
mental history—in a tomb of silence, in part because of their pain,
but also because they believed that in sealing off the subject they
were shielding their surviving child. When I was an adolescent,
that was fine with me; I was more concerned—consciously, at
least—with getting on with my own life than with exploring the
family mausoleum. But as I grew older I began to want answers,
to feel that the facts of Stephen's short life, and its aftermath,
might help explain aspects of my parents' personalities I didn't
fully understand and illuminate corners of my own emotional life
as well.

I put off this investigation for many years, until, in 1969,
when I was thirty-five years old, I decided the time had come to
go see Bruno Bettelheim. I did not tell my father of my decision;
he had recently suffered a minor stroke, and though it had not left
his body impaired he was deeply shaken psychologically, and I did
not want to burden him further. I did tell my mother, albeit with
considerable trepidation. It meant revealing my curiosity to her
for the first time, and I had feared for years that bringing up the
subject of Stephen might undo her. We were in the sunny living
room of my parents' Chicago apartment when I told her of my
plan. She showed not the slightest emotion, as if I had just announced that I had an appointment at the dentist's that afternoon.
She sat on the sofa and quietly encouraged me, like a responsible
mom who felt strongly that dental hygiene was important for her
son. She said nothing about Stephen, nothing about Bettelheim;
she simply said, in effect, "Go, you have my blessing."

The Sonia Shankman Orthogenic School, as it is formally
called, is housed half a mile from the block where I grew up in
the university neighborhood of Hyde Park. In my youth, it was
always That Place: a special institution with an ominous name
whose meaning I did not comprehend, a bedlam of strange children, including Stephen. I walked past the home going to and
from Hyde Park High School for three years after Stephen's death.
The buildings, a red brick former church and its rectory, did not
look at all forbidding from the outside, and I often wondered what

it would be like to go up to the big wooden door and ring the bell. Once inside, would I find a Dickensian nightmare; would the children crowd around and poke at me as if *I* were the freak? More important, would such a powerful and important figure as Bruno Bettelheim see me if I asked? And if he did, would he tell me what had been wrong with my brother, or was such information for grown-ups only?

Walking to my meeting on that June day in 1969, I felt almost as intimidated as I had in high school. In the nearly twenty-five years since Bettelheim had become director of the school, he had achieved an international reputation as a defender of and spokesman for mentally wounded children and, because of his incarceration in Dachau and Buchenwald, singular status as an authority on the psychological impact of the concentration camps. He had written three acclaimed books about his work at the school—*Love Is Not Enough* (1950), *Truants from Life* (1955), and *The Empty Fortress* (1967)—and just that spring had been called, in a typical encomium, "one of Freud's few genuine heirs of our time . . . [a man who had] sought to think through all of human psychology for himself."[1] I entered his office not as an experienced, adult journalist, which I was, but as anxious supplicant looking for Stephen and not knowing quite how to begin.

Bettelheim was sixty-five years old, almost twice my age, and his heavy Viennese accent and the thick lenses of his glasses made him all the more formidable as he sat behind his desk and waved me to a chair. He did not invite small talk, so I fumbled right to the point by asking if I could look at Stephen's records, explaining that this might help me frame more informed questions. He brushed aside the request, saying he wasn't sure the school still had the file after twenty-one years and that, even if it did, I probably would not understand what was in it. He then leaned forward and asked me to vow that I would not discuss our session with my mother and father. This struck me as an odd request, but I was willing to abide by whatever ground rules he demanded if they helped me get the history I had come for. I told him this, and he immediately went on the attack.

My father he dismissed as crude and somewhat simple-minded, a "schlemiel" who paid the bills and stayed out of emotional problems. My mother was the villain. He said she paraded as a saint and a martyr when, in fact, she was almost entirely responsible for my brother's problems. With astonishing anger, he said she had rejected Stephen at birth and that to cope with this lockout he had developed "pseudo-feeble-mindedness." He said that my brother was a "lovely child" who manifested a sensitivity my mother wished she possessed, and he castigated her for never conceding that she was responsible for Stephen's distress and for insisting, against the school's wishes, that he be allowed periodic home visits. As his guttural assault filled the small room, I recalled how often my mother had cried after dealing with Bettelheim, her tears accompanied by bitter accusations that he hated her and, for that matter, all mothers. As these memories returned, I heard him saying, in particularly acid terms, that my mother had been under the sway of Mortimer Adler, a guiding force of the university's Great Books project, where she had worked during some of the time Stephen was at the school. "Adler has contempt for the emotions and is only interested in the intellect," he said, maintaining that, under the philosopher's "pernicious" influence, my mother had yearned for Stephen to be successful intellectually, which he could not be at the time. "What *is it* about these Jewish mothers, Mr. Pollak?" he asked. I was stunned by this casual anti-Semitism, coming as it did from a Jew who had suffered in the camps, and by the ferocity of his antagonism two decades after Stephen's death. I had thought hard about my mother over the years, including during three years of psychoanalysis. I was under no illusion that she was Mrs. March, but I knew, too, that she was not the Medea of Bettelheim's tirade.

Having demolished my mother, he went on to state, categorically, that Stephen had committed suicide. I timorously ventured to explain that Stephen and I had been romping happily in the hay and that I had nearly slipped down the loft's hidden chute myself, but the director had long ago made up his mind. In 1956, I would discover, he had written that the school had warned my parents that a home visit for Stephen was ill-advised because he might harm himself. "Despite our objection the visit took place . . . [and] the child died in a carefully contrived accident."[2] Bettelheim told me with utter confidence that Stephen had once purposely fallen out of a speedboat near the propellers and that it was only a matter of time before he found a situation like the loft in which his efforts at killing himself would succeed. In fact, my brother had never fallen out of any boat. The day after he died, however, the eleven-year-old granddaughter of our host at the farm *was* thrown from a speedboat, and died after the propeller cut through her heart. I did not remind Bettelheim of this coincidence because, at the time of our meeting, I did not know of it, my ignorance yet another consequence of my parents' determination to protect me as much as possible from the trauma of that grim August weekend.[3]

Over the years, I had tended to dismiss my mother's complaints that Bettelheim hated parents as the understandable hyperbole of a woman who had given up her son to his care and the prolonged separations that required. Now I saw that, if anything, she had been understating his hostility. As I stared across the director's desk, I could not comprehend his anger. We were meeting for the first time, I had come for help; yet he seemed determined to vent his spleen and draw me into a conspiracy against my mother. This world-renowned healer appeared interested only in wreaking vengeance on her more than two decades after Stephen's death.

I am writing this nearly thirty years after the encounter, and it is fair to ask if I am not exaggerating, am not recalling Bettelheim in such critical terms because he bore such cruel tidings in such harsh tones. But I am not groping through the mists for these recollections. I left his office that day, walked back to my parents' apartment, and immediately set down the details of the meeting in a letter to the psychoanalyst with whom I was no longer in treatment but with whom I planned to discuss the encounter. I still have the carbons of that summary, typed on the cheap yellow copy paper my father had used since his days as a newspaperman. I can feel the touch of his old Royal standard as I sat at his desk by the eleventh-floor window; I remember looking out at the Orthogenic School in the distance and thinking it the laboratory of the evil Doctor Sivana, arch-nemesis of Captain Marvel.

I was vague with my mother, telling her the meeting had been useful and sounding, no doubt, like a White House press secretary issuing an empty communiqué after a summit meeting. She did not press for more information but did say that if I wanted to talk about Stephen further I might find it helpful to contact a psychiatrist named Irene Josselyn, who had treated my brother in conjunction with the school. I scribbled the name down but did not mention that Bettelheim had drawn Josselyn into his net of fury also, attacking her for supporting Stephen's home visits and accusing her of being more concerned with my mother's emotional well-being than with my brother's. I located her in Phoenix, Arizona, wrote to her describing my meeting, and put to her many of the questions I had tried to get Bettelheim to answer.

In two thoughtful replies, she attempted to deal with my queries. She said that her major difference with Bettelheim was over the cause of Stephen's problems, which she did not feel could be blamed simply on my mother or father. "Dr. Bettelheim, as you may know,

> has never been fond of parents! While I recognized that your mother was often over-anxious and also impatient with Stephen, and that your father made an adjustment to the situation by being somewhat aloof but patient, I could not see that they were reacting in a fashion that would explain why Stephen should show such early signs of maladjustment. . . . Your parents were always cooperative with me but I think were terrified in the presence of Dr. Bettelheim. It is my opinion that there is an inherent factor that we don't understand in some of these cases; it may prove ultimately to be a genetic anomaly. . . . I am sure that your mother was not the "Mammy" type, all-giving mother, but I always felt she was an average mother who did not as much reject Stephen as she felt frustrated in trying to react to him. [4]

Josselyn also disagreed with Bettelheim's diagnosis that Stephen suffered from pseudo-feeble-mindedness. "At that time," she wrote, "our knowledge of childhood psychosis was very limited. [Stephen's] general picture resembled what we then called schizophrenia. I suspect now we would call it Infantile Autism." Whatever the label, Josselyn had felt my brother was making more progress at the Orthogenic School than the director had. "While at the time he died he was far from well, he was quite different from when I first saw him," she wrote. She also emphatically rejected Bettelheim's view that Stephen committed suicide. She, it turned out, had been brought up around barns, where hay was fed through chutes to the cattle below. "I can recall very clearly, how we as children were warned that the chute might be covered with hay and it was a dangerous aspect of our playground! I felt Stephen fell down [the chute] accidentally. He, in my opinion, was *not* suicidal at the time."[5]

I welcomed Josselyn's supportive letters, but she was a woman I knew nothing about and had never met, even on the telephone. Bettelheim was the Stella M. Rowley Distinguished Service Professor at the University of Chicago, a man who had been widely recognized for his outstanding achievements, including by Chicago's Immigrants Service League, when my father was its president, in 1961.[6] A few months after our meeting, the leaders of the city's political, business, and philanthropic community would gather in the grand ballroom of the Conrad Hilton Hotel to mark Bettelheim's twenty-five years at the Orthogenic School and "celebrate his rare ability to bring compassionate care to children and his immeasurable contribution to the understanding of human experience."[7] This did not describe the man I had encountered; what he had said to me, and especially the way he had said it, suggested quite the opposite.

IT NEVER OCCURRED TO ME that I might attempt a biography of Bruno Bettelheim until an editor, Jennifer Josephy, suggested the idea after reading the first, tentative draft chapters of a memoir about Stephen that I began in the late 1980s. She found the material about Bettelheim and the Orthogenic School compelling and encouraged me to set aside the memoir temporarily to explore the possibility of writing about Bettelheim's life and work. I was not at all sure I wanted to embark on such a long and arduous detour, and the memory of our meeting twenty years before gave me further pause, but I agreed to write to him.

He was living in Santa Monica, California, and a few days after he received my letter he called, apologizing for doing so and explaining that, as a result of two strokes, he could no longer use pen or typewriter. He had just turned eighty-six, and the excoriating voice I recalled from 1969 was now hoarse and frail, made so, I would learn, by a recent throat operation. He was altogether cordial, saying that of course he remembered me, and talking—wistfully, it seemed—of Stephen. He asked if my parents were still alive; I said they were not, and he insisted that he, too, should be dead. When I offered some hollow response, like, "Don't be silly," he persisted, saying that he was old and sick and of no use to anybody anymore. "Nonsense," I replied, and reiterated what I had said in my letter, that I would like to come out to talk about writing his biography. He paused for a long time, then said it would be foolish of me to fly all the way from New York to see someone who looked as grotesque as he did. Our conversation lasted perhaps fifteen minutes, during which he said he was too tired to cooperate with me and, besides, he was no fit subject for a book.

Though the prospect of attempting one without interviewing him made me even more hesitant, I began reading, or rereading, his books, and I was soon struck by the fact that his writing, for all its scrutiny of other people's psychological behavior, revealed so little of his personal history. Nor was he forthcoming in private conversation, even with at least two of his three children; Naomi and Eric Bettelheim would tell me that he remained close-mouthed about his past all his life.* When a former student with whom he corresponded for several years asked him to tell her something of his early years, he dodged the question, replying that he always refused to cooperate with the "few poor souls" who wanted to write about him and made it a practice to destroy his papers and letters.[8] To a would-be biographer, a Frenchman who made a television documentary about the Orthogenic School and its director in the early 1970s, Bettelheim wrote that he knew enough about his unconscious to wish to protect himself and his family from having aspects of it exposed to the public.[9] Bettelheim's literary agent, Theron Raines, and his per-

---

* Ruth Bettelheim declined to be interviewed about her father. To honor Naomi Bettelheim's request that I not invade the privacy of her present family, I have used her maiden name throughout this book.

sonal editor, Joyce Jack, both urged him to put more of himself into *Freud's Vienna and Other Essays,* his final and, putatively, most autobiographical book.[10] He demurred, and in the introduction wrote that he eschewed such self-exposure because he believed that what Freud said about biographies "applies even more to autobiographies, namely that the person who undertakes such a task 'binds himself to lying, to concealment, to flummery.' "[11]

I don't think biographers are doomed to break up on the shoals of Freud's hyperbole, but truth was clearly a problematic issue for Bettelheim. In one of his final essays, "Essential Books of One's Life," he wrote that three of the thinkers who most influenced him as a young man were the German philosophers Theodor Lessing (1872–1933), F. A. Lange (1828–75), and Hans Vaihinger (1852–1933), and that at least part of their appeal lay in the encouragement they offered for not always hewing to the facts. From Lessing's "History as Projecting Meaning into the Meaningless," Bettelheim said he embraced the idea that the meanings of historical events "are only the projections of man's wishful thinking." Lessing had moved him to believe that fiction could play a role in ordering his life; or, as Lange put it in his *History of Materialism and Critique of Its Present Significance,* "to supplement reality by an ideal world of his own creation." This view was buttressed by Vaihinger's *The Philosophy of "As If,"* a popular work that came out in 1911 and went through several editions. The renowned Kant scholar argued that even though fictions should not be mistaken for true propositions, they can work As If true. This demonstrated to Bettelheim "the need and usefulness of acting on the basis of fictions that are known to be false," and left him with the conviction "that we must live by fictions—not just to find meaning in life but to make it bearable. . . ."[12] That Bettelheim might have encountered this pessimistic *Lebensphilosophie* at the University of Vienna in the 1920s was not surprising; it was then widely influential in German-speaking Europe, a strain of thought that owed much to Nietzsche and Schopenhauer and held, generally, that because life had no real purpose it was made livable only by pretending through fictions that it did.

I knew nothing about Lessing, Lange, and Vaihinger, and when I went to *The Encyclopedia of Philosophy* to educate myself I found that Bettelheim had been there before me. His rendition of the three philosophers' thinking drew significantly, both in language and structure, on the Vaihinger entry. Like Bettelheim, it described how Vaihinger expanded on Lange's view that man needs to supplement reality. In the encyclopedia, Vaihinger is quoted as defining mankind as "a species of monkey suffering from megalomania." Bettelheim used the same words, without the quotation marks. The entry recorded Vaihinger's belief that it "may be a great convenience to act as if the cosmos were orderly. . . ." Bettelheim turned this idea over to Lessing, writing that "to proceed on the fiction that the cosmos is an orderly place is a great convenience." [13] I was arrested by his reference to these three philosophers, and perplexed. Why had he chosen to bring them up at this eleventh hour? In mining the encyclopedia to the edge of plagiarism, was he trying to create an ex-post-facto intellectual scaffolding to rationalize a life of dissembling? Or was this the act of an ailing and despondent man who, contemplating his mortality, felt moved to offer, if not a full confession, then at least a tantalizing hint that his public persona had not been all that it had seemed? Many years earlier, he had written that lying leads to perdition but "a voice used to repent, to admit our failures and state the truth, redeems us." [14]

I knew from my own experience that Bettelheim could be dogmatic, arrogant, and cruel, and over the years had heard, if only vaguely, that such behavior was not unknown beyond his interactions with my family. But I had never heard that he lied, and even after I read "Essential Books of One's Life" and again recalled his claim that my brother had killed himself, it came as a surprise when, early in my interviewing, Benjamin Wright, a close colleague of Bettelheim's in the 1950s, told me that he did so "all the time." This assertion would be echoed often in the months to come. Jacquelyn Seevak Sanders, Bettelheim's primary assistant and hand-picked successor at the Orthogenic School, said that "you couldn't believe anything he said." Jerome Kavka, a consulting psychiatrist at the school, told me one could never tell when Bettelheim was lying, and regarded him as "a fictional artist." Josette Wingo, a counselor at the school in the late 1940s who also knew Bettelheim after he moved to California in the

1970s, said he concocted scenarios to fit the situation and that toward the end of his life he "was making up stories about everybody."

Such assessments were sometimes less harsh judgments than indulgent winks that said, in effect, "We're on to this Baron Münchhausen." And some of Bettelheim's tales did prove innocent enough, stories whipped up to make a point in the classroom, or the kind of stretchers that most of us tell once in a while, a phenomenon that in his native city is known as *Wiener Schmäh,* which loosely translates as "blarney." But as my research progressed, it became increasingly apparent that Bettelheim had lived a life of As If that was frequently not so benign.

My interest in him grew when, on March 12, 1990, he took his own life.[15] The date marked the fifty-second anniversary of the Nazis' invasion of Austria, the *Anschluss* that had ripped thousands of Viennese Jews from their homeland and sent hundreds, including Bettelheim, to concentration camps. Was his timing just a coincidence? And what family history had pushed his only sibling, Margaret, also to commit suicide in 1984? The enigma deepened further when, within a few weeks of his death, several former residents of the Orthogenic School publicly charged that he had abused them physically and emotionally, allegations soon supported by some former staff members.[16] Then a scholar accused him of plagiarizing portions of *The Uses of Enchantment,* his widely read and much-lauded book about the psychological meanings of fairy tales.[17] The charges, like Bettelheim's suicide, surprised me and triggered more questions. Why had he so angrily compared the student antiwar protesters in the 1960s to young Nazis in the 1930s?[18] And, more intriguing, why had he repeatedly, and often pugnaciously, accused the European Jews of "ghetto thinking," of refusing to fight back against their anti-Semitic tormentors and thus aiding in their own mass destruction?[19] Had Bettelheim fought back? Just who was he? I now felt impelled to find out.

In the pages that follow I have in general traced the chronology of Bettelheim's life. But because he inhabited so many different roles, and because he often played them deceptively, I have stopped my forward march at several points to investigate specific areas, among them his concentration camp experience, his directorship of the Orthogenic School, his treatment of autistic children, his interest in kibbutz child-rearing, and his views on the Holocaust. In devoting full chapters to these subjects, and in pausing along the way to explore others, I have tried to focus on what was central in Bettelheim's life without losing the sense of how that life unfolded.

Bruno Bettelheim often called his counselors "participant observers," by which he meant that they had to be both deeply involved with and at the same time detached from the children in their care.[20] Any biographer is a participant observer in relating to his subject, and perhaps I am more than most. In the following pages, I have tried to keep my personal experience of Bruno Bettelheim from unfairly darkening my portrait; I have sought to be "sympathetic yet aloof, involved yet not involved."[21] If I have not arrived at the whole truth, I hope I have come closer to it than to flummery.

CHAPTER ONE
Vienna

Bruno Bettelheim wrote that the tales of his ancestors passed on to him by his parents left a deep impression on him as a child "because they contained so many elements . . . of fairy tales." In these stories, his maternal grandfather left the small village where he was born soon after his thirteenth birthday, with a new suit on his back and only five guilders in his pocket. "To protect his only pair of shoes, the boy walked barefoot the 100 miles from his village to the big city, Vienna. There, in a very hard struggle, he eventually managed to make a great fortune." His paternal grandfather was raised in a Jewish orphanage and educated to be a rabbi, his great intelligence soon catching the attention of the "richest man in the realm," Baron Rothschild, who was seeking a tutor for his sons. The young rabbi took the post "and went from living in desperate poverty into the grand palace of the Rothschilds, in Vienna." The Rothschild sons were so impressed by his learning and grew so attached to him that when they took over the family bank "they put him in charge of many of its operations." As a result, he became extremely wealthy and a major force in Vienna's Jewish community. Bettelheim wrote that it was not these "true stories" of his grandfathers' successes that made him believe the many fairy tales he knew but the fairy tales that persuaded him that the heroic oral histories of his forebears were based in fact.[1]

The genesis of the name Bettelheim does have a fairy-tale aura. According to lore, it originated in the middle of the eighteenth century in what is now Bratislava, the Slovak capital on the Danube, about forty miles east of Vienna. Count Bethlen, one of the most powerful men in the community, so coveted the beautiful wife of a Jewish citizen that he rode into the marketplace and tried to kidnap her by lifting her onto his horse and galloping off. But her husband rushed to her rescue, fighting and vanquishing the count in hand-to-hand combat. That a Jew would confront, much less do battle with, a nobleman of such rank was so daring that the hero thereafter was known as "Bethlen-Jude." When a royal decree required that all Jews assume family names, Bethlen-Jude became Bettelheim.

Whatever the accuracy of this story, a number of Bettelheim families did rise out of this region in the eighteenth and early nineteenth centuries.[2] One descendant was Marcus Bettelheim, who lived in Budapest, and whose wife, Lewia, gave birth to Jakob Moritz Bettelheim on December 12, 1825. By 1857, Jakob was living in Vienna, and soon married Eleonore Frankel, with whom he had eleven children. The fifth, Anton, was born on April 4, 1869, and would become Bruno Bettelheim's father.[3] The fairy tale of Jakob the orphan is just as fanciful as the one about Jakob the brilliant rabbinical student who tutored Nathan, Ferdinand, and Albert, the sons of the Vienna banker Anselm von Rothschild (1803–1874). Records in Vienna offer no evidence that Jakob ever entered the rabbinate or the Rothschild home as a teacher, or that he was employed in any capacity at the bank. He did, however, work for Albert von Rothschild. Jakob Bettelheim was by profession a *Holzhändler,* a trader in wood, and served as the banker's *Domänendirektor,* the overseer of his agricultural and forest properties.[4] The only Bettelheim who appears to have worked in the bank itself was Jakob's eighth-born son, Bruno's uncle Richard, who began employment there in 1902 and was the *Prokurist,* or head clerk, from 1913 to 1938.[5]

Bruno's maternal grandfather was Adolph Seidler, the son of Abraham Seidler, a businessman, and Franziska Mühlrad. He was born on April 15, 1847, in Redschkau, a small town in Bohemia. He may or may not have still lived there when he turned thirteen, and may have walked barefoot to Vienna. However Adolph Seidler got to the imperial city, he eventually became a successful seller of sewing machines and owner of real estate, and in 1875 married Franziska Zentner. The couple had five children, one of whom, Rudolf, would establish a lumber business with Anton Bettelheim in 1907. By then, Rudolf Seidler's sister Paula had been married to Anton Bettelheim for nine years.[6] Their daughter, Margaret, was born late in 1899, and on August 28, 1903, Bruno Bettelheim arrived into "a very sheltered existence and a life of greatest ease and comfort. . . ."[7]

Over the years, he sent out mixed signals about this life, and especially about his relationship with his mother. He wrote that he had a wet nurse whom he suckled into his third year, his mother being "much too much the Victorian lady" to breast-feed her children.[8] Such arrangements were common among Viennese women in Paula Bettelheim's social circumstances, as was the presence of maids and governesses. Her son said that he would probably have preferred it if his mother had nursed him,[9] and his texts are full of passages stressing how important proper maternal breast-feeding is to the emotional well-being of children.

Still, the sketchy portrait he drew of his own mother in print is of an affectionate, devoted parent who read fairy tales to him, comforted him in her arms when nightmares woke him, took him to museums, and, especially, cared for him when he was ill. This was often, he said, for he was a sickly child who suffered from dysentery, scarlet fever, diphtheria, measles, and mumps, as well as several attacks of influenza and tonsillitis, which kept him in bed "for many weeks at a time."[10] Bettelheim said he almost died from eating poison berries, which caused such a severe reaction that he lived briefly in the home of the physician who treated him. He said that in later years, on trips to Europe, the smell of strong coffee always reminded him of this crisis, because the doctor had made him drink it as a stimulant.[11] During the many nights when he was seriously ill at home, Bettelheim wrote, "my mother sat at my bedside, sponging my feverish body and changing the cold compresses to give me relief. In moments like these I learned to understand and appreciate that a mother makes all the difference in the world when one is in need, in great pain, deeply worried, or even desperate."[12]

Bettelheim's behavior as an adult suggested that he felt a good deal more hostility toward his mother than he cared to record in print. No prominent psychotherapist of his time was as antagonistic to mothers—in private and public—as he was, insisting that they caused autism by rejecting their infants and comparing them to devouring witches and the SS guards in the concentration camps. Throughout his life he said that his own mother had not taken good care of him, leaving him in the charge of the wet nurse or a nanny; he complained that his mother had too often been busy embroidering to pay him the attention he craved. In the 1950s, he spoke to the Paul Federn Study Group, a gathering of therapists in New York City, about his work at the Orthogenic School; when a colleague who also treated disturbed children politely challenged Bettelheim's hostile view of mothers, "Bruno exploded and started to scream, 'I had no mother,' " recalled a friend, who told me he behaved like a paranoid.[13] Years later, Bettelheim would appear at a professional meeting in Philadelphia and, during a question-and-answer period, say that some women are just not fit to be mothers and that his was one of these; he also reiterated what he had said in a recent interview: that he saw no reason "why we cannot make provision for children to divorce themselves from their families, as adults divorce one another."[14]

As a boy, Bettelheim did something of this sort by spending many afternoons after school at the home of his mother's sister, Jeanette Buxbaum, who lived near the Bettelheim apartment. He sought refuge at the Buxbaums' primarily to avoid his sister, Margaret, whom he regarded as an intrusive know-it-all. "Such [escapes] were possible in the old extended family, where the bad aspects of brothers and sisters who grated on you and the authoritarianism of parents were diluted by the nearness of other relatives. . . ."[15] He said that during these years his aunt Jeanette had a greater influence on him than his mother, but he did not reveal in his writing what that influence was. Another attraction at the Buxbaums' was their only daughter, Edith, who was a year older than Bruno and became his favorite cousin; they were more like brother and sister and spent hours helping each other with schoolwork. Edith Buxbaum, who would become a leading psychoanalyst in Seattle, saw her aunt Paula not as a remote mother but as a woman who spoiled her son by smothering him with affection.[16]

The memories Bettelheim chose to set down in his books about his preadolescent years reveal few tensions with either of his "very good" parents.[17] He wrote of playing happily under the big dining-room table with his cousins, eavesdropping on the grown-ups' conversation as they pressed their knees against the tablecloth that hung almost to the floor.[18] He fondly recalled kibitzing at his father's card games, and playing cards himself with Anton for long hours on rainy vacation days.[19] He said that, when he was six years old, a four-story house across the narrow street from their apartment burned down in the middle of the night and Anton and Paula woke him so he could see the spectacle. "[T]hey were calm and talked with me about the varying colors and forms of the flames. . . . The security which I felt emanating from my parents . . . had kept me from feeling any fear."[20] Bettelheim stressed that he was never punished, describing how on one occasion he had shocked his mother by using offensive language to express his irritation with her. His father was upset when she told him of this transgression and asked his son if he really had to punish him to get him to speak respectfully to his mother. "The idea that he might have to punish me obviously distressed my gentle father," and that, Bettelheim wrote, was enough to cure him forever of using bad language in front of his parents.[21]

In 1914, when Bruno was eleven years old, his formal education began at the *Realschule* on the Albertgasse, a few blocks from his home. Over the next seven years, he took intensive instruction in German, French, English, mathematics, physics, and much else that rounded out the demanding curriculum, one that Vienna's schoolmasters taught with the strictest discipline. Bettelheim described himself as "a very good student, a quiet, introspective, even subdued youngster."[22] In his first year, he was one of five pupils in his class of fifty-four to be singled out for excellence. In his final year, 1921, his marks ranged from good to superior; he was praised for his deportment and did not miss a single day of school, reflecting a dedication to hard work that would last a lifetime. During these school days, Bruno also was singled out for his writing skills by Moritz Bauer, the rabbi who provided religious instruction to the Jewish pupils at the *Realschule*.[23] Most of the other teachers were Catholic, nationalistic, and, in many cases, "anti-Semitic bastards,"[24] as were some of his classmates. Bettelheim told of a friend with whom he walked to school every day but who one morning hit him because the Jews had crucified

Jesus. "There were the boys who extorted money: who beat us if we handed it over because we were dirty cowards, and who beat us if we didn't, because we were miserly Jews."[25]

The most detailed anecdote Bettelheim recorded about his school days turned on a teacher he chose to call Dr. X, "a simpering fool who spoke with the voice of a eunuch." So weak and inadequate was this schoolmaster that one day Bruno egged on several of his classmates and together they bodily removed the offending instructor from the room. Bettelheim recalled that he immediately began to tremble as he contemplated the consequences of this rash act; and, indeed, the next day the school's authoritarian director castigated the class, and especially Bruno, "as the leader in this unprecedented and nefarious deed." But the director did not, as the troublemaker feared, expel him. On the contrary, at the end of the scolding his demeanor suddenly softened, and, in a quiet voice, he said: "Of course I know that if Dr. X had behaved as I expect all masters of this institution to behave, nothing like this could have happened." He then merely ordered Bruno to stay after school for two hours and study the subject Dr. X should have made so compelling that no rebellion would have occurred. Bettelheim wrote that this experience made a "deep impression" on him and stayed "vividly" in his mind for more than six decades, yet he did not name the director or Dr. X, or describe what subject the teacher was presiding over so ineffectively.[26]

Whether this scenario is true or not, Bettelheim almost always employed such tales to make a point, and he extrapolated two from the story of Dr. X. In his maturity, he came to realize that the director, in acting as he had, had manifested the requirements of an incisive educator, one who examines the motives of a child so as to comprehend the reasons for his or her behavior. Also many years later, he came to understand what had moved him to such an atypical outburst. "We boys," Bettelheim wrote,

> were at an age when we had anxious doubts about our budding masculinity and needed suitable masculine figures with which to identify. Dr. X, far from offering a suitable image for identification, increased our anxieties that we might not make it as male adults; he presented us with our worst fears about ourselves—and in the flesh.

Bettelheim said that he was fifteen years old when this incident took place, and that he acted as he had because his father had recently suffered a "stroke," which made him fear that he might grow up to become a weakling like Dr. X.[27]

Anton Bettelheim may, in fact, have suffered a minor stroke when his son was a teenager, but the severe illness that so distressed young Bruno was syphilis, which Bettelheim told at least two people his father contracted in 1907, when his son was four.[28] Bettelheim speculated that his father developed the disease one summer when his mother, like many wives of successful business-men, had gone off to the mountains, leaving her husband in Vi-enna to work. He did not think his father habitually visited prostitutes, but felt he must have done so on this one occasion.[29] The disease afflicted Anton at a time when fear of the venereal plague had reached a peak, because of its spread among the troops during the Great War. Despite advances in treatment during the first years of the century—the universal blood-serum test discov-ered by Wassermann and Neisser in 1906, the development of the drug Salvarsan in 1909—a certain cure would not be found for this ugly, highly contagious infection until penicillin stopped the killer spirochete in 1943. Like AIDS, syphilis brought with it a numbing sense of doom and a cruel social stigma; also like its counterpart, it could flow quiescent in the bloodstream for many years.

Once Anton Bettelheim's syphilis was diagnosed, Paula did not have sex with him for the rest of his life—two decades, if the 1907 date of onset given by their son is correct. The atmosphere of the family's apartment at Neubaugasse 66 was melancholy, and Paula, though charming and welcoming, did not always hide the weight of her conjugal frustrations.[30] Edith Buxbaum recalled that "the poor woman knew that her husband had an ineffective anti-syphilis treatment and waited for years for something terrible to happen."[31] Decades later, Bruno would tell his own children that as a young boy he did not know what caused the oppressive climate in his home but a fear that he may have created it caused him great anxiety about his own sexuality, an insecurity that made him back away from intimate encounters with the girls who at-tracted him.[32]

Eventually, Bettelheim did learn the cause of his parents'

anguish and began to worry because "he did not know whether he was conceived before or after [his father contracted] the infection."[33] He feared that he might be what then was called a *hérédo*, that his physical defects and awkwardness might somehow be the result of syphilis and that much worse might be in store, such as blindness. Bettelheim's blue eyes coped behind thick glasses with a nearsightedness that he loathed. As an adult, he would recall that his parents and the family's eye doctor told him that his glasses fully corrected his vision. "I believed them because I had no way of knowing how other people see. I tried to play tennis and what not, like other kids, but I was always poor at it and felt pretty bad about myself. It wasn't until I was well into my forties before my eye doctor said, 'Look, even with the best correction I can give you, you have about a 30 to 40 percent loss of vision.' "[34] Miriam Williams, a psychoanalyst Bettelheim saw for about a year at the end of his life, told me that he also was "very unhappy about his looks," seeing in the mirror an image with large ears, a big nose, and thick lips that his boyish smile did not erase. This sense of being homely dogged him throughout his life, even at moments of great triumph. In accepting a National Book Award in 1977 for *The Uses of Enchantment,* he couched his remarks as a fairy tale and told his audience that his mother

> had a healthy, down-to-earth sense of reality. So when right after his birth her son was shown to her, she took in his appearance carefully and then breathed a deep sigh of relief. Thank God, she said, it is a boy.
>
> Now this mother told her children many fairy tales. And since they lived at the most remote edge of the German land, she told the fairy tales of the Brothers Grimm, not those of Hans Christian Anders[e]n. Thus the boy never got the idea that an Ugly Duckling could turn into a beautiful Swan. This was fortunate, and saved him from disappointment, because his looks remained very much the same as they had been when his mother first beheld him.[35]

Medical logic dictated that Bruno was in no danger of inheriting syphilis; it is congenital, and Paula Bettelheim never had the disease. As with AIDS, however, the terror did not come only from the scientific facts. Moreover, Bruno received scant reassurance from Freud, whose work he said he began reading as a teenager. In "A Case of Hysteria," Freud wrote that the father of his eighteen-year-old patient Dora had contracted syphilis before his marriage, adding that "a *strikingly high* percentage of the patients whom I have treated psycho-analytically come of fathers who have suffered from tabes or general paralysis." Thus, he concluded, "syphilis in the male parent is a very relevent factor in the aetiology of the neuropathic constitution of children." [36] The specter of his father's illness so traumatized Bettelheim that on the rare occasions when he managed to talk about it he often could not bring himself to say the word. At age eighty-three, he wrote to a friend of the "deathly disease, of which [Anton] knew he would die. This projected him and my mother into a state of deep anxiety which was not lost on my sister and me. . . . From this moment on the life of my parents was a nightmare for them which they kept hidden from everybody, even their parents and siblings. But they suffered quietly." [37]

Books and movies were the solace of the insecure teenager living in the shadow of his father's illness. At first he soaked up escapist fare, such as Karl May's popular adventures set in the American West, and *The Perils of Pauline,* which he saw at movie palaces like the Apollokino or the Buschkino, where an orchestra played for fifteen minutes before the films began. These diversions, he said, helped him forget for a few hours the realities of World War I, which quickly turned prosperous Vienna into a shabby, hungry city awash in refugees. "The war was rough even for the well-to-do," Bettelheim said. "We never had enough heat or enough light or enough food." He described how, when he was fourteen, he helped unload wounded soldiers from trains coming in from the front and take them to hospitals, and how he later helped disarm some of these men "so they wouldn't pillage the city." [38]

By the war's end, in 1918, an influenza epidemic was sweeping the world. It would take the lives of twenty million people, among them such notable Viennese as Gustav Klimt and Egon Schiele, whose Secessionist revolt against academic painting had revolutionized art in Vienna and beyond; Otto Wagner, who had led architecture away from the hodgepodge grandiosity of the buildings that had risen along the Ringstrasse in the second half of the nineteenth century; Sophie Freud, Sigmund's middle daughter; and Victor Adler, leader of the Social Democrats, who died just as the Austrian republic was aborning. Emperor Franz Joseph, who had ruled Austro-Hungary since 1848, had died of old age two years earlier. In the late fall of 1918, just after Bruno turned fifteen, the old Habsburg Empire fell apart, like "the downfall of a manorial family that, after living in comfort for generations, faces poverty and must subsist on dry bread and potatoes amid the faded splendor of their now unheated residence while their former retainers and tenants take over the bulk of the estate." [39]

This upheaval must have affected Anton's lumber business to some extent, but his son said that enough money remained after the war for the family to resume a comfortable life. [40] Still, he would write of how hard it was for him as a teenager to revolt against parents whose ordered world had been shattered by the war and the collapse of the Austro-Hungarian Empire. Many times Bruno had seen Franz Joseph, resplendent in bemedaled uniform and muttonchops, waving to the crowds as horses pulled his carriage through the cobblestone streets. Now the patriarchy he had presided over for almost seventy years was withering away; Bruno said that he began to see that his own father, whom he had regarded as an oppressive but protective hero, was just a "clay god," [41] and that he could no longer test his emerging values against those of his parents, because he now found theirs so lacking. Perhaps this was the vacuum that Jeanette Buxbaum and her daughter Edith helped fill when young Bruno retreated to that household after school, but it seems as likely that behind all the talk of values lay what Bettelheim would one day call the "time bomb" [42] of his father's syphilis, which was ticking ever closer to its fatal explosion.

Anton Bettelheim died on April 13, 1926, the official causes listed as tabes, progressive paralysis, a weak heart, and encephalopathy. [43] His son left no doubt in private conversation that the final stage of his father's illness had been "horrible to see." [44] Anton had been able to go to Bettelheim & Schnitzer, his lumber business, and maintain outward appearances until a few months before the end. Bruno and his mother and sister nursed him first at home and then at a sanatorium in the town of Tulln, a few miles northwest of Vienna, watching as he wasted away. He was fifty-seven at the end, his widow forty-eight, his daughter twenty-six, his son going on twenty-three; it was "much too early for me," Bettelheim wrote sixty years later.[45]

At the time of his father's death, Bruno had been enrolled at the University of Vienna for ten semesters, concentrating in art history. But because of his father's illness he also had made preparations for a business career. In 1921, the year he had entered the university, he simultaneously began courses in international commerce at the *Hochschule für Welthandel* on the Franz-Klein-Gasse. Over two semesters, he studied a prescribed curriculum that included courses in bookkeeping, commercial law, and economics and passed the required final exam on July 19, 1922.[46] With this grounding, he had worked at the lumber yard part time, but now he reluctantly dropped out of the university to assume his responsibilities full time, in tandem with his father's partner, Hanns Schnitzer. Bruno and his mother suspected Schnitzer of having cheated Anton, disdained his middle-brow tastes, and regarded him as a social inferior; moreover, the erstwhile student had little enthusiasm for the lumber business, which he found boring.[47] "If my heart had been in it," he told an interviewer many years later, "I could have made [a] fortune, but that didn't appeal to me. My family had lost several fortunes already."[48] He did not specify in this interview, or in his autobiographical writings, what form these financial setbacks took, or when they occurred. But he did tell another interviewer that in the first week of World War I, when he was eleven years old, the family's "forests, lumber and sawmills on the Austria-Hungarian border . . . went up in flames."[49] Bettelheim bridled at the prospect of being a businessman for the rest of his life; he yearned for a professional life, ideally as an academic, and in his free time always had "his nose buried in a book."[50] But Viennese men did not abandon their duties to their mothers and sisters, and whatever Bettelheim's distaste for trade, he liked the income Bettelheim & Schnitzer produced, not least because it would enable him to make a good home for Regina Altstadt.

They had met as teenagers. He had been instantly smitten,

captivated by her cheerful good nature and intelligence, and her open, smiling face and eager brown eyes; but the relationship was inauspicious from the start. Gina, as everyone called her, was still recovering from an infatuation with a handsome young artist named Dolph, whose rejection had left her brokenhearted. She was also dealing with the recent death of her father, who had come to Vienna from Poland when she was a child and gone to work in the Altstadt family's shoe business. He had traveled to Italy to recover from tuberculosis, and died after an absence of several months. "I was lonely," Gina told me. "In a sense, Bruno took care of me." This embrace was marked by a generosity that eventually included paying for her analysis and underwriting a nursery school she ran with a friend named Anni Hatschek.

Bruno courted Gina ardently throughout much of the 1920s, but her misgivings were never far from the surface. When she became pregnant after they had known one another about two years, she quickly rejected any idea of marriage and had an abortion. She also developed an ill-defined glandular condition that caused her to faint at the dinner table one evening, after which she took to her bed for several days. Gina said that each time Bruno came to visit she vomited after he left, which she regarded as a neurotic reaction to her inner struggle over the relationship. This experience led her to consult with Grete Bibring, an analyst who strongly urged that she separate from him; when she could not, Bibring referred her to Richard Sterba, a member of Freud's inner circle.

In the late 1920s, hoping distance might help end the alliance, Gina decided to go live with her brother, Leopold, who had emigrated to New York City. At the last minute, a friend there warned her that Leopold was a disturbed man and advised that she stay in Vienna. Not long thereafter, Gina learned that "Poldy" was bisexual, had been discovered in a relationship with another man, and had killed himself. With both her father and her only sibling dead, and Dolph's rejection never far from mind, Gina's loneliness began to overcome her doubts about Bruno. "I don't think I was ever in love with him," she told me, "but he was a wonderful friend who was devoted to me—and, after all, he was a very intellectual, cultivated, interesting man who offered me a great deal." On March 30, 1930, they wed, their widowed mothers, Paula Bettelheim and Mina Altstadt, enthusiastically endorsing the match. Though the two families were, like most Viennese Jews, secular in outlook, Moritz Bauer, the rabbi who had provided Bruno's religious instruction at the *Realschule,* performed the ceremony, in the Neudeggergasse Synagogue. The newlyweds went to Italy on their honeymoon, visiting the Sicilian seaside towns of Palermo and Taormina. Gina loved the bracing air and exercise of the mountains; Bruno was seldom more content than when sitting in a beach chair with a good book. With a guide, she went up into the hills on a donkey; he stayed behind reading Kantorowicz's biography of Frederick II.

The young couple settled into a spacious, second-floor apartment at Gloriettegasse 15, near the Schönbrunn Palace, in Vienna's fashionable Hietzing suburb. They had been living there about eighteen months when they took in a seven-year-old girl named Patricia Lyne. Patsy was a delicate child, with a thin face and silky brown hair, and to those who met her casually for the first time she seemed nothing more than a little shy; but she was painfully withdrawn, living most of the time in a world of her own. Her mother, Agnes Piel Lyne, had been married for several months to Patsy's father, an engineer from Kansas named Elmer Ward Lyne, when she discovered she was pregnant; she had tried to abort the baby, and had come to blame herself for Patsy's mental problems. For many months she had sought help in the United States, without success; now she hoped to find answers in the heart of the Freudian world. Money was no obstacle. Agnes was the daughter of Michael Piel, who had come to America from Germany in 1883 and with his brother, Gottfried, founded a successful brewery in New York City.

In Vienna, Agnes sought out Anna Freud, who declined to take on Patsy but recommended Editha Sterba, who specialized in treating children and who, along with her husband, Richard, was a member of the Vienna Psychoanalytic Institute. Editha Sterba agreed to work with the child, but there remained the problem of where Patsy would live. However guilty Agnes felt about her daughter's emotional state, she had not wanted her in the first place; having grown up in a patriarchal household where her family had made it clear that she was primarily fit to darn socks for her seven brothers, she was determined to have her independence. For a while, she worked as a stringer in Europe for the Associated Press, and she had some adventures as a free-lance journalist in the Balkans as well.[51] In 1928, she divorced Elmer Lyne, and when she brought Patsy to Vienna three years later she was thirty-four years old, financially secure, and not prepared to sacrifice her ambitions and footloose existence to make a home for her troubled daughter.

In the beginning, Patsy lived in the apartment of Anni Hatschek, who ran the small nursery school with Gina. Gina was drawn to the unhappy child, and Patsy soon grew increasingly attached to the teacher, who, unlike her tall, often abrasive mother, was small, gentle, and soft-spoken. When Patsy became tearfully despondent on Saturdays and Sundays because Gina was not at the school, Gina began bringing the girl home on weekends. "She was an easy, placid child, very charming; I wanted to offer her a loving, civilized home. I'm sure part of it was my need to have a child of my own," Gina said. Editha Sterba encouraged the relationship, regarding Gina's maternal instincts as an important adjunct to the child's treatment; moreover, Gina had trained at the Montessori school in Vienna, made a point of attending courses and lectures on psychoanalysis and, at twenty-five, had already been in therapy with both Sterbas. Eventually, Editha Sterba suggested that Gina take Patsy into her home full time. Bruno supported the idea, in part because he saw how attached his wife had become to the child, but also because the couple welcomed the money Agnes paid Gina for taking care of her.[52]

Gina dressed Patsy in the morning, bathed her at night, and doted on her as if she were her own daughter. She read to her at bedtime, and with this help and patient instruction at school, Patsy slowly began to read and write English, and to speak a few words of German. Gina tried to draw the child out of her emotional redoubt as best she could, playing a flute she made out of bamboo or taking her swimming in the Danube. They rode the tram downtown together, to shop at Meinl's for coffee beans and candy or visit the Prater, with its amusement arcades and *Riesenrad*, the giant Ferris wheel erected just before the turn of the century.

Occasionally, Bruno would join them for an excursion, by train to the nearby resort of Bad Vöslau, or by car for drives in the countryside. Such stimulation seldom moved Patsy out of her passivity; when not in school, she stayed mostly in the amniotic serenity of the Bettelheim apartment, spending long periods drawing or modeling tiny Plasticine figures at the dining-room table. She saw no friends, played no games, and went off to sessions with Editha Sterba three times a week.

This description of Patsy and the account of the Bettelheims' life together in Vienna depend heavily on Gina's recollections. I first met her in 1991, when she was eighty-five years old, and I tried to bring to that encounter the same detachment I did to most other interviews for this book, but it was not to last. She is a handsome woman with an inquiring countenance beneath a cap of white hair, and her vigor and cheerfulness belie the ordeal of open-heart surgery she suffered in the early 1980s. Her garden apartment in San Francisco was a warm haven of books and artifacts attesting to her Vienna past, steeped in Schubert, Mozart, and Beethoven, which she worked at on the baby grand in the corner of her living room with the perseverance of a dedicated amateur who, five years later, at age ninety, was still taking regular lessons. I liked her immensely from the start, and our relationship eventually developed beyond my need for the information she could supply to a friendship resting in part on our shared love of music, which we indulged together at the opera and in the concert hall. The hazard here was all too apparent: I was drawn to the only living person who could provide intimate details of my subject's Vienna years, a crucial window that could easily become distorting if I let it.

Patricia Lyne offered another window, but it was clouded by a strong desire not to remember. Now in her seventies, she lives alone with many cats in a large house in northwestern Connecticut. She rejected my requests to come and talk to her, but for a while did respond to letters I wrote and tried to answer some of the questions I put to her and to describe life at Gloriettegasse 15. She called me "Dear Visitor," and in the handwriting of an earnest fifth-grader eager to get her penmanship right, wrote that "Bruno hated to get going in the morning but Gina felt that no matter how you feel in the morning you should get going, be active." In short, often unrelated sentences that offered few details, she wrote of how she, Bruno, and Gina regularly ate lunch together ("Meal skipping is not approved of in Europe"), of how she had been used to drinking cocoa at breakfast in the United States but had learned from Gina to drink coffee and milk, of the modern furniture in the apartment, of the household's devoted maid, Hedwig, of Gina's love of skiing, hiking and swimming, of Bruno's interest in art and old buildings, of the elevator that took her up to her sessions with Editha Sterba. Often, the letters wandered off the subject, to the Spanish Civil War or how *Cosmopolitan* magazine taught you to conduct yourself.

It was clear from the outset that Patricia Lyne's efforts to help me were gallant but painful. "Please be understanding if I do not want to talk about Bruno Bettelheim," she wrote in her first reply, and later: "I hope you realize dear Visitor that I do not like talking about CHILDHOOD—it has forced me to think about my past which I want to forget." Gina told me that Patsy was very fond of Bruno, who returned the affection, encouraged her artistic bent and sometimes brought her gifts. But the child was Gina's charge from the beginning. "Bruno did not play any role in bringing me up," Patricia Lyne wrote.[53] Like most other Viennese men of the time, he knew little about rearing a child and was fully occupied outside the home. Agnes Lyne supported Patsy by sending money to Gina, but what made it possible for the couple to afford their well-appointed ten-room apartment, a live-in maid, and the comfortable life they led was Bruno's half-interest in Bettelheim & Schnitzer, to which he went six days a week.

He was a devoted, hardworking husband, "a very sweet and obliging person, wanting to give the impression of being helpful whenever possible," recalled Maria Piers, whose mother gave Gina voice lessons.[54] But the lingering trauma of Anton's syphilis was never far from his mind. In his final book, Bettelheim wrote elliptically of his "depressive tendencies," and of the "[p]ersonal experiences" within his family that, combined with the horrors of World War I, made him feel "deeply pessimistic" about life and himself.

Bettelheim wrote that after the war he abandoned escapist

literature for texts that "would suggest how the horrors of the world at large could be rectified. . . ."[55] Among the first publications that impressed him was *Anfang,* which means "beginning" and was the organ of Freie Schulgemeinde, a school-reform movement that held, among other tenets, that teachers and students should participate in the learning process more or less as equals, a heretical notion in the authoritarian precincts of the Austrian *Realschulwesen.* Like most inquiring German-speaking students, Bettelheim read Goethe, Schiller, and the other lodestars of his parents' generation. But however great he found their works, he was looking for new intellectual heroes, and he found them in the likes of Theodor Lessing, F. A. Lange, and Hans Vaihinger and their varying messages in support of the uses of fiction to make life tolerable. Bettelheim wrote that he was also attracted to Vaihinger's argument that pessimism provided moral strength and helped one see the world more objectively—a view that seemed to justify his own dark assessment of life as an outlook he could use constructively.[56] (Bettelheim may also have been drawn to Vaihinger because he, too, suffered from extreme nearsightedness, limiting his ability to be a man of action and moving him toward scholarly endeavors.[57])

Bettelheim's despondency was one reason he entered analysis with Richard Sterba, though just when he first lay down on the couch and for how long is unclear. In one version,[58] he put the year at 1929, saying he had sought therapy because of continued feelings of depression and inferiority as well as a crisis in his marriage. (He did not wed Gina until 1930, though it is possible the crisis was over whether she would finally agree to his proposals.) More likely is another version, in which he said he completed his analysis in 1936,[59] by which time the marriage had developed serious strains. Nowhere in his books did he state precisely what the duration of the analysis was, though at one point he implied that he was in therapy for at least two years[60] and elsewhere wrote that he "underwent several years of intensive analysis."[61] Gina told me that he saw Richard Sterba for no more than a year, in the mid-1930s.

Sterba, who was only five years older than Bettelheim, was in the first generation of trained analysts. He had received his medical degree from the University of Vienna in 1923 and had followed up with three years of postdoctoral studies; he was an accomplished amateur violinist and that rarity in Vienna's psychoanalytic community, a Catholic. Bettelheim said that he sought out Sterba because he himself was friendly with so many young therapists and wanted to find an analyst with whom he was not well acquainted. But Sterba could not have been too much of a stranger: Bettelheim had paid for Gina's sessions with him, Patsy's mother was in treatment with him when in Vienna, and Patsy herself was seeing Richard's wife, Editha. Bettelheim wrote that in the beginning, like most new analysands, he fenced with Sterba, trying to get him to say whether psychoanalysis would help reduce his anxieties. Sterba would only say that time would tell.[62]

The patient did not reveal in any detail what took place in his sessions, but he did invite us into the waiting room, where another of his oft-told scenarios unfolded. Both Sterbas, like most of their colleagues, used the living room of their home as a waiting room for their patients, and Bettelheim wrote that he occasionally encountered a withdrawn and frightened child waiting to see Editha. Small, potted cacti rested on the windowsill, and Johnny, as Bettelheim called the boy, "had the disconcerting habit of plucking one of the leaves full of sharp thorns, putting it into his mouth, and chewing it." Bettelheim said that once in a while he saw Johnny's lips bleed from the prickly spines, and that watching him wound himself was upsetting. Finally, after many months of witnessing this self-mutilation, Bettelheim could restrain himself no longer and, against his better judgment, expressed his dismay that after all this time Johnny was still chewing the cactus leaves. "In response," Bettelheim wrote,

> this scrawny little boy suddenly seemed to grow in stature—I still do not know how he managed to give me the impression that at this moment he was looking down on me—and said with utter disdain: "What are two years compared with eternity?" It was the first time he had uttered a full sentence, and it left me flabbergasted.

Bettelheim wrote that he later learned that the origin of Johnny's misery had been "extreme traumatization" at an early age, a shock of some kind to his "oral cavity." [63] Bettelheim did not explain how he found out what normally would be privileged information about a patient. Jacquelyn Seevak Sanders, who worked with Bettelheim at the Orthogenic School for thirteen years, heard variations of this scenario several times; like other Bettelheim colleagues, she likened such stories to fairy tales, "more important for their message than their reality." Bettelheim spun the tale of Johnny so convincingly that only after hearing it one last time, not long before Bettelheim died, did Sanders stop to wonder why Editha Sterba, who must also have seen the boy's mouth bleed over those many months, did not remove the cactus plants on the days of his sessions. "Anyone at the Orthogenic School would have been accused by Bettelheim of child abuse had they not done so immediately," Sanders said. "But as I listened to him elaborate on the many lessons that could be learned from this incident, I remembered that Bruno's ability to mesmerize with example and style was so profound that one tended to become caught up in the power of the point he was making." [64]

Bettelheim said that Johnny's seven words constituted an epiphany, some of which hit him immediately, some of which came over time. He said that as soon as he lay down on Sterba's couch he realized that the question he had put to Johnny did not really reflect concern about the boy's bloody mouth but flowed from doubts he had about the efficacy of his own analysis. "[I]n a flash Johnny had taught me how inclined we are to believe that the wellspring of our action is concern for the other rather than self-involvement." Bettelheim said his reading of the psychoanalytic literature had taught him that one could learn about oneself through the behavior of others; Johnny's stern admonition had made this abstract concept real, and confirmed for him "that only through one's personal experience can one fully understand what psychoanalytic theory is really all about." He said that this understanding became central to his work with disturbed children when he came to the United States. He had viewed Johnny's cactus-chewing as a sign of craziness, but later experience taught him to be ashamed of his "readiness to see such things as strange or even nonsensical when in truth they conveyed deep meaning." [65]

The *Übermensch* who provided the key to such meaning was

Sigmund Freud, who Bettelheim said was at first nothing more than the frustrating obstacle to his earliest love. In a scenario he told many times, he described how he and his compatriots in the Jung Wandervogel, a youth movement with a socialist and pacifist tinge, would go on Sunday outings to the Vienna Woods.[66] On one of these excursions, thirteen-year-old Bruno was pursuing his first girlfriend, only to be upstaged by Otto Fenichel, who was six years older and then attending Freud's talks at the University of Vienna, which would become *A General Introduction to Psychoanalysis*. Fenichel's enthusiastic account of the arcane new world of dreams and their sexual connotations fascinated the girl but mostly angered Bruno, who saw his quarry gravitating toward this intellectual interloper, not only an older man but a medical student who wore the uniform of the Austrian army, from which he was on leave. Bruno wrote that his fury at psychoanalysis was so great that Sunday night that he could not sleep, but by morning he had decided on a strategy to win back the girl: he would learn as much as he could about this man Freud and the following Sunday impress her with his own knowledge of psychoanalysis. On Monday, after school, he went to Deuticke, the bookstore in Vienna that carried works about psychoanalysis, bought as many of them as he could afford, and began to read. "The more I did," he wrote years later,

> the more surprised I became. . . . I soon realized that my Victorian family, although personally acquainted with members of the Freud family, would be utterly shocked to find me perusing such obscene literature. My solution was to hide it from them by taking it to school and reading it there surreptitiously while I was supposed to be attending to studies which, by comparison, were utterly boring.[67]

Bruno was now armed for his next encounter with the girl, but when he began dispensing his newfound wisdom she was no longer interested in the topic. One Sunday of Freudian instruction had been quite enough.

Gina, who met her husband-to-be a few years after this tale of the Vienna Woods, told me she did not recall his ever telling her this account of how he discovered psychoanalysis. Bettelheim said that his romance with the girl soon died but they remained good lifelong friends, though he did not name her in his published renditions of the story.[68] We do have Otto Fenichel's identity as the catalyst that sent Bruno running to Deuticke; but after coming to this country in 1938 and practicing as a psychoanalyst in California, he died in 1946. He was, in fact, a leader of the Jung Wandervogel during the years of World War I, so Bettelheim's account may have spun out of a certain reality. But the yarn has the creativity of others that he told, especially the aside about his parents' acquaintance with members of the Freud family, a claim for which there is no supporting evidence and that Gina said is not true. Yet, however Bettelheim's exposure to Freud came about, it did make him a convert; beginning at age fourteen, he said, he read all that Freud had written and was "hooked for life."[69]

CHAPTER TWO
The Anschluss

D ESPITE THE IMPACT of the worldwide depression, which had pushed Austria to the financial brink in 1931, the Bettelheims led the life of a typical upper-middle-class Viennese couple. They immersed themselves in the rich culture that burgeoned along the Ringstrasse: performances of *Reigen* at the Burgtheater, of *Die Zauberflöte* at the Staatsoper, of *Don Juan* at the Musikverein. Both Bruno and Gina loved art and regularly attended new gallery shows and exhibits at the vast Kunthistorisches Museum or at the Secession Pavilion, Joseph Maria Olbrich's lavishly oriental, domed shrine to Schiele, Klimt, and the movement's other breakaway modernists. Occasionally, on a weekend evening, the couple invited friends in, and Hedwig would set out an informal but elegant supper, concluding with the desserts that Bruno so loved, especially the golden, foamy baked egg soufflé called *Salzburger Nockerl*. When not socializing at home, they gathered at the Herrenhof and other coffeehouses, often with Hans Willig and Walter Neurath, Bruno's classmates from the *Realschule,* and Fritz Redl, the friend from his aborted university days.

Yet, despite this comfortable and cultured existence, Bettelheim felt doubly the outsider: he was a Jew—an ugly one, in his view—who daily had to face the sneer of Austria's Catholic majority, and also a merchant with no standing in the remarkable Jewish intellectual elite that managed to thrive in Vienna's oppressive anti-Semitism and that gave the city so much of its luster during the years when Bruno came of age.

He sat at the Herrenhof and read the *Neue Freie Presse,* but he was not a *Kaffeehausliterat,* did not travel with the influential Jewish writers of that liberal publication or with the literary crowd that gathered around Karl Kraus's satirical journal, *Die Fackel*. He sat in concert and theater audiences, but that is as close as he came to the realms of Robert Musil or Max Reinhardt, Arnold Schönberg or Richard Strauss. Most of the time he could only peer through the glass at the heady world of Sigmund Freud and his disciples—a world in which Gina participated far more than he did. He especially envied Fritz Redl, only a year his senior, who had gotten his degree in 1925, the year before Anton Bettelheim's death thrust the lumber business onto his reluctant son. Redl's training analyst was Richard Sterba at the Vienna Psychoanalytic Institute; Anna Freud supervised him in psychoanalytic counseling. Bruno's cousin, Edith Buxbaum, also only a year older, was making her way as well, a graduate of the university in training to be an analyst, and active in socialist politics. But without a diploma, even a routine career in law or medicine was out of Bettelheim's reach, at a time when both professions remained open to a man of his intelligence. As late as 1936, 62 percent of the lawyers and 47 percent of the doctors in Vienna were Jewish.[1]

Adolf Hitler was seventeen when he first arrived in Vienna in 1907, while Bruno was just beginning to play beneath the dining-room table. The would-be artist from Linz was full of optimism about what moving to the pulsing imperial city would mean for his future, but his drawing was found wanting and his efforts to become a student at the Vienna Academy of Fine Arts were twice rejected. In *Mein Kampf,* he wrote that the next years were the saddest of his life. He lived only a short tram ride away from the Bettelheim family's apartment at Neubaugasse 66, first in a furnished room in the Simon Denk Gasse, near the Franz Josefs Bahnhof, then in a series of flophouses or the run-down men's hostel at Meldemannstrasse 27, a few blocks from the Danube. Between meals at soup kitchens, he roamed the city in a shabby black overcoat draped to his ankles, working occasionally as a construction laborer or picking up odd jobs shoveling snow, beating carpets, or hauling luggage at the Westbahnhof.[2] The frustrated artist immersed himself in the anti-Semitic literature widely available in Vienna, tracts that kindled his belief in a great Aryan master race. In 1913, the year before Bruno entered the *Realschule,* the "bookish vagrant"[3] left inhospitable Vienna for Germany; two decades later, on January 28, 1933, Nazi storm troopers jack-booted through Berlin shouting "Sieg Heil!" as Hitler declared himself chancellor of what he promised would be a thousand-year Reich.

That Austria would be part of it, Hitler had no doubt. It was just a matter of when, and in March 1933, the Austrians obliged him by starting down the road to fascism on their own. The country had struggled with the idea of democratic government since the war's end in 1918, with no party ever gaining the upper hand for long. The workers gave the Social Democrats a solid majority in "Red Vienna," where about a third of the Austrian people lived; the Christian Socialists ruled among the Catholic peasants and conservative classes in the provinces. The Pan-German Nationalists drew some supporters from both of these camps, and many more from the urban middle class. All these parties made democratic noises from time to time, but they never abandoned preparations for the possibility of civil war. The Social Democrats' Schutzbund (Defense League) and the Christian So-cialists' Heimwehren (Home Defense Forces) collided regularly throughout the 1920s, and by the early 1930s, with the economy in tatters from the failure of the Creditanstalt, Austria's most im-portant bank, and Nazism on the rise in Germany, both the Aus-trian Nationalists and the Social Democrats saw a chance to take control of the parliament by demanding a general election. Both failed, but only by one vote, which is all the majority that Engel-bert Dollfuss could muster when he formed a Christian Socialist government in May 1932. Ten months later, the thirty-nine-year-old federal chancellor, known as "Millimetternich" for his fierce political ambition and diminutive stature, solved this awkward problem by suspending parliament and initiating rule by decree. The First Republic had lasted fifteen years.

For Bruno Bettelheim and the rest of Vienna's Jews, the slide toward catastrophe had begun. Though Dollfuss opposed annexation with Germany and had no sympathy for the Austrian Nazis, they soon began to thrive in the totalitarian atmosphere he created. "[T]hey released tear gas in department stores to frighten off shoppers, smeared housewalls with pro-Hitler graffiti, set off firecrackers and petards in many places to cause panic, and eventually started outright bombings."[4] In October 1933, Dollfuss was grazed by a single shot fired by a Czech Nazi named Drtil. Four months later, civil war erupted when "[m]ilitant groups of the social democrats rank and file, long impatient with the cautious attitude of their party's leadership, started fighting on their own." Dollfuss had dissolved the left-wing militias, but some twenty thousand underground members rallied to the cause around the country. Ultimately, almost a thousand people died in the outbreak, many of them around the Karl Marx Hof, the massive red brick complex of some sixteen hundred apartments opened in 1930 by the Social Democratic city government for working-class families. Holed up in these fortresslike superblocks, less than five miles from the leafy quiet of Gina and Bruno's suburban neighborhood, defenders held out for four days before Dollfuss's forces, using artillery, overcame their resistance. "The power of Red Vienna . . . was broken," and the new mayor of the capital, a Christian Socialist politician named Richard Schmitz, took over the Social Democratic institutions that had provided a considerable measure of democracy. "Instead of taking on the illegal Nazi networks, Austro-Fascism had crushed the sole force that might have offered serious resistance to Hitler."[5]

On July 25, 1934, a force of 154 Nazis overwhelmed government headquarters in the Ballhausplatz and shot Dollfuss in the neck and shoulder. He was placed on a couch in his office, where he bled to death, his murderers refusing him either a doctor or a priest. News of the assassination exhilarated Hitler, who received it in Bayreuth, where he was attending a performance of *Das Rheingold* at the annual Wagner festival.[6]

In his books and other writing, Bettelheim did not relate in any detail how he and his family, or his friends, reacted to these developments, how they coped on a daily basis with the politics of thuggery and gunfire that had begun to subvert the once serene world of cafés and culture they inhabited. Gina told me that her husband toyed with the idea of leaving, and at one point urged her to ask her father's wealthy brother, Moritz Altstadt, to give them the money to emigrate to the United States. On one of their Sunday visits to his villa outside Vienna, she did so; but Uncle

Moritz turned her down. It is not clear, however, that they would have packed up even if he had provided the cash. Bruno did not need anyone else's money to leave Austria; he had more than sufficient funds to get himself and Gina across the Atlantic had they really wanted to go. Bettelheim & Schnitzer continued to provide a good income, and, despite the looming political crisis, in early 1937 the partners began to expand, turning out finished products like paneling and furniture as well as the raw lumber that they had sold for years.[7] Like hundreds of thousands of European Jews who contemplated leaving their threatened homelands, Bettelheim hesitated: because Austria and Vienna were what he knew, because German was his language and his culture, because Gloriettegasse 15 seemed a safe haven at the end of the day, and, most of all, because not even the most pessimistic of souls could imagine what was to come.

Some Austrian Jews, of course, did sense it was time to leave, among them Edith Buxbaum, who fled to New York City in 1937, after the police began threatening her with jail for her left-wing political beliefs. The year before, Fritz Redl, though not Jewish, also had emigrated to the United States. Not everyone had the connections—or, like the writer Stefan Zweig, the fame—to persuade reluctant governments around the world to grant them visas. But, though Bruno Bettelheim was by no means famous, he did have a connection, a far better one than most Jews in Vienna had.

In the summer of 1936, Gina had taken Patsy to the United States for two and a half months. She spent six weeks as a counselor at the camp on Cape Cod that the child attended; the rest of the time she stayed with the Piel family in Connecticut or toured New England with Agnes and Patsy, stopping at elegant inns. Agnes had urged her not to return to Vienna, but she had; now, as the situation in Austria worsened, Agnes began pleading with her to come back to America for good. Her plan was simple, the kind a willful and wealthy woman could afford to hatch: the Piel family, with its thriving beer business, had more than enough resources to provide a sanctuary for the Bettelheims; Gina and Bruno should bring Patsy home, and Agnes would take care of them all. Bruno could pursue his dream of becoming a teacher, and Gina would become the child's permanent caretaker. Despite the political temblors shaking Austria, the Bettelheims rejected the proposal. Gina had already watched over Patsy for six years and had no intention of doing so indefinitely, however much she loved her. She also feared Agnes had ulterior motives; on her summer visit in 1936, she had detected in her hostess what she regarded as lesbian tendencies toward her. For Bruno, there remained his responsibilities as son and brother, and to the lumber business. He also had begun an affair with a young woman named Gertrude Weinfeld.

She, too, was a regular visitor to the Sterbas' waiting room in the mid-1930s. In 1914, when Trude was three years old, her father, an officer in the Austrian army, abruptly left home for five years, four of which he spent as a prisoner of war in Siberia. At about the same time, she was made to watch her brother's circumcision in the family dining room. For a long time thereafter, Trude would wake up screaming because of terrifying nightmares that no amount of comforting could banish. She had sought out Editha Sterba to try and confront these childhood traumas, which she felt were at least partly responsible for her shyness and re-pressed sexuality. She had been encouraged to seek therapy by her close friend Emarina Vischer, the daughter of a Swiss minister who had just married Editha Sterba's brother, Hubert.

Both Trude and Emarina were in their mid-twenties and taught at a three-room school operated on the Montessori princi-ples, which were then being established throughout Europe. Weinfeld had already taken courses in social work for two years, but most jobs were closed to her because she was Jewish; when the opportunity opened at the Montessori school in the mid-1930s, she seized it with enthusiasm. The work was hard but rewarding and exciting, and involved much interaction with the Vienna world of psychoanalysis, including a course on teaching led by Anna Freud herself. Trude and Emarina also made a trip to Rome, where they met Maria Montessori and visited her original school. Soon Trude was teaching both first and second grades, finding great joy in the Montessori method of treating children as individuals by drawing on their creativity. Many of her pupils were the sons and daughters of Americans, and most of them were emotionally stable; but one was Patsy.[8]

Trude Weinfeld met Bruno Bettelheim in the mid-1930s, when he and Gina gave a birthday party for their troubled ward. By now, the Bettelheims' marriage had begun to fray, in part because of the strain in their sexual relationship, which Gina said, without casting blame, was never comfortable; they were sleeping in separate bedrooms. Though she felt a growing desire to have a child of her own, both she and Bruno resisted this because of their shaky partnership.

Gina had already had a brief affair with a married doctor and had now fallen in love with another married man, a research associate in the dental department of the University of Vienna named Joseph Weinmann. An oral pathologist whose friends all called him by his middle name, Peter, Weinmann had pursued the kind of serious academic life Bruno had so often envied from behind his desk at the lumber yard; he was *Dr.* Weinmann, a modest, dedicated scientist whose reputation was such that he had been called in to help treat Sigmund Freud's cancer of the jaw and palate. He was also Patsy's dentist, which is how he and Gina met, and before long he and his wife, Bertl, were exchanging social visits with the Bettelheims. Gina's strong attraction to this handsome, pipe-smoking professional man, who was more than six years older than her husband and in so many ways his opposite, created an emotional vacuum for Bruno that Trude Weinfeld began to fill.[9]

Bruno started to ask Trude out occasionally when Gina was otherwise occupied, to take walks in the Schönbrunn Palace gardens or visit the arcades at the Prater, sometimes with Patsy in tow. Gradually, they grew more daring and went off alone into the Vienna Woods, where Bruno sometimes let Trude practice driving his gray Fiat. When Trude had a break from her duties at the Montessori school, she would rush across the Grünentorgasse to a small store that had a telephone and call Bruno—always at the office, so as not to arouse Gina's suspicions. Still, she continued to visit the Bettelheim apartment, on one occasion to help Gina make up Patsy and other children for the pre-Lenten *Fasching* festivities. When it became quite late, Gina invited her to spend the night in a small bedroom. "I couldn't sleep," Trude recalled, "and I began to realize that I was in love with Bruno." While Gina was away in the United States during the summer of 1936, Bruno and Trude spent more and more time together, their affair "fraught with guilt, exciting as it was forbidden." [10]

Though neither the Bettelheims nor the Weinmanns had children of their own, in the beginning neither couple seriously considered divorce, a rare solution to marital dissonance at the time. With both romances agitating beneath the surface, domestic life went on much as usual at Gloriettegasse 15, which had the appearance of a warm, loving home, one filled with the comfortable modern furniture that Bruno bought or had made by his workmen at the lumber yard. Both he and Gina had sensitive eyes for art, and even before they were married had purchased a Käthe Kollwitz lithograph of a working woman wearing a black shawl. To this Bruno added, among other paintings and objects, a 1914 Egon Schiele called *Vorstadt I,* a painting of dark suburban houses on a white field that had been exhibited at the Hagenbund/Neue Galerie in Vienna in 1928. "He did everything so I would love it," Gina told me, recalling that Bruno always made a point of giving her two presents at Christmas because her birthday fell on Christmas Eve. He continued to earn a good living in the lumber business, going off each morning to Bettelheim & Schnitzer, returning at noon for the main meal of the day, then taking the tram or driving back to the office at Gaudenzdorfergürtel 3a, near the Matzleinsdorf freight station. Gina ran the nursery school with Anni Hatschek and hovered over Patsy at home, and also took in, on separate occasions, a Canadian woman in her mid-twenties whom Gina described as neurotic, and an older, wealthy Chinese woman who she said was seriously depressed. Both were patients of Richard Sterba, who asked Gina to house them for short periods and to provide supportive counseling. Often Bruno, Gina, Patsy, and one of these singular guests took the evening meal together, a quartet of disparate psyches served by Hedwig.

IN 1936, Bettelheim resumed his studies at the University of Vienna, prodded by Trude, who sensed how important a degree would be for him if events did force him to emigrate. He had been deep in the study of the humanities in general and art history in particular when his father's death had forced him to quit ten

years before. His great passion was Italian art, a world opened up
to him, he would write, by an early reading of Jacob Burckhardt's
1860 masterpiece, *The Civilization of the Renaissance in Italy*. He
said that in the summer of 1922, following his first year at the
university, he had traveled to Italy, primarily because of the Swiss
historian's writings. "His *Der Cicerone*," Bettelheim wrote of
Burckhardt's comprehensive guide to Italian art, "was my vademe-
cum; it is not exaggeration to say that for more than a decade it
became my bible. I tried to make every year at least one and
sometimes two prolonged trips to Italy, the *Cicerone* at all times in
my hand. It was this experience that helped me to switch my
major from German language and literature to art history, and
finally to aesthetics, in which I took my degree." [11]

Bettelheim managed to take nine courses while continuing
to comanage the lumber business with Hanns Schnitzer. He also
began work on his dissertation, "Das Problem des Naturschönen
und die moderne Ästhetik" ("The Problem of Nature's Beauty
and the Modern Aesthetic"). [12] In it, he wrote five decades later,
he "tried to integrate a psychoanalytically informed approach to
the psychology of art with a philosophical understanding of beauty
(based mostly on Kant) and with the history of art." [13] The dissertation does take the Kantian view that it is the mark of a good
soul to take an unmediated interest in the beauty of nature, but the
claim that the work was psychoanalytically informed is overstated.
Essentially, Bettelheim argued that the aesthetics of nature were
not sufficiently appreciated compared with the aesthetics of art.
This was so for both historical and systematic reasons: historical
because the history of art is older than aesthetics and therefore
what is really an art-historical evaluation gets confused with an
aesthetic one; systematic because a work of art is much easier to
grasp conceptually than a natural landscape.

Bettelheim saw the aesthetic experience as a correlative
relationship between the "I" and the "thing," with the latter representing the outer world. Here he used the German word *aufgeho-
ben*, a Hegelian term notoriously difficult to translate. It combines
two meanings: to postpone, or keep for later, and to lift up, or
make nonexistent for the moment. When one is experiencing
such a relationship with nature, Bettelheim wrote, thinking and

will are switched off in the aesthetic experience, the significance of one's own personality is erased, and there is no division between the inner and the outer world. In order for such a melting together to happen, the aesthetic object must represent the existential world —a real view of a landscape rather than a framed rendering, which puts it one step removed. Bettelheim maintained that the aesthetic experience of nature makes greater demands on the psyche than does a work of art, because the viewer experiences the object— the Vienna Woods or a bend in the Danube—without the mediation of the artist. In his conclusion, he wrote that people who do intellectually demanding work seek out the aesthetic experience of nature because they need it for the harmony of their psyches. Only in nature, he said, are we freed from the requirement to think. In literature we must think about the words, in the fine arts about what is represented. Music comes closest to nature, in requiring only an emotional response. In an aesthetic experience of nature, we feel the world rather than think it.

Bettelheim's thesis examiners were Robert Reininger, a Kant scholar, and Karl Bühler, by then a well-known psychologist who, with his wife, Charlotte, ran a psychological institute in Vienna. Bettelheim told his son that the two examiners made him rewrite his dissertation several times, urging him to sharpen the focus by shortening each version. He regarded their instructions as one of his most important writing lessons, and although his future manuscripts would often prove repetitive and overwritten, the dissertation experience helped make him eager for good editing all his life.[14] The thesis ran 145 double-spaced typewritten pages; Reininger graded it very good, Bühler found it excellent. On May 31, 1937, the university approved the work, and on February 2 of the following year awarded Bettelheim a degree in philosophy, which signified his general study of the humanities.[15]

Bettelheim's academic record shows that he took three courses in general psychology, two just before his father's death forced him to leave the university in 1926 and one in the winter of 1936–37.[16] All were taught by Karl Bühler, who in 1918 had published *Die geistige Entwicklung des Kindes (The Mental Development of the Child)*, the first systematic treatment of the developmental psychology of the child, and who, together with his wife, was at the center of child study in Austria. Fritz Redl also studied with Bühler at the university. Bettelheim would eventually say that, like his friend, he had been in training analysis with Richard Sterba. He made it clear that these sessions were interrupted by the *Anschluss,* but in a tale he told many times about applying as a candidate for the Vienna Psychoanalytic Institute he said he had had the stamp of approval of the Master himself. He said he was interviewed by three people: Paul Federn, the psychoanalyst and member of Freud's inner circle; Anna Freud; and a person he could no longer remember. Bettelheim told one enthralled audience that, when he was interviewed by Anna Freud,

> it happened that her father entered the room in which we were talking. She introduced me to him and he was very gracious and said a few words, which was a lot because he already had cancer of the jaw, which made speaking very difficult and very painful. At the end he asked me what my background was, in which field I had taken my Ph.D. And I told him that I had come originally from the study of literature, then to the study of art history and philosophy, and I finally had taken my doctor's degree in esthetics. To which Sigmund Freud said: This is exactly the person we need for psychoanalysis to grow and develop. We need people with a broad humanistic background much more than we need people with a medical background.[17]

In another version of this encounter, Bettelheim said that, when Anna introduced him to her father, Sigmund declared: "[A] Bettelheim does not need any introduction to me." He explained that Freud, "as a student, frequently came to the house of my grandfather, and he became friendly with an uncle of mine who shared military service with him."[18] If this meeting did take place, Bettelheim never reported the happy anointment to Gina. Nor do records at the Vienna Psychoanalytic Institute offer any evidence that Bettelheim was ever in training analysis with Richard Sterba or anyone else, or that he was a candidate for the society, even briefly.

•

On February 11, nine days after Bettelheim received his diploma from the University of Vienna, Dr. Kurt von Schuschnigg left the capital by special train for a secret meeting with Adolf Hitler. Schuschnigg, a Jesuit intellectual, had presided over Austria's clerical-fascist state since becoming chancellor after Dollfuss's assassination in the summer of 1934. Now he had been summoned by the super-fascist to his "Eagle's Nest" in the Bavarian mountains at Berchtesgaden. The next day, between luncheon boasts about the huge skyscrapers he planned to build in the Third Reich and strolls past the picture window that looked down into Austria, the Führer advised Schuschnigg that he was on "a historic mission" to unite the German people and that nothing would stand in his way. By afternoon, Schuschnigg had in his hands a two-page typewritten set of demands that Hitler said must be signed on the spot if the Austrian leader wanted to avoid an invasion by the German army. In effect, he had been told to hand over his government to the Nazis within a week. After some inconsequential modifications, Schuschnigg signed and retreated down the mountain.[19]

Within four days, Schuschnigg lifted the ban on the Nazi Party, whose hooligans had been seething just beneath the surface of Austrian political life for months, and granted a general amnesty to the party's jailed members, including those who had murdered Dollfuss. At Hitler's insistence, Schuschnigg named the pro-Nazi Viennese lawyer Artur von Seyss-Inquart minister of the interior, with control over security and the police. On February 20, the ecstatic Führer addressed the Reichstag in Berlin and made it plain that the future of Austria's seven million citizens (as well as three million Sudeten Germans in Czechoslovakia) was now in his hands. The fiery speech was broadcast throughout Austria and set off Nazi demonstrations from Vienna to the Tirol. "In the Alpine provinces," wrote Paul Hofmann,

> Nazis took over the schools, many government offices, and the army and police barracks. Swastika banners were seen everywhere, and jubilant crowds were parading. In Vienna, hundreds and then thousands surged into the streets, shouting "Heil Hitler!" and "One People, one Reich, one Führer!" The police no longer interfered.[20]

The hapless Schuschnigg tried to answer the Führer in a speech of his own to the Austrian Bundestag on February 24. In impassioned words, he told the cheering deputies that the country was determined to remain independent. Summoning the colors of the Austrian flag, he concluded, "Until death, red–white–red!" This speech, too, was broadcast to the Austrian people. In Graz, ninety miles south of Vienna, a mob of some twenty thousand Nazis took over the town square, tore down the loudspeakers and the Austrian flag, and ran up the swastika. Schuschnigg, now desperate, contacted the underground leaders of the outlawed Social Democrats, whose workers his Christian Socialists had been shooting at for years. He promised to legalize the party again; it promised to join him in opposing the Nazis.

On March 9, Schuschnigg astonished almost everyone by announcing a plebiscite for the following Sunday, March 13, in which Austrians—or at least those allowed to vote in a country that had permitted no free elections for five years—would decide *Ja oder Nein* on independence. William L. Shirer was an American radio correspondent based in Vienna at this tense moment. "I emerged from the subway to the Karlsplatz," he wrote in his diary for March 11–12:

> . . . Before I knew it I was being swept along in a shouting, hysterical Nazi mob. . . . The faces! I had seen these before at Nuremberg—the fanatical eyes, the gaping mouths. . . . What had happened? I was still in the dark. I shouted my question into the ears of three or four jammed against me. No response. Couldn't hear. Finally, a middle-aged woman seemed to get me. "The plebiscite!" she yelled. "Called off!" [21]

An enraged Hitler had ordered the referendum canceled; when Schuschnigg acquiesced, his tormentor then demanded that the beleaguered chancellor leave office, which he promptly did on March 13, ending his resignation broadcast, "God save Austria." Within four hours, German troops invaded the country at Salzburg, Kufstein, and Mittenwald, and the "Horst Wessel" song rang over the airwaves from Vienna for the first time. The next day, Hitler made his triumphal entry into the city. "I'll never forget the noise of those boots on the street," recalled Trude Weinfeld.[22] The largest crowd in the city's history, estimated at upward of half a million people, crushed into the Heldenplatz, the vast Hero's Square, in front of the Hofburg; Hitler addressed his frenzied adherents from the balcony of the former imperial residence, declaring: "As Führer and Chancellor of the German nation I report now, before history, the entry of my native land into the German Reich."[23]

Over the weekend, "an orgy of sadism" began in Vienna that Shirer said was worse than anything he had witnessed in Germany itself up to that point. The Luftwaffe sent low-flying aircraft over the city to terrorize the population while Nazi bully boys in swastika armbands roamed the streets, assaulting Jews and forcing them to scrub the gutters on their knees, sometimes with toothbrushes. The police began arresting hundreds of monarchists, socialists, labor leaders, and others, among them the banker Baron Louis de Rothschild and Otto Loewi, who two years before had been a corecipient of the Nobel Prize for Medicine. Many found themselves incarcerated in the vast Hotel Metropol, which overnight had become Gestapo headquarters, with many rooms converted into holding cells. Throughout the city, the new rulers began a systematic plunder of Jewish businesses and homes.

Suicides, always high in Austria, rose dramatically. On March 16, Emil Fey, vice-chancellor under Dollfuss and a prominent leader of the Heimwehr, shot his wife, his son, and himself in their Vienna apartment. "Let's go to another place," Edward R. Murrow said to his radio colleague Shirer after they entered a quiet bar off the Kärntnerstrasse. Perplexed, Shirer asked why. "I was here last night about this time," Murrow said. "A Jewish-looking fellow was standing at that bar. After a while he took an old-fashioned razor from his pocket and slashed his throat."[24] One journal reported that, in the first year of Nazi rule, 3,741 Austrian Jews killed themselves.[25] Almost all were Viennese, among them Trude Weinfeld's aunt.

Though Bruno Bettelheim would write thousands of words on the Holocaust, his books and articles tell us virtually nothing about how he reacted to the *Anschluss,* or to the events leading up to and following that cataclysmic weekend. He did, however, talk about his behavior and describe it in letters. At the Orthogenic School, he told stories of his activities in the Austrian underground, of how he sometimes hid out at night while working with the resistance. "He was very down on the interest certain boys had in toy guns," recalled Ronald Angres, a resident of the school in the 1960s. "He would talk about how guns foster violence and then say, 'Even when I was in the underground, I never carried a gun, because I feared I might be tempted to use it.' " Bettelheim told the author James T. Farrell, with whom he corresponded on and off throughout much of his life in the United States, that he stood watch at a Vienna gas works that he and his socialist compatriots expected the fascists to blow up. He wrote that the attack never materialized and that the sentinels finally abandoned their post after burying their weapons. He then walked ten miles home.[26]

Bettelheim told an interviewer that his primary role in the underground was to supply money and false papers to Austrians seeking to escape the Nazis.[27] Later, he would tell a colleague that he had been "an officer in the underground army" and that he had remained in Austria long enough "to demobilize his men" before escaping to Czechoslovakia, where he was detained until the Nazis arrested him.[28]

In recounting such stories, Bettelheim was sometimes explicitly critical of Jews who had not joined the resistance, telling his young charges at the school that more Jews should have acted as he had and drawing a parallel between himself and the hero of Alexander Solzhenitsyn's autobiographical novel, *A Day in the Life of Ivan Denisovich.*

In 1945, in a sworn affidavit solicited for use in the Nuremberg war-crimes trials, Bettelheim told yet another story of his attempted escape. "[O]n or about March 12, 1938," he said, "it became apparent to me that I would not be permitted to live in peace in Austria. Therefore, I resolved to leave the country. My wife and I left Vienna on about 12 or 13 of March and were stopped at the Czechoslovakian-Hungarian border that night." He implied that they were seeking to flee by car, for he said that the next day they tried to leave Vienna by train. He said that this time Gina Bettelheim was permitted to proceed but that he was detained by the police, who confiscated his passport. Bettelheim did not say where he and Gina hoped to go if they had gotten across the border by car, or where his wife did go when officials allowed her to board the train. Nor did he mention Patsy.[29]

Records at the archive of the Austrian resistance provide no evidence that Bettelheim played any role in the underground, and Gina told me that he did not. "Bruno was not interested in politics," she said. "Of course we were upset by the advent of Dollfuss in 1933 and the rise of Nazism thereafter, but we were not active politically." She said that even when her husband talked of emigrating to the United States it was less because of Hitler's shadow than because he was frustrated in the lumber business and yearned more than ever for an academic career, which might be available to him in America, especially if he managed to get a university degree. As for their actions on that mid-March weekend when the unleashed Austrian Nazis rampaged through Vienna's streets, Gina gave the following version of events:

That Sunday evening, Peter and Bertl Weinmann came to dine at the Bettelheim apartment. Afterward, Gina and Bruno drove them home and en route saw hundreds of their Gentile countrymen in the streets, rejoicing over Austria's inclusion in the Third Reich. The Weinmanns had been prepared to leave for England if Hitler came, and now they decided to go. "Bruno said to me: 'You have to leave with Patsy; I can manage more easily by myself. You go with Peter and Bertl.' " Gina had already told Patsy's mother that if the Nazi threat reached a crisis point she would leave everything and bring the child to the United States; on Monday morning, Gina again spoke by phone with Agnes. As she had been urging for months, Patsy's mother said yes, of course Gina should come, and as soon as possible; Bruno should come, too, and neither of them should even think about ever going back.

Ordinarily, Gina would have had as much trouble getting away as the thousands of other Jews who were now clamoring for visas of escape, but three weeks before the *Anschluss,* Agnes had managed to gain the attention of Cordell Hull, the U.S. secretary of state, on behalf of her daughter and Gina. In a letter to the American consul in Vienna, a copy of which went to Hull, she wrote:

[I]n view of current political developments in Austria, Mrs. Bettelheim, who is Jewish, may have need of your help in bringing my child to a place of safety.

I am particularly concerned, lest, in case of any emergency, my daughter should be separated from Mrs. Bettelheim, who has been virtually a mother to her and on whom she has a child's emotional dependence.

The need for Mrs. Bettelheim's continued nearness to and care of my child is, however, even more pressing than the above statement implies. Six years ago, upon the advice of a Viennese psychiatrist, to whom I had brought my child for treatment when specialists in this country had said that her condition was hopeless, I put her in the care of Mrs. Bettelheim. During these six years my child's condition has steadily improved until now it seems that she may grow up to live a normal life. A prime factor in this improvement has been the work of Mrs. Bettelheim who is a trained worker with problem children. I have been warned by two psychiatrists that any emotional shock such as would result from her sudden separation from Mrs. Bettelheim might well undo the work of the past six years and make her a permanent mental invalid.[30]

On March 12, the consulate granted Gina a six-month visitor's visa.[31] Her plan was to take Patsy first to Paris, along with the Weinmanns. Her marriage was broken, she was traveling with her lover and his wife, but all that seemed secondary as she said goodbye to Bruno, whom she had known for seventeen years, eight of them as his wife, and who, whatever the strains in their relationship, always had treated her with generosity and kindness. As they parted at the Westbahnhof, where the ragged Adolf Hitler had once made a few coins lugging suitcases, both feared that they never would see one another again.

"The train left at midnight," Patricia Lyne recalled, "and I tried to sleep by sitting up and hiding behind a coat."[32] The next day, as they rolled toward France, young Nazi inspectors came through the carriages checking passports, papers, and the amounts of money passengers had taken with them. Gina, fearful that they would discover she was taking more out of Austria than regulations permitted, went to the lavatory and flushed away most of the cash she was carrying. She and Patsy did not share a compartment with the Weinmanns, and when Gina went in search of them in the morning they were not on the train. One of Peter's dental assistants, a Nazi sympathizer, had reported him, and he and his wife had been detained in Vienna. But they managed to board a later train and arrived in Paris only a few hours after Gina and Patsy. All of them stayed with Emarina Vischer, who, with her husband, Hubert Radanowicz-Harttmann, was now living in Paris and providing temporary quarters for an increasing stream of refugee friends and friends of friends. On March 17, Gina and Patsy sailed from Le Havre on the S.S. *President Roosevelt,* which docked in New York Harbor nine days later.[33]

Bruno Bettelheim's compulsion to exaggerate the facts with tales of dashes to the border and adventures in the Austrian underground embellished behavior that, if left unvarnished, would seem altogether worthy, and, in the catastrophe of the *Anschluss,* selfless. He might well have been able to obtain a visitor's visa along with Gina, given that Patsy had lived with both of them for seven years and that Agnes was offering refuge to him as well as to his wife. But he chose to stay in Vienna at that critical moment, in part because he felt he could not walk away from Bettelheim & Schnitzer, but primarily because he would not abandon his mother and sister. When he discussed the possibility of emigrating in the days after the Nazi maelstrom began sucking at Vienna's Jews, Margaret grew hysterical and begged him not to leave.[34]

For a number of years, his sister had pursued a career as an actress, studying in Germany and on a few occasions performing at provincial theaters there and at Vienna's Deutsches Volkstheater. A publicity photograph shows her in the white toga she wore as Iphigenie, a handsome but somber-looking woman with dark, soulful eyes and brown, wavy hair who used the stage name Margaret Roederer. Her career was middling at best, and by the end of the 1930s she was dabbling in journalism for the Vienna daily *Der Morgen,* and often seen with its editor-in-chief. She was still living at home with her mother, not a typical arrangement for a woman nearing forty. While her younger brother supported the household by working at a job he disliked, she led the life of a dilettante, hobnobbing with Vienna's newspaper crowd at the Café Herrenhof into the small hours and sleeping until noon.

Gina Bettelheim found her sister-in-law arrogant and judgmental, in part because Margaret made plain her disapproval of
what she regarded as the grand life her brother and Gina led at
Gloriettegasse 15. In Gina's view, Margaret was jealous of her
brother, who had always been Paula Bettelheim's favorite child.
What Bruno himself thought of his sister at this stage he never set
down on the page; as with his other relatives—even including his
parents—he did not even give her name on the few occasions
when he mentioned her.

In the days following the *Anschluss,* Nazi predations in Vienna grew more and more terrifying. Now that the annexation
was a fait accompli, Hitler resurrected the plebiscite in a whirlwind of pro-Reich propaganda. While Jews by the thousands continued to scrub streets and latrines, the Viennese archbishop,
Cardinal Theodor Innitzer, fell into goose step with the new
regime. He had welcomed the Führer with the Nazi salute on
March 14; now he instructed his Catholic flock that it was their
"national duty" to vote the country into Germany. On April 10,
rejoicing Austrians did so by an official tally of more than 99
percent. Jews were not permitted to vote. When not forced into
the streets to do the Nazis' bidding, they continued their frantic
efforts to obtain visas before the knock came at their doors. "One
lived in a state of permanent anxiety," recalled Maria Piers; during
this post-*Anschluss* period, she encountered Bruno at a social gathering and he told her he planned to take a vacation at some resort
town and swim the Rhine to safety, a feat that would require his
first making it to the eastern shore of the river, where it flows
between Austria and Switzerland, or traveling to Germany itself
and swimming to France. "It was all so naïve; we were incredibly
stupid," Piers said.

By April 20, ten days after Hitler's rubber-stamp plebiscite,
Bettelheim had begun to focus seriously on trying to leave his
homeland. On that day, he went to the American consulate and,
like hundreds of other Viennese Jews, applied for a visa as a quota
immigrant to the United States. He told Donn Medalie, the vice-
consul who typed up his application, that he intended to settle
permanently in America and that he would pay for his own passage. He had not arranged it yet, but said that when he did sail he

planned to join Mrs. Agnes P. Crane in Greenwich, Connecticut, where Patsy's mother now lived with her new husband, Percy Hatfield Crane. She had already sent the required affidavit for Bruno on April 8 and had been assured by John C. Wiley, the American consul in Vienna, that all was in order. But Medalie told the desperate applicant that the affidavit was not in his file; moreover, he said Bettelheim should not return to the consulate until it had received word from the U.S. Department of Labor that Gina had acquired an immigration visa, as opposed to the six-month visitor's document she had been granted to accompany Patsy across the Atlantic.[35]

This now became the principal sticking point, as Agnes Crane plunged into the State Department labyrinth with growing dismay and frustration. In mid-May, hoping that her efforts at last might have produced results, she cabled Bettelheim, urging him to return to the consulate. He went immediately, he replied, but to no avail. The consular officials told him Crane's affidavit was not in his file and refused to look for it. "I was told that it would be superfluous to search, since my case is considered closed," he told his sponsor.[36]

Somehow, Agnes Crane succeeded in keeping Cordell Hull at least marginally interested in helping her, a remarkable achievement given that the secretary of state had a good deal else on his mind as Hitler threatened to devour Europe and the Japanese expanded into Asia. On May 20, he cabled Vienna seeking a status report on the Bettelheim visa application. Three days later, John C. Wiley, who had reassured Crane on April 8, cabled back, "[S]upport [for Bettelheim] believed inadequate because apparently contingent on wife's permanent entry into the United States."

In the days that followed, Crane received a maddening recommendation from A. M. Warren, chief of the State Department's visa division. He said that the only way Gina could obtain an immigration visa was to leave the sanctuary she had just found. She need not return to Vienna, Warren told Crane, and suggested that Gina try the consulate in Cuba and that Bruno could join her there, after which they could apply together for entry as quota immigrants. Warren did not speculate on how long this process might take, or discuss whether Cuba would prove any more sympathetic to Bettelheim's plight than the United States.

On May 31, Wiley sent another communiqué to Hull, this time outlining the bureaucratic obstacles that prevented the consulate from issuing a visa to Bettelheim; he said he appreciated "the inconvenience caused the American citizens interested in this case as well as the inconvenience caused the applicant and his wife."[37] Two days later, Bettelheim was on a train for Dachau.

CHAPTER THREE
Dachau and Buchenwald

I<small>N</small> M<small>AY OF</small> 1938, the Austrian authorities arrested some two thousand Viennese Jews on special orders from Berlin.[1] Some of these "asocial elements," as the Nazis called them, were communists, Social Democrats, anti-Hitler journalists, and other opponents of the regime; but many, like Bruno Bettelheim, had not been active politically and now found themselves swept up for real or manufactured minor infractions such as traffic violations, or charged with participating in the resistance whether they had or not. The most cynical classification was *"Schutzhäftling Jude,"* a Jew incarcerated for his own protection.

That was Bettelheim's label,[2] though from the outset he maintained that he had been singled out for his anti-Nazi deeds, saying, in the words of one fellow prisoner, that he had been seized "for his clandestine activities in the social assistance section of the resistance movement against the Austrian fascist government."[3] In the years to come, he would promulgate this fiction, often insisting that he had been arrested not because he was Jewish but for his "radical political beliefs."[4] But in the sworn affidavit he gave to the war-crimes tribunal in 1945, he said that the Austrian police questioned him for three days about his political activities and found "no basis whatever" for a legal action against him. He said that after this interrogation he was released and then, two weeks later, arrested again, and this time jailed.[5] On June 2, the police loaded Bettelheim and some six hundred other prisoners into vans and took them to the Westbahnhof, where members of the SS *Totenkopfverbände,* the Death's-Head Units, herded them onto a train for Munich.[6]

Even before this transport pulled out that afternoon, the

gray-uniformed conductors with skulls on their caps began terror-
izing their captives, barking commands at the "dirty Jews," who,
even if they obeyed, were slapped, punched, kicked, and in some
cases bayoneted. "We were beaten constantly from Vienna to Salzburg," recalled Ernst Federn, then a twenty-three-year-old Marxist who had served as a secretary to his father, the psychoanalyst
and Freud intimate Paul Federn. Another passenger was Bruno
Heilig, a fifty-year-old journalist who had been editor-in-chief of
Die Stimme, the principal organ of the Austrian Zionists, which
had published many anti-Nazi articles, including some about Dachau, based on reports of released prisoners. In Men Crucified, his
book about his incarceration, he would call the transit a "moving
hell." [7] Despite the summer weather, the heating systems stifled the
carriages; the guards, two or three in each car, forbade the removal
of jackets and provided no water. The prisoners sat dripping with
perspiration, forced to keep their hands in their laps and to stare
into a blinding light as the train rolled through the night. [8] If a
prisoner failed to remove his hat in the presence of a guard, the
guard knocked it off with a rifle butt.

      Bettelheim wrote that he received several blows to the head,
and was puzzled as to why the SS did not kill him and the others
outright; he wondered, too, how they could endure so much
without committing suicide, "though some prisoners did, by
jumping out of the train windows." [9] He said that the guards shot
or otherwise killed twenty prisoners during the night, and that
few remained physically unscathed after the twelve-hour train trip
and the ten-mile truck ride from the Munich station to Dachau.
He said that he himself arrived at the camp suffering a loss of
blood from the blows to his head and a slight bayonet wound. [10] As
a result, he wrote, the following morning he was among the
wounded taken to the camp clinic, where a doctor examined him
and allowed him a few days' rest and a week of preferred treatment. This gave him a chance to recuperate, and also to take stock
of his situation. Bettelheim counted himself relatively lucky to
have suffered no permanent physical damage. [11]

      By the late spring of 1938, the concentration camp at Da-
chau, a small town northwest of Munich, had been in operation
for five years. [12] In the beginning, its inmates were not primarily

Jews but socialists, communists, labor leaders, and other outspoken antagonists of the Nazis. The original reason for incarcerating these "politicals," aside from taking them out of circulation for "re-education," was to spread terror throughout Germany, a message that grew louder and more effective as the Nazis added categories to their enemies list: among them Jesuits, who balked at the regime's manipulation of the church; Jehovah's Witnesses, who resisted the draft; monarchists; freemasons; homosexuals; Gypsies; and, increasingly, Jews. More than a quarter of Germany's Jewish population had fled Hitler's Aryan utopia by 1938; now the lightning success of the *Anschluss* had saddled the Nazis with nearly two hundred thousand more Jews.[13]

The abandoned World War I munitions factory that had been converted into the camp was designed to hold five thousand prisoners; by the time Bettelheim's trainload pulled in, the population threatened to overflow, and guards were driving inmate labor gangs toward the summer completion of thirty-four more barracks. These twin rows of wooden or stone blocks, as they were called, sat surrounded by a wall, a water-filled ditch, and an electrified barbed-wire fence; seven watch towers manned by guards with machine guns looked down on this stockade.

The commandant of the camp, the first of its kind, was a former police officer named Theodor Eicke; he was determined to make Dachau the prototype for all future *Konzentrationslager,* and, indeed, soon became inspector general of the entire burgeoning Gulag. It was Eicke who whipped the ill-disciplined young SS volunteers into a cadre of fearsome guards, demanding that they feel no pity for the enemies of the Third Reich in their corral. "At Dachau the SS created the models of incarceration, organizational structure, codes and policies, medical experimentation, and officer/guard training that served as the basis for the years of punishment, destruction, and killing that lay ahead for the inferior peoples of Europe."[14] Adolf Eichmann spent time at Dachau under Eicke's tutelage, as did Rudolf Höss, who would become a commandant at Auschwitz.

Bruno Bettelheim, wrenched from the comfortable life that he had led for thirty-five years, now found himself prisoner number 15029, with his thinning brown hair cropped short. Most inmates bore a single color-coded triangle on the breast of their gray-striped fatigues: pink for homosexuals; black for criminals, sex offenders, and other so-called asocial prisoners; red for German politicals. Bettelheim did not indicate, in writing about his camp experience, what color triangle he wore, but it was probably red; whatever color his primary triangle, superimposed on it was a yellow one, creating a Star of David and marking him as one more hated Jew. He was quickly segregated and, with some two hundred other Jewish prisoners, crammed into a wooden barrack, stone being reserved for Aryans. Each morning the targets of this degradation fell out for roll call onto the Appellplatz, the camp's central square. From there they marched off to labor details, which lasted from sunup to sunset and sometimes longer. They excavated in gravel pits, built roads, and converted marshes to arable land; but with the new barracks almost finished, their toil also included much make-work, such as hauling stones from one end of the camp to the other and then bringing them back, pulling and pushing wagons like so many oxen. An inscription above the main gate read *"Arbeit Macht Frei"* ("Work Will Make You Free").

The guards spewed out a constant stream of verbal abuse. " 'Shit' and 'asshole' were so standard that it was rare when a prisoner was addressed otherwise," Bettelheim wrote.[15] They sometimes forced an entire block to stand at attention on the Appellplatz for hours in the hot sun, each man with his hands behind his head. Weaker inmates collapsed and died on this baked parade ground; anyone who tried to help a fallen comrade risked solitary confinement or worse. Guards imposed punishments capriciously and often for the slightest transgressions; an inmate who failed to make his bed tightly enough or who did not polish his eating utensils or boots to the liking of the SS could find himself strung from a tree, the rope tied to his wrists behind his back, the weight of his body sometimes dislocating his shoulders. The cries from these hangings, which often lasted for hours, pierced the camp daily, as did the screams of inmates strapped across the wooden "horse" and whipped until blood poured from the gashes in their backs. Others suffered in the notorious *Wirtschaftsgebäude,* the farm building, where guards hung inmates from stakes in the showers and flogged them.

Bettelheim did not write that he suffered this kind of punishment, or any other severe physical abuse, once he left the transport from Vienna; nonetheless, he may have, and certainly he witnessed these barbarities. He wrote that he saw the guards plunge prisoners into the latrines, suffocating them in excrement.[16] Guards shot inmates or hanged them by the neck in front of their fellow prisoners, usually alleging they had tried to escape; some inmates hanged themselves in the barracks or found other ways to commit suicide, cutting open their wrists or running against the electrified fence. Dachau never became a mass extermination camp like Auschwitz or Treblinka, but of the more than 206,000 prisoners registered by the camp between 1933 and 1945, when it was liberated by the Allies, 31,591 died inside the barbed wire, most of them after the war began, in September 1939.[17]

Despite the mistreatment and constant threat of torture and death, inmates who humbled themselves before the SS and did as they were told stood a good chance of making it. For all Commandant Eicke's savage catechism, "[T]he S.S. leaders split into two groups in 1938: one group wished the inmates to be treated fairly; the other favored cruel measures." [18] Moreover, the Austrians who arrived with Bettelheim brought a new atmosphere to the camp; many were resolved, wrote Bruno Heilig,

> to meet the rude German methods with passive resistance and attack Nazism by their easy-going Viennese ways. Five thousand men united in the determination not to work could not be coerced even by the S.S. men. There were men strolling through the camp with wheelbarrows only half full, and even returning with them at a walk when they were empty. In the afternoon there was treatment at the infirmary for prisoners working in the camp who were not confined to bed. Hundreds of people turned up who had nothing wrong with them. One stood there, perhaps for an hour or two, then slipped away quietly just before it came to one's turn.[19]

Bettelheim himself wrote, "After one had learned how to live in the camps, the chances of survival increased greatly." [20] If prisoners had the energy at the end of the day's hard labor, they could make use of a well-stocked library; the SS also permitted soccer and other sports and arranged concerts, films, theatricals, and lectures, usually drawing on talent among the prisoners. Bettelheim recalled that when he first arrived at Dachau he could not swallow the food "because of physical pain and psychological revulsion," but he took heed when a veteran inmate admonished him: " 'Listen you, make up your mind: do you want to live or do you want to die? If you don't care, don't eat the stuff. But if you want to live, there's only one way: make up your mind to eat whenever and whatever you can, never mind how disgusting.' " [21] Meals at Dachau consisted of bread, cheese, soup, and occasionally sausage and other meats. Bettelheim testified many years later that this fare, though badly prepared, was "relatively sufficient" and of "adequate nutrition," and that he supplemented it with food from the camp canteen, "which was quite adequate if you had the money to buy it." [22]

The SS allowed each inmate to send two letters or two postcards a month to relatives. This ration was among the regulations spelled out in twenty-nine lines printed on both the envelopes and stationery that the camp required inmates to use. When Bettelheim's first letter to his mother and sister arrived at Neubaugasse 66, they read, under the boldface heading *"Konzentrationslager Dachau 3 K,"* that they, too, were limited to two letters or postcards per month, that their writing had to be in ink and clearly legible and could not exceed more than fifteen lines per page. They were to use normal-size stationery, and envelopes only one layer thick. The envelope could contain their letter and a maximum of five twelve-pfennig stamps for Bruno's use; all else was forbidden and would be confiscated. Photographs could not be used as postcards, which were limited to ten lines. Newspapers were permitted but had to be ordered through the camp post office; packages were not, because, the regulations assured, inmates could buy everything they needed in the camp. The fifth and final warning in this enumeration was aimed at both sender and recipient: *"Entlassungsgesuche aus der Schutzhaft an die Lagerleitung sind zwecklos"* ("There is no point in pleading to the head of the camp to be released"). [23]

However, the rules specifically stated that prisoners could receive money *("Geldsendungen sind gestattet")*; if Paula and Margaret Bettelheim were initially surprised by this permission they would soon understand that at Dachau Reichsmarks were a matter of "life itself."[24] The steady flow of money they began sending Bruno allowed him not only to buy additional nourishment at the canteen but to ease his plight with payoffs to camp officials and their *Kapos*, inmates on whom the SS bestowed subordinate power. Bettelheim wrote that he was "lucky in having relatively stable work assignments (sometimes through bribing the foreman) . . . ."[25] On July 3, a month after he entered the camp, he wrote to his mother and sister: "I gratefully received your letter and the money. Please send RM15 in the same regular intervals.* If that is too much for you, maybe Trude will lend you the money."[26] Two weeks later he asked them to send $126 immediately and then $63 every eight days."[27] On July 31, he wrote again, asking that they send $63 more on August 20 and the same amount every week thereafter. The letters do not indicate how Paula and Margaret were able to grant his request for a supply of Reichsmarks every week or so and still mail only two letters per month. Perhaps they sent the money twice a month despite his pleas; or the SS, eager to oil the bribery gears, did not strictly enforce the rule; or the funds arrived separately in money orders. Whatever the case, Bettelheim's nineteen letters and postcards to Neubaugasse 66 make it clear that he received much of the money he sought.

Since censorship was a given, the letters reveal nothing specific about camp life and little about the prisoner's true condition; but the reality is constantly implicit between the lines of Bettelheim's methodically neat penmanship. ". . . I think of [Gina] and you all with the greatest longing," he wrote in the July 3 letter, after assuring Paula and Margaret that he remained physically well. "You have to make all your plans without any consideration of me because my future is completely uncertain. . . . Please don't worry too much because it makes no sense, there is no point. All my thoughts are busy only with Gina and you all because I don't want to think about myself. . . . Are you all and Mina [Gina's mother]

---

* *In 1938–39, a Reichsmark was worth $0.40, which adjusted for inflation was worth $4.26 in 1996. To give a clearer indication of how much money Bettelheim received in the camps and to better measure other financial transactions, all amounts are given in 1996 dollars hereafter.*

healthy? I kiss and embrace you all, unfortunately only in my mind. You and Gina just have to be brave. Many kisses, Bruno." [28]

On July 17, Bettelheim gave his mother power of attorney to declare his assets. Just after the *Anschluss*, Hermann Göring, Hitler's economic dictator, had announced in Vienna that Aryanization must be quickly implemented throughout the Third Reich. "To prevent the Jews from saving their property by fictitious sales and token registration under the names of non-Jewish associates, Göring issued the Order Against the Support of the Camouflage of Jewish Businesses on April 22. Four days later, in conjunction with the Ministry of the Interior, he published the Order Requiring the Declaration of Jewish Property, whereby all Jews—including those married to non-Jews—were enjoined to declare their holdings in Germany and abroad." [29] The systematic extermination of the Jews would not begin until 1942, but the notorious engineer of that slaughter was already hard at work honing his bureaucratic skills. Karl Adolf Eichmann, who, like Hitler, had spent his youth in Linz, was in charge of the Central Office for Jewish Emigration in Vienna. This was the euphemism for an agency that dealt exclusively in blackmail: permission to leave the country in exchange for all the worldly possessions of Jews and any other "undesirables" the Nazis sought to banish. By the time the war started, half of the city's 180,000 Jews had managed to purchase their freedom to emigrate by turning over their assets to their persecutors. [30]

The new regime moved in on Bettelheim & Schnitzer even before Bruno was arrested. A sheaf of documents charts the Aryanization of the business Bettelheim's father and uncle had founded in 1907. [31] The Nazis assessed the firm's worth at $117,600, which was likely a significant undervaluation; as a rule, the Nazi bookkeepers forced Jews to sell their businesses for 60 to 75 percent of their worth, reducing the amount further with taxes and rigid payment terms. "[I]n the best of circumstances, the Jewish seller received from 30 to 60 percent of the value of his property." [32] In many cases the seller received nothing at all, which may have been the fate of Bettelheim and his partner, Hanns Schnitzer—the record is not clear. What is plain is that little was overlooked in setting down the details of this official theft. Listed among the confiscated items were two gold watches, one signet ring, one painting, two carpets, table silver, and one Steyr Baby 50 automobile. The documents also record that in 1937 Bettelheim & Schnitzer's four employees included one Jew; by June 9, 1938, less than a week after Bettelheim entered Dachau, all four employees were Aryans.

Their new boss was one Nikolaus Lackner, a bank accountant with whom the partners had done business in the past and who had "bought" the firm. "I hereby declare . . . that both I and my wife are of pure Aryan descent," Lackner assured Berlin on new firm stationery, his name printed at the top in large letters; he signed this warranty under a neatly typed "Heil Hitler!" [33] For its part, the Nazi Party certified that Lackner had been a member since 1933 "and was in good standing even in the illegal time." [34]

Bettelheim's first letters from Dachau show him frantic about the Aryanization of the business; they urge his mother to work hard with his lawyer cousin, Norbert Bettelheim, to see the transaction through to a quick resolution and to salvage what money they could, in part because she and Margaret needed it to live on. [35] But by July 31, he was writing that getting his tax matters and other private affairs in order was far more important than any business payout, which by then he may have concluded was a chimera, and not only because of the Nazis. "About the business and Hanns [Schnitzer] write little, it's all his fault but we need him until I am back so try to get along with him and I will take revenge." What Schnitzer had done to trigger this vow the letters do not disclose; it is possible that, once Bettelheim entered Dachau, Schnitzer, who never much liked his disdainful younger partner, tried to claim for himself whatever assets the Nazis allowed the former owners to keep. Schnitzer did sign the Aryanization papers on July 14, 1938, and the following month pleaded with the authorities to leave him enough money to get to the United States. [36] He and his wife, Alice, who was not Jewish, emigrated to New York City in 1939 and settled in Queens, where he worked in an export-import business until his death in 1971. The couple had no children, so any opportunity to hear their version of these post-*Anschluss* events ended with Alice Schnitzer's death.

Bettelheim did not have many assets to declare beyond his interest in the lumber business. In instructing his mother and sister to settle his personal financial affairs as quickly as possible, he wrote that his life-insurance policies were nearly valueless, because he had mostly cashed them out. He speculated that his automobile might be worth something but was not optimistic: not only had the Nazis appropriated it but he owed $5,460 on the vehicle. He had also accumulated between $8,400 and $10,500 in other debts, and though the ten-room apartment at Gloriettegasse 15 was valuable, he and Gina had rented, not owned it. He told his mother to ask Gina what household goods she wanted and, whatever her wishes, to move all the freestanding furniture into storage. If the buffet, cupboards, and other built-ins could not be sold to the next tenant, he wanted them dismantled. "From the boards I will then be able to make something for myself," he wrote, as if he somehow might construct a new life from this used lumber. A subsequent letter implies that Paula, in consultation with her sister, Jeanette, and Gina, raised the possibility of selling all the furniture, which moved Bruno angrily to reiterate his original instructions.[37]

The prisoner also worried about two lawsuits against him. One sought to recover what he owed on the automobile; the other claimed unpaid insurance premiums. On October 13, he told his mother that the suing company should take the car, whose value was more than the debt; if the insurance firm insisted on getting its money, it should come from Bettelheim & Schnitzer, by then an unlikely alternative given that the business had been in the Aryan hands of Nikolaus Lackner since July. The car, too, was Nazi property by then. The premiums owed were for fire, accident, and theft insurance on the lumber business; Bettelheim instructed his mother to cancel these policies and reassured her that he had a contractual agreement with the company, Anglo-Danubian Lloyd, that said he at least did not have to pay back the discount he had been given.

IN THE DAYS immediately before and after Bettelheim's imprisonment, Agnes Crane labored to persuade her government to grant him a visa. Among other things, this required that she sign an affidavit saying that, if necessary, she would support him so he would not become a public charge. On June 9, a week after Bettelheim entered Dachau, Cordell Hull cabled John Wiley in Vienna:

> . . . [Bettelheim's] admissability does not appear to be dependent on [his wife's] immigration status as he apparently will not be supported by her. Mrs. Agnes Piel Crane, whose child is being attended by Mrs. Bettelheim, has promised to support both Dr. and Mrs. Bettelheim.
>
>   There would be no objection to your acceptance of Dr. Bettelheim's visa application if he can be released from incarceration for such purpose. . . .[38]

The same day, the American consul cabled back, "Visa application Bruno Bettelheim approved today and may be issued immediately on his release." [39] The State Department's A. M. Warren in Washington relayed this tardy good news to Crane in Greenwich, but when she pleaded with him to help gain Bettelheim's release through the U.S. Embassy in Berlin, he told her that the State Department could not make such inquiries because Bettelheim was not an American citizen. Warren suggested that she pursue Bettelheim's release through the American Society of Friends, whose London office had already told her that he was well and might be freed before the summer was out.[40] Warren also received a plea from Lawrence S. Kubie, secretary of the American Psychoanalytic Association, who had been asked to help by Bettelheim's cousin, Edith Buxbaum, who was now pursuing her psychoanalytic career in Manhattan.[41] But the summer waned and Bettelheim remained in Dachau, going through "severe mood swings, from fervent hope to deepest despair, with the result that I was emotionally drained before the day even began, a day of seventeen long hours that would take all my energy to survive it." [42]

   This fluctuation between deep despondency and desperate optimism surfaces again and again in the letters. "Now I have been in the camp for three months and you can imagine my mood on this day . . ." Bettelheim wrote on August 28, his thirty-fifth birthday. He told his mother and sister to send his condolences to a woman named Erica and her family; apparently, her husband had recently died, moving the prisoner to write that he envied him. But the birthday letter also reflects Bettelheim's determination to survive; he asked his mother to get him instead of or as well as Vienna's *Presse* a subscription to the *Frankfurter Zeitung,* saying that though he only read newspapers on Sundays, they chased away "a little of my dark thoughts." He assured Paula that she should not worry about his ingrown hair because it caused him little complaint, reminded her to send him $63 every week, asked once again whether the furniture had been put in storage, and urged her to keep trying to retrieve at least some portion of her assets as well as an advance on his own.

On September 1, he told her that before his arrest he had ordered six sets of shirts and pants of the same material from a tailor named König. He asked his mother to pay for the clothes with funds from the business or, failing that, to loan him the cash. From another tailor, whose name he had forgotten but whose address he recalled as Postgasse 13, he had ordered a suit, on which he had already paid $360, as well as a lightweight suit and a *Winterulster,* a short overcoat. He asked his mother to pick up these garments as well, then wondered if he would ever have a chance to wear them.

By now, Margaret was investigating an opportunity to emigrate to Colombia, and her brother urged her to take it, stressing that she must not stay in Vienna because of him. He added that Trude should also make sure that she got away, and sent her warm greetings. But it was Gina who preoccupied his thoughts. His mother had written that his wife was hoping to travel from New York to Cuba in an attempt to re-enter the United States on a permanent visa rather than the temporary one she had been granted. Bruno urged that Gina get to Cuba as soon as possible. "Is she well?" he asked. "Edith [Buxbaum] has to take care of her. . . . [T]ell her that the only thing that keeps me going is the hope for a better future on which she is working and she should keep at it."[43] Such passages throughout the letters leave no doubt that, despite Gina's affair with Peter Weinmann and Bruno's with Trude Weinfeld, he remained devoted to his wife and yearned to resume their marriage in the United States. "Please tell Gina how endlessly I long to see her again," he wrote in one letter;[44] in another he declared that it was his "only and most longing wish to be with her as soon as possible and forever, but she must be prepared that this is still very uncertain. Tell her that so she doesn't have any false hopes. . . ."[45]

In Vienna, Paula and Margaret Bettelheim had implored various Nazi officials for weeks to release Bruno, and feared for his life constantly. So did Trude, but though she loved him she was neither his wife nor a blood relative and could only stand on the sidelines and hope. Moreover, like all other Jews in the city, she and her parents faced their own peril. Her father, a successful accountant, was in Switzerland on business at the *Anschluss;* stranded with no money, he wanted to return, but Trude discouraged him and instead urged her mother to join him. Frederika Weinfeld was at first reluctant, but when forced to scrub the street on her knees she took her twenty-six-year-old daughter's advice. Soon the Nazis closed in on the Montessori school where Weinfeld taught, scorning its progressive principles and the Jews who worked there and demanding that it vacate the public building it occupied on the Schubertstrasse. Emma Plank, the director of the school and a Jew, managed to find a sympathetic Gentile substitute, and under his protection classes continued in new quarters until the school year ended. This was little comfort for Weinfeld, especially after the suicide of her aunt, who felt abandoned by her brother and his wife.[46]

Each morning, all Vienna's Jews awoke to the possibility that they would be summoned to Gestapo headquarters at the Hotel Metropol, and in late spring Weinfeld received the command. "They didn't tell me what they wanted, but like a good little girl I went." They took away her passport and locked her in a bathroom, interrogating her on and off all day, subjecting her to "an absolutely gruesome experience." They released her by the evening and, after a few days, returned the passport. Determined now to leave the country, she found a young man who said he would take her over the mountains into Switzerland. Some Montessori parents, grateful for the dedication she had shown their children, gave her money to pay him and to buy provisions for the trip. She also received a few gold coins from the new head of the school, to

whom she entrusted a letter to Bruno. She packed what possessions she could in trunks and sent them ahead to Edward Vischer,
her friend Emarina's brother, a teacher in the Swiss canton of
Glarus, just across the border.[47]

In mid-September, with a knapsack on her back and posing
as a mountain climber, she and the guide left Vienna by train for
the Tirol, the Alpine countryside that six months before had been
the western part of an independent Austria. From there they
walked for several days, staying in hostels at night, until they
reached the edge of freedom. The Swiss guards proved friendly
and gave them a room until the next morning. "It was a terrible
night for me," Trude recalled, "because the young man wanted to
take advantage of the situation; it took all my crying and pleading
. . . to keep him from molesting me." The next day, she took a
train to Edward Vischer's home, paying for the ticket with the
gold coins, which she had hidden in her stockings.[48]

Bettelheim remained at Dachau, but on the morning of September 23, as the prisoners marched out of the Appellplatz to
their details, the commandant suddenly called them back over the
loudspeaker. "All labor detachments to be dismissed!" came the
next order, followed by "All Jews to form up in Blocks!"[49] For
several weeks, a trickle of prisoners—including Jews—had been
freed once they had demonstrated to their captors that they had
the visas and the wherewithal to leave the Third Reich immediately. Now Bettelheim and the other Austrian Jews gathered in
the mustering area, hoping that the mass release so long rumored
was about to take place. They stood there for almost six hours,
until seven in the evening, when the SS guards marched them out
the main gate.

"We were driven into cattle-trucks, which were standing in
readiness on a railway-line," Bruno Heilig wrote. "There were
more than twelve hundred of us, and we were packed into four
trucks. We stood tight against each other and by the time we
reached the station at Munich we were half-stifled."[50] Once again,
the SS prodded the inmates onto a train, this time headed north
through Nuremberg into the heart of Germany. As on the transport from Vienna to Dachau in June, the guards carried rifles with
fixed bayonets. But they employed less brutality this time, since

the weeks in Dachau had left their passengers properly cowed. After a night of fearful speculation, the prisoners arrived in Weimar, once the intellectual and cultural cradle of Germany, the home of Goethe and Schiller. Five miles to the north, beech trees covered the slopes of the Ettersberg; when Heinrich Himmler, the SS overlord, had established a concentration camp on the site the previous summer, he called it Buchenwald.

Bettelheim was now prisoner number 9036. Almost everything about this new camp was worse than Dachau. The food rations were smaller, the work was harder, mail and money from home were more restricted, the guards more imaginative and quicker in their punishments, and killing was more common. In Weimar, the Ettersberg was called "Totenberg," the Mount of Death. A Gypsy who tried to escape was put in a wooden box so small that the nails driven through it pierced his flesh whenever he moved. For two days and three nights, the box sat on the parade ground for all to see, as the caged victim screamed in pain. On the third morning, he was put out of his misery with a lethal injection. The man who ordered this cautionary exhibit was Karl Otto Koch, commandant of the camp and husband of Ilse Koch, the notorious "Bitch of Buchenwald," who beat prisoners with her riding crop, staged sexual orgies for her own amusement, and had lampshades made from the tattooed skin of dead inmates.

Buchenwald was also far less hygienic than Dachau. "The huts were dirty, the prisoners were dirty and all the tools were sticky with the filth that had dried on them."[51] Strictly enforced rules prohibited defecating or urinating during the twelve-hour workday, and even during the periods when prisoners were allowed to relieve themselves, indoor toilets were useless because there was no flush water. Latrines, Bettelheim wrote, "were usually nothing but a trench with logs on either side on which prisoners had to balance."[52] The stench of these pits filled the air, mingling with the thick mist that often shrouded the Ettersberg, enveloping the camp in a fetid soup that soaked through clothes and boots.

It was in this dank, murderous climate that Bettelheim met Ernst Federn, as they passed bricks along a human chain. Because of his poor eyesight, Bettelheim dropped many of the bricks Federn threw to him, fumbles that could land on one's foot or, worse, move a guard to thrash them both. Federn recalled making a snide remark about this ineptitude.

> "Is that your brick?" [Bettelheim said.] In the ensuing exchange of words I called to my opposite: "You nobody!" "Who is a nobody for you—are you an anybody? I am Bettelheim." "And I am Federn." "Are you a relative of Paul Federn?" "I am his son."

The two prisoners then shook hands "and remained friends from that hour—I think even friends of a very special kind . . ." said Federn.[53] Bettelheim, in recalling the meeting, also remarked on the long-standing friendship that developed, adding that he had been inwardly amused by Federn's initial irritation and had told him that he "never had the slightest intention, nor any desire, to be a competent brick-catcher or brick-thrower. . . . [I]t was my very particular, and highly narcissisticly [sic] invested self-image, that permitted me to consider funny a situation in which I was cursed out and depreciated, not only by the guards but even by Ernst Federn. They viewed as degrading my lack of competency in the catching of bricks, I experienced it the other way round."[54]

Bettelheim and Federn lived in a wooden barrack with about 125 other Jews, getting what sleep they could on mattresses and pillows stuffed with straw. At the end of the long, arduous days, they would gather around these bunks or in the small living room that, with six tables and a few chairs, passed as a recreation area. "We bought thousands of books," Federn told me. "We collected money, gave it to an SS officer, and he ordered them. But you needed time and energy to read them after working all day, and we didn't always have it." Mostly, Bettelheim wrote, the inmates indulged in their favorite free-time activity, "exhanging tales of woe and swapping rumors about changes in the camp conditions or possible liberation."[55] Bettelheim wrote that it was during one of these sessions that "it suddenly flashed through my mind, 'this is driving me crazy,'" and that he decided to study camp behavior as a way of giving himself something to do to help him maintain his sanity.

"Bruno had the wonderful idea that whenever we had a chance we should exchange ideas," recalled Hans Bandler, who was a twenty-four-year-old socialist and engineering student when he befriended Bettelheim in Dachau, and was also among the Austrian Jews transferred to Buchenwald in September. On work details when they hoped the guards were not watching, or in the evening if they had strength left, Hans would explain the principles of engineering to Bruno, and the older man would talk of Freud and psychoanalysis and make tentative stabs at interpreting the psychology of camp life. "It was a wonderful oppportunity to escape from a devastating situation, if only for a few minutes. Bruno seemed to have the intellectual ability to rise above the physical restraints that encased us."

Ernst Federn wrote that Bettelheim owed his survival in Buchenwald "to the chance of finding work in the stock[ing]mending shop, where he could live in relative safety."[56] This *Kommando*, as the workplaces or details were called, was next to their barrack, and the SS officer in charge was "a very nice man, no question," Federn told me. Bettelheim himself never wrote of this person, but he did say that among the SS devils there were "at least a few angels. . . ."[57] Federn said he did not know how Bettelheim had been treated in Dachau, but when he met him in Buchenwald "he seemed somehow protected." Hans Bandler had the same impression and called the indoor assignment "a very, very rare situation." Herbert Zipper, a Viennese conductor-composer who knew Bettelheim in the camps, also concluded that he had a guardian *Kapo;* he said that Bettelheim managed to keep in comparatively good physical condition because of his sock-mending assignment, which spared him the crushing outdoor labor most other prisoners faced daily.

Bettelheim wrote that it could not be stressed enough that survival "depended foremost on luck. . . ."[58] He said he himself had been lucky, though he did not elaborate on his special treatment at Buchenwald in his published writing; nor did he reveal what may have been the main reason for his good fortune: his poor eyesight. Ernst Federn wrote that, for reasons he could never quite fathom, "the SS guards showed some respect for [Bettelheim's glasses]."[59] Like other prisoners who did not see well, Bet-

telheim wore a special three-pointed insignia on his sleeve. "Twice
during my time in the camps I hid, which I could do very well
because I had the armsleeve that declared me as blind," Bettelheim
wrote to Federn three decades later, not specifying how or where
he had hidden. He said he did not regard going to ground as
cowardice but as a temporary defense, and that in each instance,
after less than two weeks, he had emerged and taken the insignia
off because he found it "too self-destructive, and had watched the
destruction it wreaked in others." [60]

When Bettelheim wrote publicly about his glasses, he said
that they had not protected him but had put him at serious risk.
They marked him as an intellectual, he said, and on the transport
to Dachau aroused the antagonism of the guards, who smashed
them.[61] He wrote that, after arriving at Dachau, he told an SS
officer that his glasses had been broken during the transport.

> When the SS officer heard this he began to deliver a beating and
> screamed, "*What* did you say happened?" I corrected myself, saying
> I had broken them accidentally. At this he immediately said, "Okay,
> just remember that for the future," and matter-of-factly sat down
> to give me written permission to receive glasses.[62]

On another occasion, Bettelheim wrote that, since he was
near-blind without his glasses, the physician who attended him at
Dachau—not the SS officer—permitted him to write home for
new glasses.

> Having learned my lesson, I requested—and a while later received
> —glasses of the simplest and cheapest kind. Even so, I found it best
> to hide my glasses and do without them whenever the SS went on
> a rampage; I was much safer this way. This is but one of the many
> precautions a prisoner had to learn to take if he wanted to increase
> his chances for survival.[63]

In a third telling, Bettelheim wrote that the camp physician
who had treated the bayonet wound he said he had received on
the train to Dachau had given him permission to work indoors
because of his broken glasses, an authorization that had to be

renewed every other day by certain officers. "They decided to find out whether I was really unable to see by throwing beer bottles past my head. I managed not to move my head, nor to blink my eyes." [64]

It is certainly possible that Bettelheim was attacked on the transport because his glasses labeled him an intellectual in the eyes of the guards, but his letter to Federn and his published accounts of the incident do not support his claim that "to enter the camp with hornrimmed glasses was tantamount to a death warrant." [65] Moreover, his camp letters make no mention of broken glasses until more than six months after the June 2 transport to Dachau. On December 20, he told his mother in a letter from Buchenwald that his glasses were broken and asked her to get a new pair from an optician named Schlieffelder in the Graben. He did not ask for glasses of the simplest, cheapest kind but for "good glasses . . . in a good case," and told his mother to write on the package, "Permitted Mail."

In writing about his camp experience over the next four decades, Bettelheim never referred to his letters, and he mentioned those he received (which have not survived) only once, in an anecdote aimed at showing how prisoners often willfully misinterpreted good news. He said his mother wrote him that a colleague of his had delivered a paper in Vienna using some of his ideas, and that the presentation had been well received. On one level, he knew his mother and the associate meant well and had hoped to buoy his morale with word that his ideas had been accepted. However, the letter sent him into "a cold fury to think that my colleague was enjoying success with my ideas while I lived in such misery." [66] Bettelheim's nineteen letters do not allude to this hurt, and, with a vagueness that would prove typical of his written work, he did not identify the colleague or reveal the nature of the ideas he had borrowed or the audience that had embraced them.

Much of what Bettelheim wrote about the general conditions in Dachau and Buchenwald during his time there corresponds to the accounts of Ernst Federn, Hans Bandler, Herbert Zipper, and others, especially Bruno Heilig, whose *Men Crucified* covers the same months Bettelheim was imprisoned. What Bettelheim wrote

about his own torment—how camp life impinged on him personally; how he dealt with the daily rigors; how, in fact, he did survive
—must be taken almost entirely on his word, since little of what
he said and wrote about his actions and reactions in the camps can
be corroborated.

The difficulty, after so many years, of locating among the
thousands of inmates those few living survivors who might have
known Bettelheim was compounded by his failure to name his
fellow inmates. He did identify Ernst Federn eventually, possibly
because he, too, wrote about the psychology of camp life, after
spending seven years in Buchenwald; but Bettelheim did not mention Hans Bandler or Herbert Zipper. He wrote that he asked
"hundreds of German Jewish prisoners" why they had not left
Germany rather than submit to the degradation inflicted on them
by the Nazis;[67] that he asked "more than one-hundred" older
political prisoners if they would reveal the horrors of camp life if
they were freed and managed to reach safe territory;[68] that, in
collecting data for his psychological observations, he "came into
personal contact" with "at least" fifteen hundred prisoners in the
two camps.[69] He was able to interact with so many inmates, he
said, because he worked in at least twenty different labor details
and slept in five different barracks. Given his sock-mending assignment, the first claim seems unlikely; the second is untrue. Pris-
soners were required to write their block numbers on their
correspondence, and Bettelheim marked all his letters from Dachau Block 22 and from Buchenwald Block 17. However many
inmates he did interview, with the exception of Federn and the
passing mention of a man named Alfred Fischer, his subjects always
remained nameless and faceless.

Bettelheim himself, however, was always a central presence,
and nothing in his accounts put him in a brighter spotlight than
his tale of dealing with frostbite. On November 7, 1938, Herschel
Grynszpan, a seventeen-year-old Polish Jew, fatally shot Ernst vom
Rath, the third secretary of the German Embassy in Paris. As is
well known, this act led, on the night of November 9–10, to the
rampage of anti-Semitic murder, arson and vandalism in the Third
Reich that came to be called Kristallnacht, an explosion mirrored
in Buchenwald by a ferocious crackdown on Jewish prisoners.[70]
One new order barred them from the camp clinic, the only place

they could obtain treatment for frostbite, which afflicted many inmates because they worked outdoors in freezing weather with neither gloves nor overcoats. Bettelheim said he, too, suffered from frostbite, and the fear of amputation finally drove him to the clinic.

When he arrived, he found that some twenty others had come to have their extremities treated and that most of them had devised an approach to the officer in charge that they hoped would get them admitted. They would stress their meritorious World War I service, or tell some tall story that another officer had ordered them to come. "The prisoners seemed convinced that the Gestapoman on duty could not see through their schemes," Bettelheim wrote. "Moreover, they neglected to take into account the fact that he might be an individual with personal biases and that it might be advantageous to appeal to these."[71] Bettelheim said he himself had no story and saw no gain in inventing one, because he could not anticipate the admitting officer's personality and prejudices. He said his fellow inmates were derisive and accused him of harboring some secret plan or of eavesdropping and stealing some of their ploys. When their time came to use those stratagems, the officer became increasingly vicious and turned most of them away, making clear that *he* certainly could not be taken in by Jews. "When my turn came," Bettelheim wrote,

> the Gestapoman asked me whether I knew that work accidents were the only reason for admitting Jews to the clinic, and whether I came because of such an accident. I replied that I knew the rules, but that I could not work unless my hands were freed of the dead flesh. Since prisoners were not permitted to possess knives, I asked to have the dead flesh cut away. I made these statements in a matter-of-fact way, avoiding pleading, deference, or arrogance. The Gestapoman replied: "If this is really all you want, I am going to tear the flesh off." He started to pull with force at the festering skin. Because it did not come off as easily as he might have expected, or for some other reason, the Gestapo soldier ordered me to enter the clinic.
>
> Once I was inside the clinic he gave me a malevolent look and pushed me into the treatment room. There he told the orderly to attend to the wound. While this was being done, the Gestapoman watched me closely. I succeeded in suppressing signs of pain. . . .[72]

Bettelheim published this story for the first time in April 1947, in "The Dynamism of Anti-Semitism in Gentile and Jew," which appeared in the *Journal of Abnormal and Social Psychology*. Ten months later, he covered the same ground in *Commentary*, this time identifying the tale's insightful and stoic hero only as "N." and describing him as "a trained psychologist, capable of observing the mental processes at work [in the camps] with substantial objectivity."[73] By 1960, when Bettelheim retold the account once more in *The Informed Heart*, he had returned to center stage.[74] In all versions, the message was the same: that he (or N.) had achieved his goal at the clinic by treating the guard as a person instead of a Nazi beast; thus, Jews should understand that they stereotype the anti-Semite at their peril, whether in the concentration camps or in the world at large. To comprehend anti-Semitism, he wrote in 1947, "one must concentrate as much on the study of the Jew as on the study of the anti-Semite. The complementary character of their respective roles makes it apparent that the phenomenon is an interlocking of pathological interpersonal strivings."[75]

It is impossible to know for certain whether Bettelheim or the pseudonymous N. was the brave protagonist of the Frostbite Story, or whether the tale was another As If. There is no question that conditions grew much harder on Jewish prisoners in the wake of the vom Rath assassination and that many Buchenwald inmates suffered from frostbite in the winter of 1938–39. One of them was Ernst Federn—who said that he could not be the model for N., because his own experience with frozen hands and feet was "completely different" from that described in Bettelheim's account. He did not recall that Bettelheim had suffered from frostbite at any time, primarily because he was indoors, warm, mending socks. "I think he made the person up," Federn told me. Hans Bandler, who also did not recall anyone going through such a heroic medical episode, found Bettelheim's tale "fairly unlikely." Bettelheim's statement in the *Commentary* article that during the fall and winter Jews were worse off than the other prisoners at Buchenwald because they "were not allowed to work indoors" makes the anecdote further suspect, given that he was able to work inside much, if not all, of the time. Other inmates—both Jews and Gentiles—drew similar soft assignments; in Buchenwald, even more than at Dachau, the Nazis gave *Kapos* and block elders (prisoners who oversaw the barracks) considerable sway over their fellow inmates, and bribery was widespread.

ON NOVEMBER 3, 1938, Agnes Crane telephoned A. M. Warren at the visa division in Washington saying that because of Bettelheim's transfer to Buchenwald Gina was "on the verge of a nervous breakdown." [76] When the refugee had first arrived in the United States with Patsy in March, Agnes had installed her in a small hotel near the Crane home on Steamboat Road in Greenwich. Each morning she went to the house to take care of her fourteen-year-old charge and hear her patroness again urge that she make this job her life's work.

Gina quickly realized that this was no world for her, caring for the troubled child by day, "living in an elegant hotel, spending my evenings singing Gilbert and Sullivan and going around in long dresses, while I got letters from Vienna pleading for affidavits." In July, she and Patsy had moved to Manhattan and into a house in Greenwich Village belonging to Paul Piel, one of Agnes's brothers. During these weeks, Gina occasionally went out in the evening with Paul and also with Fritz Redl, who had found work with the Rockefeller Foundation after coming to New York City in 1936. When Agnes was in town, she often waited up, knitting furiously, until Gina came home, fueling further the émigrée's suspicion that her sponsor had lesbian tendencies. [77]

In September, as Bettelheim entered Buchenwald, Patsy returned to Steamboat Road, and Gina at last was able to gain some distance from her suffocating protector; she moved into the servants' quarters of an apartment in Manhattan and found a job at the Community Service Society, a leading social agency. Still, after work on many afternoons she would board a train at Grand Central Station and visit Patsy in Connecticut. Meanwhile, Peter Weinmann, who had made it safely to London, wrote Gina almost daily, saying he was trying to get to the United States and that he would leave his wife and marry her if she would have him. This and all the other pressures and worries in Gina's new life, including a brief stay in Cuba that allowed her to return with a permanent visa, soon produced a severe bleeding ulcer, what she called her "immigrant's disease." After one collapse, Agnes Crane, though she donated blood, refused to visit her child's surrogate mother in the hospital: she was angry about Gina's affection for Peter, which was upsetting her fantasy of a happy extended family with Patsy, Gina, and Bruno.[78]

Despite Agnes's growing disenchantment with Gina, she did not let up on her efforts to help her husband. In early November, Cordell Hull again intervened in the case, setting up an interview at the U.S. consulate in Vienna for Paula and Margaret Bettelheim.[79] Officials there assured them that the Nazis had been told on several occasions that the United States was prepared to grant Bruno a visa. This had produced no movement, so Raymond Geist, the American consul in Berlin, entered the case.[80] On November 12, in the wake of Kristallnacht, Crane wrote a desperate letter to Warren in Washington, D.C., expressing her fear that "the current wild persecution of all Jews in Germany may entangle [Bettelheim] in such confusion and red tape that he might not gain his freedom for many months or even years."[81]

In Vienna, Paula and Margaret cowered in anguish as the marauding Nazis closed some four thousand Jewish-owned shops and ransacked hundreds of apartments; Nazi hooligans destroyed forty-two synagogues in the city, including the one on the Neudeggergasse where Bruno and Gina had married in 1930. They arrested hundreds of Jews, and scores committed suicide.[82] On November 26, Geist sent a coded cable from Berlin telling Hull that he had formally asked the head of the Gestapo to free Bettelheim. It concluded: "Believe in view of arrest having taken place last May, release will be difficult."[83] By Christmas, a holiday that the Bettelheims, like most of Vienna's secular Jews, normally embraced with candles on the tree and generous gift-giving, snow and ice had turned Buchenwald into a frigid nightmare.

In the days after Kristallnacht, the Nazis sent more than ten thousand Jews to Buchenwald, bringing the total population to eighteen thousand.[84] Many of the newcomers were bankers, industrialists, merchants, and other wealthy entrepreneurs whose homes and businesses in Berlin or Frankfurt had been pillaged, torched, or both. Now this human prey was robbed again. As the inmates looked on, "the SS men plundered in the most shameless fashion those who had been beaten to the ground, murdered, or trampled to death, stealing watches, rings, money, and other objects of value out of their pockets."[85] Some seventy Jews went insane during this pogrom within a pogrom and wound up in chains on the cement floor of a barrack that had served as a washhouse. Guards took them in groups of four to a cellblock ruled by the "Hangman of Buchenwald," a sergeant named Martin Sommer who beat them to death.[86]

Though the Kristallnacht Jews offered welcome targets for such orgies of sadism and theft, they also presented a problem. By the end of November, the chief of the SS health department was complaining that as a result of the mass arrests the camps were so crowded that an epidemic could break out at any moment.[87] As a result, Heinrich Himmler soon decreed that all Jews would, in principle, be released if they guaranteed to leave the Third Reich, and announcements began blaring almost daily over the camp's loudspeakers: "Attention Barracks 1a to 5a! The following Jews to the gate with their belongings!"

In November, December, and January, the Nazis freed more than eleven thousand prisoners, most of them Jews, who came down from the cold, fog, and terror of the Totenberg and straggled away.[88] The call came for Herbert Zipper and Hans Bandler, but not Bettelheim. For those not summoned, there was "The Buchenwald Song" by Fritz Löhner-Beda, an inmate who had written librettos for Franz Lehar's operettas and who would die in Auschwitz. The chorus rose on hope:

> . . . *O Buchenwald we do not lament and wail,*
> *whatever our fate might be.*
> *But we want to say yes to life,*
> *for someday the time will come when we are free!* [89]

As several thousands of his Jewish fellow prisoners left the camp during the winter of 1938–39, Bettelheim kept up the pressure on his mother and sister. His concern with getting his financial house in order had by now given way to a frantic effort to satisfy the bureaucrats who held the keys to his release. On October 2, he granted his mother another power of attorney, this time to get the still-missing papers and passport he needed to leave the country. He said his sister must take copies of these documents to Berlin "immediately," underscoring the word twice. Once in the capital, she should deliver the papers to the Hilfsverein der Deutschen Juden. Founded in 1901, this German Jewish aid society initially helped the persecuted Jews of Eastern Europe, but in the early 1930s began concentrating on the plight of German Jews; by 1941, when it closed down, the society had secured exit visas for some ninety thousand persons. Bettelheim urged his sister to find her way to a good lawyer recommended by the society, and also to take copies of his papers to the *Kultusgemeinde* in Vienna. "Letters to the Buchenwald command are forbidden," he reminded his correspondents—a redundancy on Buchenwald stationery, which declared in small Gothic type that such pleas were pointless.

"Thanks for the money, please keep it coming," he wrote in a postcard on November 22, urging them again to arrange for his passport, and also to procure his ship ticket. On December 22, he asked for more money and reported that the Gildermeester Emigration Aid Society was helping him with his passport.[90] He wondered if his mother and sister had gotten him the ship passage he wanted, telling them that if the Paris-Cuba-New York-San Francisco route wasn't possible, he was willing to go directly to New York and then San Francisco. Paula Bettelheim marked her sixty-first birthday on December 21 and her son sent her greetings and wished one and all a Merry Christmas. On January 8, he wrote again, enclosing photos to be used for his passport and visa. If they needed notarization, he urged his mother to go to the Gildermeester operation in Weimar and have it done.

In the same letter, Bettelheim instructed his mother to send $630 to a Frieda Goldstein at Fehrbellinerstrasse 19 in Berlin. "This transfer is a matter of honor for me and because of that very important." On January 15, he asked Paula to confirm that she had sent the money: "[n]ot more but $630 for certain!" On February 5, he asked: "Did you transfer the $630 or not? Please make sure!" He also told her to transfer $210 to a Dr. Klein at Hohenzollernstrasse 1 in Saarbrücken; he said Klein would pass this payment to a woman named H. Wagner-Sender at Passagestrasse 6 in the same city. By March 19, he was telling his mother that she had misunderstood his directions and that she should send only $420 to Berlin and $210 to Saarbrücken. "Under all circumstances, these are debts that, if they are not paid by you, will have the most unpleasant consequences for me!" This cry strongly suggests that the money was required not to settle any debts of honor but to lubricate whatever Nazi hands were holding up the prisoner's release.

Bettelheim said years later in an interview that "a large sum of money" changed hands before his captors set him free.[91] He supplied no specifics, but Maria Piers told me that some kind of payoff may have been made. She and her husband, Gerhart Piers, had known the Bettelheims slightly in Vienna. By the time Bruno was transferred to Buchenwald, the Pierses had managed to take refuge in Switzerland; Gerhart, a fledgling analyst who had served as a resident in a Viennese mental hospital, found employment in Basel as an assistant to Heinrich Meng, a German minister turned psychoanalyst who had published two books with Paul Federn. At the time, Bettelheim was the only person the Pierses knew personally who remained in a concentration camp. Maria said that through Meng her husband contacted a woman named Vogeli, a Swiss lawyer with connections in the Gestapo, and enlisted her help in trying to ransom Bettelheim out. She charged Meng for her services and he paid Gerhart's salary money directly to her. Maria Piers said she did not think the ransom money itself came from Meng but was passed through him, possibly from Agnes Crane or Paula Bettelheim or one of the several rescue committees operating in the United States at the time. It is certainly possible, even likely, that Frieda Goldstein in Berlin and Dr. Klein and Frau H. Wagner-Sender in Saarbrücken played a role in this transaction.

Maria Piers said that she and her husband never learned whether the money actually triggered Bettelheim's release and that, though both he and they eventually settled in the same neighborhood in Chicago, he never talked to them about how he got out of Buchenwald or thanked them for their efforts.

On March 4, Bettelheim wrote that he now assumed from his mother and sister's reports that his papers were at last in order. "One must have very much patience and not lose hope," he told them; one indication that he had not lost hope was his request that they send him a book called *Colloquial English,* which they succeeded in doing. He referred to Gina in almost every letter from Buchenwald, always urging his mother to write to her saying how much he loved and missed her. He was pleased to learn that she had found work in New York City and asked how much she earned per month and whether she could live well off her salary. "How are my other friends?" he added. "Do I have any left at all? So far, I am not bad, and happy that the winter is over; hopefully there will be nicer and better times." Bettelheim's final letter from Buchenwald, dated March 19, contains his plea that the money be sent to Berlin and Saarbrücken lest he face "the most unpleasant consequences," and instructs his mother to renew his ship ticket at fourteen-day intervals and keep everything ready for his immediate departure.

Bettelheim would write that on three occasions during the winter and early spring of 1939 Buchenwald officials told him that he would be released. The first time, most of the inmates called up with him were freed but he was sent back. The second time, almost all the prisoners were returned to their blocks. Bettelheim said that when he was beckoned the third time he refused to be put into civilian clothes, "because I was convinced it was just another effort of the SS official to break me. But this time the call was authentic." [92]

Buchenwald records show that Bettelheim was scheduled to be freed on February 23. The most likely reason he was not was that on that day the authorities declared the camp infected with typhus. [93] Normally, Nazi doctors did not get overly concerned about the disease, which they often recorded merely as "catarrh of the stomach and intestines." [94] But the fever had spread to nearby communities, and the district doctor in Weimar had insisted on a quarantine, which, under German law, could not end until no new cases had been reported for six weeks. Bettelheim did not touch on this development in writing of his camp experience, though it was a topic of passionate speculation in Buchenwald, as prisoners seized on every rumor that there were or were not new outbreaks of the infection. Meanwhile, Bruno Heilig wrote, hundreds of inmates "were pricked in the breast with the same needle, which was not sterilized even once. No one was so much as asked whether by any chance he was suffering from syphilis." [95]

For Hitler, the typhus at Buchenwald was a definite inconvenience. He had decided that on his fiftieth birthday, April 20, he would reduce overcrowding in the camps by freeing more prisoners in an act of amnesty. In early March, an order went out that the typhus must be stopped, and not long thereafter commissioners appointed by the Reich Ministry of Health proclaimed that the epidemic was abating. As word spread through the camp about the April 20 pardon, prisoners began thinking of their tormentor as their savior and started wishing him happy birthday in advance. On the evening of April 11, word began circulating that the quarantine had at last been lifted and that another wholesale exodus would start soon. The next morning, the news came, and from "that time onwards, with the exceptions of Sundays, not a day went by without releases, varying in number between twenty and a hundred." [96] The Nazis freed Bruno Bettelheim on April 14, warning him, as they did all Jews, that he faced rearrest if he did not leave the country within a week. [97]

All the details of how Bettelheim's release came about may never be known. Agnes Crane's determined efforts on his behalf can be traced through documents in his visa file at the National Archives in Washington, but only until the end of 1938. It seems safe to assume that she did not give up after that, but either the archives or the U.S. Department of State has misfiled, lost, or destroyed the records that would help illuminate her effort as it continued through the first three and a half months of 1939.

In 1945, Bettelheim told the war-crimes tribunal that his "release was effected through the aid of some influential friends of [his] in America who were able to enlist the assistance of the State Department of the United States." [98] But for more than thirty years thereafter, he chose not to discuss—in his articles about his concentration-camp experience, or in *The Informed Heart,* his 1960 book on the subject—how he managed to get out of Buchenwald.

In 1979, Bettelheim wrote that he had "no idea" why he was among the lucky ones who were released, speculating that it "may have helped that one of the most prominent American public figures intervened personally" on his behalf.[99] He never credited in his writing either Cordell Hull or Agnes Crane by name, possibly because he never learned of the former's efforts and because he feared that naming the latter would risk identifying her troubled daughter. Sometimes he left the impression that he had been all but abandoned after entering Dachau, saying that few of his friends at the time "did anything more than write a note how sorry they were." [100]

Other times he said that the intercession of Eleanor Roosevelt and Herbert Lehman, then governor of New York, had helped free him, a story that over the years took on mythic proportions as he repeated the claim to family members, colleagues, and journalists. "Mrs. Roosevelt asked the American ambassador in Berlin to intervene for me," he told one interviewer in 1988.[101] No supporting evidence exists in either the Roosevelt or Lehman papers to show that they helped Bettelheim in any way, though it is possible some indication of an involvement is, or was, contained in the absent visa documents. In later years, Bettelheim would maintain that the intervention of notable people in his case actually could have delayed his release, because the Gestapo might have concluded that he would "be useful as a hostage. . . ." [102]

In his published work, Bettelheim wrote nothing about the days immediately following his release. However, toward the end of his life, he offered some details to his literary agent, Theron Raines, who was working on a book about his client. He told Raines that the deprivation in the camps had left him totally bald, and that he had lost half his body weight, emerging from Buchenwald at seventy-five pounds; he had been so starved that for a while after his release eating too much at any one time brought on nausea. Bettelheim said that when he arrived back in Vienna he found his mother living with a friend, the Nazis having thrown her out of her apartment at Neubaugasse 66 and taken it over, as they had hundreds of other residences. When officials came to evict her, she had already disposed of almost all her possessions but had kept three packing cases of crystal and Dresden china that had been in the family for years and that she hoped to take with her if she ever managed to obtain an immigration visa. Bettelheim told Raines that, when his mother urged a police officer inspecting the cases to be careful, he picked one off the table and inverted it, so that its contents shattered on the floor.

Bettelheim's visa had come through ten months before, largely thanks to the persistence of Agnes Crane. But, he told Raines, when he went to the U.S. consulate in Vienna officials said that the quota under which he had been accepted was now filled; they held out the possibilities of immigration to the Philippines or Shanghai, but not to the United States. Bettelheim said he left the building and went to the central post office and cabled Crane; the next day, he returned to the consulate and a different official approved his application, pending a physical examination and a visit to the Gestapo. Bettelheim told Raines that when he went to that headquarters the officer who interrogated him was Adolf Eichmann. Bettelheim said that the Nazi asked him to sit down, but that he had learned what such offers really meant and stayed standing while Eichmann asked a few questions, stamped his papers and dismissed him.[103]

In a 1988 interview that touched on the same days in Vienna, Eichmann made no appearance. This time, Bettelheim said that he had had to report to Gestapo headquarters every day before he left the country, and that he had had to sign a paper saying he had not been mistreated in the camps. He said one officer conceded that this was not true and then told him that when he got to the United States he should "never forget that [the Nazis] didn't have any Negroes in Germany—implying that they treated the Jews, you know, as the Negroes."[104] Bettelheim wrote that he did not tell people about life in Dachau and Buchenwald, "not so long as I or my mother was still on German soil. All I did tell others was to get out of Germany in a hurry. That is how little my conscience spoke as long as I had to fear being returned to the camp."[105]

YEARS AFTER Bettelheim's ordeal, he would write about the agony of survivor guilt and of how the realities of camp life "induced me (in my more optimistic moments I like to think, forced me) to do things . . . that would not stand up too well under closest scrutiny."[106] Beyond disclosing that he paid bribes, he never revealed in his published work what these acts were. His deception about the role of his glasses and his failure to describe the sock-mending assignment suggest that he felt ashamed because his poor eyesight, which had so embarrassed him since childhood, had won him a warm refuge for at least part of the winter of 1938–39, while most other prisoners worked in the death-dealing cold.

In general, Bettelheim's published accounts of his ten and a half months in Dachau and Buchenwald deserve skepticism; but doubts about their veracity do not mean that what he suffered was anything less than hellish. Just to be separated from one's family, to have one's worldly possessions stolen, and to be robbed of one's homeland was bad enough; to be sent into the Nazi Gulag, even before the war had started and when the ovens were more than three years away, was cruelty unimagined. No one who did not go through the experience is in any position to criticize Bettelheim's behavior at the time, to judge him for seeking to improve a desperate situation by using to best advantage his poor eyesight, the money he received from home, or any other strategies he could devise, including those he did not reveal because they "would not stand up too well under closest scrutiny."

If, after settling in the United States, he had become just one more obscure survivor, telling his camp stories to friends and neighbors only, his distortions would not matter much. But the accounts became the foundation on which Bettelheim would construct an international reputation as an expert not only on the camps but on the Holocaust itself, a role he pursued aggressively all his life, often with an I-was-there pugnacity. His writing and speaking on the subject brought him much publicity and made him, in the minds of many, a leading authority on how one survived the camp ordeal. In arguing his positions, he often claimed the high moral ground, attacking the views of others and delivering stern indictments of Otto Frank and his family and the European Jews in general for not resisting their Nazi persecutors, an accusation dealt with at length in Chapter Fifteen.[107]

Now Bettelheim was on the verge of freedom. From Vienna, he made his way to Antwerp, and on April 29 sailed on the S.S. *Gerolstein,* of the Red Star Steamship Co. One hundred and eighty-one passengers crammed the liner, the largest number it had ever carried; 116 of them were refugees from the Third Reich, many, like Bettelheim, listed on the ship's manifest as "Hebrew"; thirty-eight others were natives of Spain fleeing Francisco Franco's fascist regime. Bettelheim described his mental and physical health as good, put down his occupation as "merchant," and said he planned to reside with Agnes Crane on Steamboat Road in Greenwich. In answer to the question whether he planned to return to Austria, he said no, adding that he intended to become a U.S. citizen. At noon on May 11, 1939, the *Gerolstein* docked in Hoboken, New Jersey, across the Hudson River from Manhattan.[108] "I remember the exhilaration of walking the streets of New York," he recalled years later. "It was a hot summer day, with blue skies; the sun was shining. At that moment, I felt . . . I would make a new life for myself very different from the old one."[109]

CHAPTER FOUR
Chicago and Rockford

B Y THE TIME Bruno Bettelheim arrived in New York Harbor, Trude Weinfeld had been living in Australia for five months. She had quickly discovered she was unable to earn a living in Switzerland and had tried to immigrate to the United States; but even a letter of support from Anna Freud and the Freud family intimate Dorothy Burlingham, both of whom she had known in Vienna, failed to move the American consul in Zurich, who tore the document up and made it clear to the stateless young woman that she should forget about becoming an American. The Australian government was more welcoming. With a shortage of potential wives in the country, it was courting women and making immigration a relatively easy process, requiring little more of Weinfeld than that she show she had a small amount of money. Her father arranged for a letter of credit in Sydney, and the family of her friend Emarina Vischer gave her the cash for the passage, a month-long voyage that took her by ship from Naples to Sydney via the Suez Canal. She arrived in December 1938, just before the most peculiar Christmas she had ever encountered—one celebrated in the hot sunshine of the Australian summer.[1]

Richard and Editha Sterba had given her the name of a psychoanalyst, Roy Coupland Wynn, and through him she found a job at Crest Haven, a progressive boarding school in the suburb of Mona Vale. She had brought her Montessori instructional material in the trunk with her belongings and soon was doing again what she loved, working with children. She lived at the school, where her colleagues immediately discovered her good nature and energetic competence. Her teaching, and the novelty of living by the ocean in this expansive land of kangaroos, aborigines, and inverted seasons, distracted her some of the time; but mostly she worried about the fate of her parents and Bruno thousands of miles away. She also had to deal with the growing anti-German sentiment in Australia, which she tried to do by telling everyone that her name was Trude Field, a ruse that could hardly have disguised her accent.

When Bruno emerged from Buchenwald in April, one of the first things he did was send her a cable saying he was free. Though he addressed it to Trude Weinfeld and got the name of the school slightly wrong, she received it. "It is hard to describe my joy when I got that wire," she recalled. "I told everybody about it. I pretended that Bruno was my fiancé."[2] Despite the wire, he was not ready to assume that role. After the *Anschluss,* he had urged Trude to get to Australia if she could, not just to rescue herself from the Nazis but because he had wanted to end the affair. More than five decades later, he would confide to an acquaintance that he had always felt ashamed that he had treated her so badly by encouraging her to settle so far away.[3]

As soon as he cleared immigration in New York Harbor, he went to Gina, who was now living in a small apartment on Manhattan's Upper East Side. She was surprised to see that he looked physically well, not like someone who had lost half his body weight, though by the time of their reunion he had had almost a month to put on pounds. "He was not for one moment unsure that we would resume our marriage," Gina told me. He suggested that they might run a children's school together, perhaps with their friend Fritz Redl, who was now dividing his time between teaching psychology at the University of Michigan in Ann Arbor and working in research at the University of Chicago. She said he also talked of how he might make a political career in the United States—exhibiting a grandiosity she found altogether new. Bettelheim saw his immediate salvation in helping Gina care for Patsy under the benevolent umbrella of Agnes Crane until he managed to establish himself.

But the Bettelheims of Vienna, with their commodious apartment in Hietzing and their income from the lumber business, were now refugees with almost no money; the mercurial Crane, for all her efforts on their behalf, no longer saw the couple as her social equals, and had already made it clear to Gina that she planned other arrangements for Patsy. This cooling had been compounded by Agnes's disapproval of Gina's growing affection for Peter Weinmann, who had made it from England to Chicago and was now trying to resume his career at the University of Illinois College of Dentistry. Bruno quickly saw that the Crane safety net he had counted on as he crossed the Atlantic was in tatters, and by the end of his first day with Gina in fourteen months he knew that his marriage was, too.

Once again, as he had so many times as a boy after school in Vienna, Bettelheim found a welcoming refuge with the Buxbaums. His cousin Edith and her mother, his aunt Jeanette, were now living in the German-American community of Yorkville, a few blocks from Gina. They gave him a small room in their apartment and agreed to help support him until he could find work. Bettelheim immediately wrote Trude, telling her that he and Gina were getting a divorce and asking her to come join him. He also sent a letter to A. M. Warren, the visa official in Washington whom Agnes Crane had repeatedly asked to help gain his release from the camps. "My dear Mr. Warren," he wrote in his neat hand five days after his ship docked, "I think that only if you knew fully out of how desperate a situation the intervention of the State Department rescued me even at the last moment, could you realize how deeply I appreciate the help which you were able to give me. Yours very sincerely, Bruno Bettelheim." [4]

In the weeks that followed, Bettelheim slowly began to gain his equilibrium. He took long walks to explore Manhattan, visiting museums and seeing the few émigrés he knew, among them his *Realschule* classmate Hans Willig and his wife, Wanda. Mostly he wrote letters and went from agency to agency, trying everything he could think of to help his mother and sister get to the United States, and also to find work for himself. In June, the Committee on Relief and Immigration of the American Psychoanalytic Association, which at Edith Buxbaum's urging had written the State Department after Bettelheim entered Dachau, sent out several letters to academic institutions recommending him for "work in art history or along psychological lines in the field of art." [5] But no job had materialized by July.

Edith Buxbaum proposed to her cousin that they spend the summer driving to the West Coast and back in her old Cadillac convertible. He agreed to the trip, seeing it as a good opportunity to explore his new country and also to make contacts and follow up job possibilities. The outdoor life had never been one of Bettelheim's enthusiasms, but because money was short they camped out in sleeping bags much of the time. Every few days, the travelers would check into a tourist court for a bath and a good night's sleep. Edith had long been jealous of Gina's relationship with her favorite cousin, and now that his marriage was over she hoped her fantasies might be realized. "My expressed intention was to show him the country, to divert him . . . ," Buxbaum wrote many years later. "But my unexpressed intention was to have him for a lover." Bruno was not interested, which left Edith "plenty angry" as the Cadillac rolled across America.[6]

Bettelheim never published an account of the trip, but he told Theron Raines that on the West Coast he visited the University of Redlands, a small Baptist school east of Los Angeles, to which he had applied from New York. After an interview, he was offered an instructor's position—in what subject, he could not recall for Raines. Bettelheim was grateful for this opportunity, even in so remote a town as Redlands, and considerably relieved at the prospect of a berth in academia and a regular income. Thus buoyed, the two Viennese cosmopolitans drove north through the farmland, mountains, and sequoias of California and into Oregon, where Bettelheim said he was offered a better job teaching German at Reed College, in Portland, to which he had also applied from New York. He said he accepted instantly and wrote a letter to Redlands asking them to release him and offer the teaching post there to another Jewish refugee.[7]

Despite Bettelheim's relief at finding a steady job so quickly, "he had his heart on Chicago."[8] On the drive west, they had stopped there to visit Fritz Redl, Bettelheim's Vienna friend; in Hyde Park, the university community on Chicago's South Side, Redl introduced Bettelheim to George Sheviakov, who had come to the United States from Russia around 1920 and would eventually teach psychology for twenty years at San Francisco State University. Both Redl and Sheviakov were involved in a project called the Eight-Year Study, an exploration of how thirty secondary schools around the country might make teaching more progressive and effective by planning their own curricula instead of adhering to traditional standards. Bettelheim said he and Sheviakov hit it off immediately, and that the Russian émigré promised to alert him if any jobs opened up on the campus.[9] The prospect tantalized Bettelheim as he walked through the placid quadrangles, whose neo-Gothic buildings, despite their Indiana limestone, offered a certain European embrace. They also housed a nationally renowned faculty, presided over by Robert Maynard Hutchins, the avatar of progressive education who had become the University of Chicago's president in 1929, at the age of thirty. This was the academic big time, where the chances for advancement might be great, not a small college in a provincial city at the far edge of the country.

On September 1, 1939, the Nazis invaded Poland and World War II began. Bettelheim told one interviewer that he and Edith were passing through Chicago over that Labor Day weekend, on their way back east. He said he went to a meeting of the Modern Language Association at the Palmer House in the Loop, where a letter from Reed College was waiting; it advised him that because of the war few students wanted to take German, so the job was no longer available.[10] In a different version, he told Raines that he returned to Manhattan in late August and that Reed rescinded its offer by telegram a few days after the war broke out.[11]

Wherever he received this setback, it was ameliorated by news that his mother had at last obtained a visa and booked passage for the United States. On September 25, two days before Warsaw fell to the Germans, Paula Bettelheim sailed from Antwerp aboard the S.S. *Pennland,* and she arrived in New York Harbor on October 6.[12] Bettelheim told Raines that on the day his mother docked he received a letter from George Sheviakov saying a job was available at the Eight-Year Study; it offered no salary but would provide him with a desk, a secretary, and the good possibility of pay in the future. Bettelheim settled his mother in Manhattan with her sister, Jeanette Buxbaum, and headed back to Chicago.

At about this time, Trude Weinfeld was in a hospital in Australia. Not long after she had received the April cable from Bruno telling her that he was out of Buchenwald, she met Hans Bandler, the young engineer whom Bettelheim had befriended in the camps. Bandler had told his fellow inmate that he hoped to get to Australia; when Bandler had been released in January, Bettelheim asked that, if he did make it, he try to find Trude, whose where-abouts he knew from his mother's letters.

One day, Trude recalled, "this young man appeared, telling me a lot about Bruno and how he had managed to keep people interested in life and alive by telling them about his life. Bruno's analytic training, his warmth and understanding apparently helped others to manage that absolutely gruesome experience." [13] Bandler was twenty-four, Weinfeld twenty-seven—two Viennese refugees far from the familiar world of the Ringstrasse and still coping with the emotional reaction to their narrow escapes. "She was a very wonderful, very brilliant person," Bandler told me, the memory of their encounter still fresh in his seventy-eighth year. They soon became good friends, exploring their new surroundings together, taking hikes in the bush, boiling the billy to make tea.

"I think it was almost inevitable that, with my longing for Bruno, and our being such strangers in a strange country, that we should become intimate. I don't think I really was in love with him, maybe he not with me either; it was just a matter of circum-stances and loneliness." [14] Their romance continued for weeks, until one day Trude experienced severe pains in her pelvis, indi-cating an ectopic pregnancy. She required an immediate operation, one that could leave her unable to have children. The surgeon, aware that his patient was eager to raise a family someday, suc-ceeded in saving one of her ovaries. "I will never forget the words the doctor said to me after the operation: 'You can still have thousands of children.'" She recuperated in a sanatorium outside Sydney for three weeks, visited by Bandler and her colleagues from Crest Haven, and worrying constantly because she now wanted nothing more than to join Bruno in the United States.

She had begun trying to get her papers together to persuade the American consul to let her emigrate. Her hospitalization had interfered with that process, and with the outbreak of the war on September 1, she had become an enemy alien as well, her Austrian passport now "not worth a penny." Any authorization to leave

Australia was up to the military, and when Trude finally emerged from the sanatorium she took a taxi to a military headquarters and asked for permission to sail for America. When the officer hesitated, she began to cry and beg him, telling him that her fiancé had just come out of a concentration camp and was waiting for her in the United States. He granted her the papers.

To pay for her passage, she borrowed money from friends, and in early October, about the time Bruno was welcoming his mother in New York, she sailed from Sydney. After stops in New Zealand, the Fiji Islands, Samoa, and Hawaii, she arrived in San Francisco on October 31, to discover that the United States was a place where people put grinning candlelit squashes in the window and children dressed up as witches and ghosts traveled in packs at night ringing doorbells.

Weinfeld was greeted by Emma Plank, who had been one of her superiors in the Vienna Montessori system and would eventually become a professor of child development at Case Western Reserve University in Cleveland. She had fled Austria after the Nazis closed down her school and had already established herself in a similar undertaking in San Francisco. Plank urged her former employee to stay with her, in part because she valued her teaching skills, but also because she thought Trude should not run to Bruno's arms. Weinfeld would speculate that Plank was taking her cue from Richard and Editha Sterba, who disapproved of the relationship. Though she did not say why, it may have been because Richard, who had analyzed both Bruno and Gina, and Editha, who had analyzed Gina and Trude, felt that Bruno and Trude were not suited for one another. Whatever the reason, under Plank's influence, Trude sent Bettelheim an ambiguous wire that read: "Arrived safely, letter follows." But early the next morning, she went down to the wharf and arranged to have her baggage shipped to Chicago.

Within a day or two, she told Bruno she was coming, boarded a train east, and for an endless two nights and three days fantasized about her reunion. When she arrived, she was dismayed to be greeted at the station by Gerhart and Maria Piers, the Viennese couple who had tried to help Bruno by passing money to the Nazis from Switzerland and who were now living in Hyde Park.

They explained that Bruno, whose new and uncertain position at the Eight-Year Study paid no salary, was out of town investigating the possibility of a job that did. The Pierses checked her into a hotel not far from the campus and told her that Bruno was expected to return by bus in a few days. On the morning he was due, Trude walked to Stony Island Avenue and 63rd Street, on the South Side, where she had been told the bus would unload passengers. But it passed through without stopping and headed for the main depot downtown, nine miles away. She took a taxi to the terminus and found Bruno pacing the floor wondering where she was. "I leave to everybody's imagination," Trude recalled, "what that meeting meant to both of us, and how we experienced it." [15]

FEW CONCEPTS are more Viennese than *Protektion,* the feudal system that outlived the Habsburg monarchy and continues to hold that the best way to get ahead in the world is to find a powerful patron. Sigmund Freud himself owed his professorship at the University of Vienna to a devoted and influential patient, the Baroness Marie Ferstel, who bribed the minister of education with a painting for a gallery he was planning. [16] "When I first came to this country," Bettelheim said, "I did the smartest thing in my life. I tied myself to a truly great man—Ralph Tyler. . . ." [17]

In 1939, Ralph Winfred Tyler was chairman of the department of education at the University of Chicago and also the institution's examiner, having been brought in by Hutchins to reform testing and make the four-year college strictly exam-based. In addition, the energetic thirty-seven-year-old educator was research director of the Eight-Year Study's evaluation staff and needed someone to help assess how well art was being taught in secondary schools. He quickly spotted Bettelheim, with his strong University of Vienna credentials in the subject, as the man to help do the job. By December, Tyler was sufficiently impressed by the newcomer's work so that he started paying him a small salary. Bettelheim had been in the United States only seven months and in Chicago less than three; already he had driven across the country and back, been reunited with Trude, and landed a paying job in the academic world he so desired, and at the very university he had aimed for.

He and his fellow evaluators met regularly to discuss their findings, and these gatherings almost always turned into bull sessions. At one of them, someone brought up the Great Books, the syllabus of Western thought that Hutchins believed should be at the core of a liberal education; he taught seminars in the subject himself, usually together with his intellectual alter ego, Mortimer Adler. Bettelheim's reaction to the Great Books project would eventually become part of campus folklore.

He told Theron Raines that he saw the program as no big innovation and advised his astonished colleagues, most of whom he still barely knew, that in Germany and Austria Plato, Aristotle, Kant, and many other masters on the Hutchins-Adler roster were required reading at the *Realschule* level. He said that the university was foolishly teaching Homer, Dante, Melville, and the other great texts without providing a historical context so the books would make more sense to undergraduate readers. The attack irritated Joseph Schwab, a biologist on the faculty and an enthusiastic advocate of the Great Books idea, and soon George Sheviakov was signaling his friend, realizing that Schwab knew Hutchins well and would doubtless tell him how this presumptuous, job-seeking newcomer had denigrated his prized project.[18]

At the Eight-Year Study, Bettelheim worked immediately under Paul Diederich, who had come to the project the year before and would eventually serve for many years with the Educational Testing Service in Princeton, New Jersey. Together, they concocted a test to measure the appreciation of the visual arts, one that employed ten large framed reproductions of modern paintings that they arranged to have hung in the central halls of various senior high schools around the country. They sought comments about the works and received hundreds of replies, which they broke down into categories: demands for photographic realism, special sensitivity to color, etc.

Bettelheim also developed a test of his own, in which he showed students a large cardboard sheet on which forty colored, postcard-size prints were mounted and asked them to pick out pairs that impressed them as being alike, such as two works by Rembrandt or paintings by different artists that dealt with the same subject. Bettelheim "was very competent and very sensitive," recalled Diederich. "He was quite close to the youngsters and could get them to talk about what they liked." One of the first things that impressed Ralph Tyler about his new evaluator was that he believed that the project's investigations should begin with the problems of the students, not, as so often happened in academia, with the demands of the researchers. "Bettelheim was very effective. We received many reports from the schools telling how they were helped by his insights," Tyler told me.

Bettelheim's work for the Eight-Year Study required that he visit high schools out of town from time to time, but mostly he stayed close to the campus and nursed his "badly wounded soul."[19] He had suffered no major lasting physical afflictions in Dachau and Buchenwald but, like many survivors, was plagued by "horrible nightmares."[20] Trude said she spent many of their first days together in tears because of Bruno's depression. She tried to persuade a psychoanalyst to help him, but the woman refused, for reasons Trude did not give; she doubted, however, that Bruno would have agreed to enter therapy even had the analyst been willing. To add to the tension, Trude, who had a scar from the operation in Sydney, had to reveal her affair with Hans Bandler, a confession that pained her greatly and left Bruno, who had asked Bandler to find her, "very upset."[21] Soon he was gravitating toward another woman, a research assistant he had met at the Eight-Year Study.

Jean Friedberg was not long out of Vassar College, slim and dark-haired with a thin, high nose and blue eyes, a countenance as patrician as her background. Her father, Stanton—who died just after World War I, when she was seven—had been a prominent ear, nose, and throat doctor in Chicago. Jean had grown up in the assimilating liberal-intellectual atmosphere of Chicago's German Jewish elite, of which her mother, Aline, was a member in good standing. She had been instrumental in helping several German Jews come to the United States, among them her cousin, Helen Dukas, who was Albert Einstein's secretary.

Bruno was powerfully attracted to the twenty-seven-year-old Jean and asked her to marry him.[22] He may have turned away from Trude partly in anger, because he felt she had betrayed him with Hans Bandler, and because he feared she might never be able to have children after the ectopic pregnancy; but he may also have seen in Jean Friedberg a more propitious match. Trude loved him deeply and had traveled thousands of miles to succor him, but she lacked the sophisticated wit and intellectual charm of this well-born American. Jean may also have reminded Bruno of Gina, who was slim, dark-haired, blue-eyed, and cultured as well, and whose name sounded the same. For the moment at least, Trude's devotion was overshadowed by the opportunity Bruno saw for carrying off such a prize as Jean Friedberg and splicing himself into a world that would instantly enhance his prospects and greatly ease his struggle in America.

It is impossible to know if Bruno would have walked away from Trude had Jean said yes to his proposal, but she did not. She already was betrothed to a lawyer named Samuel Block, who was twenty-nine, eight years younger than Bettelheim. Block had demonstrated quick promise as an undergraduate at Yale and at Harvard Law School, from which he graduated in 1936, and would become a partner in one of Chicago's leading law firms, Jenner and Block. His university credentials and obvious ease in his fiancée's social circle moved Bruno, again rebuffed, to lash out. He told Jean she had turned him down because Block brought status more fitting for her class, a remark that so enraged her that she never completely forgave him, though they lived within a few blocks of one another for the next thirty-three years.[23]

When Bettelheim first arrived in Chicago, he had moved into a small apartment at 6033 Dorchester Avenue, hard by the Midway Plaisance, where, in 1893, millions of Americans had been awed by the sixty-five thousand exhibits from forty-seven countries that made up the World's Columbian Exposition; it now was a grassy, tree-lined corridor linking Washington Park, on the western edge of the campus, to Jackson Park, by Lake Michigan on the east. Bettelheim shared his bachelor quarters with Fritz Redl, who used them when he came to Chicago from Ann Arbor. Trude stayed in the apartment for a while, but eventually rented a room across the street. "The first thing the landlady told me," she recalled, "was that I was to leave the door open if I had any male visitors."[24] Nevertheless, the Australian surgeon's assurances too soon proved correct: Trude became pregnant. Not only was she unmarried but the prospective father was not yet divorced from Gina. Desperate, Trude confessed her condition to Helen Martinson, a neighborhood acquaintance, who steered her toward an abortion. Years later, Trude told at least one of her children that the baby was stillborn. Whichever account is true, the pregnancy only added to the trauma the two refugees faced as they tried to adjust to their new life.

Trude eventually found a job supervising the study hall in an institution for Jewish children; she later did similar work for an Episcopalian organization and also administered play therapy in various parts of the city. But it quickly became apparent that she would have to go back to school, because the social-work degree she brought from Vienna was not recognized by the local agencies. Nor did she have the luck Bruno had had with the University of Chicago: the School of Social Service Administration refused to grant her credit for any of her education or training, in part because Montessori methods were not yet accepted, or even widely known, in the United States. Ultimately, a Jewish organization gave her a loan so she could attend classes at Loyola University, on the North Side, and this opened the door for a long career working with children in Chicago. The loan came about in part through the intercession of Jean Friedberg—whether before or after Bruno's proposal is unclear.[25]

In early February 1940, Bruno's sister, who had made it safely from Vienna to England, was finally able to join their mother in New York. She had sailed from Liverpool on the S.S. *Lancastria,* listing herself on the passenger manifest with stage name appended: Margarete Bettelheim-Roederer. According to a story her brother related to his children and others over the years, Margaret had left a fiancé behind in Vienna. To this businessman she and her mother had entrusted some valuable jewelry as well as money to be deposited for them in a Swiss bank account. He planned to come to the United States and marry Margaret as soon as he could arrange for the necessary papers; but at the end of 1940, he was found dead of a coronary in his limousine. The family never recovered the jewels or the money. Still, with Hitler now preparing to take over Norway and Denmark and growing bolder by the day, all three Bettelheims had reason to be grateful:

they had managed not only to survive but to find sanctuary in the same country.

Trude Weinfeld's family was not so fortunate. Her parents, Paul and Frederika, had found temporary safety in Tours, where Trude had been able to visit them once before sailing for Australia. By September 20, 1940, their thirtieth wedding anniversary, France had fallen to the Nazis; unable to leave the country, they sought refuge in Limoges, living in a small room with an outside toilet, little heat, and a hot plate on which they prepared meager meals. That winter, Paul Weinfeld suffered some kind of intestinal obstruction; after weeks of terrible pain, he died on April 19, 1941. His widow's letters were such "that one [could] hardly read them without crying." [26] Trude sent her mother what little money she could, and Frederika wrote letters pleading with French officials in Marseilles to grant her an exit visa for Spain or Portugal, from which she hoped to get to the United States. Finally, the consulate summoned her to Marseilles, only to tell her that all exit visas had expired. She returned in defeat to the small French town where she was living, and in a letter to her daughter said that if taken to the camps she would commit suicide. "I have no idea whether this happened," said Trude, who never heard from her mother again. [27] In August 1942, Frederika Weinfeld was arrested and taken to a French camp called Stepfonds. On the morning of September 9, 1942, she and about one thousand other Jews, more than one hundred under the age of seventeen, were loaded onto a train at the Le Bourget/Drancy station on the outskirts of Paris. Two days later, this convoy No. 30 arrived at Auschwitz, where most of the victims died in the ovens. Whether Trude's mother killed herself before suffering this fate is unrecorded. [28]

Headlines daily charted the march of the Wehrmacht across Europe, and reminders of the conflict would soon fill the neighborhood as well: children skipping classes to collect tin foil and newspapers for defense industries, victory gardens sprouting in backyards, windows hung with gold stars signifying the death in action of a son or husband. Officers in Eisenhower jackets stepped smartly through the doors of the Chicago Beach Hotel, which had been converted into Fifth Army headquarters for the duration. On the campus, sailors trained in semaphore, wigwagging as perplexed undergraduates looked on, and marching to and from their barracks to the staccato beat of drummers on their flanks. In the summer of 1942, Stern Park Gardens, a predominantly Czech housing project, was renamed Lidice, after the Bohemian village the Nazis had wiped out on June 10.

Bruno and Trude did their best to distract themselves from the war by focusing on their work and slowly putting down roots. Though they both had incomes, the money did not go far; Bruno regularly sent some of his salary to his mother in New York, and Trude had done the same for her mother in France. They lived frugally, eating at home or on rare occasions at the Hutchinson Common cafeteria on the campus. They strolled Hyde Park's quiet, shaded streets, admiring many of the architecturally ambitious houses, including several designed by Frank Lloyd Wright. Their neighborhood enclave boasted no Hofburg or Schönbrunn palaces but did offer the Museum of Science and Industry, which remained from the World's Columbian Exposition and sprawled like an oversize Greek temple in Jackson Park. On steamy summer days, they went swimming at the 57th Street beach, in a lake that dwarfed those they had known in the mountains of Austria. Hyde Park provided no *Stammcafé,* a coffeehouse where Bruno and Trude could gather regularly with friends, as they had in Vienna, and the watery java at Stineway's drugstore, a popular campus hangout at Kenwood Avenue and 57th Street, was no match for the mochas and mélanges served by obsequious black-tie waiters at the Herrenhof. This was the land of the soda jerk. To remind themselves of home, Bruno, Trude, Fritz Redl, Gerhart and Maria Piers, and several other recent arrivals, among them a striking dark-haired Viennese psychiatrist named Emmy Sylvester, nourished their spirits with Wiener schnitzel and Sacher torte at one another's homes. "We had great times in that apartment," said Trude, of the parties at 6033 Dorchester.[29] By the spring of 1941, she and Bruno had taken over the lease, Redl having settled in Detroit full time as a professor of social work at Wayne State University.

By now, Gina was also living in Chicago, together with Peter Weinmann, who had become an assistant professor of oral pathology at Loyola University. They remained friendly with Bruno and

Trude, a relationship that soon extended to shared Thanksgivings and Christmases. Neither Bruno nor Gina had any desire to contest a divorce action, but one of them had to bring it. This Bruno gamely did, testifying in March 1941 that he had been a dutiful spouse for almost a decade in Vienna, that he had wanted to continue the marriage in the United States, but that Gina had refused to live with him. George Sheviakov, a witness in the brief proceeding, confirmed his friend's abandonment. Bettelheim's attestation was mostly a pro-forma legal maneuver to simplify the disentanglement and get it over with. Nonetheless, it must have been painful for the rejected husband to speak the words; doubly so, perhaps, since his lawyer was Sam Block, who had married Jean Friedberg four months before. Bruno and Gina amicably divided up what little property they had managed to bring out of Austria. She told him to take *Vorstadt I*, the Schiele painting he had bought for her, because Peter found its dark colors depressing —a reaction not without financial consequences for the future. The divorce decree was entered in the Superior Court of Cook County on May 7, 1941. A week later, Bruno, now thirty-seven, and Trude, twenty-nine, were married by City Court Judge John J. Wallace, who on December 30 would perform the same rite for Gina and Peter Weinmann.

Bettelheim continued to benefit from Ralph Tyler's *Protektion*. When the Eight-Year Study ran its course in 1941, the American Council on Education asked Tyler to set up the Cooperative Study in General Education to explore the quality of teaching and curricula at twenty-two colleges around the country. Again, Tyler needed someone to assess art instruction and tapped Bettelheim for the position. But the job was only part time and the salary inadequate, especially since Bettelheim continued sending some of it to his mother and because the newlyweds were planning to have a child. In August, Tyler wrote to Mary Ashby Cheek, the president of Rockford College, recommending Bettelheim for an opening in the school's art department. Ulrich Middeldorf had already told Cheek she had an opportunity to hire "a brilliant man"[30]—no minor endorsement, coming from the former curator of the German Institute for Art History in Florence and now chairman of the University of Chicago's art department. In seconding Middeldorf's view, Tyler said Bettelheim "came from a wealthy Viennese family who have had fine art collections of their own," a burnish that could only have been supplied by the candidate himself.[31]

THE CITY OF ROCKFORD was the third largest in Illinois, an industrial center of eighty-four thousand people ninety miles northwest of Chicago, just south of the Wisconsin border. The community, heavily Swedish and Irish, tended to be politically conservative, and the board of trustees of the small all-female college was highly so, taking its cue, as thousands of Midwesterners did, from the reactionary signals pulsing out of Robert Rutherford McCormick's Chicago *Tribune*. Mary Ashby Cheek, however, was an internationalist, an open-minded educator who had come to Rockford from Mount Holyoke College in 1937 and was trying to make the campus a haven for several refugee scholars every year. She offered Bettelheim a post teaching art courses two days a week for six hundred dollars a year, plus free lodging and meals in the campus dining room, which she estimated made the job worth two hundred more a year.[32] Bettelheim was not enthusiastic about the long commute, and the college was no University of Chicago, but he was glad to have the income, and on September 22 he arrived in Rockford by train and began teaching two courses, an introduction to art and the history of ancient art.[33]

"I met him the first day," recalled Mildred Berry, who taught speech and American history and had been asked by President Cheek to share her office in John Barnes Hall with the new instructor. "He came in a tattered old raincoat and cap. He said, 'I'm Bruno Bettelheim,' and I introduced myself. He sat down at his desk, unpacked a few books, and then left without saying goodbye. He came to the office every morning but seemed not to want to talk. He was chilly; he never visited or made small talk. He seemed not to want to tell me anything about his past." He kept his distance from most other faculty members as well, reading in his room on the nights he stayed over and concentrating on his teaching. In the classroom, however, he was anything but reticent, assuming his duties with relish. "He was stern, yet goodhearted and kind," recalled one student. "In class you hung on his every word." By the end of the first semester, Cheek was telling Tyler that Bettelheim was "an excellent and genuine teacher as well as a scholar of parts,"[34] and by June 1942 was eager to have him return to Rockford for the following academic year. In a letter to Bettelheim, she praised him for being "such a versatile person and at home in so many fields . . . ," and asked if he would send her any credentials he had in subjects outside the field of art, including psychology.[35]

Bettelheim had already embellished his past by telling *The Purple Parrot,* the student newspaper, that he had worked "at the Kunsthistorisches Museum and in the University [of Vienna] as a lecturer in the extension division until coming to the United States in 1939."[36] Now he sent Cheek a two-page letter and four-page curriculum vitae that gave his Vienna years a radiant academic glow. He wrote that "due to fortunate circumstances" he had been able to devote fourteen years, instead of the usual six, to his studies at the University of Vienna, not mentioning that he had dropped out of school for a decade. He said he had passed separate doctoral examinations *summa cum laude* in philosophy, the history of art, and psychology, whereas he had taken a doctorate only in philosophy, without honors. He described how he had painted, modeled in clay, and done woodwork at Vienna's Kunstgewerbeschule, taking instruction from leading artists. Because the courses in musicology he had taken at the university had not exposed him to contemporary music, he "became a member of the society for modern music, where studies were conducted under the personal leadership of [Arnold] Schoenberg." He declared that he had worked for two years as an assistant at Vienna's Kunsthistorisches Museum; excavated Roman antiquities for six months at an archeological dig; served as a member of Vienna's housing board from 1927 until all antifascist members were dismissed; conducted seminars for freshmen and supervised their work in art history and philosophy at the university, where he taught adult education courses as well—courses he adapted for art studies in settlements for the poor; ran the art department of Lower Austria's library; served as a research associate of the Society for Research in the History of the Theater; and supervised the art teaching in Vienna's progressive Montessori schools. Bettelheim also got his bibliography off to a promising start, assuring Cheek that he had already published two books, one of them his dissertation.

To these handsome credentials, Bettelheim added that he was "well trained in all fields of human, and social psychology, and [had] taught courses in them, as well as in normal and abnormal psychology," and had been "a member of an association of professional psychologists and educators which studied the developmental problems of children and adolescents."[37] Nowhere in the vita did the former partner in Bettelheim & Schnitzer mention that he had been a lumber dealer in Vienna from 1926 to 1938, the years of his impressive achievements. In his covering letter to Cheek, Bettelheim wrote that the résumé had been "prepared some time ago for another purpose."[38] What that purpose was, when he first wove the embroidery, and for whom, are unclear. Bettelheim did supply a résumé of some kind to Ulrich Middeldorf, who enclosed it in a 1941 letter of recommendation to Cheek. Ralph Tyler may have seen it as well, for he was under the impression before his protégé went to Rockford that his doctorate was "in the field of psychology."[39] By 1945, Bettelheim would claim, in his sworn deposition for the Nuremberg tribunal, that for about twelve years prior to the *Anschluss* he had "conducted research work in psychology and education."[40] (As Bettelheim inflated his academic record, the Nazis expunged the real one; on July 3, 1941, administrators at the University of Vienna reported to their masters in Berlin that they had rescinded his degree, as well as those of several other Jews, because of their "crimes" against the Third Reich.[41])

Bettelheim's ambition to become a respected figure in the academy doubtless moved him to dress up his vita, well knowing that Ralph Tyler, Mary Ashby Cheek, and others would hardly be inclined to investigate his credentials in the middle of the war, even had that been possible. He had other, more practical reasons for dispatching the fabricated pages to Rockford in the summer of 1942, however. He had been in the United States for three years, but, for all the praise his research and teaching had received, he remained constantly short of cash.

On the strength of the vita, Cheek invited Bettelheim back

to Rockford, this time to teach courses in German literature, philosophy, and both general and advanced psychology. This heavier load required that he spend four full days on campus; his yearly salary went up to nineteen hundred dollars, and at his request the college granted him the rank of associate professor.[42]

Bettelheim taught at the college for the next two years, so mesmerizing the young women with his Viennese accent and confident classroom style that he became something of a cult figure on the campus, with "a very large following of students who spent a lot of time with him, really adoring him."[43] Many of these acolytes saw him as a "father figure," a fount of European wisdom that flowed as easily with Dante as with Freud, with whom he said he had studied.[44] Mary Jane Wilcox, whose father sent her to Rockford because he didn't want her exposed to the liberal infection of Eastern education, soon caught the Bettelheim bug. "He was one of the world's ugliest men; he looked like a frog, really, because his eyes bulged out so," she told me. "But I found him very attractive, and he was a wonderful teacher who knew how to make every girl in his class feel important. He was the first person who ever made me feel like an intellectual." When a student told Bettelheim she liked to draw, he offered to pose for her, and she painted an oil portrait of him, "larger than life." She estimated that a half-dozen of her classmates switched their majors from English to psychology so they could study with him.[45]

Bettelheim used the Socratic method to challenge his students to think for themselves. He usually sat within a circle of young women, asking them probing questions, drawing out their answers, and instructing them not to take notes, explaining that professors who asked their classes to record their pronouncements slavishly were overly fond of their own ideas.[46] His reading lists excited these neophytes, most of whom were not yet twenty-one and had never read, or even imagined, such works as *The Psychopathology of Everyday Life*. Most other courses at Rockford were traditional and routine; Bettelheim's crackled with surprises every day. In his psychology classes, he turned his students into their own subjects, asking them to write short psychological autobiographies that mined their early dreams, their first memories, their view of their parents. Then, playing analyst, he would help them interpret their young lives. He did the same with Rorschach tests. "In my case," recalled Aimee Isgrig, who with Bettelheim's guidance looked for herself in the inkblots, "he was very profound. He said I had a great many responses and had to work on disciplining a mind that had so many ideas." She and other Bettelheim psychology students also went about the campus plumbing psyches with the Rorschachs, as well as with the Thematic Apperception Test, a series of nineteen relatively unstructured pictures aimed at getting the viewer to project her emotional needs and anxieties. Not a few of these guinea pigs "felt kind of invaded."[47]

As often as he was warm and understanding, Bettelheim turned sarcastic and dismissive. "When he liked you and felt you somehow met his standards, your relationship with him was almost collegial," Aimee Isgrig told me. But if a student showed weakness, he often moved in for the kill, as with one timid girl in a philosophy course. She brought to the class the orthodox religious values with which she had grown up in a small Illinois town, and which, like most of her classmates, she had never examined. Bettelheim kept pushing her until "he almost destroyed her; it was terrible to watch," Isgrig recalled. Sobs came often when Bettelheim dropped the role of kindly Viennese uncle and strode the classroom like Erich von Stroheim. "He literally reduced me to tears three or four times, and I would stomp out," said Veronica Dryovage, another student. "He kept challenging me in a way I wasn't used to, and I didn't know how to deal with it." Yet most students never doubted his commitment to them. When he was hospitalized in Chicago with pneumonia in January 1944, he asked Trude to write and tell the young women to read their term papers aloud in class until he was able to return.[48]

Bettelheim eventually became chairman of the college film committee and further entranced his followers by screening European movies in the evenings and leading discussions. He sometimes sat up late into the night at Maddox House, where seniors gathered over coffee and Cokes, talking of Secessionist Vienna or the Italian Renaissance and prodding them with guttural insistence to shake off their provincial thinking. Once in a while, he would talk about the war and his months in Dachau and Buchenwald, moving Aimee Isgrig to compose a poem about him:

Two lives
Have I lived.
Two sets of roots
Have been nourished
In two soils.
The old roots,
Cut without warning,
Linger on. . . .[49]

Occasionally, he invited students up to his room. One of them, Mary Jane Wilcox, went several times. "We discussed psychology and philosophy," she told me. "I was very attracted to him but was innocent and naïve, and never in my wildest dreams would have thought of having any physical contact with him. He never touched me, but I do remember the overpowering feeling of sexual vibrations." Wilcox said rumors eventually began circulating that Bettelheim had invited a student and her best friend to his apartment and that while the latter studied in one area the former was alone with her host. The girl who had stuck to her books was disturbed enough to report to the dean what she thought she saw. Whether or not this "incident" ever happened, something did cause the administration to sour on Bettelheim by the spring of 1944.

On May 4, President Cheek, whose letters to Bettelheim had always been cordial and who up to then had been an enthusiastic supporter, advised him coolly that he could not "look forward to a permanent appointment to the staff."[50] Several of Bettelheim's disappointed students deputized Aimee Isgrig to go see Cheek to find out why Dr. B, as his devotees now affectionately called him, was not coming back in the fall. Isgrig said Cheek told her only that "it was unfortunately necessary" that he leave. Mary Jane Wilcox recalled that at one point Bettelheim organized a rally in the chapel on his own behalf, showing a film on Nazi persecution and implying that, once again, he was being victimized. If so, the reason was less likely sexual misconduct than campus politics.

Bettelheim may have had a claque of young women, but many faculty members envied and disliked him, viewing him as "an intellectual Pied Piper" who had lured away their students.[51]

Their irritation cannot have been much soothed by his belief that, after only three years of teaching, he had earned the rank of full professor, a request rejected by Cheek.[52] Then there were the trustees. The president was "constantly battling" the conservative board, which regarded any teacher with progressive leanings as a heretic.[53] Also in 1944, one trustee, Grace Roper, decided that a professor named Levenstein was too pink because he taught communism as an economic philosophy; she refused to renew the money she had been giving to support his salary.[54] In this pinched community, which doubtless simmered with a measure of anti-Semitism, the long-term prospects for an ambitious, magnetic Viennese Jew—who was not bashful about saying what was on his mind and who sometimes made his students cry—would not have been great.

Bettelheim was not crushed by his failure to land another year at Rockford. He liked teaching and needed the income, but Rockford was a pretty dull place, especially compared with the vigorous intellectual atmosphere of the University of Chicago, whose faculty by now boasted such star émigrés as the German political scientists Hans Morgenthau and Leo Strauss; the Italian novelist, literary critic, and professor of romance languages Giuseppe Antonio Borgese, whose wife, Elisabeth, was Thomas Mann's youngest child; and the Italian physicist Enrico Fermi, who had won the Nobel Prize in 1938, and in 1942 had famously led the team that achieved the first nuclear-fission reaction, conducted in great secrecy beneath the stands of the university's Stagg Field. In the summer of 1944, Bettelheim's employment future remained uncertain, but he was happy that he no longer faced the long trips to and from Rockford and hoped that, with luck and perhaps the good offices of Ralph Tyler once again, he would find full time work at the university, for a steady job was imperative: on December 4, 1942, Trude had given birth to their first child, Ruth Colette.

CHAPTER FIVE
Extreme Situations

Bruno Bettelheim wrote that, from the moment he came down the gangplank of the S.S. *Gerolstein* in 1939, he began describing the horrors of Dachau and Buchenwald "to everybody willing to listen, and to many more unwilling to do so." Despite the pain of recalling his incarceration, he said, he felt duty-bound to the thousands still imprisoned to make as many people as possible aware of the Nazis' calculated inhumanity. But, as has long been well known, even after the war broke out most Americans refused for many months to believe that the nation of Beethoven and Thomas Mann was capable of the atrocities Bettelheim and others were describing. "I was accused of being carried away by my hatred of the Nazis, of engaging in paranoid distortions. I was warned not to spread such lies." His listeners said he was giving the SS "much too much credit for being intelligent enough to devise and systematically execute such a diabolic system, when everybody knew they were but stupid madmen."[1] In 1940, hoping that if he could publish his alarm it might prove more persuasive, he began setting down his observations.

At the time, little had been written by former inmates about the two camps he had been in. The two principal accounts—Bruno Heilig's *Men Crucified* and Peter Wallner's *By Order of the Gestapo: A Record of Life in Dachau and Buchenwald Concentration Camps*—were both published in England in 1941 and did not reach a wide readership there, much less in the United States. Bettelheim gave no indication that he had ever read these books; but whether he had or not, their highly personal, heavily anecdotal portraits of camp life, however valuable and moving, did not focus on what interested him most: the psychological impact of the concentration-camp experience.

The writing went slowly, in part because of the freighted subject, in part because Bettelheim had to fit it in around his busy research and teaching schedules in Chicago and Rockford. He did not finish the paper until 1942, by which time the United States had entered the war, anti-Nazi fever was running high, and reports of concentration-camp brutality no longer met with quite the disbelief Bettelheim had first encountered. Still, a certain skepticism continued; he wrote later that for well over a year he sent the manuscript to one psychiatric or psychoanalytic journal after another, only to have it rejected. He did not name the journals, or the editors who turned the paper down, but he did list their reasons for doing so: his failure to keep a written record in the camps, his inability either to verify or to replicate his data, or the seeming improbability of his facts and conclusions. Bettelheim said that some of these editors added, "probably correctly, as judged by my experience when I tried talking about these matters to professional people. . .that the article would be too unacceptable to their audiences."[2] The editor who did finally find it acceptable was Gordon W. Allport, a Harvard psychology professor who had spent time studying in Germany, and whose well-known views on personality emphasized the individual; he also oversaw *The Journal of Abnormal and Social Psychology,* which published Bettelheim's paper in the fall of 1943, under the title "Individual and Mass Behavior in Extreme Situations."[3]

In some twenty thousand words, the former prisoner sought to show how the concentration camp was not primarily a place where the SS indulged its appetite for random ruthlessness but a carefully organized and calculatedly cruel operation designed to make the prisoners more useful subjects of the Nazi regime. He said at the outset that it was not his intention "to recount once more the horror story of the German concentration camp,"[4] with which he assumed his readers were by now roughly familiar; instead, he was determined to present his case in a "scientific fashion."[5] He gave the paper a statistical underpinning, reporting that as a result of sleeping in five different barracks "he came to know personally at least" fifteen hundred inmates in the two camps. As noted, he had in fact slept in only two barracks, one in each camp; but even if he had been housed in five, establishing a personal relationship with fifteen hundred prisoners in ten and a half months would have meant getting to know and interview five new inmates every day, in a setting hardly conducive to such research. Whatever the number, the interviewees provided "an adequate sampling" to study the "case material."[6] Bettelheim wrote in the third person, the academic tone made more stilted by his struggle to master the nuances of his new language. He said he took this approach hoping to achieve an "objectivity" that would disarm those who insisted that he was exaggerating his findings out of a desire for revenge. He also cautioned that he regarded the paper as a preliminary report that did not "pretend to be exhaustive."[7]

In Bettelheim's view, the Nazis had established four major goals in the camps: to break the prisoners as individuals, to spread terror among the rest of the population by example, to give the Gestapo a training ground, and to create a human laboratory where the SS could gauge the maximum amount of hard labor the prisoners could withstand and minimum amount of food and medical care required to keep them alive.[8] Bettelheim divided the inmates into new prisoners, those who had spent no more than a year in the camps, and old prisoners, those who had been confined at least three years. He said that new prisoners retained a measure of hope for release and managed to keep their personalities intact, so that they had a good chance, if freed, of emerging much the same as when they were arrested. Old prisoners were mainly concerned with how best to cope with daily life inside the camp, had accepted their grim conditions, and "were afraid of returning to the outer world."[9] Old prisoners also tended to direct their aggression against one another, so as not to get in trouble with the guards; new prisoners aimed their aggression at their keepers, at least when they felt their angry words would not be heard.

The essay's core contention was that most prisoners eventually developed "types of behavior which are characteristic of infancy or early youth." To support his contention, Bettelheim wrote that "the prisoners were forced to say 'thou' to one another, which in Germany is indiscriminately used only among small children." [10] In fact, the term *du* was used at the time not just among small children but between lovers, good friends, and between adults and children within the family. The SS insisted that inmates use *du* not to make them childlike but to humiliate them, to rob them of their status as *Herr Doktor* or *Herr Professor* or the dozens of other honorifics or titles in which Germans and Austrians put such store. Still, Bettelheim pressed his case, writing that, like children, inmates found satisfaction in daydreaming instead of action, lived always in the immediate present, fought furiously with one another one minute and then made up moments later, and felt no shame when they were caught exaggerating their manliness. "During the day the prisoners who wanted to defecate had to obtain the permission of the guard. It seemed as if the education to cleanliness would be once more repeated." [11] New prisoners were often required to do make-work they regarded as childish, like digging holes in the ground with their bare hands even though tools were available, or carting stones from one end of the camp to the other and back for no useful purpose.

Bettelheim argued that widespread regression to childlike behavior eventually reduced most prisoners to an undifferentiated mass and "more or less willing tools of the Gestapo," whose values the inmates soon began accepting as their own.[12] Instead of using the "verbal aggressions" of the sort they had employed before entering the camp, they aped the foul vocabulary of the guards. "It was not unusual to find old prisoners, when in charge of others, behaving worse than the Gestapo, in some cases because they were trying to win favor...but more often because they considered this the best way to behave toward prisoners in the camp." [13] Bettelheim said that *Kapos* and block elders helped the Gestapo torture and kill inmates regarded as weaklings or traitors. This was certainly true, but not because these prisoner-overseers had undergone a unique psychological metamorphosis. As Bettelheim well knew but did not say, camp officials purposely chose as *Kapos* thugs like themselves, "former SA men [Storm troopers], Foreign Legionnaires, and professional criminals—those who knew how to use a whip. . . ." [14]

Bettelheim wrote that old prisoners eventually became so enthralled by their keepers that they "tried to sew and mend their uniforms so that they would resemble those of the guards." They even copied one of the guards' favorite off-duty games: hitting a comrade to see how much punishment he could take without crying out. Bettelheim found it "appalling" to see how far even politically well-educated prisoners went in identifying with their captors.[15]

By way of measuring this phenomenon, he said, he asked "more than one hundred old political prisoners" the following question: " 'If I am lucky and reach foreign soil, should I tell the story of the camp and arouse the interest of the cultured world?' "[16] Bettelheim did not consider, at least in the essay, that a prisoner might well pause before answering such a question in the affirmative, given that his reply could easily reverberate to the ears of his keepers. Instead, he said that only two inmates in his sample felt everyone escaping Germany should fight the Nazis by sounding the alarm; all others hoped for a German revolution but rejected the notion of other countries' interference in the fatherland's internal affairs. He said these inmates even "expressed their hatred" of the international press when foreign correspondents tried to help them by reporting on conditions in the camps.[17]

Bettelheim wrote that what happened to prisoners in Dachau and Buchenwald—the reduction of the individual to a slavish, childlike member of the group—happened in less grotesque terms to the inhabitants of greater Germany, and he warned that it might happen to the populations of France, Belgium, Holland, and other occupied countries if they failed to organize resistance movements. He maintained that the best way to fight the Nazis' systematic plan was through the formation of democratic groups in which independent and mature people reinforced one another's ability to oppose the oppressor. If such groups were not formed, it would be difficult to counter "the slow process of personality disintegration." Bettelheim concluded that this disintegration should be studied by all people interested in learning what happens to the individual caught in a totalitarian regime's psychological vise, especially if those who managed to survive were to be resurrected "as autonomous and self-reliant persons."[18]

Bettelheim wrote that he had tried to check his research with other inmates, but "[u]nfortunately. . . found only two who were trained and interested enough to participate in his investigation." [19] He said one was a doctor named Alfred Fischer, about whom he told his readers nothing save that he was now in England; the other was Ernst Federn, though Bettelheim did not risk identifying his friend at the time because he was still in Buchenwald. He said both men were "less interested" than he was in exploring the psychology of camp life. [20]

"Perhaps he thought so," Federn told me. Federn, who was liberated from Buchenwald in 1945 and eventually became a social worker in the United States, wrote that in the camp he and Bettelheim "had noticed the degree to which the mechanisms of defence that Sándor Ferenczi and Anna Freud have described as identification with the aggressor could be observed amongst the camp inmates." [21] Federn did not recall whether he or Bettelheim came up with this observation first, but Bettelheim avoided fully crediting their collaboration; nor did he suggest anywhere in his essay that his observations owed anything to the thinking of Anna Freud and her father's close colleague Ferenczi. Federn, who was in Dachau and Buchenwald for a total of seven years, told me that there is no question that regression of the kind Bettelheim described took place among some inmates, a few of whom did desperately ape the guards. But he said this phenomenon differed markedly from man to man, and called "nonsense" the notion that it was universal. Throughout much of his paper, Bettelheim implied that it was; toward the end, however, the generality seemed to make him uneasy, and he wrote that the "same old prisoners who identified with the Gestapo at other moments defied it, demonstrating extraordinary courage in doing so." [22] He supplied no examples.

If he had second thoughts about the many other generalities in his essay, he did not state them. He said flatly that criminals and political prisoners "did not feel too badly" about their incarceration; [23] that none of the many inmates he talked to dreamed about the terror of the transportation to the camps; [24] that the longer a prisoner spent in the camps the less realistic were his daydreams. [25] Describing a winter night when the SS forced prisoners to stand outside without overcoats for hours, during which many died of exposure or suffered frostbite that led to amputations, Bettelheim wrote:

> A feeling of *utter indifference* swept the prisoners. They *did not care* whether the guards shot them; they *were indifferent* to acts of torture committed by the guards. The guards no longer had any authority, *the spell of fear and death was broken*. It was again as if what happened did not "really" happen to oneself. There was again the split between the "me" to whom it happened, and the "me" who really did not care and was just an interested but detached observer. Unfortunate as the situation was, [the inmates] felt free from fear and therefore *were actually happier* than at most other times during their camp experiences.[26]

Recasting this passage for a 1947 volume of the *Encyclopaedia Britannica,* Bettelheim wrote that a "quasi-orgiastic happiness spread among the prisoners. . . ."[27] He maintained, also without qualification, that the inmates neither dreamed about their ordeal nor attached particular emotions to it.[28] If he himself stood through that terrible, freezing night, he did not say.

In another generalization, Bettelheim wrote that prisoners deluded themselves into thinking that beneath the rough exteriors of some high camp officers a certain sympathy existed for the prisoners' plight.[29] In fact, as Ernst Federn and other former inmates have testified, and Bettelheim himself would write, not all camp officials and guards were hell-bent on inflicting punishment, and some did try to treat the inmates with a certain decency.[30] Moreover, many of the prisoners the SS chose to put in charge of barracks and *Kommandos,* far from copying SS brutality, did the best they could in an almost impossible situation to protect their charges.[31] Better treatment also came through bribes. "Old prisoners," Bettelheim wrote, ". . .used [their money] for securing for themselves 'soft' jobs, such as. . .work in the shops where they were at least protected against the weather while at work."[32] He did not disclose that he had held such a job during his winter at Buchenwald; that he was, by his own definition, not an old prisoner at the time; or that his poor eyesight had helped protect him. Nor did he reveal that he himself had paid bribes, a disclosure that would not come for seventeen more years.

Bettelheim did not mention that the Gestapo freed thousands of prisoners during the ten and a half months he was incarcerated, and revealed nothing about what led to his own release. With the exception of the mysterious Alfred Fischer, he named no fellow inmate, and offered no examples of the toughness and often bravery with which many withstood the daily barbarity, or of the kindness and selflessness exhibited by some of his fellow prisoners.

One such inmate was Herbert Zipper, the Viennese composer-conductor Bettelheim had met in Dachau. Soon after arriving at the camp, Zipper began recruiting other musicians who, using two or three violins and guitars plus some makeshift instruments, formed a small orchestra. They rehearsed in the barracks on Sunday afternoons, while other prisoners stood watch, and performed concerts in an unused latrine with room enough for about twenty-five listeners to file in at a time. They played compositions by Zipper, written late at night in the barrack's latrine, which the composer had made his "studio" by volunteering to clean it—after a full twelve-hour working day—for the duration of his stay in Dachau. Sitting among the toilets, he wrote on margin strips of Nazi propaganda newspapers, cut and pasted together for him by "patrons" of the concerts. Zipper told me that Bettelheim's writing on the camps unfairly accented the meanness of the guards and prisoners, and not just because it ignored his own behavior. He recalled a man named Tillinger, a poor, uneducated Jew who barely had managed to eke out a living running a small grocery shop in Vienna. In Dachau, Tillinger made it his daily crusade to counsel his fellow inmates to persevere, and especially to reject the option of suicide. This fifty-year-old storekeeper, who could hardly read, became the "little hero" of the barracks.[33]

Bettelheim found no room in his account for such stories. In his determination to be the objective scholar, he made himself omniscient and his comrades, if not invisible, identityless stick figures whose sole purpose was to support his "scientific" findings. Yet Bettelheim's prose was less clinically neutral than eerily detached and superior, as if he had not been a prisoner at all but had merely hovered over Dachau and Buchenwald taking mental notes. What he saw when he looked down were prisoners he seemed to hold in contempt, men he called "pathological liars. . .unable to restrain themselves,. . .unable to make objective evaluations, etc." Having implied with his "etc." that these pathetic creatures manifested other weaknesses as well, Bettelheim then posed what he regarded as the central question for his survival: " 'How can I protect myself against becoming as they are?' " His answer, he said, was to study these guinea pigs to find out what was happening to them and to him, an intellectual exercise that also would allow him to occupy his spare time with "interesting problems. . ."[34] This tone would characterize much of Bettelheim's writing about his fellow prisoners over the years, but occasionally a certain self-awareness surfaced. In 1947, writing about the concentration camp as a class state, he said that "looking down upon lower class prisoners was an important psychological defense against one's own fears."[35]

When the essay appeared in the fall of 1943, with World War II at full pitch in the Pacific and Europe, and reports of the Nazi crematoriums mounting monthly, its omniscient voice riveted readers. Few of them had access to any other perspective on the camp experience, and they were disinclined to question the views of a man who had suffered as Bettelheim had while they had sat safely an ocean away debating whether even to go to war against Hitler. Meyer Schapiro, the Columbia University art historian, was so struck by "Extreme Situations" that he pressed it on several friends, among them the author James T. Farrell, whose starkly realistic Studs Lonigan trilogy, about an Irish-American youth growing up in Chicago, had been a major literary event of the 1930s. Farrell found the essay "a brilliant study"[36] and soon told Bettelheim so, beginning an on-and-off correspondence that would last for many years.

"Extreme Situations" also impressed Dwight Macdonald, the sometime Trotskyist, pacifist, and anarchist who had just quit as an editor at Partisan Review to found his own publication, Politics. In the first issue of this soon-to-be-influential magazine of the left, Macdonald called attention to the essay, and then wrote its author, praising him and inviting him to expand on the subject of concentration camps for the new journal.[37] Bettelheim was duly flattered, but replied that he was too busy to write anything new on his camp experience. Moreover, he was applying for U.S. citizenship, during which process the government barred him from any actions that would influence U.S. politics.[38] Bettelheim suggested that Macdonald excerpt "Extreme Situations" in *Politics,* which he did, introducing it in July 1944 with an announcement that identified Bettelheim as a psychiatrist. In a handwritten letter, Bettelheim politely corrected his new admirer: "I am *not* a psychiatrist, I am only a psychologist. I just feel that one should not make claim to a professional standing which one does not have."[39]

"Extreme Situations" also attracted the notice of a number of prominent émigrés, leftist intellectuals like Theodor Adorno and Max Horkheimer, who had gathered in New York City to reconstitute Frankfurt's Institut für Sozialforschung. In 1944, the exiles organized a series of lectures on National Socialism, the final one touching on Bettelheim's essay. The session's theme was that "Fascism produced something similar to a psychological collapse in the inmates of concentration camps—an analysis that paralleled the Frankfurters' bleak view of mass culture and its lobotomizing effect on the public."[40] Leo Lowenthal, the German sociologist and a prime mover at the institute, would soon quote Bettelheim's essay liberally and approvingly in the new political and intellectual organ of the American Jewish Committee, a monthly called *Commentary.* Abstracts of or references to "Extreme Situations" appeared in several other publications, including *The Journal of the American Medical Association,*[41] and it would soon be anthologized and hailed as a classic psychological study, to become required reading on many campuses for at least two decades.

Early on, Bettelheim began saying that General Dwight D. Eisenhower had made the essay required reading for U.S. military-government officers in Germany, a claim likely based on a letter from Gordon Allport, who had first published "Extreme Situations" in the *Journal of Abnormal and Social Psychology,* saying that Eisenhower had sought reprint permission from him.[42] Neither the Eisenhower library nor U.S. Army historians can find any evidence that the general followed through and that "Extreme Situations" was ever used by the military in postwar Europe.

•

By 1944, BETTELHEIM had developed a growing reputation at the University of Chicago as something of a Renaissance man, whose rigorous classical education at the *Realschule* and the University of Vienna and the breadth of his reading had supplied him with an impressive depth of knowledge. As with other émigrés who had begun attracting attention at American colleges and universities, his thick accent and intellectual exoticism gave him star potential in an insecure land where Europe equaled better. Even though Mary Ashby Cheek had refused to rehire Bettelheim, she gave him the highest marks for his teaching of art history, psychology, and philosophy at Rockford. Ralph Tyler, too, continued to be impressed by his protégé, whose byline had appeared not just in *Politics,* along with those of George Orwell, Paul Goodman, Simone Weil, Daniel Bell, Meyer Schapiro, and Macdonald himself, but in other publications as well.

In reviewing a book for the *College Art Journal,* Bettelheim criticized the author for making his text "forbidding for the college student" by using the clotted language of philosophy when simpler terms could have expressed more clearly what he had in mind.[43] This impatience with obfuscation would become a hallmark of Bettelheim's teaching, and over the years his commitment to accessible—if not always honest—prose would set his books and articles apart from much of the glutinous writing turned out by others in the profession he would soon embrace.

Bettelheim's genuine accomplishments during his first five years in the United States played nicely on the Austrian stage the erstwhile lumber dealer had carpentered for himself, with its splendid backdrop of polymath achievements: fourteen years at the University of Vienna, studies with Arnold Schoenberg, *summa cum laude* in three disciplines, two books published, training in all fields of psychology, and membership in an organization that studied the emotional problems of children and adolescents. Ironically, Bettelheim invented these credentials needlessly. America was not Europe, where lack of status so often suffocated ambition; anyone with wit and drive could get ahead in the land of opportunity, as thousands of Jews had. Moreover, from its founding in 1892, the University of Chicago had never been as stuffy about faculty appointments as the Ivy League bastions of class and privilege, with

Bruno Bettelheim at about age ten and a decade later in his early student days at the University of Vienna, from which he had to drop out, at age twenty-three, to enter the family lumber business after his father died of syphilis in 1926.

Above left, Margaret Bettelheim, Bruno's only sibling. An actress, she used the stage name Margaret Roederer.

Above right, Bettelheim and Gina Altstadt, whom he pursued ardently for several years before she finally consented to marry him in 1930.

Below, Gloriettegasse 15, in Vienna's fashionable Hietzing suburb, where the newlyweds settled in the spacious second-floor apartment and lived during the 1930s with Patsy Lyne, the disturbed American child whom Gina cared for from ages seven to fourteen.

Above left and right, Richard and Editha Sterba, Freud intimates and members of the Vienna Psychoanalytic Society. Both Sterbas treated Gina; Editha treated Patsy for several years; Richard treated Patsy's mother, Agnes Piel Lyne, as well as Bruno, who saw him for several months in the mid-thirties.

Below left, Joseph Peter Weinmann, the dental pathologist with whom Gina began an affair in the months before the *Anschluss* and whom she married after divorcing Bruno in the United States in 1941, the same year he married Trude Weinfeld.

Below right, Patsy Lyne with her mother, Agnes, in New England, where they lived together for many years.

Prisoners marching on the *Appellplatz*, the area between the barracks at Dachau, in the summer of 1938. Bettelheim entered the camp on June 3 of that year and would remain there and then in Buchenwald until April 14, 1939, when the Nazis freed him during the release of several thousand inmates.

Konzentrationslager Dachau 3

Folgende Anordnungen sind beim Schrift-
verkehr mit Gefangenen zu beachten:

1.) Jeder Schutzhaftgefangene darf im
Monat zwei Briefe oder zwei Karten von
seinen Angehörigen empfangen und an sie
absenden. Die Briefe an die Gefangenen
müssen gut lesbar mit Tinte geschrieben
sein und dürfen nur 15 Zeilen auf einer
Seite enthalten. Gestattet ist nur ein Brief-
bogen normaler Größe. Briefumschläge
müssen ungefüttert sein. In einem Briefe
dürfen nur 5 Briefmarken à 12 Pfg. beige-
legt werden. Alles andere ist verboten und
unterliegt der Beschlagnahme. Postkarten
haben 10 Zeilen. Lichtbilder dürfen als
Postkarten nicht verwandet werden.

2.) Geldsendungen sind gestattet.

3.) Zeitungen sind gestattet, dürfen aber
nur durch die Poststelle des K. L. Dachau
bestellt werden.

4.) Pakete dürfen nicht geschickt werden,
da die Gefangenen im Lager alles kaufen
können.

5.) Entlassungsgesuche aus der Schutzhaft
an die Lagerleitung sind zwecklos.

6.) Sprecherlaubnis und Besuche von Gefangenen im Konz.-Lager sind grundsätzlich
nicht gestattet.

Alle Post, die diesen Anforderungen nicht
entspricht, wird vernichtet.

Der Lagerkommandant.

Meine Anschrift:

Absender:
Name: *Bettelheim Bruno*
geboren am: *28 August 1903*
Block: *22* Stube: *3*

Dachau 3 K, den: *31. Juli 1938*

Meine Lieben. Dank

für Brief und Geld. Schick

erst wieder am 20. VIII. RM 15.— und dann wieder

alle Wochen. Ich habe mir einst vom Prokuris-

ten Gina Papi RM 5.— ausgeborgt, und konnte sie

nicht mehr zurückgeben. Erkundigt Euch nach

Bettelheim wrote at least nineteen letters to his mother and sister from Dachau and Buchenwald, all of them strictly limited by the rules enumerated on camp stationery. In this letter, written two months after Bettelheim entered Dachau, he asks for money and says that all his hopes rest on hearing that Gina, now in the United States, is preparing for their future together. But the marriage was over, as he would discover soon after his release.

Portions of the letter and curriculum vitae that Bettelheim sent Rockford College president Mary Ashby Cheek in the summer of 1942, in which he exaggerated or invented his academic credentials.

I am well trained in all fields of human, and of social psychology, and I have taught courses in them, as well as in normal and abnormal psychology. I would hesitate to teach courses in animal psychology, and in experimental (physiological) psychology. I am well familiar with Gestalt psychology.

Due to fortunate circumstances I was able to devote fourteen years (instead of the conventional six) to the study of the arts, of philosophy, and of related fields. During this period of study, I completed course requirements and passed separate comprehensive doctoral examinations summa cum laude in each of three major fields, namely: Philosophy, history of art, and psychology. I also completed a "minor" in Germanic languages (which included German literature and English language and literature). I elected to write my dissertation in the field of aesthetics.

Since I always enjoyed music I tried to integrate this art, too, into my studies, and since the courses in musicology which I took at the university of Vienna did not bring me in contact with contemporary musical developments, I became a member of the society for modern music, where studies were conducted under the personal leadership of Schoenberg.

I worked for two years as an assistant at the museum in Vienna (Kunsth-historisches Museum). I participated for six months in archeological field work, excavating Roman antiquities. I was a member of the advisory board of the housing authority of the city of Vienna (Gesiba) from 1927 up to the time when all anti-fascist members of this board were dismissed. I travelled extensively in Europe and in Asia Minor and added to my experience by working in a number of different art institutions.

THREE PHOTOS BY MYRON DAVIS/COURTESY SONIA SHANKMAN ORTHOGENIC SCHOOL

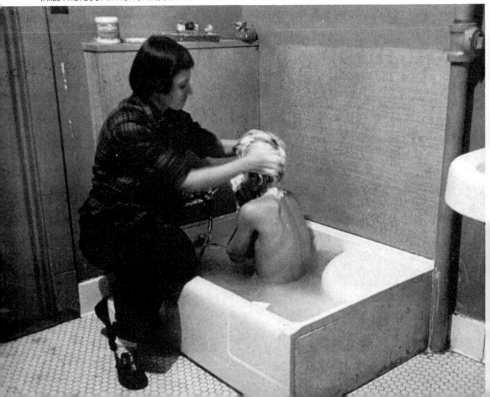

In 1944, Bettelheim became director of the Orthogenic School, the home for emotionally disturbed children at the University of Chicago, and in the first decade the young counselors worked long, exhausting hours playing with the children on the dorm floors, giving them shampoos, reading stories, and tucking them in at night. Bettelheim worked even harder and showed a particular interest in the children's artwork, which he said revealed Freudian truths and he often reproduced the drawings in his books and articles.

The Orthogenic School as it looked when Bruno Bettelheim became director in 1944.

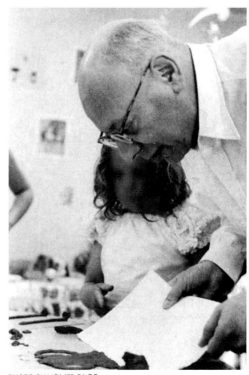

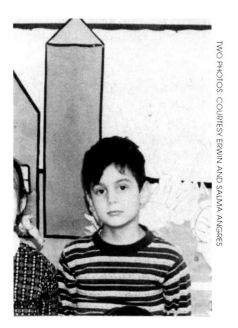

Ronald Angres, at about the time he entered the Orthogenic School as a seven-year-old in 1959, and in his twenties. Angres lived at the school for twelve years and was among the children Bettelheim misdiagnosed as autistic. In 1971, Angres's parents withdrew him against Bettelheim's advice; after the director's suicide in 1990 Angres wrote a trenchant critique of Bettelheim and the school in *Commentary*.

Tom Wallace Lyons on the sandbox at the Orthogenic School not long after he entered at age nine in 1951, and as a young man. He left at twenty-one and feels in general that the school helped him, primarily because of the counselors' devotion. Lyons's 1983 novel about the school, *The Pelican and After,* did not please Bettelheim, in part because it made clear that he sometimes hit the children.

PHOTO BY DAVID JOEL

Above left, the author (with flashlight) and his brother, Stephen, and their parents, Robert and Janet Pollak, in their Hyde Park home, circa 1941, two years before Stephen entered the Orthogenic School and seven years before he died in a barn accident that Bettelheim insisted was a suicide.

Above right, Jacquelyn Seevak Sanders became Bettelheim's chief deputy during her thirteen years as a counselor at the Orthogenic School and was among the most dedicated members of the staff. In 1973, Bettelheim chose her to succeed him as director, and she ran the school for two decades.

Young mothers and a few fathers gather around Bettelheim (top, center) at the University of Chicago to hear his advice on how to raise their children. Transcripts of these weekly sessions became the basis of his 1962 book, *Dialogues with Mothers,* and, later, a column for *Ladies' Home Journal* that he wrote for a decade.

THE UNIVERSITY OF CHICAGO MAGAZINE

By the late 1960s, Bettelheim's strong aesthetic sense and gift for fund-raising had given the Orthogenic School an embracing ambiance that stood as a model for homes of its kind. The main door welcomed visitors with panels of carved figures and colorful murals graced the building's façade and stairwells. In the dorms, comfortable beds had replaced the double-decker bunks and each child had his or her cozy corner. In the playground, the young residents clambered over "The Lady," a stone sculpture of a supine woman.

Eric, Naomi, and Ruth Bettelheim (rear) with Bruno and Trude in front of 5725 Kenwood Avenue, the house where the children grew up in the University of Chicago neighborhood of Hyde Park.

Clara Claiborne Park and David Park with their autistic daughter Jessy. The Parks disdained Bettelheim's insistent claim that autistic children must be removed from their families because mothers caused the illness by rejecting their infants with a ferocity akin to that of concentration camp guards and infanticidal kings. The Parks raised Jessy at home, an experience Clara described in her 1967 book, *The Siege.*

Bettelheim at a press conference on January 31, 1969, at which he called the students who had taken over the University of Chicago administration building sick and paranoid and compared them to young Nazis in the 1930s. He would soon repeat this view in other forums, including before a House subcommittee in Washington, D.C., investigating student unrest.

Bettelheim receiving an honorary doctorate at Tulane University in the spring of 1987.

Bettelheim's jacket photo from *The Uses of Enchantment*, his popular 1976 book about the meaning of fairy tales.

Bettelheim with his grandchildren Matthew and Aurelia, the children of his daughter Ruth, from whom he was estranged at the end of his life.

Trude and Bruno Bettelheim in 1975, two years after they moved to California.

their donnish emulation of Cambridge and Oxford and their gentlemanly anti-Semitism. Chicago was far less hostile to Jews, in part because its first president, William Rainey Harper, had been a distinguished Hebrew scholar. If anything, Chicago in the 1940s had more in common with the great German universities before the rise of Hitler, where the search for truth was the highest academic goal. Robert Maynard Hutchins and his disciples believed that education was an end in itself and needed no excuse for existence; the chancellor regarded credentials as less important than how smart a person was and how well he taught. "In a very profound sense," recalled a Chicago dean, "they didn't give a damn where you got your education as long as you were educated."[44]

Still, it didn't hurt if that learning had been acquired on the Ringstrasse and carried the aura of psychoanalysis. Bettelheim had arrived in a land where "the cause" so transfixed the populace that in 1941 a singing analysand and her dreams starred on Broadway in *Lady in the Dark;* Hutchins and Adler's Great Books project began with Homer and marched along the shelf through Plato, Aristotle, Aquinas, Shakespeare, Kant, and Darwin, the final volume sanctifying *Civilization and Its Discontents* and seventeen other works by Freud. As W. H. Auden had eulogized in 1939, Freud had become less a person than "a whole climate of opinion. . . ."[45] Peter Blos, like Bettelheim a Viennese refugee, was astounded by the enthusiastic reception he received as a novice analyst, and would come to see in the open opportunity the profession offered in America a parallel to Frederick Jackson Turner's frontier thesis, suggesting that perhaps the covered wagon had been replaced by the couch.[46]

Despite this receptive atmosphere, Bettelheim seemed compelled to continue fabricating. He started saying and writing that it was he who had cared for and treated Patricia Lyne during the seven years she had lived with him and Gina, either minimizing the roles played by his former wife and by Patsy's analyst, Editha Sterba, or—far more often—obliterating them altogether. Once he discovered that no one challenged this useful new achievement, he began polishing it to a higher sheen. In *The Informed Heart* (1960), he wrote that he had lived with "two autistic children" in Vienna as part of their treatment.[47] In *The Empty Fortress* (1967)[48] he made the same claim, as he did when interviewed by *Newsweek* after the book came out. "I became fascinated with their problems," he told the magazine.[49] In *Surviving and Other Essays* (1979), he wrote that he had worked and lived with "some autistic children" before the *Anschluss*.[50] In *A Good Enough Parent* (1987), he wrote that, by employing what he regarded as sound child-rearing practices based on psychoanalytic principles, he had "tried to heal one and, for some time, two autistic children who lived with [him] in [his] home for many years."[51] Sometimes he told the story as if daring those closest to him to catch him out. In *A Home for the Heart* (1974), he conflated his first and second wives:

> Before our own children were born. . .my wife and I brought in a child who suffered from infantile autism (a "hopeless" case) in order to find out whether [psychoanalysis] could help her. Something within the little girl, and within myself, made me become deeply involved with her.[52]

Patricia Lyne was the only child the Bettelheims took into their home in Vienna, and she was never diagnosed as autistic. She could not have been by Editha Sterba, who treated her in the 1930s, because it was not until 1943 that the term "autism" was coined, by the Johns Hopkins psychiatrist Leo Kanner, to describe the condition of small children trapped inside their thoughts and unable to relate to the world around them. "Though Patsy was by no means normal, I don't think she was what you can call autistic," said Gina, a view shared by Emarina Radanowicz-Harttmann, who, with her friend Trude Weinfeld, had taught at the Vienna Montessori school that Patsy eventually attended. Unlike most autistic children, Patsy was able to manage certain complex actions by herself, like taking the tram to and from school each day. Most autistic children do not speak at all, or utter words and sounds that make little or no sense to the listener. Patsy, though withdrawn, was speaking coherently when she arrived in Vienna, which was what made it possible for Editha Sterba to try to help her three times a week with the talking cure.

Bettelheim would eventually write that Patsy had been "virtually mute" all her life and that she spoke her first words only after living under his watchful eye for a year and a half. He said this breakthrough resulted from a simple game he played with her, a combination of peek-a-boo and "Where's the baby?," in which he pretended not to see her and then would discover her. He wrote that as the game progressed over the weeks she took increasing delight in it and finally began allowing him to hug her when he "found" her. It was during one of these affectionate embraces that she uttered "her first sentence," which was: " 'Give me the skeleton of George Washington.' " Bettelheim explained the sentence by stating that the tragedy of Patsy's life

> had originated in the fact that her father was completely unknown, not just to her but also to her mother. . . .[I]n her sentence she told that what she needed was a father, and as an American girl with no known father she could think only of the father of her country as a solution to her problem. Since the unknown father was "the skeleton in the closet" of her life, she asked for his skeleton.[53]

Patsy may well have longed for her father, but if so it was most likely because she did remember him, as did her mother. Patsy was not the child of a "one-night stand" her mother had had while drunk, as Bettelheim would tell one interviewer.[54] Her father, Elmer Ward Lyne, had married Agnes Piel on September 19, 1922, and their daughter was born eighteen months later; the couple divorced in 1928, when Patsy was four years old.[55]

The Patsy card greatly strengthened the hand Bettelheim had dealt himself in the early 1940s. Ralph Tyler and others in the university community believed that not only did this hardworking newcomer have strong credentials in psychology from the University of Vienna but that he had treated at least one emotionally disturbed child in his home for several years, a child who—at least in some tellings—suffered from the newly named affliction of autism. Bettelheim wrote that it was "because of [his] experience with this autistic child" that the university asked him to take charge of its home for emotionally troubled children, the Orthogenic School.[56]

•

THE ORTHOGENIC SCHOOL had been in operation in one form or another since 1912, when Rush Medical College, then affiliated with the University of Chicago, had established a clinic to treat children of "doubtful mentality" and to instruct medical students in handling such patients.[57] In the mid-1920s, the school had attracted the attention of Charles Hubbard Judd, who had run a psychology laboratory at Yale University and under whom Ralph Tyler had gotten his doctorate at the University of Chicago, where Judd became chairman of the department of education in 1909. Judd was interested in establishing a program to explore the development of abnormal children, believing, Tyler told me, that in this area "you didn't go to books to learn but to where the phenomenon was." By 1930, the Orthogenic School had moved through three unsatisfactory homes; at Judd's urging, the school formally became part of the university that year and settled permanently at 60th Street and Dorchester Avenue, in a three-story, red brick Georgian building that had belonged to the Saint Paul Universalist Church.

To oversee the school, Judd chose an ambitious Chicagoan named Mandel Sherman, who held a medical degree from Rush and a doctorate in experimental psychology from the university and taught educational psychology. Sherman would remain in charge for more than a decade, working with the school's principal, Helen Mansfield Robinson, a psychologist and reading specialist. They presided over an enrollment of about thirty children, most of whom lived at the school full time. Their diagnoses ranged from generalized emotional problems and reading disabilities to epilepsy and mental retardation. On average, these disparate and difficult children stayed at the school less than a year; thus Sherman and Robinson placed a good deal of emphasis on helping them make the transition to other schools. Sherman's main interest was research. He established a laboratory on the premises for psychological testing and a committee to look into the causes of reading disabilities; the school also conducted neurological examinations, sometimes attaching wires to the heads of the children to take electroencephalograph readings for brain-wave studies.

By the early 1940s, serious criticisms of Sherman's stewardship were being raised by both university officials and the parents of some of the children at the school.[58] "The complaints were that the children were not getting any better," recalled Ralph Tyler, who in 1939 had succeeded his mentor, Charles Judd, as head of the department of education, which oversaw the school. Sherman also was unable or unwilling to control many of his young residents, whose destructive behavior frequently created chaos at the institution.[59] Tyler had already appointed a faculty committee to investigate the school and make recommendations for its future, and in a report that ran six double-spaced pages the committee worried most about the school's educational shortcomings, citing its inadequate teaching equipment, its lack of an indoor gymnasium, and the teachers' low pay. The report urged expansion of the school's research program, suggesting that Sherman be put in charge of a special interdisciplinary committee to that end. As for the school's "eclectic" therapeutic program, the report called it "sound"—a finding that may have owed something to the presence of Mandel Sherman on the committee.[60]

Despite the report, criticism of the school continued, including charges in some circles that Sherman was at times "horribly sadistic."[61] By 1944, one of the principal fund-raisers lamented that the school was in such financial distress that it no longer could serve enough milk and food to keep the children properly nourished.[62] Tyler and the university were grappling with these problems when Sherman unexpectedly announced that he planned to leave Chicago and go into private practice in Los Angeles. Over the years, Bruno Bettelheim told his family and several others the following story of the events that led up to what happened next.

In 1942, Ralph Tyler had asked Bettelheim to draw up a memorandum on the Orthogenic School, but Bettelheim ignored the request: he was reluctant to tell his mentor that he thought the school was such a dump that it should be burned down. He said the place was dirty and stank of urine. Several months later, when Tyler pressed him for the report, he confessed his view, which only made Tyler more eager for his thoughts on how to rescue the school. Bettelheim made it clear he had no interest in running the home, but agreed to write the memorandum.

In putting it together he sought the help of his émigrée

neighbor Emmy Sylvester, who held a medical degree from the University of Vienna, had worked in that city's Children's Hospital, and recently had become a certified psychiatrist in Chicago, specializing in the treatment of children. Bettelheim said they drew on the work of their fellow Viennese August Aichhorn, who had applied psychoanalytic understanding to child development and was widely known for his 1925 book *Verwahrloste Jugend (Wayward Youth)*, for which Sigmund Freud had written the foreword. Aichhorn believed, "The more the life of the institution conforms to an actual social community, the more certain is the social rehabilitation of the child."[63] His approach, combining permissiveness with large doses of understanding, met with mixed success as he treated the delinquents he took in at Oberhollabrunn, the home he had developed after World War I for these sometimes dangerously aggressive youths. Bettelheim said that the memorandum also leaned on the ideas of his friend Fritz Redl, who had studied with Aichhorn in Vienna, and who would apply some of his techniques in 1946, when he started a home called Pioneer House in Detroit. Bettelheim told Theron Raines that in drawing up the report for Tyler he also was heavily influenced by what he had learned in caring for two autistic children in his Vienna home.[64]

A few weeks after Bettelheim delivered the memorandum, Tyler invited him to lunch at the Quadrangle Club, the university's vine-covered faculty sanctuary. Tyler, who was something of a raconteur, kept his protégé entertained with jokes and stories, but dessert and coffee came and went with not a word about the report. After lunch, his host asked Bettelheim to walk him to his office, but Tyler guided him instead into the chancellor's office, where the memorandum lay on Robert Hutchins's desk. Bettelheim said that Hutchins liked his ideas and asked him to take over the school; the refugee angrily protested that he had agreed to write the memo but that was it. Hutchins said he knew that but wanted Bettelheim to take the job anyway, because he was the best man for the post. There followed a good deal of flattery and cajoling by both Tyler and Hutchins, who finally asked for Bettelheim's conditions. He was so annoyed that he decided to make demands he assumed they would never meet: tripling the Orthogenic School's budget, and no questions asked or answered for five years. Bettelheim said his patrons huddled for a moment and then Hutchins declared the conditions fair.[65]

No version of the memorandum exists in the Bettelheim or Orthogenic School papers at the University of Chicago, nor is it among Emmy Sylvester's papers in California. Whether or not Bettelheim actually wrote a memorandum, and regardless of whether it led to the climactic scene in the chancellor's office, there is no question that Ralph Tyler wanted him to take over the Orthogenic School. And at least one other influential faculty member may have put in a good word for him with Hutchins. University folklore holds that Joe Schwab, the biology teacher and Great Books enthusiast who had been at the Eight-Year Study bull session when Bettelheim dismissed Hutchins's favorite project, admired the émigré's outspokenness and told Hutchins so.[66]

Despite these endorsements, the candidate remained reluctant. Ulrich Middeldorf, the head of the art department, who had called Bettelheim "a brilliant man" in recommending him to Rockford, had held out the possibility of making him an assistant professor of humanities, with emphasis on teaching art history. It was a job for which his credentials and training were far stronger than they were for running a home for emotionally disturbed children, and the post appealed to him. But Middeldorf could not yet make an offer, and the Orthogenic School proposal was there for the taking. By the fall of 1944, Bettelheim needed a steady job more than ever; his daughter, Ruth, was now almost two, and he and Trude were trying to have a second child.

After some agonizing, he finally bowed to Tyler's blandishments and, on October 1, became principal of the Orthogenic School, with a one-year contract at a salary of thirty-six hundred dollars. Looking back at the decision near the end of his life, Bettelheim said that the school he inherited was a shambles, full of children the community regarded as "hopeless cases." Because of this, if he failed no one would really blame him; but if he succeeded everyone would be more than pleased. "So it was a no-lose situation, which I liked."[67]

CHAPTER SIX
The Orthogenic School

GAYLE SHULENBERGER was twenty-two years old when she arrived in Chicago, not long off the farm in South Dakota. Like many career-minded young women in the 1940s, she thought vaguely that she might like to be a social worker; but although she had taken some college courses she had no degree, and attending classes now was out of the question, because she was broke. Desperate for a job, she applied for typing work at a home she had heard worked with children, a place called the Orthogenic School at the University of Chicago. When an interviewer asked if she had any teaching experience, she said she had been a high-school substitute on a couple of occasions back in South Dakota. The school hired her immediately as a substitute night nurse.

Shulenberger slept at this "nutty place" every night for the next two weeks, charged mainly with looking after a teenage boy who wandered the halls and scrubbed his hands so often that they were red and coarse. He also refused to take food from anybody's hands, so she was told to leave it for him, as if for a terrified puppy. "My job really was to stay up until he was in bed, sometimes one or two in the morning," Shulenberger told me. "The night nurse whose place I took was an old prune, a wicked woman, I thought. She complained that the boy had a full set of keys to the school's locks but that the principal would not let anyone take them away from him. I didn't know much about mental illness, but I thought, *Good for him.*" At one of her first staff meetings, Shulenberger learned that this principal was a Viennese émigré with the resonant name of Bruno Bettelheim, that he had just taken over the school, and that he knew everything that was wrong with it and what changes had to be made. "I walked out on air; it was the most exciting day of my life."

This exhilaration soon spread as Bettelheim began purging much of the staff assembled by his predecessor, Mandel Sherman, and hiring his own people, almost all young women like Shulen-berger with little or no experience. When Veronica Dryovage, who had been one of Bettelheim's devoted students at Rockford College, wrote him seeking a scholarship reference to continue her education, he called her and convinced the twenty-year-old she should come work at the school. Two other Rockford disci-ples, Marjorie Jewell and Betty Lou Pingree, were also among the recruits in those first weeks. "The whole idea of working at the school seemed interesting," Pingree told me. "But I didn't know a thing about emotionally disturbed children. I think he hired us because he didn't want a staff with its own ideas, people who had been trained by someone else."

On her first day, Pingree and another counselor took a few preadolescent boys out to play football on the Midway, the grassy expanse across the street from the school. Pingree recalled ruefully that she acted less like someone dealing with delinquent and un-predictable children than like a Girl Scout leader eager to join in the fun, with the result that the boys soon swirled out of control, turning on both women and ripping Pingree's blouse. In tears, the neophytes somehow managed to round up their charges and get them back to the school, where Bettelheim waited. He delivered the boys into the care of another counselor and took the two young women around the corner to his apartment, where he and Trude served them tea. Bettelheim told them they had gone wrong by acting too much like the children, and that this had frightened the boys, who needed more than anything else to feel protected by him and the staff.

Bettelheim set out to create this sense of refuge from the moment he took over the converted church property at the corner of 60th Street and Dorchester Avenue. But he knew he could not do it with the kind of population he had inherited from Sherman, a mix of about three dozen patients, many well into their teens, that included children suffering from epilepsy, encephalitis, hydro-cephalus, and other physiological maladies.[1] Bettelheim told the parents or social agencies responsible for placing these children in the school that they must be withdrawn as soon as possible. From now on, newly admitted patients would range in age from about six to fourteen, must be of normal or greater intelligence, and must be "free of physical disorder, but suffer from severe emotional disturbances that have proved (or are expected to prove) beyond the reach of the common therapeutic techniques."[2] Under Sherman, the average stay at the school had been just short of eleven months;[3] Bettelheim felt that to make any significant progress a child needed to remain in his care for at least two years.[4]

"Bruno said our job was to give the children a childhood," recalled Josette Wingo, who arrived at the school at age twenty-three, a gunnery instructor just out of the navy. Overnight, she and the other novices became instant mothers, most of them living at the school. In the morning, they coaxed the children out of their dorm beds, down to breakfast, and off to the school's classrooms. In the afternoons, they took the children on outings in the neighborhood, to the Museum of Science and Industry, or on shopping expeditions beneath the "El" tracks on 63rd Street, or to the 57th Street beach for a swim. For the long, summer twilight hours, they encouraged intense games of tag or kick-the-can on the Midway, sessions Shulenberger called "Take 'em out and run 'em till they drop." These workouts were supposed to leave the children so played out that, after a bath and a soporific chapter of *Swiss Family Robinson,* they would readily nod off, a theory tested nightly by children who saw myriad demons in the dark. While the counselors comforted them, sometimes for an hour or more, impatient boyfriends and future husbands sat in the living room downstairs leafing through a stack of dog-eared *New Yorkers* and exchanging wary glares with Bettelheim as he passed by the doorway.

The counselors coped with lost teddy bears, overflowing bathtubs and toilets, and misbuttoned pajamas, but mostly with the mysterious and sometimes frightening range of behavior manifested by the more difficult children. They sat mute for hours, soiled themselves nightly, exploded with rage seemingly without provocation, vomited at mealtime for no apparent reason, smeared food in their hair and feces on their clothes, gorged themselves or refused to eat, ran away and rode the "El" to the end of the line, lashed out with fists or kicks, and sometimes threatened to kill themselves, another child, or a counselor. One evening, Shulenberger took the boys in her dorm down to the kitchen for a snack; Harry, perhaps the most violent child at the school in the late 1940s, clambered up onto a counter, grabbed a carving knife from its hook, and threw it at the counselor, narrowly missing her head.[5]

Such incidents were not common, but the mere possibility of them, combined with the routine pressure of caring for the children, left the young women physically and emotionally exhausted at the end of the day, and nagged by a fear that they were out of their depth working at this "last-chance ranch," as Shulenberger came to call the school.[6] Yet, at the same time, recalled Joan Little, who had come to the University of Chicago from Kansas and had just crossed into her twenties when she gravitated toward the school, "we had a feeling of doing pioneering work, of being connected with ideas and movements from Europe."

New notions of how to treat emotionally disturbed and delinquent children had crossed the Atlantic throughout the 1930s, not least those put forth by August Aichhorn in *Wayward Youth,* which had come out in an English translation in 1935. Others who contributed to this ferment in child therapy included Jean Piaget, Maria Montessori, Anna Freud, Melanie Klein, and Editha Sterba, as well as Bruno Bettelheim's psychology professor and dissertation reader Karl Bühler and his wife, Charlotte. One result of these fresh ideas was that institutions that for years had been primarily custodial began cautiously moving toward treating their patients. By 1930, the American psychiatrist Harry Stack Sullivan was attempting to show that schizophrenics could be understood, no matter how difficult their behavior. The Menninger Clinic's Southard School in Topeka, which had been housing retarded and brain-damaged children, started taking those with emotional troubles instead. Other institutions followed the same path, among them the Ryther Child Center in Seattle, Hawthorne Cedar Knolls near New York City, and Bellefaire in Cleveland. World War II put this "residential-treatment" movement on hold, but once the fighting stopped in 1945, tremendous energy poured into all areas of civilian life, including the care of children like those now entering the Orthogenic School.[7]

Bettelheim's approach was mainly psychoanalytic. He often riveted the counselors with his photographic knowledge of the Freudian canon when they gathered in the basement kitchen after the children finally went to sleep. "It was the most exciting thing I had ever done in my life," recalled Jean O'Leary, who was nineteen when she became a counselor soon after Bettleheim took over. She was thrilled to be part of the university community and living at the school instead of in the stifling family atmosphere of her South Side home, where she had slept in the living room. "Bettelheim gave me a religion, which I laugh at now, because psychoanalysis doesn't play a big part in my life any longer; but at the time it gave me a system, a way to judge things." At the informal kitchen gatherings, the staff began calling the director "Dr. B," the truncation Pingree, Dryovage and Jewell had brought from Rockford, and that Bettelheim readily accepted. The counselors brought him their questions and anxieties about the children's behavior, and their personal woes inevitably spilled out as well. "Whenever anybody was in trouble," recalled Josette Wingo, "it turned out that Bruno had a friend back in Vienna who had the same kind of problem. Someone would be about to kill herself over a broken love affair and he would tell us of a friend who had decided *not* to kill himself at the last minute. Only later did we realize that these were Bruno's scenarios, his teaching stories, and that nobody had that many friends go through so many crises."

Bettelheim sometimes embroidered his refugee experience as well. At one session, he said that in the 1930s he had made anti-Nazi speeches not only in Austria but in Germany itself, and that, at the *Anschluss,* he was on a plane with the motors running when Hitler Youth kept it from taking off, leading to his arrest and incarceration in the camps. O'Leary recalled that when they asked him how he had escaped from Buchenwald he replied that nobody escaped, but did not answer the question. Over coffee, tea, and cake, he combined such grandiosity and evasions with wistful descriptions of Vienna, only recently the target of Allied bombers. As the counselors sat, like children at story time themselves, Dr. B told of seeing the Emperor Franz Joseph's funeral procession in 1916, of walking in the Vienna Woods and the Prater, of the art revolution wrought by Klimt and Schiele and the other Secession- ists, of sitting for hours in the coffeehouses along the Ringstrasse, of a time that seemed to swim in *Kultur mit Schlag*.

Emmy Sylvester also awed the counselors, and to a degree Bettelheim himself. He had hired this capable Viennese doctor, who he said had helped him write the report for Ralph Tyler that got him his job, as the school's psychiatrist, and when she arrived for her weekly visits he greeted her "as if she were royalty," scurry- ing down the steps to meet her and ushering her into the living room, where he served her coffee.[8] In her mid-thirties, she was seven years his junior, but far better educated and more experi- enced in the treatment of troubled children. She held a psychology doctorate and medical degree from Vienna, and had interned at the Children's Hospital there; she was an associate in the depart- ment of neuropsychiatry at Chicago's Michael Reese Hospital, and she also had trained at the psychoanalytic institutes in both Vienna and Chicago. By the time Bettelheim took over the school, Sylvester was already a life fellow of the American Psychi- atric Association. She seemed always in command, a robust, ener- getic woman with a determined stride whose sculptured features beneath a swirl of dark curls gave her a dramatic countenance. Her legs drew surreptitious wolf whistles from the few men on the staff, and her stylish clothes made the female counselors feel all the more dowdy in their faded jeans and rumpled blouses and skirts.

Each week, Sylvester saw one or two children in private and then met with Bettelheim and the counselors to discuss what she had learned. The youthful staff sat wide-eyed as the two Viennese accents parsed the wounded psyches of the children with what seemed like laser insights. Both therapists sometimes expressed frustration that they could not find the English words and phrases to characterize a child's behavior. After struggling together to de- scribe one depressed boy, they finally laughed, threw up their hands, and decided that he looked "like a canary that had fallen into a bowl of soup."[9] But their relationship was not always so collegial. Sylvester held more orthodox psychoanalytic views than Bettelheim and was not bashful about stressing them, or about noting, when they disagreed in staff meetings, that she was better trained than he was.[10]

Few American women stood up to men in public in this way, and the counselors drew strength from Sylvester's self-confidence. Whenever they felt discouraged, she buoyed them up, assuring them that even the smallest act—buying a boy a new pair of corduroys, helping a girl make fudge—had important therapeutic value. Her principal message was that psychiatrists who dipped in once a week could not really be very helpful; if anyone could rescue the children it was the counselors, who stood watch twenty-four hours a day. Bettelheim adopted that view, structuring the school so that he and the consulting psychiatrists acted as mentors for the counselors, who became the children's primary therapists. He eventually would write:

> Without doubting the merits, for less disturbed children, of institutional settings relying on psychiatric or casework sessions for therapy, we have found that such a separation of function between houseparent or residential worker and therapist does not work well with extremely disturbed children. . . . Being repeatedly bitten, kicked, defecated upon or otherwise abused results in defensive or punitive actions, cold indifference, emotional distance . . . [and] such attitudes interfere with rehabilitation. They can be avoided only if staff members know it is their responsibility, and only theirs, to help these children, if they receive all the narcissistic and interpersonal rewards that derive from being the children's main therapists.[11]

Sylvester collaborated with Bettelheim on six journal articles that went a long way toward defining the new Orthogenic School for the profession and establishing Bettelheim's early reputation in the field of residential treatment. They were the first authors in the American literature to use the term "therapeutic milieu" to describe the kind of all-encompassing healing atmosphere they sought to develop.[12] Bettelheim and Sylvester wrote that one-on-one therapy was adequate for adults but had only limited efficacy in treating troubled children, and maintained that such children could not be helped successfully while still living with their parents. They argued that "real personality change is best initiated in an environment where the child faces the realistic consequences of his acting out and is protected at the same time from the self-destructive implications of his behavior." [13]

Emmy Sylvester "was absolutely crucial for the beginning of the school," said Gayle Shulenberger, who became head counselor in the early years. Bettelheim himself singled out his countrywoman for developing and shaping therapeutic practice at the school and for influencing "the actions and the viewpoints of staff members so extensively that it would be difficult to acknowledge each of her contributions specifically." [14] Despite this recognition, Sylvester felt that Bettelheim never adequately credited her for helping him establish the Orthogenic School's new direction, and for years harbored bitter memories of her involvement with him. "He was a very bright guy, no doubt about it," she told me. "But he was also a bad character, full of a lust for power, an absolute monarch, always manipulating people: the kids at the school, the staff, his collaborators. He was a typical Viennese. In Chicago, he got in touch with the university crowd and all of a sudden he became the boy who knew everything about analysis. He used people, sponged off them intellectually. As long as he needed you, he was very nice; then he would cool off."

In 1950, Sylvester left Chicago to pursue what would become a successful career in the Bay Area, in private practice and as a professor of clinical psychology at Stanford Medical School. Her successor as the school's principal psychiatrist was a mild-mannered Bostonian named George Perkins, a competent therapist whom everybody liked and respected but who gave off no competing Old World sparks.

Whatever the contributions of Emmy Sylvester and others to the therapeutic milieu at the Orthogenic School, Bettelheim soon gave it an interpretation very much his own. He said repeatedly over the years that his commitment to saving the children stemmed from his camp experience, from his anger at the idea of wasted lives, whether trapped behind metal or emotional barbed wire. [15] He was determined to give the children a good life and hoped that by promoting their integration he could promote his own, that by serving the living he could, as much as possible, meet his "obligation to the dead. . . ." [16] He said he recognized that mental patients, particularly troubled children, lent themselves easily to the gratification of infantile and megalomanic rescue fantasies, but he assured his readers that this pitfall was minimized by his "psychoanalytic training. . . ." [17]

The former prisoner wrote that he had entered Dachau believing that nothing compared to psychoanalysis when it came to freeing the individual and guiding him toward an integrated and happier life, but had emerged from Buchenwald with serious doubts. He had come to question one of the discipline's main tenets, "that the personality shaping influence of the immediate family is all important, and that society in the broader sense is relatively negligible by comparison." [18] He said that, once inside the camps, he quickly came to believe that an environment could turn personality upside down, producing more radical change than psychoanalysis, and more quickly. If the personalities of prisoners disintegrated in the cruel atmosphere of the camps, Bettelheim argued, then a loving milieu could play a key role in reintegrating the broken personalities in his care. Thus, he sought to re-create the Orthogenic School in the reverse image of the camps, to make it a place where the doors were locked *against* the outside but the children could walk away at any time. Inevitably, some did from time to time, but the school's policy was to understand this impulse and to welcome back runaways without punishment.

Bettelheim's camp-school construct would become a permanent edifice on the landscape of his thought and would eventually lead him to compare the children themselves to the prisoners, maintaining that the parallels "were so startling and unexpected" that he initially hesitated to publish what he had discovered. [19] He did so in 1956, echoing his 1943 essay on the camps with an article titled "Schizophrenia as a Reaction to Extreme Situations." He maintained that childhood psychosis was due to spontaneous developmental forces that produced "mortal anxiety." When he asked himself what set this process in motion, he answered that he had seen the whole range of autistic and schizophrenic reactions among his fellow camp inmates, behavior he attributed to the fact that they found themselves totally overpowered. So, too, were the school's schizophrenic children. He said that he had found "again and again" that the cause of childhood schizophrenia was "the child's subjective feeling of living permanently in an extreme situation, that is, of being totally helpless in the face of threats to his very life. . . ."[20] Bettelheim would come back to this theme many times over the years, in one case invoking "Todesfuge," Paul Celan's poem about the death camps, with its recurring reference to "black milk":

> Black milk of dawn we drink you at night
> we drink you at noon death is a master from Germany[21]

Most critics interpreted this image as an allusion to the "clouds of smoke issuing from the crematories. . . ."[22] Bettelheim felt it represented a mother destroying her infant: whether one was a prisoner required to drink black milk from dawn to dusk in Auschwitz, or a child in a luxurious crib facing the unconscious death wishes of his mother, "a living soul has death for a master."[23]

Bettelheim sought to support this conclusion and his other "findings"[24] in the 1956 article much as he had his observations in "Individual and Mass Behavior in Extreme Situations," with ex-cathedra pronouncements, generalizations, and anecdotes. He said that he had observed "practically all types" of schizophrenic adaptations and symptomatology in the camps, including illusions, delusions, catatonia, depression, megalomania, suicidal tendencies, and suicides themselves. He stated flatly, "Loss of memory was universal, as were shallow and inappropriate emotions."[25]

When confronted by the literature on camp psychology that had accumulated since he had staked his claim to the subject in 1943, he looked away. In 1949, the psychoanalyst Edith Jacobson published a clinical study of women prisoners that came to far less sweeping and dogmatic conclusions than Bettelheim did; she found that, in general, those citizens who arrived in camp with stable personalities did not disintegrate. Her observations appeared in *Searchlights on Delinquency,* a collection of thirty-four psychoanalytic studies that the *American Journal of Sociology* gave Bettelheim to review. He wrote in passing that he found Jacobson's article rewarding, but neither engaged its content nor allowed her research—or anyone else's in the years to come—to impinge on his 1943 assessment of camp behavior.[26]

Readers had to take him on faith, as they did when he said

that the Orthogenic School children were schizophrenic and had become so because, like the inmates, they feared for their lives. As the only evidence to buttress this thesis, he supplied three excerpts from case histories: one about a boy whose parents talked in his presence about sending him to an institution and who fantasized about how he would torture and kill others before they could kill him; another about an adopted boy who, before the age of three, chanced to see a man in an adulterous situation with his mother, who threatened to kill the child if he ever revealed what he knew; and a third about a boy with delusions of persecution that stemmed from the fact that his older brother and some friends had made him the object of a hanging game, after which he had to be revived by artificial respiration.[27]

The idea of rebirth was central to Bettelheim's camp-school equation. He saw regression in autistic and schizophrenic children as their plea to be reborn, to start over on a road to a better life; he compared this to the daydreams of his fellow prisoners, who, in their own regression, frequently fantasized about starting life over should they be lucky enough to gain their freedom. Bettelheim maintained that only those former prisoners who were able to establish a new beginning "fully overcame the damaging influence of the camps."[28] Thus, as D. Patrick Zimmerman, the coordinator of research at the Orthogenic School, would suggest in a 1993 assessment of Bettelheim's thought, his work with children was both shaped and limited by his own experience as a man who, in his early years as director of the Orthogenic School, was "transforming himself in the eyes of the public from a Viennese upper-middle-class businessman to a self-trained 'psychoanalyst.' "[29]

Bettelheim's apodictic style and the lack of hard evidence for most of his claims came to characterize much of his writing. This would bring him criticism from the therapeutic establishment over the years, especially from psychiatrists, but he waved it away. He told his friend the Hungarian-born psychologist David Rapaport that he felt hemmed in by psychoanalytic theory and that he learned more about the children at his school by carefully observing them.[30] He said repeatedly that he regarded psychoanalysis less as a science than as an art, and when an interviewer asked him, late in his life, about his lack of scientific rigor, he replied that after observing a patient he trusted his unconscious to supply an idea that could be refined into a way of treatment. He said the abstractions that science requires are contrary to the uniqueness of the human being. He saw himself as a psychologist of the soul, as something of a poet: "Not without reason," he asserted, "has it been said that the poets understand man more deeply, more penetratingly than the so-called scientist."[31]

The poet in Bettelheim likened the Orthogenic School to the sanatorium atop *The Magic Mountain,* an institution also run by a Dr. B. with an eye for art. Thomas Mann's Dr. Behrens takes in the tubercular young German engineer Hans Castorp, who stays more than seven years, breathing the cleansing air in a time-less universe high above the ominous politics of Europe before the Great War. Bettelheim said that he, too, aimed to create a home out of time and away from the world's concerns, where both the children and the staff could gulp the unique curative powers of his therapeutic milieu.[32]

Central to this process were regular staff meetings, sessions that usually proved a good deal less *gemütlich* than the cozy, late-night gatherings in the basement kitchen, and that reverberated with Bettelheim's conviction that "a man's work must be perme-ated by his personality."[33] Often in the early years, Dr. B presided over these meetings from an easy chair at one end of the over-stuffed, first-floor living room, sometimes pulling tissues from a box at his elbow and folding them neatly on the arm in anticipa-tion of an attack of hay fever. ("He said once that he didn't know why he was so allergic, but figured it was cheaper to buy [antihista-mines] and Kleenex than suffer the expense of being analyzed again," Josette Wingo recalled.) He required that all counselors regularly dictate descriptions of the children's behavior, and their reactions to it, into tape recorders, and he usually arrived at the staff meetings with typed transcripts, which rested in his lap like so many sentencing decrees. "Well," he would announce, his mother tongue converting the "w" to a "v," his thick lenses scanning the pages and then sweeping the room. If no one spoke, he often plunged into a passage of dictation. For example, Josette Wingo had reported:

Pete walked into the dormitory and threw his model airplane on the floor.

I said, "If you don't like it anymore, I'll be glad to keep it for you." He kicked the pieces to flinders.

Daniel said, "He's always breaking things. He's just trying to *uproar* you, Josette."

The other kids gathered around the table for their snacks. "Want a piece of cake, Pete?"

"You know I hate cake. You know I hate chocolate. It's shitty, shitty, shitty!"

I shrugged my shoulders. . . .

"Why did you shrug your shoulders?" Bettelheim asked Wingo. Her tongue was pinioned by the question. She thought she had done well not to let Pete get to her. "He was being hostile to you," Bettelheim insisted. "Why?" Wingo beat back an impulse to shrug again. The matter unresolved, Bettelheim changed the subject to Pete's hat. "Our most neurotic parents would never let a child go out in a hat that makes him look like Happy Hooligan out of the funny papers," he said. He seemed furious, and it was now quite clear to Wingo that she must do something about the hat, "but whether the sound psychological reasons were Pete's self-image or Dr. B's dislike of arsenical yellow-green plaid wool caps with ear flaps was beyond the scope of the discussion. Lots of things were. When to shut up, when to speak up, when to put up: I put up my finger and held it up to the wind, trying to decide whether to tack or jibe. . . ."[34]

Such heavy sailing was routine at the staff meetings throughout the three decades Bettelheim ran the Orthogenic School. Just before he retired as director in 1973, he allowed Daniel Karlin, a French filmmaker, to shoot a documentary at the school. A scene at a staff meeting shows Bettelheim sitting on a couch, a stern father talking while the counselors, most of them young women, look about apprehensively. His tone says, "Why don't you understand this, you dummies?" His acolytes look chastened as he dismisses their minds; there are many pauses, during which everyone seems afraid to talk, to risk saying the wrong thing and being savaged by the master.[35] "He was very cruel to the staff," Karlin told me. Fae Lohn was about to turn twenty when she joined the school's staff in the late 1940s. "You never knew what the agenda would be," she recalled. "You weren't sure whether you were going to get a kudo or a brickbat." Bettelheim occasionally praised a counselor, for an insight in her dictation or the way she had calmed a child's tantrum in the dining room, but mostly he was the Viennese taskmaster, sitting in judgment of how the counselors handled the children, making the staff feel stupid when they failed to see what to him was the obvious reason for a child's behavior. If he thought a counselor lacked control in a situation, he would ask, "Are you trying to make this kid crazier?," his sarcasm drenching the room. "You had the feeling you were a piece of shit, that you didn't know anything," said Mary Cahn, who, at twenty-two, became a counselor for about a year in the 1950s. Some staff members realized that Bettelheim's growls were occasionally an act, a one-ring circus put on by "one of the greatest performers of all time" to get them to remember what he was trying to teach them.[36] Still, The Big Bad Wolf, as he sometimes called himself, could be a very convincing beast when he employed his "instruction through terror,"[37] or what Robert Bergman, who spent six months at the school when he was a psychiatric resident, called his "Nazi-Socratic method."[38]

One reason the staff meetings were frequently upsetting was Bettelheim's determination to dissect not just the children's behavior but the counselors' as well. He saw the sessions "as instruments for challenging staff members to confront themselves,"[39] insisting that they could not help the children unless they understood their own psychopathology. He also saw the school's therapeutic milieu as "an eminently suitable"[40] setting for helping the counselors resolve childhood conflicts. "He would get into your parents, your brother, your whole personality," recalled Shelton Key, a counselor and teacher at the school from 1953 to 1962, who often was so shaken after evening staff sessions that he could not sleep. Few of the staff meetings ended without at least one of the women in tears and several others fighting them back. "When there was a staff meeting before lunch," recalled one former resident, "you would see many staff members come into the dining room with eyes red from crying."[41]

Yet most of the tearful young women remained in his thrall,

turning the Orthogenic School into something of a harem. He relished having "young, pliable, agreeable, passionate women around," said Ann Morrissett, a counselor for eighteen months in the late 1940s. Leslie Aranow, a counselor during Bettelheim's last years at the school, felt that he had an intense need to be "unambivalently adored" and that many of the female counselors reciprocated by making him their father figure. When these dutiful daughters repaired to the neighborhood's Cornell Lounge for a restorative drink or two after a long day with the children, they seemed unable to talk of anything but Daddy, who, they joked, was eavesdropping on every word through microphones he had hidden in the plastic flowers near their dark booth. In Mary Cahn's view, most of the counselors were "madly in love with him. He was a cult figure for them. The atmosphere was always exciting and tense, sexually charged. The school was known as the nunnery, because you were married to Bettelheim but never had sex with him."

What many counselors did have with him was individual therapy. In the first years, Gayle Shulenberger, Fae Lohn, Patty Pickett, and several others spent an hour or two a week in his small office pouring out their troubles, and in the decades that followed many more, most of them young women, would do the same, some for many months. Even before they put themselves in Bettelheim's hands, he had accessed their emotional vitae. When hiring, he often asked for psychological résumés, like those he had solicited from his students at Rockford; he urged would-be counselors to skip their student-council and glee-club triumphs and tell him instead of their childhood traumas, of their sexual anxieties, of how they felt about their parents. For many, Bettelheim's offer to let them unpack still more such baggage in his office was irresistible; he did not charge for the sessions, and it was "exciting" to tell all to such a magnetic personality,[42] a man many of the counselors believed held a degree in psychology from the University of Vienna and was a trained analyst who had traveled in Freud's circle.

That the confessors worked for their analytic priest gave some of them pause, but in the early years especially, there seemed ample precedent for rationalization. After all, hadn't Freud analyzed his

friends Max Eitingon and Sándor Ferenczi, and Ferenczi his professional associate Ernest Jones? It was in this intramural atmosphere that Melanie Klein analyzed her children and Freud his
daughter Anna. Besides, many of the counselors believed that the
sessions shored them up. "I don't know what I would have done
without his help," said Patty Pickett, who credits Bettelheim with
showing her how to cope with a critical family problem when she
was at the school. "I did lie down on his couch," said Ugo Formigoni, a counselor in the 1960s who would become a mental-
health professional. "I had confidence that he would understand
what I had to say, that he could help me solve problems. He made
you feel that you deserved to be put together." Those who justified
the sessions argued, like Bettelheim himself, that working at the
Orthogenic School was so charged emotionally that the counselors needed a regular opportunity to decompress, to air out their
psychological conflicts, like the guilt that often overwhelmed
them when they grew angry at the vulnerable but difficult children they were supposed to love and nurture. When such anxieties
proved counterproductive at more conventional residential-
treatment centers, the staff member was usually dismissed. Bettelheim provided a sympathetic ear instead.

Few disputed that the counselors needed some kind of therapeutic hearing, but not everyone thought the best place for it was
in the Freudian shadows of Bettelheim's inner sanctum. Bertram
J. Cohler, who attended the Orthogenic School in the 1950s and
subsequently became a counselor and, briefly, associate director
under Bettelheim, was appalled that the all-powerful, charismatic
master saw his young, insecure employees in treatment. Cohler,
who would become a professor of education, psychology, and
psychiatry at the University of Chicago, told me that Bettelheim
dismissed his concern, insisting that what he was doing was not
treatment but "dynamic supervision."

By whatever name, the practice inevitably set the staff roiling
with sibling rivalry as counselors basked in the status of being on
Bettelheim's couch or sulked because he had not found their neu-
roses worthy of his inspection. "I don't really know how he carried
it off, because it aroused so much ambivalence among the staff,"
recalled Karen Carlson, who became one of Bettelheim's favorite

counselors in the 1950s and 1960s and would co-author *On Learning to Read* with him in the 1980s. She, too, feels he helped her in therapy, especially in dealing with her relationship to her father; now an experienced therapist herself, however, she looks back with a certain reluctant disapproval on her mentor-healer-employer's performance. To Cohler, who infuriated Bettelheim by refusing to lie down on his couch, the director's main motivation was control. Counselors inevitably discussed what went on at the school at their sessions with Bettelheim, who was not above using what he learned in confidence to confront other counselors, sometimes in staff meetings. "I so idealized him at the time," said Robert Bergman, "that I was not sophisticated enough to realize the practice was a big mistake. Like Freud with Anna, Dr. B thought he could carry it off because he was a genius." To former counselor Ben Wright, Bettelheim was an obsessed puppet master who lived through many of his women counselor-patients—and they through him.

Few staff members would dance as loyally on Bettelheim's strings as Jacquelyn Seevak, who arrived at the Orthogenic School in 1952 fresh out of Radcliffe College. About the only good thing Bettelheim had to say about her at their first meeting was that she did not wear red fingernail polish, which he said frightened adolescent boys. "I came to his office dressed and groomed as I thought appropriate for the first interview with a new employer," recalled Seevak. "He evidently didn't think so; he told me I should leave off my Radcliffe manners; my voice was too soft, it was full of holes; [he] complained that I had changed since the picture that I had sent to him had been taken. . . . To add clear emphasis to his perspective, he called into his office and gave me as a guide [for a tour of the school] a young woman who was the caricature of a typical University of Chicago student—a chainsmoking, unkempt, uncombed, unlipsticked brilliant philosopher."[43]

Like many prospective counselors, Seevak had been drawn to Bettelheim after reading "Individual and Mass Behavior in Extreme Situations," which had made her cry. She managed to muster her courage and return to the wolf's den the next day in part because she was curious about how such a "heartless maniac" had been able to move her so with his writing. At the second interview, Bettelheim won her over completely by telling her "what almost every 21-year-old secretly wants to hear—that everything that might be wrong with me was dear old mommy's fault." He allowed that she was now looking more like her picture, apologized for being so critical the day before, and said that her soft voice was doubtless a reaction to her mother's loud and harsh one. At the time, these insights seemed almost magical to Seevak. How could this man possibly know so much about her and her family? In her thrall, she had forgotten that only a few months before she had sent him, along with the photograph, the requisite psycho-autobiography, which told him a good deal about her "poor maligned mother." [44] Seevak would stay at the school for thirteen years, becoming one of its most dedicated counselors and before long Bettelheim's principal deputy, the workhorse of the staff. She turned her life over to both the school and its director, working endless hours and spilling out her tearful emotions in sessions of dynamic supervision that stretched over many months.

Bettelheim's penchant for exploitive and often tyrannical behavior was seldom far from the surface, yet from the beginning he demonstrated a parallel capacity for insight and empathy. Not long after Seevak arrived at the school, she came into the dining room with a group of children, several of them out of control. She was unable to handle the situation and felt deeply distressed that her incompetence was on display not only for her new employer but for the children and staff as well. She left the room in tears. "Jacqui," Bettelheim said when he caught up with her, "you have a very important decision to make." Prepared for the worst, the twenty-one-year-old newcomer tried to pull herself together. "Will you have beer or an ice cream cone?" he said. [45]

Bettelheim had "a shark-like smile" that made more than one staff member feel that he cruised the school like a wrathful god and that even if she could not recall having done anything wrong there was always the possibility she had forgotten about something. But he also had "a much more tentative, interested grin" that beamed on at the late-night informal bantering sessions. [46] He also had a big laugh. Sandy Lewis, who attended the school in the fifties and remained entwined with Bettelheim for years afterward, recalled how he made self-deprecatory remarks about his homeliness. "But to me as a child the man was beauti-ful," Lewis told me. "When he laughed his big laugh the whole school was happy." This mood often came with corny one-liners, like his oft-repeated observation that he only knew three things but could remember just two at any given time, or his suggestion to Seevak that she open a fund-raising talk by referring to a new book about the school as *Love Is Not Enough, It Takes Money Too.*

The director came to the rescue of his anxious staff again and again, often in unexpected and unorthodox ways. Harry, the boy who had thrown the carving knife at Gayle Shulenberger, also manifested his violent streak by making a shambles of his dorm room. The son of a drunken father, he tried to copy his parent's alcoholic rampages by repeatedly toppling the furniture, including the bunk beds. One afternoon, he returned to the dorm and discovered to his amazement that the tables, chests, and bunks— everything but the chairs—had been bolted to the walls or floor. He was infuriated, Bettelheim wrote,

> but this very frustrating experience turned out to be also quite constructive. For the first time Harry found himself prevented from committing a misdeed without having been physically restrained, threatened by punishment, or actually punished. Despite his anger, he realized that at the School people were so concerned with his and the other children's well-being that they were ready to go to some length in safeguarding it, while at the same time they made special arrangements to avoid the use of restraint.[47]

Another case that demonstrated Bettelheim's rejection of conventional solutions involved a boy who refused to go to the toilet and had become so constipated that he no longer moved his bowels at all. In desperation, several counselors took him to the university's Billings Hospital, across the Midway, where doctors reamed him out with mineral oil as he screamed in pain, a trauma not only for the child but for the helpless young women as well. Bettelheim listened to their agonized account at a staff meeting and then asked: Did it occur to anybody to tell the poor boy that he could go in his pants, or in his bed? It had not—to the counsel-ors or to Jerome Kavka, the psychiatric consultant present at the session. "He demonstrated to us," Kavka told me, "that we were, like the rest of the world, too preoccupied with cleanliness, which kept us from doing the right thing in this case." Bettelheim liked to remind the staff that in Vienna shopkeepers always greeted customers by asking, politely, "How may I serve you?" That was the message he wanted the children to get, maintaining that too often psychotherapists in the United States assumed they knew it all and their patients knew nothing.

Bettelheim insisted that staff members put themselves in a child's place, try to understand his seemingly incomprehensible behavior by imagining what *they* might be feeling if they were to act in a similar fashion. Robert Bergman recalled a counselor who reported that a child had become upset over the way she had touched her. "Bettelheim teased out that she had touched the child tentatively and with some anxiety. He got her to think about how she would feel if she were with a young man she liked and he had touched her that way." One of his favorite questions was: How would you feel if you discovered someone you loved sitting on top of a flagpole? Fledgling counselors looked at one another in bewilderment, not eager to hazard a reply; few of them guessed that the answer their teacher sought was that they should have faith in the climber's reasons for being up there.[48]

Bettelheim also liked to say that "the end is in the beginning," by which he meant that the attitudes counselors brought to their interactions with the children often determined how those interactions would play out. One child, Sammy, walked hesitantly to his sessions with a counselor named Diana Grossman, and paused before the door of the room where they were about to talk. Bettelheim explained that the session had actually begun when Grossman picked up Sammy in the classroom, and that every step he took lagging behind her while she impatiently preceded him had communicated to him whose session it was and who was in charge. Thereafter, Grossman began waiting for Sammy to go ahead of her at every step, giving him a chance to make clear that he wanted to come to the session; if he continued to hang back and never reached the room, then that became the session.[49]

Several times over the years, Bettelheim described how he

had come into his office one morning soon after taking charge of the school to discover a huge meat cleaver on his desk, with a note that he said read: " 'This time it's on your desk; next time it'll be in your head.' " In one telling, the cleaver had been used to break into the candy closet, which his predecessor, Mandel Sherman, had kept locked, doling out the contents as he saw fit.[50] In another version, Bettelheim said he had already taken the lock off but the children had not felt free to come in and help themselves because the closet was behind an imposing desk in Sherman's large and intimidating office, which Bettelheim was still using. He said he had planned to take a more modest space, but in the crush of the transition had decided the move could wait; the meat-cleaver incident convinced him that the size of the chamber, its muscular furniture, and the location of the candy symbolized the oppressive atmosphere of the previous regime.[51]

Bettelheim soon settled into a small office just off the entrance to the building and re-established the store of sweets outside his immediate orbit. Any child could raid this trove whenever she wished and was free to carry off as many Hershey bars, Chuckles, Baby Ruths, cookies, and assorted other confections as she liked, no questions asked. "We have found," Bettelheim wrote, in a characteristic rejection of orthodox parental thinking, "that candy eaten shortly before main meals only rarely spoils the children's appetite, and that even when it does, the children's health does not suffer. We do not care when or what they eat, whether they eat mainly at meals, or in between; our chief concern is that eating itself become a pleasure to them."[52]

The daily fare at the school was ample and nourishing, and the children themselves chose the menu several times a month.[53] At dinner, bowlsful of steaming mashed potatoes and peas and carrots poured forth from the kitchen, along with platters of chicken or meat loaf, plenty of bread and butter, and often cake or ice cream for dessert. Bettelheim had nothing but disdain for the trays and cafeteria lines of most institutions. The kitchen staff served boarding-house style, shuttling to and from the dining room's several tables, at each of which sat a counselor or teacher with about half a dozen children. No diner had to fear being treated like Oliver Twist; if he wanted more, empty serving bowls were quickly replenished. Bettelheim was determined that the dining room, like the rest of the school, have a homey atmosphere; he insisted on the use of quality china at every place setting and eventually would choose the wallpaper himself as well, dark-skinned ballerinas dancing in blue tutus against a gray background. He was fond of saying, *"Die Liebe geht durch den Magen,"* "Love goes through the stomach." But, like so many therapists of his generation, he seemed compelled to make such commonsense observations carry a heavy Freudian load. He wrote that psychoses were often caused by a regression to early oral fixations; thus it was at mealtime that these old traumas could be countered by corrective emotional experiences that would help rebuild the personality.[54]

At no time did a warmer atmosphere envelop the school than at Christmas, a holiday that grew increasingly lavish over the years and usually turned Bettelheim into a doting paterfamilias. He relished going downtown to Marshall Field's and acquiring the most expensive Santa Claus suit for a counselor to wear, or to another favorite store in the Loop where he spent generously on hundreds of foreign-made toy soldiers.[55] As December 25 approached, weary counselors stayed up night after night sewing stuffed animals and dolls, making marzipan from scratch, and transforming the playroom into a fairyland hung with bulging stockings. Bettelheim believed that anyone "who cannot thoroughly enjoy buying a gift for somebody who plays an important role in his life . . . had better give up working intimately with people."[56] But he could be an irritating stickler for making sure a present was just right, sometimes criticizing counselors for getting a child a Raggedy Ann doll when, in his view, a toy stove would have been more psychologically appropriate. If he felt strongly enough, he would run to his office and rummage through the store of gifts he kept there and come up with what he regarded as a fitting substitute.

Not long before one Christmas in the fifties, Bettelheim and Sanders were commiserating about two difficult children the school had had to give up on. They decided that everyone needed cheering up and arranged for a secret Santa Claus to arrive early at critical moments with presents to boost the staff's morale. When a counselor arrived to decorate the front hall banister she found a corsage waiting for her. On the night before the children's Christmas party, when the staff worked into the morning making preparations, one exhausted member found an Easter bunny costume with instructions that he dress up in it and distribute Easter presents to his fellow elves. And one year, Bettelheim decided that the secret Santa should leave a stocking and a present for each staff member to find in the living room before he or she went to the playroom for the children's gift opening. Bettelheim himself provided funds for the presents and many of the ideas and the secret Santa became a tradition that lasted several years, signaled by the mysterious appearance of a large stuffed reindeer in the director's office chair.[57]

Lou Harper, who ran the teaching staff at the school for two decades, told me that no one he had ever known captured the spirit of Christmas better than Bettelheim. As he would spell out when writing about fairy tales, Bettelheim saw "magical thinking" as a boost to a child's development, and that very much included the belief in Santa Claus. When a mother told her five-year-old boy that there was no such person and instructed him instead in the abstract spirit of giving, Bettelheim pointed out that Santa is a good elf who wants nothing in return, which is why he comes in the middle of the night. "We need to realize, as our children do, that there is a great difference between accepting presents from some sprite who wants no gratitude, and exchanging presents with thank-you's all around."[58]

AT THE END OF 1947, Bettelheim reported that twenty-five boys and eight girls boarded at the school, organized in dormitories of four to eight beds. He listed the principal reasons for their referrals as delinquency (eighteen), feeble-mindedness or severe retardation (seven), behavior disorders of a schizophrenic nature (four), neurotic deafness (two), and an inability to read (two). He said that eleven of these children produced regular and severe temper tantrums, fifteen showed academic retardation, twenty-eight displayed psychosomatic disturbances ranging from bulimia and anorexia to stuttering and tics, and four had attempted suicide. The quarterly fee for boarding students was $750, and the full-time staff now numbered thirty-three, among them a psychiatrist, a psychologist, a social worker, ten counselors, four teachers, a registered nurse, a seamstress, and the kitchen, maintenance, and office workers. Most of the children came from the Chicago area, an increasing number from middle- and upper-class families, several of them wealthy and most of them well educated. As a result of Bettelheim's new admissions policies, the collective intelligence of the residents had begun to rise; he said their IQs now ranged from 90 to 157 (normal to gifted), with the preponderance (eighteen) just above average.[59]

Academic education took place every weekday between 9:00 A.M. and 3:00 P.M. in what amounted to a one-room schoolhouse. The teachers not only had to tailor lessons for children of varying ages and abilities but to cope with the paroxysms of rage and other emotional shrapnel that flew about the classroom almost daily. The children worked at their own pace, one boy struggling with simple addition while a girl of the same age raced through the multiplication tables. Whatever a pupil's capacity for learning, his emotional well-being came first; if a task proved too frustrating, Lou Harper would assure him that it was not the most important issue in his life at the moment. A child who felt the work too threatening could, without fear of censure, spend his time in class playing on the linoleum floor with blocks or, in some cases, skip school altogether until he felt confident enough to return. To reduce pressure, no homework assignments were made; to minimize competition, no marks were given. With some amusement, Myrna Adams, who entered the school in 1948, told me that she and her classmates never knew what grade they were in. In this relaxed atmosphere, the progress was always uneven but occasionally "almost magical." One twelve-year-old boy who refused to read suddenly became entranced by *The Yearling,* which Lou Harper had been reading to him. "When I was finished he asked me to read it again. I said: 'No, you have to read it yourself now.' And so he began."[60]

In 1948, R. Wendell Harrison, the dean of faculties at the University of Chicago, asked F. Howell Wright, head of pediatrics, for his assessment of developments at the Orthogenic School. Wright, who at Bettelheim's request had agreed to treat the children's medical problems and would continue to do so for almost forty years, replied that on the basis of limited observation he had found the new principal's stewardship "far superior" to Mandel Sherman's and described him as "an intense, hard working, intellectually honest individual who has a considerable interest in children. . . ." Wright felt something "very important and valuable" was taking place at the school and lamented that no mechanism had been established to permit medical students, pediatric interns, residents, and the attending staff at Billings Hospital to observe the school's milieu therapy regularly.[61] Wright did note that he had heard Bettelheim had a volatile temper and sometimes lost control of himself. He told me that he himself was never on the receiving end of such outbursts, stressing that Bettelheim always treated him with immoderate respect, a deference Wright suggested stemmed from a refugee Jew's insecurity in the presence of a Gentile who held an important post at the university and was also a medical doctor. Though Bettelheim installed "Dr." in front of his name soon after taking over the Orthogenic School, when Wright greeted him with that honorific he sometimes corrected him by saying, with self-deprecating sarcasm, "*Mr.* Bettelheim."

Wright felt that anyone overseeing a residential-treatment center for emotionally disturbed children had "every conceivable alibi" for exploding from time to time, but some actual targets of the new director's wrath were less understanding. A year after Bettelheim took over the school, Robert M. Hutchins received a letter from a mother after she and her husband had met with Bettelheim to discuss whether they should enroll their son, who they felt had a reading disability. "We were completely astonished," she told the chancellor,

> by the discourtious [sic] reception and his rude, sarcastic answers to our question[s]. When we finally asked to see the school, he became violently angry, burst into a tirade about the place not being a zoo, and acted like a man who thought he was being spied upon. We came to the quick conclusion that the school with such a principal was no place for our child or any other child.
>
> Now perhaps he has nothing to conceal, but puts on such an exhibition to subdue inquisitive parents. But he is evidently un-

aware that American parents consider it their right to be inquisitive about an environment in which they may put their child. However, the important part of the affair is that [it] seems inevitable that his lack of emotional stability, his sadistic determination to make us uncomfortable must be present in his dealing with the children under his care.[62]

Bettelheim defended his behavior by telling Hutchins, who had asked him how to respond to the mother, that she had insisted not only on touring the school but on talking to the children, in order to persuade herself that they were "much inferior to her son"; he said he refused to let her see the children because he feared she would upset them.[63] Hutchins let the matter slide.

The mother's behavior may have been as demanding as Bettelheim suggested, and his decision not to let her invade the children's domain a valid one; but his antiparent assaults were not limited to this woman, and early on they troubled some campus administrators. A 1948 confidential memorandum reported that the dean of the university's School of Social Service Administration had found, along with her staff, that Bettelheim was "incapable of appropriate parent orientation, or not interested in it." The staff was reluctant to recommend financial support for the Orthogenic School because of the "shock" treatment he inflicted on parents: telling them when they enrolled their child that it was his decision, and his alone, as to when they would next see their son or daughter, and whether they would have to settle for a few hours over a weekend or could hope for a longer reunion in their home.[64] Bettelheim generally opposed the latter, maintaining that such home visits often unraveled, if only temporarily, the progress the child had made.

This was undoubtedly true in some cases, but the prolonged separations inevitably had other traumatic consequences as well. Myrna Adams recalled being taken to the school by her mother in 1948 and having no idea why. After entering the front door, the terrified eight-year-old was told to wait in a room, where a counselor eventually explained that she would be staying. "That was the last time I saw my mother for at least a year," Adams told me. Helen Martinson, whose daughter Dorothy attended the school

during Bettelheim's first years there, said that he seemed determined to make mothers feel guilty, "and if he could make us weep
that was better." He viewed parents, particularly mothers, not only
as the cause of children's emotional difficulties but as the chief
obstacle to overcoming them; he regarded himself as the children's
advocate. "I consider my role as attorney for the child, let the
parents get their own attorney," he said.[65] Even some of his most
devoted counselors came to regard his policy as at best misguided
and at worst cruel. But as Joan Little pointed out, when they first
began working at the school they were growing away from their
own mothers and fathers; blaming parents in general for the psychological woes of their offspring had a certain easy attraction,
especially if it was encouraged during one-on-one sessions with
the boss.

Bettelheim's conviction that parents were at the root of most
childhood mental disorders found a good deal of support in the
psychoanalytic tradition. Sigmund Freud had never met the
mother of his famous hysteric, Dora, but in his 1905 monograph
about the teenager he wrote that he was "led to imagine" by her
and her father's testimony that the mother was an uncultivated and
foolish woman who had no understanding of children because she
concentrated on domestic chores, a preoccupation Freud called
her "housewife's psychosis."[66] This sort of patronizing position,
rarely buttressed by any evidence, would harden into received
truth in the decades that followed, sometimes offered in the
thoughtful, sympathetic language of such experts on the family as
D. W. Winnicott, John Bowlby, and Benjamin Spock, other times
delivered as stern indictments by psychoanalysts like David Levy
and René Spitz. As late as 1965, Spitz would write in his book
The First Year of Life that phenomena like colic and eczema were
"psychotoxic diseases of infancy" provoked by the mother's personality.[67] At about the same time, a doctor at Harvard Medical
School argued that having children deeply distressed women because it confirmed their femaleness, which they secretly abhorred;
thus, they felt compelled to disown motherhood by destroying
their offspring. He conceded that most mothers did not murder
or even totally reject their children but contended that death per-
vades the relationship.[68]

Such mother-bashing grew in intensity after World War II, reflecting "a widespread anxiety that something was going wrong with America—or Americans."[69] In the 1920s, the concept of permissiveness had entered the nursery and begun to replace the nineteenth-century belief that properly raising children required strict discipline. Some two million men had been rejected or discharged from the military for psychiatric reasons; a few experts suggested that the new permissiveness just might be responsible for their inability to cope. When the war ended, millions more servicemen came home to face an uncertain job future and to discover that women, who had helped build warships and airplanes, had also run the household quite well on their own. This had left these "housewives" standing tall behind the wheel of the great consumer freighter just getting under way on advertising's seductive sea. As Barbara Ehrenreich and Deirdre English point out in *For Her Own Good,* their trenchant analysis of *150 Years of Experts' Advice to Women,* the idea that women had achieved any real social or economic power was an illusion, that "if anything [they] had reached a nadir for the twentieth century."[70] Nonetheless, many men saw women as the cause of postwar America's problems; they felt emasculated and regarded women as a growing threat, "afflicted very often with penis envy," in the words of Ferdinand Lundberg.[71] In his 1942 bestseller, *Generation of Vipers,* Philip Wylie had turned "Mom" into an accusative, writing that "megaloid momworship has got completely out of hand."[72]

It was in this atmosphere that Bettelheim picked up the megaphone that would make him, over three decades, the profession's loudest advocate for the Mom-as-villain diagnosis. There was and is no shortage of evidence showing that some parents or their surrogates mistreat children in myriad ways, and that their behavior, whether willfully cruel or merely misguided, can have a profound impact. Gayle Shulenberger recalled that Harry, the boy who had thrown the knife at her, had been held from a third-floor window in his foster home and told that he would be dropped if he kept misbehaving. Other children at the Orthogenic School had come from dark backgrounds as well; but many were raised by basically affectionate parents who did the best job they knew how, only to discover that something they could not explain had gone wrong with their children. By the time they arrived at Bettelheim's door they usually were desperate, and when he told them to leave their children and go away they sheepishly withdrew, always confused and sometimes quaking.

Erwin and Salma Angres, whose son Ronald entered the school in 1959 at age seven, recalled Bettelheim telling them soon afterward that a Rorschach test had indicated he was a very sick boy. Angres, a psychoanalyst, told the director that he and his wife were well aware of that, which was why they had come to him. As was his practice, Bettelheim told them that they could not look around the school and that they might not see their son again for many months. "I remember standing by the window of his office, and for the first time in maybe twenty years, I cried," Erwin Angres told me. Bettelheim gave him a tissue and consoled him, said that the sharp break was necessary and the situation would look better after some time had passed. After several months, Salma Angres asked if Ronald could come home to be with his siblings for Easter, when they were out of school; Bettelheim agreed to the visit but not before reminding the couple that, though their three other children might be in *school,* Ronald was in a "booby hatch." He would remain there for twelve years, after which the Angreses withdrew him against the director's advice.

Carl Devoe, a Chicago lawyer and businessman, and his wife, Naomi, went to Bettelheim seeking help for their troubled teenage daughter. Devoe had helped raise thousands of dollars for the Orthogenic School and had come to revere Bettelheim as a gifted therapist. He knew the director could be difficult, but nothing had prepared him for the onslaught that came after the couple laid out their daughter's emotional difficulties for the man they saw as her savior. "He practically ruined Naomi," Devoe told me. "He told her in so many words that she was the cause of [our daughter's] problems, that our child must enter the school, and that he couldn't possibly tell us when we might see her again. He was an absolute brute, there is no question about it." Nonetheless, their daughter was soon living under Bettelheim's care.

A FEW MONTHS after Bettelheim took over the Orthogenic School in 1944, he laid out ambitious plans to create "the outstanding

nationally known center for the treatment and study of emotionally disturbed children."[73] He called for research programs, scholarships for families who could not afford full tuition, fellowships
to pay some staff members, and a new building to house the
institution. These and additional goals would eventually require
thousands of dollars, and the cash began to flow in immediately.
In his first year, the school's budget almost doubled, to sixty-four
thousand dollars, largely as a result of a twenty-thousand-dollar
gift from the Sonia Shankman Foundation, a memorial fund established by the family and friends of a Chicago woman who had
died in 1936, at the age of forty-two, after many years devoted to
helping children.[74] Carl Devoe was a prime mover in the foundation, as was Philip Pekow, a wealthy Chicago hotel owner whose
daughter had attended the Orthogenic School during the Sherman years. Pekow had sent out the fund-raising letter in the summer of 1944, warning that the school was in parlous financial
condition and that, as only one consequence, the children suffered
from malnutrition. He was determined that the institution should
survive, and regarded the hardworking Bettelheim, with his confident style and Freudian aura, as its redeemer.

By 1949, the new principal's performance had so impressed
the foundation that it agreed to make the institution its sole bene-
ficiary and pledged forty thousand dollars or more for 1950 and
each succeeding year, a commitment that moved the University of
Chicago to designate the home formally the Sonia Shankman
Orthogenic School.[75] The family fund renamed itself the Foundation for Emotionally Disturbed Children and began devoting itself
exclusively to raising money for the school. Gifts came in from
companies as well as individuals, and additional funds flowed from
special events, such as a benefit performance of *Fiddler on the Roof.*
On Clark Street, just north of the Loop, the FEDC's women's
auxiliary opened a thrift shop, an enterprise staffed by dedicated
volunteers who would eventually raise upward of a hundred thousand dollars annually, mostly for scholarships. Bettelheim gratefully
accepted the auxiliary's checks at its luncheons, telling his benefactors how crucial their work was for the school and how beautiful
they all looked in their hats. He always stressed how successful he
was in restoring his charges to healthy, productive lives. "Ninety

percent was his theme song," recalled Nell Pekarsky, who helped oversee the FEDC fund-raising for many years. "He got whatever he wanted from them; they were in such awe of him that being in his presence was like having some kind of spiritual experience." To most of the women, and many of their husbands, he was both God and a genius, and the money rolled in. "He was terrific," said Ben Wright, who sometimes accompanied Bettelheim on fund-raising forays. "He just made people feel good about giving him money."

With the FEDC established, Bettelheim was now in a position to push hard for his goal, spelled out in his 1945 memorandum on the needs of the institution, of improving and expanding the physical plant. By 1950, the church and adjoining minister's house, never intended for use as a school in the first place, had deteriorated badly for lack of money to make repairs. Architectural plans already existed for the construction of two additional dormitory units and more space for classrooms, and ground was soon broken.

Bettelheim believed that a good residential-treatment center should fit the children's lives like "a very comfortable, old shoe,"[76] and to achieve that homey feeling, the new dormitory building was integrated into the rear of the rectory, with three dorm rooms for boys on the second floor and two for girls and one for boys on the first. A night counselor lived adjacent to each dorm; in all, the enlarged house now accommodated fourteen counselors in small but comfortable rooms, most of them singles. Six or seven children slept in each dorm room, now in beds instead of the double-decker bunks that had been used to create more play space in their old, cramped quarters. Each child was free to arrange the furniture in her area as she liked, and dormmates decided collectively on their room's decor, choosing from a variety of cheerful curtain patterns and paint colors laid out for them by their counselors and sometimes Bettelheim himself. If the children failed to reach consensus, painting one wall bright red, another pale blue, a third yellowish green, and the fourth purple was an altogether acceptable compromise, a multihued reflection of the art-historian-turned-psychologist's belief that "[n]o one can feel that he is master of his fate if he cannot decide even such simple matters as the color of his walls or the design of his curtains."[77]

The church, too, was substantially renovated, its sanctuary divided to create a rumpus room below and a gymnasium above. The two-story building now contained four classrooms, five small rooms for individual play sessions, and a craft shop and wood-working area. The school also boasted three playgrounds, two between the house and the church and one across Dorchester Avenue, with a jungle gym, sandbox, seesaw, baseball diamond, and tennis court. By one estimate, the cost of expanding and repairing the school exceeded three hundred thousand dollars, a considerable sum in those years, especially for an institution limited to some forty children.[78]

The renovation was completed in 1952, and the following spring, the Bettelheims themselves moved into more spacious lodgings. They had been living near the school in a railroad flat at 6103 Kenwood Avenue, to which they had moved from the small Dorchester Avenue apartment when they needed to make room for their second child, Naomi Michele, who was born on November 19, 1945. When Eric Christopher, their last child, arrived on January 27, 1952, Bruno and Trude followed the path of millions of other American families in the postwar boom and went looking for a house. They found it across the Midway from the school at 5725 Kenwood Avenue, a three-story, detached, red brick home built in 1892 that they bought by scraping together $2,000 in cash and borrowing the rest of the $24,500 purchase price from a local bank and the university. "[W]e don't own it, rather the mortgage company owns us, but it is nice for the children," Bettelheim told James T. Farrell.[79] The dwelling, with a backyard in which Trude would indulge her love of gardening, sat in a neighborly, architecturally discordant line of wooden, brick, and stone houses and apartment buildings on a block graced with large trees and small front lawns. At the north end, the block gave into 57th Street, where Stineway's drugstore, Woodworth's and the Red Door bookstores, and a march of row houses bursting with students pulsed with campus life well into the evening.

Except when the winter weather roared off the lake, turning the Midway into a windswept steppe, the house was a pleasant ten-minute walk from the school. Bettelheim arrived there each morning around nine-thirty, as he had from the beginning, for a day crammed with administrative tasks, staff meetings, and interventions in crises large and small. Few details were too small for his personal attention. When the school had a chance to buy a seventy-nine-dollar junior-size billiard table, he dispatched a memo to Ralph Tyler asking that he bring this need to the attention of the FEDC's women's auxiliary, which the chairman of the department of education promptly did.[80] When Karen Carlson came to Bettelheim frantic because one of her children had the stomach flu and was getting sicker and sicker, unable to keep any food down, Bettelheim suggested she make the girl some chamomile tea, a beverage unknown to Carlson. "Where do my counselors come from that they've never heard of chamomile tea?" said the dismayed principal, who went and brewed the tea himself and spoon-fed it to the child.

Most days, Bettelheim ate lunch at the staff table in the dining room, on his way in or out sometimes placing a penny by a child's plate and asking for her thoughts. He went home for dinner, but was usually back at the school by eight or eight-thirty, making rounds of the dorms, dropping in on the staff bull sessions, or disappearing into his office with a counselor to hear his or her problems. He spent many hours at the school on weekends, and early on Trude realized with some resentment that she had not married Bruno Bettelheim but the Sonia Shankman Orthogenic School. Gayle Shulenberger recalled at least two occasions when Trude arrived at the school in tears, pleading with her husband to come home. He would put his arm around her and take her into the office, and a while later she would emerge, the flow staunched, and return to her motherly duties. Most nights, Bruno didn't arrive home until one or two in the morning: when the children, and then the counselors, finally drifted off to sleep, and the school was at last quiet, he would closet himself in his office and write.

CHAPTER SEVEN
The Feast-Day Garment

Bruno Bettelheim said that as a young man he had been deeply impressed by *Palestrina,* the early-twentieth-century romantic opera about the Italian Renaissance master of vocal polyphony. Like Wagner's *Die Meistersinger* before it and Hindemith's *Mathis der Maler* later, this musical legend by the German composer Hans Pfitzner honors the struggle of the artist against a society that would make him compromise his creative integrity. In Pfitzner's libretto, the world-weary Palestrina vows he will never write another note after hearing that the Council of Trent plans to ban all sacred music except Gregorian plainsong. But the spirits of nine composers urge him to take up his pen again, and, inspired by a theme sung to him by an angel, Palestrina composes his celebrated *Missa Papae Marcelli.* All, including the pope, hail him for this masterpiece, a mass so sublime it rescues the art of contrapuntal music from the hostile forces within the church. Bettelheim said that what moved him was an aria in which Palestrina's son, Ighino, sings of how his father's great fame accrued to him quietly and unobserved—enveloping him slowly over a lifetime, like a feast-day garment. In his seventies, Bettelheim confided to a friend that this was his private psychology, what he had secretly striven for all his life.[1] His enthusiasm for Ighino's hymn to his father's humility was strikingly similar to Thomas Mann's delight in the same "blessed-lyrical moment" as expressed in a 1918 appreciation of the opera.[2] Whether or not Bettelheim cribbed the passage, from the moment he attracted attention in 1943 with "Individual and Mass Behavior in Extreme Situations" he understood that the fabric for his own feast-day garment would be his writing.

By the end of 1950, hunting and pecking in his second

language late into the night and on weekends, Bettelheim had produced at least thirty published articles, co-authored eleven more, seen "Extreme Situations" reprinted three times, and turned out two books. Much of this writing was about the Ortho- genic School or the treatment of emotionally disturbed children in general, such as "Closed Institutions for Children," which ap- peared in the *Bulletin of the Menninger Clinic.* He also wrote about the Nuremberg trials and Palestine for *Politics,* about anti-Semitism for *Commentary* and *The Journal of Abnormal and Social Psychology,* and about the concentration camps for the *Encyclopaedia Britannica* and *Modern Review.* He reviewed Alexander Mitscherlich's *Doctors of Infamy* and Marie Bonaparte's *The Myths of War* for the *American Journal of Sociology,* addressed "Somatic Symptoms in Superego Formation" for the *American Journal of Orthopsychiatry,* and found time, when asked by a colleague at the University of Chicago for a contribution to a collection on the teaching of the humanities, to set down his views on "What Students Think About Art."

From the outset, Bettelheim wove his garment of prose with the constant and devoted help of skilled seamstresses, women he hired over four decades to rescue his manuscripts. He could write well when he tried, as his letters sometimes showed, but the rush of words that he produced each night that he spent holed up in his office usually lacked structure and concision; and he sometimes stumbled over the hurdles of English grammar and idioms, per- sisting for many years in writing "times immemorial" instead of "from time immemorial." Throughout his life, he felt profoundly insecure about his style, which he knew was at best cumbersome;[3] he feared that readers would laugh at his thinking, would "reject his most personal and important offerings as not worth anything, and make him feel miserable."[4]

In the mid-1940s, he met a young woman who lived in Hyde Park named Ruth Soffer, an editor at the *Encyclopaedia Britannica* who had been impressed by "Individual and Mass Behavior in Extreme Situations." She soon became his personal editor, shaping his drafts for more than fifteen years under her married name of Ruth Marquis; again and again, he gratefully credited her labors, writing in *The Informed Heart* that most of his ideas took their final form in print thanks to her. "She not only edited [the book], as many other of my publications, but she helped me plan it, from the title down to the last entry of the index." [5]

Marquis declined to share her recollections of this process, but others did describe it, among them Linnea Brandwein, who joined the Orthogenic School staff as a typist in 1959 and would become an editorial needlewoman herself, remaining so even after she left the school in 1965. In the beginning, each day she arrived for work seemed like Christmas morning; once again Santa had worked deep into the night and had left a gift by the side of her typewriter, usually a translucent green disk onto which he had dictated a first draft that needed transcribing, or a typescript she had made from earlier disks that now bore the bright-blue traces of his fountain pen, a labyrinthine scrawl posted with arrows and hieroglyphs that few besides Brandwein could decipher. When a substantial number of cleaned-up pages accumulated, Ruth Marquis would go to work on them. "He trusted her absolutely," recalled Brandwein; still, after the pages were retyped with Marquis's emendations, the blue ink would flow again, and the cycle would be repeated.

Bettelheim was as receptive to outside editors as to those he employed. When, in 1948, he submitted the article on Palestine to *Politics,* Dwight Macdonald praised its "skill and boldness" in reproaching American Jews for their unwillingness to bring more displaced European Jews to the United States instead of working so hard for their settlement in a land of hostile Arabs; [6] but the editor complained that the piece was overwritten and asked Bettelheim to trim three or four of its ten typewritten pages. The author complied immediately, saying when he sent back the revised manuscript that he trusted Macdonald to make any additional minor changes without further consultation. In criticizing Bettelheim's original submission, Macdonald had said that for an academic journal "it is perhaps (and perhaps not) necessary to state things as heavily and carefully as you do here. But for a general magazine, it is not necessary, and just loses the reader's attention." [7] Bettelheim took this instruction seriously, understanding early on that he would more likely reach a large, lay readership if he made sure to approach it with accessible, jargon-free prose.

Bettelheim called the belief that the Jews and Arabs could

live in peace "a pipe dream." [8] Whether that phrase was his, Marquis's, or Macdonald's, the refugee's early letters show him slipping comfortably, if sometimes not quite accurately, into the vernacular of his new tongue. He told James T. Farrell he felt "like a heel" for not replying to a letter sooner.[9] He told Macdonald that earning a living kept him "plenty busy," [10] that if the editor wanted him to review a certain book he would be glad to "try my hand on it," [11] and that if *Politics* could come out more often than once a month "that would be swell." [12] Bettelheim said that so many people must be telling Macdonald how good the magazine was that the editor probably thought *he* was just trying to "jump on the band wagon." [13]

In the spring of 1945, on a visit to New York to see his mother and sister, Bettelheim greatly enjoyed an evening with Macdonald, his wife, Nancy, and their politically engaged friends. Before long, the two men were beginning their letters "Dear Bruno" and "Dear Dwight," and Macdonald was urging Bettelheim to rent a vacation cottage in Wellfleet, the Cape Cod community of writers and artists where the Macdonalds summered. Wellfleet proved too expensive, but, beginning in August 1949, Bruno and Trude and their two small girls did rent a cottage for several summers in the town of Truro, just up the road from the summer salons of Wellfleet.

By the mid-1940s, Bettelheim was also on a "Dear Jim" basis with James T. Farrell, who had praised "Extreme Situations" and would seek Bettelheim's advice about his retarded son, John Stephen. Farrell's Lonigan trilogy, which Bettelheim admired,[14] was set in an Irish neighborhood not far from Hyde Park, but the "Chicago writer" now lived in the thick of literary Manhattan. "The East is [Europe], but the Middlewest, [let's] not talk about it," Bettelheim wrote to Ernst Federn, who was living in Brussels after his liberation from Buchenwald in 1945 and had sought his former campmate's views on life in the United States. "In New York you will find many intellectuals, interesting and very lovable people. Only outside of the New York area things get pretty barren. And I mean barren. [The University of Chicago] is one of the many oas[e]s, but even here it is very difficult to remain in contact with things." In an earlier letter, Bettelheim had told Federn that he liked his work at the Orthogenic School, especially because university administrators did not interfere with him.[15] But now he said that his dream was finding a job in New York, and lamented that nobody had offered him one.[16]

A group of New Yorkers did, however, offer him the opportunity to publish his first book. In 1944, Max Horkheimer, who had been director of Germany's Frankfurt Institute in the early 1930s as well as of its successor at Columbia University, joined the American Jewish Committee, where he established a department of scientific research to produce a five-volume series called "Studies in Prejudice." The project sought to examine the impact on the individual and community of racial, religious, and ethnic prejudice in general, and of anti-Semitism in particular. Horkheimer recruited several of his Frankfurt colleagues as contributors, among them the sociologists Paul Massing, Leo Lowenthal, and, not least, Theodor Adorno, whose *The Authoritarian Personality* became the best-known book of the series.

Bettelheim had first attracted the attention of these powerful leftist intellectuals with "Extreme Situations," which would appear in Germany in the mid-1950s as the only essay by an outsider in a collection by Frankfurt-school writers. "Extreme Situations" had also impressed the American Jewish Committee, to whose magazine, *Commentary,* Bettelheim soon would become an occasional contributor; he seemed to Horkheimer a good candidate to direct one of the studies. The two men discussed various investigations, among them comparing the prejudices of psychotics with those of a normal group of people with like intelligence, education, and family background, with the aim of finding out if the disintegrated personality was more prone to bigotry or less. But with the Allied victory in 1945, what began to intrigue them and their colleagues was the opportunity to measure how returning servicemen, who had just fought in a four-year war against fascism and were now trying to find their way in the peacetime economy, felt about minorities.[17]

About this time, a young teaching assistant named Morris Janowitz had begun work on a doctoral dissertation at the University of Chicago that involved interviews with former soldiers. Janowitz had been drawn to Chicago in part because he, too, had been impressed by "Extreme Situations," and was delighted when Edward Shils, a leading light in the sociology department, recommended him to Bettelheim as just the man to help with the Horkheimer project.

Bettelheim and Janowitz soon became good friends. With the young doctoral candidate taking on the major responsibility for the collection and analysis of data, they and their small staff conducted extensive open-ended interviews with a random sample of 150 army veterans from the Chicago area, all of them white, Gentile former enlisted men.[18] Bettelheim and Janowitz excluded officers from their study, because their war experiences differed sharply from those of Willie and Joe, though why and how this distinction might play a role in officers' attitudes toward minorities Bettelheim and Janowitz did not make clear. They conceded that their decision skewed their sample to the lower and lower-middle classes, but maintained that this was "not unrealistic," since Nazism had shown that the most ardent anti-Semites came from such social ranks.[19] Such reasoning, along with other aspects of the survey, would lead to criticism that it was "seriously flawed."[20]

Bettelheim and Janowitz's initial findings appeared in 1950, in *The Dynamics of Prejudice: A Psychological and Sociological Study of Veterans,* the second volume in the "Studies in Prejudice Series." They stressed that their research showed that "intolerance is always an outlet for hostility, but that it depends for its intensity on the degree of hostility accumulated, and on the strength of the controls which restrain it,"[21] a conclusion some readers may have reached on their own without requiring so much buttressing. The book is heavy with appendixes, charts, and tables ("Social Correlates of Anti-Semitism"[22]), quotations from the interviews ("I just couldn't stand being near a nigger . . ."[23]), and more than a few passages suggesting that Dwight Macdonald's admonition about clear, jargon-free prose had not yet sunk in ("Eissler has pointed out that in those cases where tendencies rejected by the superego are displaced on members of an outgroup, the rationalizations for persecution of the outgroup induce the superego to join its energy to the id's asocial impulses"[24]).

The co-authors planted Freud's flag with the book's epigraph: "The limitation of aggression is the first and perhaps the hardest sacrifice society demands from each individual."[25] They set out to see if dynamic theories of human behavior could be applied to group interaction and concluded that interethnic hostility could be reduced if personalities were better integrated.[26] This, in turn, required that individual tension be diminished, and one of the best ways to accomplish that was in the bedroom. "According to psychoanalytic theory," they wrote,

> the main adult avenue for the discharge of tension is that of inter-personally gratifying sexual relations. The same body of theories maintains that anxiety (which was found to be strongly associated with intolerance) is a direct or indirect consequence of inhibited sexuality. It may seem doubtful, in a society as complex as ours and with its countless sources of anxiety, whether all tensions can actually be discharged in sexual activity. But there seems little doubt that if two people enjoy a mutually gratifying sexual relationship, under normal circumstances the remaining tensions can be integrated with relatively greater ease.[27]

Even in 1950, before the Freudian grip on the nation's collective psyche had begun to loosen, this was too much for some. One reviewer found incredible the authors' "blind acceptance" of what was at best a sexual hypothesis that could hardly "throw any further light on the whole problem of intolerance."[28]

Bettelheim and Janowitz concluded from their data that intolerance was primarily a function of feelings of economic deprivation and downward social mobility. As an antidote, they prescribed an increased annual wage and an extension of Social Security and called for a change in the country's economic ethos, so that self-respect and respect for the community were not tied to the prevailing notion of upward mobility, the media-driven lust for ever-larger cars and bigger television sets that was gathering momentum in the postwar boom.[29] On this score, Bettelheim practiced what he preached, living modestly on his university salary plus the occasional speaking fee, maintaining a deep commitment to his work at the Orthogenic School, and always rejecting the idea of a lucrative private practice, which he could have established at any time.

•

WHILE *THE DYNAMICS OF PREJUDICE* was still in the making, Morris Janowitz introduced Bettelheim to an ambitious young Hyde Park neighbor, Jeremiah Kaplan, who in 1947 started a publishing house called The Free Press of Glencoe. Eager to build a list and impressed by what he was hearing about the Orthogenic School, Kaplan signed up its principal to write a monograph on his work, and the indefatigable writer set about producing it. When Kaplan saw the final manuscript, he was astonished. He had expected a scientific work, a dry psychological study aimed at a limited, professional readership; what he had in his hands was the opposite, a richly anecdotal account in which Bettelheim took the reader on an unhurried tour of the school, pausing again and again to give detailed and often moving descriptions of the children and to explain his treatment philosophy.

Bettelheim also supplied Kaplan with pictures taken by Myron Davis, a University of Chicago graduate and *Life* magazine war photographer who had spent two weeks capturing the children playing games on the dorm floors, planing boards in the woodworking shop, splashing in the bathtub, and frolicking in the pool at Sunny Gymnasium across the Midway. The book came out in 1950, the same year as *The Dynamics of Prejudice,* but its impact proved far greater and gave a quantum boost to Bettelheim's reputation, not least because of its provocative title, *Love Is Not Enough*.

"Modern living conditions," Bettelheim wrote in the introduction, have made it much more difficult for parents to create a setting in which both their own legitimate needs and the needs of their children can be satisfied with relative ease. That is why love alone is not enough and must be supplemented by deliberate efforts on the part of the parent.[30]

By way of an immediate example, he wrote that, instead of keeping a child penned up so he wouldn't be able to burn himself on a hot stove, parents should fence off the stove itself, thus enlarging the space in which the child could play safely. Moreover, parents should campaign for the redesign of gas ranges so that toddlers would not be able to reach their knobs. Bettelheim argued that the alternative to such sensible approaches was too often the angry parental "No!," which convinced children that exploring their world was either dangerous or against Mom and Dad's wishes, or both. In preparing readers for what lay beyond the introduction, Bettelheim wrote that his observations about parents might sound unduly harsh but emphasized that they were drawn from his treatment of emotionally disturbed children and were meant to help conscientious mothers and fathers better understand and raise their normal children.[31]

Bettelheim drew heavily for *Love Is Not Enough* on Orthogenic School records, which he said elsewhere typically totaled some seven hundred single-spaced, typewritten pages for a child who had been at the school for two years.[32] These thick dossiers included family histories, psychiatric evaluations, IQ scores, the results of Rorschach and Thematic Apperception Tests, and reports on classroom progress; transcripts of the counselors' dictation took up scores more pages, and to these descriptions and assessments of the children's behavior Bettelheim brought his considerable storytelling skills, drawing pseudonymous sketches of the unhappy children in his care: tales of Richard, who believed that animals protected him and who had to talk to his teddy bear in the morning before he could talk to people;[33] of Felix, who felt that, to be loyal to his father, who had died when the boy was very young, he must make sure never to acquire an education as good as his stepfather's;[34] of Emily, who after some time at the school grew less rigid about cleanliness but then began to see ghosts whenever she went to the toilet.[35]

Bettelheim set down these psychological snapshots and all else in the book in a tone of psychoanalytic sweet reasonableness, a disarming voice at once all-knowing ("it is common knowledge that the difficulties of almost all emotionally disturbed children have originated in the relationship to a parent . . ."[36]) and modest ("we are [not] always a match for our tasks, because unfortunately we make mistakes"[37]). In soothing and reassuring prose, he wrote about the children's first encounter with the school, their dreams, their efforts to learn in the classroom, their eating and bathroom habits, and about their ventures into the immediate neighborhood. In the final chapter, he took the reader into the dorms at bedtime as he tucked in Jack, who dreaded falling asleep because he feared he might not be alive in the morning;[38] and Ann, who thought babies came out of penises and had a long history of bed-wetting and night terrors;[39] and eleven-year-old Ronnie, who, with a severely depressed mother who had contemplated killing both herself and her children, now worried that once he fell asleep he might kill.[40] With the reader entranced, Bettelheim quietly turned out the light and tiptoed from the room. "I would like to go on with my story of the School," he wrote in this nocturne, "but in a manner of speaking it is past midnight and all the children are asleep."[41]

Bettelheim noted his debts to Emmy Sylvester, his friend Fritz Redl, and the work of August Aichhorn, among others, and in footnotes on many pages he credited the efforts of individual counselors, calling each a "participant observer," a concept developed in the 1930s by Harry Stack Sullivan, who believed that the therapist is inextricably bound up in the information he draws from his patient. He also acknowledged Ruth Soffer's "untiring help" in editing the book, the first of seven she would make whole for him. Jeremiah Kaplan told me that these manuscripts arrived at The Free Press needing little further editing; in that respect, "Bettelheim may have been the best author I ever published."

Bettelheim planned three books about the school,[42] inspired in part by the example of his friend Jim Farrell's ambitious Lonigan trilogy. In 1955, The Free Press published the second, *Truants from Life: The Rehabilitation of Emotionally Disturbed Children.* Unlike *Love Is Not Enough,* which was full of vignettes and anecdotes, brief descriptions of the behavior and treatment of numerous residents, this volume offered four extensive case histories that Bettelheim said fairly represented the school's forty patients.[43] There was Paul, who entered after ten and a half years in other institutions, where he had demonstrated both homicidal and suicidal tendencies; Mary, who had a history of petty theft and of hurting both animals and other children, in one case attacking a playmate with a knife; John, who was fragile and anorexic, in part the result of the thrush mouth infection he had developed in the days after his birth; and the delinquent Harry, a constant truant who first ran away from home at age four and who often spent his days riding streetcars or the "El" trains, sitting in movie theaters, and occasionally visiting taverns, where patrons rewarded his childish antics with drinks or gifts.[44] To tell these stories, Bettelheim again mined the reams of dictation supplied by his mostly female staff—in one case "several thousand pages, typed single-spaced"[45]—and again leaned on the organizing and editing skills of Ruth Soffer Marquis, as well as three other women.[46]

He devoted 428 of the book's 511 pages to the histories, and though space limitations makes it impossible to summarize them fully, a common pattern is clear. All four portraits of the children's parents or foster parents are unflattering. Paul's father was an immature man who showed no interest in his son; the boy's mother was a gold-digger whose in-laws called her "that witch" and who rejected her son by dumping him in one institution after another.[47] Mary's parents had both died by the time she was three and a half, leaving her to be raised by a cruel, rejecting aunt who could not deal with her wildness and who constantly compared her actions with the good behavior of her own two children. John's mother and father demonstrated "an emotional inability" to deal with his physical and mental abnormalities, not only before they put him in the school but throughout his stay there.[48] Harry's father was weak and an alcoholic; when drunk, he often abused the boy, who himself demonstrated great hostility at an early age. When he frustrated his mother's desire to have a model son, she punished him severely and called him " 'the meanest child in the world.' "[49]

Each child was extremely difficult to handle, especially in his or her first months at the school, and Bettelheim and his staff showed heroic and patient dedication in dealing with this behavior. Paul grew enormously fat from overeating and frequently sucked his thumb, smacked his lips, and made loud clucking noises with his tongue. He said he was a "crazy killer" who didn't want to live himself and threw fearsome tantrums, during which he destroyed toys and even set fires, first to his own pajamas and then to a pile belonging to his dormmates.[50] Mary screamed constantly, her rages pushing her caretakers to the emotional edge. But, Bettelheim said, they never left her to cry alone, and never became so upset or frustrated that they lost touch with her.[51] John was literally a foul child: homely, disheveled, often smeared with spittle, mucus, and dirt, vomiting at almost every meal. When he seemed least likable, one counselor reported, she concentrated on his appealing dark eyes as a way of maintaining her affection for him.[52] Harry was the child who had thrown the carving knife at Gayle Shulenberger, when she had taken her boys to the basement kitchen for an evening snack. "At this," Bettelheim wrote,

> the other boys turned on him in a fury, and he grew paralyzed for a moment. But before he had time to turn and run, [Shulenberger] went up to him, took his hand and held it firmly; then she told Harry and the other boys that no one was to blame but herself. She said she knew Harry could not control his temper and so she should not have taken him to a place where there were knives lying around, or have let him out of her sight for even a minute.[53]

All four children made steady progress at the school, and each one left much better able to cope with life. Bettelheim reported that a year after Paul departed he graduated from high school seventy-third in a class of 305 and was making a good adjustment in the outside world. Mary, too, did well academically after she left, and though she initially had to deal with a rigid foster mother, she eventually moved to a more accepting home, where she felt "happy, well-liked and understood. . . ."[54] John left the school "vastly improved,"[55] returned to live with his parents, and in time attended a "well-known private school . . . [with] very high academic standards."[56] Harry chose to live with his mother; when she continued to criticize him, he moved in with his father. His life remained difficult, but he received good grades in high school and "despite all hardships . . . was able to turn his life toward success."[57]

In the pages of *Truants from Life,* the four graduates all endorsed Bettelheim and his methods. He wrote that he asked Harry to talk about himself and his experience at the school at his farewell party, but instead the boy chose to talk mostly about Dr. B, whom he described as "a very cautious man" who did not want anybody to hurt himself or others.[58] Paul, during a return visit to the school, told the director that it was the little things and time that had helped him. In concluding Paul's case, Bettelheim wrote that he had told him that "Little Things and Time" would make an ideal title for his history. He said Paul replied, " 'Good title, and add *understanding and patience.' " [59] When Mary, too, returned to the school for a visit, Bettelheim said he asked her if they had done anything wrong in treating her. She said that she had not liked it when the counselors had, in fact, ignored her occasionally during her screaming spells, but that was her only complaint. "Although I encouraged her and told her how much I wanted to know what we did wrong, she could not think of any other mistakes we had made in handling her." He then asked her if he should continue conducting the school as he had when she was a resident. "She answered with great conviction, 'Sure!' and added that she thought we did the right thing for children like her." [60]

The main thing all four case histories had in common, which made each so compelling, was Bettelheim's gift for storytelling, which riveted the reader from the moment each broken child entered the school until he or she emerged much repaired. The profiles in *Truants from Life,* wrote one reviewer, read "as fluently as a good novel." [61] Bettelheim's friend and model Jim Farrell agreed; in assessing the book for *The New York Times Book Review,* he called it "a brilliant study" and said that the case histories made the children "become as real as characters in a good novel. . . ." [62] By the 1980s, fiction is just what such histories had come to be regarded as by most of the therapeutic profession, which had ceased to consider them at all evidentiary but more a literary form, a heuristic "series of exemplars of the author's ideas." [63] But in the 1950s, most psychotherapists still regarded case studies as science, as they had since the histories of Anna O. and Dora entered the Freudian canon at the turn of the century.

Still, the profession generally believed that theory should come first, a position Bettelheim rejected. While working on *Truants from Life,* he wrote to his friend David Rapaport, a psychologist on the staff of the Austen Riggs Center in Stockbridge, Massachusetts, saying that he felt "hemmed in by an over-growth of psychoanalytic theorizing on infantile development and schizophrenia which for years led [him] to misunderstand the meaning of observations. . . ." [64] He argued that case histories should come first, that the time had come to re-examine and perhaps replace "some worn out theoretical concepts with some better ones" based on clinical experience. He did not specify in the letter what theories had led him to misunderstand his observations, or even what those observations were; nor did he indicate which worn-out theoretical concepts needed replacement. Sometimes he also sent out contrary messages about psychoanalysis. Though he often said that it was an art and not a science, and likened himself to a poet, he wrote that he had striven for "scientific honesty" in setting down the histories in *Truants from Life,* in part as a way of guarding against the hazard of "narcissistic pride" in having been the person best able to help the children.[65]

After *Love Is Not Enough* came out in 1950, Bettelheim told Dwight Macdonald that he "surely would appreciate it" if he would review it, ideally for *Partisan Review.*[66] Macdonald wrote a review, though it never saw publication anywhere. In the manuscript, he conceded that Bettelheim had some important things to say, but questioned whether, as the book implied, "the Freudian-Deweyan mountie" always got his man:

> [T]he many fascinating stories in the book invariably have happy endings, the child is helped, the source of his trouble is located. But surely there must have been some failures, some kids who just didn't respond to treatment, or else shifted their symptoms to new hide-outs as the mounties closed in? It would be refreshing to hear about the big ones that got away, and perhaps instructive as well. . . . As a success-story, *Love Is Not Enough* is an impressive and instructive book in the modern scientific tradition, in whose bright lexicon there is no such word as failure. It might have been something even more useful if its author had risen above, or sunk below, the foible of omnipotence.[67]

That was not Bettelheim's style. In a long footnote at the end of *Love Is Not Enough,* he reported that in the five years he had run the school forty children had graduated and that nearly all of them had reached their grade level in academic achievement and were now doing well in public or private school. He conceded that it was too soon to make any long-term guarantees about these successes, noting that lack of funds had made it impossible for him to conduct any systematic follow-up study. From a "casual" one, however, it appeared that "better than eighty percent of our former students have been doing very well during the years since they left the School, sometimes far better than we dared to expect in view of the severity of their initial difficulties."[68] He did not explain how he made his casual study or how he had calculated the 80-percent figure; nor did he describe, even using pseudonyms, the lives being lived by any of the thirty-two graduates who were now doing so well, or indicate what their severe problems had been when they came to the school.

By the time *Truants from Life* came out in 1955, five years after the first book, a follow-up study of former residents had still not been undertaken, but money no longer seemed the main obstacle. Now Bettelheim argued that "statistical analysis [was] not sufficiently refined to shed much light on the questions of treatment success."[69] He also wrote that, because the school's children depended so on others to take over their care after they left, "forecasts are virtually impossible." None of these obstacles discouraged him from making broad claims of success based on his "subjective impressions," which he asked his readers to accept. He reported that, from 1948 to 1953, thirty-one children who had been at the school more than twelve months had left. He said two showed no lasting improvement, three were somewhat improved, eleven were much improved, and fifteen were "fully rehabilitated."[70]

A systematic, long-term follow-up study of the children at the Orthogenic School would not begin until the late 1980s, some fifteen years after Bettelheim retired as director. D. Patrick Zimmerman, coordinator of research at the school, started the investigation by organizing the admissions and outcome records into a database. It shows that Bettelheim often buttressed his success claims by conjuring up numbers that best made his case. Between 1944 and 1949, the first five years he ran the school, eighty children left, not forty, as he had written in *Love Is Not Enough*. Thirty-two children did leave the school between 1948 and 1953, only one more than he stated in *Truants from Life;* but the Zimmerman database indicates that Bettelheim's claim that half were "fully rehabilitated" and eleven more much improved is not true. Using each child's records, Zimmerman employed the Timberlawn Level of Function Scales to gauge how well the resident was coping with life at the time he or she left Bettelheim's care. This measure assesses the child in three categories—how he interacts with his peers, how he relates to his parents, and how he manages in school or in a job—and rates him good, fair, or poor in each. None of the thirty-two children received three good ratings, four received two, and two received one; the remaining twenty-six ranged from fair to poor.

Tom Wallace Lyons, who attended the Orthogenic School from age eight to age twenty and wrote a novel about his experience called *The Pelican and After,* likened Bettelheim to Big Jule, the crapshooter from Chicago in *Guys and Dolls* who insists on using his own dice. These, it turns out, are blank, leading Nathan Detroit to ask Big Jule how he knows he has just rolled a winning seven. The Windy City gambler tells him not to worry—*he* knows just where the spots are. Lyons, who after leaving the school in 1963 would eventually graduate from the Columbia University Graduate School of Journalism and become a reporter, saw the case histories in Bettelheim's books as Big Bruno's dice, all-white bones that allowed the director to come up a winner on every throw. Moreover, the dice were loaded even before he scooped them up. Some counselors, like Gayle Shulenberger, worked hard on their dictation and made a point of doing it, as Bettelheim wanted, at the end of each day, when the children's behavior and their reactions to it were fresh in their minds. But many were exhausted after finally getting the dorms quiet at night and often let the burdensome task slide for a week or more, by which time the complex psychological interactions with their charges were inevitably blurred. Whether the dictation arrived on time or not, it almost always came from a counselor who was young and inexperienced, or who, if she had been at the school for a while, had received all her training from Bettelheim. Regardless of the quality and accuracy of the dictation, Bettelheim scrambled it in his hat and out rolled the steady stream of optimistic case histories: dramatic, readable stories of troubled children, "hopeless" cases he said everyone else had given up on[71] but who, in most instances, had made major progress in his unique therapeutic milieu.

Most counselors did not see how Bettelheim had shaped their reports until after *Love Is Not Enough* was published. Patty Pickett, for one, wished he had consulted her first. "It wasn't exactly how I had dictated it," she told me. "I felt like saying: You don't have to exaggerate, Dr. B, it was dramatic enough." Ann Morrissett, who was a counselor at the school for eighteen months in the late 1940s, felt that Bettelheim carefully chose cases to make the school look good "and sometimes made the reports sound better than they really were." In *Truants from Life,* Bettelheim wrote that all four case histories "were read by all staff members who in some major capacity worked with the child described."[72] In fact, several of the counselors had left the school by the time the manuscript was in preparation, and at least one of them, Betty Lou Pingree, who had worked with John, said she read the history for the first time only after the book was published. Her recollection, however, was that it was a fair reflection of the boy's time at the school.

Other former counselors also said Bettelheim was true to their dictation. Karen Carlson said she dictated copious notes on the child Bettelheim called Marcia and described at length in *The Empty Fortress,* his third book about the school, and the one that focused on autism. Carlson said that after Bettelheim wrote up that case history he showed it to her and was open to corrections of facts as well as to challenges of some interpretations that he had made. She said Bettelheim was skeptical when she told him that Marcia had used the pronoun "I"; when Carlson insisted that this was true, he included it in the case history.[73]

It would be helpful, of course, to compare the dictation and other raw material on several former patients with Bettelheim's use of it in his books, but the information is part of personal files that the Orthogenic School holds in strict confidentiality. This limitation and the absence so far of any long-term follow-up studies produce a singular irony when trying to gauge the efficacy of Bettelheim's work: for the most part, his claims can only be assessed through interviews with former residents and their families and the occasional public statement, which produce just the sort of anecdotal "evidence" that critics often accused Bettelheim of using to make his cases.

Of the four residents Bettelheim described in *Truants from Life,* only Paul was available for an interview. He was almost sixty years old when I talked to him, a successful Chicago businessman and husband and father living in one of the city's prosperous northern suburbs. A boy of ten when he entered the Orthogenic School in 1946, he recalled Bettelheim working long hours. "I saw him exhausted, I saw him unhappy, but when I found things too tough or I wanted something special I would go to him and he always seemed to know what to do. When I had an anxiety attack at bedtime and would go into a crying jag, a counselor would take me downstairs and say, 'Wait here, Dr. B is coming.' He would sit on the couch, his hands folded, and say, 'What were you thinking, what frightened you?' " He said Bettelheim combined this ability to empathize with a strong sense of authority. "It never fazed him if you liked or disliked his decisions; there was no appeal."

In the beginning, Paul found some of Bettelheim's policies confusing. He wondered why, given the director's strictness, the children who ran away were almost never punished. Only after he had been at the school for a while did he come to understand that Bettelheim and the staff were trying to show him and the other residents that truancy was for some a logical reaction to their first weeks at the school, that it was nothing to be ashamed of, and that they would always be welcomed back with relief and affection. Paul also was struck by the explanation given when protective gates went up on the windows of the upper floors. The school installed these bars to keep the children from falling out, but many saw them as imprisoning. To counter this fear, Bettelheim explained that the gates were there to keep people from getting in. "This was reassuring, because many of us suffered from what you could call the 'bogeyman syndrome.' " Paul's primary counselor was Gayle Shulenberger. As a child, she had feared losing her parents and being placed in an orphanage, so she quickly identified with her young charge. But she also felt that Bettelheim should not have admitted him, that he was too "entrenched in his disturbance and infantile in his reactions" ever to get well.[74] Once he was admitted, however, she labored day and night to guide him toward integration, and as he began to improve found him "the most thrilling child to work with." [75] Paul told me that at the time he did not really know what a mother was, but that, looking back on Shulenberger's efforts, it is clear that she was his surrogate mother. "The stability that she and Bettelheim instituted at the school finally engulfed me."

Paul stayed for four years. Bettelheim wanted to keep him longer, but, though residents would eventually be able to stay beyond age twenty, in 1950 the upper age limit was fourteen. Paul was terrified by the prospect of leaving the place that had cosseted him more than any other; in the weeks before his departure, he tried to inhale everything the school had to offer, primarily food. He gained ten pounds in his last month, Bettelheim wrote, and left forty-four pounds overweight. [76]

In the next few years, Paul struggled, with mixed results, to adapt in two foster homes, and also tried, without success, to establish a relationship with his mother. He continued studies for a while at the Art Institute of Chicago, developing a gift for painting that he had demonstrated with his drawings at the Orthogenic School; but he soon gave up his brushes, discouraged by his caseworker, his foster parents, and his peers at Roosevelt High School, who in differing degrees regarded painting as sissified and an obstacle to his efforts to become a well-balanced, conventional citizen. He never resumed painting. "It was one of those crossroads-of-life decisions," he said, sounding wistful.

After high school, Paul spent two years at Shimer, a small liberal-arts college associated with the University of Chicago, and then finished his undergraduate work at the university itself, concentrating in science and math. He worked in engineering sales and at other jobs until the late 1960s, when his father-in-law died and he took over the family business; he continues to run the company. "Here I am, some forty years down the road, for all intents and purposes a functioning adult. But I've had lots of crises in my life," Paul told me. "When I face a crisis, I don't see myself in quicksand or drowning or hiding underneath a rock. I see myself on a tightrope, trying to get from point A to point B. I don't really get frightened by the abyss, because if I have doubts about my footing I concentrate on the bar in my hand that keeps me balanced until I have the confidence to move forward to get to that safe point. That balancing bar is the influence that Dr. B gave me. What makes up that balancing bar is every moment I had with him. One of his techniques was a simple mother's technique: to be in the room when you needed him."

F. Howell Wright, the head of pediatrics at the University of Chicago, who treated the children's medical needs throughout Bettelheim's three decades at the school, said there is no question that the director was dedicated to creating a special therapeutic atmosphere for children like Paul. But he also felt that quite a few of the patients did not need such radical treatment and never should have been removed from their families in the first place. In Wright's view, one such case was Bertram Cohler. As a child, Bert Cohler was, in his own words, "a pain in the ass to live with," a boy who got into constant fights with his parents and did poorly in school. His father, Jonas Robert, was a law partner of Edward Levi, a member of Chicago's German Jewish elite and a gifted teacher who would become dean of Chicago's law school and, in 1968, president of the university. After Roy Grinker and George Mohr, prominent Chicago psychoanalysts, recommended the Orthogenic School for Bert, Levi checked it out for the Cohler family. "Bettelheim was delighted to admit someone so well connected," Cohler told me. "He was buying into good, high-class German stock, which was important to him." The new resident's grandfather ran a men's clothing company called Kuppenheimer's, and Bettelheim greatly enjoyed going downtown and ordering one of the elegant dark suits he favored.

Cohler entered the Orthogenic School in 1950, at age ten and a half, and stayed until he was seventeen, moving on to achieve a success Bettelheim frequently pointed to as a measure of the school's effectiveness. After getting his bachelor's degree at the University of Chicago, Cohler earned a doctorate at Harvard and eventually became, like Bettelheim himself, a professor in the departments of education, psychology, and psychiatry at Chicago. Along the way, he spent periods at the Orthogenic School as a counselor, associate director, and, in the early 1970s, as director for several months when Bettelheim was on leave. Recalling his years as a resident, Cohler said it was clear to him from the outset "that Bruno knew who I was and cared what happened to me,"

187

hat his "singular genius" was in creating an envelope around the
children that made them feel safe, what D. W. Winnicott called "a
holding environment."[77] Cohler said that there were some extremely disturbed children in the dorms, but he agreed with Howell Wright that many others were just basically delinquent kids as
he was, children who weren't getting along with their families.
"Bruno was always loose with his diagnoses; that's how he could
make great success claims." Though about 220 residents of all
kinds passed through the school while Bettelheim was director
between 1944 and 1973,[78] in the mid-1960s he wrote that "several
hundred" schizophrenic children, all with "an unremitting fear for
their lives," had been in his care since 1944.[79]

William Blau, a counselor in the late 1940s who quickly
came to regard Bettelheim as a bullying cult leader and his women
counselors as a slavish Roman cohort, said none of the children
seemed to him to be nearly as disturbed as the director proclaimed
them to be at staff meetings and in his writings. "It amazed me,"
Blau wrote, "that Bettelheim, a man from another culture, could
look at the same child as I and see a 'schizophrenic' while I saw
another rambunctious American kid. What did a forty year old
Viennese intellectual really know about the inner (or outer for
that matter) life of a ten year old West Side Chicago Irish kid who
had no one to care for him?"[80] Twenty years after Blau worked at
the school, David Dempsey toured it while researching a profile
of the director for The New York Times Magazine;[81] he told me
that he could not believe, when he talked to some of the children,
that there was anything wrong with them: "I couldn't understand
why they were there." One reason was that Bettelheim planned it
that way. Nina Helstein, a teacher at the school during the brief
period Bert Cohler ran it, recalled a staff meeting just before he
assumed control at which Bettelheim told him that he should
make sure to admit some children that he knew were not too
disturbed. Helstein told me that Bettelheim said: " 'You need to
develop some credibility in the community, and the way to do
that is to show some successes.' "

To Alida M. Jatich, who was a teenager at the school during
these final years of Bettelheim's tenure, the institution was, for the
most part,

a dumping ground for young people who were "different" in some way or, for whatever reason, didn't match their parents' expectations. Many parents were given bad advice by "experts" and did not know that there were alternatives. Some of the young people needed to be in special classes for gifted youth or for those with disabilities in specific areas. Some needed treatment for medical problems. . . . To label all of these people as "psychotic," as Bettelheim repeatedly called us, was a truly evil act. It also put him in a position to inflate his success rate by "curing" people who were not actually psychotic in the first place.[82]

Bettelheim's penchant for making severe diagnoses was cruel and self-serving but not unique. In a summary of the literature on childhood mental pathology, Barbara Fish and Edward R. Ritvo found that by the 1950s such stark assessments were widespread in the United States and that "[m]any disturbed children, whom one would consider today to have only borderline or even no psychotic symptoms, were lumped together in an ill-defined category of childhood psychosis."[83]

MOST REVIEWERS IN the lay press were as dazzled as James T. Farrell by Bettelheim's optimistic accounts in his books about the school. The Chicago *Sun-Times* called *Love Is Not Enough* "a book no intelligent parent should miss," stating that "Bettelheim and his associates have been able to discover just where many parents go wrong in raising their youngsters."[84] The Chicago *Tribune* said the author told a "fascinating story,"[85] a view also expressed in *The New York Times Book Review*.[86] The San Francisco *Chronicle* called the book important and challenging "for all who are concerned about the mental health and welfare of children."[87] The sociologist David Riesman, whose influential study of the changing American character, *The Lonely Crowd*, also came out in 1950, praised his University of Chicago colleague in *The Nation*, writing that "the fabulously great efforts put in by those who work with the more extremely disturbed constitute among other things a political protest of great promise for the future."[88] (Several months later, Bettelheim lauded *The Lonely Crowd* in *The University of Chicago Magazine*.[89])

What published criticism there was of the books surfaced mainly in professional journals and received little attention. Though conceding that *Love Is Not Enough* represented a pioneering effort, Norman V. Lourie, Bettelheim's counterpart at Hawthorne Cedar Knolls, a leading residential-treatment center for children in New York's Westchester County, wondered just what kind of training, if any, Orthogenic School counselors received; he also faulted Bettelheim for not making clear just how he employed psychotherapy.[90] Others questioned Bettelheim's belief that abnormality was just normality exaggerated and his consequent contention that the behavior and treatment of troubled children necessarily carried a useful message for parents trying to raise their average kids.[91] Therese Benedek called *Love Is Not Enough* "a brilliant attempt" to describe treatment at the school; but the Hungarian-born psychoanalyst, a member of the Berlin Institute who had come to Chicago in the 1930s, felt, like Lourie, that Bettelheim's explanations of his methods fell short, and she went so far as to warn mothers *not* to use the book as a guide for rearing their children because the vignettes might prove too upsetting.[92]

Donald W. Fiske, in his favorable Chicago *Tribune* review of *Love Is Not Enough,* had observed that the "patience, fortitude and ingenuity of the whole staff as described by Dr. Bettelheim are almost beyond belief." Most likely he meant this without skepticism, but some professionals did find the confident prose and smooth anecdotes a little too neat. One pointed out, correctly, that the book was full of passages that claimed to know what the children were thinking and asked just how Bettelheim and his counselors could be so certain what the children "wondered" and "felt" in given situations. Bettelheim wrote that one boy

picked up a sandwich at his first meal, bit into it and then put it down. Provocatively, he picked up another one, took a little bite, and put it down. And this he continued with another and another until he had bitten into eight altogether. By then *he began to wonder* if we might not, contrary to his expectations, be more interested in allowing him the freedom to behave in line with his emotional need to waste food, than we were in saving food or in enforcing good manners at the table.[93]

That is a remarkable insight, the critic suggested, for an emotionally disturbed child to have at his first meal in a strange new institution.[94]

By the mid-1950s, Bettelheim had made a good start at weaving his Palestrinian feast-day garment of fame. Many who saw it from a distance were impressed by its colors and what seemed its fine stitching; but those who saw the fabric up close knew the robe served partly as camouflage. The counselors liked their cameo roles as participant observers in *Love Is Not Enough* and *Truants from Life,* and relished the cachet of being associated in print with their charismatic employer-therapist, whose self-propelled reputation for curing was beginning to spread well beyond Hyde Park. But even at the time, and certainly later, many recognized that he prettified life at the school, that he rarely captured what it really was like in the emotional trenches with the children day after day, or revealed the traumatic interactions of the staff meetings, where psyches quivered and tears flowed regularly in the face of his "Nazi-Socratic method."

This reality roiled invisibly beneath the tranquil, inspiring pages of the books, something soon discovered by future staff members who had been drawn to the school by the "sweetness and light" of Bettelheim's seductive prose.[95] One of them was Dennis Duginske, a Wisconsin farm boy who was a counselor and teacher in the 1960s and went on to teach psychology at Northeastern Illinois University in Chicago. "After I was at the school for a while I saw that [*Love Is Not Enough*] was full of nice stories," Duginske told me. "But Dr. B left out the dark side of running a place like the Orthogenic School. You could not construct an institution out of his book; there was no sense of what happened when the children acted out, no sense of the repercussions and the punishment."

CHAPTER EIGHT
The Big Bad Wolf

IN HIS BOOKS AND ARTICLES and in speaking to parents and professional groups, Bruno Bettelheim made one thing clear: hitting, slapping, or spanking children—physically abusing them in any way—was *verboten*. "I'm against [slapping] because it's a brutal and illogical method, a method based on superior force, not on superior reasoning," he told a group of young Hyde Park mothers who met with him regularly into the early 1950s to hear his counsel on how to raise their toddlers.[1] He said that a child "will learn to stop hitting only if we set an example of never using physical aggression in relation to him, not even in what we consider a just cause."[2] He wrote that, "in any psychotherapy, the setting must militate against the therapist's exercising an unwarranted dominance over the patient, and against the patient's falling into the trap of accepting such dominance."[3]

Bettelheim stated this message again and again over the three decades he ran the Orthogenic School, including for attentive journalists. "A spanking achieves a short-range goal, but it has a price tag—degradation and anger—that I am not willing to pay. My task is to build up self-respect. And I believe people do the right thing not because they are scared to death but because their self-respect requires it," he told *Time* magazine.[4] "I'm absolutely against [spanking]; it shows only that the stronger one can be brutal," he told David Hartman on ABC's *Good Morning America*.[5] His viewers often included the school's residents, who at the urging of the staff would assemble around the TV set to see their famous therapist. Joe Suchman, who spent his teenage years at the school in the 1960s and early 1970s, recalled watching when Bettelheim was asked if he ever punished the children. "He said, 'No,' and we all started laughing. Little did they know."

Virtually no one outside the school did know that Bettelheim sometimes struck his young patients until David Dempsey hinted at it in his *New York Times Magazine* profile, which appeared in 1970, twenty-five years after Bettelheim became director. Dempsey wrote, parenthetically, that Bettelheim "has been known to spank a youngster," but he pursued the matter no further.[6]

The first former resident who publicly communicated this side of Bettelheim's temperament was Tom Lyons, who did not do so until a decade after Bettelheim retired. In *The Pelican and After,* Lyons's 1983 *roman à clef* about his life at the Orthogenic School, he is the character Tony and his school director a concentration-camp survivor with thick glasses and a heavy accent named Dr. Vorlicten. "Tony winced," Lyons wrote,

> as Dr. V.'s left hand caught Ronny on one side of the face, then returned with a swift backhand across the other. SMACK! SMACK! SMACK! SMACK! SMACK! Dr. V.'s left hand moved quickly, methodically back and forth across Ronny's face. Then: SMACK! SMACK! SMACK! SMACK! with both hands on the back of the head as Ronny ducked forward. Dr. V. grabbed a small tuft of his hair and shook. And with both hands he caught Ronny by the shirt and hauled him halfway out of his chair.[7]

The Pelican and After made little impact, gathering a handful of mixed reviews, few of them in major publications, and quickly sinking from sight. But the book infuriated Bettelheim, even though it was by no means all negative about him and the school, and despite the fact that Lyons had dedicated it to the former director "with gratitude and affection." Augusta Lyons, who so believed in Bettelheim and his work that she gave a half-million dollars to the school over the years, told me he called her and said she should never speak of her son's book in his presence again— ever. When a reporter writing an article about the book and the issue of corporal punishment called Bettelheim for comment, he reiterated that he did not believe in physically disciplining children.

When asked whether he slapped Lyons or other children, Bettelheim said, "That's between me and the children."

But he said, "I cured them. And I cured [Lyons], who was hopeless." [8]

Lyons's fictional account stood alone until 1990, when, in the weeks after Bettelheim's suicide, several former residents publicly attacked his abusive behavior in articles and letters. Charles Pekow, who attended the school for a decade beginning in 1965, wrote in the *Washington Post* of "The Other Dr. Bettelheim," describing him as often cruel and hypocritical and the school as "Orwellian." [9] The grandson of Philip Pekow, the Chicago hotel owner who was one of Bettelheim's biggest financial supporters, and after whom the school's adolescent unit was named in 1966, Charles conceded that some former residents felt they had been helped by Bettelheim; but he said that, regardless, many were physically and emotionally manhandled in the process. Pekow said that, when he skipped classes one day, Bettelheim slapped him across the face and dragged him downstairs; when, on another occasion, he refused to participate in group therapy, the director slapped him again. He said Bettelheim whipped children with his belt for dancing naked on a table, and became furious when some patients violated a no-sharing rule and divvied up a box of Cracker Jacks. "On one level it was funny, on another quite serious," Pekow said. "In our off hours we'd laugh about it and imitate him and his accent, slapping people around. We had a set of puppets and one looked just like Bettelheim. We'd have the Bettelheim puppet beating up all the others." [10]

Alida Jatich wrote that she lived in terror of the director, who, when she was fifteen, pulled her naked out of the shower and beat her in front of a room full of dormmates and counselors. [11] She said that he was angry because she was withdrawn and did not want to socialize with her peers and because she generally disapproved of him and the school. "He started slapping me over and over, dragging me out by the hair. I tried to grab a towel to cover myself but was not able to do that." [12] Another former resident, who signed his name "Winston 1984," wrote that there was "*always—always—*a visceral, stomach-tightening . . . terror in all when [Bettelheim] made his nocturnal and afternoon approaches." [13] Ronald Angres wrote in *Commentary* that during the twelve years he attended the school he, too, lived in constant fear of Bettelheim's beatings, "in terror of his footsteps in the dorms —in abject, animal terror." When the children came down to meals, they often sat on a bench outside the dining room until a counselor arrived to lead them in. "As the bench was normally quite crowded," Angres recalled,

> sometimes I would sit in an armchair just inside an adjacent room, to steal a few moments of darkened serenity before the glare and din of the meals. One day, Bettelheim found me there and dragged me back to the bench by the hair. "Do you know what they call people like you?" he thundered. "A megalomaniac!" Later, when our group returned to the dorm, the counselor harried me to find the word in the dictionary: "Don't you want to know what he called you?" I did not. With perfect zeal, she made me look it up anyway. Supposedly, as with the other terms they freely hurled at us—narcissistic, paranoid, anal-retentive, obsessive, psychopathic —no moral blame was to be inferred since the terms themselves were "scientific," value-free. Thus did they force us to pour out with our own hands the salt they proceeded to rub in our wounds. [14]

Inevitably, these and similar charges caused an international media spasm, with *Newsweek* asking in its headline: " 'Beno Brutalheim'?" [15] For the many thousands who had never crossed the threshold of the Orthogenic School—who knew Bettelheim only through the reassuring prose of *Love Is Not Enough* and his other writing about the school and emotional disturbance—the very question seemed impossible to credit. The accusations, said Nell Pekarsky, made no sense, had knocked her out of her boots. She had come into contact with the director for years through her fund-raising work with the Foundation for Emotionally Disturbed Children and had always found him considerate and frequently charming. The public outburst also dismayed many former staff members, men and (mostly) women who had fallen under Bettelheim's spell at an impressionable age, who in many cases saw him as a father figure and had been in therapy with him, who had put in long hours, sometimes for years, genuinely trying to help these difficult children, and who knew Bettelheim had done the same. Some suggested that the former residents making the allegations were still unbalanced, or had been so upset by the suicide of the man who had been their healer, their protector, that they were lashing out in a furious cry of despair.[16]

After the Chicago *Sun-Times* published an article about the charges,[17] fifteen former staff members signed a letter to the paper saying they were appalled by the image of Bettelheim as a brute and a sadist who preached understanding while acting out his own uncontrolled impulses.[18] The letter, which also ran in the Washington *Post* in response to Charles Pekow's article,[19] said Bettelheim cared passionately about the children, who were regarded as "hopelessly untreatable" when they arrived at the school and would have become "castaways of society" were it not for his and their efforts. Nowhere, however, did the letter engage the actual allegations. Instead, the signatories asked, rhetorically: "Is the public to believe that Dr. Bettelheim perpetrated child abuse for over 25 years in a laboratory school of the University of Chicago . . . [and] that he successfully concealed the existence of this 'concentration camp' environment . . . within one of the world's great research universities?"

The answer is yes. Certainly the Orthogenic School was no concentration camp, as one former resident had implied,[20] and was in many ways a loving, healing environment, made so primarily by the devotion of the letter's signatories and other staff members. But it was also a house of fear, as Bettelheim's principal assistant and successor suggested in the same *Sun-Times* article to which the letter selectively responded. Jacquelyn Sanders, whose name was conspicuous by its absence from the letter, told me that Bettelheim had indeed raised his hand against the children and sometimes had brought it down with frightening effect. "The people who are so surprised," she said in the *Sun-Times,* "are the popular media and people who believe in fairy tales. People who knew him knew he could be a bastard. He could be charming, scintillating, extraordinarily [empathic], but also a goddamned bastard who could say horrible things."[21]

It was true that Bettelheim's suicide had upset some former

residents, especially those who had heard him say repeatedly when they were residents that killing oneself was never an option, that they owed it to others to affirm life. "I couldn't believe that, after all the years he preached to us, he would kill himself," one ex-resident told me;[22] "I got awful mad at him; it shook me right down to the core that he should disappoint us so," said another.[23] It is fair to say, too, that not all the former residents who went public with their anger have adjusted well to life as adults. However, almost without exception, others confirmed that, whether they themselves were struck or not, physical and emotional abuse was a part of everyday life at the Orthogenic School, an institution run by a man who was devoted to helping the children but who also admired *Patton,* the 1970 film about the narcissistic, monomaniacal, and cruel World War II general, finding in it a vision "that can sustain us."[24]

"That he hit children is unquestionable," said William Sugden, a counselor in the late 1960s, who recalled Bettelheim's reaction when one girl, who had been diagnosed as autistic, struck another child. As a rule, Bettelheim did not permit staff members to punish a resident physically, so the girl's counselor went to get the director, who took her into the hall and demanded that she apologize to the child she had hit. Sugden said that when the child showed reluctance Bettelheim began slapping her and continued until, in tears, she agreed to his command. Victor DeGrazia, a counselor at the time Bettelheim was writing *Love Is Not Enough,* recalled the principal "balling up his fist and hitting a kid while he was lying in bed." When the surprised DeGrazia, who was nineteen at the time, went to the office to ask about the act, Bettelheim was rubbing his hand and complaining that he had missed the child once and struck the metal bunk. Ann Zener, who was Alida Jatich's counselor in the late 1960s, was present when Bettelheim pulled the terrified teenager out of the shower; Zener told me that Jatich's description of the incident is accurate, and that the former resident is also justified in rejecting the "psychotic" label Bettelheim sought to pin on her.

Nina Helstein, who worked as a teacher at the school during Bettelheim's final years as director, told me of a seven-year-old girl who had become upset about an older boy who was leaving because the school had been unable to help him. At lunch, the girl was sitting next to Helstein when Bettelheim came through the dining room. Helstein told him that the child had been obsessing about the boy all morning, wanting the director to reassure her, to say, "But I'm not sending *you* away." Instead, Bettelheim exploded and, in front of the children and staff in the dining room, began slapping the child across the face. "I'd seen him lose it with staff members, be absolutely outrageous at staff meetings; but I'd never seen him hit the kids. It was shocking, it was terrible." At a staff session after lunch, Helstein recalled, Bettelheim asked her: " 'Well, Nina, what do you think was going on with this child?' " When she reiterated her feeling that the boy's imminent departure was making the girl quite anxious, Bettelheim said: "That's right. So, when a child is upset, why would you have me hit her?" Helstein was numb with dread at the prospect of challenging her world-famous employer, but somehow she managed to say: "Dr. B, you do not hit children because I tell you to, *you* did that." She said he was enraged by her effrontery. "It was insane. A lot of what went on at the school was, and the staff members went along with it."

To Philip Goldbloom, who entered the school at age eleven and emerged at twenty-one, Bettelheim in the midst of one of his furies was like a frustrated mother in a department store, an out-of-control parent railing and hitting at her child for some misbehavior, real or perceived. Joe Suchman said he was on the receiving end of such tantrums several times, in one instance after he had pushed another boy down and a counselor had carried out the ever-present threat to "tell Dr. B." What followed varied little. The dorm would fall silent as Bettelheim arrived on his rounds, his approach signaled by the squeak of his crepe-soled shoes. When he entered the room, a counselor would say: "May I speak to you in the hall, Dr. B?" After several minutes, both would return; Bettelheim would glare and say (here Suchman, like so many others when describing the Viennese émigré, mimicked him), "Joe, vill you come wiz me, pleeze." Once in the hall, Bettelheim would be quiet but Suchman always kept his peripheral vision alert for the retributive hand, which soon arrived, usually open but occasionally as a fist. After the incident in which he had knocked the boy down, Suchman told me, Bettelheim "pushed me, kicked at me, and slapped me. I didn't scream or anything. I just took it. And he kept on doing it harder and harder. And it finally occurred to me that I'd better say something or he's going to keep bopping me around."

Charles Marks, Jr., entered the school when he was almost eleven, in 1955, and stayed until he was twenty-seven, far longer than other residents. He told me that during his first five years or so he was "absolutely terrified" of the director. Like everyone else, Marks was never sure when his behavior would ignite Bettelheim's rage. He went rigid when the director walked in on him and a friend as they splashed around in water from a bathtub they had allowed to overflow; Bettelheim merely asked if they were having a good time and moved on.

On another occasion, Marks's throw went wild when he was playing catch, and the soft rubber ball accidentally hit counselor Karen Carlson in the head. She was more startled than hurt, but Marks was "numb with fear" as he contemplated what Bettelheim would do when he learned of the incident. He knew he should have apologized, but he did not, and later in the day told another counselor that he felt bad about his failure to do so. She listened sympathetically and said that perhaps she should mention the episode to Dr. B.

At dinner that evening, she did so, and Bettelheim called Marks into the hall and asked if he had apologized. When the fourteen-year-old said no, the director struck him two or three times in the chest with his fist and ordered him to find Carlson in the dining room and tell her he was sorry. He looked but did not see her, which in retrospect he feels was because he was so tormented by what was happening to him in full view of everyone gathered for dinner. Marks told me that when he returned to his table Bettelheim escorted him out into the hall once more, pushed him down roughly onto a bench, struck him in the chest, and again demanded the apology. Marks said that only after this scene played out one more time did he finally spot Carlson at her table and go up to apologize. The next day, he complained to the woman he saw in private therapy sessions at the school that his upper left arm was black and blue from where Bettelheim's nails had dug in. He said she replied that what Dr. B was trying to teach him was far more important than a mark on the arm.

In the early 1980s, about ten years after Marks left the Orthogenic School, he entered treatment with Arnold Tobin, a Chicago psychoanalyst who was astonished and enraged by the accounts of Bettelheim's abuse. "It was something I didn't want to believe," he told me. He said Marks told him that on at least one occasion Bettelheim struck him as punishment for masturbating. Stories like these persuaded the analyst that Marks had so feared Bettelheim that instead of making steady progress he had retreated and become passive, which explained in part his abnormally long stay of sixteen years. Tobin feels that Bettelheim was exploiting both the children and their parents, that instead of doing the hard work of treating the family he had taken the easier way by simply removing the kids from their homes. "This gave him an opportunity to play out his megalomanic and authoritarian fantasies, which was a terrible violation of his position."

Marjorie Weaver discovered when she broke a dish just how brutal that violation could be. In his writing and lectures, Bettelheim said he used china rather than plastic plates in the dining room because the latter sent out a message that the school worried about breakage. He maintained that if you showed the children you trusted them enough to provide quality tableware they would respect and not smash it. He also wrote that when a resident did break a dish counselors should demonstrate that they were "not annoyed with him for giving vent to pressures he feels unable to contain. . . ."[25] Few former patients or staff members disputed the therapeutic value of the warm environment Bettleheim sought to create, but the impression he left in his books that things could be destroyed with impunity was, as Bert Cohler put it, "nonsense." When Weaver, who attended the school in the sixties, broke the dish, Bettleheim soon appeared in her dorm and dragged the frightened teenager off to an adjacent room. She said he pulled her pants down and whipped her with his belt. "I was afraid of him the entire nine years I was there," Weaver told me.

Mary Moyers, who entered the school at age seven and emerged at twenty-one, received the same treatment. She said Bettelheim slapped and spanked her frequently over those fourteen years, for behavior that she concedes was at times disruptive. Her transgressions ranged from fighting to breaking windows to flunking chemistry. She was twenty years old when she brought back the offending report card from Hyde Park High, the public school a few blocks away that some residents attended. Moyers said Bettelheim took her down to the sewing room in the basement, as he had on other occasions, and told her to lie across the table. "He would take my panties down and take his belt and wear my backside out. I remember having to slip into the stalls in the girls dorm, or keep my back to the wall, so nobody would see the bruises," she recalled.

Barbara Kojak, who attended the school from age eleven and a half until she ran away in 1972 at age twenty-two, said that when Bettelheim wanted to strap her, he would order her into the night counselor's room near the girls dorm on the first floor and make her bare her bottom and lie across the bed. "Dr. B would take his belt off and his beatings would literally leave welts. We're not talking about a smack, we're talking about a really bad beating," Kojak said, estimating that Bettelheim delivered such beltings to at least eight other girls when she was there. Did the counselors know about this? "Absolutely, because when you took a bath you could see the marks. But you have to understand, the counselors were brainwashed to believe that what Bettelheim did was right. What makes me the angriest today is that the staff did not come forward and tell him, 'No, stop it!' "

Mary Moyers told me that Bettelheim also fondled her breasts on several occasions. She said he would call her into his office and yell at her for some transgression and after she was in tears would hug her. "When he was letting go, that's when he would do it," she said, adding that Bettelheim's behavior left her so traumatized that she refused to let her first husband touch her breasts or even hug her closely. She said she did not know whether other girls suffered the same degradation because she was so afraid of Bettelheim and ashamed of the incidents that she could not bring herself to discuss them with anyone. Talking about this history was clearly painful for Moyers, who said she was doing so because she hoped a public airing would help others who may have been similarly treated overcome their trauma.

Barbara Kojak said Bettelheim fondled the breasts of other teenage girls at the school, she among them. "He could beat you and humiliate you in the dining room and then when he made rounds he would call you into the hall," Kojak told me. "You had no way of knowing what he would do. But sometimes he would say, 'I love you, I beat you because I love you,' and then he would touch your breasts." Kojak said Bettelheim also sometimes came into the dorm after midnight, sat on her bed and let his hand roam over her body under the covers. She said that "the sexual abuse was much worse than you think. Much more than just fondling. I began to wear underwear to bed because I didn't want Dr. B to touch me. Not that it always worked."

Bettelheim was initially drawn to Kojak because she was a German refugee whose parents had died in the camps. She had been brought to the United States by the United World Church Service when she was three and a half and lived in various institutions until Bettelheim admitted her at age eleven. He talked to her all the time about how he had rescued her. At the Monday afternoon meetings in the playroom, he sometimes belittled and yelled at the children. Kojak said that when her turn came he would say, " 'What do you do when you save a girl from the camps and she won't cooperate, she won't go by the rules?' I can't begin to tell you how damaging it was. He really took all your hope away, all your dreams away. The mind games were very bad: 'Your parents don't want you, so I saved you; but I don't want you, nobody wants you, you're no good.' He was very, very cruel; caustic, like lye."

After leaving the Orthogenic School, Kojak suffered from posttraumatic stress syndrome and eventually entered into therapy with a Chicago analyst named Aaron Hilkevitch. She was sent to him by Jacquelyn Sanders, who told him that the young woman was not delusional and that he should believe what his new patient told him. Hilkevitch said that he has no doubt that Kojak's stories of abuse are true and that one clue was her initial reluctance to open up to him because he was a Russian émigré who, like Bettelheim, had an accent. Hilkevitch also treated two Orthogenic School counselors, both of whom also left him a clear picture of Bettelheim's tyrannical and exploitative behavior.

The sincerity and anguish with which Barbara Kojak, Mary Moyers, and Marjorie Weaver told me of Bettelheim's sexual abuse invites belief. Nonetheless, it is possible that they imagined he touched their breasts, or exaggerated his actions. His acts, if they did take place, had no witnesses, or none who spoke to me. Of the twenty-seven other former Orthogenic School residents I interviewed, none even hinted that Bettelheim indulged in such behavior, including several whose continuing antipathy to him is such that they would not have hesitated to reveal his sexual abuse had they known of it. No former staff member suggested that Dr. B had lost control in this way either, including Jacquelyn Sanders, who, despite telling Aaron Hilkevitch that he should believe what Kojak told him, feels confident that Bettelheim, for all his violence, did not cross the sexual line. I enter these caveats in an effort to be fair but also with a certain reluctance. The tendency to dismiss accounts of those who were, and may even still be, "disturbed," and to accept as gospel the contrary and often smug word of their healers is psychotherapy's cruelest bias. This starkly uneven power equation kept many residents of the Orthogenic School from speaking out when they were there and after they left, and to cast doubt on three women whose stories sound truthful in favor of a man who regularly gave truth a wide berth seems particularly unjust.

Bettelheim wrote that privacy was an unqualified right, to be safeguarded "under all circumstances,"[26] but at the school it was invaded daily. The children's periodic sessions with counselors or outside therapists were not refuges, where they could reveal their most troubling anxieties without fear that these would go further, but conduits through which their often deeply personal problems —or criticisms of their treatment—flowed straight back to the Big Bad Wolf; and much of this "material" also found its way into his books about the school. The children could never be sure whether their mail was censored; sometimes it was.[27] Mary Moyers said she was driven to making up a code of Greek and Hebrew letters when she discovered that her counselor was reading her diary. When Charles Pekow's parents sent him a book about Abraham Lincoln, Bettelheim decreed it inappropriate and sent it back because it contained a picture of a hanging. A therapeutic case might be made for such a decision, but other infringements seemed altogether arbitrary. When Pekow arrived at the school with an enthusiasm for *Mad* magazine, Bettelheim immediately declared Alfred E. Neuman off-limits; when Mary Moyers said she wanted to study Spanish in high school, he told her that only "scum and trash" took Spanish; when an adolescent girl hung a picture of the Beatles in her dorm, he called her a slut.[28] Ronald Angres wrote that even school papers

> became grist for further dissection of our characters, and were thrown back in our faces with accusations about our motives and the "symptoms" that were supposedly revealed by our ideas. Writing even a factual essay was risky; writing fiction was downright reckless. Grammar itself became fair game for psychologizing/moralizing: "It's 'he and I,' not 'me and him,' but then, you always think of 'me' first."[29]

Angres told me that he came to feel that Bettelheim was like a permanent solar eclipse, casting his dark shadow over all aspects of the children's lives, and the staff's as well.

What humiliated many of the residents most, especially the teenagers, was the lack of physical privacy. Bettelheim believed it was important that the residents not be ashamed of their bodies, an embarrassment he traced, citing some unspecified cases, to parents who made "threatening or provocative jokes, or disparaging remarks about their [children's] genitals. . . ."[30] To counter such pernicious history, he encouraged the residents to dress and undress in front of one another and the counselors, and required them to bathe or shower in tubs without curtains. "He would walk into the bathroom anytime he felt like it," Mary Moyers told me. "If you happened to be in the tub when he was making his nightly rounds you were stuck; he would just stand there and look at you, even when we were in our teens." Marjorie Weaver was a teenager as well when he stood around while she was bathing and questioned her about a movie she had just seen. "I hated it, having this old man look at me," she recalled. It was no better for the boys. "We were encouraged to sit around and masturbate and talk about it," recalled Charles Skinner, who attended the Orthogenic

School throughout the 1960s. "It was very, very strange. When I was thirteen or fourteen, two students could take a bath at the same time in the two dorm bathtubs; we would masturbate and the counselors would come in and look at us and say, no problem. We would ask them about women's anatomy; they wouldn't show us anything, they would just smile."

In the 1960s, when the Orthogenic School population included many teenagers and several older residents, some of the women counselors were only three or four years older than the boys in the tubs, sometimes less. "Bettelheim maintained for far too long the fiction that the kids had not entered puberty," said Arnold Granville, who attended the school during Bettelheim's final years, who returned there to teach, and then went on to earn a master's degree in teaching and a doctorate in American history. "You had a whole bunch of really horny boys and these nubile postcoeds on the scene, seeing us nude in the dorms and in the bath. It complicated issues in a way that was not really necessary." Jacquelyn Sanders came to agree. For many years she shared her mentor's view about physical openness, but she eventually concluded otherwise, and shower curtains went up.

Arnold Granville regarded the invasion of privacy and occasional beltings as mild problems compared with the overwhelming sense of menace that seemed fundamental to the director's therapeutic philosophy. "His favorite weapon when he was trying to instill discipline was to indicate quietly, with a kind of moral disdain, that you would wind up in the back ward of a mental institution if you didn't shape up." Charles Pekow wrote that Bettelheim would bring children to tears by saying, "You get better here or you go to the nuthouse."[31] Jerome Kavka told me that Bettelheim regarded some of his charges as potential murderers and would say at staff meetings, and sometimes directly to the resident, that if he weren't at the school learning to live properly he would be in jail because he would have murdered somebody. Or, he might become a murder victim himself. In the 1960s, when crime began to increase in the neighborhood, the body of a woman turned up in the alley behind the school, the corpse easily visible from one of the dorm windows. "Bettelheim came running into the room and started ranting and raving about this woman in the alley," Philip Goldbloom told me. "Suddenly, he grabbed me by the hair and dragged me over to the window and said that if I didn't get my shit together that's what would happen to me. Then he walked out, and no one said a word."

Bettelheim said and wrote repeatedly over the years that he sought to shape the Orthogenic School in the reverse image of the concentration camps, to create a haven where the children felt protected and safe. Much of the time he strove to do this; but he also was prey to the dark impulses he had felt and witnessed in Dachau and Buchenwald. In *The Informed Heart,* where, in 1960, he first expanded on his camp ordeal, he wrote that prisoners

> were often mistreated in ways that a cruel and domineering father might use against helpless children. But just as even the cruelest parent threatens physical punishment much more often than he actually inflicts it, so childlike feelings of helplessness were created much more effectively by the constant threat of beatings than by actual torture. During a real beating one could, for example, take some pride in suffering manfully, in not giving the foreman or guard the satisfaction of groveling before him, etc. No such emotional protection was possible against the mere threat.[32]

No passage in all of Bettelheim's writing better describes the role of fear at the Orthogenic School. He did not hit or invade the privacy of every child, and he was easier on some counselors than on others at staff meetings; but everyone saw or heard about his frightening explosions, and no one was exempt from the anxiety they produced, an anxiety that in some cases did make the children feel like terrified prisoners.

Bettelheim reserved a special disdain for those who saw any value in such operant conditioning. He insisted that a regimen of reward and retribution reduced patients "to the level of Pavlovian dogs" and mainly satisfied a need of those in control to punish.[33] He said and wrote that he ran the Orthogenic School in a much more humane fashion, hewing to the psychoanalytic approach. But his readiness to strike and threaten the children—and to tyrannize the staff much of the time—owed more to the operant notions of B. F. Skinner than to the views of Sigmund Freud.

"[S]o far as I could see," said David Dempsey of his visit to the school for *The New York Times,* "he did not put [his psychoanalytic beliefs] into practice. . . ." Dempsey overstates the case, because Bettelheim often did find his bearings in psychoanalytic thought; but the journalist was not far off the mark when he suggested that the director's iron rule prefigured what came to be known as "cognitive behaviorism," where just the anticipation of reward or punishment was enough to change a child's, or a counselor's, behavior.[34] Others, too, came to believe that Bettelheim's methods shared "disquieting similarities" to Skinner's.[35]

IN 1950, NOT LONG AFTER *Love Is Not Enough* came out, Fritz Redl visited the Orthogenic School. He had worked with delinquent children in Austria under August Aichhorn, who along with Anna Freud was one of his advisers at the Vienna Psychoanalytic Institute. After settling in Detroit, Redl had directed Pioneer House, a home for such children; it closed in 1949, in part because he lacked the fund-raising skills of his Chicago friend. Like Emmy Sylvester, Redl had been of immense help in developing the Orthogenic School's working philosophy, so much so, Bettelheim wrote, that their many conversations and constant exchange of ideas "had created a situation in which I no longer know exactly where his ideas end and my own begin."[36] Redl, sitting in the school's dining room having lunch with Bettelheim and several staff members, asked his grateful countryman why he had not been forthright in *Love Is Not Enough* about how he maintained discipline at the school. "Fritz knew from his experience running Pioneer House," recalled Benjamin Wright, one of the young counselors at the table that day, "that you sometimes had to take pretty definite physical positions with the kids, and he felt Bettelheim had dodged that issue."

Bettelheim said that, had he told the truth in *Love Is Not Enough,* his readers would not have believed him or, worse, would have taken him to mean that he was recommending that they use physical punishment in dealing with their normal children's misbehavior—which he was not.[37] Publicly, Bettelheim never abandoned this rationale for not disclosing the climate of fear he fostered or his practice of striking the children, just as he never abandoned his conviction that if the school were to integrate the residents' troubled personalities successfully someone had to provide the superego, or—as the director liked to say—to play the Big Bad Wolf. Barbara Kaplan, who spent the summer of 1953 as a substitute counselor at the school, was stunned when Bettelheim slapped a nine-year-old boy hard after he had pushed another child into the street. "His explanation was that he could do this because he was the children's superego, that he had to externalize the superego until they could internalize it," she told me.

Bettelheim's defenders, though critical of the lack of candor in his writing, support this general view. They argue that no residential-treatment center can hope to help its patients unless there is a strong authority figure to make sure that these patients do not hurt themselves or one another. They insist that this was especially true at the Orthogenic School, where Bettelheim rejected physical restraints, isolation rooms, and, in particular, psychotropic medication, which he regarded with utter disdain. To those who recommended it, he was apt to say, "I am not interested in working with druggists." [38] Ugo Formigoni, one of Bettelheim's more devoted counselors, told me that "it was important to show that order could be re-established quickly, that destructive impulses would not go unchecked." Former counselor Mary Cahn recalled Bettelheim's hitting a boy until he was crying hard. The director was frustrated because the child was holding back, keeping secret what was bothering him. "This was in a dorm where other kids were watching. I felt totally unseen by Bettelheim, and I remember being shocked," she told me. But Cahn also felt that the message was mixed, that Bettelheim's anger flowed from a feeling that he could not help the boy unless he revealed his inner life. "I got the impression of how eager Bettelheim was to rescue these kids. And my feeling is that these kids knew it and loved him for it."

Charles Skinner recalled teasing a boy who was about to have heart surgery. "I made a drawing, a stick figure, with a little heart jumping out of it with a big grin on its face, and I showed it to [him]. It was not a very nice thing to do, because it made him more upset. Jacqui [Sanders] told Dr. B, who came over and clobbered me. He slapped me, boom, boom, across the face, one-two," Skinner told me. He said that he had had his "ass whipped" on other occasions as well, but Bettelheim always explained why, always said it was not because he hated him but because he loved him and wanted him to get better. "He believed in disciplinary action for the things you did wrong, and I think that's right. I had great love for Dr. B and terror of him at the same time, because he was the total authority; he was rock strong, he was a pillar of strength for all of us, and I think it was important to the process of getting well. I am very, very grateful that I was sent there."

James Ely, who also attended the school in the 1960s, became angry one day at the dinner table, stormed outside, and threw a roller skate through a window. When Bettelheim confronted him, Ely was still fuming. "I told him: 'You can hit me or do anything you want, but I'm not going to repent or change or anything.' " Ely said Bettelheim did not hit him, but showed a sympathetic understanding of what was bothering him. "I generally thought he was right, which is what made me respect him and fear him; I knew I couldn't fool myself in his presence, or him."

Some have suggested that Bettelheim's abusive behavior must be judged in the context of his time and Germanic background, one steeped in a "poisonous pedagogy" that readily endorsed the abuse of children for their own good.[39] Austrian parents of Bettelheim's generation were not shy about slapping and spanking their children, and although he wrote that his own father was a gentle man who found even the prospect of punishing him painful, in private Bettelheim hinted that discipline at Neubaugasse 66 had not always been so benign. In 1976, he would write to a friend that children needed to be slapped around from time to time, to give them some tangible basis for dealing with the antagonism they feel toward the inescapable power of their mothers and fathers. "But of course I cannot afford to say that out loud, because it runs against all child psychology. But I know: boy does it feel good to be once in a while mistreated by a parent."[40] He offered no specifics, but, however young Bruno was punished by Anton or Paula Bettelheim, the grown man was not reluctant, in private, to suggest a good walloping.

Charles Feldstein, with whom the director worked for many years in raising funds for the Orthogenic School, told me that he and his wife had agreed to care for the daughter of friends while the friends were away. The girl, who was in the process of leaving the Orthogenic School, lived with the Feldsteins for three or four weeks and was something of a trial. "When I complained to Bruno, he said, 'Smack her right across the face.' " Jerome Kavka, who served as a psychiatric consultant at the school in the 1950s, recalled attending a professional meeting at which he had lunch with a young man who had worked at the school and now ran a home for disturbed children in Pennsylvania. He told Kavka that one of his patients had come from Bettelheim and that, when the child spun out of control one night, he had called Bettelheim to seek advice. Kavka said the young man had told him that Bettelheim said, "Beat the shit out of him." At the time Bettelheim arrived in this country, many Americans, too, believed sparing the rod was a mistake that would lead not only to spoiled children but to ill-disciplined ones as well. By the 1960s, that notion had begun to fade; but by most accounts Bettelheim grew more, not less, abusive during that decade, in part because the school by then housed residents well into their adolescence, some of whom were especially difficult to handle.

During the thirteen years that Jacquelyn Sanders worked for Bettelheim, she shared his view that hitting the children in certain circumstances was therapeutically justified. She had struck them occasionally herself, and screamed and yelled at them as well. And she would continue this behavior for several years after she succeeded her mentor as director. But she eventually came to see that such tactics were counterproductive for at least four reasons:

> (1) we became the abusers of abused children; (2) children who had aggressive tendencies identified with this aspect of our approach; (3) we became actors in sexual-sado-masochistic fantasies; and (4) we sent out negative messages that we were not aware of.[41]

Under Sanders, discipline eventually centered on the idea of "transgression," the hope being that a rule-breaking resident would see himself not as "bad" but as having crossed a line established for everyone's good. In particular, anyone who intentionally hurt himself or others—or tried to—received a "transgression," and everyone knew that a certain number of transgressions resulted in a reduced allowance.[42] Sanders feels that Bettelheim believed his scary disciplinary demeanor was in the best interest of the children; but she now thinks he was wrong a lot of the time, in part because he was not nearly so deeply in touch with his unconscious as he thought he was. "A lot of what he did could be considered acting out, but I don't think he was aware of it," she told me.

Among the many professionals who were surprised to learn of Bettelheim's abusive practices was Joseph Noshpitz, a former president of the American Association of Children's Residential Centers, an organization Bettelheim helped found in the 1950s and that in 1990 established an award in his name, of which Noshpitz was the recipient the following year. In 1987, Noshpitz, a psychoanalyst, psychiatrist, and editor-in-chief of the *Basic Handbook of Child Psychiatry,* had contributed a paper on the history of residential treatment to a *Festschrift* for Bettelheim at the University of Chicago. The two men had been warm colleagues for many years, but the revelations dismayed the holder of the Bruno Bettelheim Award. "You can't have a public service of any kind which involves hitting children," he said. "You cannot treat someone and hurt them at the same time. It involves a sense of humiliation, rejection; sometimes a sense of exploitation, sadism, all sorts of qualities that, to say the least, are antitherapeutic."[43]

REVIEWERS WHO ACCLAIMED *Love Is Not Enough* in 1950 had no idea that behind the calm prose was an author who sometimes struck the children and often terrified both them and the staff with his ferocious outbursts, behavior that frequently brought their targets to tears. Or that some of the sobbing counselors regularly repaired to Bettelheim's office for private sessions of dynamic supervision. Nor did the book's readers have any inkling that the author had become principal of the Orthogenic School in part because he had falsely claimed to have treated one or more autistic children in Vienna and because of invented credentials that, among several other inflations, gave him a substantial background in the study and teaching of psychology. Even those few readers who found the case histories, for all their clinical fascination, a little too facile and, like Dwight Macdonald, found the book as a whole unpersuasively optimistic, would have been barred at the door had they sought a closer inspection.

From the day Bettelheim took over the school in 1944, he

set it off-limits to almost all outsiders: to parents like the mother who had complained to Hutchins about the director's anger and imperiousness in refusing to let her and her husband tour the school before deciding to enroll their son, and who felt that Bettelheim "acted like a man who thought he was being spied upon"; to scores more parents who did enroll their children but were barred for many months from seeing where and how they lived and had to depend almost entirely for knowledge of their child's treatment on the periodic reports the school sent them; to the school's wealthy fund-raisers, whom Bettelheim assured he was achieving a very high cure rate[44] but to whom he made it as clear as "the word from Mount Sinai" that on their visits to the school they could not see the children.[45]

Bettelheim's colleagues at the university fared little better. Though Chicago had a tradition of giving faculty members wide latitude, most semi-autonomous centers—like the medical school or the Court Theater or even the athletic program—had boards of visitors or some other kind of oversight. The Orthogenic School had virtually none; no one in the education department, of which the school was a part, professed any expertise in the psychopathology and the care of disturbed children, and such informal committees as sprang up from time to time were "really window dressing," recalled Philip Jackson, who joined Bettelheim in the department in 1955 and ultimately became its chairman. "Everyone knew that the Orthogenic School was Bruno's castle," Jackson told me. "All the sounds that came out of it, at that time at least, were very positive. No one wanted to do anything but applaud. And it was across the Midway. Everyone was just delighted that Bruno was running the place and bringing fame to himself and to the university and also attracting all kinds of money." Like other universities, Chicago was always on the lookout for stars; to people in the development office like Charles Feldstein, who soon would befriend Bettelheim, the author, with his growing national reputation, his Viennese charisma, and his magnetic ability to attract money, was beginning to look like a "hot commodity."

CHAPTER NINE
The Terror of Judd Hall

B RUNO BETTELHEIM'S STOCK at the University of Chicago was rising not only because of his work at the Orthogenic School and the success of his books. By the early 1950s, he had become one of the most popular teachers on campus; his classes on the Dynamic Theories of Personality or his seminars on psychoanalysis were packed with students who, like the young women he had mesmerized at Rockford College and the counselors he transfixed in staff meetings, sat awed and apprehensive before him. No one was neutral about his courses, which former students recalled either as marvelous, evanescent experiences, or as terrifying and brutal, or sometimes as both—as battlegrounds that were almost classes in emotions themselves. "It was a bit like Dungeons and Dragons," recalled David Gutmann, a graduate student in human development in the 1950s. "There was this ogre. You had to go up against him in his lair. If you could survive, then maybe you'd be a man."

Bettelheim's primary den was Room 126 in Judd Hall, home of the department of education. A spacious, wood-paneled classroom with chandeliers and mullioned windows and columns interspersed among the chairs, Judd 126 accommodated well over a hundred students, and that many and more had often crowded in by the time Bettelheim took his chair on the platform. He remained seated most of the time, because a circulatory disease that plagued his legs often made standing painful. In his dark suit and conservative tie, he looked every bit the formidable Herr Professor Doktor, especially when bent in the Mephistophelian position, yardstick in hand. As he smoothed back his wisps of hair, fussed with his tie, and swept the faces from behind his thick lenses, silence choked the room. What would he do today? Whom would he call on? Would someone actually sacrifice himself by asking a question or chancing an observation, risking a salvo of derision? Would a young woman again leave the room in tears? In the hope of avoiding Bettelheim's eye, most students made sure not to sit in the first two or three rows. "The sense was," recalled Marc Lubin, a former graduate student in human development, "that if he could see you he would cut you to ribbons."

By the middle 1950s, Bettelheim's reputation for dicing had taken on mythic proportions with the Knitting Story. Just the mention of his name now prompts many people who may know little else about him to say, "Well, of course, you know that he once spotted a woman knitting in the first row and told her that what she was doing was a sublimation for masturbation, and that she shot back, 'Dr. Bettelheim, when I knit, I knit; when I masturbate, I masturbate.' " Others have her saying, "You do it your way, I'll do it mine."[1] David Riesman said the riposte is "wholly apocryphal" but that Bettelheim did make the masturbation-knitting equation when speaking to a large group of sociology students in Mandel Hall, the university's main auditorium. Riesman, who was hosting the class, found Bettelheim's behavior so outrageous that, though his junior by six years, he felt compelled to call him on it and to comfort the young woman, who he said was far too crushed by the remark to make any response whatsoever.[2] Phyliss Steiss, a former student, recalled Bettelheim attacking a knitter during a class in Judd 126—"He really lit into her; it was unbelievable"—but she, too, said the woman made no snappy comeback. Theodor Sterling, however, told me that the exchange did take place as the legend has it. He said he was a student in human development in the early 1950s, the class was Dynamic Theories of Personality, and the knitter was an Asian woman in the first row who did indeed coolly respond, "When I knit, I knit; when I masturbate, I masturbate."

After David Dempsey rehearsed the Knitting Story, riposte and all, in his *New York Times Magazine* profile, Bettelheim wrote a letter to the paper putting his own spin on it. He merged the incidents into one generic tale, making no mention of his masturbation remark or the impact it had on the young target or targets; instead, he suggested that this interpretation had its genesis in

Vienna, when Lou Andreas-Salomé brought her knitting to meetings of Freud's inner circle and someone teased her by comparing the movement of her needles to coitus. Bettelheim went on to explain that knitting distracted him because it reminded him of how frustrated and upset he had become as a boy when his mother concentrated on her needlework instead of giving him the attention he craved, adding that when he told the offending student this she "very graciously put her knitting away." He wrote that he introduced his mother into the story in the hope of teaching the class how lingering the aftereffects can be of even small childhood rejections, adding that as he became more sure of his teaching skills knitting ceased to bother him.[3]

As at Rockford and in the Orthogenic School staff meetings, Bettelheim taught mostly by throwing his students into the deep end of his Socratic pool. Normally, he handed out extensive reading lists at the beginning of the term, with standard works like Aichhorn's *Wayward Youth* and Freud's *Totem and Taboo* complemented by material from contemporary books and journals, including some of his own writing. He rarely lectured, and told Jacquelyn Sanders that he prepared for his classes during the few minutes it took him to walk across the Midway from the school to Judd Hall;[4] he seemed to regard the papers he assigned and the exams he gave less as measures of his students' abilities than as bothersome requirements of the academic bureaucracy, often handing these exercises back with no comments and occasionally with no grades. As at Rockford, he opposed note-taking, regarding such stenography as a distraction from the learning process; when he suddenly asked a student what he was writing, pens dropped around the room.[5]

So did the self-esteem of anyone unwise enough to try and impress the professor with Freudian orotundities or jargon of any kind. He felt most graduate students hid behind their texts instead of observing the psychological phenomena around them. In one class, an earnest student referred to a "male child." Bettelheim barked: "You mean 'boy'?" and then, in his thick accent, "Speak English!"[6] Anyone foolish enough to use a term like "oral libido" was instantly asked to define it, not a comfortable task after Bettelheim had advised the room that, well, he ate every day, sometimes six times, but did not have sex with nearly that frequency.[7]

Even use of such an accepted word as "ego" drew his wrath. One student after another would scramble bravely to come up with a definition, offering up such college tries as "an ego is that part of the psyche that controls the relation to reality and the control of impulses." "No!" Bettelheim would shout. As others tried with equal desperation, his guttural rejections echoed through Judd 126. "Finally," Marc Lubin recalled, "some courageous soul would say: 'The ego is a concept.' Bettelheim would say, with this affirming Viennese certitude, 'Zat's right!' " Gutmann told me Bettelheim asked one class: " 'Why do you think I make you hate me? Because if you hate me you will remember everything I say.' And he was right, the son of a bitch." Many students called him "Brutalheim" or "the terror of Judd Hall,"[8] and occasionally one would summon up the nerve to ask him about his ferocity. "Why are you so cruel?" a young woman hazarded in the 1960s. "Don't you like us?" She said he replied: " 'I'm not cruel and angry with you people, you don't mean enough to me. I only get cruel and angry with people I really care about.' "[9]

Bettelheim frequently showed short movies on depression, schizophrenia, and other mental-health subjects produced by the National Film Board of Canada. Knowing they had to be prepared to respond to these films or to the assigned readings, and risk Bettelheim's withering put-downs, caused anxiety enough; but what made his classes uniquely intimidating was his frequent use of the students' own behavior to score his psychological points, the same technique he so often used in staff meetings at the Orthogenic School. Karen Carlson, who took his course on the Theory of Group Work while she was a counselor at the school, recalled once arriving late for the class, in which about two dozen students already had gathered around Bettelheim. The only empty chair in the circle was next to him, so Carlson sat down in a back row, whereupon he said: " 'Kar-en, can you think of a way of joining us.' " She had a choice: she could get to the chair next to him by pushing directly through the circle, or she could go out into the hall through one of the classroom's two doors and come in the other and sit in the vacant chair with a minimum of disturbance. Carlson chose the doors, and when she had finally sat down next to Bettelheim he devoted the rest of the class to the maneuver, saying her initial decision to sit on the fringes indicated that she was reluctant to join the group, and that the group itself, by not immediately making a path for her, had demonstrated its own hesitancy to let her come sit next to him. "He did a whole analysis of group processes based on this one little incident. I was utterly fascinated by it," Carlson told me.

In his seminar on psychoanalysis, Bettelheim required that each student make a presentation. Marc Lubin chose to describe what happened when he took Ralph, a schizophrenic boy with whom he had just begun to work at a residential-treatment center in Chicago, to his therapy session. Lubin's colleagues had warned him that Ralph would try to manipulate him into buying an ice-cream bar. After the appointment Ralph did just that and Lubin said no; when Ralph asked why, Lubin said, Because it's not a good idea. "So Dr. B said, 'Why didn't you get him the ice-cream bar?' And I felt this terrible ignorance and anxiety; I was embarrassed to admit that I was very much worried about the opinion of my peers, that I would look like a jerk if I bought Ralph, who was the most blatant manipulator in the world, an ice-cream bar." Lubin, who went on to become dean of the Illinois School of Professional Psychology, sees Bettelheim as a paradox, an authoritarian personality bearing an anti-authoritarian message. He credits Bettelheim with making him realize that he had to let his relationships with his clients unfold slowly, that he had to be honest with himself about his own reactions and not try to hide behind someone else's directives, even it if meant doing what seemed like the wrong thing.

This ability to make everyday experience the grist of his classes is what, to Bettelheim's admirers, made him a great teacher, "a Socrates of the unconscious life . . . [who] was able to effect substantial progress toward understanding just by getting everyone to be against him."[10] Charles Saltzman, another former graduate student in human development, told me of one class in which a young woman asked a question growing out of her experience trying to teach ballroom dancing to handicapped children. The notion infuriated Bettelheim, who said it was a crime to make children attempt tasks at which they were doomed to fail, to rub their noses in their limitations. The woman fled the room in tears. "There were times," Saltzman said, echoing the view of other former students, "when I felt I was witnessing education at its most emotionally intense."

That is how Eric Schopler experienced Bettelheim when he first encountered him as an undergraduate in the late 1940s. Schopler was drawn to the Viennese refugee not only because of a budding interest in the treatment of disturbed children but because he, too, was an émigré, having fled Germany for the United States in 1938, when he was eleven years old. His career would intersect with Bettelheim's for many years, as Schopler developed into a leading authority on autism, becoming the head of a pioneering program at the University of North Carolina and the editor of the *Journal of Autism and Developmental Disorders*. Initially, Schopler wondered if Bettelheim's intent in class was to evoke original thinking in his students by caricaturing the theories he was teaching with overstated applications to personal behavior, like Karen Carlson's reluctance to sit next to him, or knitting as onanism. "[C]ould this be a brilliant and original teaching approach?" Schopler asked himself at the time. He would decide no, and came to regard Bettelheim as an important "negative role model."

Schopler now sees Bettelheim as the "Don Rickles of psychoanalysis," a performer who kept his audience tyrannized and off-balance with sarcasm, insults, and psychological interpretations often aimed primarily at gaining the upper hand. Schopler soon recognized Bettelheim as a "florid invention of himself" and blames the University of Chicago for not putting him in the humanities, where his exaggerations and metaphorical flights would have done little harm. "He would say the most outrageous things," Schopler told me, recalling an exchange at Chicago's Jewish Children's Bureau, where Bettelheim was a consultant for a time. A young attendant presented a case in which a child was threatening others with a knife. "Bruno said, 'Well, what do you think the knife means?' The young man said, 'It's a phallic symbol and the boy is showing his aggressiveness through the knife.' And Bettelheim roared at him and said, 'Vat, a phallic symbol? Have you ever heard of a penis that could cut a loaf of bread?' He would hit you over the head with his Freudian symbols if it was convenient for gaining control of the conversation; if it was convenient for knocking you down, then he'd take that tack, showing how silly you were."

Like Schopler, others look back on the *frisson* in Bettelheim's classroom with a certain embarrassed bemusement, men and women no longer in their late teens and early twenties and high on the Freudian ether that intoxicated much of society into the 1960s, especially on university campuses. Like many of the once equally impressionable young counselors at the Orthogenic School, they now realize that Bettelheim often "shot from the hip,"[11] dazzling his wide-eyed listeners by saying whatever popped into his head. He liked to demonstrate that when a child added numbers incorrectly it had meaning, so he occasionally asked several students to pick the first number that came to them and then to tell him the size of their immediate families. Sometimes the numbers matched, implying psychological significance; when they did not, Bettelheim was unfazed. One student said that the first number he had thought of was twelve but that he was an only child; well, Bettelheim explained, the one stood for the student and the two for his parents. This numerology left this seventeen-year-old undergraduate so amazed that after class he ran back to his dorm to try it on his friends, with disappointing results.[12] Marc Lubin, who, like many others who came under Bettelheim's sway, continues to hold him in a certain esteem, concedes that he had idealized him hopelessly. "I think he was a man who wanted to be seen as being profoundly wise, and certain of every opinion. He never exposed to me that he was unsure of himself, so for many years I accepted everything he did as being absolutely unquestionable."

Once, after showing a film depicting aggression, Bettelheim asked the students why they, too, had so many aggressive tendencies; before they could answer, he deflated them by saying they all feared that they were small and ridiculous. "Some power impelled me to my feet," David Gutmann told me. "It was like moving out under machine-gun fire. I said: 'Dr. B, when you make fools of your students, aren't you defending against the same thing?' That got him. He sort of reeled back dramatically. You could see that he wanted to tear me apart, but he knew that would prove my point. He looked around rather slowly and said: 'Does anyvun care to anzer zis young man?' In short, either defend Daddy or join the camp of the father-eating rebellious brothers. Nobody spoke." Gutmann said that a few classes later Bettelheim showed another film, in which an angry inner-city boy smeared paint or paste over his image in a mirror before going out and committing some provocative act. Gutmann said that the boy was trying to destroy himself in the mirror, and Bettelheim looked at him and said: " 'Ver did you get zat? Did you get zat from me?' I had arrived; this was the tap on the shoulder, the 'Rise, Sir Knight.' " For Gutmann, Bettelheim fit the epigram about the Huns: he was either at your throat or at your feet.[13]

MOST WOMEN STAYED at his feet, among them the young mothers who gathered at least once a month to hear his advice on how to raise their children. In the 1940s, after the war, when these sessions began, most of the women were married to former servicemen studying under the GI Bill and, together with their infants and toddlers, coping on less than a hundred dollars a month in the "prefabs," temporary housing on campus. The meetings began at eight in the evening, when as many as forty mothers, and occasionally a father or two, pulled up their folding chairs around the hexagonal table in Blaine Hall and poured out their concerns about bed-wetting, bottle-weaning, and toilet training.

"He gave us so much to think about that it sometimes took several sessions to digest," recalled Helen Ratzer, who with the other mothers pondered Bettelheim's counsel almost daily in their cramped apartments or as they pushed their strollers around campus. Occasionally, Ratzer and her husband, Earl, invited their exotic instructor over for coffee and cake after the sessions and with one or two other couples stayed up talking about everything from politics to concerts they had recently attended. "Bettelheim seemed to enjoy our company, and we found him to be incredibly intelligent and thoughtful about all subjects—not just psychiatry," said Helen, who was particularly impressed when Bettelheim told them he had a Ph.D. not only in psychology but in art history as well. "He was God, we idolized him," said Ruth Bemak, another recent bride at the time. Their deity returned the compliment. In 1948, he and his editor, Ruth Marquis, had begun recording the sessions and would use the transcripts, as they had the Orthogenic School counselors' dictation for *Love Is Not Enough* and *Truants from Life,* as the basis of another book, this one called *Dialogues with Mothers.* In the introduction, Bettelheim wrote that "only a limited percentage of all mothers in the prefabs took part in the meetings, [but] they were the mothers most interested in child rearing, and hence the leaders in everything pertaining to children." [14]

His basic instruction to these young, biddable women was, for the most part, the same as the one he gave the counselors at the Orthogenic School: that in seeking to deal with a child's behavior it was crucial first to find out what was on his mind, to comprehend why he felt compelled to act in a certain way. His exchange with one mother, who reported that her son had come home from school complaining that another child had hit him and had asked if he should hit back, typified his approach. The mother had told her son that retaliation was not such a good idea.

> DR. B: The issue is to *ask* him. Not, "That's a good idea, that's a bad idea," or you wouldn't like him to do that. The question is, "What did you feel like doing?"
>
> MOTHER: Well, I think . . . gosh . . . it seems . . .
>
> DR. B: You impose your choices on him whatever you do— whether you say, "Hit" or "Don't hit," or "Call the teacher." You say, by implication, "I'm convinced you can't handle the situation on your own." He already knows that, or feels it, and you hit right back into it. Therefore it's immaterial whether you say, "Hit back," or "Defend yourself," or "Run away." You hand him your opinion, without asking him for his. [15]

In general, Bettelheim urged the mothers to be permissive, telling them their children knew their own needs and that parents should adjust accordingly, as did one family in the prefabs whose infant stayed up all night and slept all day. "This was our job," Ruth Bemak told me. "He made it seem so beautiful, so right."

Bettelheim wrote that in giving advice he was not seeking to establish hard and fast rules but instead hoped to get the mothers to start thinking intelligently about how they should respond when faced with everyday child-rearing dilemmas, and he cautioned them not to follow expert recommendations slavishly, including his.[16] Nonetheless, a lot of his instruction came out sounding like dogma, especially when delivered with the same sarcastic, anxiety-producing disdain that so often permeated his other teaching venues.[17] He told the mothers that spanking and hitting was the wrong approach to discipline; that kissing their children was ill-advised because it stimulated them in an adult way and might tempt them to start having intercourse when they became teenagers; that one of their children's greatest fears was that their sex could be changed; that little boys hoped their baby sisters would eventually grow a penis; and that pets should not be neutered, because children feared that the same would happen to them.[18]

Some of Bettelheim's pronouncements were par for the Freudian course on which most psychotherapists played in the 1940s and 1950s, but occasionally he sliced the ball deep into the woods of incredulity. He told the mothers that he did not believe "that a child who is regularly fed with a propped bottle will have too easy a time in establishing decent relationships to other human beings,"[19] and went on to stress the importance of attentively feeding their infants.

> As we know from many famous examples, very gregarious people like Churchill and Roosevelt were fed very long and very extensively; not necessarily by their mothers, but by their nurses. They turned out to be very optimistic people. They enjoyed food and drink, they enjoyed company, and they sat very long at the dinner table, chatting and having a good time.[20]

Such a passage, like much else in *Dialogues with Mothers*, suggests that Bettelheim was not being falsely modest when he wrote that, though he drew on "a great backlog of experience with normal and very difficult children" to help him guide the young mothers, there was hardly ever time at the sessions themselves "to reason out" what he said, and that he offered solutions "semi-consciously, almost automatically."[21] He told one mother, who was worried about the slow growth of her child's vocabulary, that "[i]t's a fact in our society that you can get very far if you can talk well and fast. And there are many successful, even famous, people who get far because they're glib. . . . You can even find them in the universities!" [22]

Bettelheim's gift for spiel made him much in demand as a speaker, one who seemed to have a bottomless briefcase of instant insights and therapeutic nostrums. In 1946, he urged a group of high-school teachers to study the jitterbug phenomenon as a way of understanding the insecurities of adolescent males. "The boy's action in throwing the girl around suggests hostility to the opposite sex—or else fear!" he explained. [23] From various platforms, he declared that competitive sports were psychologically ill-advised; [24] that a man's unhappiness in his job might stem from his having played cowboys and Indians as a child; [25] that world government and not disarmament was the way to universal peace. [26] Questioners sometimes found themselves under the same machine-gun fire as his students. One professor recalled Bettelheim speaking thoughtfully about James Strachey's translation of Freud, then dismissing follow-up queries with a shabby superciliousness; [27] an audience of public-high-school teachers eager to hear his views on how to handle their difficult students got more contempt than answers, leaving one to conclude that he was a "terrible, egocentric, vain, sadistic, vicious, power-mad person." [28]

On October 20, 1959, Bettelheim spoke to a parent-teachers meeting in River Forest, a Chicago suburb, telling his listeners that they should stop worrying about juvenile delinquency, because it was no worse than it ever had been. J. Edgar Hoover was deceiving them by painting a bleak picture of the blackboard jungle, distorting crime figures so Congress would give the FBI more money; everyone knew the bureau's director was corruptible for the right price and would get his appropriations "by hook or by crook." To lighten the proceedings, Bettelheim assured his audience that none of this really mattered much, because the communist Chinese were going to take over the world anyway.

Hoover was not amused. An FBI informer who had been in the audience reported Bettelheim's remarks to the director, who within days ordered a file opened on the unwitting émigré—described on one page as "probably Jewish." [29] In a memorandum to Clyde Tolson, Hoover's associate director, an agent named C. D. De Loach wrote: "Bettelheim has not only challenged our crime reporting program but what is more important has challenged the Director's morals. He obviously should be called to task for this and should be told to put up or shut up." De Loach recommended that the bureau's Chicago office confront Bettelheim on his "slandering" of Hoover; the nonredacted portions of the file offer no indication that this was done, but Bettelheim did eventually learn that the FBI had opened a dossier on him.[30] It contains the usual mundane revelations produced by the bureau's snooping on innocent victims: summaries of Bettelheim's clipping envelopes in Chicago newspaper morgues, reports that he had written for the "pacifist" magazine *Politics* and that he had spoken on the problem child to the Women's Educational League of the Workers Party. The file also notes that Trude Bettelheim had apparently not been active "in any type of criminal or subversive activity. . . ."[31]

Throughout the 1940s and 1950s, Bettelheim was a conventional Democrat, like most of his liberal neighbors and faculty colleagues. "Like everybody else, I am doing everything I can to get [Adlai] Stevenson elected," he wrote to James T. Farrell just before the 1956 election, adding that he feared it unlikely that the Democrat would prevent Dwight D. Eisenhower's re-election.[32] He seldom got involved in electoral politics, but he did take progressive public stands from time to time. In 1959, he testified before a U.S. Senate subcommittee investigating juvenile delinquency and attacked the "class justice" meted out to youthful offenders. "If you are a rich man's son and get caught violating the law, you get a psychiatrist as a reward, but a poor boy gets sent to [reform school]."[33] Rather than send delinquents to such institutions, he said, the nation should devote more money and resources to rehabilitation programs and less to the military and moon shots.[34]

Bettelheim made these last remarks on February 19, 1963, when the University of Chicago named him Stella M. Rowley Professor of Education at a celebratory press luncheon at the Tavern Club downtown. Among those present high above Michigan Avenue were the university's President George Beadle, Provost

Edward H. Levi, Education Department Chairman Francis S. Chase, and Mrs. Rowley, the eighty-nine-year-old former public-school teacher who had endowed the chair. The citation praised the honoree for books that had moved colleagues to more fruitful work and instructed parents to sounder insights into their own and their children's behavior, for his theoretical contributions, and for the development of a milieu therapy at the Orthogenic School whose quality and efficacy exceeded "any other contribution to the field."[35] In accepting the honor, Bettelheim saluted his staff and again said that about 80 percent of his residents were leaving the school emotionally whole.[36] The next day, the university's public-relations office proudly reported that seventeen journalists had attended the luncheon and that one had been moved to observe, " 'Now I've seen the canonization of a saint.' "[37]

The Chicago psychoanalytic community took a somewhat less hagiographic view of their colleague on the Midway, an attitude in which envy surely played a part. While they labored mostly in obscurity, dutifully listening to their patients, attending their meetings, and publishing in the requisite intramural journals, Bettelheim's headlines grew ever bigger. Despite Bettelheim's celebrity and his willingness to take on the difficult cases at the Orthogenic School, the city's Institute for Psychoanalysis never made him a formal member; he felt like a second-class citizen from the start, and in the minds of many local psychoanalysts he was. They bridled at his dismissal of theory, and his tendency to be aggressive and sarcastic was obnoxious to some, including the institute's president, Gerhart Piers.

It was Piers and his wife, Maria, who, when escaping from Austria through Switzerland in 1939, had helped pass money to the Nazis in the effort to free Bettelheim from Buchenwald. Maria Piers said Bettelheim never thanked them after they had all settled in Hyde Park, which doubtless fueled her husband's antipathy; but he also regarded his fellow Viennese as mean and intellectually dishonest, a con artist who had misrepresented his credentials to get where he was, took credit for other people's work, and inflated his achievements at the Orthogenic School.[38] Honoring the *omertà* that prevails in most professions, Piers and other Bettelheim critics in the psychoanlytic community usually only whispered their disapproval. But even if one or two had attacked him openly, he was now so well known and respected by the lay public that any challengers risked being accused of sour grapes—precisely the fear Gina Weinmann felt whenever, after reading her former husband's repeated claims to have treated Patsy, she contemplated telling *anyone* that in fact she had cared for the child.[39]

Bettelheim's lack of status with the psychoanalytic establishment infuriated him. In 1949 and 1950, he had co-authored with Emmy Sylvester two articles that appeared in *Psychoanalytic Study of the Child,* but after that he never appeared in any of the five leading psychoanalytic journals again.[40] In 1961, he submitted a manuscript about an "autistic" girl to the *Journal of the American Psychoanalytic Association.* Several members of the editorial board found his portrait interesting, even "masterful"; one reported that despite its eighty-page length it read "almost like a novel. . . ." But they criticized his lack of theoretical underpinnings for his conclusions, which one called "very risky." The editor rejected the paper, but held out the possiblity of future publication if the author "would supply more details as to how he rea[c]hed his formulations. . . ."[41] In response, Bettelheim wrote that the difference between him and the critical editorial-board members was that he believed in "pushing against the limitations of a science so as to forever enlarge on its scope," and told the editor he had arranged to have the paper published elsewhere.[42]

In 1974, after Bettelheim stepped down from the dais where he had been honored before a large and enthusasitic audience along with Anna Freud and Erik Erikson, among others, a former student named Kay Field reminded him that he had agreed to let her interview him. She had expected him to be warm and receptive after basking in so much acclaim, but she said he yelled at her: " 'You're from the institute in Chicago. I wouldn't give an interview to anyone from that place. They don't recognize that I am the outstanding child analyst in the country, if not the world.' "

Bettelheim's relationships with his faculty colleagues at the University of Chicago were better than with the analysts, but he never felt fully accepted on campus either. He knew that some of the professors he chatted with in the corridors of Judd Hall or in the dining room of the Quadrangle Club regarded his books about the school with a certain disdain, popularized "potboilers," as one called them.[43]

After the success of *Love Is Not Enough,* he had tried taking the approved academic high road with *Symbolic Wounds: Puberty Rites and the Envious Male.* In it, he wrote that he had "observed" four adolescent children at his school—two boys and two girls— agree to a pact in which the boys would prick their fingers and mingle their blood with the girls' menses. The staff intervened, but the incident moved Bettelheim to ponder what the act meant, and to suggest that circumcision and similar genital mutilations in preliterate society did not necessarily stem from the father's pathological, sadistic need to dominate the son in the latter's rite of passage, as both anthropologists and psychoanalysts generally believed at the time. Instead, he cautiously argued, perhaps such rituals reflected the male's envy of the female's ability to menstruate, give birth, and breast-feed. Bettelheim buttressed his arguments with considerable research, most of it carefully attributed in numbered endnotes.

The book received a mixed reception in several scholarly journals, some anthropologists and sociologists complaining that Bettelheim was poaching on terrain he did not altogether understand. But the reviews did treat *Symbolic Wounds* as a serious book that sought to advance a novel interpretation of puberty rites. Bettelheim was disappointed that it received nothing like the attention accorded "Individual and Mass Behavior in Extreme Situations" and *Love Is Not Enough,*[44] and would never again go the academic route.

Bettelheim was also uneasy on campus because he suspected that, like Gerhart Piers, some of his colleagues questioned his credentials and were on to his As Ifs, such as his claim that Eleanor Roosevelt had rescued him from Buchenwald. Yet, no matter how big a star he became, he seemed compelled to recirculate such deceptions year after year. In a routine 1964 memo to the dean of education, he wrote that he had a degree in psychology from the University of Vienna and had trained at the Vienna Psychoanalytic Institute, "with work in child analysis, and in the treatment of psychotic and delinquent children."[45]

The university had given him a refuge in the 1940s and he

had risen to become one of its most widely known professors, but he continued to feel the outsider, as he did among the psychoanalytic hierarchs and as he had as a merchant in Vienna. Those on campus who "belonged" were men like Robert M. Hutchins and Ralph Tyler, with their impeccable pedigrees and their ability to offer him *Protektion;* or like Howell Wright, the head of pediatrics, who watched over the medical needs of children at the Orthogenic School, and who Bettelheim insisted call him "Mr." He gave these well-born Gentiles total deference, as he did anyone he regarded as his social or official superior. If he felt, rightly or wrongly, that he was intellectually out of his depth, his confidence evaporated. He occasionally confided in Benjamin Wright, who worked closely with him at the Orthogenic School in the 1950s. Wright recalled going to a professional meeting with Bettelheim, who soon found the other participants intimidating. "Say something smart, say something smart," he kept whispering to his junior colleague. "No matter how successful he became," Wright told me, "no matter how much people praised him, no matter how obvious it was that they were terrified of him and were willing to let him be the whole cheese, he continued to believe that he was ugly, small, and Jewish."

IN THE LATE 1940s, Bettelheim revealed for the first time in public how uncomfortable he felt in his Jewish skin. He had come to speak on "Anti-Semitism Today" at Hillel House, the university's Jewish center. The room was packed with Jewish students and some faculty members eager to hear from this man who actually had been imprisoned by the Nazis and who had written "Individual and Mass Behavior in Extreme Situations." He astonished the gathering at the outset by asking: "Anti-Semitism, whose fault is it?" Eric Schopler, who was in the audience, recalled what came next:

> He paused as if expecting every student to volunteer his own thoughts to this emotionally burdened question. Finally, the silence was pierced by Bettelheim's pointed finger drawing an arc, encompassing all of us. "Yours!" he shouted. "Because you don't assimilate, it is your fault. If you assimilated, there would be no anti-Semitism. Why don't you assimilate?"

Schopler said Bettelheim answered his rhetorical question with a passionate denunciation of "this hopeless vice of Jewish identity . . . [trying] every trick of persuasion in his Germanic repertoire of sarcasm, guilt, and shame," finally asking how many of his listeners saw themselves as Jews for religious reasons.

> He regarded the absence of any answers with a triumphant smirk, then shifted to sarcasm. "If it is for cultural reasons, what is this Jewish culture? Who are the great Jewish composers? Who are the timeless artists? Who are the great writers? Shalom [sic] Asch?" This Yiddish writer, popular at the turn of the century, often wrote about the common spiritual heritage of Christians and Jews. He might have been used as support for the assimilating argument, but instead, Bettelheim dismissed Asch with a retching "Yech," indicating a writer not worthy of a tile in the shabby mosaic of Jewish culture.

At the end of the talk, as the audience blinked in numb silence, the young Schopler braved the machine-gun fire and raised his hand to ask for clarification. He said that he understood Bettelheim's remarks to mean that Jews could end anti-Semitism if they relinquished their religious and ethnic interests and had their identifying noses altered. If that was the case, then what was the difference between the speaker and the anti-Semite?

In red-faced anger, Bettelheim shouted, "I am only the doctor prescribing the cure."

I followed up, "You mean by identifying with the disease?"

"Yes, by identifying with the disease," he shouted.[46]

Bert Cohler said that Bettelheim was "avowedly anti-Semitic" in the days when he knew him. Many of the wealthy Chicagoans who supported the Orthogenic School through the Foundation for Emotionally Disturbed Children were descended from Eastern European Jews. Cohler, who came from the elite German Jewish stock that Bettelheim so admired, occasionally accompanied the director on fund-raising missions in the 1960s and recalled the Austrian's muttering imperiously about how he resented having to put on a dinner jacket and oil his Viennese charm for people he regarded as his inferiors.

Early on, Bettelheim also criticized Jews in print on a variety of issues. In *Politics,* his article "Exodus, 1947" attacked the American Jewish community for pushing to settle European refugees in Israel instead of working harder to bring them to the United States. And he had chided Jews for stereotyping anti-Semites, supporting his case with the Frostbite Story, in which he or N. bravely tore off flesh to impress the hostile infirmary guard in Buchenwald. He also instructed Jewish parents on how they could best arm their children against anti-Semitism. He said little could be done to prepare children of four or five against the realities of prejudice and told parents not to try, instead urging them to set a good example for their offspring and to provide them with the education and security they needed so that they would be strong enough to deal with prejudice when they grew older. He told Jewish parents they were too preoccupied with building community centers, that Jewish institutional life was becoming "a vast system of psychological fortifications" behind which they hoped to live without incurring the emotional scars of anti-Semitism. They overstated the amount of anti-Semitism in American society, and their "irrational fear of the *goy*" was in danger of becoming a psychological necessity.[47]

To support this thesis that too many Jews were afflicted with a ghetto mentality, Bettelheim revised one of the "findings" he had reported in "Individual and Mass Behavior in Extreme Situations" in 1943. In that essay, he had written that he had asked "more than one hundred old political prisoners" if they would sound the alarm about the camps if they should be lucky enough to reach freedom. He said only two indicated that they would, the rest preferring to put their hope in revolution and rejecting the idea that other nations should meddle in Germany's internal affairs.[48] By 1963, speaking to the Chicago chapter of the American Council for Judaism, Bettelheim was telling the story this way: The Gentile inmates were nearly unanimous in wanting to tell the world of the Nazi atrocities, but the Jews were divided. Some agreed with the Gentiles; others preferred caution, then and in the future. "Thus," he said, "it was Jewish procrastination, in the face of their annihilation as self-respecting persons, that gave the Nazis time to develop a policy of physical annihilation."[49] Such

reasoning moved Severn Darden, a student at Chicago who with
Mike Nichols, Elaine May, and others, was a prime mover in
establishing the "Second City" comedy cabaret, to begin a mock
lecture on *Oedipus* by saying: "I see you're all here, which means
that some of you are missing Dr. Bettelheim's lecture on 'Some
Positive Aspects of Anti-Semitism.' "[50]

Bettelheim was a professed atheist who felt God was a fiction
and who kept his birth religion behind the Gentile scrims of
Christmas and Easter, as had his parents and most of their Jewish
friends in Vienna. For more than twenty years, he was adamant
that the many Jewish children and staff members at the Orthogenic School do the same. "He would not tolerate even a discussion of Hanukkah or the High Holy Days," Karen Carlson told
me. Bettelheim had been granted U.S. citizenship in 1944, just a
few weeks after taking over the school; to those who asked him
why he rejected the Jewish celebrations, he often said, "This is
America and we celebrate American holidays." Philip Goldbloom,
a resident during the 1960s, told me that, when he asked Bettelheim if a seder could be held in the dining room, the director told
him that it would not be good for his psychological well-being.
Bettelheim's public instruction to all Jews remained what it had
been at Hillel House: "assimilate, assimilate, assimilate."

But he sometimes sent out a contradictory message in private. In his books, Bettelheim often leaned on the work of Erik
Erikson,[51] and after receiving a grant in the mid-1950s to study
autism, he invited Erikson, then at the Austen Riggs Center in
Stockbridge, Massachusetts, to spend regular periods consulting at
the Orthogenic School so that all hands could benefit from his
"great knowledge and insight."[52] Erikson did pay one or two
visits, but, whatever his contribution, Bettelheim would develop
an angry hostility to this man who had used his stepfather's name,
Homburger, when studying, teaching, and being analyzed by
Anna Freud in Vienna, but who became "Erikson" once he took
up his profession in the United States in the 1930s. In a letter
attacking Erikson for claiming that he and parents in general were
unselfish, Bettelheim wrote, "Erikson tries to pretend to be the
magnanimous goy, the god damn Jew. I know I am a selfish Jew,
so help me god, so I can afford to look at things [as] they are. All

this god damn pretense."[53] A year later, Erikson was "a miserable so and so, who was a Jew in Vienna, when it paid, and is now a Viking in the States, when that pays."[54]

When Philip Goldbloom's sister was about to marry a Gentile, the Goldblooms, who, like many parents, were in awe of Bettelheim because of his reputation, sought his advice. He told them that such mixed marriages were ill-advised, a position Karen Carlson told me he took when she advised him she planned to marry a Jew. In letters and private conversation, he said that fear of the goy was anything but irrational and overstated, though by the early 1960s he and Morris Janowitz were updating *Dynamics of Prejudice* with statistics indicating that anti-Jewish sentiment in the United States had shown a "pronounced and striking" decline since the end of World War II.[55] He told one friend that he felt Jews were not really safe anywhere and that they owed what relative security they had found in America to the greater prejudice against Negroes, which distracted anti-Semitic impulses.[56] In this, he echoed the German officer who he said had told him, when he was gaining his freedom in 1939, that the Nazis had victimized the Jews because they had no Negroes to persecute. How seriously Bettelheim believed that this explanation applied in either Germany or the United States is difficult to say, but that he feared anti-Semitism in his adopted country is clear. After speaking at Harvard University during the height of the protests against the Vietnam war, he had dinner with Marc Lubin and his wife, Kathy, who had been a counselor at the Orthogenic School. Lubin, who is Jewish, recalled Bettelheim saying to his wife that she was lucky not to be Jewish, because when the fascists took over the country in reaction to the antiwar zealots she would not be taken away.

Bettelheim's struggle with his Jewishness was just one of the burdens that contributed to the deep pessimism and depression that had sent him into analysis with Richard Sterba in Vienna. Gina Weinmann said those sessions had lasted no more than a year; the analysand himself said several years. Whatever the duration, he did not again enter therapy for more than fifty years. Trude had tried to persuade him to seek professional help when they first settled in Chicago, primarily to deal with the persistent memories of his camp experience. Gina told me that the psychoanalyst Kurt

Eissler had also urged therapy on him, saying that no one should operate a school for emotionally disturbed children without a thorough analysis himself—a recommendation consonant with Bettelheim's own insistence that many of his counselors could profit by regular sessions with him or therapists outside the school. But Bettelheim said that Sterba had taken him as far as he could go and that "no more was possible. . . ."[57]

Toward the end of his life, Bettelheim said that during his analysis "there were probably tremendous areas of mutual misunderstanding. But my analyst made an *effort* to understand, which was enough even if it may have misfired. We get an *E* for effort, not an *A* for achievement."[58] He did not describe in his writing what he meant by "misfired" or offer a detailed account of what he had managed to accomplish in therapy with Sterba, but in private he said that through analysis he had become aware of how oppressive his father's syphilis had been for him.[59]

He said that his concentration-camp ordeal had helped make clear that analysis was not the panacea he had once thought it was. At the time of his arrest, he wrote in *The Informed Heart,* he had regarded psychoanalysis as the best route to understanding the "true" nature of man, though he was no longer convinced such therapy could produce the "good" man. He said that psychoanalytic theory at the time of his incarceration was inadequate to explain fully what happened to the prisoners, that it gave little guidance for understanding what made the "good" life or the "good" man, that it told much more about the "hidden" man than it did about the "true" man. Such blurry language, used by a student, would have set Bettelheim snarling, as would some of the contradictions that marked his explanation. He wrote that, to his surprise, he found that psychoanalysis, which by 1938 he had come to view as the best key to all human problems, offered no suggestions for surviving in the camps. Four pages later, he said that psychoanalysis gave him a deeper comprehension of what went on in the unconscious of the prisoners and guards, an understanding that on occasion "may have saved my life, and on other occasions let me be of help to some of my fellow prisoners, where it counted."[60]

He made this same point again two decades later when describing the few days rest he received upon arriving wounded in Dachau. He wrote that psychoanalysis had reminded him

> how psychologically reconstructive it is to try to comprehend one's mental responses to an experience, and how helpful it is to fathom what goes on in the minds of others. . . . Had I been projected immediately into the dreadfully destructive grind of deadly mistreatments and utterly exhausting labor, as were my comrades, I do not know whether I would have succeeded equally well in reestablishing some parts of my psychological protective system.[61]

In a single paragraph of *The Informed Heart,* he wrote that his "years" with Richard Sterba had resulted in a "quite successful" analysis, and then that life in Dachau "within a few weeks" had done for him what all his sessions with Sterba had not.[62] He did not reveal just what this was. He did concede that, in making this last statement, he had laid himself and Sterba open to criticism that his analysis had provided him with insight but had not led him to a working through of his emotional problems. "Perhaps," he wrote, "it is to the credit of my analysis that the prospect doesn't trouble me. . . ."[63]

CHAPTER TEN
The Other Family

THE DEPRESSION that plagued Bruno Bettelheim as a young man in Vienna and that ultimately drove him into his brief analysis with Richard Sterba dogged him all his life. In Chicago, he rejected the kind of professional therapeutic help he constantly urged on others, and only rarely disclosed his demons to the outside world. But within the sanctuary of his home, he often gave in to his dark moods, sometimes seeking refuge in bed, where his daughter Ruth, when still a young girl, would find him when sent upstairs by her mother to try and cheer him up.[1] His nightmares about the concentration camps abated over the years, but never disappeared, and reminders of his ordeal were never far away.

In 1954, he saw *The Life and Death of Colonel Blimp*, the wartime propaganda film written and directed by the celebrated British team of Emeric Pressburger and Michael Powell. The movie traces the lives of two fictional military men, the British Clive Wynne Candy and the German Theodor Kretschmar-Schuldorff, who become fast friends after fighting a duel in 1902. By 1939, Kretschmar-Schuldorff is seeking political asylum in England as an alien. He is subdued and apprehensive, leaning on his black cane as he makes his plea to the interrogating officer, who is discouraging and suspicious, implying that the supplicant might well be a spy. Kretschmar-Schuldorff makes a poignant speech about how evil the Nazis are and how much he loves England. Moved, the official asks if he has any friends in the country, and in walks Candy, who embraces his old comrade and says that he will vouch for him "with everything I have."

Bettelheim told James Farrell that he well knew the feeling of such desperation, recalling the frantic letters he had written after the *Anschluss* and later, in the camps, and of all the letters written for him to British and American friends. "And the waiting: will they know me any longer now that I really need them, will they answer, will they come to the rescue. Now I am secure as any mortal can be, well known in my field, supposedly friend, close friend, to some of the most influential persons—but there it was, as real as ever, when just seeing a movie, this past experience of 14 years ago, of being deserted. . . . [But] I better become friends with it, since it'll stay with me as long as I live."² Bettelheim rarely spoke of this burden with his children, whom he and Trude were determined to protect as much as possible from the impact of their exile. But no such catastrophe could be made to disappear. When Eric Bettelheim needed money in 1967 for his high-school junior prom, he contemplated shoveling manure at the Chicago stockyards, a job he had heard paid twelve dollars an hour. " 'You don't want to do that; I've done that,' " Eric recalled his father saying, clearly referring to the human excrement the guards had forced him to muck.

Bettelheim continued to feel that people regarded him as ugly, small, and Jewish, that he would forever be the outsider despite his successes, fears that fed on painful memories of his several childhood illnesses; his poor eyesight and the pop bottle glasses he wore to correct it; his father's prolonged struggle with syphilis and the gloom it brought to the Vienna household, a pall so lasting that Bettelheim rarely spoke of the affliction outside of his family, and then not by name; his feeling that his mother had often been distant and cold when he was a boy; his resentment at having to drop out of the University of Vienna and go into the family lumber business after his father died; his knowledge that, even had he been able to pursue his formal studies, an academic or professional life would have been difficult to achieve because he was a Jew. He had struggled with these entangled emotions while the house of Europe collapsed around him, starting with the breakup of the Austro-Hungarian Empire and followed by the disillusionment and carnage of World War I, the Depression, the rise of the Nazis, and, finally, the *Anschluss,* Dachau, and Buchenwald. When freed, he had rushed to Gina, but the woman he had pursued so ardently in the late 1920s, with whom he had lived for eight years in their comfortable apartment in Hietzing, and with whom he had hoped to resume his life, told him that their marriage was finished, that she planned to wed Peter Weinmann. Only a few months later, in Chicago, Trude had revealed her affair with Hans Bandler in Australia and the ectopic pregnancy that had resulted, and when this had pushed him toward the striking and well-connected Jean Friedberg, she, too, had turned him away.

Various physical ailments compounded Bettelheim's dark emotional state. He suffered from chronic hay fever and was plagued by digestive problems, which he traced to the illness that he said had almost killed him as a child, and which had left his stomach scarred;[3] he stayed away from raw vegetables, fresh fruit, and cereal, and tried to be careful about the rest of his diet. Worse than his stomach disorder was the circulatory disease that gripped his legs, which eventually made walking even the short distance between his home and the school painful. In 1971, he would undergo a lumbar sympathectomy, a surgical interruption of the sympathetic-nerve pathways; the procedure reduced the pain, but standing and walking would remain difficult for him for the rest of his life.[4] Bettelheim was so convinced this disease would kill him that he told Ruth that she would have to be responsible for putting Eric through college, because *he* would not live long enough to do so.[5]

In part, it was this same fear that moved him to sell *Vorstadt I*, his prized Schiele. The painting needed restoring, but Bettelheim had neither the money nor the inclination for such a project; he either sold or consigned it to the Marlborough Gallery in London for its 1964 Schiele exhibition. The following year, the Staatsgalerie in Stuttgart purchased the work for 180,000 Deutsch marks (forty-five thousand dollars in 1965); at Bettelheim's death, in 1990, it was worth at least twice that amount.[6] He knew the painting was a good investment, but his enthusiasm for collecting turned more on his love of art than on financial motivation. Moreover, he did not want Trude to inherit the Schiele, because he felt she was ambivalent about it since he had bought it as a present for Gina. In 1965, with the proceeds of the sale, he took the family on a trip through Europe, saying he wanted to show his children the Continent before he died.

As the superego at the Orthogenic School, Bettelheim rejected—had to reject—suicide as an alternative to getting well, but outside the school he made clear that he regarded it as a viable option. *Suicide,* by the French sociologist Émile Durkheim, often appeared on his reading lists. "The book is based on a lot of statistics, and Bettelheim made them applicable," recalled John Ransome Phillips, who encountered the teacher as an undergraduate in the late 1950s. "As he explained suicide, it became understandable and acceptable, because it was such a human act. He made me see that it was a legitimate choice, because it came out of a deep need." That deep need had been answered by scores of Viennese Jews, including Trude's aunt, in the days after the *Anschluss;* and by the prisoners who had jumped to their death from the Dachau-bound train, or who, once in the camps, cut their wrists, hanged themselves in the barracks, or ran against the electrified fences. Suicide was more common among Austrians than most other nationalities, and a number of prominent figures had resorted to it, among them Sigmund Freud's disciple, Victor Tausk; Stefan Zweig, who killed himself in Brazil after a long depression; the spy Alfred Redl, the philosopher Otto Weininger, the physicist Ludwig Boltzmann, three brothers of Ludwig Wittgenstein, a brother of Gustav Mahler, a son of Hugo von Hofmannsthal, the daughter of Arthur Schnitzler, and, most famously, the Emperor Franz Joseph's only son, Archduke Rudolf, who killed himself with his mistress at the imperial hunting lodge of Mayerling in 1889.[7] Gina Weinmann's brother, too, had committed suicide.

Benjamin Wright told me that Bettelheim talked of killing himself from at least 1950 on. "For one thing, he was afraid he was losing his sight. At one point, I was in the hospital with a blood clot in my leg and he was on the phone saying his eyes were bothering him and that he might commit suicide and here's what I should do at the school. I said, 'Couldn't you wait until I get out of the hospital?' He said, well, he was sure he was going blind, and he didn't want to be a burden to anybody." In the late 1960s, he would have a cataract operation on his left eye, and for many days lay recovering at home in bed with sandbags immobilizing his head, unable to read, unable to work but with hours to contemplate the worst.

Bettelheim criticized therapists for too often concentrating on psychopathology, for emphasizing the tragic and spectacular and slighting the common aspects of normal life; he urged his colleagues to "free themselves from their fascination with morbidity. . . ."[8] But he himself could not. In the late 1950s, Itamar Yahalom often sat alone with Bettelheim late into the night at the Orthogenic School. Yahalom had come to the United States from Israel, where he had worked with disturbed children, and, like so many other staff members, found the director both fascinating and trying. He was reluctant to disclose the details of the director's postmidnight unburdenings, but said: "I can tell you one thing: Bettelheim had a desperate desire to be immortal and was terrified of dying."

In late 1953, Paula Bettelheim died. She was almost seventy-six years old and had been living in Newark, New Jersey, where Margaret, Bruno's sister, now married to a hotel maître d' named Peter Abbot and living in Manhattan, could easily visit her. Days after the funeral, Bettelheim wrote to James Farrell that though his mother was old and tired her death had been unexpected and had caught him unprepared. "[I]ntellectually I'm quite realistic that it was probably best for her," he told his friend, "[but] emotionally it hit me quite hard."

Trude bore the brunt of her husband's emotional and physical complaints. She listened patiently for months, frequently in tears, as he struggled with the immediate aftereffects of his imprisonment in Dachau and Buchenwald. What spilled out in those days, or what else he revealed of his fears and insecurities over the years, remains locked in the couple's deeply private marriage of more than four decades, but her therapeutic ear was always open. "She was absolutely devoted to him," their friend Gusti Kollman told me, echoing the universal view of how the marriage worked. "She took care of him, like European men are taken care of by their women. She saw to it that he had food just the way he liked it, and made sure that when he slept nobody made a sound."

Over the years, she became as much his selfless mother as his devoted wife. Though Bruno had initially hesitated to marry this woman who had adored him almost from their first meeting in Vienna, he soon became totally dependent on her, and they grew extraordinarily close. In the eyes of some neighbors, they seemed deeply romantic, an Old World couple often seen strolling along

Kenwood Avenue arm in arm, like lovers in the Tiroler Garten, Trude sometimes in a dirndl. Bruno never let a special occasion pass unmarked and always kept his eye out for gifts he knew would delight her, sometimes buying a piece of antique jewelry months in advance and hiding it in a drawer until her birthday.[9] They did not share a bedroom, however. Trude slept in the second-floor master bedroom, Bruno down the hall, an arrangement explained partly by the late hours he kept and his need for air conditioning to combat his persistent allergies. But he and Gina had not shared a bedroom either, because of their uneasy sexual relationship, and Bruno's nightly isolation from Trude suggests a similar tension. Trude had entered therapy with Editha Sterba in Vienna in part to deal with what she regarded as her repressed sexuality; Bruno had grown up traumatized by his father's syphilis, in a home where his parents had slept apart for years.

In temperament, Trude was in most ways her husband's opposite, a sturdy woman who exuded the athletic strength of someone who had walked across mountains to freedom. Most of the time, she looked on life through a lens of cheerful optimism, even though she, too, had been robbed of her homeland, her aunt had killed herself, her parents, unlike her husband's mother and sister, had died in the Holocaust. Bruno may have listened sympathetically to Trude's anguish and helped her through these and other difficult times, but, whatever his attention, there was never a doubt about who came first. In moments of despair, Bruno often sighed, "Oh, God." Trude never ignored the sign. "If it turned out to be something that didn't seem to be so important really, she'd say, 'Now, come on, Bruno, don't be silly,'" Eric Bettelheim told me. "But there was never any doubt about the person who was uppermost in her mind on all occasions, including when she dealt with us children; we just knew, and if we didn't she told us, that in certain circumstances we just had to shut up and let her deal with our father. She would always come back to what our need was. But his needs always came first, and I think this was very, very important to him; it was essential." Emarina Vischer, who had known the couple since she worked with Trude at the Montessori School in Vienna, said Trude kept her hand on the floor where Bruno could stand on it.

Bettelheim's overpowering need was his work, which he told

his faculty colleague David Riesman provided the only real meaning in his life.[10] Fatherhood did not engage him, even as a subject;
his dialogues were with mothers, and on the few occasions he did
write about fathers he warned that they shouldn't try to be mothers. Husbands who shared infant care with their wives did so at
their peril, "because the male physiology and that part of his
psychology based on it are not geared to infant care." Fathers were
better advised to stay away from the changing table and instead
stand tall as models for their children by pursuing "man's function
in society: moral, economic, political."[11] When he wrote these
words, in 1956, he felt that the father had become too much of an
"also-ran" in the American family; eleven years later, he spelled
out the consequences in the *Ladies' Home Journal:* "We read about
all this increase in homosexuality and drug addiction, particularly
among boys, and you begin to wonder if that's not the result of
being born in a time when they're still expected to be strong, but
never had a very strong father."[12] In 1951, when Ruth was eight,
Naomi five, and Eric's birth not quite a year away, their father told
an audience that he had certain minimal standards that he expected his children to meet, "and that's all there is to it." When a
questioner asked what made him think his rules were necessarily
right, he said that did not matter: he had earned a certain obedi-
ence "because of the services [he had] rendered."[13]

Growing up under such a patriarch, who was often as despondent as he was dogmatic and stern, was not easy. By the time
Bruno came down to breakfast on most weekday mornings, Ruth,
Naomi, and Eric had departed for school, and Trude for the
Chicago Child Care Society, the neighborhood foster-care and
adoption agency where she worked from 1946 to 1965. For years
his breakfast consisted of cornflakes, but when cereal proved to be
a cause of his indigestion the menu changed to a soft-boiled egg,
toast and tea. These were served by Lillian Brown, who arrived
from the nearby Negro ghetto to clean the house and over more
than twenty years would become a second mother to the children,
especially Naomi. It was Trude, however, who left work each day
early enough to comb the aisles of the Hyde Park Co-op or to
pick up some fish at Jesselson's or some pastry at Nachmann's and
come home to prepare dinner, which Bruno expected to be on
the table at 7:00 P.M. sharp.

A friend of Ruth's, who occasionally had dinner with the family, said that Bruno arrived at the table like a general, and the troops saluted.[14] He and Trude regarded the evening meal as sacrosanct, the one period when they could be together to hear about their children's day and talk about their own. Mostly, the dialogue turned on their own work, Trude describing her cases and Bruno discussing the Orthogenic School and the other facets of his demanding professional life. This conversational lopsidedness led Naomi to cease speaking at the table, an "absolutely willful" shutdown prompted by her feeling that her father had no real interest in what she and her siblings had on their minds. Martha Friedberg, Jean Friedberg's sister-in-law, lived across the street from the Bettelheims and was friendly with the family; she recalled that during Naomi's high school years she never opened her mouth at the table, "as if she were in a Bergman film. Bruno and Trude thought she was crazy. She wasn't. She had a fine record at school and lots of friends; she just didn't want to talk to her parents."[15] One thing Naomi feared, like the children and staff at the Orthogenic School and her father's students, was attack. "By and large with women, and many men whom he did not see as his equals or superiors, my father could be quite brutal in arguments, and could devastate people without regard to the merits of their position," Noami told me. "I probably had experienced this at an early age, or saw it with my sister or my mother or others, and I had no interest in going through the same thing myself. Perhaps it was overcompensation for his insecurity, but he had to come out looking the best; the object of the game was always to make the other person look like a fool."

After dessert, Bruno would ascend to his small bedroom, where he had a desk, and read counselors' reports or lie down for a brief rest; then he would return to the school, leaving Trude to get the children to bed. It was she and Lillian Brown who infused the household with warmth, twin female engines who, like the mostly female Orthogenic School counselors, were expected by their foreman to do the heavy lifting, emotional and otherwise. In public, Bruno occasionally made sympathetic noises about the plight of women in a male-dominated society.[16] Privately, he said that the "stupidity" of the women's liberation movement appalled him. Women should serve their men in bed like Scheherazade, and should concentrate on their purpose in life, which was to have and raise children, whether they worked outside the home, like Trude, or not.[17]

Trude was "strudel herself,"[18] a sometimes disheveled *Hausfrau* with seemingly bottomless energy who served up hearty meals of meat loaf, pork chops, and beef Stroganoff, brought flowers to the table from her cherished backyard garden, and welcomed her children's friends with snacks at the kitchen table, seldom complaining about their boisterousness. Her husband's arrival home was "like a cold front blowing in," recalled Matthew Piers, Gerhart and Maria's son and one of Eric's high-school friends; Trude would warn the boys to settle down, and after Bruno entered a pall often enveloped the house. "Eric was a very bubbly, lively kid; his manner would change, and he instantly would become subdued; the whole household would. I don't ever recall Bruno sticking his head in the door and saying, 'Hi.' "

Deirdre English, who, like the Bettelheim children, attended the Laboratory School, the University of Chicago's elite academy for the primary and secondary grades, babysat for Eric on several occasions when he was about twelve. Trude would greet her and say that Dr. Bettelheim was upstairs in his study and was not to be disturbed unless there was an emergency; she would then tell the teenager what to make Eric for dinner and leave for the evening. "I found it very peculiar," recalled English, who wondered why a twelve-year-old needed a sitter with his father in the house, a father who did not emerge from his labors to join them for dinner or take a break to say good night when Eric went to bed.

In eulogizing his father, Eric Bettelheim said that being his son had been a "challenge," but it was probably less of one than his sisters faced. They were nine and six years his senior, and grew into adolescence during their father's struggle to establish himself and make the family financially secure; by the time Eric turned ten, in 1962, Bruno was known throughout the world. Ruth was in college at the University of Chicago and no longer living at home, and Naomi would soon be off to the University of Wisconsin, leaving Eric prince of the roost. He fondly recalled playing pounce, canasta, and double solitaire with his father, as Bruno remembered playing cards with his father at Neubaugasse 66; Eric also developed an interest in collecting old coins and went with his father to stamp and coin exhibitions. He would eventually become a lawyer, but in high school he was briefly drawn toward medicine, and Bruno found him a used microscope and an old lab table. "It was very handy and exciting to have them. He encouraged me whenever I expressed an interest. I was not a particularly good student when I was younger; I only began to become serious at university age. But he didn't push me. What he communicated was not demands but just a wonderful sense of confidence."

Such understanding is reflected in a letter Bettelheim wrote to his friend Morris Janowitz when Ruth was trying to choose a college. He had urged her to go to the University of Michigan, but she opted for the University of Chicago. "I guess that her old man wanted her to go [to Michigan] was enough to have her decide against it. After all, we too revolted against our parents, and a revolt against the school they suggest is so relatively minor that one must hope that it will stop there." [19] He clearly took a fatherly pride in his children, telling his friend David Rapaport, who had encouraged Naomi's interest in chess by sending her a book on the game, that "pretty soon she will be able to beat me if I don't watch out." [20] At the end of his life, he told another friend, "My three kids are so bright that they would have made it whatever their parents did." [21] Still, he rarely spent the kind of time with his children that many other neighborhood fathers did with theirs; the Lincoln Park Zoo or White Sox games at Comiskey Park or family picnics were not on his crowded agenda. He and Trude occasionally took the children to a concert or the ballet, where Bruno would comment for their amusement on audience members whose fancy dress he thought unusual or striking; and on long car trips he sometimes distracted them by finding pictures in the cloud formations. But for Naomi at least, the overwhelming experience of her childhood was that "he was not there." In an oft-told family story, the Bettelheims are visiting friends in California and Bruno is left to mind Naomi while the others go out. When she begins to paint the walls with the contents of her diaper her father is unfazed and remains in his rocking chair happily reading until Trude returns to deal with the young artist and her canvas.

Benjamin Wright said that Bettelheim kept Ruth, Naomi, and Eric away from the Orthogenic School because he feared it would make the young residents envious, a feeling inevitably reciprocated. Eric told me that he felt great sympathy for the troubled young residents at the Orthogenic School, and admired his father's dedication to them; but he also felt jealous, especially when Bruno would buy an expensive antique or a piece of furniture for the school.

The Bettelheims initially furnished their own home in the Scandinavian modern style popular in the 1950s, but as the émigrés grew more confident in their new country, and more prosperous, the Spartan blond look gave way to the rich texture of their European roots. Perhaps nothing symbolized this transition more than the late-eighteenth-century Dutch display cabinet in the living room, a vitrine reminiscent of Freud's and similarly full of *objets,* like small Egyptian vases and Ashanti coins. Many of these and other pieces Bettelheim acquired while poking around antique shops and galleries, an avocation that by his death had produced a trove of more than 360 items.

By the early 1960s, Bruno had replaced the windows flanking the brick fireplace with bookcases, dimming a living room already darkened by an Oriental rug and the somber mood of *Helping Hands,* a signed Käthe Kollwitz lithograph, and the soon-to-be-sold Schiele. Bruno did not collect records, but he carefully selected those he had: Beethoven and Schumann, Schubert *Lieder* sung by Dietrich Fischer-Diskau, Bach played by Pablo Casals, performances by the Budapest String Quartet, works by Schoenberg and Mahler. A baby-grand piano in the living room, which Naomi played for a time, added to the Old World flavor. Occasionally Bruno descended to a workbench in the basement where he repaired an electric switch or did some modest woodwork. His years in the lumber business had made him quite good with his hands, but he was not a person who bought tools. His extracurricular passions were reading and scouting for antiques.

Because Bettelheim spent so many evenings at the Orthogenic School, he and Trude had less time for social engagements than most of their neighbors, but they did attend the Chicago Symphony at Orchestra Hall and performances at the Civic Opera

House. Even after these events, Bruno sometimes returned to the school and, still in his tuxedo, gathered with the staff until nearly midnight, talking of the Verdi or Mozart he had just heard and comparing it with an *Otello* or a *Don Giovanni* he had seen at the Staatsoper in the 1930s.[22] Despite his sensitive stomach, he relished sitting down at The Bakery, a restaurant on Chicago's Near North Side where his friend Louis Szathmary, the Hungarian chef-owner, seduced him with such tasty hazards as smoked-pork soup with liver dumplings, a boiled-beef dish called *Tafelspitz,* crisp home-fried potatoes, and thin crepes filled with creamed spinach and Swiss cheese. "Cabbage did not agree with him," recalled Szathmary, "but he loved it, and when he smelled red cabbage he would say, 'Can I have a little plate? If I live three weeks less for a wonderful plate of good cabbage, the world will not lose too much.' " He took the same position on desserts, calling Szathmary in advance to say he would like to be surprised with *Salzburger Nockerl* or *Kaiserschmarrn,* an "emperor's trifle" made of large, buttery pancakes scrambled into bite-size pieces and then piled high with raspberries and powdered sugar.

When the Bettelheims entertained at home, Bruno was the charming Viennese host, hovering over the guests and ensuring that all glasses were full, while Trude, whom he called his "good wife," labored in the kitchen preparing a sumptuous meal, which she often served as a buffet. Such evenings were *gemütlich* in part because Bruno was usually more benign with friends than in his classes, in staff meetings, or on the lecture platform. "He was considerate, kind; you didn't feel that he was playing Herr Professor Doktor," said Sophie Bloom, whose husband, Benjamin, was a fellow faculty member whom Bettelheim highly respected. However welcoming he was, however, his parties rarely passed without his taking the floor. "Even in his house he tended to dominate, with his Erich von Stroheim look; he loved argument, loved exchanges," recalled the novelist and English professor Richard Stern, another faculty colleague. Trude seemed to have an innate sense of when her husband had held forth too long and, with a roll of her eyes and a gentle, "Oh, Bruno," usually managed to end his monologues.[23]

The high point of the Bettelheims' socializing came at

Christmas, a holiday that always closed the distance between Bruno and his children. The family went downtown to Marshall Field's to see the tree and have lunch or tea and on the annual expedition to pick out their own tree. It was the talk of Kenwood Avenue because it was decked not only with unique ornaments that Bruno had picked up in his travels but with candles, a Viennese tradition some neighbors found "hellishly dangerous."[24] On Christmas Eve, Trude lighted the wicks and the children were hustled out of the living room while their parents surrounded the trees with presents. At the sound of the Vienna Boys Choir or some other music emanating from the phonograph they rushed in to find electric trains, ice skates, Steiff animals, skis, or straw donkeys that Bruno had carried on his lap on a plane ride back from Mexico. Once wrapping paper covered the floor and the candles had flickered down, the family repaired to the dining room for Christmas dinner, after which Bruno returned to the school to help prepare for his other children's celebration the next morning.

The family also gave an annual Christmas party for the school's staff, in advance of which Trude cooked for what seemed like days. As his guests arrived, Bruno plied them with fish-house punch, a potent mix of fruit juices, rum, and gin that worked to banish whatever anxiety they felt at being under their master's roof, and the conviviality usually lasted until well past midnight. These Americans were also impressed by the candles. "This is remarkable, Dr. B," Dennis Duginske told his boss; "you have to come to a Jewish home to see what a real Christmas tree looks like." In the 1960s, Bettelheim sometimes feted the staff at The Bakery, taking over the restaurant at lunchtime, when it wasn't open to the public. After singing carols in English and German, the gathering sat down to a menu of venison, *Hasenpfeffer,* Wiener schnitzel, and roast goose as Bruno table-hopped like everyone's "wonderful daddy."[25]

After Bruno celebrated Christmas morning at the school, all the Bettelheims drove to the North Shore suburb of Highland Park and continued the holiday with Gina and Peter Weinmann and their daughter, Catherine. "I knew the Weinmanns up until age sixteen," Eric told me. "They were another Austrian couple of my parents' generation, obviously old familiars from Vienna. We went to their house on Christmas Day, they came to us on

Thanksgiving, and on other occasions. Cathy and Naomi were good friends. Then, one day at dinner, someone said something en passant and finally the penny dropped and I realized that Gina had been married to my father. I was angry that I hadn't been told. Naomi said to me, 'Well, of course you knew, everyone knew.' But the fact is, nobody had bothered to tell me. They just assumed I knew, and it was no longer a matter of concern to anyone." The two couples, whose reconfigured marriages had been performed by the same judge several months apart in 1941, established a relationship right from the start, when the Weinmanns had settled in Hyde Park for a few years before moving north. Bruno had "always gotten along very well"[26] with Peter in Vienna, and despite Gina's defection the two men remained friends, bonded, like their wives and many others who had fled the Nazis, by an upheaval that dwarfed any marital awkwardness. When Naomi was born in 1945, it was Peter who took Trude to the hospital. In 1947, the couples took a summer vacation together, traveling to Estes Park in Colorado with their three small girls.

Naomi and Catherine, who were the same age, often pretended they were cousins, and on many overnights giggled over Bruno and Gina's former status, thinking the whole business quite risqué.[27] As Bruno had gravitated to the Buxbaum's apartment in Vienna to be with his cousin Edith and to escape his sister and the oppressive atmosphere of the Bettelheim home, the two girls looked for comfort in each other's families. Naomi, caught between a father who favored her older sister and a mother who doted on her younger brother, envied Catherine's position as an only child; she sometimes fantasized about living with the Weinmanns, where she was always welcomed by Gina, who was impressed by her precocity, and where the soft-spoken Peter was the antithesis of her self-involved, often domineering father. "When I was a child, I always viewed it as if I had three mothers: Trude, Lillian, and Gina," Naomi said. "We both idealized what the other had," Catherine Weinmann told me. She felt intellectually inferior as a child and admired Naomi's considerable verbal skills, an articulateness that it seemed to her all Bettelheims possessed as a matter of birth. "I felt I just couldn't keep up with them."

By the time the Weinmanns moved to Highland Park in

1950, Gina had begun to practice psychotherapy, and Peter was well on his way to becoming a distinguished oral pathologist at the University of Illinois. But by the end of the decade he was dying of cancer, and during the months of his illness Gina and Catherine often stayed with the Bettelheims to be closer to the hospital. When Peter died in 1960, just after his sixty-fourth birthday, Bruno was eager to fold Gina and Catherine into his extended family and encouraged them to move to Hyde Park, where he could better look after them. They didn't, and Gina soon settled in San Francisco, but Bruno kept in touch, bestowing the kind of generosity that had long been typical of him and that for many mitigated his more difficult behavior. Both he and Trude made substantial contributions to Catherine's support when she was in training as a child therapist at Anna Freud's clinic in Hampstead in the late 1970s. She had been fifteen when her father died, and in the months that followed she sometimes hoped that the strong man who sat at the head of the family she so envied would take over Peter's role. Like so many others, she saw Bruno as larger than life, a forceful father-therapist who knew the answers and could envelop her with care. But as she grew older, she began to see that he was not always right, and that he found it impossible ever to admit he was wrong. "I loved him, but he was a very flawed man."

CHAPTER ELEVEN
Autism

IN THE SUMMER OF 1955, Bruno Bettelheim asked the Ford
Foundation for $673,200 to study autism and the dynamics of
early ego development. He proposed admitting to the Orthogenic
School up to fifteen autistic children between the ages of six and
eight and following them for seven years. He argued that most
studies of such children had been based either on adult patients'
memories of their early years or on interpretations of infant behavior based on intermittent observations in psychiatrists' offices. By
treating autistic children around the clock for several years, he
hoped to learn what therapy worked best to break through their
armor and build their egos. He told the foundation that he also
planned to study his counselors with equal intensity, the better to
understand their role in the therapeutic process.[1]

The use of the term "autism," from *autos,* the Greek word
for "self," dates back at least to 1912, when the Swiss psychiatrist
Eugen Bleuler used it to describe schizophrenic thinking divorced
from both logic and reality. It was not until the mid-1940s, as
Bettelheim was taking over the school, that the word came to
be applied primarily to children with certain specific abnormal
behavioral characteristics. This was the result of coincidental investigations by two Austrian psychiatrists: Hans Asperger, whose
work in Vienna would remain largely unknown outside Europe
for more than four decades, and Leo Kanner, who had emigrated
to the United States in 1924. Kanner, who settled in Baltimore
as director of the children's psychiatric service at Johns Hopkins
Hospital, first attracted wide professional attention in 1935 with
the publication of *Child Psychiatry,* a textbook that would go
through four editions and fourteen printings by 1972.

Kanner's signal contribution came in 1943, in a paper that described eleven children who had come to his clinic over several years and who, from infancy, had seemed cut off from their parents. These strange youngsters existed in their own, often impenetrable world, and Kanner was the first clinician in the United States to make the case that this behavior constituted a unique syndrome, which he called "early infantile autism." The three main features that Kanner saw in his eleven patients continue to define autism today: (1) a social impairment characterized by an aloofness and lack of reciprocity; (2) a failure to communicate manifested by muteness, echolalia, or an inability to get intonations right, and (3) repetitious, stereotyped behavior, like rocking and twiddling in small children and the preoccupation with, say, railroad schedules in older ones. In the 1980s, as Hans Asperger's research and ideas became more widely known, some clinicians extended the definition of autism to include children who could talk fluently, albeit oddly, by age five, and who became at least superficially well adapted and occasionally quite successful adults, though such "Asperger syndrome" cases "tend to remain supremely egocentric and isolated."[2]

Today, both the medical and therapeutic communities agree that autism is a developmental disorder originating in genetic fault, brain insult, or brain disease.[3] Both Asperger and Kanner suspected that the illness might prove to have such a neurological root; but they lacked conclusive proof, and in the beginning Kanner felt that a child's psychological environment might also play an important role. His initial findings convinced him that almost all parents of autistic children were highly intelligent, self-absorbed, preoccupied with their careers, and emotionally cold, keeping their autistic children "neatly in a refrigerator that did not defrost."[4] He came to regret this chilling metaphor, because it gave rise to a persistent belief that he blamed so-called refrigerator mothers for causing autism. He never took such a hard line; in fact, in 1941 he had published *In Defense of Mothers: How to Bring Up Children in Spite of the More Zealous Psychologists*. Still, during the three decades when Bettelheim ran the Orthogenic School, the belief that parents were the devils in the netherworld of autism held wide sway, partly because of Kanner's early research but also because parents, and especially mothers, had come to be demonized by many psychotherapists. Bettelheim told the Ford Foundation that, besides treating his autistic patients, he intended to explore what their parents had done "wrong" in raising them.

In his grant application, Bettelheim acknowledged Leo Kanner by name but cited none of his research, which by 1955 included at least five more papers on various aspects of autism, including a report on the first hundred cases he had seen. Bettelheim said he knew of no intensive longitudinal studies of children with the syndrome, this despite the fact that in the summer of 1954 Kanner and a Johns Hopkins colleague had presented a paper with follow-up data on forty-two autistic children who had reached an average age of fourteen years.[5] Bettelheim did not specify in his proposal, the substance of which ran seven double-spaced typewritten pages, how he planned to pursue any of the research goals he had set for himself, nor did he offer any evidence to support his claim that he had already succeeded in helping a few autistic children in the decade he had directed the school. He did not say, as he had so many times, that he had treated one or more autistic children who had lived with him and his first wife in Vienna; but he did employ Editha Sterba, Patsy's analyst, in his cause.

In 1933, Sterba had published "Ein abnormes Kind" in the *Zeitschrift für psychoanalytische Pädagogik;* three years later, this two-part monograph about a boy she called Herbert, who had come to her when he was five years old with a diagnosis of infantile psychosis, appeared in English under the title "An Abnormal Child."[6] Bettelheim told the foundation that this article was the result of studies in which he had participated in Vienna, a claim for which there is no confirmation and which Gina Weinmann said is not true. By manufacturing this latest credential, the former lumber dealer and student of art history now succeeded in appropriating the work and prestige of a woman whose care for Patsy —along with his former wife's—he had long ago commandeered as his own. Ford officials could have checked Bettelheim's assertion about "An Abnormal Child" by contacting Sterba in Detroit, where she had settled with her husband, Richard, after they emigrated to the United States. But few were likely to question the claims and credentials of the author of *Love Is Not Enough* and the just-published *Truants from Life,* especially after Lawrence A. Kimpton, who had succeeded Hutchins as chancellor of the University of Chicago in 1951, told the foundation that Bettelheim's work with disturbed children was "almost unmatched in this country."[7]

In November, the foundation sent two members of its advisory group on mental health to the Orthogenic School: Merton Gill, a training analyst from Berkeley, California, who would become a much-honored academic psychoanalyst, and Seymour Kety, associate director in charge of research at the National Institute of Mental Health. Kety, who wrote the report on this site visit, found Bettelheim "a charming and sagacious individual with a great capacity of human understanding which must make him an outstanding therapist."[8] He said that the director believed that proper training based on human relationships can reverse the autistic process and bring about remarkable improvement. Kety was convinced, on the basis of what he saw, that such gains did take place at the school, though in his report he gave no indication of what it was that persuaded him; he said he took Bettelheim's word that without such intervention autistic children either died or ended up in mental institutions. That Bettelheim had no research design to test this hypothesis did not trouble his visitor, who felt the grant proposal's value lay in active observation and "the formulation of hunches" that could be tested by others. Kety was, however, bothered by the makeup of the staff. "I would be happier," he wrote,

> if there were a greater amount of scientific sophistication and rigor among them. They appear to me to be highly motivated and devoted youngsters, some of them with training in the natural sciences, but I did not perceive a carry-over of scientific rigor . . . to their own work and I feel that much of what they see is selectively seen on the basis of their own hypotheses or those which they absorbed from Bettelheim. For these reasons, I do not believe that this group is capable of objectively testing their own hypotheses.[9]

After stating this misgiving, Kety urged the foundation to make a grant.

In June 1956, Ford gave Bettelheim $342,500, to be spread out over five years. Though the gift reduced his original request almost by half, it was a considerable boon—the equivalent of $1.3 million in 1996—to a school with some forty children. The university announced the grant in a press release that was picked up by both the *Sun-Times* and the *Tribune;* the latter ran Bettelheim's picture. "Your success in obtaining this support, and additional substantial support from other sources, is indeed notable," Francis Chase, chairman of the department of education, wrote to his colleague. "It is not often that a distinguished scholar is also a gifted administrator and fund-raiser. . . . We are proud to have you as a member of the Department of Education." [10]

The Ford Foundation required that Bettelheim submit annual summaries describing his progress, and in July 1957 he reported that, during the grant's first twelve months, the school had examined fifty children and admitted six boys and six girls who "no doubt [suffered from] childhood schizophrenia, autistic type." The neatness of this gender distribution offered grounds for suspicion, since Kanner's research had shown that autism occurred primarily in firstborn males and that the ratio of boys to girls afflicted was about four to one,[11] a disproportion that still obtains.[12] Nonetheless, Ford accepted Bettelheim's numbers, though school records show that he had actually admitted ten new children, seven girls and three boys. Of this group, one nine-year-old boy and one seven-year-old girl arrived classified as autistic.[13]

Despite this diagnostic legerdemain, two years into the grant Bettelheim was lamenting to David Rapaport that he had "so little to show" the foundation.[14] Still, he told his friend that he remained "quite excited" about the possibility that, given enough time to work with the children, he might be able to provide a solid body of clinical evidence to support Erik Erikson's theoretical formulations about human growth and the life cycle, as expressed in his 1950 book, *Childhood and Society.* Bettelheim hoped that he might even be able to do for early development what Erikson had done for adolescence, and did his best to indicate that he was making at least some progress in what he called, in his 1958 report to Ford, his "intensive study of twelve autistic children."

In this second annual summary, Bettelheim supplied vignettes describing the behavior of several children and offered tentative clinical observations. He suggested, for example, that the dish towel twiddled by one boy offered a kind of dream screen that represented the hallucinated breast; or, alternatively, that manipulating the towel allowed the child to pretend "a megalomanic self-sufficiency of the body and its organs." He also reported that George Perkins, the school's principal psychiatric consultant, and the anthropologist Jules Henry, had found in studying the families of autistic children that the literature on the subject needed revision.[15] He did not specify what literature, or even generalize about the direction the revisions should take. Nor did he provide any details of Perkins and Henry's joint investigation, beyond quoting his colleagues as saying that the characteristic attitude of mothers was one of either "towering rage" against everyone in their families, or "humiliation run rampant" and directed mostly against the children who became autistic. As for fathers, they seemed to show "uniformly an implacable paranoid distance from their wives." Where Perkins and Henry made these statements, and on what evidence, Bettelheim did not say.

However genuine Bettelheim's desire to help autistic children may have been, he recognized from the start that the novelty and mystery of the disorder gave it considerable allure,[16] and that his gift for retailing case histories only augmented this glamour. To help bring his stories alive, he often illustrated them with the children's drawings. In 1952, well before the appearance of his lengthy account of Mary in *Truants from Life,* he had published "Schizophrenic Art: A Case Study" in *Scientific American.* The magazine ran twelve of Mary's drawings, which took up more space than Bettelheim's text, and which he said depicted her march toward health; i.e., picture three contained no people but only a house against a dark background and was thus "gloomy," whereas picture twelve, which Mary drew not long before leaving the school, portrayed children at play in the sand and water, was called "Fun on the Beach," and showed that "Mary could now have fun as normal children do."[17] In 1959, in his third Ford report, Bettelheim told the tale of a twelve-year-old, nonspeaking autistic girl who after "a decade of deepest regression" progressed from purposeless scribbling to the clear representation of faces and figures after only a few months at the school. He illustrated this extraordinary headway by interspersing ten of her drawings throughout the report, the last one of a child made whole.[18] More drawings accompanied the fourth annual summary, these made by a child Bettelheim called Dick; they putatively demonstrated his "utter autism" upon entering the school and the steady improvement that followed.[19]

Few of Bettelheim's cases proved more riveting than "Joey: A 'Mechanical Boy,' " which also appeared in *Scientific American*.[20] The magazine's editor, Gerard Piel, was Agnes Piel Crane's nephew and Patsy's cousin, but Piel would not meet the man he regarded as his relative's healer until the mid-1950s, when he came to the University of Chicago on a lecture visit and sat in on one of Bettelheim's classes in Judd 126. "What he did was explore all the horrendous pop ideas of why people study psychology," Piel told me. "Did they think that an understanding of how human beings behave will give them more power over other human beings? The students began to get madder and madder and demonstrated to him all the points he was making. Was there anyone in the classroom, he asked, who was interested in the sanctity and agony of the individual? It was a fabulous experience, and none of the people in that room will ever forget it. I had never seen a teacher perform like this; I felt a moral force emanating from a really great man." When Bettelheim raised the possibility of an article about Joey, Piel was receptive; it appeared in March 1959.

"Joey was a child who had been robbed of his humanity," Bettelheim declared in his opening paragraph. His parents had "completely ignored" him. His mother did not want to nurse him or take care of him in any other way; his father punished him when he cried. He was healthy at birth but soon became frail and irritable. Once he learned to speak, he talked only to himself. "At an early date he became preoccupied with machinery, including an old electric fan which he could take apart and put together again with surprising deftness." He developed compulsive defenses, which he called his "preventions," and began drinking through elaborate piping systems made of straws, saying liquids had to be pumped into him. Bettelheim said that three months before Joey entered the Orthogenic School, at age nine, he had attempted suicide. By this time, he had frozen himself in the image

of a machine, presenting what Bettelheim called "a classic example
. . . of infantile autism."

Bettelheim described how Joey could eat only when his digestive system was electrified by an imaginary wire plugged into
an imaginary outlet; how he often turned himself on and shifted
into higher and higher gears; how a machine called the "criticizer"
kept him from saying words with unpleasant connotations; and
how, during his first year at the school, he could defecate only
while squatting on top of the toilet and touching the wall with
one hand, in which he held the vacuum tubes that powered his
bowels. Joey rigged his dorm bed as a kind of car machine that
would "live him" as he slept. A photograph accompanied the
article showing this complex support system, with its makeshift
"battery," "carburetor," and "wheel" taped about the boy's bed. As
with Mary, the magazine published several of Joey's drawings,
three of which Bettelheim said demonstrated his growing autonomy: the first showed an unoccupied electric car, the second a
similar vehicle with a passive driver, the third a figure at the wheel
who had "gained control of the machine." The final drawing in
the text was of a tree that appears to have birds in it; the caption
described this as a gentle landscape painted by Joey at age twelve,
"after his recovery," when he had learned to express his feelings
and no longer felt he was a machine.

The same month that Bettelheim recounted this latest triumph, he also diagnosed some children he had never treated or
even met. He said that, in the fall of 1957, William Fielding
Ogburn, a professor of sociology at the University of Chicago,
had sent him a manuscript about a six-year-old Indian boy named
Parasram whose parents claimed he had been stolen from them at
eighteen months by wolves. Ogburn had read about this child
while in India and—after visiting him, interviewing his parents,
and talking to the man who had actually found him—had concluded that Parasram had not been raised by wolves. "Since he was
familiar with the work of the Orthogenic School," Bettelheim
wrote, "he wondered if this child might be like some of the
children we work with, and he invited my comments." [21] In March
1959, the *American Journal of Sociology* published Ogburn's "The
Wolf Boy of Agra," followed by a Bettelheim article maintaining

that such children, whom the literature called "feral," in fact suf-fered "from the severest form of infantile autism." [22]

Bettelheim said that as he read Ogburn's manuscript "the blinders fell from [his] eyes" and led him to reinterpret the famous case of the wolf girls of Mindapore. In 1929, the Reverend J. A. L. Singh had reported finding these "hideous beings" in a wolf den inside a white-ant mound two stories high. He named them Amala and Kamala and kept a diary describing their behavior as he tried to raise them at his orphanage in Mindapore, India. After reading Ogburn, Bettelheim decided that Singh's accounts of the girls' behavior were accurate enough but that his attributing it to wolf-rearing was not. He likened Singh's story of finding Amala and Kamala in the lair to "the wild fantasies we spun about the pasts of our autistic children when we first met them—speculation originating in our efforts to find emotionally acceptable explanations for [their] nearly inexplicable and wholly unacceptable behavior." Bettelheim maintained that this conjecture flowed from the psychological need for explanations as well as a narcissistic un-willingness to admit that children who exhibit animallike behavior could have pasts similar to those of normal human beings. Because of these defenses, he said, everything Singh wrote about the girls' wolf-den origins was believed; critical voices were silenced, the mind became an "unreliable instrument." [23]

Bettelheim now gave his readers an eye-popping tour of the Orthogenic School. His autistic patients had not been raised by wolves, he pointed out, but many of them exhibited animallike behavior: urinating and defecating in their pants "without so much as knowing it"; tearing off their clothes and running about naked; screaming or howling instead of talking; insisting on raw vegetables at meals and throwing violent tantrums if denied them.

> Others lick salt for hours, but only from their own hands. Others
> . . . build dens in dark corners or closets, sleep nowhere else, and
> prefer spending all day and all night there. Some build caves out of
> blankets, mattresses, or other suitable objects, . . . and at least two
> of them would eat only if they could first carry their food into
> their self-created caves or dens, where they would then eat without
> using utensils. [24]

He said that some of the children, upon seeing an animal in the neighborhood, responded "as though they had found a dear, long-lost friend." On spotting a dog, one girl fell on all fours and began howling "like a wolf" and snapping her teeth.[25] He said most of the children bared their teeth when angry and that one counselor, unnamed, had to seek medical treatment more than a dozen times in a year because of bites by a child he called Anna.

Bettelheim often dismissed requests to visit the Orthogenic School by saying that he was not running a zoo.[26] "Feral Children and Autistic Children," as his article was titled, described a school that was a menagerie of often dangerous child-beasts. That most children bite occasionally, or eat with their hands at some point, or reject clothes, or build dens of blankets and card tables, or bark back at dogs and treat kittens like long-lost friends did not impede Bettelheim's theoretical advance. He wrote that, like the wolf children, "psychotic" children have acute sensations of smell and touch, that "autistic" children rely little on sight, and that "schizophrenic" children often behave as if they were insensitive to heat and cold. Standing on this pontific foundation, he maintained that, since "The Wolf Boy of Agra," the wolf girls of Mindapore, and other such creatures in the literature behaved so much like the autistic bipeds in his care, they must be autistic as well. His "guess" was that they had been emotionally, and perhaps physically, abandoned.

> Our own experience suggests . . . that [Amala and Kamala] were probably utterly unacceptable to their parents for one reason or another. This is characteristic of all autistic children, no matter of what age; the parents manage to disengage themselves from them by placing them in an institution (as is the usual case in the United States today), or by setting them out to fend for themselves in the wilderness, or, the most likely explanation, by not pursuing when they run away.[27]

In short, Bettelheim concluded, "feral children seem to be produced not when wolves behave like mothers but when mothers behave like non-humans." [28]

Along with published tales of mechanical boys and children crawling around the Orthogenic School on all fours, Bettelheim made his case with film. In 1960, the *Armstrong Circle Theater,* a popular CBS television series, portrayed life at the Orthogenic School in a nationally broadcast docudrama called *The Hidden World.*[29] Actors played Dr. B and two of his key staff members, Florence White and Anna Lukes; the writer visited the Orthogenic School while preparing the script and Bettelheim himself coached the actress who played the deeply disturbed child on whom the story focused. The tenor of the film is typified by its ending, an exchange between a new counselor, Martie, and a resident named Andy.

MARTIE
Where are you going?

ANDY
Home . . . for a week.

MARTIE
Good, Andy.

ANDY
I told you I'd go home some day.

MARTIE
Yes . . . you did. The first day I was here.

ANDY
Well, I know this place . . . that's all.
It's good for everybody.

MARTIE
I guess it is.

ANDY
Did you hear about George Waring?

MARTIE
I don't think so.

ANDY
He was here before you came. For six
years. Now he's a junior in Michigan
. . . and the second in his class. It's
just a good place here. . . . that's all.
Even for the counselors.

Dr. B was soon screening this hour-long testimonial as part of an optimistic progress report at a fund-raising gathering.[30]

Bettelheim also had hired moviemakers to photograph some of the children on a regular basis[31] and in 1957 he asked the Ford Foundation to let him make this film project "a significant part" of his research;[32] the foundation agreed, and by early 1960 he was in New York City presenting a slide-and-film show for Ford officials, hoping in part that this depiction of his work would persuade them to give him additional money after the original grant expired in the summer of 1961. The films and stills shot at the Orthogenic School during Bettelheim's years as director repose in his archive at the University of Chicago. It is impossible to assess them, because his estate, though it has made most of his papers available, decided that the photographic material raised questions of privacy for former residents, and closed it to researchers.

One of the films in the archive is *Doris,* a sixteen-millimeter black-and-white sound portrait that Bettelheim showed at the Ford Foundation and also screened in the following weeks at a Chicago Psychoanalytic Society meeting and at the American Psychoanalytic Association's annual gathering in Atlantic City, New Jersey. "Stirrings of life and self-consciousness in a girl of 7 were dramatically portrayed here today by a noted psychologist," a *New York Times* reporter wrote after seeing the film at the APA conference. The film showed a pretty, sturdy child who Bettelheim said had been emaciated and dehydrated when she arrived at the Orthogenic School, a waif "frozen in immobility, isolation and desperation." The cause of this autistic state, Bettelheim told his audience, was the total rejection of Doris by her mother. He said that the child had come to him from a mental institution and was so passive that she had not fed herself for four years. Within two days at his school, however, she was picking up and eating raisins placed on her bedspread by her counselor. Once again he cited artwork to show progress, telling his audience that Doris initially painted only in black, covering up intricate patterns she had made, but gradually began painting in colors.[33]

Ford Foundation officials said they liked the films and Bettelheim's work in general, but their approval did not translate into additional funds.[34] The foundation did accede to his compromise request to spread whatever money remained from the original grant over an additional two years, so he could follow his autistic children through what he said were "very important steps in their development."[35] This extension was a mixed blessing, for Bettelheim had come to regard Ford's demand for annual reports as a burdensome nuisance and often groused that never again would he get himself into such a bind.[36] The director had never had to put up with accountability before, and would never have to again —not from parents, most of whom were awed, if not terrified by him; not by social agencies, which were similarly cowed by his reputation and personality; and not by the University of Chicago, which over three decades never established a board of visitors or any other formal oversight committee to monitor Bettelheim and the Orthogenic School. Bettelheim's sixth report, which ran less than two double-spaced pages, noted, "While we made no startling new discoveries during this year, we were able to collect and consolidate further evidence to support the theoretical statements previously formulated and to refine them considerably."[37] Six months after the seventh, and final, report was due in the summer of 1963, Bettelheim apologized for being tardy in a one-page letter. He enclosed another case history, which he hoped would do until "it shall be my privilege to present you with a book length printed report."[38]

THE EMPTY FORTRESS appeared in 1967. Subtitled *Infantile Autism and the Birth of the Self,* it was Bettelheim's summa theologica on the subject, and he assured his readers at the outset that he was well qualified to lead them through the complex terrain ahead. He told them that, in the 1930s,

> I had living with me one, and for a few years two, autistic children. To make this a therapeutic experience for them, many conditions of life in our home had to be adjusted to their needs. This was my initial experience with trying to create a very special environment that might undo emotional isolation in a child and build up personality.[39]

Having once again said that Patsy was autistic, a diagnosis that no qualified medical doctor or trained psychotherapist had made, and multiplied her by two, Bettelheim next told his readers that the volume they held in their hands did not derive primarily from introspection but was "based on the findings of trained observers. . . ."[40] Just the opposite was true, as Seymour Kety had worried in his site-visit report for the Ford Foundation over a decade before. Throughout the years of the grant and beyond, Bettelheim continued to hire counselors and teachers in their early twenties or younger; at best, most of these initiates had read a psychology text or two as undergraduates and, as Kety had put it, much of what they recorded about the children was based on their own best guesses or the instruction they received at their master's knee. The school did employ professional consultants, like the psychiatrists George Perkins and Jerome Kavka; but whatever their credentials and skills, they had little or no experience with autistic children and also tended to take their cue from their employer.

To further establish his expertise, Bettelheim reiterated the equation that he had first set down in 1956 in "Schizophrenia as a Reaction to Extreme Situations" and which by now had become his diagnostic mantra: autistic children behaved much like many of his fellow concentration-camp inmates because they, too, were responding to an extreme situation. They suffered from the kind of helplessness that characterized the "moslems," a camp term for those prisoners who had given up all hope.[41] The children who lacked muscle tone and shuffled about the dorms were just like the moslems; those who suffered from infantile marasmus and were wasting away for lack of nutrition were like prisoners who refused to eat; those who constantly averted their gaze evoked inmates who tried to avoid eye contact with the guards; those who twiddled and indulged in other forms of self-stimulation were akin to prisoners who constantly daydreamed. Both the children and the inmates were trying to blot out an immediate, threatening reality—the SS in the camps, their mothers in the home.

Bettelheim underscored this point by taking the reader into the forest with Hänsel and Gretel. Some years before, his friend Rudolf Ekstein, a psychologist who worked with children at the Reiss-Davis Child Study Center in Los Angeles, had argued that the fairy tale's rejecting-mother figure became the paranoid projection of the devouring witch. Bettelheim said this reasoning anticipated his own in *The Empty Fortress,* which was that "the figure of the destructive mother (the devouring witch) is the creation of the child's imagination, though an imagining that has its source in reality, namely the destructive intents of the mothering person." [42] This passage typifies Bettelheim's own wizardry at having it both ways: out of the smoke, the fantasy of Mom the Destroyer reappears as the real thing. "Indeed the theme found in this and other fairy tales . . . still haunts our children today. Like Gretel, there is Martha, one of our schizophrenic girls who was convinced that her mother wanted to bake her in the oven and eat her." [43]

As in his two previous books about the school, Bettelheim made sure there was no shortage of such dramatic tales. The story of Joey and his preoccupation with matters mechanical now spread over 106 pages and included twenty of his drawings; the history of Doris, now called "Laurie," covered fifty-eight pages. Running seventy-eight pages was a portrait of "Marcia," who Bettelheim said was mute, autistic, and unable to relate to objects when she arrived at the school at age eleven.[44] In a thirty-nine-page section called "The Persistence of a Myth," Bettelheim expanded on his belief that wolf children were autistic, now enlisting Shakespeare's "uncanny insight" to help make his case. In *The Winter's Tale,* Leontes, the king, cannot bring himself to kill his child and orders Antigonus to do it. When the lord pleads for the girl's life, Leontes agrees that she should not be burned to death but just set out to die. Antigonus prays that wolves and bears, "casting their savageness aside," will rescue the child. "Thus," wrote Bettelheim, "Shakespeare understood that behind a belief in feral children stands the fact that some parent wishes his child to be dead, but too afraid to kill it he exposes the child to a fate just as deadly." [45]

Few subjects preoccupied Bettelheim more than maternal breast-feeding, which comes up again and again in *The Empty Fortress.* He felt that nursing was central to an infant's ability to shape his life around his own needs, and the failure of a mother to respond properly to this demand invited psychological catastrophe, including schizophrenia and autism. Bettelheim saw evidence for this notion everywhere. He said that, just as an infant must connect to his mother's breast, so Joey had to plug himself in before he could function. He reported that Marcia liked to lie in her bed with a large, lightweight ball or balloon touching her mouth, adding in a footnote that "one can hardly walk down the street without seeing some child fondly handling a ball, the perfect sphere and an object often made of what was once skin." Marcia also played with a bottle that she called "lady," which Bettelheim said could be seen—"with some imagination"—as having breasts. When Marcia was asked why she wanted to smash the school's circular ceiling lights, she said, "Baby needs breakfast." This made no sense, Bettelheim said, until she began saying "break breast" instead. "Break breast," he explained, "is probably an idea more readily available to a baby fed from a breakable bottle than to one nursed from the breast." Quite a few of his patients thought of the light fixtures as breasts, he wrote, adding parenthetically that many felt the same way about automobile headlights. Laurie was one such fawn jacked in these Vienna Woods, "caught eternally between her overwhelming desire for the good breast (the good mother) and her despair because, in spite of all her efforts there seemed nothing there for her, not even a 'bad breast,' but just an empty nothing." Bettelheim conceded that this interpretation was speculative, but did not resist giving it further weight by reproducing three of Laurie's drawings that he said "probably" represented breasts.[46]

Many years later, a woman named Donna Williams came across Laurie's drawing in *The Empty Fortress*. She, too, was autistic, but by her mid-twenties had made progress so remarkable that she was able to write an autobiography, *Nobody Nowhere*. In it, she told of how she had drawn identical pictures over and over in her diary: a white square inside a black square, surrounded by the stark whiteness of the paper. When she saw Laurie's comparable efforts and read Bettelheim's bad-and-good-breasts decoding, she "laughed [herself] stupid. . . ." She viewed Laurie's drawings as like her own, which to her represented the terrifying blackness both faced as they struggled to pass into the nonautistic world. It is impossible to prove that Williams's interpretation is right and Bettelheim's wrong; but her observation that Freudian explanations stem more from what she calls the "worlder's," or therapist's, reality than from the autistic one speaks to one of Bettelheim's persistent inconsistencies.[47] He constantly admonished his staff and students not to depend on the experts and the textbooks when trying to comprehend disturbed behavior; instead, they should put themselves in a child's place and try to imagine what forces would make her so unhappy and act so strangely. Yet Bettelheim himself often wrote and behaved "as though he had a private line to the Truth,"[48] and he filled *The Empty Fortress* with the kind of Freudianism represented by his breast fixation, which, to Williams, reflected the egotistical and culturally biased arrogance of much psychoanalytic thought.[49]

To Bettelheim, Joey's fascination with rotating blades stood for the circle of emotion "he was helplessly caught in."[50] His enthusiasm for drawing dinosaurs was typical of many psychotic children because, "in addition to being dangerous and huge, [dinosaurs] are something that was once alive but is now dead, much as some of these children view their stools."[51] For a spell, Joey frequently played a game he called "Connecticut papoose," the papoose being a person with glass around him. "He was no longer a collection of wires in a glass tube but a person, though still encased and protected by glass, connected and cut off at the same time (Connect-I-cut)."[52]

Bettelheim said Marcia had an intense interest in the weather, which stemmed in part from her fear that her mother, and later the staff at the Orthogenic School, intended to devour her, as in "we/eat/her."[53] When Marcia eventually spoke, saying "ud-der" and then "mud-der," he thought the words related to nursing. "But with her slurred pronunciation the word could equally well have been taken for 'mother' or 'murder.'"[54] Bettelheim was full of this kind of language play at staff meetings as well. "He was wonderful with words," recalled one counselor who was at the school in the mid-1950s and is now a therapist herself. "He would talk about the psyche's puns and their meanings, and it was dazzling. But now I do this every day; it's fun, it's easy; but there's no profundity there."[55] And no insight into autism. It is exactly the capacity for the metaphorical and symbolic thinking that Bettelheim attributed to Joey and Marcia that is impaired in autistic children, whose thinking is almost always literal and concrete.

Gayle Shulenberger felt that Bettelheim "tried to do the

impossible" when he began admitting autistic children. Though she left the school in 1951 after several years as head counselor, she settled in Hyde Park after marrying Bettelheim's friend and co-author, the sociologist Morris Janowitz, and she remained close to the director and the school. She saw the autistic behavior as an insuperable challenge to the young staff, which spent month after month trying to puzzle out and pierce the muteness, the twid-dling, the flapping, the rocking, and myriad other mysterious symptoms that made these children so difficult to reach.[56] The commitment required not only long hours and bottomless energy but often a suspension of the middle-class instincts the young caretakers had been raised to regard as fundamental to civilized living. For weeks, Marcia refused to move her bowels voluntarily; when she finally began to defecate in the bathtub, her counselor, Karen Carlson, was overjoyed.[57] She had every reason to be; such progress was rare and came only after the most exhausting dedication.

Jacquelyn Sanders, who was chief counselor during the years of the Ford grant, told me that Bettelheim imbued the staff with a sense of hope and esprit, leaving her and his other acolytes con-vinced that with enough hard work they could accomplish mira-cles. Viewed from this optimistic perspective, their effort to help the autistic children was "a dismal failure." Sanders feels, in retro-spect, that if the counselors' expectations had been lower they might have been willing to settle for slow development instead of naïvely looking for dramatic breakthroughs. "The autistic kids were the most difficult to deal with and yielded the poorest re-sults," recalled the consulting psychiatrist Jerome Kavka. "I super-vised one counselor for a year in trying to get an autistic child to talk; we did not get one word." By the mid-1960s, the school's records show,[58] Bettelheim had given up on autism, largely, in the view of F. Howell Wright who cared for the children's medical needs, because the treatment became too expensive "and the re-sults were never sure." A far rosier picture emerged in *The Empty Fortress*. Bettelheim wrote that the autistic child had the same growth potential as the normal child,[59] that the school had restored some children, like Marcia, "to full functioning" in society,[60] and that he had worked with forty-six autistic youngsters, "all of whom showed marked improvement."[61] In his classes across the Midway, he often told his students of these gains. "He talked of miraculous cures; there was lots of self-congratulation," recalled one of them.[62]

The study of Orthogenic School admissions and discharge records begun in the late eighties by D. Patrick Zimmerman, the school's research coordinator, shows that between the summer of 1956, when the Ford Foundation gave Bettelheim the $342,500 to study autism, and 1963, when the grant ran out, the school admitted forty-eight children, six of whom—four boys and two girls—were labeled autistic by the referring parents, social agency, or therapist. Of the 220 children who entered the school between 1944 and 1973, Bettelheim's years as director, only thirteen arrived with a diagnosis of autism.[63] Without access to the counselors' dictation and other material in each child's complete folder, especially the evaluations of consulting psychiatrists, it is impossible to make even an educated guess as to whether all thirteen were in fact autistic. Conversely, no accurate assessment can be made of those who entered with other diagnoses, such as schizophrenia, atypical development, depression, or "none given." Were some of them reclassified as autistic, either because Bettelheim genuinely believed they were or because he needed the numbers? "We identified the autistic kids by mutual agreement," recalled Sanders, who said that the director sometimes made "a kind of retrospective diagnosis."

He did this with both Joey and Marcia, whose diagnoses were schizophrenia and brain damage, respectively, when they entered the Orthogenic School in the fifties.[64] Thus, of the three children whose histories formed the vivid, 242-page core of *The Empty Fortress,* only Laurie came to the school diagnosed as autistic, a fact that did not deter Bettelheim from writing that "we rarely erred in our initial evaluation of a patient. . . ."[65] Again, an independent assessment cannot be made without seeing each child's full record, but at least in the case of Joey, Bettelheim's most publicized portrait of an autistic child, the diagnosis does appear dubious. "I never considered Joey an autistic child, because there was always a directness in his relationships," said Sanders, who was at the school throughout the boy's nine years there. "Bruno could speculate about the meaning of an autistic kid's behavior; but Joey told us what his fantasies were, and what they meant"—i.e., that he needed motors, wires, and other mechanical gadgetry to keep himself functioning, to live. Both Bert Cohler and Philip Gold-bloom, who knew Joey as a schoolmate, said he did not seem autistic, and Patrick Zimmerman would write that "a reading of Joey's history in *The Empty Fortress* reveals a number of autistic-like behaviors, but also raises serious doubts about whether the formal diagnosis of infantile autism should have been applied in this case at all." [66]

Bettelheim's diagnostic fliers tended to be dramatic, but often that was all that distinguished them from what was going on in the rest of the field. In "Psychoses of Childhood," the 1979 summary of the literature, Barbara Fish and Edward R. Ritvo wrote that during the years Bettelheim ran the Orthogenic School there was a spreading tendency in both Great Britain and the United States to label children autistic on the basis of inadequate criteria. One result was that researchers chose samples of profoundly retarded children who suffered primarily from organic brain disorders. Fish and Ritvo stressed that Leo Kanner's definition of autism in the 1940s was an important advance because it established a distinct set of symptoms; but, as Kanner himself put it, his concept of early infantile autism "was diluted by some to deprive it of its specificity, so that the term was used as a pseudodiagnostic wastebasket for a variety of unrelated conditions, and a nothing-but psychodynamic etiology was decreed by some as the only valid explanation. . . ." [67]

During the 1950s and 1960s especially, many disturbed children, "whom one would consider today to have only borderline or even no psychotic symptoms, were lumped together in an ill-defined category of childhood psychosis." [68] At the Orthogenic School, this sometimes had painful consequences. Myrna Rowe was frightened and embarrassed by her schoolmates who had been identified as autistic. She and other nonautistic children "spent a lot of time trying to figure out what it was that *we* did that made these strange kids lash out and do things like bite us." Joe Suchman was an unhappy eleven-year-old who entered the Orthogenic School because of troubles at home, but he soon began to fear that he might be autistic; if not, why was he living in a place that treated such children?

Ronald Angres recalled that Bettelheim and the staff often suggested that the autistic children were not so different from the rest of the population. "It was as if the Raj had abolished the caste system—at the same time that they denounced and humiliated any Indian who seemed to think he was better than an Untouchable. . . ."[69] Angres himself carried the dreaded label for most of the twelve years he attended the school, and Jacquelyn Sanders used this case of "a brilliant autistic boy" as the core of her master's thesis at the University of Chicago in 1964. "It still embarrasses me that I swallowed so easily Bruno's diagnosis of Ronald," she told me three decades later. "He had some autistic tendencies, but he was not an autistic kid. I forgive Bruno to some degree for being so broad in his diagnoses, because everybody else was, too. However, his whole interpretation was wrong. I was young, but I really should have known better."

By the time *The Empty Fortress* appeared in 1967, a number of professionals had begun to suspect Bettelheim's "poetic interpretations"[70] and to complain about what one later called his "often freewheeling reflections, and extravagant speculation . . . [and] his lack of circumspection when applying rules of evidence."[71] When under such assault, Bettelheim often fired ex-cathedra salvos in return. In 1962, a psychologist and a pediatrician assessing the education of emotionally disturbed children wrote that it was not possible to ascertain from Bettelheim's writing whether graduates of the Orthogenic School were able to cope in a typical school setting.[72] "A hundred have done so," Bettelheim decreed, sarcastically dismissing the authors in the *Harvard Educational Review*.[73] When a sociologist named Gary Merritt questioned the statistics in *The Empty Fortress* and suggested that the children might not be as severely autistic as claimed,[74] Bettelheim replied that he had not found any cases in the literature "that could be viewed as more severe than those of Laurie, Marcia, Joey, Anna, Eve or Andy," the last three also described in the book. As for his follow-up claims, Bettelheim wrote that he had not been as explicit as he might have been but insisted that his negligence had been deliberate.

I wanted the reader to form his opinion on the basis of the clinical material. This he can evaluate by his own empathy, and in terms of its inner logic, and not by any reliance on figures which, *however carefully checked by my associates, and against our records,* would still have to be accepted on my say so.[75]

Almost everything in *The Empty Fortress* had to be accepted on Bettelheim's say-so. Like *Love Is Not Enough* and *Truants from Life,* the book offered no systematic source notes—a fact that did not trouble a Chicago reporter who, in a respectful series about the school's work with autistic children, wrote that its director was "a relentlessly exact scientist and an uncompromising critic of careless, shallow research."[76]

To Merritt, *The Empty Fortress* was a good deal less than the "heroic accomplishment"[77] most reviewers called it. But, like the few dissenting reactions to Bettelheim's earlier books about the school, Merritt's analysis appeared in a professional journal and was drowned out by the very endorsements in the lay press that he lamented. *Newsweek* gave over the better part of two pages to an enthusiastic feature on the book, reproducing three of Laurie's and Joey's drawings and noting that Bettelheim's interest in autism dated to the 1930s, "when he took two such disturbed youngsters into his Vienna home."[78] *Time,* which reported that Bettelheim had studied under Freud, gave a précis of Joey's history incorporating the director's claim that the school had rescued him from autism.[79] Writing in *Commonweal* about "The Holy Work of Bruno Bettelheim," William Ryan, a Connecticut mental-health physician, called *The Empty Fortress* "a brilliant piece of work."[80] *The New Republic* headlined its review, a glowing recommendation by the Harvard psychiatrist and author Robert Coles, "A Hero of Our Time."[81] In an unsigned review, *Scientific American,* which had given the story of Joey its first prominent attention in 1959, now called Bettelheim's work with autistic children "demonstrably successful" and his theory linking autism and wolf children "brilliant."[82] Newspapers across the country celebrated *The Empty Fortress,* among them the Chicago *Tribune*[83] and both the daily and Sunday *New York Times,* the latter calling it "a pioneering analysis. . . ."[84] As Christmas 1967 approached, the *Times* listed the book among the year's twenty outstanding nonfiction works.

In *The New Yorker,* Yale historian Peter Gay wrote that Bettelheim had analyzed autism "with exhaustive care. . . ." [85] He called the stories of Laurie, Marcia, and Joey beautiful and heart-rending and summarized them at considerable length. [86] He embraced the author's unique explanation of what caused the children's affliction, writing that their families "were efficient machines for dehumanization—little, unwitting concentration camps putting the small inmates at the mercy of extreme situations," so that in rage and despair they withdrew into autism. [87] Gay was so impressed by *The Empty Fortress's* authority that he felt no need to cite Bettelheim's claim to have made major headway with forty-six autistic children; he let *New Yorker* readers assume, as he did, that in general the director had achieved "spectacular successes." [88] He concluded that these were due primarily to Bettelheim's willingness to work within a Freudian framework, and suggested—in his only quibble—that the director might have profited by hewing even closer to the Viennese line. By way of example, he suggested that the unremitting apprehension Bettelheim detected in autistic children might stem from an extreme fear of castration, [89] an interpretation not altogether surprising from a writer who two decades later would produce an admiring biography of the man who gave us this phobia.

Bettelheim sallied forth from *The Empty Fortress* as the nation's leading expert on autism. He recast material from the book for *The New York Times Magazine,* writing of his "studies" that showed that autistic children had the potential for good or even superior intelligence, [90] and on January 10, 1967, he appeared on NBC's *Today* show, talking about the book. As a result of such self-promotion, and the media's credulous reading of the book, the notion spread that the Orthogenic School was primarily a home for autistic children, though Bettelheim himself wrote that fewer than a quarter of the residents fit that description at any given time. [91] The Zimmerman database suggests that even that percentage was exaggerated; regardless, it was overshadowed by the author's success claims and the mesmerizing case histories of Laurie, Marcia, Joey, and others. In 1984, more than a decade after

Bettelheim retired, Tom Lyons appeared on Studs Terkel's radio program in Chicago to discuss *The Pelican and After,* his novel about the school. When the usually savvy Terkel opened the interview by saying Bettelheim had run a school for autistic children, Lyons quickly corrected his surprised host.[92] In 1993, the editors of an anthology of essays reprinted "Joey: A 'Mechanical Boy,' " describing its author as the former director of "the Orthogenic School for autistic children. . . ."[93] A book about Jews in Chicago, published in 1996, praised Bettelheim as "a pioneer" in the treatment of austistic children.[94]

BY THE END OF 1969, *The Empty Fortress* had sold more than fifteen thousand hardcover copies, a respectable number at the time for a book on such a daunting subject. Hundreds of parents of autistic children turned to its pages in desperation, hoping that this Viennese therapist with "Dr." so often preceding his name, this widely sung author who was achieving such "spectacular successes," would help them understand and cope with their children's terrible isolation and the devastation it so often brought to their families. What they found instead was a cascade of blame: *they* had caused the autism by rejecting their children—by acting like witches, like feral animals, like infanticidal Shakespearean kings, like the SS guards in the concentration camps. When not offering analogies, Bettelheim said it straight: "Throughout this book I state my belief that the precipitating factor in infantile autism is the parent's wish that his child should not exist."[95] Thus, Joey was "simply and completely" ignored by his mother.[96] Thus, when Laurie was six weeks old, her mother gave her over entirely to a young nursemaid; later, when the child started making what sounded like loud, animallike noises, the mother spanked her and she stopped talking.[97] Thus, from what Marcia's parents told the school, it seemed "reasonable to speculate" that they wished her out of the way and that she kept on living only because "it seemed the worst revenge she could take on her parents."[98] After four hundred pages of such finger-pointing, Bettelheim wrote that it served no good purpose "to make the parents of autistic children feel guilty as having caused the disturbance."[99] For Peter Gay, those words signified how remarkably free the author was of egocentricity and aggression; for Robert Coles, Bettelheim deserved high praise for this refusal to characterize mothers as rejecting or schizophrenogenic. For Molly Finn, whose autistic daughter was eleven years old when *The Empty Fortress* came out, the passage only confirmed her view that Bettelheim was a charlatan.[100]

Finn was a twenty-five-year-old New Yorker working toward a master's degree in philosophy at the New School for Social Research and married to her first husband, William Esty, when, in 1956, she gave birth to a girl the couple named Abby. The baby showed signs of precocity, was quite musical, and developed a large vocabulary at an early age; but she quickly lost it all, and by the end of her third year had ceased talking and was given to tantrums and rigid behavior, definite signs of autism. No treatment over the ensuing years was able to bring major improvement, and at age eleven Finn entered Abby in a Camphill community. These mostly rural havens for mentally handicapped adults are the outgrowth of a movement begun by a disciple of Rudolf Steiner named Karl König, an Austrian pediatrician and educator who, like Bettelheim, fled the Nazis in 1939. Soon thereafter, he and his followers established the first Camphill sanctuary on a twenty-five-acre estate near Aberdeen, Scotland, and there are now more than ninety worldwide, seven in North America. Abby, who is entering her forties but still rarely speaks, now lives at Camphill Village, a self-supporting farm community on six hundred acres in upstate New York, and leads a productive life together with some two hundred other adults, about half of them mentally impaired.

Molly Finn, a Camphill trustee, sees her daughter regularly. She told me that one reason she never considered the Orthogenic School for Abby was Bettelheim's well-known hostility to parental visits. When *The Empty Fortress* appeared, just as Abby was moving into the Camphill program, Finn read it, largely out of curiosity; but she soon began making angry notes about its dubious success claims and its scientific vocabulary, which she found risible at best. When she reached page 403, where Bettelheim advised her she should not feel guilty, her notes burst into outrage: "Those who will suffer the most from B's book are the parents & these children. After saying repeatedly and at length that [parents] have caused . . .

this horrible illness he throws them a bone. . . . He must surely be ready to read these unfortunate people out of the human race . . . if he thinks that they would not feel guilty if they believed what he says. . . ."

Such fury typified the reaction of many parents of autistic children when they read *The Empty Fortress.* "Bettelheim really sowed seeds of evil," Josh Greenfeld told me. "Intellectual evil is the worst kind, especially when it is self-aggrandizing. As his reputation grew and grew, I just came to hate the man, hate him. He was not the philospher-poet-prince; to me he was a fucking fraud." In 1966, Greenfeld's wife, Foumi, had given birth to *A Child Called Noah,* as Greenfeld would call their son in the first of three books he wrote about the family's struggle to raise the boy. Noah, like Abby, had at first seemed to progress normally, but by age four could not feed himself, was not toilet-trained, seldom spoke, and spent most of the time absently lint-catching, thread-pulling, blanket-sucking, and pursuing myriad other repetitive actions typical of autism. The Greenfelds then lived just outside New York City, where they had friends in the psychoanalytic community, several of whom said that if anyone could rescue Noah it was Bruno Bettelheim. Greenfeld wrote to him and was told that the Orthogenic School did not take children until they were five or six. Then he read *The Empty Fortress,* and Bettelheim quickly became the enemy, someone "who didn't tell you what to do but just threw guilt at you." Foumi Greenfeld in particular rejected this slap of blame. Her husband, an American Jew, had initially been susceptible to psychoanalytic solutions, but she was Japanese and had never fallen under the Freudian spell. Bettelheim's condemnation of her as the cause of Noah's affliction made no sense. For one thing, the couple's older son, Karl, was normal, and they had embraced Noah with equal affection.

Judy and Ron Barron also had a normal child, a daughter named Megan. But in 1965, when Sean, their firstborn, was four, a neurological pediatrician told them that he was autistic, a word they had never heard. They were living just south of Youngstown, Ohio, in a small community with limited informational resources; but the pediatrician had named Bruno Bettelheim as the avatar of expertise on the boy's affliction, so when his book appeared in

1967 Judy Barron read it in one day. "I was horrified," she told me. "It was everything I didn't want to hear. I had a child on my hands who responded to nothing that I did, and I thought I was doing all the right things; Bettelheim told me, in effect, that I wasn't doing any of the right things, that *I* wasn't the right thing, and that only if Sean was taken from me might he stand a chance of being helped." As Barron read deeper into the book, she grew increasingly dismayed. "I wasn't a scientific reader, and I certainly wasn't a researcher; I was a twenty-four-year-old mother; but I just didn't see any evidence to support his pronouncements." In particular, she found ludicrous his notion that improper or inattentive breast-feeding might trigger autism. Mothers through the centuries had suckled their infants in fields, in jungles, in war zones, sometimes in the most unsanitary and poverty-stricken conditions, without causing autism. Epidemiological studies showed in the 1960s, and still show, that the syndrome afflicts no more than five out of ten thousand persons.[101] The notion that this aberration, with its predominance in first born males and its appearance in about four boys to every one girl, could occur because of something as universal as breast-feeding seemed laughable to Barron; yet she thought: *Why is Bettelheim's thinking laughable to me but taken seriously by a whole profession that is supposed to help parents with their autistic kids?*

The answer, as the Barrons and many other families would learn, was that many in the profession shared Bettelheim's view. In the fields of autism and schizophrenia, leading investigators such as Louise Despert, Margaret Dribble, Beata Rank, and S. A. Szurek, all better trained than the director of the Orthogenic School, had argued with varying degrees of conviction that these disorders could be laid in the lap of parenthood.[102] Leo Kanner's refrigerator mother had retained a tenacious hold over the years, despite his disclaimers that he had not meant to condemn parents and the fact that he always remained open to the possibility that autism might have an organic basis.[103] What set Bettelheim apart and made him the lightning rod for parental anger was his popular reach. Most therapists discussed childhood mental illness in the muted pages of professional journals, making their scholarly cases in articles with titles like "Intensive Study and Treatment of Preschool Children Who Show Marked Personality Deviations or 'Atypical Development,' and Their Parents." [104] These were no match for "Joey: A 'Mechanical Boy,' " which *Reader's Digest* excerpted, [105] or for a title like *The Empty Fortress,* or for a TV dramatization like *The Hidden World,* or for an author who confidently promulgated his views on autism and many other subjects not only in his books but in newspaper interviews, on the *Today* show, for Dick Cavett, in *Redbook,* and in a column for the *Ladies' Home Journal* that he wrote for a decade beginning in the mid-1960s.

Clara Claiborne Park did not seem much of a match for such a luminary either, even though she wrote well, and the moving story she told was every bit as compelling as Bettelheim's case histories. In a book she aptly called *The Siege,* published in 1967, the same year as *The Empty Fortress,* Park recounted the first eight years of her struggle to raise her daughter Jessy, who by twenty-two months was still not walking, talking, or responding to speech and would ultimately be diagnosed as autistic. Both Clara and her husband, David, were teachers—she of English, he of physics—at Williams College in Williamstown, Massachusetts. They spurned for its lack of science the idea that somehow Clara was to blame for Jessy's plight, a rejection bolstered by the fact that she had given birth to three healthy, happy children before Jessy arrived in 1958. "This knowledge and this pride," Clara Park wrote, "sustained us as we read the formulations of the Bettelheims of this world—this, and a certain natural skepticism which had been with us even before [Jessy] made us need it." [106] The Parks, like Foumi Greenfeld, had never come under the sway of Sigmund Freud and his disciples, despite growing up in New York City. "Anglo-Saxons from way back," they regarded the Oedipus complex and the rest of the Freudian kit as implausible, and psychoanalysts as "a bunch of failed poets." [107] Clara Park was not immune to the pain of the mother-blaming she encountered as she and her husband sought help for their sequestered daughter, but she alleviated it with the anodyne of her conviction that the accusation simply was not true.

The Siege was the first book-length account by any mother in the United States describing the practical and emotional burdens of raising an autistic child; but its eloquent narrative was buried beneath the huzzahs for the wisdom and expertise of *The Empty Fortress.* Dick Cavett did not phone. Neither the daily nor the Sunday *New York Times* reviewed *The Siege.* Except for favorable notices in *The Nation* and the Washington *Post's Book World,* the latter by the same Robert Coles who had so praised Bettelheim, the book was largely ignored by the press. After Peter Gay's paean to Bettelheim appeared in the *The New Yorker,* friends of the Parks pressed the magazine to review *The Siege* as well, to no avail. Park then wrote a letter to the editor, knowing that the magazine did not routinely publish them but on occasion did run a response under the rubric "Department of Amplification." She hoped her effort to redress the credulity of Gay's essay would qualify. It did not.

However, if *The Siege* failed to achieve the neon display of *The Empty Fortress,* it slowly began to provide inspiration and encouragement for many parents who found themselves in the same difficult situation as the Parks. Not only did Clara and David refuse to blame themselves for Jessy's affliction, they were determined to raise her in Williamstown, at home, where she lives today, an accomplished artist who holds down a regular job at the college post office, a lithe, blue-eyed woman approaching forty who in many ways still relates to her family and others as if she were a small child.

Bruno Bettelheim ignored *The Siege,* but a book published three years earlier would eventually prove more difficult to slough off. Its author, Bernard Rimland, was twenty-five years Bettelheim's junior and had just earned a doctorate in experimental psychology and research methodology from Pennsylvania State University when the older man was riding the success of *Love Is Not Enough* and *Truants from Life.* Rimland had come across "Individual and Mass Behavior in Extreme Situations" and a few other Bettelheim works as an undergraduate, but they had made little impact on a student whose main interest was in statistics and experimental design, and who, in 1953, began a thirty-year career with the U.S. Navy Personnel Research Laboratory in San Diego, California. Still, his education had trained him to accept the view that Bettelheim would write so large: that psychosocial forces were the principal cause of mental illness. He had also been taught that the few who questioned this position were irrational and inhumane, evil clinicians whose belief in organic causes slammed the door on the possibility of ever really helping the mentally ill.[108] He was surprised when he occasionally stumbled on such wrongheaded thinking in the literature, and, as schooled, dismissed it. Then, in 1956, Rimland's wife, Gloria, "after a picture-perfect pregnancy . . . [gave birth to] a picture-perfect baby, except for the screaming."[109]

Mark Rimland screamed many hours a day throughout his infancy and into early childhood. He seemed totally unaware of his parents, and rocked constantly in his crib, often banging his forehead on the headboard; during the day he bounced incessantly in his jump chair, wearing three of them out over the months. By age two, he could repeat with clarity anything said to him, including words like "hippopotamus"; but, recalled his father, his speech came as if from a tape recorder, "just repetition of words, sentences, and even nursery rhymes, without any real idea of what they meant." Change infuriated Mark, and he threw frightening tantrums when Gloria came near him in a new dress, a problem she solved by buying from the Sears Catalog several dresses of the same pattern, not only for herself but for her mother and mother-in-law, the only babysitters willing to cope with the boy. The Rimlands' pediatrician, a physician with thirty-five years' experience, had never encountered such a child, and the couple often felt they were doomed to struggle in darkness forever. But one day Gloria remembered reading in one of her college textbooks a description of children like her son. Her husband found the volume on a shelf in their garage and quickly discovered that it described a syndrome called "early infantile autism" that characterized Mark's behavior almost exactly.

Rimland began reading everything he could find on the subject of autism, including many articles in German, Dutch, and other foreign languages that he had translated. He found that, despite Leo Kanner's view that autism was a unique clinical entity, many in the profession, including Bettelheim, often used the term as an alternative to "childhood schizophrenia" and sometimes applied it to children who only remotely fit Kanner's quite specific definition. More unsettling to Rimland was the widespread conviction that autism had a psychogenic basis. He himself had been primed for that view by his university education; but now, like Molly Finn, the Greenfelds, the Barrons, the Parks, and scores more such parents, he felt it made no sense. "I remembered how Mark had screamed implacably in the nursery, even before he was brought home from the hospital, and wondered why these highly trained professionals, psychiatrists, neurologists, pediatricians, and psychologists, were so convinced that autism was caused by bad parenting rather than by an unknown biological factor." [110] Over a four-year period, while working at his navy job and helping his wife cope with their difficult son, Rimland kept reading and taking notes; he also started writing, and in 1964 produced *Infantile Autism: The Syndrome and Its Implications for a Neural Theory of Behavior.*

In 217 pages of measured prose, all of it carefully sourced to a bibliography of more than 450 titles, Rimland offered an exhaustive survey of the literature on autism and related subjects, an exploration that eschewed dramatic case histories for close scientific scrutiny. From this investigation he concluded that no hard evidence existed to support the position that autism was caused by bad parenting or any other environmental factors; he argued that assuming such an etiology was "not only unwarranted but actively pernicious." [111] He also found significant research suggesting that autism was an organic disorder, and tentatively proposed that the dysfunction might be seated in the reticular formation, a small but highly complex set of nerve cells in the brain stem. [112] Rimland laid out scientific data to support this supposition, but frankly conceded its speculative nature, and ended *Infantile Autism* with specific recommendations for further research. [113] This call was endorsed by Leo Kanner, who, in his foreword to the book, wrote that Rimland had offered a logically cohesive chain of theories that deserved sober scrutiny. [114] This they received. By 1981, *Infantile Autism* had been cited more than 425 times in the professional literature and had been recognized as a classic work by the Institute for Scientific Information. [115]

Rimland's book also brought him a fellowship at the Center for Advanced Study in the Behavioral Sciences in Stanford, California. Among Rimland's colleagues at this social-science think tank during the 1964–65 academic year was Benson E. Ginsburg, a geneticist at the University of Chicago who knew Bettelheim slightly as a faculty colleague. A woman Rimland knew was trying desperately to reach Bettelheim, whom she hoped could help her autistic child where all others had failed, and Rimland asked Ginsburg if he would urge the director of the Orthogenic School to talk to her. A three-way conference call was arranged, with Bettelheim in Chicago, Ginsburg and Rimland on the line together in Palo Alto, and the woman at some other location. Bettelheim was polite but firm: he would not take her child. Ginsburg told me that he gave no reason and that when the mother became distraught and said, " 'You're my only hope, what should I do?' Bettelheim replied, 'Lady, you have done enough.' He said it in a tone that implied that she was the cause of the child's problems. After that I could never look at him with respect in terms of just his humanity."

During their stay at the center, Rimland discussed with Ginsburg the difficulty of conducting chromosome studies on autistic children, in part because so many of their families had been driven into hiding by the stigma they felt. Ginsburg suggested that a cytogeneticist at Chicago might be willing to conduct such tests, so Rimland wrote Bettelheim seeking to enlist his help in finding some candidates in the Chicago area.[116] He received the following reply: "I regret to inform you that I am very critical of the approach you are using to study infantile autism. In my opinion your book contains gross errors and misstatements. I therefore shall give you no help in a study of autistic children which I consider ill-conceived and based on erroneous and biased judgements." [117]

In 1966, back in San Diego, Rimland wrote Bettelheim again, this time asking for data that might help him evaluate the success of the Orthogenic School program in general.[118] In response, the director said he saw little point in discussing his treatment results because Rimland insisted that autism was an inborn disease (which, in essence, he did) and that it was incurable (which he did not, as he had made clear in his book by noting that if autism did turn out to be an organic disorder it was as susceptible to a cure as diabetes or cretinism).[119] "Suffice it to say," Bettelheim wrote, "that better than eighty-five percent of our former students have made an adequate adjustment to life, including some who are your and my colleagues as Ph.D.'s in psychology. . . . Whether or not this and similar facts [sic] permit evaluation of our work I leave up to you to decide." Bettelheim went on to advise his correspondent that his own book on autism was due out in 1967 and that it contained an assessment of *Infantile Autism* that, "though critical, I trust is more objective in the evaluation of your work than you were of ours."[120]

Bettelheim made that evaluation in the final pages of *The Empty Fortress.* If autism were caused by a dysfunction in the reticular formation, or any other part of the central nervous system, he asked, then how was it that the Orthogenic School had been able to "reverse" the course of the disorder through psychotherapeutic treatment; how was it that Joey "and others" had been freed of "all those symptoms" typical of the illness?[121] In *Infantile Autism,* Rimland had speculated, as had Kanner in the 1940s, that children stricken with autism might be genetically vulnerable as a consequence of an inborn capacity for high intelligence.[122] To refute this idea, Bettelheim summoned his forty-six autistic children, reporting that thirty-four sets of their parents were of average intelligence and eleven sets were of better-than-average or superior mind, and only one of them of high achievement. This was, he wrote, "hardly an impressive validation of the alleged superior intelligence of parents of autistic children."[123] Bettelheim saw as little need to explain how he had measured the acuity of all these parents as he did to reveal that he had rolled their forty-six autistic children with his spotless dice. Nonetheless, it was a lucky throw. Eventually, research of a more exacting nature would establish that intelligent parents were not, in fact, predisposed to have autistic children.[124] Bettelheim did concede that an organic explanation for autism might materialize someday and that research in that direction deserved pursuit.[125] But, he insisted, "even if a specific neurological dysfunction should some day be found to correlate highly with the syndrome of infantile autism, it would still be compatible with the psychogenic hypothesis."[126]

Infantile Autism received even less attention in the lay press than Clara Park's *The Siege,* but like that book it quickly became a resistance manual for parents of autistic children, and Rimland their guerrilla leader. In an eighteen-page appendix, he had set down a diagnostic checklist of eighty questions for parents of disturbed children: "Did you ever suspect that your child was very nearly deaf?"; "At what age did the child say his first words . . . ?" etc. These questionnaires poured back from all over the world and helped create the critical mass of families who, in late 1965, under Rimland's prodding, formed the National Society for Autistic Children (later the Autism Society of America). The organization would not hold its first annual meeting until 1969, on the July weekend when most of the nation was transfixed by the U.S. astronauts' moon landing; while Neil Armstrong set foot on the dusty surface near the Sea of Tranquillity and announced one giant leap for mankind, some four hundred registrants gathered at the Sheraton Park Hotel in Washington, D.C., to hear presentations by leading authorities in the field of autism. Bruno Bettelheim was not among them, but Leo Kanner was. He was now seventy-five years old and looked fragile when he stood to speak at the gathering's banquet; but his message was anything but feeble. He reminded his audience that from the beginning in the 1940s, he had suspected that autism had an organic basis and with feeling said, "I herewith especially acquit you people as parents." He further gladdened the room by referring to Bettelheim's much-lauded treatise as "The Empty Book." [127]

Also present at this singular event was Eric Schopler, the German émigré who as a young man, in 1948, had been drawn to the University of Chicago in part because of Bettelheim's reputation, but who, by the time he received his doctorate in child clinical development in 1964, had come to regard the director of the Orthogenic School as a negative role model. Schopler was now deeply involved in autism research at the University of North Carolina, where in 1972 he would found TEACCH, a center for the Treatment and Education of Autistic and related Communication Handicapped CHildren that would receive much praise for its innovative approaches, not least the involvement of parents as cotherapists in the efforts to help their autistic children. "There were a good many years," David Park told me, "when Eric Schopler was our main defense against Bettelheim." A few weeks after the heady convention at the Sheraton Park, Schopler was back in Washington for an American Psychological Association symposium where he gave a paper entitled "Parents of Psychotic Children as Scapegoats." Ironically, he took as his model a mono-graph by Gordon Allport, the Harvard social scientist and psychol-ogist who, as editor of the *Journal of Abnormal and Social Psychology* in the early 1940s, had given Bruno Bettelheim his first major break in the United States by publishing "Individual and Mass Behavior in Extreme Situations," the concentration-camp essay that he would draw on repeatedly in his mother-blaming.

Reviewing the motives and conditions that Allport said led to scapegoating, Schopler reminded his audience that one of the chief frustrations in the field of mental health was the lack of any clear understanding of what caused mysterious disorders like autism, an opacity that often made clinicians feel guilty about their inability to help their patients. This left the therapists prone to projecting their guilt onto the child himself; but this would not do, since he was, after all, the patient, so his mother and father became the convenient substitutes for the therapists' aggression. Such parents were almost always confused and desperate, which allowed the clinician to maintain his role as powerful authority and to keep his sense of self-enhancement intact, though his prog-ress with their child was uneven at best and sometimes nonexis-tent. For the psychoanalytically oriented therapist, there was also the comfort of conformity, of knowing that in emphasizing paren-tal pathology he was striding safely along a popular therapeutic trail. Bruno Bettelheim's personality and behavior can be seen to some degree in all these aspects of scapegoating, and in particular in what Allport called tabloid thinking: the inclination to give complex subjects easy explanations, to oversimplify by blaming the snafu at the motor pool on the brass hats, the high cost of the social safety net on welfare queens, the greed in Wall Street on money-grubbing Jews, autism on mothers.[128]

It would be tabloid thinking to insist that Bettelheim's obses-sion with maternal pathology can be traced entirely to his relation-ship with his own mother, but this clearly was a factor. In what little he wrote about Paula Bettelheim, toward the end of his life, he described a generally caring woman; but when talking about her over the years, in public and in private, he repeatedly stressed that she had turned him over to a wet nurse and had not been as accessible as he would have liked.[129] The depth of this feeling sometimes proved astonishing, as Ernst Federn had recalled in describing his friend's behavior at a meeting of the Paul Federn Study Group in the 1950s, when, during a discussion of mothers, Bettelheim had angrily exclaimed, "I had no mother." [130]

In 1974, he sent out a similar message to hundreds of fellow professionals in the packed ballroom of a hotel in Philadelphia. They had gathered to hear from and honor "The Great Pioneers," a panel of refugees from Nazism that included Anna Freud, Erik Erikson, René Spitz, and Margaret Mahler, as well as Fritz Redl, Rudolf Ekstein, Peter Blos, and Bettelheim, who had retired as director of the Orthogenic School the year before. He opened his remarks by observing that "psychoanalysis has taught us that nothing is more important than the care a mother can confer on her infant. Nothing can take the place of this most intimate of all relations." He then told his rapt audience about the unmarried peasant girl his mother had handed him off to, a teenager "so devoid of motherly feeling" herself that she had willingly abandoned her own baby shortly after its birth to suckle the infant Bruno for pay. This she did for three years, boosting her milk supply with a steady flow of beer that left her "happily half inebriated" most of the time. When her nursling cried or otherwise showed unhappiness, a development that might endanger her employment, this "sex delinquent" stimulated him erotically, Bettelheim said; he called such fondling "early seduction," assuring his listeners, to much appreciative laughter, that it quickly calmed him down.[131]

Who had told Bettelheim of this adventure in cribland, which was not without a certain tabloid tingle itself, he did not reveal. But as with most of his tales, he used it to make a point, which was that Paula Bettelheim was at least a good enough mother to know her limitations. During a question–and–answer session, he added that some women are just not fit to be mothers, and that his mother was such a person. "He didn't say this with anger," recalled Clara Park, one of the few parents of autistic children in the audience. "He simply said that that was the way she was." Another questioner asked whether recent developments in the field of autism had moved him to qualify his views about mothers. Park told me he replied that no one should ask such a question, because it challenged the very foundation of his life's work.

CHAPTER TWELVE
The Kibbutzim

Bruno Bettelheim was fond of saying that there "is no reason why we cannot make provision for children to divorce themselves from their families, as adults divorce one another."[1] Beginning in the 1950s, he grew increasingly interested in the kibbutzim, where thousands of children had, in fact, grown up in significant ways divorced from their parents. Most of these agricultural settlements in Palestine and then Israel had required that parents turn over their infants to a *metapelet,* a caregiver charged with looking after a child's daily needs. In most cases, these *metaplot* helped raise the children through high school. The youngsters grew up in special houses apart from their parents and spent most of their time together. They visited with their mothers and fathers at the end of most working days and on weekends, and parents sometimes came to the children's house to read a story at bedtime and say good night; but the center of each child's daily life was his *metapelet* and his *kevutza,* the peers with whom he lived.

The kibbutz pioneers had established this separation in the second decade of the century as part of their movement to create a new society on the land, one of humane and just socialist collectives that would put an end not only to capitalistic materialism but to the patriarchal and often smothering family life of the urban ghettos and the shtetls of Eastern Europe and Russia, from which most had come. They had migrated to Palestine to build a Zionist utopia where women and men could work as equals. In this Sparta, the bone-wearying demands of farming and the constant threat from hostile Arabs left little time for the ordinary hug of family life. In the early years especially, the children were kibbutzniks first and sons and daughters second, a message they absorbed as they drifted off to sleep each night in a roomful of agemates overseen by a night guard.

This unique social experiment attracted the interest of several American social scientists and psychotherapists, among them Bruno Bettelheim's friend David Rapaport. In 1957, at a workshop on kibbutz child-rearing at the annual meeting of the American Orthopsychiatric Association, the Austen Riggs psychologist delivered a paper lamenting the paucity of research dealing with the kibbutzim, which by then numbered about two hundred and twenty, with a total of about eighty thousand inhabitants, roughly 4 percent of Israel's population. Rapaport, like others at the gathering, saw in the radical departure from ordinary upbringing a rich field of study, creating a "burning need" to learn how these kibbutz sabras fared. The anecdotal evidence suggested that, on the whole, they were growing up to be healthy and well adjusted, a hardworking and loyal cohort devoted to perpetuating the founders' ideals.[2] But John Bowlby and others, adherents of attachment theory, were warning that they faced a future of depression and other emotional problems because they had not received enough conventional mothering.

Bettelheim had never been to Israel, but he discussed these issues with Rapaport and others, and corresponded with Nechama Levi-Edelman, a member of Ramat Yohanan, a kibbutz about ten miles east of Haifa. A social worker and teacher, she had been impressed by *Love Is Not Enough* and was eager to spend time at the Orthogenic School. In 1956, when the counselor Fae Lohn told Bettelheim she needed to take some time off and was planning to spend a month in Israel, he asked her to look up Levi-Edelman, who both thought was a man. "He was playing *shadchen,* fixing me up, because I was having problems with a relationship," recalled Lohn, who disembarked from her ship in Haifa to be greeted not by a potential spouse but by a big-boned earth mother. Lohn spent two weeks at Ramat Yohanan and was drawn to her warm hostess, whose peasant features and concern for children made her something of the matriarch at the kibbutz, where she had lived since 1940. "I told Dr. B, 'Invite this lady, she's only wonderful.'" In 1957, Levi-Edelman spent about two months observing at the Orthogenic School and came away full of admiration for the therapeutic milieu Bettelheim and his dedicated staff had fostered; like others, she found the director difficult, but felt that in order to learn from him it had been worth putting up with his "hard side." [3]

In 1959, the year Bettelheim first wrote about "Joey, the 'Mechanical Boy,' " he also staked his claim as an expert on kibbutz child-rearing. The year before, Melford Spiro, a professor of anthropology at the University of Washington, had published *Children of the Kibbutz,* a book based on fieldwork he and his wife had conducted while living on one for thirteen months in 1951– 52. Bettelheim, without ever having visited a kibbutz, reviewed *Children* for *The Reconstructionist,* at once deriding Spiro's "weaknesses" and "limitations" and using the author's considerable research to advance his own agenda. The kibbutzniks, Bettelheim wrote, had created a system that "pays off and pays off handsomely," one that had produced children who view their parents "casually and amiably, but with neither much love nor respect." These parents, or at least those who had been reared on the kibbutzim themselves, had given up their babies to the *metaplot* "[w]ithout any doubt or hesitation" and, having a full life of their own, "[did] not miss having their children's emotions centering around them. . . ." The lesson, Bettelheim said, was as obvious as it was at the Orthogenic School: "If we remove [parents] from the lives of our children, our children are not necessarily the worse off for it, perhaps even much better off. . . ." Bettelheim did report that some members of the founding generation had come to question their original impulse and had begun pushing for closer familial ties; but, he predicted, this was not likely the wave of the future. [4]

In 1962, Bettelheim stepped forward again as an authority on the kibbutz, lifting passages from his *Reconstructionist* article and setting them down virtually unaltered in *Commentary:*

> The relations of Kibbutz educated children to each other and to their parents are amazingly uncomplicated, straightforward, unneurotic, although Spiro often claims the reverse is true; *but,* and here's the rub, therefore quite lacking in intensity by comparison. [*The Reconstructionist.*] [5]

> But though the relations of kibbutz-educated children to their parents and to each other are amazingly uncomplicated, straightforward, and unneurotic, they are at the same time—and here is the rub—comparatively lacking in intensity. [*Commentary.*] [6]

Bettelheim reported in both articles that this putative lack of intensity was "viewed with alarm" by both researchers and kibbutz parents, but that he saw little cause for concern. As he put it in *The Reconstructionist,* "Blood simply is not thicker than the shared emotional experiences; it is these which tie people together." [7] To his *Commentary* readers he explained: "Blood simply is not thicker than shared emotional experiences; it is the latter that tie people together." [8]

In *Commentary,* Bettelheim expressed a certain sheepishness about never having been to Israel, conceding that his knowledge was not firsthand. He listed a few journal articles and books that he said he had consulted, among them Spiro's study. "In addition," he wrote, "I have had conversations over a long period of time with persons who spent some years as educators in the kibbutz movement. Some, still active in their posts, visited with us for months at a time at the . . . Orthogenic School. . . . Others, who had left the kibbutz, worked with us. And others still, who had been originally with us and left to teach in a kibbutz, later returned to report their experiences." [9] At the time Bettelheim wrote these words, the only kibbutznik who had been at the school for more than the few weeks that Nechama Levi-Edelman had visited was Itamar Yahalom, who had worked with disturbed children in Israel. Yahalom, who joined Bettelheim's staff in 1956 and stayed for four years, did not retain his kibbutz position after he arrived in Chicago. If any staff members left the school to teach on kibbutzim, whether to return or not, neither Yahalom nor Fae Lohn can remember them.

To Bettelheim, "all available evidence" demonstrated that kibbutz education was an "unequivocal" success; reports to the contrary by American observers like Spiro were fatally flawed by a bias in favor of traditional child-rearing practices and their own notions of correct personality development. Some therapists, like Bowlby, did make a strong case for the orthodox family; however, nowhere in *Children of the Kibbutz* did Spiro express approval or disapproval of the settlements' child-rearing practices. Bettelheim wrote in *Commentary* that his "examination of the whole body of data" had convinced him that what the kibbutzniks had accomplished should lead Americans to reconsider their own assumptions and values "throughout the entire field of education." [10] He did not specify what should be re-examined or make any recommendations, and by the time he reached his final paragraph seemed to have developed misgivings about the sweep of his conclusions. He wrote that he was not urging that the United States adopt the system of education he had just finished lauding, only proposing that Americans take education as seriously as the kibbutzniks. [11]

By 1963, Bettelheim was planning a book about kibbutz child-rearing, and after receiving a grant from the New World Foundation, he arranged with Nechama Levi-Edelman to visit Ramat Yohanan. Few of the kibbutz's three hundred members besides her knew much about Bruno Bettelheim, and when she discussed the purpose of his visit with the leaders they were wary of stepping into his petri dish; nonetheless, at her urging, they agreed to open doors for him. He arrived in March 1964 and, with Levi-Edelman as his guide, began five weeks of nonstop investigation. He observed the children in their classrooms, in their special houses, and at mealtimes. He handed out questionnaires and recorded daily interviews with kibbutzniks young and old, mailing the tapes back to Linnea Brandwein and other transcribers at the Orthogenic School. Early on, Bettelheim made it clear how he viewed the kibbutz system of raising children; in an interview with the Israeli navy's chief psychologist, he said he had little patience with the notion "that kibbutz education is so bad because the dear mothers are not all the time with their dear little ones. . . ." [12]

At sixty, Bettelheim was older than Levi-Edelman and hardly as robust as this sabra who had lived the hard kibbutz life for twenty-four years; but at the end of each day it was she who was exhausted from trying to match his pace and meet his constant demands. "There were days when he made me really nervous," she recalled. "When he wanted something, the wishes of others didn't exist." One Friday afternoon, his typewriter broke down, and he insisted on going to Haifa the next day to have it repaired. Levi-Edelman explained that everything would be closed because of the Sabbath, but he was determined, and she knew that if she refused to take him he would only make her life more difficult. They went, and after much searching found someone to fix the machine, a triumph of the single-mindedness that Bettelheim often brought to even the most mundane task.

During social evenings in Levi-Edelman's home, her guest assured her that despite his sometimes exasperating behavior he loved and appreciated her. To others, he complained that she was an inferior teacher and therapist who had been "unable to learn" under his tutelage during her brief stay at the Orthogenic School in 1957.[13] Levi-Edelman herself had been "really frightened" of, and deferential to, the famously intimidating author of *Love Is Not Enough* during her weeks at the school. But she was seven years older now and on her own turf, and as Bettelheim went about his research at Ramat Yohanan he found her bossy and manipulative.[14] During a meeting of educators in her home, he said several times that it seemed to him the Israelis were proud of the capitalist advantages they had achieved since becoming a nation in 1948. Levi-Edelman demurred, insisting that the pride was in the Histadrut, the country's labor federation. "Yes," said Bettelheim, "but I cannot see any difference if the factory is owned by the Histadrut or by a private capitalist." "Well," replied Levi-Edelman, "then you have to learn the difference."[15] On another occasion, while they were talking with several teachers, she asked what he would do if his son, Eric, who was then twelve, decided he wanted to have a bar mitzvah. The question upset him, and he demanded to know who gave her permission to raise such a matter.[16]

This exchange exposed what Levi-Edelman saw as "the tragic" aspect of Bettelheim's visit, his impulse to bury his Jewishness, even—or perhaps especially—in the haven of the Promised Land. From the moment he arrived, he had resisted seeing anything of the country; finally, his hostess decided that he needed to put his work aside for a few hours and go with her on a tour of the Galilee. When she hired a taxi, he reluctantly agreed to the trip, and they set out together with Charles Dee Sharp, a filmmaker who had shot movies at the Orthogenic School for several years and had come to Ramat Yohanan to record footage that Bettelheim hoped to use with lectures when he returned to the United States. Their first stop was at Capernaum, the site on the northwest shore of the Sea of Galilee where, the New Testament records, Jesus established a ministry and found St. Peter and several other disciples among the community's fishermen. Levi-Edelman wanted to show Bettelheim and Sharp this place—called Kefar Nahum in Hebrew—because of its rich archeological store of both Christian and Jewish symbols, among them the traces of fresco work at the House of St. Peter and the ruins of an imposing synagogue dating to the second or third century A.D. The morning was clear and cool, the setting idyllic and peaceful, and there was no shortage of artifacts to intrigue the student of art history from Vienna, who normally delighted in exploring antiquities when he traveled. But Bettelheim seemed to be going through the motions at best, like a recalcitrant teenager on a high-school field trip. "I had such a hard time," recalled Levi-Edelman. "If it hadn't been Bettelheim, I would have thrown him out of the taxi." They argued constantly as she rubbed his nose in the Jewish past all around them; again and again, he pleaded with her to leave his feelings on this subject alone. At Nazareth, Bettelheim made a point of visiting several churches, prompting Levi-Edelman to twit him for his desire to become a Christian, an aspiration it seemed to her he manifested further when, on the drive back to Ramat Yohanan at day's end, he announced that Jesus Christ was the greatest educator who had ever lived. Levi-Edelman was appalled that a Jew could feel this way, and once again Charles Sharp found himself dodging the ricochets as his companions' furious quarrel filled the taxi. "They were shouting at each other," he told me. "It was the goddamnedest fight."

Passover began at the end of March, not long after Bettelheim arrived, and as happened every year several hundred members of the kibbutz and their guests packed into the main dining hall for a giant seder. Bettelheim resisted attending, but when Levi-Edelman pressed him he relented, and sat with her and her family to drink the Kiddush wine, break the matzo, eat the bitter herbs, and ask what made this night different from all other nights. When exuberant song filled the hall at the event's end, Levi-Edelman was astonished to hear her reluctant celebrant hesitantly join the others in "Hava Nagila," which salutes the Jews' return to their ancient soil. She told me that when the voices died down he confided that when he was a boy he had studied at a *heder,* the traditional school where instruction in Judaism was given in the home of the teacher, usually a *rebbe.* This revelation was at odds with everything he had ever said about his intensely secular upbringing in Vienna, and likely was produced, like his tentative singing, both to mollify his proselytizing hostess and to make himself feel less alien in the festive crowd.

Whatever Bettelheim's private strategies, there was no question in Levi-Edelman's mind that he had been touched by the ceremony, and that he was moved further several days later when members of Ramat Yohanan reconvened in the dining hall to mark Yom ha-Sho'ah, the annual Holocaust and Heroism Remembrance Day, which the government had established as a formal holiday only five years before. Again Bettelheim pulled back, and again his self-appointed tutor pushed him forward. "I said, 'Dr. B, you have to come; this is the one day that every Jew is at one with Israel.' " She took him to the hall, and the former inmate of Dachau and Buchenwald sat quietly with his head bowed as solemn music filled the room and survivors rose to tell their stories. "He did not say a word, but I saw tears in his eyes," Levi-Edelman told me.

Bettelheim would never write or declare publicly that his experiences in Israel had put a crack in the assimilationist carapace that so long ago had hardened around him; but, if only a hairline, it was now there. Among those who came to sense it was Leonard Atkins, who had arrived in Israel from his native Cape Town in 1951 at age twenty-three, attracted to the utopianism of the kibbutz movement. By the time of Bettelheim's visit in 1964, the idealistic South African had become codirector of a residential-treatment center for emotionally disturbed kibbutz children. Bettelheim spent a day there observing them and was impressed by Atkins's dedication; that evening, at a meeting with the staff, he announced, without looking at the codirector and with typical dramatic flair, that a position awaited him at the Orthogenic School if he wanted it. Two years later, Atkins, his wife, Miriam, and their two children resettled in Hyde Park, where he became a teacher and therapist at the school for the next five years.

Atkins admired much about Bettelheim but found offensive his insistence on celebrating only Christian holidays at the school. They never entered a dialogue on the matter, because the director did not invite dialogue; but the subject of Jewishness did surface occasionally. "He would say," Atkins told me, "that there is a sort of arrogance in remaining different from the people in your host country, and that assimilation was the solution. And I would say that I didn't think cultural suicide was the answer. Bruno listened; he didn't engage, but he listened." He also seemed to hear when Atkins talked wistfully of the beauty and vigor of Passover services in Israel. Finally, after twenty-five years as head of the school, Bettelheim permitted a celebration of a Jewish holiday on the premises. This seder, which Atkins organized in 1969, was a major undertaking that involved the entire school, Jew and Gentile alike. Since Bettelheim had given the observance his tacit blessing, Atkins assumed he would participate; but the director begged off, saying in an offhand fashion that a previous commitment made it impossible for him to attend—an excuse that would have been unthinkable at Christmastime.

Atkins told me he was deeply hurt by the director's absence but feels nonetheless that his willingness to countenance the seder at all flowed from his experience in Israel, where for the first time he had seen "a different Jew," a tough and confident citizen who was nothing like the subservient or overcompensating stereotypes that had filled his head since childhood and had been given terrifying reinforcement in Dachau and Buchenwald. At Ramat Yohanan, he came face to face with Jews who were determining their own fate, often under difficult circumstances. Paradoxically, it was assimilation that had helped give these Israelis their strength; they had created a nationality and had developed a culture of their own, and within the borders of their new state they no longer faced daily reminders, as did Bettelheim and all other Jews in even such tolerant corners of the diaspora as Hyde Park, that they belonged to a minority.

Bettelheim would become a strong supporter of Israel. When the Six-Day War broke out in 1967, he rushed to Hillel House with a check for five hundred dollars.[17] In subsequent years, he worried more and more over the country's future, an agony reflected repeatedly in his correspondence with Nancy Datan, a former student who had lived in Israel, and Carl Frankenstein, a psychoanalyst and teacher who had emigrated to Palestine from Berlin in 1935 and whom Bettelheim befriended during his 1964 visit. "There seems to be no end to the trials of the Jews," he wrote to Frankenstein just after the Yom Kippur War in 1973, in a typical lament.[18] A year later, he told Datan that Israel's plight in a hostile Arab world reminded him too much of his experience at the hands of the Nazis. "I feel very hopeless in the long run. . . ."[19]

IN 1969, BETTELHEIM published *The Children of the Dream,* his book about child-rearing and education on the kibbutzim in general and at Ramat Yohanan in particular. He acknowledged that his research had been hampered because he spoke and understood only a few words of Hebrew;[20] however, he insisted that this deficiency was not a significant drawback in communicating with adult Israelis, because many of them spoke English and he had communicated with others in German, French, and the smattering of Yiddish that he understood. He conceded that his lack of Hebrew was a "serious handicap" in interviewing the children, that even those who spoke some English did so haltingly and were inevitably unresponsive to the nuances of this foreign language.[21] Nevertheless, he maintained that it did not faze him that these youngsters were his principal subjects and that his mostly translated interactions with them provided the primary grist for many of his observations. "I hope," he wrote,

> that what I lost out on by my ignorance of Hebrew was compensated for by an intimate knowledge of the rearing of children away from their parents. As a matter of fact, one of my many initial reasons for wanting to study kibbutz rearing was the reports on how destructive it is for children to be reared away from their mothers. These reports I could not accept, having for some twenty years directed a center where children are brought up not by their parents, but by professional educators, and to the children's advantage. Thus I felt I was in a better position than most to evaluate the assets and liabilities of group rearing and that this, in the long run, might be as important for understanding such a method of education as it would be to command the language of the children.[22]

In this boast of expertise, Bettelheim made no distinction between the normal farm kids he interviewed and observed on the kibbutzim and the emotionally troubled children at the Orthogenic School.

On page 8 of *The Children of the Dream,* the author termed the book "a very personal, impressionistic report"; on page 13 he described it as "a study in depth"; and in an appendix entitled "The Data" he wrote of the considerable objective information that he had collected. He placed "objective" in quotation marks, by which he seemed to be signaling that such detachment is an unachievable ideal; the emphasis also suggests the conscious or unconscious irony of a man who knew that once again he was plowing the fields of As If.[23] In the book's first sentence, he wrote that he had studied the kibbutzim for seven weeks,[24] though by his own word, and Nechama Levi-Edelman's as well, he spent only five weeks in Israel.[25] The evidence in his papers at the University of Chicago shows that during those thirty-five days he interviewed about fifty individuals and participated in several meetings with groups of both children and adults, most of which, like the interviews, he recorded on tape. In all, these encounters produced some eight hundred pages of transcripts, and they confirm Levi-Edelman's description of the busy pace Bettelheim set for himself. For the book, though, it was not busy enough; there he wrote that he had interviewed "several hundred persons," some for more than twenty hours,[26] and that he had come home to "thousands of pages" of transcripts.[27]

Such exaggeration bobs on a sea of prose that, like most of the author's previous works, lacks any systematic source notes, producing a vague scholarship blurred further by the dense fog of anonymity that envelops the book. Bettelheim disguised Ramat Yohanan by calling it Ytid, which means "future" in Hebrew. He maintained that his interviewees had requested such protection,[28] and some may have, but Levi-Edelman told me that neither she nor the other leaders had asked their guest to mask either their or the kibbutz's identities. Bettelheim thanked Levi-Edelman for her generous help but identified her only as his "interpreter" and "[t]his person,"[29] nor did he name anyone else among the "several hundred" kibbutzniks he encountered in Israel, except for Len

Atkins, whom he thanked in the acknowledgments for having read portions of the manuscript.

By 1969, such camouflage had become a standard Bettelheim technique, allowing him to call the dots on his blank dice, to make it seem, as Charles Rycroft had put it, as if he had a private line to the truth; or, as Dwight Macdonald had written in reviewing *Love Is Not Enough,* that the mountie always got his man. For more than a quarter of a century—from his descriptions of the nameless prisoners in Dachau and Buchenwald in "Individual and Mass Behavior in Extreme Situations," to his dialogues with unidentified mothers, and through his three books about the Orthogenic School, with their dramatic pseudonymous vignettes and case histories—he almost never identified the subjects of his psychological scrutiny. He argued, as did most of his professional colleagues, that the patient's privacy must be maintained at all cost; but he, like they, rarely discussed the temptations of the canvas of anonymity.

In *The Children of the Dream,* Bettelheim didn't bother with pseudonyms; instead, he attributed the more than sixty quotations he deployed to such sources as an "educator" (page 79), a "leading educator" (page 40), a "kibbutz-born social worker" (page 272), or a "left-wing metapelet who had cared for many generations of babies from birth to six months" (page 95). On page 106, he offered the veiled voices of a young woman, one of her agemates, and a mother. In another passage, he supplied a quotation from "a group" of educators that ran to 205 words (page 102). The book is made all the more opaque by its inconsistencies, contradictions that moved one frustrated critic to ask, "Will the *real* Bruno Bettelheim please stand up?"[30] He wrote, for example, that by and large "kibbutz-born youngsters seemed to show considerably less emotional disturbance, both in number of cases and severity, than would a comparable group in the United States." Yet his next paragraph begins: "My judgment however rests on shaky grounds, because of the uncertainty of what would be a comparable group in America."[31] Elsewhere, he stressed the importance of studying the kibbutz because "it proceeds within the framework of a democratic society, involving people very much like ourselves."[32] Thirty-six pages later, he wrote that "it is hard to visualize how we could duplicate [the kibbutz] in our pluralistic society."[33] On the one hand, Bettelheim liked what he saw at Ramat Yohanan, concluding that group child-rearing away from mothers seemed quite successful.[34] Yet he maintained that the babies born in the settlements developed into adolescents with emotionally flat[35] and "depleted"[36] personalities, especially compared with their forceful, path-breaking parents.

To support this view, Bettelheim offered scant evidence; instead, he most often made his case with the kind of aggressive apriority that by now had become his trademark. In a principal conclusion, he maintained that the youngsters had repressed their feelings in part because of the leveling impact of kibbutz education and in part because their communal upbringing had given them a collective rather than an individual ego. "Without the peer group they are lost," he declared,[37] explaining that the *kevutza* had made the second generation emotionally dull (page 232), had made them reluctant to touch or be touched (page 239), uneasy in marriage and with their children (page 246), estranged from the world of ideas (page 285), even "downright xenophobic" (page 230). He often buttressed such pronouncements with his blind quotations, like that of "[a] teacher" who he said had been a kibbutznik and now taught in the city as well as at a kibbutz. He said this ephemeral source told him: "I tried all kinds of methods of teaching [the adolescents] to be spontaneous, to be creative in their writings. The methods that worked in the city schools did not work in the kibbutz. When I encouraged them, the children in the kibbutz wrote eagerly, but they would never read out what they wrote in front of the class, nor would they show it to the other youngsters."[38] Even on the rare occasion when Bettelheim supplied statistics, he didn't reveal where they came from, as with "a nationwide study" that made the leveling impact of kibbutz education "quite apparent. . . ."[39]

At the time *The Children of the Dream* appeared, the kibbutzim offered fertile ground for such freewheeling analysis. No large, meaningful studies existed from which significant conclusions could be drawn about the overall impact of the settlements' child-rearing practices,[40] creating a seductive tabula rasa for the anecdotal approach. Bettelheim seemed to recognize this hazard when he wrote, toward the end of his book, that any useful judgment about the efficacy of kibbutz education would have to wait until the third generation matured, that until then his observations must be regarded as "tentative, very open to question, beset by uncertainties."[41] This caution may have been well meant, but, coming as it did after almost three hundred pages of seat-of-the-pants research couched far less humbly, it registers much like the author's last-minute sop to guiltless mothers at the end of *The Empty Fortress.* Certainly it did not mollify many in the kibbutz movement, who found *The Children of the Dream* filled with, in the words of Mordecai Kaffman, a lot of "blah, blah, blah."

When Bettelheim visited Israel in 1964, Kaffman was director of a special clinic for disturbed children at Oranim, the kibbutz teachers' college near Haifa. A native of Santiago, Chile, where he attended medical school, he had come to Palestine in 1947 at age thirty and helped found Ramot Menashe, a kibbutz near Tel Aviv, where he and his wife still live and their three children grew up. By the time I interviewed him, Kaffman had become a leading authority on kibbutz children, the medical director and chief psychiatrist of the Kibbutz Child and Family Clinic in Tel Aviv, and the author or co-author of some 150 articles in professional journals and books.

Kaffman had first met Bettelheim during a brief visit to the Orthogenic School when studying child psychiatry in the United States from 1958 to 1961. Like most others, he had found the director a man hard to ignore, a true believer who seemed to have "no place for doubt." Still, the confident sweep of *The Children of the Dream* had left him astonished and dismayed. When we talked in his small office, he had the book in hand and turned at random to several passages that he called "nonsense," such as Bettelheim's contention that there was great community pressure on mothers to cease nursing when their infants reached six months of age (pages 75–76); that the kibbutz founders would feel enslaved by the re-establishment of deep emotional family ties (page 94); that, unlike children elsewhere, kibbutz youngsters did not push and hit one another from time to time (page 175); that there were no schizophrenics among the kibbutz-born (page 196). Kaffman also dismissed Bettelheim's generalized thesis that second-generation kibbutzniks were emotionally shallow compared with their parents, reiterating what he had written not long before we spoke: that studies made both before and after Bettelheim's 1964 stay demonstrate that kibbutz children and adolescents "revealed neither a homogeneous characteristic personality type nor any distinctive psychiatric problems." [42]

Beyond that, Kaffman stressed that comparing the two generations at all was at best a dubious enterprise. The pioneers were a unique cohort, a group of strong-willed Jews from a distinct shtetl or ghetto culture in Russia or Europe, settlers imbued with great socialist idealism and a willingness to break the land; this self-selected band constituted no more than 4 percent of the thousands of migrants who had come to Palestine in the first half of the century. Their children, inevitably, were unselected, a homogeneous population raised in a common system that was bound to produce adolescents less varied and engaged than their founder-parents. With the agitation of a scientist frustrated by having to point out the obvious, Kaffman told me that it was "impossible, totally impossible, for any human mortal" to write a thoughtful, book-length study of kibbutz child-rearing after a visit of only a few weeks, even if he had spoken fluent Hebrew. What further angered Kaffman—and not a few other kibbutz leaders, including Nechama Levi-Edelman—was the conviction that Bettelheim had arrived in Israel with his mind made up. "He didn't need the few weeks, the book was already constructed, nothing could change his views," Kaffman said.

By the time *The Children of the Dream* appeared in 1969, it had been ten years since Bettelheim had declared, without any firsthand investigation, that the kibbutz system of child-rearing and education had paid off handsomely, producing healthy youngsters who regarded their parents with neither much love nor respect, parents so focused on the needs of the kibbutz that they had given up their babies to the *metaplot* without any misgivings. *The Children of the Dream* is less reductive, but its message is essentially the same: that, in terms of importance to the child, "the peer group comes first, the kibbutz itself second, and the parents only last." [43] The literature on kibbutz child-rearing makes clear that the reverse is true, that even in the early years of the movement it had become apparent "that relations between members . . . could not substitute for family ties." [44] Or, as another observer put it the year after *The Children of the Dream* came out, parents and children "are deeply attached to each other and comprise a distinct and recognizable social group." [45] Chai Lador, the wife of an Israeli consulate official in Chicago, had been a *metapelet* at a kibbutz in the western Galilee for twenty-seven years, in a settlement where the couple's three children grew up. In a 1969 newspaper interview, she waved away Bettelheim's picture of kibbutz mothering as unrecognizable, a judgment the headline writer summed up as "A Jewish mother replies: 'Oy!' " [46]

When Bettelheim was still writing his book, in the late 1960s, the desire of kibbutz parents to have their children sleep at home had begun to grow. This impulse, which in 1959 Bettelheim had predicted would fade, continued to gain momentum throughout the 1970s and 1980s; by the beginning of the 1990s, collective sleeping arrangements remained the practice at only three of Israel's 260 kibbutzim. [47] To Bettelheim, such burgeoning familialism was anathema; when he spoke to the general meeting of Ramat Yohanan at the end of his stay, he criticized the parents for constantly looking over the shoulders of the *metaplot*. [48]

Getting mothers and fathers out of the picture had long been central to Bettelheim's treatment philosophy at the Orthogenic School, but his visit to Israel gave him a new agenda. At the outset of *The Children of the Dream,* he suggested that poor children in the United States might well profit from a similar divorce. The feeling is "widespread," he wrote, citing no one, "that if we are to help the culturally deprived child—whether in city slums or impoverished rural areas—he had best be reared in an environment different from his home, since his home life often makes him unfit for the world he must later enter." [49] He conceded that America's poor mothers might prove more reluctant than their kibbutz counterparts to part with their offspring; nonetheless, he felt that, given the kibbutz success, such a "radical change would best resolve the problem of our slums, and in short order." [50] In promoting the book, Bettelheim bruited this idea about in speeches and interviews, attacking Project Head Start in particular. This federal enrichment program for deprived pre-schoolers was a popular and often successful ingredient of the Great Society's anti-poverty effort in the 1960s, but Bettelheim argued that a "terrible strain is created when you take children out of the ghettoes for a few hours each day and teach them how to adapt to a middle-class learning pattern which is entirely different from the skill they need to survive in the jungle of their home environment."[51] As an alternative, he proposed taking infants from poor parents just after birth and placing them in an American version of the kibbutz children's house, where they would remain until age eighteen. He recommended that two such institutions be established as an experiment, each caring for 100 to 150 children and staffed by specially trained caregivers; parents would be able to visit their offspring for a few hours each day, he assured one interviewer.[52]

Not only were the kibbutzim fast moving away from such arrangements but Israelis who came to observe Project Head Start left particularly impressed by the heavy parental commitment. Sylvia Krown, a research psychologist at Hebrew University, noted approvingly that the program required that one staff member work with parents at each center and that parents make up half of each center's advisory committee; she regarded this and other efforts to get parents more involved in their young children's education well worth emulating in Israel.[53] In 1969, Sarah Gluck, chief inspector of nursery schools and kindergartens in Israel, toured several Project Head Start centers and also came away with the conviction that her country would do well to encourage the kind of parental involvement she had witnessed.[54]

Bettelheim's contrary view of how to save the children of the inner-city "jungle" did not originate or end with him. In the mid-1990s, the fractious, right-wing Republican leader Newt Gingrich, citing Boys Town as a model, urged a nationwide resurrection of orphanages so that impoverished children could be separated from the pernicious influence of their parents and the crime- and drug-infested neighborhoods where they live. For a conservative politician, such a proposal has an easy attraction: it sounds simple and humane ("We just want to help these kids!") and it avoids facing the racial and economic injustice that created the crisis, not to mention the heavy taxation required to ameliorate it. As early as 1946, Bettelheim had made clear that he well understood this dimension of the problem, writing that good housing, full employment, and a feeling of financial security in general were crucial in any fight against intolerance.[55] He echoed this theme four years later in *Dynamics of Prejudice,* and again, in 1964, when that study was reprinted—with new, introductory material—as *Social Change and Prejudice.*[56] When writing *The Children of the Dream,* Bettelheim doubtless understood that economic reform remained a key factor in any effort to reduce racism and thus raise the status of African Americans; but as he urged the kibbutz approach for ghetto children, he gave such hard correctives scant attention, even though economic leveling is at the socialist heart of kibbutz life.

Bettelheim also seemed to have forgotten, in criticizing Project Head Start, that on at least two occasions he had urged the creation of just such a program. In 1958, he proposed that five-year-olds from poor homes attend small preparatory classes in which they would be encouraged to learn by the very best teachers.[57] In 1964, he insisted that there must be radical reform in the school lives of children between the ages of two and five. Why, he asked rhetorically, "are we so blind to the fact that all our educational planning for the underprivileged begins when for all practical purposes it is too late?"[58]

Bettelheim's 1969 dismissals of Project Head Start's attempt to address just this question would seem baffling, were he not so often inconsistent. He was not the scholar who had revised his ideas in light of new information and after careful thought, and who offered reasons for his change of mind, but one of those university professors who, he himself had suggested, "get far because they are glib."[59] He "often talked in half-ideas,"[60] but they carried like the pitch of a barker who knows what will draw a crowd to his tent on the midway. The wide-eyed fairgoers had seen the feral mothers, the mechanical boy, the miraculous cure for autism; now they could step inside and watch ghetto kids have a parentectomy.

Most reviewers who knew anything about Project Head Start, the kibbutzim, or child psychology in general saw through the pitchman. They found much in *The Children of the Dream* "grossly oversimplified"[61] and criticized its author for trying to force his unsupported conclusions into "a Procrustean bed of the-ory." [62] Menachem Gerson, director of Oranim, the kibbutz move-ment's teaching seminary, observed that Bettelheim's "easy generalizations give the reader no knowledge about the records of kibbutz youngsters' diaries, group conversations [and] . . . artistic achievements. Despite his great appreciation of the kibbutz, the author is doomed to mislead his readers." [63] Gerson laid out his views in *Israel Horizons,* and most other criticism of Bettelheim's book surfaced in publications of similarly low profile, such as *Children, Conservative Judaism,* and *The Hudson Review.*

Meanwhile, the mainstream media once again gathered out-side the author's tent and amplified his spiel. He promoted the book on the *Today* show, and gave numerous newspaper inter-views, including two to *The New York Times,* one of which intro-duced him as "one of the world's outstanding authorities on childhood emotional development. . . ." [64] In Chicago, the *Sun-Times* treated the book favorably [65] and the *Tribune* published a review by the short-story writer Hugh Nissenson that called the work "a brilliant contribution to the study of communal child-rearing on the Israeli kibbutz." [66] Christopher Lehmann-Haupt, the daily book critic of *The New York Times,* called Bettelheim a "pioneer" in the exploration of childhood emotional development and disorder, and his book a "painstaking examination" of kibbutz children's growth; he concluded his review by noting that the book, like the author's proposal for resolving the problems in the slums, was "something to think about." [67] In *The New York Times Book Review,* the social and political scientist Paul Roazen called Bettelheim "an ardent clinician" who stood as "one of Freud's few genuine heirs of our time." Perhaps no one, he wrote, was "more equipped to assess the effects of kibbutz society on personality formation than Bruno Bettelheim." [68]

Like a number of people initially dazzled by the man and his prose, Roazen would have second thoughts. Not long after he reviewed *The Children of the Dream,* he became a parent for the first time and "grew a good deal more skeptical about Bettelheim's outsider approach to traditional family life. . . ." Roazen admired Freud and recognized that Bettelheim was acting in the master's wake, and he conceded that there were times when a child and his parents could benefit from the intervention of a neutral observer. But as a father himself he became suspicious of all the pretense to expertise "in an area of thinking so filled with conflicting ideological convictions." [69] Others came to share Roazen's reservations, but in 1969 *The Children of the Dream* only increased Bettelheim's visibility as a seer with unique insight into the troubled psyches of the young, a visibility that would grow even greater as he took on the students protesting the Vietnam War and the inequities of American society.

CHAPTER THIRTEEN
Young Nazis Redux

I N MID–NOVEMBER 1968, some two thousand guests gathered at a black-tie dinner to celebrate the inauguration of Edward H. Levi as the eighth president of the University of Chicago. The scene was the Conrad Hilton Hotel, which less than three months before had been the headquarters of the Democratic National Convention, around which, in a haze of tear gas, the city's club-wielding police had battled hundreds of young demonstrators protesting U.S. involvement in the Vietnam War. To millions of older Americans, the seething images on television represented just the latest eruption in a nation that seemed to be coming apart in an inexplicable frenzy of violence, one summed up by the youth movement's troubadour, Bob Dylan, when he sang, "Something is happening here / But you don't know what it is / Do you, Mr. Jones?" Already that year, Robert F. Kennedy and Martin Luther King, Jr., had been assassinated, and in the wake of the latter's death, on April 4, racial disturbances had broken out in more than two hundred cities. In Chicago, authorities had called in five thousand federal troops and sixty-seven hundred Illinois National Guardsmen to bolster the police. In the first half of the year alone, 211 demonstrations had erupted at 101 campuses, and on at least sixty occasions students had occupied one or more buildings, most notoriously at Columbia University.

As Chicago's aristocracy entered the Levi fête that night in November, about one hundred pickets organized by the Students for a Democratic Society chanted, "One-two-three-four, McGeorge Bundy made this war," a reference to the evening's main speaker, then president of the Ford Foundation but, until 1966, a principal architect of U.S. policy in Vietnam as national security adviser to Presidents John F. Kennedy and Lyndon B. Johnson.[1] Among the pickets was a thirty-two-year-old assistant sociology professor named Marlene Dixon. A month later the university notified Dixon that she would not be reappointed. The administration and Dixon's colleagues in the sociology department maintained that they based their decision on her failure to meet academic standards, but a core of students and a few faculty members insisted that she had been denied because of her leftist politics and because she was a woman. They turned down an administration offer to convene a seven-member commission to re-examine the teacher's dismissal, and on January 23, 1969, demanded that she be rehired and that the university grant students equal say with the faculty in the hiring and firing of teachers; if these conditions were not met by January 29, "militant action" would follow.

Edward Levi was a son of Hyde Park with a deep and protective affection for the university; his grandfather, a prominent rabbi, had been on the original faculty in 1892, his father-in-law was a trustee, and Levi had attended the institution's primary and secondary schools before entering the college. The new president was also a lawyer, a former dean of Chicago's law school, whom President Gerald R. Ford would name U.S. attorney general in 1975; he did not believe in negotiating under threat and, to the surprise of almost no one, rejected the ultimatum. At noon on Thursday, January 30, some four hundred Dixon partisans invaded the administration building, setting up camp throughout its six stories, including in the president's office.[2]

The next day, Bruno Bettelheim arrived at the scene and conducted an impromptu press conference, announcing to the crush of reporters and onlookers that the protesters, like those who had fought with the police around the Hilton in August and who had been rebelling at Columbia, Berkeley, and dozens more campuses for months, were in the grip of mass paranoia.[3] The incidence of paranoia among the young had not increased, he assured the crowd, but the climate of the 1960s had given the paranoiacs too much public attention; many were just emotionally sick, and "society should start calling the nuts nuts." The protesters were anarchic and nihilistic and reminded him of the university students who had supported Hitler: "I see exactly the same thing happening here from the so-called left as happened in Germany from the right," he said,[4] an assertion that made WHPK-FM, the student radio station, regret that it had not managed to tape his remarks and prompted an immediate invitation to repeat them in the studio.

Bettelheim accepted, and on February 2, the sit-in's fourth day, his familiar guttural voice went out to several thousand listeners throughout Hyde Park and adjacent South Side communities. He reminded his interviewer at the outset that because of "certain convictions" he had spent a year in the concentration camps. He said he had fought fascism all his life, though it had not been his "style" to do so on the barricades; instead, he had fought with words, written and spoken, and through teaching and political action. But even in his "own group" he had insisted that they had no right to impose their will on other people; they could only try to persuade, educate, and convince, because resorting to force would have meant accepting the Nazis' strong-arm tactics against him. Bettelheim followed this blend of reason and make-believe about his anti-Nazi activities by again comparing the demonstrators to young Nazis, adding that he was opposed to giving them any role whatsoever in running the university. He suggested that the "hard-core idealists" who didn't like their teachers or the administration needed more education and that they try universities in the Soviet Union or China, offering to "start a collection among [his] colleagues to help them a little bit."[5] Four days later, in a letter to the *Maroon,* the student newspaper, Bettelheim castigated all softheaded adults who applauded, condoned, or excused the sit-in and repeated the Nazi analogy,[6] as he did at the daily three o'clock meeting in the Orthogenic School playroom, where he told his captive audience that he had fought in World War I and the antifascist Austrian resistance.[7]

By now, Ed Levi had taken refuge in his home, from which he was running the university with the advice of trusted faculty and administration colleagues. Threats arrived daily, including a package containing a dead dog; "We were afraid someone was going to shoot him," recalled Michael Claffey, a member of the kitchen cabinet.[8] From the start, Levi made it clear to the occupiers that they faced disciplinary action; but he also was determined not to call in the police to force them from the building. Columbia University had done so the previous spring, resulting in injuries to twelve policemen, four faculty members, and 132 students. The bloodier clash between the antiwar forces and the Chicago police around the Hilton was even fresher in Levi's mind. Bettelheim endorsed the president's restraint, albeit in his inimitable fashion. At his press conference he had said that bringing in the cops was just what the dissidents wanted and would play right into their hands; instead, what they needed were psychiatrists.[9]

Bettelheim's opposition to the sit-in was shared by almost the entire faculty and the majority of students, but his hostility rose from a unique well of fury. The protesters had attacked not only the institution that had given him a haven and a new career but also his friend and co-author, Morris Janowitz, who was head of the sociology department and who stood squarely behind the decision not to reappoint Marlene Dixon. Moreover, Ed Levi was not just the chief officer of the university but the kind of well-born German Jew the Viennese émigré so admired and envied, and one who had become his latest *Protektor*. In 1962, as provost, Levi had made Bettelheim the Stella M. Rowley Professor of Education, and in a few weeks he would add "distinguished service" to that title. The demonstrators' behavior was an insult that Bettelheim seemed to take personally and both Janowitz and Levi understood his rage. But they and the other negotiators were trying with some desperation to end the occupation peacefully and were dismayed that one of their own was calling the demonstrators mentally ill and making incendiary comparisons to Germany in the 1930s.[10] They kept their distance from Bettelheim's fractious language, but also held firm, and by mid-February the sit-in had collapsed; after disciplinary hearings, the university expelled forty-two students, suspended eighty-one, and placed three on probation.

Bettelheim would tell at least one colleague that he regretted his public pronouncements in the siege's first days, that he had not expressed himself carefully enough.[11] But his noisy stand, combined with his reputation as an expert on the behavior of troubled children, now thrust him onto the national stage once again, and he quickly inhabited the role. Well before the sit-in, he had begun speaking out: to a committee of the New York state legislature investigating student disorders; at the University of Rochester, where his son entered as a freshman in the fall of 1968; in his *Ladies' Home Journal* column, a distillation of his dialogues with mothers, which had resumed on campus in the 1960s. But it was his Nazi analogy that focused the spotlight on him.

Five weeks after the demonstration ended, he was in Washington testifying before a special House subcommittee on education, at the invitation of Representative Roman C. Pucinski. A six-term Democrat and decorated veteran of the Army Air Corps who had flown with the first B-29 bomber raid over Tokyo, Pucinski represented Chicago's heavily ethnic Northwest Side, a district that, like the congressman himself, had grown increasingly impatient with the unwashed radicals' contempt for the established order. Pucinski endorsed Bettelheim's notion that many of the demonstrators were emotionally sick and found his Nazi parallel "most timely," saying that the therapist's diagnosis offered for the first time some professional guidance for dealing with the dissidents.[12]

Bettelheim spelled out that guidance in a statement of about eight thousand words that he read to the rapt committee. He said that many of the young protesters were bright but "remained fixated at the age of the temper tantrum," which was what they were throwing on the campuses. From his expert's chair, he told the representatives that the protesters were indulged, "guilt-ridden," middle-class kids drawn to figures like Ho Chi Minh and Mao Tse-tung because they desperately needed strong father figures; he assured them that psychiatric study had shown the demonstrators to be emotionally immature and that psychologists "always found" that such people hated themselves as much as they hated the establishment. Bettelheim offered no evidence to support these observations, and the committee members asked for none. He had "no doubt" that the protest movement included would-be Stalins and Hitlers, though he conceded that there were "vast differences" between Germany in the 1930s and the United States in the 1960s. He felt that the rebelling students undermined university and intellectual life but that they themselves did not pose a serious threat to the nation; what he did fear was that the

Students for a Democratic Society and other disruptive guerrillas of the New Left would trigger a fascist backlash of the kind he had witnessed in Austria and Germany against the communists and Social Democrats.

The urge to revolt, Bettelheim told the committee, could be significantly reduced by a year or two of required national service for high-school graduates, either in the military or in a domestic peace corps working on socially useful projects for pay and vocational training. American society kept adolescents dependent for too long, encouraging puerility; the cure for this was "to age them a little bit," he said, to appreciative laughter. In Bettelheim's view, national service would give many in their late teens both a sense of confidence and a stake in rebuilding society while persuading a significant number to skip higher education. This was a good thing, for too many high-school graduates attended colleges and universities even though they did not belong there, students who had neither the discipline nor the intellectual curiosity to benefit from the curriculum. Bettelheim said he also was convinced that if a program of national service were established enough young people would want to serve in the armed forces to end the draft. A volunteer army, in turn, would obviate the need to continue the college exemption, which he regarded as a major cause of campus unrest. If students are excused from service when others are not, he said, then they can live in peace with themselves only if they regard the Vietnam conflict as "a vile war." [13]

Bettelheim's statement made headlines across the country. " 'Nazi Parallel,' " announced the *Mercury-News* in San Jose, California, over the Associated Press's widely distributed report on his testimony.[14] "Student Protests Tied to Guilt Idea," declared *The New York Times* above its news story.[15] Two days later, the paper excerpted a portion of Bettelheim's statement on its editorial page,[16] and the Washington *Post* published a larger extract in its Sunday "Outlook" section.[17] The Chicago *Tribune* ran a news story ("Bettelheim Hits Lack of Self-Discipline"),[18] an approving editorial ("The Devil Finds Work for Idle Hands")[19] and the entire statement as an article in its Sunday magazine ("On Campus Rebellion: A New and Potentially Dangerous Rite of Manhood.")[20]

In mid-May, Bettelheim returned to Washington and repeated his views, this time before a Senate subcommittee investigating civil disorders. Throughout 1969 and beyond, he rode the issue, in his *Ladies' Home Journal* column, in interviews, in lectures, and in articles. In *Playboy,* he wrote, "[I]f some modern boys engage in rampages, I believe we can trace it to the virtual abdication of their dads from any sort of clear-cut position in the family." [21] In *Encounter,* he recommended that the angry young follow the example of Melville's Ishmael, who did not succumb to the hypos when faced with the damp, drizzly November in his soul; instead of knocking off people's hats or reaching for pistol and ball, he escaped the establishment and tested his mettle against Ahab and Moby-Dick, thus achieving manhood. [22] In *The New York Times Magazine,* Bettelheim advised weak-kneed parents and educators that children must learn fear. "What was wrong with old-fashioned, authoritarian education was not that it was based on fear," he wrote. "That is what was right with it." [23]

One mother who read these lines was Ruth Bemak, who had idolized Bettelheim when she had sat with other wide-eyed young brides at the University of Chicago in 1948 drinking in his wisdom on how to rear their small children, advice that reached thousands more in his popular book *Dialogues with Mothers.* Then his repeated instruction had been that the child best understood his own needs and that permissiveness should be the parental rule. Bemak and many of the other new mothers had accepted this advice as gospel, and now some of their sons and daughters, including her boy, were dropping out and trashing the establishment. Well, Bettelheim now lectured them in the *Times,* what did you expect if you indulged them so? He wrote that he knew mothers of "extreme campus activists who, when the children were infants, fed them cookies against inner resistance because that is what good mothers were supposed to do. And soon even the child's pleasure evaporated as he realized he was being indulged to make the mother feel good about herself." [24] Bemak told me that after reading the piece she "never believed another word he wrote."

Like many men in their mid-sixties, Bettelheim disdained the prevailing youth culture, with its loud rock, hippie clothes, and long hair, and at the Orthogenic School often treated it as a personal affront. Charles Pekow told me that when he pointed out that Jesus had unshorn locks, Bettelheim said, "Look at him, he's dead." Joe Suchman loved bellbottoms and yearned to play the guitar; he said Bettelheim permitted neither. Suchman did have a ukulele, and the director came into the playroom one day when he and a friend were singing a Beatles song that included the phrase "Baby, I love you." Suchman recalled that everyone applauded when they were done except the director, who gave them one of his hard looks and asked, Just who is this baby? "It was ridiculous," Suchman said. "It ruined a good time for everyone." Eric Bettelheim and his friends received similar treatment during a party at 5725 Kenwood in the mid-1960s. The teenagers had gotten into the liquor; the dancing was slow and close, the music loud, the room semidark; then, suddenly, the lights were on. "I remember the heart-in-the-throat feeling when Bruno appeared," recalled Eric's Lab School friend Matthew Piers. "He chewed out Eric in front of all of us and sent everyone home." Later, Bettelheim described the incident to Charles Saltzman, principal guidance counselor at the Lab School, saying that more parents should stand up to their children.

Inevitably, Bettelheim's high profile and blunt opinions made him a target for demonstrators. Two weeks after he appeared before the House subcommittee, he was in New York City for the annual meeting of the American Orthopsychiatric Association, an interdisciplinary organization founded in the mid-1920s that regards itself as representing progressive thinking in the U.S. psychotherapy movement. At this 1969 convention, the association was at pains to address the issues consuming the nation, scheduling panel discussions and symposia on hippies, student revolt, drugs, black power, the ghetto child, and a lunch marking the first anniversary of Martin Luther King, Jr.'s assassination. There was also a roundtable in which the dissident young had a chance to make their main argument, which was that the profession's concentration on psychology was misplaced, because social factors like poverty, racism, and lack of education were the primary causes of mental suffering.

Despite the AOA's efforts at inclusiveness, the bulletin boards at the New York Hilton blossomed with announcements of rump meetings and caucuses, and several panels commenced under the threat of a "break-in" by the dissidents, not least the workshop on autism and schizophrenia in which Bettelheim was the star participant. Marion Langer, the association's executive director at the time, told me that when she warned Bettelheim he faced a potential invasion he resisted the Levi strategy that had worked so well at Chicago and demanded that she call the police in advance. She refused, telling him, "It hardly looks good to the public if a great mental health expert can't handle these kids and that he should deal with them."

Shortly after the workshop began, in the Rotunda Room on the third floor of the hotel, about a dozen protesters marched in. They wore Che Guevara berets, carried one or two toy machine guns, and chanted, "Ho, ho, Ho Chi Minh/The paranoids are gonna win." Irwin C. Rosen, who was chief psychologist at the Menninger Clinic at the time and also on the panel, told me what happened next. "When they got to the well of the room, where we were sitting, one said, 'Dr. Bettelheim, you are on record as saying that students who demonstrate are paranoid.' Bruno said, 'That's right,' and the kid said, 'Well, was this diagnosis the result of a full examination? Because if you call them paranoid without a full psychiatric examination you're irresponsible. And if you went public and said they were paranoid after you examined them, then you're unethical. Which are you, irresponsible or unethical?' " Bettelheim reddened and then simply "lost it"; he said he didn't have to stand for such harassment and stalked out of the room. Still, the demonstrators refused to leave, and soon a hotel security guard arrived and asked if the remaining panelists wanted them evicted. "All of us wanted to prevent that, to avoid a serious confrontation," Rosen said, so the panel offered to let the dissidents have their say if they would then depart so the workshop could continue; they agreed, and the afternoon played out peacefully. "They were very angry at Bruno, but I think he overreacted," Rosen said. "I kind of liked the kids. They were not thuggy, and the one kid framed the question about Bruno's paranoia charge very well."

Bettelheim may have lost it on the steps of the administration building and at the AOA meeting, but his response to the militant young in general was not always unreasonable. Some of the protesters doubtless could have benefited from a year or two of national service. "I think Bettelheim had a point about us," recalled Jerald Lipsch, who was among the more moderate students who sat in at Chicago. He concedes that many of the undergraduate dissidents did lack maturity. Bettelheim's argument that the university should be a haven for intellectual debate and not a battleground was shared across the political spectrum, including by the leftist philosopher Herbert Marcuse, whose radical teachings had made him an idol to the demonstrators at Columbia but who told them that violence had no place on the campus. Bettelheim was hardly alone, too, in observing of youthful mind-blowers that when "you can't face life without drugs, you're already in very bad shape."[25] What set him apart from most other critics of the rebellion was his failure to engage the main issue that was driving it. To students who thought the Vietnam War "vile" for reasons other than rationalization of their draft deferments, who called the U.S. intervention immoral, he replied that all wars are immoral and left it at that.[26] "And don't tell me," he wrote in *Ladies' Home Journal,* "[that] the children can do something about the war in Vietnam, because that's been tried, too. It was tried in the children's crusade, and all those children died. Well, they no longer die physically. They die mentally; they die psychologically."[27] Of intellectuals like Paul Goodman, Leslie Fiedler, and Edgar Friedenberg, who had become culture heroes to the protest movement for encouraging its opposition to the war, he said: "They have a tremendous need to be loved by the young. I have absolutely none."[28]

Almost from the moment Bettelheim arrived in the United States, he began criticizing Europe's Jews for their passivity in the face of the growing Nazi threat, for not doing precisely what many in the 1960s antiwar movement, for all its excesses, were now doing. In 1963, he had criticized the nation's willingness to spend billions of dollars on the military and the space program while devoting so little money to rehabilitating juvenile delinquents and the mentally ill.[29] He had subtitled *The Informed Heart* "Autonomy in a Mass Age," and repeatedly decried technological society's threat to the individual, writing that mankind's greatest hope lay in a "sizable minority" that would resist this oppressive trend.[30] Now such a minority had risen, attacking the military-industrial complex and other manifestations of the corporate culture that were pushing the United States in the direction that Bettelheim said he deplored.

But now, while he conceded that, yes, things were wrong with the country, he insisted that there was also "plenty right" with it, and that one should go along with the establishment if it is half-way reasonable because "any establishment is only half-way reasonable."[31] The day after Bettelheim testified before the House subcommittee, the Washington *Post* reported on page one that 351 U.S. servicemen had died in Vietnam the week before. Bettelheim did not examine whether such lethal facts represented a halfway reasonable response to the civil war in Southeast Asia; instead, he urged parents to raise their children "on the British [sic] statement, 'My country, right or wrong.' "[32] If he pondered how that rallying cry might have struck him on the train to Dachau, he did not say; nor, in calling all wars immoral, did he wrestle, in print at least, with the philosophic complexities posed by "the good war" that had crushed a master race bent on turning him to ashes.

Bettelheim's attitude toward the student revolt reflected his growing political conservatism. The man who in 1956 had told James Farrell that he was working for the election of Adlai Stevenson now dismissed such a liberal as unable "to see a problem when it is in front of his nose."[33] Liberals had become helpless before the threat of "mob rule" and were making "all too much of a fetish out of formal democratism."[34] Bettelheim would rail at the intellectual establishment's "empty deep down vicious 'progressivism' "[35] and accuse the New York Jewish intelligentsia and its Gentile fellow travelers of promulgating a sick and destructive literature about "paranoic nihilists." He cited no specifics, but said that the enthusiasm for such writing flowed from a deep, unwitting anti-Semitism.[36]

It was the plight of Israel, however, that brought down his greatest wrath on the liberals. He saw them as working subtly against the Jewish state, in part by making sure that the media countered news of that nation's suffering with reports on the oil shortage in the United States and the need to appease Arab suppliers. Privately, he called the oil shortage a chimera and charged the liberals, "Jews foremost among them," with blocking construction of the Alaska pipeline; if it were built, he said, U.S. dependency on Arab oil would end.[37] By the early 1970s, Richard Nixon was his man, a true friend of Israel; ten months after the president fell in August 1974, Bettelheim was still blaming the liberals, in a letter to his Jerusalem friend Carl Frankenstein. "Our 'Watergate' was the worst pseudo battle of the most amoral men who camouflaged themselves as guardians of virtue and, by pointing at Nixon as the embodiment of everything vile, avoided looking at themselves. Nixon was their sacrif[i]cial scape goat. . . ."[38] (Speaking to a meeting of social studies teachers, Bettelheim lamented America's value-free society, suggesting that it was a function of the nation's educational system; he said the Watergate scandal might have been avoided if the co-conspirators had been required in school to use McGuffey readers, which taught ethical behavior.[39])

Bettelheim's concern for the Israelis and for beleaguered Jews in general did not extend to the plight of African Americans in the land that had rescued him from an annihilating prejudice. In March 1962, the Cook County Department of Public Aid named the Orthogenic School one of six children's institutions that barred blacks and said it would no longer make placements there.[40] Bettelheim publicly denied the allegation, but in fact he enforced an all-white policy throughout his three decades as director of the school, where a heroic depiction of John Henry, the legendary black steel-drivin' man, still graces a stairway, and another mural shows a pregnant woman with a black-and-white belly, meant to symbolize racial equality. Bettelheim's stated reason for his policy was that one or two African-American residents would feel uncomfortable because of their minority status and the disturbed white children would feel somehow threatened by the presence of blacks.[41] The latter concern did not extend to the men and women who cooked and served the children's meals and cleaned their toilets, almost all of whom were black throughout Bettelheim's tenure. The rest of the staff was white. Bert Cohler told me that in 1971, when he ran the school for several months while Bettelheim was on leave, he hired a black counselor, a young middle-class woman with a master's degree from the University of

Chicago. This enraged the director, as did Cohler's proposal that a preschool center funded by one of the school's big donors take in some children from ghetto families. "Bettelheim was furious that I wanted to bring in these black kids," Cohler said. "He was a snob and a racist, what can I tell you?"

Race relations was a contentious issue in Hyde Park, where throughout the 1950s the university led one of the most ambitious urban-renewal efforts in the nation, one its detractors called "Negro removal." By 1960, the project had pushed scores of businesses and hundreds of families out of the neighborhood, and bulldozers had razed acres of aging homes and stores, which were replaced by town houses and other upscale amenities in a successful attempt to seal off the campus from the black poverty that encroached on three sides. The radical organizer Saul Alinsky was publicly critical of the university and worked hard in the early 1960s to improve the lot of poor blacks in Woodlawn, the neighborhood on the northern edge of which sat the Orthogenic School. One day Alinsky was walking near the school with his organizing colleague, Nicholas von Hoffman, when they ran into Bettelheim. "There was the briefest hello," von Hoffman told me, "and then Bruno went into a harangue about how Saul was bringing in these savages and gorillas and animals and letting them loose on the university community."

Though Bettelheim wrote of the anti-Semitism that had crimped his life in Vienna and, with Morris Janowitz, published two books that sociologically charted the pain of prejudice, he gave the notion of racial equality his hard eye in print as early as 1956. In a review of Kenneth Clark's *Prejudice and Your Child*, he wrote that it is "obviously untrue" that all children are harmed by prejudice, and dismissed as "blatantly untrue" the African-American psychologist's belief that meeting children of different races and religions leads to better relations. Bettelheim cited as evidence his own experience as a Jewish boy in the non-segregated schools of Germany (sic) and Austria, where, he said, racism and ultranationalism had taken root; whereas "most children who went to [segregated] Catholic parochial schools turned out (even under the Nazis) to be much less prejudiced, not only against Jews but Poles and Czechs as well." How he knew this he did not say, but he did suggest that slavery was not always such a bad thing, since without it in ancient Greece "there would have been no leisure, and hence no Plato or Aristotle." [42]

Bettelheim's conservative politics, and especially his stern judgment of the youth culture, moved *The New York Times Magazine* to headline its 1970 profile "Bruno Bettelheim Is Dr. No." (Not long before, *Time,* in a laudatory article about his work with autistic children, had called Bettelheim "Chicago's 'Dr. Yes.' " [43]) The director had cooperated with David Dempsey, author of the *Times* article, sitting for long interviews and giving the writer access to staff and, in a rare breach of his rule, the children as well. After the journalist departed, his subject had what Bert Cohler called a major attack of paranoia. "He told me that as a result of what he had said someone was going to discover some awful truth about him, which, if known, would discredit his work and the work of the school," Cohler said. He did not tell his protégé what this awful truth was, but enough false information appeared in the piece to embarrass Bettelheim seriously if anyone had checked the facts. Dempsey reported that Bettelheim had been a practicing analyst in Vienna; that he had taken two autistic children into his home; that Eleanor Roosevelt and Herbert Lehman, who "knew of his work," had helped snatch him from Buchenwald; and that Eisenhower had made his 1943 essay on the camps required reading for his officers in Europe during the war. These As Ifs had been buoying up Bettelheim for years, but never in so prominent a place as the paper of record's Sunday magazine, on whose cover he appeared listening intently to a resident at the school.

By coincidence, Dempsey returned to New York from Chicago with the director, who was flying to a speaking engagement. The reporter found "none of the stiffness and formality or ideological bluster" he had encountered at the school, but instead a seatmate who now was friendly and companionable. In this chatty atmosphere, Bettelheim disclosed that he played in a regular poker game that included his faculty colleague Saul Bellow,[44] a diversion the novelist told me was imaginary, though he held out the possibility that the game may have included a ringer who had assumed his identity.[45] At the school, Bettelheim also had told Dempsey that he had been approached to treat Marilyn Monroe's emotional problems. To Bettelheim's likely relief, neither the Monroe nor the Bellow story appeared in the profile, which gave readers a caring if crotchety Dr. No in a portrait that was, on balance, positive, though the subject did not think so: "I am smarting from the deliberate distortions and outright lies which Dempsey put in his article,"[46] he wrote to James Farrell.

ON APRIL 7, 1970, many of the community leaders who had gathered at the Conrad Hilton Hotel to salute Edward Levi sixteen months before were back in the grand ballroom to honor Bruno Bettelheim for his twenty-five years of dedication to the Orthogenic School. Robert Finch—Richard Nixon's secretary of health, education, and welfare—was the principal speaker, and the list of sponsors for the fund-raising event ranged from Chicago Mayor Richard J. Daley and Illinois Governor Otto Kerner to Karl Menninger and Anna Freud, and included not only Levi but Robert M. Hutchins, Lawrence A. Kimpton, and George W. Beadle, the three former presidents of the University of Chicago under whom Bettelheim had served. The program for the black-tie dinner, attended by some four hundred guests, saluted a refugee who had come from Vienna as a "[p]sychoanalyst and art historian" and found a new life and career in Chicago, a "[t]herapist and teacher, author and humane philosopher . . . [who had] restored hundreds of children to useful lives." In his speech, Finch said that, "all across the board, it can be said that the influence of Dr. Bettelheim's insights and of his disciples is pervasive."[47]

In 1967, the university had received a pledge of five hundred thousand dollars from the Foundation for Emotionally Disturbed Children, the Orthogenic School's committed fund-raising arm, to establish a professorship to be held by future directors.[48] At the dinner, Levi announced that the plans would go ahead for this Bruno Bettelheim chair, and to a hushed room the honoree, clearly moved, said that he had now been relieved of one of his greatest worries: "Will it be possible to carry on our work after I had to withdraw from it? The endowed professorship assures that in each coming generation the very best man will shed light into what then will be the darkest recesses of the human mind, the most severe disturbances of the soul. To our university, and to you all, I am more grateful than I can put into words for the most unusual, the most unexpected honor that you attached my name to this chair." [49]

A chair of a different kind already rested in the corner of the Orthogenic School living room, a stately seat of carved wood that symbolized as much as anything what Bettelheim had created in the past quarter-century. When he was growing up, one of the dramatic new sights in Vienna was the Kirche am Steinhof, the centerpiece of a mental hospital high on the western edge of the city. Otto Wagner, Austria's master of Jugendstil, had been invited to design the institution, a remarkable request given that world-famous architects were then, as now, rarely if ever asked to bother with buildings for the mentally ill. For centuries, society had cast these embarrassing citizens into prisons and asylums as ugly and mundane as they were dark and cruel, buildings carefully stashed away from the daily traffic of the general population. But the glistening copper dome of Wagner's church could be seen from much of the city, and beneath it residents of this Institution for Care and Cure, so named to avoid the connotation of insanity, walked in spacious quiet, shafts of light suffusing the tranquillity through stained-glass windows by the Secessionist Kolo Moser. "The patients knew that this building, one of the most beautiful and impressive in the city, was there only for them," wrote Bettelheim,[50] who by 1970 had transformed the buildings that housed the Orthogenic School into his own Steinhof on the Midway.

Dr. B may often have been the Big Bad Wolf, but anyone waiting for him did so in a den whose welcoming decor set the tone for a children's institution that smiled physically more than any other in the nation. Besides the elegant, thronelike chair, which the art-loving director had unearthed in a university storeroom, the living room featured a carousel horse of polished wood that Bettelheim had picked up during a vacation on Cape Cod, a wooden cradle he had found on a trip to Austria, and a three-story Victorian dollhouse. "He chose everything with great care," Jacquelyn Sanders told me—the paint for the walls (light blue with white trim), the sturdy, comfortable sofa, the pastel rug with its border of trees. Bettelheim insisted that the school order the finest produce and meats for the dining room and always paid close

attention to the table settings. At one point, he wanted new stem-
ware but was concerned about the children's safety. He and a staff
member descended to the basement and smashed several sample
glasses until they found a make that splintered into small fragments
instead of dangerous large shards.[51]

The dorms were large, cheery rooms with walls of different
hues, patterned curtains, and multicolored ceiling lights that shone
down on polished floors and throw rugs. The days of bunk beds
were long gone; now each child had his or her own wooden bed
and dresser, each embellished with a floral or other figure. The
former lumber dealer worked with a furniture designer to create
these pieces and insisted they be well made. He also insisted that
the beds differ in size, to fit the various corners of the dorm and
to give each child a sense of individuality; if that meant the extra
expense of custom-made mattresses, so be it. The children's drawings adorned the walls around many of the beds. "Bruno recognized the void in many of the kids' lives," said Jerome Goldsmith,
Bettelheim's counterpart at Hawthorne Cedar Knolls. "He sensed
they were reluctant to hang stuff on the walls themselves, so he
put up pictures first and then let kids replace them. He said that if
you start barren it stays barren. That is a very simple but a very
subtle understanding that he taught us."

The school's hallways were not the drab corridors of most
institutions but colorful passages of painted stairs and wall art,
which Bettelheim likened to the stoa, where Greek philosophers
walked along decorated colonnades.[52] On one stairway, a mural by
the Hyde Park artist Harold Haydon featured, besides John Henry
with his hammer, scenes of Tom and Huck rafting down the
Mississippi, Paul Bunyan and his blue ox Babe, pilgrims at Plym-
outh Rock, and pioneers moving west. Another mural, by Jordi
Bonet, graced the façade of the adolescent unit, opened in 1966
and named the Pekow Wing, after one of the school's principal
benefactors, Philip Pekow, whose grandson, Charles, would stun
the family in 1990 by publicly accusing Bettelheim of abuse. The
four panels of Bonet's ceramic mural represent, in the director's
interpretation, the search for self-realization, from birth (the
black-and-white belly) to rebirth (three birds symbolizing the victory of spirit over matter).[53] Like the Steinhof, the school now

had its own stained-glass window, through which light filtered into a corridor fronted by the Bonet mural and twelve romanesque arches. In the garden area, children clambered at will over *The Lady,* a twice-life-size sculpture of a supine female figure. In an interior court, a statue of a girl being cared for by her older sister stood in the center of a fountain pool.

The unique aesthetic ambience of the Orthogenic School owed itself entirely to Bettelheim's vision and constituted a singular achievement, one that parents, children, staff, and visiting professionals like Goldsmith sensed immediately upon entering the front door with its colorful panels of infants, angels, and flowers in bas-relief. The welcoming artwork spoke eloquently for itself, but Bettelheim could not resist giving his Steinhof a thick Freudian overlay. In *A Home for the Heart,* his final book about the school, published in 1974, he wrote that the playground's circular sunken pool and a circular sunken sandbox represented urination and defecation, respectively, and that the children also saw these areas as comforting breasts.[54] They had named the supine woman *The Lady* because if they had called the sculpture *Mother* they would not have felt as free to jump and step on its breasts, abuse that gradually abated as they learned to express their affection and rest their heads on the stone bosom.[55] The heavenly bodies at the top of one stairway also represented the nurturing mother, as in the Milky Way.[56] Animals along another stairway stood for thoughts of instinctual freedom (monkeys in trees), protection (lions), failure to face hard facts (an ostrich with its head buried); a unicorn gave up its phallic power for true love, and the phoenix rose from its own ashes, "thereby of its own free will shedding its former existence to gain a new and better one."[57] Five pages after saying that the children saw pool water as urine, he abandoned that interpretation; now, discussing the statue of the two sisters, he wrote that the "quietly playing fountain, the music of its rising and falling, remind us not only of what should be (the easy flow of human life) but also of the origin of all life in the liquid element . . . the 'oceanic' feeling [Freud] traced back to the earliest phases of ego feeling. . . ."[58]

By the end of 1970, Bettelheim was facing the inevitability of giving up his Steinhof. Two years before, when he had turned sixty-five, the university began extending his contract on an annual basis; but retirement was mandatory at seventy, and, regardless, he knew he could no longer maintain the killing pace he had for so many years. For all the long hours at the school and his heavy schedule of teaching, writing, and speaking, he had never been robust; moreover, there was the disease in his legs, which continued to plague him. Trude was urging him to slow down and to consider moving to a warmer climate, to help his circulation and because she had grown weary of Chicago winters and was tantalized by the prospect of living a more outdoor life where she could garden year-round. The Europeanized nest on Kenwood Avenue was now empty: Ruth had gotten her bachelor's and master's degrees from the University of Chicago and, in 1972, would earn a doctorate at the University of California at Los Angeles, and settle in the area as a therapist; Naomi had gone to the University of Wisconsin and the University of California at Berkeley as an undergraduate and, in 1971, took a master's degree in regional planning from the University of North Carolina at Chapel Hill; Eric was an undergraduate at the University of Rochester and would go on to study law at Oxford in England and the University of Chicago Law School, graduating in 1976 and entering practice in San Francisco.

Free to experiment with a new environment, Bruno and Trude decided to try California. In 1953, Bettelheim's old *Protektor* Ralph Tyler had left Chicago to start the Center for Advanced Study in the Behavioral Sciences, the think tank near Stanford University where Bernard Rimland had been a fellow in the mid-1960s. In the fall of 1971, Bruno began a fellowship there for the academic year, taking up residence with Trude in a cottage just off the center's sunny veranda and working on the manuscript for *A Home for the Heart*. The decision to go west meant that Bettelheim had to tap a successor, or at least a temporary one. He had dangled the directorship before Benjamin Wright as early as the mid-1950s, urging the counselor to become a professor at the university and then come back and head the school; by the mid-1960s, Wright was a professor of statistics and Bettelheim again was pressuring him to return. Wright told me that he rejected the idea because he feared the director would meddle behind his back and that he would wither and die in the great man's shadow. In 1968, Bettelheim also offered the succession to Robert Bergman, who had worked for six months as a counselor in 1965 when he was a psychiatric resident at the university; he, too, declined, preferring to continue his work with the Indian Health Service in New Mexico. By the late 1960s, the director was desperate and began pleading with Bert Cohler to come back and prepare to take over. Cohler was bound for a teaching post at Yale, but at the last minute turned it down and, in 1969, returned to the Orthogenic School as associate director.

Cohler had left the school in 1957 as a teenager to become Bettelheim's star graduate. He had now begun to publish and was an assistant professor at Chicago, where he would rise, as had Bettelheim, to full professor in the departments of education, psychology, and psychiatry. As a former resident and counselor, and now associate director, he understood the Orthogenic School culture as few others and seemed, even though he was only thirty-three, the logical choice to become the next director.

Cohler felt the school had saved his life after he entered as a confused ten-year-old in 1950, and admired much that Bettelheim had accomplished; but he also recognized Dr. B's shortcomings, among them his snobbery and racism, his penchant for instruction by terror, his tendency to indulge in loose diagnoses and exaggerated cure claims, and his practice of luring staff members into "dynamic supervision." Cohler not only disapproved of Bettelheim's couch-work but saw it as an indication that he had come to have more interest in the staff than in the children. Mostly, Cohler felt the school had to be brought up-to-date; he had no intention of overseeing it as if he were "the head of a turn of the century Viennese family."[59]

Papa's departure for the center relieved a good many of the residents. "The days of his marching into the dorm, of everyone falling silent, of people getting clobbered—that stuff ended," Arnold Granville told me. John Schnebly, another resident during this transition period, recalled that when Bettelheim made rounds he and his dormmates had been afraid to talk to him. "We simply would say, 'I'm fine,' when he asked how we were. We wanted him out of the room. When Cohler made rounds, he was more friendly and would stay longer, and he took our side more than Dr. B did. . . . sometimes he would give us a stern lecture, but there was no longer the pervasive sense of fear."

Among some counselors, however, there was a pervasive sense of nostalgia. The women in particular missed their father figure and the certainty he conveyed, for all his growling and the tears it brought, and many counselors resented any push Cohler made to alter the old ways. Mark Blechner, an undergraduate at the university who worked briefly at the school when Bettelheim was in California, was struck by the pecking order in staff meetings. "There was a hierarchy as to who had known Bettelheim the longest," he told me. "The talk was constantly peppered with 'Dr. B would do this' or 'Dr. B would do that.' You felt that for whoever was taking over it was an impossible situation."

As Ben Wright had predicted, Bettelheim began meddling immediately. "From the moment Bert walked in the door, Bruno was undermining him," recalled Leslie Aranow, who arrived as a counselor in the teeth of the transition. "Bruno went to his syco-phants and would depreciate Bert. 'Bert is not me' was the message." The "little girlies," as Cohler's wife, Anne, called these acolytes, complained constantly to their guru by long distance, even about Cohler's decision to remove Quik from the dining-room tables. The children had been imbibing so much of the chocolate-flavored drink each morning that many had stopped eating breakfast; by midmorning they were hungry, so their teachers had to interrupt class to prepare a snack, after which the children weren't hungry at lunch but would be again by midafter-noon. "At a staff meeting we agreed that we would stop putting Quik on the tables, but when I came in the next morning there it was. I looked around and said, 'I thought we'd decided to remove the drink.' 'Yes,' said Elaine or Julie or Joan, 'but we called Dr. B and he said you were depriving the children.'"

Bettelheim second-guessed in more serious crises as well. When a counselor who had been in therapy with Bettelheim slashed her wrists, Cohler hospitalized her in the psychiatric unit of the university's Billings Hospital. "Bruno was furious," Cohler recalled. "He said I should have cared for her in the way she needed to be cared for, that it was my fault. I told him, 'I'm here for the kids, not the staff. The staff have to be grown-ups.' I was glad to talk to them, and did six nights a week, but I was not going to have them sitting in my lap."

Just before Christmas 1971, Cohler got into a dispute with Steve Herczeg, an able, experienced counselor whom Bettelheim called "footballer" because of his lineman's physique and athletic history. Bettelheim had insisted that Cohler accept Herczeg as his principal assistant, in part because he was popular with the children but also because he was a Gentile in a school that Bettelheim told Cohler was top-heavy with Jews. Herczeg had promised to visit his son over the holidays, and did so despite Cohler's demand that he stay at the school, where he was needed. When Herczeg returned after Christmas, Cohler fired him. In Herczeg's telling, Bettelheim refused to intervene in the matter; according to Cohler, the director did just that, calling the university administration from California and furiously demanding that Herczeg be rehired, which he was not. The incident ended with anger all around and both men realizing that by yoking them Bettelheim had set them up to fail. The situation was compounded by the fact that Cohler was, by common agreement, a poor administrator who, unlike Bettelheim, with his background in the lumber business, lacked experience with numbers. By the time the director returned from the center in the spring of 1972, the school's budget had begun to spin out of control. Back in charge of his Steinhof, Bettelheim "was really vicious to Bert,"[60] who soon resigned.

By now, the director had turned to Jacquelyn Seevak, who had been his devoted aide-de-camp until 1965. That year she had married a furniture designer named Billy Woodrow Sanders and left the school to move to Los Angeles, where the couple had a son, Seth, and his mother pursued a doctorate at UCLA. She received it in 1972, but by then the marriage was ending, and when Bettelheim invited her back to succeed him upon his retirement the following year, she accepted. Unlike Cohler, Sanders understood the administration of the school, where, over thirteen years, she had not only worked as an indefatigable counselor but done everything from food ordering to bookkeeping. Also unlike Cohler, she had been in therapy with her anointer, who had hopes that his loyal former analysand would keep the flame alive and run the school as he had. "I am absolutely convinced that he didn't look on me as his successor, but as someone who simply was taking care of the school while he was away; with me, he could have the fantasy that if he ever came back the school would be his again," Sanders told me.

In the summer of 1972, she and her mentor began operating the school together, and by December he had left again, this time to teach for several weeks at Hebrew University in Jerusalem, a step he took in part "to remove myself from my life's work—the School." [61] At the university, Bettelheim renewed his acquaintance with Carl Frankenstein, the Berlin-born psychoanalyst and philosopher who had welcomed him warmly during his 1964 stay in Israel, and the two men soon would begin a steady correspondence that lasted until a few weeks before Bettelheim's death in 1990. Also in Jerusalem, Bettelheim received an unexpected phone call from Paris.

Daniel Karlin wanted to come to Chicago and make his film. He had recently read the French edition of *The Empty Fortress* and found it fascinating. "I was very young, thirty-one, so I just picked up the phone and called Bettelheim and told him I wanted to make a documentary about him and his school," recalled Karlin, who at the time had been working in French state television for several years. Bettelheim would eventually tell Karlin that he had loathed all his life "those who used patients to make themselves famous," [62] a distaste that apparently ebbed during the late-night hours when he had woven "Joey: 'A Mechanical Boy' " and the other dramatic case histories that became central to his reputation. Bettelheim himself had hired Myron Davis to take the photographs of the children that appeared in *Love Is Not Enough,* and Charles Sharp to make films that Bettelheim sometimes showed when lecturing, or when trying to persuade the Ford Foundation to reopen its purse strings as his autism grant was running out. Nor had he ever been shy about sitting down with Dick Cavett or other TV hosts and discussing the children on TV. He was scrupulous, however, about not revealing their real names, and over the years had rejected requests by U.S. producers to bring cameras into the school, in part because he feared they might not be so careful about concealing identities. But Karlin's pitch flattered him; now that he was on the verge of retiring, he was drawn to the prospect of a film that would sum up his work there, a documentary that would appear not on the vulgar American airwaves but in the highbrow, commercial-free precinct of French government television.

By March 1973, Karlin was at the school with a crew, much to the dismay of Jacquelyn Sanders and several other staff members, who were concerned, as had been Bettelheim up to then, about the children's privacy. But Karlin was adamant; he had not come all the way from Paris to shoot the backs of heads, and Bettelheim, in one of his last acts of authority, insisted that the Frenchman have a free hand. Eventually, a compromise was worked out: Karlin could film just as he wished, but the result could never be shown in North America.[63] When the film appeared in France in the fall of 1974, it would become a *cause célèbre,* the focus of what one Paris newspaper headlined as the "scandal of the 'traffickers' in autism." [64]

That brouhaha was more than a year away. With the filming finished, Bettelheim now began his painful withdrawal from Hyde Park. He and Trude had considered moving to Europe, possibly to Switzerland. Trude's friend from her Montessori days, Emarina Vischer, now lived in Basel with her husband, Hubert Radanowicz-Harttmann, Editha Sterba's brother; in 1970, the couples had made a happy three-week trip together through Italy, with Bruno acting as "a great guide" to the country's art.[65] The friendship was a powerful lure, as was the Old World in general, but the Bettelheim children were a greater one. Ruth already lived in southern California, and Eric was attracted to the idea of practicing in San Francisco once he graduated from law school. Bruno had enjoyed his stay at the center in Palo Alto, and had made major progress on *A Home for the Heart,* but he disliked California's laid-back atmosphere and perpetual sunshine. "You can't do therapy outdoors, it's not an outdoors sport," he would tell a friend, adding that California was for fruits and nuts.[66] He knew, however, that the warm climate was good for his health, and Trude adored it.

Reluctantly, they sold the house on Kenwood Avenue, in which they had raised their family, and which had represented such stability in the New World. The buyers were a couple named

Childers, and as Bruno showed them around he wondered aloud how he would manage without the seasons, which he felt primed his creative energy.[67] He agonized, too, over how he would survive without the Orthogenic School, and especially without the University of Chicago, which had succored him almost from the moment he had arrived in the United States in 1939.

Bettelheim bought a house in Portola Valley, a development of rolling hills about a ten-minute drive from the Stanford campus. In this strange new land of freeways and open collars, would anyone know or care who he was, the way his Chicago colleagues did when he entered Judd Hall or the dining room at the Quadrangle Club? In 1971, Bettelheim had been named to the American Academy of Arts and Sciences, and the American Academy of Psychoanalysis had presented him with its Frieda Fromm-Reichman Award for his distinguished contribution to the understanding and treatment of childhood psychosis. The next year, the American Orthopsychiatric Association made him a life fellow, and just as he left the school in 1973 he appeared on *CBS Reports* to talk about autism.[68] He feared that he would disappear among the palm trees, that the honors would cease and the media would stop calling to tap his views on children, concentration camps, the kibbutzim, and the myriad other subjects on which news desks had come to regard him as expert. And even at age seventy, Bettelheim still felt the need for a *Protektor.* Would he find a Ralph Tyler or Ed Levi at Stanford? Would the university, where he knew almost no one, even bother to ask such an old man to teach there, especially an old Freudian who, like many other therapists of his generation, was increasingly regarded as irrelevant by a profession turning more and more to family therapy and psychotropic-drug treatment?

CHAPTER FOURTEEN
California and Fairy Tales

B<small>Y THE BEGINNING OF</small> 1974, Bruno and Trude Bettelheim had settled into their new home in Portola Valley. Though they had purchased it from an Austrian couple, it was a long way from the Ringstrasse, and from Hyde Park as well. The address itself, 1 Sierra Lane, bespoke the alien terrain. The couple now had stunning views of the hills from their terrace and picture windows, but the one-story, two-bedroom wooden structure was set apart; there were no easy sidewalk chats with neighbors here, no strolls to the corner to buy a newspaper or browse in a bookstore, no encounters with colleagues on walks to the campus—only that ubiquitous California carapace, the car, permitted escape from this suburban isolation. The Bettelheims rewrapped themselves in their carefully acquired European mantle: the Oriental rugs, the Kollwitz and Daumier lithographs, the Matisse tapestry, the reproductions of Rembrandt and Goya etchings, the vitrine filled with objets. Trude was soon digging her trowel in the sloping earth surrounding the house, planting roses and alpine strawberries, and doing battle with rabbits and deer, which seemed determined to remind the newcomers that they were indeed now living in a much different place. "We are finding the move to California quite difficult, in parts traumatic," Bettelheim wrote to his former student Nancy Datan just after taking possession of the house. "Life is so very different here, and I miss the University, School, Hyde Park and all our friends very much. I simply haven't found my bearings in a world where the most important thing . . . is the weather—it pours most of the time." [1]

Two weeks after that lament, a local headline announced, "Famed Psychologist on Stanford Faculty." The story reported that Bettelheim had been appointed a visiting professor of psychiatry at the university's medical center and would also teach summer classes in the education department. The article, based on a Stanford press release, left little doubt that landing this therapist "renowned for his work with autism" was a major coup. "Before World War II," one paragraph read, "[Bettelheim] and his wife took into their European home an autistic American girl aged 7 who had been diagnosed as hopelessly feebleminded. This was a decade before autism was even described in the medical literature."[2]

Before long, Stanford students were ducking the machine-gun fire that had raked Judd 126 for so many years. "He lectured and asked intimidating, confusing, Socratic questions," recalled Jonathan Farber, who sat in the packed hall of Bettelheim's Psychoanalysis and Education that first summer. "His style of interacting with the students was really contemptuous, really disdainful and rude. He cowed the whole group." But when, toward the end of the course, the visiting professor began showing films of the children at the Orthogenic School, he changed completely, Farber told me. "The instant there was a child on the screen, his voice softened and he became warm and affectionate. I came away thinking that he hated students but loved these children."

Initially, Bettelheim retained a vicarious connection to his former charges. The phone rang often at 1 Sierra Lane with calls from Jacquelyn Sanders seeking advice on how to handle various crises or administrative problems that arose in the weeks after she took over the school. Though she was now forty-three years old and a mother, and had been away from Chicago for seven years, she remained locked in the dependency on her mentor-therapist that had developed over her thirteen years in his employ. Around this time, however, she resumed therapy, with a Chicago psychoanalyst who viewed Bettelheim and his work with a certain skepticism. Over the ensuing months of analysis, Sanders slowly began to realize the degree to which she had allowed herself to be manipulated and exploited, especially in "dynamic supervision," and she would eventually accuse Bettelheim of unethical practice in placing her on his couch, noting bitterly that the therapeutic situation had given him an unfair hold over her.[3] Sanders's breakthrough made her so angry that she not only stopped calling Bettelheim about school matters but ceased speaking to him for several years. They had a rapprochement before he died, but the subject of their relationship would remain so painful that she refused to talk about it in detail, telling me only that she felt acutely embarrassed that it had taken her so many years to make peace with how blind she had been.

Ruth Marquis, Bettelheim's longtime manuscript doctor, had also come to see him in a new light by the late 1960s. A political liberal, she had been dismayed by his my-country-right-or-wrong view of the Vietnam conflict and had found repellent his dismissal of the antiwar protesters as paranoiacs who deserved to be compared to Nazi youth. Marquis had an experience with a woman neighbor that altered her perspective on Bettelheim's writing as well. "I did it all wrong," the mother told the editor tearfully after reading several pages of *Love Is Not Enough*. Marquis explained that Bettelheim had not meant that everything in his book should be taken as gospel, but at the same time she began to see how his works could have a negative impact on readers and felt a degree of responsibility. In *The Children of the Dream*, which came out in 1969, Bettelheim had once again gratefully acknowledged his "friend and collaborator" for the "loving care" with which she had shepherded the manuscript into print.[4] But after twenty-five years, eight books, and scores of articles, Marquis had now had enough, and despite Bettelheim's sometimes desperate pleadings she would play no role in the editing of his future books beyond supplying titles for the next two.[5]

The loss of the woman who had shaped his prose for so many years was a serious blow, but Bettelheim had a backup in Linnea Brandwein, who as his typist at the Orthogenic School had worked in harness with Marquis. Brandwein had continued to do editorial tasks for him after she left the school in 1965, among them boiling down the dialogues with mothers' transcripts for his *Ladies' Home Journal* column. These, in turn, were edited by Marquis's successor Joyce Jack. She was a secretary at the magazine when she first encountered the publication's prized columnist, and she was as impressed by him as Marquis had been in the 1940s. In 1967, Jack had taken the Radcliffe College publishing course after graduating from Ohio Wesleyan University, where she had minored in psychology, and when the *Journal* offered her the chance to oversee the column she was thrilled. Bettelheim communicated with Jack by phone and mail, as he had with Marquis, who lived in Ann Arbor, Michigan, and Brandwein, who lived in South Bend, Indiana; and as with them, he soon came to depend on her pencil. On a visit to Manhattan, he asked her to join him for breakfast at the Algonquin Hotel, where he often stayed, basking in the European atmosphere of its rooms and dark-paneled lobby. "I was about twenty-six, from the Midwest; it was all terribly glamorous," recalled Jack of that first meeting, at which Bettelheim told her how pleased he was with her work and then stunned her by asking if she would take on his books and articles as well. "There was quite an age difference and I was in awe of him. I felt that he was a really great intellect, a giant," said Jack.

Bettelheim had also now acquired for the first time a literary agent, an experienced New York representative named Theron Raines. During the 1960s, the author had grown increasingly disenchanted with The Free Press, despite his close friendship with its founder, Jeremiah Kaplan, who had seen the possibilities of *Love Is Not Enough* in the 1940s and had published all his works to date. In a common writer's grievance, Bettelheim complained that his books had not been vigorously promoted, at one point railing at a Free Press editor that the company had "ruined" his "life's work" by not getting behind his output;[6] he told the house that its failure properly to publicize and distribute *Dialogues with Mothers* and *The Informed Heart* constituted "a raw deal" and angrily threatened to take his books elsewhere.[7] He finally did so after signing with Raines, who moved him to the prestigious house of Alfred A. Knopf and into the hands of one of publishing's most respected editors, Robert Gottlieb, who counted among his many authors the biographer Robert Caro, the historian Barbara Tuchman, and the novelists John LeCarré and John Cheever. Gottlieb inherited the manuscript in which his new author was trying to sum up his work at the school, the first book that Joyce Jack worked on as well.

Knopf published the book in early 1974 under Ruth Marquis's title, *A Home for the Heart,* and, like Bettelheim's three previous books about the school, it received a warm reception. Elizabeth Janeway, writing in *The New York Times Book Review,* described the author as "a natural parabolist, capable of seeing the universe in a grain of sand and passing it on."[8] In *The New York Review of Books,* child psychoanalyst Elsa First wrote that Bettelheim's "clinical resourcefulness and the unfailing respect he showed his psychotic children were remarkable."[9] Christopher Lehmann-Haupt of the *New York Times* praised the author for creating a "hospital that specializes in the treatment of autistic and severely schizophrenic children," a nurturing milieu that urgently needed to be replicated throughout the country, as Bettelheim proposed. Lehmann-Haupt lamented that "there is only one Bruno Bettelheim, and only a handful of people who approach him in perceptiveness and courage. . . ."[10]

In its plea for more humane children's treatment centers, and in its angry attack on a society that tolerates the dark and impersonal warehouses that were and remain all too common, *A Home for the Heart* carries a strong and valuable message, though one that dates back at least to Dickens. Bettelheim's portrait of the Orthogenic School is of a loving refuge for troubled children whose physical embrace—vividly depicted not only by the prose but in color plates of the dorms, the murals, the statuary, and the carvings on the welcoming front door—does indeed deserve replication as widely as possible. But much in the book is little more than self-promotion, just the result that the author claimed he was "terrified" would be the case unless Joyce Jack kept him from pushing himself into the foreground.[11] As Bert Cohler would put it, the book reads less like a thoughtful summation of a life's work than "a public relations report. . . ."[12]

Once again Bettelheim wrote of his "psychoanalytic training" (page 11) and of Patsy, the "hopeless" case he had treated for autism in Vienna (page 12). He reported that over twenty-five years only two prospective residents had decided not to attend the Orthogenic School (p. 186) and once more maintained that better than 85 percent of those who did were "restored to full participation in life" (page 6). As in the past, there was no evidence for this claim, since he had commissioned no follow-up study during his twenty-nine years as director.

Bettelheim explained that the first principle of treatment was that the children were always right (page 425) and left no doubt that he regarded their privacy as sacrosanct (page 152). He wrote that physical restraint was rarely necessary (page 58), and how important it was to "avoid the enticement to dominate the patient, one of the most hazardous temptations to the psychotherapist" (page 18). He stressed, too, how crucial it was that the staff demonstrate "a deep commitment not to push others around" (page 418). The self-described Big Bad Wolf said that he had reorganized the school in the 1940s so there would be no hierarchy (page 216), and made it clear that supervision, which he in fact had practiced over three decades on Jacquelyn Sanders and many other staff members, did not "fit the reality of the therapeutic milieu because it assumes that one person knows more than another, and therefore can direct his work" (page 402).

Besides such revisionism, Bettelheim indulged his gift for dramatic vignettes. There was the mute schizophrenic child who refused to defecate in the toilets and stuffed them with paper instead. Engineers spent "days on end" reaming out the pipes, "sometimes all the way to the city sewer," to make sure that the toilets worked again the next morning, thus allowing the child to see that he (or she; Bettelheim did not provide name, gender, or age) could again stuff them up. "The real payoff came

> when this up-to-then mute patient not only suddenly commenced defecating into the toilet, but also started to talk. Now all the stuffed-up words overflowed, as the toilets had before. . . . [I]t seemed such a miracle to those who had worked so hard at unplugging the toilets that it was as though through their patient labor they had unplugged the patient which, in a way, they had. [Page 305.]

Eric Schopler, for one, found this oral-anal breakthrough somewhat lacking in science but nonetheless felt compelled to salute his old professor, observing that, as a rationale for keeping janitors and counselors happy on latrine duty, the equation of bowel movements and language development was "sheer artistry." [13] It was also familiar artistry, turning as it did on the magic

arrival of speech: like the tale of Johnny, the cactus-chewing boy
in Richard and Editha Sterba's Vienna waiting room who after
weeks of silence suddenly spoke profound words about psychoanalysis; or the story of Patsy, who had been mute until one day,
under Bettelheim's therapeutic care, she made the roots of her
anguish clear by asking for the skeleton of George Washington.

A Home for the Heart kept its author's name before the American public but did not significantly modify his reputation one way
or the other. In the fall of 1974, however, the name Bettelheim
would become a household word in France. A strike against
ORTF, the state broadcasting monopoly in a nation then with no
commercial TV, had left the government in desperate need of
programming, and among the people it turned to was Daniel
Karlin, whose documentary about Bruno Bettelheim and the Orthogenic School was now ready. The unions asked Karlin to with-
hold his film, a request they had every reason to believe he would
honor since he was an avowed communist; but the prospect of his
work appearing in prime time moderated whatever solidarity he
may have previously felt with the workers. The documentary appeared in October in four installments, virtually the only television
available in a nation of more than fifty million.

The films, called collectively *Un Autre Regard sur la Folie (A
Different View of Madness),* take their viewers on an extensive tour
of the school, showing its physical warmth, the children in the
playground, at volleyball, drawing, walking on the Midway.[14] A
girl of about twelve tells Karlin that the school is a good place and
that she is glad that the film will appear in France, so the French
will see that disturbed people are not so terrible. A teenager says
that she would not have survived had she not come under Bettelheim's benevolent wing. In another scene, a kindly Dr. B leans
against a piano talking to two other teenage girls, patting them on
the head with avuncular affection. Only at a staff meeting is there
any tension, as the counselors' eyes dart about nervously under
Bettelheim's (and the camera's) gaze.

One segment is devoted to Marcia, using film that Charles
Sharp had shot in the 1950s that shows her discovering balance on
a seesaw, feeding her dolls cups of water, hugging one of her
counselors. Bettelheim appears, telling Karlin that when he was in

the concentration camps he discovered what an impact environment could have, so he decided to create one at the school that would have a positive effect on children like Marcia. He explains that the school was least successful with such autistic children, helping only 50 percent; overall, however, his results were better than 85 percent. He talks of the importance of privacy and of how, before he took over in the 1940s, children were slapped and beaten, a practice he put a stop to immediately. He tells Karlin that when the children on his watch got violent and abusive the school did nothing to restrain them. Harpsichord music plays in the background.

Throughout the four installments, Karlin challenges almost nothing Bettleheim says. Nor does he bring on Jacquelyn Sanders, Bert Cohler, or any other present or former staff members to give their views of what it was like to work at the school; he talks informally with several children, but does not interview any who had left and might have felt freer to talk about their experiences. The viewer hears from no parents, none of the mothers of autistic children who had been devastated by *The Empty Fortress*. There are no interviews with Bettelheim's faculty colleagues or former students at the University of Chicago, or with psychotherapists, French or American, who might have brought some perspective to the portrait. Karlin, who regarded his subject as "kind of a genius," told me that he never considered broadening the documentary's scope. "In a way, Bettelheim was my master. I had a great deal of admiration and love for him, and I wanted to do these films as a tribute."

Much to the filmmaker's astonishment and delight, his homage quickly became the talk of the nation, as the press gave it the kind of running coverage usually reserved for the Tour de France. After the first installment appeared, *Le Figaro* interviewed Roland Huméry, the psychiatrist who had translated *The Empty Fortress* into French; he said the naïve Karlin had been seduced by Bettelheim, whose theories on autism were shaky at best but who was deft indeed in the art of *"relations publiques."* [15]

After the second segment, which had offered the portrait of Marcia, *Le Figaro* sought the reaction of Pierre Debray-Ritzen, director of the children's psychiatric service at the Necker Hospital, a major medical center in Paris. He called Bettelheim an excellent example of *"esbroufe psychanalytique,"* the braggart side of psychoanalysis, and suggested that, in pushing his 50 percent and 85 percent success claims, he was something of a crook, and that Karlin's film offered false hope to the parents of autistic children. Debray-Ritzen noted that Bettelheim was not a doctor and had no idea what role neurological factors might play in autism, yet pretended to know the cause of and therapy for the illness while trained child psychiatrists and pediatricians remained mystified by it.[16] When Léo Sauvage, *Le Figaro*'s New York correspondent, telephoned Portola Valley to get a response to this attack, Bettelheim asked who was this man Debray-Ritzen and then dismissed his criticisms by pointing out that his statistics were published under the auspices of the University of Chicago and had been accepted by Stanford, where he was now an honorary professor. "It is on my results that I ask to be judged, on my works, my practice, my books," he told Sauvage.[17]

Bettelheim defenders quickly surfaced. In *L'Express,* the popular newsmagazine, a columnist wrote that his cure results could not be seriously questioned.[18] A psychoanalyst named Jean Filhol called Debray-Ritzen a complete fanatic in his unshakable belief that the seat of autism was neurological and praised Bettelheim as the uncontested master of his Chicago empire.[19] On October 17, ORTF's first channel, where the documentary had made its debut, broadcast a live debate on infantile autism and the methods of Bruno Bettelheim. Among the participants in this evening program, again the only TV fare for millions of viewers, was Roger Misès, a neuropsychiatrist who believed, like Filhol, that biology did not explain everything, and Debray-Ritzen, whose anti-Bettelheim views now spilled out at every opportunity. He said it was monstrous and clownish for state television to devote so much time to this purveyor of Freudian mythology, whose parent-blaming was *"la tarte à la crème de la pensée contemporaine,"* the cream pie of contemporary thought.[20]

This being France, the debate was politicized in some quarters. In *L'Humanité,* the communist daily, Tony Lainé, a child psychiatrist who like his friend Daniel Karlin was a communist, called Bettelheim a courageous man whose belief that autistic children could be rescued placed him in the Marxist tradition that held that all nature was transformable.[21] On the far right, the weekly *Minute* reveled in Debray-Ritzen's assault, not only implying that Bettelheim was an impostor but branding him an extreme leftist and sarcastically suggesting that Karlin had made a flattering documentary because, as a communist, he did not dare criticize a Zionist.[22]

Some of the pie-throwing that followed the airing of *Un Autre Regard sur la Folie* was just that, and, in the case of *Minute,* worse, but what is striking about the coverage, which went on for days in papers throughout the country, is how serious much of it was. In many instances, the complex subject of autism and Bettelheim's views on it were given thoughtful treatment by informed specialists, and a large population was drawn into an intellectually challenging discussion of a profoundly enigmatic illness. This debate marked the first time that Bettelheim's work had been scrutinized in a wide public forum. No such examination had ever occurred in the United States, where broadcast and print journalists had been complicit in building Bettleheim's reputation ever since he had published his concentration-camp report in 1943. Almost without exception, the American media had viewed him through a heroic filter, the same one Karlin had used in shooting a documentary that, ironically, had finally provoked a loud dialogue.

WHATEVER BOOST BETTELHEIM may have gotten from all the attention in France was dampened by the fact that he was facing another cataract operation at the time. The one in Chicago five years before, after which he had had to lie with his head immobile for so many days, had left him with good corrected vision in his left eye; but for months now he had been virtually unable to see out of the right one, which was steadily deteriorating.[23] He contemplated the new operation, as he had the first, with considerable anxiety; he was now seventy-one years old and knew that merely going under the anesthetic at his age was risky. The operation was scheduled for December 2, and as the date approached he called Joyce Jack on the East Coast. "I think he was afraid he was going to die and wanted to say goodbye," she recalled. The procedure was a complete success, giving the patient 20/25 corrected vision once the eye had healed. Bettelheim told Carl Frankenstein of being blindfolded for a period after the operation and of how it gave him time to reflect that, even in old age, one tends to take one's body for granted despite daily reminders of its shortcomings. "[N]ot being able to see for a time was quite an experience," he told his Israeli friend. "I doubt it has made me wiser, as it should. But it was a big step in the direction of accepting the end when it will finally come."[24]

Nine months after the operation, Bettelheim's body gave him reason to fear that the end might be near. He and Trude had undertaken a demanding summer trip through Europe, first visiting Eric in London and then traveling to Normandy for a meeting of French Jungians. After lectures in Geneva and Basel, Bruno returned to France for a ten-day seminar in Lyon, during which he experienced periodic shortness of breath and pain in his chest that radiated into his left arm. "I had my com[e]uppance," he would tell Nancy Datan. "Teaching in French all day long proved too much of a strain for my heart and I suffered an insufficiency. . . ."[25] A Lyon cardiologist had ordered an electrocardiogram and then prescribed nitroglycerin and one other antianginal medication and urged hospitalization; but the patient agreed only to bed rest for several days, until he was deemed well enough to fly home. There his doctor ordered absolute rest for a week and cancellation of all engagements for a month.

While Bettelheim recuperated, he had other bodily betrayals to contemplate. The severe arteriosclerosis in his legs continued to make walking painful, and he now suffered as well from a mild case of adult-onset diabetes and from Zenker's diverticulum, an abnormal pouch in his upper esophagus that at many meals made him feel as if food was sticking in his throat. Initially these episodes caused discomfort for a few minutes and then passed; but they steadily worsened, occasionally causing gagging spells that drove their victim from the table in frightening coughing fits. There was no medication to alleviate the problem, so Bettelheim did his best to control it by avoiding meat and other coarse foods.[26] Despite this precaution, there was no predicting the onset of a serious attack, and he felt increasingly anxious about going to dinner parties and restaurants, fearing he would embarrass himself. "This

really was a torment, an unbelievable torment," recalled Eric Bettelheim, whose father eventually taught him how to force open
his throat if he began to choke.

Bettelheim coped with his medical crises as he did with most
other setbacks, by forging ahead with work. He was not only
teaching at Stanford but in the mid-1970s spent the spring semester doing the same back at the University of Chicago, immersing
himself in the familiar precincts of Hyde Park, seeing old friends,
and occasionally visiting the Orthogenic School. He continued to
accept speaking engagements, and his talks often drew on the
project that was now his central focus, an exploration of the psychological meaning of fairy tales that would become his next and
most popular work, *The Uses of Enchantment*. In a letter to Carl
Frankenstein, Bettelheim wondered if perhaps he had entered into
his second childhood, because he was now finding such enjoyment
in rereading the stories and speculating about their message. But
he also gave his interest a darker interpretation, suggesting that it
flowed from a semiconscious feeling that only a Brothers Grimm–
like miracle could "save the Jews in the long run. . . ."[27]

Robert Gottlieb at Knopf was enthusiastic about the book,
and "Bruno was very excited about it, wanted it to be really
good."[28] However, the literary luster of his new publishing house
intimidated him, as did the scope of this new undertaking. His
mother had read fairy tales to him, but he had not done likewise
very often for Ruth, Naomi, and Eric, explaining that he had
accepted the prevailing view at the time that the scary tales were
bad for children. He blamed psychoanalysts for pushing this idea,
which some had.[29] He knew the literature was vast, but in a
moment of bravado told Frankenstein that it was "astonishing"
how little had been written on the topic.[30] With some trepidation,
he now plunged into this imaginary void, and as the manuscript
developed he repeatedly expressed almost obsequious gratitude to
Joyce Jack for rescuing his "coarse material."[31] He urged her to
make the book succinct and interesting from start to finish. "As I
suggested on the phone, he wrote, "I would like very much that
you let yourself go much more, critici[z]ing, suggesting what
needs to be changed, added. But what I did not say on the phone
is that I would be delighted if you add some spontaneous writ-

ing of your own. I know you are an excellent writer, so why not write some passages to include in the manuscript, the more the better. . . .[32]

Jack did not take up this invitation, but, like Ruth Marquis before her, she played a crucial role in organizing the manuscript and making Bettelheim's prose read, help for which he usually paid her double what she billed him.

Despite this editorial first aid, the manuscript still needed work after it arrived at Knopf. At one point, Gottlieb sent Bettelheim a letter recommending a number of specific changes and in general urging him to curb his repetitiveness and his tendency to give the fairy tales simplistic, dogmatic Freudian interpretations, defects that had worried Jack as well but that she had managed to ameliorate only in part. In one passage, Bettelheim had written that, absent a certain kind of fairy tale, a child is subject to Oedipal anguish without relief. Gottlieb told his author that he was loading the dice, making it appear as if no other comfort were possible; he was taking too much for granted and was bound to put off the reader.[33] As with Jack, Bettelheim was abject in his response. "You are so very right with all you point out, that I am worried that you did not find more to criticize," he wrote to Gottlieb. After offering a tentative modification of the passage, he told his editor to feel free to "rewrite it in any other and better way to meet your most justified objections" and worried that because he was deemed an expert on children Gottlieb might hesitate to be rigorous in his criticism. "Please remember my reputation was not made as a writer, but as a therapist. I need your help badly as an author."[34]

Bettelheim had also needed help while researching the book, and one place he found it was in *A Psychiatric Study of Fairy Tales: Their Origin, Meaning and Usefulness.*[35] This 1963 volume, by a clinical psychiatrist named Julius Heuscher, was rich with psychological gingerbread, and, like the hungry Hansel, Bettelheim helped himself.[36] For Heuscher, fairy tales were a key to understanding human development (JH, page 53); for Bettelheim, "fairy stories represent in imaginative form what the process of human development consists of" (BB, page 12). In *The Uses of Enchantment,* Bettelheim stressed that parents should bring a certain attitude to the telling of the tales.

> One must never "explain" to the child the meanings of fairy tales.
> However, the narrator's understanding of the fairy tale's message to
> the child's preconscious mind is important. . . . It furthers the
> adult's sensitivity to selection of those stories which are most ap-
> propriate to the child's state of development, and to the specific
> psychological difficulties he is confronted with at the moment.
> [BB, page 155.]

More than a decade before, Heuscher had written:

> While one must never "explain" the fairy tales to the child, the
> narrator's understanding of their meaning is very important. It
> furthers the sensitivity for selecting those stories which are most
> appropriate in various phases of the children's development and
> for stressing those themes which may be therapeutic for specific
> psychological difficulties. [JH, page 186.]

Bettelheim criticized children's literature as "one-sided" (BB, page
7), a term that Heuscher used a dozen times to mean materialistic
(JH, page 51 and elsewhere). He restated Heuscher's view that
fairy tales become "refined" by years of retelling (BB, page 5; JH,
pages 5–8) and, like Heuscher, defended the tales as a good means
for a child to comprehend his destructive impulses (BB, page 55;
JH, page 188). Each author set up distinctions between fairy tales
and myths and between fairy tales and dreams (BB, pages 26, 36;
JH, pages 4, 10). To Bettelheim, "The Frog King" was in part
about women getting over the sex taboo and frogs puffing themselves up like erections (BB, page 290), which was how Heuscher
saw the tale (JH, page 138). Both authors criticized what they
regarded as the prettified version of "Sleeping Beauty" handed
down by the seventeenth-century French fairy-tale collector
Charles Perrault (BB, page 230; JH, page 99), and both attacked
Disney and television (BB, page 24; JH, pages 189–95). In a
passage discussing how an individual's growth depends on the
relationship to another person, Heuscher wrote, "Without a
'thou' . . . there is no real existence" (JH, pages 58–59). Bettelheim wrote that, on however high a plane one's life proceeds, "the
I without the *Thou* lives a lonely existence" (BB, page 278). This
dichotomy was a major precept of the philosopher Martin Buber,

set down in 1923;[37] Heuscher credited Buber and other existentialists, Bettelheim credited no one.

In exploring the psychology of fairy tales, Heuscher chose to interpret "Hansel and Gretel," "Little Red Riding Hood," "Snow White," and "Briar Rose" (also called "Sleeping Beauty"); Bettelheim analyzed the same tales in the same order, adding "Jack and the Beanstalk," "Goldilocks and the Three Bears," and "Cinderella." Bettelheim appropriated the three-phase childhood-development scheme that Heuscher loosely attributed to psychology, philosophy, and religion and also used Heuscher's examples when linking certain fairy tales to certain phases of development. In both books, "Little Red Riding Hood" and "Snow White" are about latency, "Sleeping Beauty" is about adolescence, and "Hansel and Gretel" is about the developing infant's relationship to his parents, of which Heuscher wrote:

> The oral frustrations inherent in early childhood training lead to an emotional interaction between the child and the parents in which the latter (at least unconsciously, at night) are experienced as unloving, selfish and rejecting. Since they need their parents desperately, children attempt to counteract, to deny this rejection. In fact, Hansel succeeds in finding the way back from the forest in which they were abandoned the following day. . . . [JH, pages 63–64.]

Bettelheim put it this way:

> It is the child's anxiety and deep disappointment when Mother is no longer willing to meet all his oral demands which leads him to believe that suddenly Mother has become unloving, selfish, rejecting. Since the children know they need their parents desperately, they attempt to return home after being deserted. In fact, Hansel succeeds in finding their way back from the forest the first time they are abandoned. [BB, page 159.]

Heuscher went on:

> . . . Hansel and his sister Gretel appear successful at first. But the frustrations at home continue. The mother seems to become more shrewd in her plans for rejecting the children, [and] finally convinces the father again to abandon them. . . . [JH, page 64.]

Bettelheim wrote:

> The children's successful return home does not solve anything.
> Their effort to continue life as before, as if nothing had happened,
> is to no avail. The frustrations continue, and the mother becomes
> more shrewd in her plans for getting rid of the children. [BB, page
> 160.]

In discussing "Snow White," Heuscher wrote:

> Not wishing to deprive anyone too much, she eats just a little from
> each of the seven plates and drinks just a drop from each glass (how
> different from Hansel and Gretel who, rather disrespectfully, start
> eating the gingerbread house). [JH, page 85.]

Bettelheim's Snow White

> eats just a little from each of the seven plates, and drinks just a drop
> from each of the seven glasses, so as to rob none of [the dwarves]
> too much. (How different from Hansel and Gretel, the orally fix-
> ated children, who disrespectfully and voraciously eat up the gin-
> gerbread house!) [BB, page 208.]

Bettelheim did not list Heuscher's book in his bibliography,
more than half of which consisted of German titles, and he acknowledged him only once in his 122 endnotes, in an aside about
Jungian interpretations of fairy tales (BB, page 314). Nor is
Heuscher the only source that Bettelheim failed to credit. In 1941,
Géza Róheim, a Hungarian psychoanalyst noted for his interest in
fairy tales, wrote, "A folk-tale is a narrative with a happy end, a
myth is a tragedy." [38] Bettelheim wrote that the ending "in myths
is nearly always tragic, while always happy in fairy tales" (BB, page
37). Six years after Bettelheim was born, Freud's protégé Otto
Rank, who had applied psychoanalytic theory to legend and
myth, wrote, "The fictitious romance is the excuse, as it were, for
the hostile feelings which the child harbors against his father, and
which in this fiction are projected against the father. . . . The child
simply gets rid of the father in the neurotic romance, while in the
myth the father endeavors to lose the child." [39] Bettelheim wrote

that "the wish to be rid of the parent arouses great guilt. . . . So in a reversal which eliminates the guilt feeling, this wish, too, is projected onto the parent. Thus, in fairy tales there are parents who try to rid themselves of their child. . . ." (BB, page 204.)

Even when Bettelheim did cite a source, he was sometimes offhand, as when he noted that the psychoanalyst and social philosopher Erich Fromm, in his book *The Forgotten Language,* "makes some references to fairy tales, particularly to 'Little Red Riding Hood' " (BB, pages 313–14). In fact, as the novelist, critic, and children's-book author Alison Lurie observed in her review of *The Uses of Enchantment,* Bettelheim "repeated most of Fromm's points in his discussion of the story." [40]

Bettelheim had been in this forest before, scrambling for nuts and berries that would give him something to say about concentration camps or parenting or autism or the kibbutzim or the youth culture, but seldom digesting his pickings before announcing their meaning to a waiting world. His message this time, as it had been so often in the past, was unequivocal. "The overwhelming bulk of . . . so-called 'children's literature' attempts to entertain or to inform, or both. But most of these books are so shallow in substance that little of significance can be gained from them." However, "nothing" was as enriching and as satisfying to child and adult alike as fairy tales. More could be learned from them "about the inner problems of human beings, and of the right solutions to their predicaments in any society, than from any other type of story within a child's comprehension." [41]

To buttress this claim, Bettelheim again resorted to his favorite device, the anonymous anecdote. In a typical example, he wrote of how the bottled-up giant in "The Fisherman and the Jinny" grows increasingly angry the longer he is confined, until he finally announces that he will slay whoever releases him. "This is exactly how a young child feels when he has been 'deserted,' " explained Bettelheim, who then told of a three-year-old boy left in the care of a woman while his parents traveled abroad for several weeks. First the child looked forward to his mother and father's return, then he grew angry with them for staying away, and when they finally did come home he froze into a silence that took several weeks of compassion and understanding to melt. This child did not speak to his parents because the idea that "forces may reside within us which are beyond our control is too threatening to be entertained," wrote Bettelheim. To reinforce this point, he summoned up a "seven-year-old" who said, when his parents told him that his emotions had carried him away, " 'You mean there is a machine in me that ticks away all the time and at any moment may explode me?' "[42]

Bettelheim maintained that children almost always drew benign instruction from fairy tales and that psychoanalytic principles readily explained these responses, a reductive view that neither Joyce Jack nor Robert Gottlieb had been able to keep in check. Dogs symbolized the ego, hunters the father figure, apples mature sexual desire, and the three bears "the penis and the two testes in the male; vagina and the two breasts in the female."[43] To one reviewer, the reader wasn't in the nursery but in what Vladimir Nabokov called "the fundamentally medieval world of Freud, with its crankish quest for sexual symbols (something like searching for Baconian acrostics in Shakespeare's works) and its bitter little embryos spying, from their natural nooks, upon the love life of their parents."[44] In another critic's view, Bettelheim looked at fairy tales as if they had no history, analyzing them "flattened out, like patients on a couch, in a timeless contemporaneity."[45]

For all his borrowing, he seemed largely ignorant of or at least unwilling to consider the vast exploration of literary romance that predated psychoanalysis and that offered alternative explanations for what a tale might mean. As the fairy-tale scholar Jack Zipes has pointed out, "the symbols and patterns of the tales reflect specific forms of social behavior and activity which often can be traced back as far as the Ice and Megalithic Ages."[46] In eighteenth-century France, the peasantry heard a "Little Red Riding Hood" in which the wolf kills the grandmother, pours her blood into a bottle, and slices her flesh onto a platter; he invites his young visitor to partake of this repast, and when she does a cat calls her a slut for devouring the remains of her elderly kin. She is then forced to do a striptease by the wolf, lured into bed by him, and eaten.[47] No father-figure hunter arrives to save the day; no one cuts open the wolf's belly to free grandmother and granddaughter for the happy ending that Bettelheim had heard as a child in Vienna and that he now found so salutary because children saw "in the opposite figures of the wolf and hunter the conflict between the id and the ego-superego aspects of their personality." [48] Even had the French peasants been able to riffle through the "The Psychopathology of Everyday Life," they might be pardoned for feeling that the main lesson of the bloody tale was that wolves are best avoided, a pragmatic message that a six-year-old snug in her pajamas in Shaker Heights might also draw from the happily-ever-after version. But for Bettelheim the tales were first and foremost psychoanalytic prisms; through them "the child begins to understand—at least on a preconscious level—that only those experiences which overwhelm us arouse in us corresponding inner feelings with which we cannot deal. Once we have mastered those, we need not fear any longer the encounter with the wolf." [49]

No doubt Bettelheim could have made much of Lewis Carroll's rabbit hole. But he rejected with his usual ex-cathedra certainty the possibility that a young twentieth-century reader might find Alice's adventure as instructive as Cinderella's, that her encounters with the Red Queen and the Mad Hatter might prove at least as intriguing as (and less sexist than) a distant world of pumpkins, palaces, princes, and proper slipper sizes. He did not speculate on whether Dorothy's terrifying tornado ride to Munchkinland, the remarkable characters she met there and in the Emerald City, and her safe return to Kansas might be just as delightful and therapeutic for a child as Jack's greedy chases up and down the beanstalk after eggs and harps of gold. For Bettelheim, the large body of modern children's classics was invisible, as if hidden in the shadow cast by a Grimm, culture-bound giant. There were not only no uses for *Alice In Wonderland* and *The Wizard of Oz,* but none for *The Wind in the Willows; Winnie-the-Pooh; Charlotte's Web; A Wrinkle in Time; The Lion, the Witch and the Wardrobe; The Yearling; The Little Prince; The Lord of the Rings; The 13 Clocks; The Phantom Tollbooth; Willy Wonka and the Chocolate Factory; Curious George; Little Women; Heidi;* or the fantastic world of Dr. Seuss, where Bartholemew Cubbins faces beheading because he cannot take off his hat before the king, and Horton the elephant hatches an egg. There was no place for *Bambi* either, even though the popular 1923 story of the steadfast young deer was written by an Austrian novelist, Felix Salten, and offered just the kind of dramatic coming-of-age lesson Bettelheim applauded in fairy tales: that the struggle against severe difficulties in life is unavoidable but if one meets these often unjust hardships bravely "one masters all obstacles and at the end emerges victorious." [50]

Bettelheim was so confident that contemporary children's literature was vacuous that he didn't need to read it. In *Where the Wild Things Are,* the mother of an obstreperous boy named Max calls him a wild thing, and when he threatens to eat her up she sends him to bed without any supper. In Maurice Sendak's perennial bestseller, winner of the Caldecott Medal in 1964, Max not only meets an assortment of monsters in his banishment but controls these hairy, horned beasts. He has fun with this power but eventually grows weary of it and longs to return home; when he does, his supper awaits him, still hot. Bettelheim had never opened *Where the Wild Things Are,* but he assured a group of mothers who asked him about it that Sendak was "obviously captivated by an adult psychological understanding of how to deal with destructive fantasies in the child. What he failed to understand is the incredible fear it evokes in the child to be sent to bed without supper, and this by the first and foremost giver of food and security—his mother." To the question "But why do children *love* this book?" he had no answer.[51] The précis he had heard from the mothers gave him enough information to suggest that Max had been on just the kind of a scary-exciting escape that appeals to most children, especially since he ends up fairy-tale safe "where someone loved him best of all." [52] But Bettelheim seemed bent on scolding Max's mother for exiling her son, saying that had he written the book he would have had her explain to him why he wanted to eat her up rather than have her send him to bed hungry.[53]

Knopf published *The Uses of Enchantment* in 1976. Several critics attacked the book for its ahistoricism, repetitiveness, and psychoanalytic template, one of them suggesting that perhaps the work demonstrated that "the truest fairy tale is Freudian psychology." [54] None of the reviews mentioned Bettelheim's uses of Julius Heuscher's fairy-tale study, a disclosure that would not come until 1978, when Joan Blos, the American editor of *Children's Literature in Education,* noted the plagiarism in an obscure professional journal.[55] Her revelations made little impact and would not surface again until twelve years later, when the folklorist Alan Dundes caused a media stir by citing them after Bettelheim's suicide.[56] "Was He Really Bruno Borrowheim?" asked *Newsweek*.[57] Blos, Dundes, and Alison Lurie thought so, as did others, but Heuscher himself was generous: "We all plagiarize. I plagiarize. Many times, I am not sure whether it came out of my own brain or if it came from somewhere else. . . . I am only happy that I would have influenced Bruno Bettelheim. . . ."[58]

Others were also forgiving. The scholar Harold Bloom noted Bettelheim's reductiveness but was nonetheless "moved, charmed, and frequently persuaded by the humane effort to clarify the dae-monic ground of romance and so to substitute the uses of enchant-ment for the uncanny actualities of the enchantment."[59] Most critics praised the author for his obvious love of the stories, and for promulgating them with such enthusiasm; in *The New York Times Book Review*, John Updike saluted him for writing a "charming book about enchantment. . . ."[60] Some parents doubt-less embraced *The Uses of Enchantment* because of its Freudian certainties, but for most it was likely the author's overall message that fairy tales were good for their children that drew them to the book. Now they had Bruno Bettelheim's imprimatur; children could well handle encounters with wolves and witches, even at bedtime. In an insightful passage, Bettelheim wrote:

> Parents who wish to deny that their child has murderous wishes and wants to tear things and even people into pieces believe that their child must be prevented from engaging in such thoughts (as if this were possible). By denying access to stories which implic-itly tell the child that others have the same fantasies, he is left to feel that he is the only one who imagines such things. This makes his fantasies really scary.[61]

The Uses of Enchantment sold steadily, and by 1995 the New York Public Library would name it one of the 159 most influential and frequently requested "Books of the Century," putting it in the company of the Bible, *Ulysses, 1984, The Joy of Cooking, The Common Sense Book of Baby and Child Care, Mein Kampf,* and,

Bettelheim might have been surprised to learn, *Where the Wild Things Are.*[62] Despite the mixed reception by reviewers, in 1977 *The Uses of Enchantment* received both a National Book Critics Circle prize (for criticism) and a National Book Award (for contemporary thought), in the latter case winning out over works by such finalists as Dostoevsky biographer Joseph Frank and architecture critic Ada Louise Huxtable. Other recipients of National Book Awards that year included Irving Howe, for *World of Our Fathers,* and Wallace Stegner, for his novel *The Spectator Bird.* At the time, the awards were administered by the American Academy and Institute of Arts and Letters, the pantheon of America's cultural elite, which included at least three of Bettelheim's early admirers, Meyer Schapiro, Dwight Macdonald, and James T. Farrell. At the black-tie presentation ceremony, C. P. Snow, the knighted British scientist and novelist, made the principal remarks, but it was Bettelheim who enchanted the august audience with his acceptance speech, which began, "Once upon a time, in a faraway land across the big sea, there was a very old city."

The seventy-three-year-old recipient, self-conscious about his countenance even at this moment of high honor, spoke first of how a mother in this very old city had wanted a second child and how relieved she had been when he turned out to be a boy because he was so ugly. He told of how, in 1914, the lights had gone out forever all over Europe, and of how an old emperor had lost his domain after ruling, it seemed to the boy, since the beginning of time. He told of how the boy, when grown, spent "years of contemplation . . . on a couch specially constructed for the purpose by a famous sorcerer," and of how even this "greatest magician of his time" could not exorcise the vicious dragon that invaded the land "soon after our hero had completed his apprenticeship on the couch." He feared he would never escape from the dragon's minions, called the SS; but, encouraged by the optimism of fairy tales, he struggled on and was miraculously carried across the ocean to the fair city where he and his audience were now gathered. In this new and free land, "his beloved soon joined him, after having traveled around the whole world. They married, had three children, and lived happily ever after."[63]

In private, the boy who grew up to win a National Book

Award regarded the accolade with a certain sourness. He complained that the book, not he, had been recognized, because what had really impressed the judges were the tales and not his treatment of them; he conceded the prize was "nice" but carped that he had had to fly "in an instant" to New York for the ceremony.[64] He also maintained that the *New York Times Book Review* had treated *The Uses of Enchantment* favorably because the editor felt guilty about not publishing an apology or correction after the review had "wrongly attacked" the author. Bettelheim did not specify the nature of the assault, but said the editor's guilt had also moved him to give Bettelheim books by Thomas Szasz and R. D. Laing to review. The assignment was the editor's "subtle way out: asking me to review two very difficult books, hoping I would fall flat on my face, either rejecting [the assignment], which showed that I was afraid to take a stand, or reviewing [the books] unfairly or stupidly."[65] Harvey Shapiro, the review's editor in 1976, called this notion "madness" and could remember no dispute with Bettelheim. He did recall the author's "marvelous" acceptance speech at the National Book Awards fête, as well as a visit the winner paid to his office. Shapiro told me he enjoyed their meeting but was perplexed by his guest's reaction when invited to sit in an easy chair. "Bettelheim said I was putting him in the grandpapa's chair. He was sort of hostile, as if I were placing him in an inferior position."

Bettelheim's sense of inferiority and a growing bitterness surfaced increasingly in the letters he wrote after moving to California. Though he continued to teach for a while at the University of Chicago, he eventually had to cut that tie and came to regard the institution as ungrateful. In a letter to Nancy Datan, he complained that he had been paid "very meagerly" and that, though he had raised several million dollars over the years and had added the luster of his reputation to the university, he had been "put out to pasture without as much as a line of thanks or good wishes." He conceded that a few Orthogenic School associates had bid him a warm farewell, but they had worked for him. "Those for whom I worked did not find it worth their while to say good bye to me. They probably felt good riddance, but did they have to make it so obvious?"[66] Bettelheim did not mention that in 1970 he had been honored by the university and the city's gentry at a formal dinner of a kind few if any of his faculty colleagues could hope for, an elegant event whose sponsors had included the president and three former presidents of the university, and at which the principal speaker, the nation's secretary of health, education, and welfare, had saluted the honoree for his work. It was in the warm glow of that evening that the Bruno Bettelheim chair had been announced, and its namesake now also felt wounded that the university had not demonstrated sufficient appreciation for his role in raising funds for the endowed professorship.

On this point, he would soon have reason to be even more bitter. As conceived, the chair was to draw a succession of distinguished psychotherapists to the directorship of the Orthogenic School. After Jacquelyn Sanders had held the post for several years, and had received an appointment in psychiatry from the university, she asked for the chair. Hanna Gray, who became president of Chicago in 1978, turned her down, saying her credentials were not strong enough—no small irony given that the inspiration for the chair had faked his own. With Sanders ensconced as director, the fund for the chair sat and grew until it approached a million dollars, money that ultimately became part of the school's endowment after the university finally decided in the 1980s that a named professorship was out of proportion for a treatment center that housed only fifty residents and historically had done no significant research.[67]

This slap only confirmed Bettelheim's belief that he was forever the outsider, as did his continued rejection by the psychoanalytic establishment. With typical if transparent disdain, he wrote to Daniel Karlin:

> [D]eep down, I really do not care about what others say, I know this is very arrogant, but it is also a defense I developed as a result of years of calumnies. For example, I am still not . . . a member of the American or the International Psychoanalytic Associations because I rejected [sic] to submit to what I considered their petty rules and regulations—which explains the guarded if not petty attitude of official psychoanalysis to my work. And the reason for all this is that I dared to say that in some points Freud ought to be corrected. . . .[68]

Bettelheim also had to contend with the young psychiatrists on the Stanford faculty, most of whom were committed to research and tended to regard seeing patients as scutwork. "They saw their job as correcting imbalances in the bodily fluids, pharmacology. You can imagine how congenial that was to Bruno. It is an understatement to say that they didn't make him feel welcome at all," recalled Alvin Rosenfeld, who in 1977 became director of training in child psychiatry at Stanford Medical School.

Not long after the Harvard-educated Rosenfeld arrived in Palo Alto, Bettelheim knocked on his office door soliciting a contribution for a Jewish charity. The young psychiatrist was immediately drawn to his famous visitor, whose intellectual achievements he would describe as "legendary."[69] Rosenfeld was more than forty years Bettelheim's junior, but he found talking to the gruff septuagenarian invigorating. He also sensed that Bettelheim was adrift in the academic community, especially after the school of education had, without asking Bettelheim's permission, assigned a student to share his small office.

Bettelheim seldom displayed warm affection, but he clearly welcomed the new friendship and was delighted when Rosenfeld suggested that they teach a weekly seminar together for psychotherapists in training. Rosenfeld knew this was a risky invitation, for more than age separated the two men. Rosenfeld was deliberate and soft-spoken, his teaching style supportive rather than confrontational. Bettelheim's reputation for abrasiveness and self-aggrandizement was well known on campus, as was his hostile attitude toward the antiwar protestors. But Rosenfeld felt strongly that young therapists could benefit from what Bettelheim had learned over three decades running the Orthogenic School.[70]

Rosenfeld came to love the older man, a devotion for which he paid "a heavy price." That he had taken up with such a notoriously unscientific partner made his younger colleagues standoffish. Committee assignments were denied him, invitations were not forthcoming. "One person tried to trick me into saying Bruno had done something wrong in helping someone with a dissertation, hoping to get him in trouble with Stanford," Rosenfeld told me.

Still, like the classes in Judd 126, the seminars were popular. They would last for six years, attracting not just aspiring therapists but practicing ones, as well as medical students and social workers. As at Chicago, some participants found Bettelheim's cutting style offensive and abandoned the sessions; but most stayed, intrigued by his dissection of the cases they presented or by his insistence that the "prime requirement for becoming a psychoanalyst is to undergo a personal analysis." [71] Soon he was "Dr. B" again, intimidating but also amusing his apprehensive listeners. "To be discovered by somebody else has never done any good to anybody," he told one meeting, stressing the importance of self-discovery. "You know, there's the story that when Columbus discovered America, the Indians said, 'We are discovered. That is the end of us.' And indeed it was." [72] In 1993, after Bettelheim's death, Rosenfeld published *The Art of the Obvious* under their joint authorship based on transcripts of the seminars, using his mentor's classic technique. He told his readers that because they would find it tedious to wade through verbatim material he had selected "parts from many different sessions that dealt with the same or related subjects, and then stitched them together and added narrative seams to create a composite." [73]

Bettelheim enjoyed the new platform Rosenfeld had provided, but it was not enough to overcome his growing depression, an obsessive focus of which had now become the plight of the Jews. In 1976, he congratulated Nancy Datan on achieving tenure, telling her to enjoy her new-won security as a professor because there was no security in the world for Jews. [74] A few weeks later, during his spring stint teaching at the University of Chicago, he stayed at the Hotel Shoreland on Hyde Park's lakefront. He again wrote Datan, saying he enjoyed being back in a real city but complaining about staying in a hotel in a neighborhood that was once his home. "Will the [J]ews never find real homes?" [75] In letter after letter, he told Carl Frankenstein of how anxious he felt about the threat to Israel and how guilty he was that he could do so little to help. "[W]hat can an American Jew who sits in relative comfort and security say to a dear friend in Jerusalem? . . . It's hypocritical when I say that no day, often no hour passes that I do not agonize about Israel, but then [what] is that compared to what you all must be going through? How can one live these days as a Jew?" [76] Frankenstein told his American friend he should face that question by being a mensch, to which Bettelheim replied, "Naturally, you are absolutely right, one can live only as a 'Mensch' but that is even more difficult, as you well know."[77]

Well before entering Dachau in 1938, Bettelheim had struggled with his manhood—in the shadow of his father's syphilis, which had left him embarrassed by his looks and unsure of his sexual powers; in a marriage to a young woman who did not reciprocate his affection; in the forced role of lumber dealer, which made him feel doubly the outsider, merchant and Jew. He had felt helpless to change these conditions, and when the SS dragon came to get him he was helpless again. Like millions of other Jews, he did not fight back, and his failure to be a mensch at this crucial moment caused him great anguish. But he did not deal with his trauma with humility and insight; instead, he became an avenging angel, telling the Jews how they should have behaved when the knock came, delivering the stern rebukes about "ghetto thinking" that run through his work like barbed wire and that caused more outrage over the decades than any other subject he touched.

CHAPTER FIFTEEN
The Survivor and the Holocaust

IN THE EARLY 1960s, Bruno Bettelheim spoke at Hillel House, the Jewish center on the University of Chicago campus, where in the 1940s he had lectured his listeners on their duty to assimilate. This time his subject was the Holocaust, and again the room was packed. For several years, he had criticized the Jews of Europe for their passivity in the face of the Nazi threat, and in recent months he had turned up the volume of this indictment, first in *The Informed Heart* and then in the Jewish review *Midstream,* where he maintained that the Jews had cooperated in their own destruction because centuries of "ghetto thinking" had conditioned them to "bow down to the *mujik* who pulls one's beard, laugh with the baron at his anti-Semitic stories, degrade oneself so that one will be permitted to survive."[1] In both the review and the book, and in an excerpt from the latter in *Harper's,* he had cited Otto Frank's decision to hide his family together in Amsterdam as a prime example of ghetto thinking and had also castigated Frank for not obtaining "a gun or two" so he could have "shot down at least one or two" of the police when they came to arrest him and his family.[2]

Much of the audience at Hillel House that Sunday afternoon arrived angry, and when Bettelheim began reiterating his ghetto-thinking accusation the hostility grew palpable. What galled many was not just his denigration of the victims but his smug, look-I-got-out tone. Both students and faculty members lined up to attack him when he finished speaking, and one professor, Hans Zeisel, seemed ready to assault him physically. Zeisel was two years younger than Bettelheim and had also grown up in Vienna, where he became a lawyer and a leading socialist until the Nazis drove him out in 1938; a respected sociologist and legal scholar, he had been at the University of Chicago since 1952. Despite his fury, he tried to explain why meaningful opposition to the Nazis had been almost impossible. He told of how in the days after the *Anschluss* many Jews—including a friend named Kate Leichter —did not sleep at their own homes for fear that the Gestapo would come and arrest them. In Leichter's case, the Gestapo went to her mother's house instead; when told the daughter was not there, they said they would wait. Soon Leichter called to ask how her mother was faring, and the Gestapo came to the phone and told her that unless she turned herself in she would never see her mother again. She came, was arrested, "and some time later was executed during a transport from one concentration camp to another." [3]

Bettelheim stuck to his position. As he had in the past when recounting the Frostbite Story and other tales of his camp behavior, he held himself up as a Jew who understood his adversary, who, unencumbered by ghetto thinking, had been able to stand up to and outsmart his keepers. He had revealed in *The Informed Heart* that he had made payoffs in the camps to get soft work assignments, [4] but he had not written about how his Hyde Park neighbors Gerhart and Maria Piers had helped pass money to the Nazis on his behalf from Switzerland in 1939, or of the critical roles Agnes Piel Crane and the State Department had played in pushing for his release and facilitating his immigration. Rather than disclose these facts, he was inclined—in conversation, at least —to make Eleanor Roosevelt and Herbert Lehman the key players in his rescue. This exaggeration only fueled the rumors about how he had survived in the camps and managed his liberation, stories that had circulated for years in Chicago's émigré community, of which the Pierses were prominent members.

Edward Lowinski, a professor of Renaissance music at the university, was one German refugee who had heard the reports. His parents had been murdered by the Nazis, and he came down on Bettelheim with such rage that some feared he would have a heart attack. He thrust himself into the speaker's face and shouted that he knew his story, knew that he had been freed from Buchenwald before the war had even begun, knew that he had been able to bribe camp officials when so many others had not, knew that influential people in the United States had helped him obtain a visa. Others echoed this cry, including Hans Zeisel, who told Bettelheim that if he continued to stand there and dishonor the Jews who had died in the Holocaust Zeisel would reveal to everyone in the room how he had gotten out of Buchenwald. It is unlikely that Zeisel could have done this, since Bettelheim himself probably never acquired a clear understanding of all the forces that had combined to free him; but the mere possibility that Zeisel knew and was about to reveal information that Bettelheim wanted kept from the public ear undid the former inmate.

He began to tremble and talk in a cracked voice. "He was very upset," recalled Benson Ginsburg, the geneticist who, on the phone a few years later with Bernard Rimland in Palo Alto, would be dismayed by Bettelheim's cruel dismissal of the woman pleading that he take her autistic daughter into his school. As Zeisel bored in with unrelenting moral outrage, his target became so shaken that Ginsburg and his wife left. "The scene was just too uncomfortable to watch," he told me. Nell Pekarsky, whose husband, Rabbi Maurice Pekarsky, had founded Chicago's Hillel House in 1940 and was its director, said the room "just throbbed" with anti-Bettelheim feeling. Ultimately, Hans Morgenthau interceded in the debate and managed to help restore a modicum of peace, but the collision reverberated on campus for days. Zeisel told Ginsburg that he knew Bettelheim had been ransomed out of Buchenwald and that his behavior in the camps had been a good deal less heroic than he had depicted it in his writing and when pushing ghetto thinking at the lectern.[5]

At the time of Bettelheim's Hillel House confrontation, one other prominent writer, Raul Hilberg, had advanced the Jewish passivity argument, albeit in a far less accusatory tone. In his three-volume *The Destruction of the European Jews,* in which he used German documents to chart the Nazi killing bureaucracy, he devoted eight pages at the end of the work to "The Victims." He maintained that most Jews tried to avoid action and when that strategy failed they automatically followed their enemy's orders. Their hope "was founded on a two-thousand-year-old experience," he wrote. "In exile the Jews had always been a minority; they had always been in danger; but they had learned that they could avert danger and survive destruction by placating and appeasing their enemies." Jews had endured the Crusades, the Cossacks, the Czarist persecution; these pogroms had brought great pain and death, but the Jewish communities always had "emerged again like a rock from a receding tidal wave. . . . This experience was so ingrained in the Jewish consciousness as to achieve the force of law. The Jewish people could not be annihilated." [6]

When Hilberg published those words in 1961, the historiography of the Holocaust was still undeveloped. But as it became more sophisticated, critics would argue that Hilberg's thesis was seriously flawed because his book was based on Nazi archives to the almost total exclusion of Jewish documents. Such documents, as Lucy Dawidowicz and others have noted, reveal that thousands of Jews resisted the Nazis in ways large and small, always against impossible odds. Of both Hilberg and Bettelheim, Dawidowicz wrote: "Neither was familiar with Jewish history or Jewish traditional life and culture. Neither understood the historian's craft in terms of critical analysis of sources and exploration of complex interacting causal factors." [7]

In the 1960s, critics of Hilberg and Bettelheim often made a blanket indictment that included Hannah Arendt. She seemed to share their passivity argument when she made the questionable charge, in *Eichmann in Jerusalem,* that "wherever Jews lived, there were recognized Jewish leaders, and this leadership, almost without exception, cooperated in one way or another, for one reason or another, with the Nazis." [8] In fact, she did not single out the Jews for their failure to resist the Nazis; rather, she pointed out in the book that "no non–Jewish group or people had behaved differently." [9] She made this same observation in a direct response to Bettelheim's ghetto-thinking article in *Midstream.* "[T]here is an abundance of evidence," she wrote, "which proves beyond a doubt that under . . . [extermination camp] conditions all groups, social and ethnic, behaved alike. There were exceptions in all groups, but they were exceptions of individual persons. Mr. Bettelheim looks for a Jewish problem where it does not exist." [10]

That Bettelheim loudly insisted that it *was* a Jewish problem is central to the denial that characterized his writing and speaking on the Holocaust for most of his life, not least in his resistance to letting other views about the concentration camps impinge on his own. In "Individual and Mass Behavior in Extreme Situations," he had written that he was offering "a preliminary report," one that did not pretend to be exhaustive.[11] He could hardly have done otherwise. When he was setting down his reflections in the months after his release from Buchenwald in 1939, only a trickle of other testimony existed with which he might have compared his own trial, information not easily available to a traumatized Viennese refugee who found himself sitting up late in a strange backwater called Rockford, Illinois, struggling to make sense of what had happened to him. Even by the time he published his essay, in 1943, no significant body of literature about the camps had accumulated, and the true evil of the Holocaust itself was only beginning to come into grainy focus for the world outside the Third Reich. But millions of words and pictures would soon start to pour forth documenting the European cataclysm, leaving Bettelheim with a unique opportunity to deepen his original report, an intellectual and emotional enterprise that might well have helped him work through some of the shame and guilt that plagued him.

Instead of rethinking and modifying "Extreme Situations" as new details and analysis became available during the late 1940s and into the 1950s, he recycled the essay—in *Politics*,[12] in the *Encyclopaedia Britannica*,[13] in *Basic Values and Human Relationships*,[14] in *Readings in Social Psychology*,[15] among other places. With each reprinting, his claims, generalities, and judgments hardened into received truth for a wider audience: he had interviewed fifteen hundred fellow inmates during his ten and a half months of incarceration; he had found that most of them had reverted to childlike behavior after a short time in the camps; many had aped the guards to the point of copying their uniforms; and they had proved, in general, to be pathological liars. By 1960, lest anyone doubt his authority, he was billing himself as an expert; when he republished most of "Extreme Situations" yet again that year in *The Informed Heart*, he assured his readers that he had "studied the problem of

the German concentration camps since they were first established," years before he became a prisoner.[16]

Bettelheim wrote that his new book offered a "much enlarged discussion" of his camp experience, one that drew on the
observations of others.[17] For the most part, however, he ignored
works that concentrated on what from the beginning he said most
concerned him, the psychological impact of the camp experience.
In 1948, his barracks-mate Ernst Federn had written "The Terror
as a System," an article about his seven years in Buchenwald.
He observed that most of the imprisoned Jews had, contrary to
Bettelheim's view in "Extreme Situations," revealed "remarkable
tenacity and ingenuity, proving that human beings preserve their
characters even in the greatest distress."[18] Bettelheim mentioned
Federn's report en passant in a footnote,[19] but did not deal with its
contents, which included almost five pages on camp psychology.[20]
(In 1946, Federn had mailed a draft of his article to Bettelheim,
who urged him to rethink the piece because it was too ambitious
and marked by uneven and redundant writing.[21])

As already noted, in 1950 Bettelheim reviewed *Searchlights on
Delinquency,* a collection of psychoanalytic studies in which he
came across Edith Jacobson's clinical investigation of women political prisoners. A doctor and psychoanalyst trained in Munich and
Berlin, Jacobson was jailed for two years before the war because
she refused to tell the Gestapo about her patients. She was confined with about one hundred other women aged twenty to sixty
in Nazi state prisons—not concentration camps, but fearsome
cages nonetheless. She found her fellow inmates generally cooperative, women who despite their desperate situation "tried to understand and to help each other over their unhappiness" and to
control the irritability so common to collective confinement, what
in World War I had been called the barbed-wire disease.[22] Bettelheim had not addressed Jacobson's study when he reviewed *Searchlights,* and he did not mention it in *The Informed Heart.*

Nor did he refer to Elie Cohen's *Human Behavior in the Concentration Camp,* at the time the most comprehensive exploration
of camp psychology. A Dutch psychologist, Cohen was betrayed
when he tried to escape to Sweden; he spent three years in the
camps, including Auschwitz, where his wife and four-year-old

child died in the gas chambers. His book, published in 1952, is a remarkably dispassionate study that devotes more than half of its 302 pages to a considered examination of the psychological behavior of both the prisoners and the SS, an exploration referenced to a bibliography of 157 entries, including "Extreme Situations." Cohen, like Jacobson and Federn, did not share that essay's pessimistic and patronizing view of prisoner behavior. Though he had come through a far more harrowing hell than Bettelheim had, what he saw in Auschwitz convinced him that the human power of adaptation, both physical and mental, was much greater than he had ever thought possible.[23]

Viktor Frankl, too, suffered much worse than Bettelheim. His mother, father, brother, and wife died in the camps, and he himself went through the agony of Auschwitz. After the Viennese psychiatrist and neurologist was liberated in 1945, he wrote a moving essay about his experience that, coupled with an explanation of the existential treatment philosophy he had developed called logotherapy, would eventually appear in twenty languages and reach several million readers. Frankl's portrait of his fellow prisoners' behavior is at once clear-eyed and sympathetic. He wrote that there "were enough examples, often of a heroic nature, which proved that apathy could be overcome, irritability suppressed. Man *can* preserve a vestige of spiritual freedom, of independence of mind, even in such terrible conditions of psychic and physical stress."[24] Frankl's book was not published in English until 1959, under the title *From Death-Camp to Existentialism: A Psychiatrist's Path to a New Therapy.*[25] This translation probably appeared too late for Bettelheim to consult it when writing *The Informed Heart,* but the original version in his native tongue—*Ein Psycholog erlebt das Konzentrationslager (A Psychologist Experiences the Concentration Camp)*—was widely known, especially among survivors, and had been available since 1946.[26] Bettelheim made no reference to the book in *The Informed Heart,* even in a bibliography, for which he saw no need.

When he did mine works on the camps that had appeared since "Extreme Situations," it was often for anecdotes he felt buttressed his own views, not least his passivity allegation. One author he cited frequently in *The Informed Heart* was Eugen Kogon, the economist and journalist who emerged from seven years in Buchenwald to write *The Theory and Practice of Hell,* widely regarded as a classic examination of the camp system. Kogon told of an SS officer who made a woman dancer perform naked as she faced death in the gas chamber. She obeyed his command and somehow managed to get close enough to seize his gun and shoot him, whereupon she was instantly shot to death. Isn't it probable, Bettelheim asked, "that despite the grotesque setting in which she danced, dancing made her once again a person?" In his admiring view, she had been momentarily transformed into her old self and had destroyed the enemy; she had been willing to risk her life to achieve a last moment of autonomy. "If we do that, then if we cannot live, at least we die as men [sic]."[27]

The millions of European Jews who had not escaped or gone underground should have behaved like the dancer, should have confronted the SS whatever the risk; instead, they first groveled, then waited to be rounded up for extermination, and "finally walk[ed] themselves to the gas chambers." Bettelheim contrasted this behavior to the stand of heroic blacks in South Africa in the 1950s. Hundreds of them had died marching against the guns of apartheid, and thousands more had been sent to concentration camps, but Bettelheim was confident that their brave fight would eventually lead to liberty. In predicting this new dawn, he did not bother to observe that the country's blacks and coloreds were not being herded into ovens, or that they outnumbered their white tormentors four to one, whereas the Jews had been a tiny minority drowning in a vast sea of Third Reich Gentiles.[28] (Bettelheim's praise for South Africa's blacks was more than a little disingenuous; he viewed the country's whites as an oppressed minority like the Jews and more than once said that despite apartheid the white government wasn't so bad, because it had created the highest living standard in Africa.[29])

To illustrate how spineless Jewish prisoners had been, Bettelheim wrote that "[o]n occasions" a mere two guards would be herding some four hundred prisoners "over lonesome roads" toward their death in an extermination camp. He conceded that a few prisoners would have been killed had the four hundred attacked the duo but assured his readers that the majority would have escaped to join partisan groups. He did not describe the terrain the lonesome roads covered, the camp or camps they were near, the condition of the prisoners, or how he knew that the ratio was two hundred to one. But, to shore up his point, he wrote that Rudolf Höss had also wondered, in his memoirs, why the Jewish prisoners had not revolted, since they could have done so easily.[30] He did not cite the page in Höss's *Kommandant in Ausch-witz* where this speculation could be found, and in fact it appears nowhere in the book.[31]

As was well known by the late 1950s, when Bettelheim was writing *The Informed Heart,* Jews were not transported to Ausch-witz and the other killing factories over lonesome roads but on well-guarded trains. Nor was Europe teeming with partisan orga-nizations, especially hard by the human slaughterhouses; and as the Holocaust scholar Jacob Robinson has noted, the few resis-tance cells that existed were often anti-Semitic or at best indiffer-ent to Jews. Even the rare group friendly to Jews would have been cautious about taking any in, especially weak and emaciated escapees whose presence would only have heightened the risk of exposure in a hostile local community, and who did not bring any weapons with them.[32]

Bettelheim did not address the matter of weapons in his lonesome-roads anecdote. But in offering the experience of Otto Frank and his family as his paradigm of ghetto thinking, he wrote that there "is little doubt that the Franks, who were able to provide themselves with so much, could have provided themselves with a gun or two had they wished." Thus, they could have killed "at least one or two" of the police who came to arrest them in their Amsterdam hideout. "There was no surplus of such police," Bettelheim argued. "The loss of an SS with every Jew arrested would have noticeably hindered the functioning of the police state." Besides, had the Franks heroically shot down one or two of the men who came for them, their fate would not have been much different, since all the family but Otto died anyway; at least "they could have sold their lives dearly instead of walking to their death."[33]

And yet it need not have come to that. Had Otto Frank been willing to break up his family and hide Anne and her sister, Margot, separately, he would have greatly increased their chance of survival. He did not do this, Bettelheim wrote, because he and his wife insisted on going about business as usual. He maintained that Anne Frank died because her parents could not get themselves to believe in Auschwitz,[34] and that the universal acclaim for her diary was symptomatic of the same denial. The doomed Anne's moving record of life in hiding above her father's food-products business on the Prinsengracht Canal encouraged millions of readers "to forget the gas chambers and to glorify attitudes of extreme privitization [sic], of continuing to hold on to attitudes as usual even in a holocaust."[35] He wrote that this exaltation of Anne's passive suffering suggested "that the Jews should have remained slaves of Egypt rather than defy Pharaoh and set out to create a new society, a new world of human experience, of law, of the dignity of man."[36]

Bettelheim broadcast these attacks widely, and not just for adults. Margo Jefferson, a *New York Times* book-and-theater critic in the 1990s, was a freshman at the Lab School in 1961 when he came to her English class with his rebuke. "What I remember best," she told me, "is the gleeful but lofty pleasure he took in mocking Otto Frank for not getting the family out, and for letting them worry, in his words, 'about little checked tablecloths.' "[37] When the 1959 movie *The Diary of Anne Frank* appeared on television, Bettelheim required that the Orthogenic School children watch and then discuss it with their counselors, after which he talked about it at one of the three o'clock meetings that regularly took place in the basement playroom. "I found the film heartrending," recalled Ronald Angres, who was about eight years old when he saw it. "However, the politically correct opinion at the school at the time was, 'Boy, were the Franks stupid not to fight back.' I was totally unprepared for that." Angres told me that Bettelheim exuded "a kind of antibourgeois message about Jews hanging on to their possessions, the implication being that what happened to them was sort of poetic justice."

The film, and the hit play that preceded it—both written by the Broadway and Hollywood team of Frances Goodrich and Albert Hackett—especially angered Bettelheim, because they stressed and commercialized even more than the book Anne's belief that despite her family's experience people were "really good at heart."[38] He maintained that this message debased the Holocaust, because if all men were good then Auschwitz could not possibly have happened.[39] Others shared his disdain, among them Hannah Arendt, who felt that the admiration for Anne Frank, especially in Germany, "was phony and that the whole business was highly unpleasant—cheap sentimentality at the expense of a great catastrophe."[40] The novelist Meyer Levin, who remained bitter all his life because his own stage adaptation of the diary was rejected in 1952, felt Goodrich and Hackett had sanitized the book, had given the world a saintly Everychild, a symbol of the abstract evils of prejudice rather than the young girl Anne was, a victim murdered like six million others because she was Jewish.[41] These criticisms have some merit, but the claim to know what millions around the world took away from the play, film, and book was tinged with more than a little intellectual arrogance, as was Bettelheim's insistence that the enormity of the Holocaust was necessarily diluted by the optimistic and humane outlook of an uncynical teenager who, in fact, did not know about Auschwitz.

More arrogant still was his refusal to let the facts intrude on his denunciation of the Franks. His blithe assurance that Otto Frank could have picked up guns as easily as tulips in an Amsterdam with ruthless Nazi occupiers on every corner and informers everywhere is the stuff of fairy tales. Just as fantastic was the notion that Jews could have put the SS and local police on the defensive had they just been brave and imaginative enough to find ways to kill them. On the night of February 19, 1941—some fifteen months before the Franks went into hiding—Dutch partisans raided a Nazi security station in a neighborhood where many Jews lived. Three nights later, this quarter was sealed off and some four hundred young Jews were arrested at random and transported first to Buchenwald, where about fifty died, and then to Mauthausen and other camps, where all but one of the rest perished. Not surprisingly, this reprisal "had a paralyzing impact" on all Jews in the Netherlands.[42]

Though Holland's Jews were more severely affected than those in any other occupied country, an estimated eighteen thousand, including forty-five hundred children, managed to survive the war in hiding.[43] By early August 1944, the Franks had remained safe in their annex for more than two years and had every reason to hope that their ordeal might soon be over. As they knew from their radio, the Allies had invaded Normandy two months before and were advancing rapidly across Europe. When the family was arrested on August 4 after being betrayed, the liberation of Paris was only three weeks away. Brussels was liberated on September 3, the day the Nazis sent their last transport from the Jewish transit camp at Westerbork to Auschwitz. Otto, Edith, Margot, and Anne Frank were on that train.[44] Bettelheim provided none of this context in *The Informed Heart*. Instead, he reproached the Franks for never trying to make their way to freedom so they could "fight their executioners."[45] Jacob Robinson called the notion of the Franks battling the Nazis *en famille* "simply silly,"[46] and it would be were it not so cruel to their memory.

Most telling in Bettelheim's attack was his failure to mention that Otto Frank had not been passive when Hitler came to power in 1933: he had read the future of Germany's Jews correctly and immediately moved his family to Amsterdam from their comfortable home in Frankfurt. Bettelheim had waited five more years without acting, despite the cautionary headlines emanating daily from Germany and the lethal growth of fascism in Austria, despite the emigration of his friend Fritz Redl in 1936 and of his cousin Edith Buxbaum the following year, and despite Agnes Piel Crane's repeated and increasingly urgent pleas that he and Gina bring Patsy home and resettle in the United States. As the *Anschluss* loomed, Bettelheim had pursued his degree at the University of Vienna, tended to and even expanded his lumber enterprise, cared for his mother and sister, coped with a failing marriage, and continued his affair with Trude Weinfeld.

He wrote in *The Informed Heart* that he had asked "hundreds of German Jewish prisoners" in Buchenwald why the Nazi terror had not moved them to flee their homeland before it was too late. "Their answer was: How could we leave? It would have meant giving up our homes, our places of business." He left no doubt that these Jews and others who got trapped in the Holocaust, including the Franks, had been foolish to allow their earthly possessions to take such hold of them.[47] However unlikely his survey,

Bettelheim was right that many threatened Jews had not found it easy to detach themselves from the businesses, homes, and belongings that had defined their bourgeois lives for years. He was one. When the Nazis invaded Vienna in mid-March of 1938, he stayed in the city instead of trying to escape with Gina and Patsy in part because of his concern for the fate of Bettelheim & Schnitzer and the income it produced. Even after his incarceration, he used precious space in his limited letters to discuss his business affairs; he worried, too, about what to do with the furniture and cabinets at Gloriettegasse 15, and told his mother to make sure to pick up the overcoat and the six sets of shirts and pants he had ordered before his arrest.

BETTELHEIM DEVOTED the first third of *The Informed Heart* to an essay on the importance of maintaining one's "Autonomy in a Mass Age," the subtitle he gave the book. He saw modern technology as a mixed blessing, providing dishwashers but also imposing a growing uniformity that stifled individuality in a way that invited dictatorship; he urged his readers to make a deeper commitment to human relations to combat the increasingly mechanized and repressive world around them.[48] By 1960, such concerns, though certainly valid, were, as one critic put it, "slightly shopworn."[49] The threat posed by mass society had been a recurring theme among leftist intellectuals since the 1920s, not least Max Horkheimer, Theodor Adorno, and other members of the Frankfurt school. A central feature of the school's critical theory was its attempt to address modern authoritarianism, and after the war Adorno explored the subject in *The Authoritarian Personality.* This became the most popular book in the American Jewish Committee's "Studies in Prejudice Series," of which Horkheimer was coeditor, and for which Bettelheim wrote *Dynamics of Prejudice* with Morris Janowitz. Among others who had raised the alarm were, most famously, Hannah Arendt, in *The Origins of Totalitarianism,* and David Riesman, in *The Lonely Crowd.* Bettelheim acknowledged the influence of his Chicago colleague Riesman but added little new to the discussion. Marc Lubin, who took graduate courses with Bettelheim at Chicago and worked at the Orthogenic School, recalled reading *The Informed Heart* as an undergraduate at

Brandeis University. "At the time I thought he was a kind of minor-league player. The stuff about mechanized society seemed kind of trite to me, because that's all we were talking about back then." Yet Bettelheim's focus on the importance of autonomy reveals, along with much else in the book, how he was grappling with the dark memory of his own crushed autonomy. For too long, he had also gone about business as usual and hoped for the best; he, too, had not gotten a gun.

Beneath his shouts of blame, he occasionally whispered that one's failure to fight back was altogether understandable. Of the night in Buchenwald when the SS forced prisoners to stand for hours in freezing temperatures, he wrote: "Open resistance was impossible, as impossible as it was to do anything definite to safeguard oneself." [50] What happened in the concentration camp showed that "the influence of the environment over the individual can become total" [51] and that "no really successful defense" was possible. [52] One was in the hands of the enemy "and powerless to do anything about it." [53] As early as 1945, he had asked: "[W]here is there a people whose average citizen is a hero . . . ?" [54] He reiterated the point in *The Informed Heart*, [55] and by 1963 was writing, in a review of Arendt's *Eichmann in Jerusalem*, that "most people are neither heroes nor martyrs," [56] that only the "extraordinary person, at great risk to himself," could retain limited freedom in a fascist state like Hitler's. [57]

Bettelheim was explaining why Eichmann had not resisted his orders to engineer the Final Solution, but he could not extend such mitigation to the dutiful bureaucrat's prey. In observing that heroism was rare among average citizens, he was writing not about the Jews but about the German citizenry's failure to oppose the Nazis actively, and in tones of understanding, not blame. He had manifested such empathy early on, writing in 1945 that in order to survive the average German "did what everyone would do in the same circumstance": tried to suppress all thoughts of the terror around him. [58] The following year, he complained to Ernst Federn of former Jewish inmates who could not be objective about their camp experience. "Again and again . . . only the fate of the Jews is bemoaned . . . as if no German Aryan prisoners had ever been in the concentration camps." [59] To Bettelheim, every German had in some way or other been an inmate of that wider concentration camp which was the Third Reich. Every German who lived under the Nazi regime, whether he accepted or fought it, had been through a concentration camp in a sense; some, the actual inmates, had gone through it as tortured slaves, others—the majority of Germans—had gone through it as trustees, so to speak.

This passage appeared in reflections Bettelheim set down in *Commentary* after visiting Dachau in 1955,[60] an essay that throws a spotlight into the depths of his denial.

He wrote that during the summer of 1955, while he was teaching at the University of Frankfurt, a German intellectual showed him a newspaper clipping he had been carrying for two years. The article described how a visitor to Dachau had been told by his German guide that only criminals had been incarcerated at the camp and that no torture had been inflicted there. Bettelheim was struck by the intellectual's carrying the clipping for so long in his breast pocket, "over his heart, as it were," suggesting to the former inmate that this man, too, "was unable to forget the concentration camps, not for a moment."[61] Bettelheim said that this encounter helped persuade him to return to Dachau, where he found a cab driver eager to give him a tour. He named neither the intellectual nor the driver, which gives his account a whiff of As If; but, however much of the scenario may be invented, the message is clear.

Bettelheim wrote that he did not reveal that he had been a prisoner but told the driver he had come to learn the truth about the camp because he had heard that people exaggerated what had gone on there. To his surprise, the driver said it was impossible to overstate the horrors. He had been a young resident of the village when Bettelheim was an inmate and had witnessed the killings and callous ferocity of the SS; he described incidents Bettelheim said he had witnessed himself, though the author supplied no specifics. The driver complained that the SS had taken over the local taverns, monopolized the girls, and made it impossible for him and his friends to talk openly. He was also furious that Hitler had located the camp outside his home town, which had acquired such a bad name that whenever he was away he preferred not to say where he lived. Bettelheim found remarkable the equanimity with which the driver faced the truth about Dachau, but soon had his explanation. It turned out that the driver had spent four years in Siberia as a prisoner of war. "This German had suffered under Hitler—so he felt—just as much as those in Hitler's concentration camps had. So he felt free of guilt." Bettelheim credited the driver with having worked through the reality of the camp so that he no longer needed to deny it.[62]

Bettelheim, however, balked at looking too hard. The U.S. military now commanded the camp, which housed refugees, and some of the area was off-limits, a fact the driver regretted because it crimped his tour. His passenger wrote that he probably could have obtained permission to make a closer inspection, "but it seemed pointless." They did manage to drive along the main street of the camp, and Bettelheim was tempted to get out when they approached the barrack where he had lived for three and a half months in 1938. But children played on the once forbidding ground, and he decided not to disturb them "for the sake of what by now was empty curiosity."[63] He had arrived at Dachau angry, in part because two clerks at his hotel in Munich had dismissed the importance of the camp and had discouraged his visit. But the displaced persons who now inhabited the barracks and the reassuring presence of U.S. soldiers had quieted his rage. "It was no use beating a dead dog, even though when alive it had mauled, maimed, and killed." Everything seemed to belong to a remote past; even the tourist graffiti on the crematorium aroused no more than "a mild disgust" in him.[64]

The crematorium was in a small grove that served as a memorial, in the center of which stood a statue of an inmate in striped uniform, physical and mental suffering etched on his face. Bettelheim wrote that at first he was oppressed by the smallness of the area; standing amid the well-kept flower beds, he found it hard to imagine that thousands of prisoners had gone through terrible degradation and deaths at Dachau.[65] Yet he wondered whether Americans would have behaved any differently had they been the vanquished, their cities in ruins and victorious foreigners stationed throughout the country. By the end of his reflections, he was suggesting that the Germans had been wise to commemorate their

Nazi history by confining it to an ever-smaller place. "[W]e can-not expect present-day Germans to have a much different attitude toward their victims than they have toward their own devastated cities. Since they are much more matter-of-fact about the ruins of their own homes than I am, I must accept their being more matter-of-fact about Dachau." [66]

By the time *The Informed Heart* appeared in 1960, Bettel-heim's willingness to understand the Germans and his angry criti-cism of their victims had become the two sides of his Holocaust coin. Yet few who reviewed the book remarked on this unique minting and the denial it represented. Almost without exception, the public critical reaction to the book was favorable. Franz Alex-ander, the Hungarian-born psychoanalyst who had founded the Chicago institute in 1932, praised Bettelheim's "unusual amount of objectivity and detachment";[67] the *New Statesman* said the book seemed "lit from within by a humanist glow." [68] Neither they nor virtually anyone else who assessed *The Informed Heart* in print addressed the author's attack on Otto Frank and Anne's diary, or even raised the subject. When Studs Terkel did introduce the topic during a talk with Bettelheim on his popular Chicago radio program, his guest said the Franks were "exactly" like the passen-gers on the *Titanic* who had not entered the lifeboats "because they had to go down to get a fur coat or some diamond bracelets left in the cabin." Terkel, deferential throughout the interview, let the remark pass.[69]

The major reason Terkel and so many others failed to look harder at Bettelheim's Holocaust writing is encapsulated in George Steiner's reaction to *The Informed Heart*. The literary critic and cultural journalist was dazzled by the book; he felt the former inmate had brought to the reality of the concentration camp a remarkable discipline of insight and wrote that "[f]iction falls silent before the enormity of the fact, and before the vivid authority with which that fact can be rendered by unadorned report." [70] That "Extreme Situations" and its permutations up through *The Informed Heart* might not be unadorned reports was something Steiner and thousands of other readers were not inclined to con-sider. Bettelheim had been there, they had not. He had gone through the terror of the camps and then the crucible of writing about his ordeal. How could they challenge what he said about such a hellish journey? Few had any way of knowing that Bettel-heim's description of life in Dachau and Buchenwald was full of questionable generalities, invented research, glib psychology, and a good deal of fiction, which instead of falling silent before the enormity of fact noisily obfuscated it. Yet, because he was the first person in the United States to stake a public claim to the Holo-caust territory, because he wrote with such "vivid authority," be-cause his reputation carried all before it, and, most of all, because he was a victim, he was sheltered from exposure, like prisoner 9036 in the sock-mending shop at Buchenwald.

This public wall of protection would remain largely un-breached until 1976, when Terrence Des Pres, an English professor at Colgate University, published *The Survivor: An Anatomy of Life in the Death Camps.* Des Pres, who died in 1987, was an American born in 1939; but though he had no personal experience of the Holocaust he was obsessed by it. In the words of a friend, he had been struck by the camp horrors "into permanent grief." [71] This grief is apparent on almost every page of *The Survivor,* but so is an articulate and unflinching scholarship, and together they gained the author a wide audience and much critical praise. Alfred Kazin wrote that Des Pres had shed "badly needed light on how well some people behaved in hell." [72] He did this by analyzing fictional treatments of the Holocaust, interviewing a number of survivors, and closely examining the written testimony of seventy-one oth-ers, including "Individual and Mass Behavior in Extreme Situa-tions" and *The Informed Heart.*

Des Pres found Bettelheim's assessments of camp life and its larger meaning seriously flawed. In particular, he criticized Bettelheim's belief, shared by Elie Cohen and others, that psycho-analysis could play a useful role in understanding prisoner behav-ior. He argued that psychoanalysis was "essentially a theory of culture and of man in the civilized state. . . . Its analytic power—which is considerable—is maximized when turned upon behavior which is symbolic, mediated, and therefore at a sufficient remove from necessity." The psychoanalytic method was one of interpreta-tion; to be effective, it had to be applied to actions that had "more than one meaning *on the level of meaning."* Des Pres maintained that this was not the case in the camps, where prisoners had to respond to direct necessity under terrifying intimidation. In such a situation "behavior has no 'meaning' at all in a symbolic or psychological sense." The survivors' experiences had to be seen in their own terms; by applying the psychoanalytic model, Bettelheim had "done more harm than good," not least because his 1943 essay and its several replays had gone unchallenged for so long.[73]

To illustrate the inadequacy of psychoanalysis as a tool for interpreting camp experience, Des Pres attacked Bettelheim's central thesis: that most prisoners reverted to childlike behavior. Yes, he wrote, inmates were obsessed with their excretory functions, as Bettelheim and many others reported; but it did not follow that this signified a return to infantilism. Des Pres pointed out that the SS constantly cowed and degraded the inmates by withholding permission to defecate and urinate. He argued that Bettelheim had failed to distinguish between just what he said he was examining—behavior in an extreme situation—and civilized behavior: "for of course, if in civilized circumstances an adult worries about the state of his bowels, or sees the trip to the toilet as some sort of ordeal, then neurosis is evident. But in the concentration camps behavior was governed by immediate death-threat; action was not the index of infantile wishes but of response to hideous necessity."[74] Ironically, Bettelheim suggested in *The Informed Heart* that he 'well understood this distinction. Though he leaned heavily on psychoanalysis in his critique of camp behavior, he noted its inadequacies as well, primarily the discipline's failure to take environment into greater consideration. He wrote that the camp experience made it clear that "we should never again be satisfied to see personality change as proceeding independent from the social context."[75] This was a useful insight, but Bettelheim never followed through on it, never developed a revised theory of psychoanalysis that drew on social psychology, never assessed inmate behavior through just the lens he was urging others to use. Instead, as Paul Marcus and Alan Rosenberg have pointed out, his camp narratives tend "to be Hobbesian-like in that the inmate is viewed more or less like a discrete entity without a social existence."[76]

Terrence Des Pres also faulted Bettelheim for the kind of oversimplification and lack of context that marked so much of his Holocaust writing. In *The Informed Heart,* he had saluted the men of the twelfth *Sonderkommando* (special squad), a team of mostly

Jews who worked in the gas chambers at Auschwitz. On October 6, 1944, they revolted, blew up a crematorium, and killed some seventy Nazis before breaking through the fence and scattering across the terrain. Most, if not all, were caught and executed, and as Bettelheim himself wrote, "all eight hundred-and-fifty-three prisoners of the *Kommando* died." Bettelheim saw this outcome as evidence that inmates in the *Sonderkommandos* had a chance of about ten to one to destroy the SS. Given such inviting probabilities, he asked, why "did millions walk quietly, without resistance, to their death . . . ?" Des Pres did not deal with Bettelheim's remarkable odds-making, but he did note that Bettelheim failed to factor into the twelfth *Sonderkommando*'s singular gamble the fact that it took years to acquire the arms and explosives used in the revolt, and that their "organization had to be forged and made trustworthy amid constant depletion of members who were killed."[77]

Des Pres saw Bettelheim's analysis of camp behavior as "rooted in the old heroic ethic." His praise for the twelfth *Sonderkommando* and for the dancer who shot the SS officer, and his disdain for Jews like the Franks who could not summon up such courage, reflected a belief that heroism "is an isolated act of defiance through which the individual *as* an individual confronts death." To Des Pres, the autonomy Bettelheim claimed the dancer achieved before being shot to death was empty, and the act he celebrated was suicide.

> What can "autonomy" at the cost of personal destruction amount to? How effective would underground activities, or any of the forms of resistance, have been on such a principle? Bettelheim's argument comes down to this: "manhood" requires dramatic self-confirmation, and in the camps this could only be achieved through some moment of open confrontation with death. Insofar as the struggle for life did not become overtly rebellious, prisoners were "childlike."

Des Pres also regarded as invalid Bettelheim's comparison of the survivor's experience with the plight of modern man in mass society; he argued that, whatever the difficulties and hazards of the homogenizing and manipulative contemporary culture, daily life does not hinge

> at every moment on the issue of life and death; pain is not constant, options abound, the rule of terror and necessity is far from total. Life for us does not depend on collective action—not directly, that is; nor is death the price of visibility. Bettelheim wishes to rouse us from our sense of victimhood; but by claiming that pressure reduces men and women to children, and by praising a heroism based on death, he tends instead to support what he fears.[78]

No one in the United States had ever attacked Bettelheim on any subject before such a wide audience; and never had his concentration-camp views been dissected with such intellectual rigor and force, least of all by an obscure English professor who had yet to be born when Bettelheim entered Dachau. The critique infuriated Bettelheim. He wrote to Nancy Datan that "some idiot" named Terrence Des Pres had published a book on survivors, and muttered that excerpts were getting big play in *Harper's* and *Dissent,*[79] referring to the latter as a Jewish magazine and implying, in a letter to Carl Frankenstein, that the editors should have known better than to publish such pernicious thinking. He told his Israeli friend that Des Pres was subtly preaching fascism and depicting the survivor as superman. In passing, he wrote, "Des Pres attacked me personally, but this is beside the point."[80] That it was precisely the point, Bettelheim would soon make clear.

At the time *The Survivor* appeared, much controversy swirled around *Seven Beauties,* the film by the Italian director Lina Wertmüller about Pasqualino, a small-time Neapolitan Mafioso and lady-killer who finds himself in a German concentration camp. To some, this black comedy offered "the most frightening vision of hell ever put on film";[81] it had propelled Wertmüller "into the highest regions of cinematic art."[82] To others, the movie was "a grotesque vaudeville show" and its box-office success "a triumph of insensitivity."[83] Bettelheim viewed the film at the request of the *New York Times,* found it appalling, and sat down in a white heat to demolish it. His article ultimately appeared in *The New Yorker,* possibly because he missed the *Times* deadline or because the piece—at some twenty thousand words—ran too long for the newspaper.

He believed that Wertmüller consciously rejected fascism, machismo, and the camp abyss but that unconsciously she was "fascinated by their power, brutality, amorality—their rape of man." He conceded that she had clearly depicted war and the camp hell but claimed she had made it possible for viewers to deny the horrors, because "what we watch is a farce played in a charnel house . . . ." Like many others who had been through the camps, and a good number who had not been, Bettelheim was dismayed that scenes of prisoners being hanged or drowned in their own feces could be regarded by the director and her film's enthusiastic audiences as a fit subject for what *Time* called a "death-house comedy." That is certainly a fair description of several scenes, chief among them the desperate seduction by Pasqualino of the camp commandant, a piggish, booted woman modeled on Ilse Koch, the Bitch of Buchenwald. She tells the desperate, starving prisoner that sexual failure will mean death, and when he does not fail she makes him a block leader. Ultimately, Pasqualino not only orders others to their deaths but shoots his best friend to save himself. Bettelheim saw in this portrait a deeply offensive message: that "survival alone counts—nothing else." [84]

This is surely one possible interpretation of *Seven Beauties,* but the film is deep enough to deserve a more nuanced analysis, which it received in several quarters. However, Bettelheim implied that because he had been in the camps his was the correct reading of the movie. He was back at *The Diary of Anne Frank.* That memoir had helped its audiences avert their eyes from the facts of camp life because it was optimistic and sentimental; Wertmüller's dark-comic approach likewise blindered her viewers. Bettelheim seemed unwilling or unable to ask the logical questions here: Why did the diary and Wertmüller's film touch so many people? Were these millions all necessarily turning *away* from the Holocaust? Nor was he willing to struggle in print with the possibility that he was the one averting his gaze, that in angrily denouncing Pasqualino's cruel opportunism he was displacing the shame he carried because of his bribing and other self-serving behavior in Dachau and Buchenwald. Moreover, he was a self-proclaimed intellectual who was unable to grant that the subject of survival, in the camps or in general, defied easy answers and needed to be approached with a good deal of care and humility.

Terrence Des Pres had done just that in *The Survivor*. But now Bettelheim did the opposite, dragging the upstart professor into his *Seven Beauties* indictment like a furious teacher taking an insolent student to the handiest woodshed. He lashed Des Pres with the accusation that he, like Wertmüller, believed that survival at any cost was all that mattered, and charged the author with presenting a small segment of the truth and claiming it was the entire spectrum, thus promulgating a "much greater distortion than an outright lie."[85] In fact, it was Bettelheim who stood astride Des Pres with the whip of mendacity. He made no effort to address the considerable research and serious analysis that Des Pres had painstakingly laid out; nowhere in his twenty thousand words did he discuss the younger man's treatment of fictional accounts of the Holocaust, his interviews with survivors, or his textual study of the testimonies of the seventy-one victims, including Primo Levi, Eugen Kogon, and Elie Wiesel. Bettelheim also saw no need to inform his readers that his own testimonies—"Individual and Mass Behavior in Extreme Situations" and *The Informed Heart*— had been sharply criticized by Des Pres.

In his final chapter, called "Radical Nakedness," Des Pres speculated that biology played a central role in the camps: that "survival depends on life literally—life, that is, as the biologists see it, not as a state or condition but as a set of activities evolved through time in successful response to crisis, the sole purpose of which is to keep going."[86] He buttressed this idea with consider-able documentation, but set it forth modestly as conjecture only, concluding

> that for all our achievements and dreams we have not, after all, defeated the body's crude claims. And this, again, is the survivor's special importance. He is the first of civilized men to live beyond the compulsions of culture; beyond a fear of death which can only be assuaged by insisting that life itself is worthless. The survivor is evidence that men and women are now strong enough, mature enough, awake enough, to face death without mediation, and therefore to embrace life without reserve.[87]

Bettelheim seized on the phrases "the body's crude claims," "beyond the compulsions of culture," and "embrace life without reserve," and flayed his impudent student with them throughout the article.[88] He maintained, to cite two examples, that Pasqualino was living by the body's crude claims in achieving an erection for the grotesque commandant; thus that was the kind of behavior Des Pres celebrated in his book. He insisted that Pasqualino embraced life without reserve by accepting fascism, murder, and rape and that he was living beyond the compulsions of culture when, as block leader, he handed over other inmates to be killed; thus Des Pres endorsed these actions as well. Des Pres supported nothing of the kind, as even a cursory reading of *The Survivor* shows; but it is altogether possible that Bettelheim never read the entire book, since his article cites only the magazine excerpts.[89]

Bettelheim's attack was a prime example of his desperate need always to, in his daughter Naomi's words, come out on top by trying to make "the other person look like a fool." He may not have succeeded in making Des Pres look like a fool to anyone who read the Colgate professor's work, but he came out indisputably on top. He was the reigning expert on the camps, again making his confident case, this time in the sacred pages of *The New Yorker,* where respectability and belief were assured; and the magazine's policy of not running letters guaranteed no response, as it had when Clara Claiborne Park tried to redress Peter Gay's valentine to *The Empty Fortress.* Des Pres eventually did reply in print, but not until three years had passed, and then in *social research,* a quarterly with a circulation of 3,000. In an essay he called "The Bettelheim Problem," Des Pres noted, among other things, Bettelheim's determination over the years to present the milieu of the Orthogenic School as the reverse of the camps. He concluded that the former inmate

will look neither right nor left but say what has to be said to keep his world free of intruders. Anyone with whom authority might have to be shared—other survivors, parents—shall be discredited. In the world of the camps, Bettelheim is the only true survivor. In the world of the School he is the only source of adequate care. By constantly crossing these worlds, planting one upon the other, Bettelheim derives an identity which, at least in his own eyes, is much like the mythical Just Man, the One who shall bear all suffering, the One on whom the existence of the human world depends." [90]

Six months after the *New Yorker* article appeared, Bettelheim stood once again as the Just Man before a conference on the Holocaust in San Jose, California. Some three hundred people had gathered to hear his address, among them most of the other speakers, including the theologian Robert McAfee Brown and Raul Hilberg, author of *The Destruction of the European Jews*. Once again, Bettelheim castigated Jews for their denial in the face of the Nazi onslaught, but this time he added a new twist. He said the words "Holocaust" and "genocide" were misnomers that failed to capture the horrors of the camps and permitted a new generation of Jews to dodge the truth, as did the term "martyr" when applied to the millions who had died. "By calling the victims of the Nazis 'martyrs,' we falsify their fate," Bettelheim lectured the audience, explaining that the term, as found in the *Oxford English Dictionary*, defines " 'one who voluntarily undergoes the penalty of death for refusing to renounce his faith.' " [91]

This exercise in semantics and Bettelheim's like-sheep litany enraged several members of the audience. One was Mel Mermelstein, a businessman from Long Beach, California, who told me he had entered Auschwitz as a teenager in 1944. He had seen his mother and two sisters driven into the gas chambers, and he resented not only Bettelheim's victim-blaming but his equation of his own incarceration before the war with that of those who suffered and died in the death camps. Before Bettelheim finished speaking, a man in the audience began shouting at him. Precisely what he yelled is inaudible on the tape of the speech, but Bettelheim's response is clear. "Whether you want to hear it or not," he shouted back, "you are going to hear it."

Two years after the speech, Bettelheim published *Surviving and Other Essays*. The collection contains several reprints that deal with subjects other than the Holocaust, but the book's title and focus are on the centerpiece essay, a replay of the author's polemic against Lina Wertmüller and Terrence Des Pres. Two decades had passed since he had sat down to write *The Informed Heart*, and thousands of books and articles had been added to the Holocaust shelf, but he referred to virtually none of this material. Besides recycling "Surviving," he again dusted off "Individual and Mass Behavior in Extreme Situations," now thirty-six years old, and also reoffered readers large swatches of *The Informed Heart*. Instead of just resupplying the few pages from that book that dealt with the Frank family, he gave a special chapter over to the expanded version of his attack that originally had appeared in *Harper's*. And he included his San Jose speech, which he called "The Holocaust— One Generation Later," a curious title given that he denigrated the word in the text. But, then, he also used the terms "Holocaust" and "genocide" throughout the rest of the volume, with apparent equanimity.[92]

Whatever Bettelheim chose to call the murderous events in Europe between 1939 and 1945, most critics outside the survivor community continued to pay obeisance when he addressed the subject. Almost without exception, the reviews that adhered to *Surviving* were favorable. Paul Robinson wrote in *The New York Times Book Review* that among Bettelheim's many virtues were "intellectual humility" and called him "one of the most rigorous of the modern Jewish intellectuals,"[93] an astonishing claim for an author who supplied neither notes nor a bibliography in the book under review. Again and again, Bettelheim's testimony on behalf of all survivors was placed on the pedestal of truth. As a victim of the camps, he was "an irreproachable witness, a steady voice in a chorus of interpreters."[94] Without doubt, wrote Rosemary Dinnage in *The New York Review of Books,* the most important essays in the collection dealt with the concentration camps and their aftermath: "here Bettelheim speaks with absolute authority."[95]

CHAPTER SIXTEEN
A Rage to Die

IN EARLY JUNE 1979, doctors in Palo Alto removed a lump from Trude Bettelheim's breast and found it to be malignant. They assured her and Bruno that the cancer had not spread and that with aggressive radiation therapy the prognosis was hopeful. The couple made trip after trip to the Stanford Medical Center for the treatments, but by the end of the summer the physicians were recommending more surgery. Trude rejected the idea of a mastectomy, and another localized procedure was performed, after which Bruno tried to be optimistic. In September, he wrote to Carl Frankenstein that as a result of this latest operation Trude was "fully restored and, as the doctors say, cured."[1] But behind his words was the realization that Trude, who was eight years younger than he was and had always been so much more robust, might die before he did.

He had leaned on this woman he called his "good wife" for forty years, ever since she ran to him from Australia in 1939. Even before that, she had loved and cosseted him in Vienna as his marriage to Gina fell apart. She had been the perfect mate for a man who demanded center stage, a partner willing to stay in the background, to listen patiently to his complaints and buoy him up through his repeated bouts of depression; she had raised the children, run the household, cooked the meals, even cut his meat. In Portola Valley she had continued to care for her *Mann,* while reveling in the California sunshine with her usual hardy enthusiasm, digging in the garden, learning tennis, hiking in the hills around Portola Valley. Now the radiation had made Trude weak and sickly. By October 1981, the cancer had spread to the bone; she underwent further radiation therapy, as well as hormone treatments and, soon, chemotherapy. At one point her third vertebra collapsed because of a tumor, causing such pain that she could not walk. She was rushed by ambulance to the medical center, where she remained through the Christmas holidays, after which she returned home on a regimen of drugs that at least made the pain bearable. She could move about the house with the aid of a walker and was able to sit up for half an hour at a time, but she needed almost constant attention. Though Bruno tried to provide it, he was not psychologically inclined to reverse the equation of care that had obtained for so many years; this reluctance was compounded by his own worsening health.

Earlier in 1981, he had been about to drive to teach a class when he noticed some clumsiness in his left hand as he tried to use the turn indicator and operate the window, and when he attempted to button his jacket. An examination at his home that night revealed no major abnormalities, nor did a CAT scan two days later; nonetheless, his doctor concluded that he had suffered a mild stroke. The diagnosis only deepened the anxiety of a man who, at seventy-seven, already had severe circulatory problems in his legs as well as heart disease. His two cataract operations had helped his eyesight, but he continued to suffer from diabetes, arthritis, a slightly enlarged prostate, and the esophagal blockage, which made eating more and more unpleasant. In 1980, he had contracted a mild case of tuberculosis and also wound up with his leg in a cast for several weeks after a bad fall, an accident that left him using a cane.[2]

In recent years, Bruno had suggested from time to time that he and Trude move into a retirement home, where someone would be available to look after them if they had to grapple with just what was now happening. She would not hear of it. She loved their house and found abhorrent the notion of moving into a home for the elderly, as in fact did her husband, who only proposed the idea as a matter of expediency. He tried to be sanguine as he faced the future. "We are determined to fight it out," he told Nancy Datan, "because we hope that we may still have a few years together."[3]

One solace the couple had was the proximity of Eric and Ruth. Their son now practiced law in San Francisco and could see them frequently; Ruth was able to visit occasionally from Pasadena, where she was a therapist and lived with her husband, an urban planner named Daniel Flaming, and their two small children. Naomi had also married, but was living in London, where her husband worked for the U.S. government. Despite the distance, after Trude's long siege in the hospital over Christmas 1981, Naomi had flown in from England and stayed at 1 Sierra Lane for many days to help care for her mother.

Though Bruno and Trude lamented that Naomi resided so far away, they were glad to see her settled. In the late 1960s, she had married a physics student with an interest in painting whom she had met in Mexico. Her parents were at best ambivalent about the match, not least because their daughter was only in her early twenties and her husband was a Catholic and spoke little English. "They were quite relieved that he wasn't dark-skinned," Naomi recalled. The couple tried to make a go of the relationship while Naomi pursued her degree in regional planning at the University of North Carolina, but by 1970 they had separated. That her new husband was a bookish professional and Jewish, with a deep interest in Israel, where the couple spent their honeymoon in the spring of 1981, particularly pleased her parents. "[W]e like him a lot," Bruno told Carl Frankenstein in a letter saying that he had urged the newlyweds to call on him and his wife, Ljuba, when they were in Jerusalem.[4]

Bruno and Trude were not so happy about Ruth's marriage. Daniel Flaming had been raised as a fundamentalist Christian, and some of his relatives looked askance at his marrying a Jew, a misgiving Bruno reciprocated. When the Flamings' first child was born, in 1975, he wrote Frankenstein that it was good to see such confidence in the future but complained that Ruth had married a Gentile.[5] Seven years and one more grandchild later, he was still upset, telling Frankenstein that his "beloved oldest daughter has a goyim [sic] for a husband." He speculated that Ruth had married him because "she was too attached to me" and had to guard against her unconscious incestuous tendencies.[6]

This Oedipal analysis is less likely the explanation than the Christmas tree at 5725 Kenwood Avenue and Bettelheim's repeated public admonitions that all Jews should assimilate. That he sometimes murmured a counter-message in private, as when he told the counselor Karen Carlson she was ill-advised to marry a Jew, made little impact at home. Naomi feels that after she and then Ruth went off and married Gentiles both of her parents may have had second thoughts about the secular upbringing they had provided for their children. Certainly her father had moved closer to his Jewishness since his visit to Israel in 1964. He did not want to live there, he was no Zionist, but his letters to Nancy Datan and Carl Frankenstein repeatedly show that he saw the Israelis as brave and heroic menschen on the barricades against Jew-hatred, which he felt was rife well beyond the Middle East.

As always, work provided the antidote for Bettelheim's anxieties. Around the onset of Trude's illness, he began writing a book on reading, in collaboration with Karen Carlson, who had not taken his advice and had married a Jewish university administrator named Joseph Zelan and was living in Berkeley. He had also been invited to deliver a paper at Stanford in connection with an exhibition of photos illustrating Sigmund Freud's life, and chose to deal with what he regarded as the misconception of Freud's ideas caused by James Strachey's mistranslations in the English-language Standard Edition. He told Joyce Jack, who continued to edit his writing from the East Coast, that giving the paper was not all that important but his thoughts on this subject were. He wanted to see them in print and once again asked her to help make his ideas publishable.[7]

While working on these projects, Bettelheim continued to accept occasional speaking engagements around the country. He was reluctant to leave Trude, and traveling had become trying, but the forays boosted both his retirement income and his morale. When he appeared at Rhode Island College in November 1979, an audience of seven hundred crammed into an auditorium that seated 550, and three hundred more watched his lecture on closed-circuit television.[8] The following summer, more than three hundred persons jammed in to hear him talk about the family at a daylong session at the University of California Extension Center in San Francisco. When speaking to such audiences, he almost always employed the unique and often unsettling brand of Socratic dialogue that had stood him in such good stead since his Rockford days; he rarely prepared his talk but instead offered a few ice-breaking remarks and then called for questions.

In San Francisco, this approach caused a good deal of muttering from a crowd that had paid thirty dollars a head to hear a world-famous Viennese-born psychoanalyst, the esteemed former director of the renowned Orthogenic School, a polymath who could shine his lamp into the darkest corners of autism as well as over the magic landscape of fairy tales. The first questioner asked, tentatively, "Would you comment on the homosexual family, and . . ." Bettelheim cut her off. "A homosexual family is not viable," he shouted; such a union was a contradiction the good Lord did not intend. This was the Bay Area, and the anger and disappointment among several gay couples in the auditorium was manifest. Bettelheim called for a dictionary. When someone brought him the American Heritage volume, he declared that he preferred Webster's but he made do, and stressed the definition of the family as a procreational unit.[9]

He conceded he was an old man with an old man's crotchets. He growled about California's exotic life-style, which he said produced more divorces than marriages in nearby Marin County, and about parents' unreasonable expectations that their children live up to their potential, that they be original and creative "and die of a heart attack at an early age." A man near the front of the auditorium asked what he could do about his twenty-two-year-old daughter, who lived in the East and refused to communicate with him. When he confessed that he had left his wife and child nine years earlier, Bettelheim shouted, "Then you deserted her." The audience sucked in its breath. Bettelheim dropped his judgmental tone yet remained forbidding, telling the questioner that his daughter had needed him and explaining that a child responds to the definite situation: if the father is present, she deals with him; if he is gone, good riddance.

Bettelheim larded his performance with reminiscences of Vienna, including an oft-told tale of a fifteen-year-old black-sheep cousin. He explained that the boy's family was the cause of his delinquent behavior but didn't realize it; thus, instead of berating themselves, as so many contemporary middle-class American parents did when their children sulked or spun out of control, they took up a collection and sent the boy to the United States, a geographic solution that drew much laughter from the audience. He said that his (nameless) cousin did well on the streets of gold, his point being that American children remained socially and economically dependent on their parents for too long.

He held out the children of the dream as exemplary products of the right alternative approach. The young kibbutzniks grew up away from their parents, so free of teenage resentments that generational conflict was virtually nonexistent, as were delinquency, drug addiction, and other pathologies of the counterculture. Once again, he was reheating dubious research and generalities over the flame of infallibility. Children were indeed raised physically apart from their parents in the first decades of the kibbutz movement; but this arrangement had never produced the emotional divide between parents and offspring that he maintained it had, and tensions within families were by no means unknown. Moreover, by 1980 most kibbutz parents were raising their children at home, and the *metapelet* system was on the verge of extinction. As for hippiedom, kibbutz teenagers merely came to it a few years later than their counterparts in the United States and Europe. By the mid-1970s, many of them, too, were puffing on joints and experimenting with LSD, their long hair falling over infrequently bathed bodies. They now took a "haughty and iconoclastic" view of the once sacrosanct kibbutzim, demanding their freedom, and drifting away in such numbers that the future of the movement was for a time in doubt.[10]

Bettelheim told his audience that parents had to know their own minds and make their standards clear to their children in no uncertain terms. By way of example, he recalled the evening in the late 1960s when he turned on the lights at Eric's high school party and sent everyone home, mortifying his son. In this telling, Eric returned to a Lab School reunion a few years later and encountered the friend who had turned out the lights. Bruno said the boy told Eric that his father had been right to turn the lights back on. Eric confirmed the story, but told me that one of the things that annoyed him about his father was his willingness to use family incidents such as this in his books and lectures.

In early 1982, Bettelheim's collaboration with Karen Zelan came to fruition with *On Learning to Read: The Child's Fascination with Meaning,* an attack on reading education in the United States.[11] Robert Gottlieb, who remained Bettelheim's editor at Knopf, had warned that the manuscript was repetitious and dogmatic and suffered from too much simplistic and often far-fetched psychoanalytic interpretation.[12] He had urged Bettelheim to expunge just such writing from *The Uses of Enchantment* with only moderate success, and he made even less headway with this latest book, as several reviewers pointed out in a critical barrage. The authors had blown what should have been a concise five-thousand-word article into a "flabby" book,[13] they had tried "to defend the magic of reading in a turgid, repetitious prose redolent of the green walls of ed-psych labs,"[14] they had lamented "the mind-numbing repetitiveness of primers, [yet] their book itself groan[ed] with the weight of ideas endlessly repeated."[15] Even a critic who lauded the book's enthusiasm for the joys of reading found it "a little repetitive and even tedious."[16]

Besides decrying the monosyllabic banality of most basal readers, the book attacked their portrayal of life as always sunny, a world full of happy families with no problems. "What vistas," Bettelheim asked in a chapter that he alone wrote, ". . . are made available to the child who is asked to develop interest in reading, not to mention literature, by learning to read: 'Janet. Mark. Janet and Mark. Come, Mark, come Mark, come. Come here.'?"[17] He said that, after he had won the confidence of children in schools he had visited, "a flood of angry criticisms" poured forth attacking such primers; "[w]ithout exception" the children said the books were "stupid," that they "hated" having to read them. With "venom" these grade-schoolers spoke of the " 'sweet little kids' " in the stories; the neophyte readers were "furious" that adults would regard them as so simple-minded as to believe that children were really like that. For all the spleen of this remakable group of mini-Menckens, their and the authors' criticisms were hardly new. As Bettelheim and Zelan themselves noted, the "fun morality" that dominated primers had been dissected as long ago as 1951.[18] One reviewer suggested that the authors had cleaned out their files "and decided to throw some old observations into a book instead of the wastebasket." [19] Bettelheim had in fact gone to his files, recycling in three of the chapters that he alone wrote material from an article he had published eight years earlier, in which he had deplored as insipid the "Janet and Mark" series of primers then popular in schools.[20]

Few argued that such readers could not usefully be made more imaginative and relevant, but Bettelheim seemed determined to dismiss altogether the importance of any instruction that stressed phonics and graphemes. "It is high time," he wrote in another solo riff, at the end of the book, "that children and teachers were freed of the yoke and the blinders that are the direct result of teaching reading as if its ultimate purpose is the acquisition of decoding skills, and as if the only way to become able to recognize a word is to be exposed to it innumerable times. The truth is that words are learned easily and fast if we are interested in what they mean to us." [21] As reading specialists have long known, the truth is a great deal more complicated than that. Just how we learn to read remains largely a mystery; what is known, however, is that for most children decoding is a crucial first step to reading, and leads to just the kinds of exciting books that Bettelheim championed. To Jerome Bruner, the Harvard psychologist and pioneer in the field of cognition, the authors seemed unable to digest the fact that, "for reasons longer than a psychoanalyst's couch, reading is a difficult intellectual process." [22]

The anonymous children in Bettelheim and Zelan's book spent a good deal of time on that couch. The authors reported that their study of three hundred children in eight schools revealed that reading errors often had deep meanings, that young readers made mistakes not because they were unable to decode the text but often because they understood it quite well, "sufficiently to reject it for what to them seemed valid reasons." [23] They buttressed this claim not with any hard research, though they had a foundation grant and six female assistants to support them,[24] but with Bettelheim's usual soufflé of anecdotes. There was the "small, very competent first grader" who read "Tigger" for "tiger," which meant that she was taking refuge from the fierce jungle cat in the benign land of *Winnie-the-Pooh*.[25] Or the "highly intelligent first grader" who substituted "dump" for "jump," which meant he wanted to dump his boring workbook, which the authors said he told them was "garbage." [26]

Bettelheim had long insisted that education should not be made easy, that children should learn to fear. He also had complained that too often the educator "who should know better fools himself and the child into believing that if something has meaning as id expression it is therefore ego correct. . . ." He warned teachers against the psychoanalytic impulse "to applaud almost any disorganized thing the child does" simply on the ground that it reveals something.[27] Now he and Zelan were giving their class a standing ovation. "We believe," they wrote, "that the ability to read is seriously interfered with when purposeful behavior—as we assume [sic] misreadings to be—is regarded to be without deeper meaning, and is ascribed to ignorance, lack of skills, or neurological deficit."[28] But surely, Robert Gottlieb had told Bettelheim with a certain frustration when working on the manuscript, "surely there must be thousands of misreadings that have no discernible underlying purpose—[that] are just plain confusions or carelessnesses."[29] The authors were not inclined to listen to their editor, or even to their Viennese deity, who is said to have observed, albeit likely in a different context, that "sometimes a cigar is only a cigar."[30]

A tribute by Bettelheim to that deity soon provided distraction from the generally negative response to *On Learning to Read.* With the help of Gottlieb, Joyce Jack, and Theron Raines, he had converted his Stanford talk on the mistranslation of Freud into a lengthy article. It ran in *The New Yorker,* which by now had done more than any other publication to legitimize the author. His attack on Lina Wertmüller and Terrence Des Pres had had the magazine's imprimatur, as had an excerpt from *The Uses of Enchantment;*[31] Peter Gay had lavishly praised *The Empty Fortress* in its pages; and a favorable review of *On Learning to Read* had recently appeared there.[32] His submissions received the careful editing for which the magazine was noted, and the Freud article emerged as one of the smoothest essays the author had ever published, one he expanded into a 118-page book, *Freud and Man's Soul.*[33]

Bettelheim maintained that the English translation of Freud's works, especially the twenty-four-volume Standard Edition overseen by James Strachey, had drained Freud of his humanism. In particular, he faulted Strachey for purging *"die Seele"* from the master's works; he wrote that in German "soul" has a deep spiritual connotation that was central to Freud's thinking. In the Standard Edition, *"die Seele"* and its variants usually emerge as "mind" or "intellect" or "mental"; Bettelheim complained, for example, that a phrase like *"überhaupt unser Seelenleben beherrscht,"* which means "dominates the life of our soul," became via Strachey "dominates our whole mental life." [34] Such mistranslations had seriously subverted Freud's intent, had made his humane ideas and insights "abstract, depersonalized, highly theoretical, erudite, and mechanized—in short, 'scientific' . . ." [35] Bettelheim had preached this to his students from the beginning at Rockford College, and at the Orthogenic School had made it plain to his young counselors that he would not stand for a lot of psychoanalytic gibberish at staff meetings or in their dictation. Instead, they had to look into themselves, deep into their souls and the souls of the children, if they hoped to understand Freud's theories and make therapeutic progress. [36]

There is a certain romanticism in this instruction, but Bettelheim was right that Strachey had scientized some of Freud's writing. For example, he took Freud's coinage *"Fehlleistung,"* which means the kind of unconscious mistake that became known as a Freudian slip, and literally turned it into Greek: "parapraxis." And Strachey gave us more Greek by translating Freud's *"Schaulust,"* which roughly means the sexual pleasure of looking, as "scopophilia." Bettelheim also criticized Strachey for his Latin words, in particular for converting direct, human terms like *"Ich," "Es,"* and *"Über-Ich"* to the cold "ego," "id," and "superego." [37] He did not concern himself much with the awkward alternative of writing and speaking in English about the "I," the "it," and the "above-I," perhaps because for forty years he had repeatedly used the Latin words in his articles and books (e.g., "that if something has meaning as id expression it is therefore ego correct") and would continue to do so.

Freud and Man's Soul offers a total of seven source notes and no bibliography, giving the unschooled reader the impression that Bettelheim was breaking new ground, a notion the author reinforced on the first page by wondering why, given the "inadequacies and downright errors in the translations," others had not criticized them long ago.[38] Many others had, among them Lewis Brandt, who in 1961 had published "Some Notes on English Freudian Terminology," and H. Frank Brull, who had offered "A Reconsideration of Some Translations of Sigmund Freud" in 1975.[39] Such examiners occasionally came up with the same criticisms Bettelheim would advance, but unlike him they made clear that they understood that translation is always at best an imprecise enterprise and recognized the heroic accomplishment that Strachey had achieved in producing what in the minds of at least seven translation scholars was "a magnificent work."[40] Moreover, as Bettelheim himself noted,[41] the Standard Edition had the approval of Freud as well as his daughter, Anna, who was deeply involved in the translation; and Sigmund's close friend and biographer, Ernest Jones, found Strachey's Freud "considerably more trustworthy than any German version."[42]

To Bettelheim, though, the Standard Edition was a conspiracy. Freud had stressed that psychoanalysis was not a medical discipline, not a codified creed; more important, he wanted it open to lay analysts. In the United States the profession was medicalized against his wishes; but it is a major leap, as Darius Gray Ornston points out in *Translating Freud,* to insist, as Bettelheim did, that Strachey and Anna Freud, who were two of the most prominent lay analysts of their day and devoted to Sigmund, "connived with the Americans against Freud's . . . explicit arguments."[43] They were motivated, in Bettelheim's words, by a "deliberate wish to perceive Freud within the framework of medicine,"[44] which was why they systematically "replaced words in ordinary use with medical terms and learned borrowings from Greek and Latin."[45] However many legitimate mistranslations Bettelheim may have spotted, his astonishing accusation suggests that what motivated him was his unabated rage at the American psychoanalytic establishment for keeping him at arm's length throughout his career.

Bettelheim's disapproval of the Strachey translation also reveals a kind of cranky wistfulness, a man nearing eighty looking back "after a lifetime of achievement in an alien culture and an alien language to the happiness and security of the Gymnasium, the city and the language of his youth." [46] Not long after *Freud and Man's Soul* appeared, he was immersed in Vienna again, this time with a long essay review of a book about Freud, Jung, and the latter's patient and lover, Sabina Spielrein. [47] Bettelheim's growing nostalgia surfaces in his letters as well. "The time to live was during the reign of Franz Joseph," he wrote to Carl Frankenstein. "How incredibly smart of Freud to see to it that most of his life, at least his creative life[,] was lived during that time." [48] A few months later, he congratulated Frankenstein on publishing a book of stories in German. "My German is gone," Bettelheim lamented, "although in my old age I practically every night dream about something in Vienna, often mixed in with something American." The two worlds were not integrated but came to him side by side. [49] Not long after moving to California, he told Nancy Datan that he guessed he was an American, or "as much as an old Viennese [J]ew ever can be American." [50]

In 1983, BETTELHEIM'S LONGING for his roots pulled him once again to Europe, this time to mark his eightieth birthday, on August 28. Both he and Trude approached the journey with some trepidation. She had now been struggling with cancer for more than four years, and though her condition was stable she remained weak and housebound much of the time, and he had suffered new medical setbacks. The previous summer, he had undergone an operation to repair a detached retina in his right eye; that procedure was a success, but the prolonged general anesthetic had led to a urinary tract obstruction that left the patient in great pain. Four days later, surgeons anesthetized him again and operated on his benign enlarged prostate gland. In all, Bettelheim spent thirteen days in the hospital and many weeks recuperating; it was now a year later, but the one-two punch, combined with his several other ailments, had left him, like Trude, feeling more frail than ever. Still, he was determined to give himself the trip as a present, fearing that it might be his last chance to touch the Old World.

They flew to New York, spent a few days with friends, regathered their strength, then went on to London for a "delightful week" seeing more friends, playgoing, and visiting with Eric, who was now practicing international law in the branch of an American firm there. They next traveled to Venice for a week, which they enjoyed even though they felt limited by their respective infirmities.[51] The last stop on the monthlong excursion was Switzerland, where both Trude and Bruno looked forward to a happy reunion with their old friends Emarina and Bertel Radanowicz-Harttmann, who lived in Basel. Trude "looked very bad" when she stepped off the train, Emarina recalled. Still, within hours they had all made the short trip to Zurich to visit their hosts' daughter, Christine. "Trude was stubborn about it; she insisted on going, in bad, rainy weather," Emarina told me. The two couples convened with Christine in a restaurant, where Trude soon collapsed. They took her back to Christine's apartment and urged her to rest; but she soon astounded everyone by demanding that they all go to a movie. She would not be denied. In the cab to the cinema she collapsed again, and this time was rushed to a hospital.

Congestive heart failure was the diagnosis, and her condition was so critical that the doctor asked Bruno if he and his wife had an agreement about prolonging life. Yes, he said, no extraordinary measures. "He was beside himself with fear," Emarina recalled. All three children flew to Trude's bedside and she began to rally when she saw them, and after nine days in intensive care the doctors said she could leave the hospital. However, getting her back to the United States would be a risky and expensive undertaking, and in desperation Bruno called Sandy Lewis in New York. Lewis, who had attended the Orthogenic School in the 1950s, was one of the former director's prized alumni; Lewis was grateful for the care he had received at the school, and had once named a family dog Bruno. He told me that Bettelheim "was in tears, like a child; he said he never should have taken Trude to Europe, that their doctor had told him not to, but he hadn't wanted to travel without her."

Lewis came from considerable Wall Street wealth and had himself made more in the market. He had given a substantial sum to the University of Chicago, instructing that the income be used exclusively to enhance Bettelheim's pension. Now, with typical command, the forty-three-year-old businessman hired a Swiss Air Rescue plane to fly Trude from Zurich to Frankfurt, a necessity because Swissair would not permit the oxygen equipment she required in its cabins. Lufthansa did agree to allow the crucial support system, so Lewis purchased a section of a nonstop flight from Frankfurt to San Francisco, and, with Bruno, Eric, a physician, and a nurse attending her, Trude returned home, first to the Stanford hospital for a few days, then to 1 Sierra Lane. After the return, Bruno made what Lewis termed a classic Bettelheim call. "He phoned me not to say thank you but to tell me that I never had to do anything for him again," said Lewis, who was infuriated by the remark but recognized that it typified the difficulty Bettelheim had in expressing appreciation.

It was now clear that Trude might die any day. Her husband felt deserted, and as often happens in such situations his fear turned to anger. Even before the crisis in Zurich, he had railed at his ailing wife, as if she had purposely allowed the cancer to invade her body to make him miserable. "He saw my mother's illness as something that was happening to him," Naomi told me. "He knew that once she died he would not be able to manage. He knew that someone would have to take care of him. Who would that be?" As he looked into this void, he lost control again and again. Naomi declined to be specific about her father's explosions, saying only that his behavior was inexcusable, as it had been on occasion years before in Hyde Park, when her mother had retreated in tears after he had angrily unloaded his woes on her. "When his own needs came first he could be blind to other people's needs, totally blind, and would do or say things that nobody in a normal state of mind would say or do," his daughter told me.

Trude's strong constitution and will to survive kept her alive for more than a year. In the spring of 1984, she and Bruno managed a trip to New York, where she went to museums in a wheelchair and attended one or two plays, though in some cases only for one act, because she tired so easily. By August, she was undergoing more radiation to relieve the bone cancer's excruciating pain; the treatment helped somewhat but left her further weakened. On October 25, Eric arrived from England for three days. After he left, on Sunday, the 28th, Bruno and Trude started their regular evening Scrabble game, but she quickly grew weary and had to lie down. Several hours later, she had a heart attack; an ambulance took her to the hospital, and by morning she was dead, twelve days after her seventy-third birthday.

Several days later, Bruno poured out his grief in a letter to Carl Frankenstein. "I owe to her all I am," he wrote, saying Trude's love had encouraged him to resume his studies at the University of Vienna in 1937 and to get his degree, and that same selfless devotion had made it possible for him to overcome his depression and make a successful career in the United States. He had tried to prepare himself for the inevitable over the last year, but "could not do it"; he had never been able to grasp the possibility that his healthy, "sportive" wife would die before he did. She had been strong for so long, which was one reason she had refused to move into any kind of retirement home. Once she fell ill, such places refused to take them. "I do not know how I'll be able to carry on, but I shall try since this is what she would have wanted."⁵²

Only a few weeks after Trude died, Margaret Bettelheim committed suicide. For fifteen years, Bruno's sister had lived at The Williams, a residential hotel for the elderly on Manhattan's Upper West Side; after her husband, Peter Abbot, died in 1974, she had moved from their suite into a small studio apartment and had led an increasingly lonely existence. Like her brother, she was prone to depression that dated back to the suffocating years of their father's syphilis; but unlike Bruno, she had not been able to create a rewarding life for herself in America. She had hoped to use her European acting experience to make a career in radio, but whereas her brother's thick Austrian accent was one of his most useful assets in the world of psychotherapy, hers was a fatal debit. She had a modest gift for playing the stock market, and was a handsome woman, regal almost, and always impeccably dressed; but essentially she had had to settle for being the wife of a hotel maître d'. A lifelong smoker, she had been plagued by emphysema for several years, and now suffered from painful dental problems as well. In mid-December, a month after she turned eighty-five, she washed sleeping pills and possibly other drugs down with a heavy dose of whiskey. Just before she did so, she called Katharine Wilheim, whom she had first met in Vienna in the 1930s and who had become one of her closest friends in New York. "I had no idea what she was contemplating," Wilheim recalled. "The only thing that surprised me was that at the end of our very conventional conversation she said, 'Thank you for letting me talk to you.' "

Margaret lingered in the hospital for about a week, during which Bruno asked his young friend Alvin Rosenfeld, who was now working in New York, to make sure that the doctors made no heroic efforts to keep her alive. Margaret had greatly admired her younger brother; she had saved magazine cover photos of him, and his cherished books lined her shelves. But Bruno had kept her at a distance since the days of their youth, when he sought refuge from her at the Buxbaums'; he had talked to her occasionally by phone, and when in Manhattan had tried to fit her in between meetings with Robert Gottlieb and Theron Raines and social gatherings with Hans and Wanda Willig and other friends. "She was resentful of that," Naomi said, "but it was typical of my father's relationships: no empathy or understanding for where she was." Margaret died on December 22, and when Bruno wrote Carl Frankenstein four days later he did not mention her; nor did he in subsequent letters to Joyce Jack and Nancy Datan. Not long after her death, he came to New York and stayed at the Stanhope Hotel, where he and Alvin Rosenfeld had dinner and then went up to his room. There he opened a briefcase and started going through his sister's effects and talking about how her promise as an actress had never flowered into a career. Margaret's life spilled from the pictures she had left behind, and as Rosenfeld sat beside his old and tired colleague on the bed, Bettelheim gazed at them with great sadness.

In the months before and after Trude and Margaret's deaths, the world seemed always ready to comfort their anguished husband and brother with recognition and generosity. He received honorary degrees from the State University of New York at Albany, the University of Santa Clara, Tulane University, and Bard College, which cited him as "one of the great twentieth-century figures in psychology and education" and saluted his "legendary record of success in treating severely emotionally disturbed children." [53] In the spring of 1983, the Goethe Institute, whose headquarters in Munich was about ten miles from Dachau, awarded Bettelheim its Goethe Medal, saying his work in child psychology "particularly embodied the spirit of German culture." [54] That same year, he appeared briefly as himself in Woody Allen's mock documentary *Zelig,* a parody about a mousy young man who mirrors the strong characteristics of people he encounters. In a cameo as a quintessential Viennese psychoanalyst, Bettelheim expounds soberly on how Zelig represents conformity.

For Christmas 1985, Sandy Lewis gave Bruno a new Mercedes, and the following spring, many of his former colleagues at the Orthogenic School and the University of Chicago gave him a *Festschrift* on the campus. That same year, the British Broadcasting Corp. aired a two-hour documentary on Bettelheim, whom the narrator called "one of the world's greatest living psychologists." He was among the last survivors of the psychoanalytic movement "to be trained by Sigmund Freud" and had worked successfully with emotionally troubled children in Vienna before World War II, including a deeply disturbed autistic child sent to him by Anna Freud. Sandy Lewis, who helped underwrite the tribute, appeared on camera, saying that Bettelheim had demonstrated that hopeless cases could be rescued. Bert Cohler also praised the former director, as did another former resident, identified only as Toni, who said she had been suicidal when she arrived at the Orthogenic School and that its enveloping milieu had saved her life. [55] In September 1987, Bettelheim returned to Vienna to participate in an international symposium on the emigration and exile of Austrian science. He was pleased to be invited, and he gave a warm speech summing up his life and work in the United States. But he minced no words about Austrian President Kurt Waldheim, the former Nazi who had been secretary general of the United Nations; Bettelheim also wondered aloud how many contemporary Viennese thought of him as "a dirty, stinking Jew," a remark that appeared in the Socialist organ *Arbeiter Zeitung* just as he said it, Rudolf Ekstein, his friend and fellow honoree, told me.

That Bettelheim had mixed emotions about homage from Austria was hardly surprising, but he sometimes seemed even less inclined to accept his domestic honors with grace, often displaying the same petulance that he had after winning the National Book Award. Instead of going along with the comic spirit of *Zelig,* he groused to his symposium audience in Vienna that Woody Allen had not allowed him to say anything deep about psychoanalysis, which he said was typical of how Americans viewed the discipline.[56] He was pleased that Bert Cohler, Ben Wright, Leslie Aranow, Bob Bergman, and his old friend Ben Bloom and others had been moved to organize the *Festschrift* in 1986, and was happy that so many former staff members and residents came to see him in his old den, Judd 126, or at the Quadrangle Club. He listened gratefully and was often touched as more than a dozen speakers praised him at Mandel Hall. But at a party for more than one hundred guests that Aranow gave in her home, he complained that the university should have arranged the event. "He was wrecking the meaning of it right in front of me," Aranow recalled. Two weeks after the gathering, Bettelheim described it in a letter to Nancy Datan. "The University . . . reacted by taking no notice of it, or me. So there you are."[57]

IN THE FALL OF 1986, a few months after the *Festschrift,* Bettelheim wrenched himself from Portola Valley and moved in with his daughter Ruth. He had resisted the idea at first. Despite his disdain "for those dumps for old people called retirement homes," he had applied to one in Palo Alto after Trude died. He felt that since his mind was still active he might even help "liven up the place" and be of some psychological help to the other residents; but the institution turned him down, "supposedly because I am too old, although there might have been other reasons why they blackballed me."[58] He desperately needed someone to take care of him, to replace Trude. Eric lived in London; Naomi and her husband were still in Vienna; that left Ruth. Originally, she and her husband planned to build a wing for him on their own house, a large, 1920s-vintage Hollywood home in the hills of Pasadena. Not long after they began construction, however, their marriage of ten years began falling apart, and now they were in the middle of a messy divorce.[59] At Ruth's urging, Bruno agreed to buy a house out of the proceeds of the Portola Valley sale and come live with her and her two children; she had chosen an imposing Spanish-style dwelling at 718 Adelaide Place, one of Santa Monica's tonier addresses. It cost her father more than eight hundred thousand dollars, part of which he borrowed from a New York bank on Sandy Lewis's guarantee.[60]

Several friends had urged Bruno to stay in the Bay Area,

including Gina, who still lived in San Francisco, had never remarried after Peter Weinmann's death, and had offered to help her first husband reorganize his life. Naomi and Eric, too, thought he should remain near Stanford, where he had found kindred spirits over the last thirteen years. "The move had disaster written all over it," Eric recalled. "It led to one of the only falling outs I ever had with my father. Naomi and I, and Gina, were dead set against the idea. Ruth was going through what was showing itself to be a very acrimonious divorce. She had a professional practice of her own, but she was not independently wealthy, so she could not provide the kind of care that someone who was rich could. For her to take on this reponsibility for a man in his eighties, very sick, was to ask too much of anyone. The house itself was inappropriate. It's really a home for formal entertaining, with large, open rooms, not discrete private rooms that would allow two adults to live separately. I was so vehement about it that I proposed that my father come to England. I'm a bachelor. I'm reasonably well off. But he would have none of it."

By Christmas, the mix of generations and personalities under the reddish tile roof at 718 Adelaide was already beginning to chafe. Bruno was eighty-three, frail, pined for his dead wife, was often deeply depressed and hated Southern California in general and the house in particular, which he regarded as ostentatious; Ruth was forty-four, still tense from the breakup of her marriage, unbending and dogmatic (much like her father), practicing psychotherapy at home as "Dr. Bettelheim," and caring for her eleven-year-old son, Matthew, and her five-year-old daughter, Aurelia. Their normal rambunctiousness frequently irritated their grandfather, whose own children had always understood that they had to tiptoe when he was working. His small study was just to the right of the front door, protected from the noisy traffic flow and the children's invasion only by a curtain. At Christmastime, he wrote with longing of the warm holidays he and Trude had made for the family on Kenwood Avenue and complained that Ruth was in revolt against everything in her past, including Christmas. "Not that I mind much, it is just another emptiness for me." [61]

As Bettelheim struggled to breathe in this alien atmosphere, he managed to publish his fifteenth book, *A Good Enough Parent,* a title whose irony would tighten like a vise in the months ahead. He had worked on and off at the book since the mid–1970s, never to the satisfaction of Robert Gottlieb. The author accused his editor of wanting a how-to book, which was to some extent true; but Bettelheim was also having trouble producing a coherent manuscript of any kind. By the early 1980s, he was on a forced march to complete the project, because he had accepted a large advance from Knopf and, as writers frequently do, had already spent it. He had had little choice but to soldier on, with Joyce Jack in close step, at a time when he felt weary and dispirited. By 1985, Gottlieb still regarded the book as unpublishable and arranged to have it extensively rewritten. "The reason is quite clear to me," Bettelheim told Nancy Datan. "[Gottlieb] has great problems as a father and must have done everything opposite of what I advocate. So in self defense he had to rewrite the book so as to justify him[self] as a parent."[62]

For all the strains between author and publisher, the book that emerged in 1987 gave readers a more temperate Bettelheim, an author who now spoke in almost grandfatherly tones. He was still polishing his As If about caring for two autistic children in his Vienna home, adding a "few other youngsters";[63] he was still working almost exclusively within the Freudian frame; and he was still writing about American families as if they were all white and affluent and had maids, and as if single motherhood were a rarity. But he was no longer sounding so much like an Old Testament prophet. Taking his cue from D. W. Winnicott's concept of the "good enough" mother, he addressed both parents, reassuring them that they "ought not try to be perfect" or expect their children to become so.[64] Instead, he reprised the central theme of his life's work, the one idea approaching a theory that he ever advanced: parents should work to understand why their children behaved as they did, try to comprehend their sons' and daughters' turmoil by drawing on their own inner experience.[65] For the first time, he revealed some details of his own youth, writing of playing under the dining-room table; of his beloved cousin, Edith; of his father's card games; of how his mother cared for him when he was sick; of his "very good parents."[66] This softer Bettelheim also was evident in his interview with the BBC, which he had taped in Portola Valley a few weeks after Trude's death. "If I have any regrets," he said, "it is that I did not emphasize the difficulties also parents have." He reiterated that he had seen his task as being the advocate for the Orthogenic School children, but now realized that it was important to be the advocate for mothers, too. He said that if he had another lifetime to live he would spend a lot of it trying to help mothers understand how difficult it had become to raise children in contemporary society, to help them have compassion for themselves as well as for their children.[67]

Bettelheim also now seemed, at least at times, to have developed some second thoughts about blaming Holocaust victims. In 1986, the same year the BBC documentary appeared, he spoke at the University of Southwestern Louisiana about Janusz Korczak, the Polish author of the 1928 children's novel *King Matt the First,* about a boy who becomes king and tries to reform his realm on behalf of children as well as adults. Korczak, born Henryk Goldszmit, had been head of the Jewish orphanage in Warsaw for many years, and Bettelheim talked with great admiration of this man precisely because he had *not* fought back against the Nazis. Unlike Bettelheim's heroic dancer, Korczak had not shot one of his captors before his death; nor had he killed the police who came for him, as Bettelheim had insisted Otto Frank should have. Instead, he had refused several opportunities to save himself so he could stay with his orphans and make their last hours as secure as possible before their—and his—extermination at Treblinka. Bettelheim quoted the last words in Korczak's ghetto diary with reverence: " 'I am angry with nobody. I do not wish anybody evil. I am unable to do so. I do not know how one can do it.' "[68]

The tone throughout the talk suggests Bettelheim deeply envied Korczak's wisdom and humanity, and not only because of his ultimate selflessness at Treblinka. Like Bettelheim, Korczak recognized that some unpleasant aspects of his personality stemmed from the way he had been raised. As a check against the kind of arbitrary and abusive behavior that can arise out of an adult's unhappy childhood, Korczak established a children's court at his orphanage. He was called before it five times in a six-month period, once for losing his temper and hitting a child who had irritated him. "He readily admitted his guilt, and that the seriousness of the provocation could not serve as an excuse for slapping the child," Bettelheim wrote.[69]

BETTELHEIM TRIED to make a life for himself in Santa Monica. He renewed his friendship with his fellow exile Rudolf Ekstein, and they spent many Saturday lunches at Marjan's at the Mart, a delicatessen near their homes, talking about their youth, trying to feel Vienna's cobblestones beneath their feet.[70] Every Thursday evening, Bettelheim supervised six local therapists in a case-study group. He complained often that he had no friends, but several people did try to get close to him, drawn both by his neediness and his reputation. One was Constance Katzenstein, who had grown up in Hyde Park and had taken Bettelheim's courses in the 1940s; her father had died when she was an infant, and her powerful teacher became, as he did for so many others, her "mentor–father figure." Katzenstein, who was about sixty when they renewed their acquaintance, made a concerted effort to bring Bettelheim out of his gloom, with distractions like a German Expressionist exhibit at a local museum and parties at her home. It was at one of these that he confided that his father had suffered from syphilis for so many years; yet, despite this rare and intimate revelation, he seemed unable to show his hostess any warmth for her devotion.[71]

In November 1987, Bruno spent four or five days with Naomi, who had given birth to her first child in Austria and with her husband had just moved back to a suburb of Washington, D.C. Her father had kept up a demanding writing-and-speaking pace during the year and had recently returned from the symposium in Vienna. He was clearly exhausted, and soon suffered a dizzy spell and later realized that he couldn't hold up his right hand. "It was obviously the beginning of a stroke, but neither of us recognized it," Naomi recalled. She urged that he see a doctor, but he was determined to honor yet another speaking engagement, in Florida. By the time he arrived, he had to be rushed to the hospital. When Ruth heard, she gathered up Matthew and Aurelia and took the night flight to his bedside, then brought him back to Santa Monica.

The stroke partially paralyzed Bettelheim's right arm and hand, which impaired his ability to write and type and drove him deeper into despair. He now became obsessed with what would happen to him if he needed full-time care. The house at 718 Adelaide Place was large, but much of it was eaten up by a two-story living room; Ruth, Bruno, and the children each had a bedroom, but there was no place for a live-in nurse. Ruth considered creating a room above the garage for her office, but refused to pay for it, in part because she did not have title to the house. It was owned by a trust her father had established, which gave him the right to sell it whenever he chose, regardless of his daughter's wishes. A substantial portion of his estate was tied up in the house, and he now decided, partly on Eric's advice, that, given his age and parlous health, this was no time to hold on to an illiquid asset. For fifteen months, Ruth had tried to be the caretaker her father demanded, and he had tried as best he could to adapt to what they both knew was an untenable situation. Over their second Christmas in the house, the tension only grew worse, and he finally announced that he was determined to sell and move to a place of his own. Ruth may well have been relieved that she would no longer have to live in such proximity to her father, but she was furious that he was pulling the house out from under her and her children.[72]

A few weeks after the decision, Bruno suffered an inflammation of the pancreas and was admitted to the hospital. He was released in the morning, but, according to Naomi, Ruth waited until she had a break from her patients in the afternoon to pick him up. In Naomi's view, this triggered a total mental breakdown. Back at 718 Adelaide, Bruno became Lear, even accusing Ruth of trying to poison him. He was soon on antidepressants and other drugs. Father and daughter barely spoke, and endless phone calls crossed the country at all hours as Naomi and others tried to heal the breach. Naomi, at forty-two pregnant with her second child, feared she would have a miscarriage and ended up with enforced bed rest. In May, Bruno moved a few blocks away to a condominium apartment on Ocean Avenue that looked out across the Pacific. Ruth and his grandchildren would take up residence only a short walk away, but he did not know their address or seem to care what it was. The trust eventually sold the house for about $1.2 million[73] to a young couple named Frankie and Barry Sholem, who told me that when they called Ruth to say that mail had come for her father she never picked it up.

A few months after giving birth to her second child, Naomi went out to Santa Monica and shuttled between her father and sister trying to effect a rapprochement. Both were intransigent. Ruth continued to seethe over the house sale, and also accused *the* Dr. Bettelheim of trying to destroy her career. He had repeatedly and publicly disparaged the house as pretentious and her southern-California life as shallow. After the break, he would say in an eventually published interview that the daughter he had raised in the cultural and intellectual incubator of Hyde Park had embraced values that he found "undesirable."[74] The interviewer, David James Fisher, a young analyst who had befriended Bruno, told me that he was far more bitter about Ruth than comes across in the interview. "He took nasty shots at her in my presence, criticizing her for not having a sliding scale for her patients but charging them all a high fee."

Fisher, an historian of psychoanalysis, was drawn to the older therapist's tales of Austria between the wars, of how as a member of the Jung Wandervogel he had lost the girl to Otto Fenichel in the Vienna Woods but found Freud, of his treatment of Patsy, of his analysis with Richard Sterba, of how Freud himself had told him that with his background in humanities he was just the kind of practitioner psychoanalysis needed.[75] Fisher visited Bettelheim often, first at the house, then in his apartment, and at least twice Bettelheim dined with the young therapist and his wife in their home. They were considering adopting a child, and their guest said emphatically that they should do so, that surrogate parenting was by no means fatal. He then described how his own mother had not given him the emotional and physical love that he needed but had turned him over to a wet nurse. "Look at me, I didn't turn out so bad," he told his hosts.

But he felt worse than bad, and talked constantly of suicide. The subject came up so often that Fisher and a friend, a professor of history at UCLA named Peter Loewenberg, persuaded Bettelheim to enter analysis. "I said, 'This will have to be a very distinguished and very old analyst.' Bruno got a kick out of that," Fisher recalled. Loewenberg suggested a woman named Miriam Williams, whose office was just down Ocean Avenue from Bettel-heim's apartment. Like her new patient, she had been born in the old Austro-Hungarian monarchy and spoke with a heavy accent. They had sessions once and sometimes twice a week, speaking in both English and German. Williams declined to divulge the details of their talks, but did say that Bettelheim rarely spoke about his parents and that his feeling of homeliness came up often. After about a year, he stopped coming. "He decided that talking wasn't enough, that he had to go out and end his life," Williams said.

When Bruno and Naomi spoke on the phone every week, he almost always talked of killing himself. At the time, her three-year-old son was going through a serious crisis about death. "I specifically told my father that this was a topic he could not discuss in front of my children," said Naomi. But he could not always keep the sluice closed, and more than once he spilled forth his consuming death wish in front of the boy. Naomi said that Ruth told her he had threatened to kill himself in the Adelaide Place house with Matthew and Aurelia present.

Bettelheim's emotional misery was compounded more and more by his physical disabilities, not least the blockage in his esophagus. At a Fisher dinner party, rice lodged in his throat and caused such a coughing jag that he had to be escorted to the bathroom. He had rejected for several years having an operation that would alleviate this problem, but his doctor now told him that he might die if he resisted surgery any longer.[76] In the summer of 1988, he entered the hospital once again. The procedure was a success, though he came out of it with a case of pneumonia. Still, he was thrilled to discover after his throat healed that he could once again enjoy sitting down to a meal. He was now able to cut into the kind of heavy fare he enjoyed, and occasionally played the courtly host to his new acquaintances at Knolls, a German restaurant on Wilshire Boulevard.

The attentiveness of these people seldom distracted him for long. His lifelong friend Fritz Redl had died in February, and Nancy Datan, whom he had known since she was a student at the University of Chicago and with whom he had carried on an intimate father-daughter correspondence for more than a decade, had succumbed to breast cancer in the summer of 1987. He continued to regard his flesh-and-blood oldest daughter as uncaring and superficial, and Ruth remained unbending. He spent long days in his apartment, enshrouded in the European artifacts he and Trude had so lovingly assembled over forty years. For many hours he sat in his familiar Danish-modern chair and read, but the pages did not always bring him peace. "I am reading Primo Levi," he wrote to Carl Frankenstein in March 1988, "and am again filled with the problems of the survivor. Hitler ruined all our lives and continues to do so, because it is only because of him that you are in Israel and I am here, and that Israel came into being and causes all Jews so much anguish."[77]

Constance Katzenstein and a sculptor named Jane Ullman hoped that sitting for a bust might help cheer Bettelheim up. They contacted Sandy Lewis, who readily agreed to pay Ullman's $6,000 fee but wanted as many people as possible to contribute whatever they could, so the bust would not just be from him. "Before I started," Ullman told me, "I called up everyone I knew who knew him, to get an idea of him so I could reflect it in the bust. Nobody had anything nice to say." She said that their half-dozen sessions were difficult, that he tended to be unpleasant and monosyllabic as she worked. To try and close the gap, she organized a dinner party around him. "He acted as if I were a son of a bitch to have bothered." The bust was meant to be displayed at the Orthogenic School, but after seeing it, Jacquelyn Sanders decided that her mentor's black, disembodied head might frighten the children, and it was relegated to the library, and now rests in the business office.

By the beginning of 1989, Bettelheim was getting specific about suicide. He talked to his young confidant, Jimmy Fisher, about taking an overdose of drugs, yet feared he might not absorb them, might vomit them up or have to have his stomach pumped; he contemplated jumping from his fifth-floor apartment, but rejected that method because it might leave him further crippled instead of dead. Fisher heard him ask a physician about the efficacy of injecting air into his veins, and also about how much Demerol constituted a lethal dose. The doctor said between one hundred and two hundred milligrams. Fisher wrote: "Bettelheim inquired of this doctor if he would be willing to prescribe the medicine. The physician declined."[78]

In April, Bettelheim began arranging to go to Holland, where doctor-assisted suicide by lethal injection was legal. Fritz Redl's widow, Helen, had given him the name of a physician, Jan Schouten, who expressed a willingness at least to meet with his supplicant if he came to Amsterdam.[79] Bruno wanted Eric to take him there, and for a while his son reluctantly entertained the idea; but he ultimately refused to participate in the plan. Naomi was strenuously opposed from the start. Their father then found a couple in Los Angeles who said they would accompany him on the trip, but they wanted some form of consent from his children. He spent Thanksgiving with Naomi and her family outside Washington, much of the time trying to persuade her to give these Los Angeles strangers permission to help him kill himself. She flatly refused, and no longer only because she had serious misgivings about the plan itself.

Some months before, she had heard from a family friend that her father had disinherited Ruth. "I was shocked," Naomi told me. "I didn't want to believe this person at first, but then I found out it was true." She had gone to Santa Monica to try and get him to reverse the decision, summoning the memory of Trude. Surely he knew that she would never have sanctioned such retribution. He was adamant. Again, she went back and forth between her father and sister trying to at least get them talking. But the break was beyond repair. Now, during the Thanksgiving holiday, she reminded her father that if he committed suicide with the will in its present form there was bound to be a very nasty court battle, through which the innocent Los Angeles couple would inevitably be dragged. "I was bound and determined that the will had to be changed back," Naomi said.

Her father was considering moving east into a nursing home near his daughter. She told him that if he did come she would give him no peace until he reinstated Ruth. When Alvin Rosenfeld came down from New York to see Bettelheim at Naomi's, she gave her father a taste of what she meant by revealing the disinheritance to his friend, who was almost as disapproving as she was. Naomi made it clear that she would also tell her father's other friends, and he knew that they would not approve, either. As 1990 began, most of those friends received a formal card announcing that he had moved to The Charter House, a home for the elderly in Silver Spring, Maryland. Before he left Santa Monica, he grudgingly restored Ruth as an heir.[80]

In early 1990, Knopf published Bettelheim's final book, *Freud's Vienna and Other Essays.* It consists almost exclusively of reprinted articles, which Joyce Jack and Theron Raines helped him assemble. He knew the book needed an introduction, but he told Jack he was burned out and managed to send her only fragments. "I wrote the introduction for him," Jack told me, saying it was the only time in their collaboration that such ghosting had occurred. "It was obvious he could no longer put down his thoughts, and it distressed him terribly." Among the essays is "Essential Books of One's Life," which he had published in a Swiss magazine in 1988. It was here that Bettelheim revealed for the first time how important the German philosophers Theodore Lessing, F. A. Lange, and Hans Vaihinger had been to him as a young man, how the philosophy of As If had taught him that living by fictions might be a way to make life bearable for someone who so often felt depressed and pessimistic.[81] That strategy had carried him a long way, but fictions could no longer help him. "I am utterly miserable here and regret the move, but it can no longer be changed," he wrote to a friend on his new Charter House stationery on February 26.[82]

IN *A Good Enough Parent,* HE HAD WRITTEN what has long been well known, that severely pathological behavior often surfaces on anniversaries of unhappy events.[83] On the night of March 12, the day when, fifty-two years before, the Nazis invaded Austria, Bettelheim swallowed some drugs and whiskey and tied a plastic bag over his head. He was found the next morning in the hallway outside his room. The note in his typewriter read: "I know you did everything possible to help me and I am very grateful to both of you for everything you did for me. The two of you were the very best that happened to me since your mother's death. But I just can not go on without her. I love you very much and want to thank you for all you did for me. Please forgive me, as much as you can. Have a good life now and in the future. Your loving father. Farewell!" The note began, "Dearest Eric, Dearest Naomi!"[84]

A NOTE ON SOURCES

All letters cited or quoted were provided by the recipients or their relatives unless otherwise noted. All interviews are with the author unless otherwise cited, and where it is obvious in the text that an interview is with the author it is not cited in the endnotes. Almost all the women interviewed who worked for Bruno Bettelheim at the Orthogenic School, or encountered him in the classroom or elsewhere, were single at the time, and, with one or two exceptions, I have used their maiden names in the text. They are listed among the interviewees below in alphabetical order by their maiden names, with their married names in parentheses. An asterisk (★) denotes a pseudonym.

INTERVIEWS

Ruth Alben; Erwin Angres; Ronald Angres; Salma Angres; Leslie Aranow (Cleaver); Leonard Atkins; Miriam Atkins; Anne Bakeman; Hans Bandler; Judy Barron; James Belch; Ruth Bemak; Robert Bergman; Mildred Berry; Eric Bettelheim; Frederick Bettelheim; Naomi Bettelheim; Ralph Bettelheim; Mark Blechner; Benjamin Bloom; Sophie Bloom; Hedda Bolgar; Alvin Boretz; Linnea Brandwein (Vacca); Jerald C. Brauer; Betty Bruce (Keegan); Mary Cahn (Schwartz); Carol Callaghan; Mary Cannon; Margaret Carey; Karen Carlson (Zelan); Elaine Caruth; Rory Childers; Michael Claffey; Sigmund Cohen; Bertram Cohler; Mary Ellen Cowan; William Crain; Preston Cutler; Charles Daly; Severn Darden; Allison Davis; Victor DeGrazia; Peter Dembowski; David Dempsey; Joan Deutsch (Herczeg); Carl DeVoe; Paul Diederich; Helen Farrell Dillon; Veronica Dryovage (Youngman); Jan Erik Dubbelman; Dennis Duginske; Sue Duncan; Gail Edelman; Rudolf Ekstein; Robert Eller-Isaacs; Sharon Ellison; Alex Elson; Miriam Elson; James Ely; Deirdre English; Fanita English; Helen Epstein; Marianne Ettlinger (Cohen); Jonathan Farber; Ernst Federn; Charles Feldstein; Kay Field; Molly Finn; David James Fisher; Richard Flacks; Richard Fogg; Ugo Formigoni; Sophie Freud; Martha Friedberg; Stanton Friedberg; Myles Friedman; Marc Galanter; John Gedo; Jacob Getzels; Judith Getzels; Benson Ginsburg; Steve Giordano; Philip Goldbloom★; Jerome Goldsmith; Robert Gottlieb; Arnold Granville★; Nora Greene; Josh Greenfeld; Natali Gump; Paul Gump; David Gutmann; Edith Bettelheim Harnik; Lou Harper; Donna Heizer; Nina Helstein; Stephen Herzceg; Elaine Herzog; Raul Hilberg; Aaron Hilkevitch; Nicholas von Hoffman; Aimee Isgrig (Horton); Joyce Jack; Philip Jackson; John Jaeckle; Dorothy Johnson; Mordecai Kaffman; Barbara Kaplan (Lee); Jeremiah Kaplan; Richard Kaplan; Daniel Karlin; Constance Katzenstein; Jerome Kavka; Oliver Kerner; Shelton Key; Daniel King; Lynda King; Heidi Kirschner; Barbara Kojak★; Gusti Kollman; Elizabeth Block Kuklick; Gertrude Kummer; Marion Langer; Nechama

Levi-Edelman; Salim Lewis, Jr.; Jerald Lipsch; Joan Little (Treiman); Peter Loewenberg; Fae Lohn (Tyroler); James Lombard; Ramon Lopez-Reyes; Gretel Lowinski; Marc Lubin; Augusta Lyons; Tom Wallace Lyons; Richard Marek; Sara Margolis; Charles Marks, Sr.; Charles Marks, Jr.; Dorothy Martinson*; Helen Martinson*; Natalie Menke (Brown); Mel Mermelstein; Harriett Jaffe Michel; Verena Sterba Michels; Otto Modley; Susanna Morgenthau Mintz; Diane Belogianis Morphos; Ann Morrissett (Davidon); Rocco Motto; June Mullins; Peter Neubauer; Gordon Northrup; Jean O'Leary (Brown); Isabel Paret; Peter Paret; Clara Claiborne Park; David Park; Paul*; Nell Pekarsky; Charles Pekow; John Ransome Phillips; Patty Pickett (McKnight); Gerard Piel; Maria Piers; Matthew Piers; Betty Pingree (Rellahan); George Pollock; Nancy Price; Helen Redl; Bernard Rimland; Dean Rodeheaver; Irwin Rosen; Robert Rosen; Alvin Rosenfeld; Jona Rosenfeld; Edward Rosenheim; Myrna Adams Rowe; James M. Sacks; Charles Saltzman; John Schenbly; Eric Schopler; Jill Schwab; Vernon Schubel; Jacquelyn Seevak (Sanders); Margrit Seewald-Graf; Harvey Shapiro; Charles Sharp; Barry Sholem; Frankie Sholem; Gayle Shulenberg (Janowitz); Lillian Silberstein; Charles Skinner; Fern Meyer Smith; Barbara Probst Solomon; Judith Stacey; Herman Staples; Phyllis Steiss (Wetherill); Theodor Sterling; Richard Stern; Louise Strouse; Joe Suchman; William Sugden; Emmy Sylvester; Louis Szathmary; Johanna Tabin; Louis Tas; Betty Goldman Thomaidis; Mary Thomas; Arnold Tobin; Toni; Ralph Tyler; Jane Ullman; Manuel Vargas; Emarina Vischer (Radanowicz-Harttmann); Marjorie Weaver; Catherine Weinmann (Isenstadt); Gina Weinmann; Mary Jane Wilcox (Rachner); Katharine Wilhelm; Clifford Wilk; Miriam Williams; Wanda Willig; David Wineman; Josette Wingo (Lowdon); Aundry Woods; Benjamin Wright; F. Howell Wright; Peter Wyden; Itamar Yahalom; Susan Yuan; Ann Zener (Edwards); D. Patrick Zimmerman; Herbert Zipper; Ari Zolberg; Vera Zolberg.

NOTES

ABBREVIATIONS

BB   Bruno Bettelheim
BBP   Bruno Bettelheim Papers, Special Collections, Regenstein Library, University of Chicago
CF   Carl Frankenstein
DK   Daniel Karlin
DM   Dwight Macdonald papers, Manuscripts and Archives, Sterling Library, Yale University
EB   Eric Bettelheim
FF   Ford Foundation archives
GW   Gina Altstadt Bettelheim Weinmann
JSS   Jacquelyn Seevak Sanders
JTF   James T. Farrell. Farrell papers, Special Collections, Van Pelt Library, University of Pennsylvania
LC   Library of Congress
NA   National Archives
NB   Naomi Bettelheim
ND   Nancy Datan
OS   Sonia Shankman Orthogenic School
PB   Paula Bettelheim
RL   Special Collections, Regenstein Library, University of Chicago
RP   Richard Pollak
SE   *The Standard Edition of the Complete Psychological Works of Sigmund Freud,* 24 volumes, edited and translated by James Strachey (London: Hogarth Press, 1953–1974)
TBT   Reminiscences tape recorded by Trude Bettelheim not long before her death in 1984
UC   University of Chicago

PROLOGUE

1. Paul Roazen, "The Children of the Dream," *New York Times Book Review,* April 6, 1969, p. 3.

2. BB, "Schizophrenia as a Reaction to Extreme Situations," *American Journal of Orthopsychiatry,* vol. 26 (July 1956), p. 508.

3. For a short account of the speedboat accident as well as Stephen Pollak's fall, see

"Two Children Killed in Accidents Over Week End," Cassopolis (Michigan) *Vigilant,* Sept. 2, 1948.

4. Irene Josselyn to RP, Sept. 8, 1969.

5. Irene Josselyn to RP, Aug. 6, 1969.

6. Chicago *Daily News,* March 15, 1961.

7. Program of the dinner on April 7, 1970, celebrating BB's twenty-fifth anniversary as director of the OS, BBP.

8. BB to ND, March 10, 1977.

9. BB to DK, Dec. 22, 1973.

10. Interview with Joyce Jack.

11. BB, *Freud's Vienna and Other Essays* (New York: Alfred A. Knopf, 1990), p. ix. The correct Freud quotation reads: ". . . is committed to lying, to concealment, to hypocrisy, to flummery. . . ." It appears in a letter dated May 31, 1936, from Freud to the novelist Arnold Zweig, in which he discourages Zweig's interest in writing his biography. See Ernest Jones, *Sigmund Freud: Life and Work* (London: Hogarth Press, 1957), vol. 3, p. 222.

12. BB, *Freud's Vienna,* pp. 106–8.

13. Paul Edwards, ed., *The Encyclopedia of Philosophy* (New York: Macmillan and Free Press, 1967), vol. 8, pp. 221–24. BB, *Freud's Vienna,* p. 107.

14. BB, *The Uses of Enchantment: The Meaning and Importance of Fairy Tales* (New York: Alfred A. Knopf, 1977), p. 14.

15. BB's suicide was widely reported. See, for example, the *New York Times, Los Angeles Times,* and the *Washington Post,* all March 14, 1990.

16. Accusations that BB abused children at the OS appeared in letters to the Chicago *Reader* on April 6, May 4, May 25, June 8, July 6, and July 13, 1990. See also Charles Pekow, "The Other Doctor Bettelheim," *Washington Post,* Aug. 26, 1990; Ronald Angres, "Who, Really, Was Bruno Bettelheim?," *Commentary,* vol. 90, no. 4 (Oct. 1990), p. 26.

17. Alan Dundes, "Bruno Bettelheim's Uses of Enchantment and Abuses of Scholarship," *Journal of the American Folklore Society,* vol. 104, no. 441 (Winter 1991), p. 4.

18. See, for example, BB's statement, March 20, 1969, U.S. Congress, House, *Hearings Before the Special Subcommittee on Education of the Committee on Education and Labor,* (Washington, D.C.: U.S. Government Printing Office, 1969), p. 258.

19. See, for example, BB, "The Ignored Lesson of Anne Frank," *Harper's,* Nov. 1960, p. 45.

20. BB, *Love Is Not Enough: The Treatment of Emotionally Disturbed Children* (Glencoe, Ill.: Free Press, 1950), p. 35.

21. Leon Edel, *Writing Lives: Principia Biographica* (New York: W. W. Norton, 1984), p. 64.

CHAPTER ONE: *Vienna*

1. BB, *Freud's Vienna and Other Essays* (New York: Alfred A. Knopf, 1990), p. 132–34.

2. For the origins of the Bettelheim name, see *The Universal Jewish Encyclopedia* (New York: Universal Jewish Encyclopedia, Inc., 1940), vol. 2, p. 256.

3. Israelitische Kultusgemeinde, Vienna.

4. Jakob Bettelheim's position with Albert von Rothschild is described in an obituary and family notice in the *Neue Freie Presse* and in an obituary in the *Neues Wiener Tagblatt,* both April 25, 1898.

5. Wiener Adressbuch—Lehmanns Wohnungsanzeiger (Vienna: Österreichische Anzeigengesellschaft, AG, 1938), vol. 1, p. 77.

6. Israelitische Kultusgemeinde, Vienna.

7. BB, *Freud's Vienna*, p. 104.

8. BB, *A Good Enough Parent: A Book on Child-Rearing* (New York: Alfred A. Knopf, 1987), p. 307.

9. Ibid., pp. 307–8.

10. Ibid., p. 306.

11. Interview with EB.

12. BB, *Good Enough Parent*, p. 306.

13. Interview with Ernst Federn.

14. "Contemporaries," interview with BB, *Modern Medicine*, Sept. 6, 1971, p. 27.

15. Ibid.

16. Edith Buxbaum, unpublished memoir written not long before her death in 1982 and made available by her executor, Herbert J. Belch.

17. BB, *Good Enough Parent*, p. 4.

18. Ibid., p. 348.

19. Ibid., p. 187.

20. Ibid., pp. 40–41.

21. Ibid., pp. 112–13.

22. Ibid., p. 80.

23. Interview with Otto Modley.

24. BB to Rudolf Ekstein, Aug. 15, 1984.

25. BB, "Class, Color and Prejudice," *Nation*, Oct. 19, 1963, p. 232.

26. BB, *Good Enough Parent*, pp. 80–87.

27. Ibid., p. 86.

28. Interview with Constance Katzenstein; BB to CF, Nov. 19, 1986.

29. Interview with EB.

30. Interview with Wanda Willig; interview with GW.

31. Buxbaum memoir.

32. BB briefly discussed the impact of his father's syphilis and his own sexual anxieties on a tape he dictated at the end of his life.

33. Buxbaum memoir.

34. BB, "Dialogue with Mothers," *Ladies' Home Journal*, April 1968, p. 48.

35. Text of BB's National Book Award acceptance speech at the American Academy and Institute of Arts and Letters, New York City, April 13, 1977, BBP.

36. Sigmund Freud, *SE*, vol. 8, pp. 20–21n.

37. BB to CF, Nov. 19, 1986.

38. Mary Harrington Hall, "The Psychology of Involvement," *Psychology Today*, vol. 2 (May 1969), p. 64.

39. Paul Hofmann, *The Viennese: Splendor, Twilight and Exile* (New York: Anchor Books, 1989), p. 162.

40. Hall, "Psychology of Involvement," p. 64.

41. BB, *The Informed Heart: Autonomy in a Mass Age* (Glencoe, Ill.: Free Press, 1960), p. 13.

42. Interview with Constance Katzenstein.

43. Anton Bettelheim's death certificate, Wiener Stadt- und Landesarchiv, Vienna.

44. Interview with EB.

45. BB to CF, Nov. 19, 1986.

46. Studien- und Prüfungsabteilung der Wirtschaftsuniversität Wien.

47. BB, *Good Enough Parent*, p. 28.

48. "Contemporaries," p. 27.

49. Hall, "Psychology of Involvement," p. 64.

50. Interview with Wanda Willig.

51. Interview with Gerard Piel.

52. Interview with GW; interview with Verena Michels.

53. Patricia Lyne to RP, Oct. 15, 1991.

54. Penelope Mesic, "The Abuses of Enchantment," *Chicago,* Aug. 1991, p. 87.

55. BB, *Freud's Vienna,* p. 107.

56. Ibid.

57. Paul Edwards, ed., *The Encyclopedia of Philosophy* (New York: Macmillan and Free Press, 1967), vol. 8, p. 221.

58. BB, *Freud's Vienna,* pp. 27–28.

59. David James Fisher, "An Interview with Bruno Bettelheim," *Los Angeles Psychoanalytic Bulletin,* Fall 1990, p. 3.

60. BB, *Freud's Vienna,* p. 32.

61. BB, *Informed Heart,* p. 18.

62. BB, *Freud's Vienna,* p. 29.

63. Ibid., pp. 31–35.

64. JSS, "Private Reflections on a Public Presentation," *Psychologist Psychoanalyst,* vol. 10, no. 3 (Summer 1990), p. 19.

65. BB, *Freud's Vienna,* p. 36.

66. Ibid., pp. 24–28.

67. Ibid., p. 26.

68. Ibid., p. 27.

69. Ibid.

CHAPTER TWO: *The Anschluss*

1. Steven Beller, *Vienna and the Jews, 1867–1938* (Cambridge: Cambridge University Press, 1990), p. 37.

2. William L. Shirer, *The Rise and Fall of the Third Reich: A History of Nazi Germany* (New York: Touchstone, 1981), pp. 16–20.

3. Ibid., p. 21.

4. Paul Hofmann, *The Viennese: Splendor, Twilight and Exile* (New York: Anchor Books, 1989), p. 216.

5. Ibid., p. 219.

6. Shirer, *Rise and Fall,* p. 279.

7. Bettelheim & Schnitzer reparation documents, Österreichisches Staatsarchiv, Vienna.

8. TBT.

9. Ibid.

10. Ibid.

11. BB, *Freud's Vienna and Other Essays* (New York: Alfred A. Knopf, 1990), p. 110.

12. BB's dissertation, BBP.

13. BB, *Freud's Vienna,* p. 110.

14. BB to Joyce Jack, Jan. 31, 1974; interview with Linnea Brandwein Vacca.

15. Registrar, University of Vienna.

16. Ibid.

17. Speech by BB to Division 39 of the American Psychological Association, Boston, April 9, 1989.

18. David James Fisher, "An Interview with Bruno Bettelheim," *Los Angeles Psychoanalytic Bulletin,* Fall 1990, p. 14.

19. Shirer, *Rise and Fall,* pp. 325–30.

20. Hofmann, *Viennese,* p. 229.

21. William L. Shirer, *Berlin Diary: The Journal of a Foreign Correspondent, 1934–41* (Boston: Little, Brown, 1941), pp. 97–98.

22. TBT.

23. Hofmann, *The Viennese,* p. 236.

24. Shirer, *Berlin Diary,* p. 109.

25. Hofmann, *The Viennese,* p. 242.

26. BB to Farrell, July 28, 1976, JTF.

27. Richard Kaplan, producer, *The Exiles,* transcript of interview for documentary film, A Richard Kaplan Production, Inc., New York, 1989.

28. Nathan M. Szajnberg, ed., *Educating the Emotions: Bruno Bettelheim and Psychoanalytic Development* (New York: Plenum Press, 1992), p. xi.

29. Affidavit, July 10, 1945, in *Trial of the Major War Criminals Before the International Military Tribunal,* vol. 37 (Nuremberg, 1947–49), pp. 818–19.

30. Agnes Crane to American consul, Vienna, Feb. 17, 1938; copy to Cordell Hull, secretary of state, Washington, D.C.; Patricia Crane visa file, NA.

31. John C. Wiley, American chargé d'affaires ad interim, to Cordell Hull, April 6, 1938, Patricia Crane visa file, NA.

32. Patricia Lyne to RP, n.d.; received Oct. 1991.

33. Manifest of S.S. *Roosevelt,* NA.

34. Interview with Wanda Willig.

35. Agnes Crane to A. M. Warren, May 18, 1938, BB visa file, NA. Crane had translated BB's cable from the German.

36. Ibid.

37. John C. Wiley to Cordell Hull, May 31, 1938, BB visa file, NA.

CHAPTER THREE: *Dachau and Buchenwald*

1. Leni Yahil, "Jews in Concentration Camps in Germany Prior to World War II," in Yisrael Gutman and Avital Saf, eds., *The Nazi Concentration Camps: Structure and Aims, the Image of the Prisoner, the Jews in the Camps. Proceedings of the Fourth Yad Vashem International Historical Conference, January 1980* (Jerusalem: Yad Vashem, 1984), p. 84.

2. Comité International de la Croix-Rouge, Service International de Recherches, Certificate of Incarceration, No. 83238, March 11, 1958.

3. Ernst Federn, *Witnessing Psychoanalysis: From Vienna Back to Vienna via Buchenwald and the USA* (London: Karnac Books, 1990), p. 3.

4. Bertram Cohler, remarks at Bettelheim Symposium, Division 39, American Psychological Association, Washington, D.C., April 16, 1994.

5. Affidavit, July 10, 1945, in *Trial of the Major War Criminals Before the International Military Tribunal,* vol. 37 (Nuremberg, 1947–49), p. 819.

6. Yahil, "Jews in Concentration Camps," p. 84.

7. Bruno Heilig, *Men Crucified* (London: Eyre & Spottiswoode, 1941), p. 13.

8. Yahil, "Jews in Concentration Camps," p. 85.

9. BB, *The Informed Heart: Autonomy in a Mass Age* (Glencoe, Ill.: Free Press, 1960), p. 126.

10. Ibid., p. 125.

11. BB, *Surviving and Other Essays* (New York: Alfred A. Knopf, 1979), p. 12n.

12. For a history of the Dachau concentration camp, see Barbara Distel and Ruth Jackusch, eds., *Concentration Camp Dachau, 1933–1945* (Brussels: Comité International de Dachau, 1978).

13. Anthony Read and David Fisher, *Kristallnacht: The Nazi Night of Terror* (New York: Times Books, 1989), pp. 26–27.

14. Konnilyn G. Feig, *Hitler's Death Camps: The Sanity of Madness* (New York: Holmes & Meier, 1979), p. 48.

15. BB, *Informed Heart,* p. 132.

16. BB, *Surviving,* p. 308.

17. Distel and Jakusch, eds., *Concentration Camp Dachau*, pp. 212–13.

18. Ernst Federn, "The Terror as a System—The Concentration Camp: Buchenwald as It Was," *Psychiatric Quarterly Supplement*, vol. 22, pt. 2 (1948), p. 62.

19. Heilig, *Men Crucified*, p. 113.

20. BB, *Informed Heart*, p. 146.

21. Ibid., p. 147.

22. Videotape of deposition in *United States* v. *Conrad Heinrich Schellong*, case 81-C-1478, U.S. District Court, Northern District of Illinois, recorded Nov. 19, 1981.

23. BB, letters from Dachau.

24. Heilig, *Men Crucified*, p. 47.

25. BB, *Informed Heart*, p. 117.

26. BB to PB, July 3, 1938.

27. BB to PB, July 17, 1938.

28. BB to PB, July 3, 1938.

29. Leni Yahil, *The Holocaust: The Fate of European Jewry, 1932–1945* (New York: Oxford University Press, 1990), p. 107.

30. William L. Shirer, *The Rise and Fall of the Third Reich: A History of Nazi Germany* (New York: Touchstone, 1981), p. 351.

31. Documents relating to the Nazi expropriation of Bettelheim & Schnitzer are in the Österreichisches Staatsarchiv, Archiv der Republik, Vienna.

32. Yahil, *Holocaust*, p. 107.

33. Nikolaus Lackner to state commissioner for the private economy, Sept. 16, 1938, Österreichisches Staatsarchiv, Vienna.

34. Affidavit of Nazi Party in Vienna to Property Transfer Authority, Vienna, Sept. 2, 1938, Österreichisches Staatsarchiv, Vienna.

35. BB to PB, July 3, 1938.

36. Aryanization documents for Bettelheim & Schnitzer, Österreichisches Staatsarchiv, Vienna.

37. BB to PB, July 17, 1938.

38. Cable from Hull to American consul, Vienna, June 9, 1938, BB visa file, NA.

39. Cable, Wiley to Hull, June 9, 1938, BB visa file, NA.

40. Cable, Warren to Crane, June 10, 1938, BB visa file, NA.

41. Lawrence S. Kubie to Warren, June 8, 1938, BB visa file, NA.

42. BB, *Informed Heart*, p. 112.

43. BB to PB, July 28, 1938.

44. BB to PB, July 17, 1938.

45. BB to PB, Sept. 1, 1938.

46. TBT.

47. Ibid.

48. Ibid.

49. Heilig, *Men Crucified*, p. 136.

50. Ibid., p. 137.

51. Ibid., p. 152.

52. BB, *Informed Heart*, p. 133.

53. Federn, *Witnessing Psychoanalysis*, p. 4.

54. BB to David Rapaport, March 22, 1957, David Rapaport papers, LC.

55. BB, *Informed Heart*, p. 112.

56. Federn, *Witnessing Psychoanalysis*, p. 4.

57. BB, "The Concentration Camp as a Class State," *Modern Review*, vol. 1, no. 8 (Oct. 1947), p. 629.

58. BB, *Surviving*, p. 108.

59. Federn, *Witnessing Psychoanalysis*, p. 4.

60. BB to Ernst Federn, Jan. 8, 1969.

61. BB, *Surviving,* p. 12n.
62. BB, *Informed Heart,* pp. 153–54n.
63. BB, *Surviving,* p. 12n.
64. BB, "The Dynamism of Anti-Semitism in Gentile and Jew," *Journal of Abnormal and Social Psychology,* vol. 42, no. 2 (April 1947), p. 166.
65. BB, *Informed Heart,* p. 206n.
66. Ibid., p. 193n.
67. Ibid., p. 258.
68. BB, *Surviving,* p. 79.
69. BB, *Informed Heart,* pp. 117–19.
70. For an account of Kristallnacht, see Read and Fisher, *Kristallnacht.*
71. BB, "Dynamism of Anti-Semitism," p. 155.
72. Ibid., pp. 155–56.
73. BB, "The Victim's Image of the Anti-Semite," *Commentary,* Feb. 2, 1948, p. 173.
74. BB, *Informed Heart,* pp. 216–17.
75. BB, "Dynamism of Anti-Semitism," p. 167.
76. Warren file memorandum, Nov. 3, 1938, BB visa file, NA.
77. Interview with GW.
78. Ibid.
79. Hull to American consul, Vienna, Nov. 3, 1938, BB visa file, NA.
80. D. D. Morris to Cordell Hull, Nov. 5, 1938, BB visa file, NA.
81. Agnes P. Crane to A. M. Warren, Nov. 12, 1938, BB visa file, NA.
82. Yahil, *Holocaust,* p. 571.
83. BB visa file, NA.
84. David A. Hackett, ed. and trans., *The Buchenwald Report* (Boulder: Westview Press, 1995), p. 113.
85. Ibid., p. 247.
86. Ibid., pp. 75, 248.
87. Helmut Krausnick et al., *Anatomy of the SS State,* trans. Richard Barry et al. (New York: Walker, 1968), p. 458.
88. Hackett, *Buchenwald Report,* p. 113.
89. Ibid., p. 140.
90. Between 1933 and 1938, Frank van Gheel Gildemeester, a philanthropist and son of a Dutch minister, supported arrested Nazis for humanitarian reasons. In 1939, Hans Fischböck, the Austrian minister for trade and economy, helped Gildemeester create an emigration operation to help the country's Jews.
91. Richard Kaplan, producer, *The Exiles,* transcript of interview for documentary film, A Richard Kaplan Production, Inc., New York, 1989.
92. BB, *Informed Heart,* p. 150.
93. Harry Stein to RP, May 25, 1992; Stein is an official with Gedenkstätte Buchenwald.
94. Heilig, *Men Crucified,* p. 280.
95. Ibid., p. 275.
96. Ibid., p. 289.
97. Comité International de la Croix-Rouge; see also Harry Stein to RP, May 25, 1992.
98. Affidavit, July 10, 1945, p. 819.
99. BB, *Surviving,* p. 14n.
100. BB to Farrell, Jan. 1954, JTF.
101. Kaplan, producer, *Exiles.*
102. BB, *Surviving,* p. 14n.
103. Theron Raines, unpublished manuscript, BBP. The manuscript is in draft

form. Raines has indicated that revisions were being made but declined to be interviewed about the material or any other recollections.

104. Kaplan, producer, *Exiles.*

105. BB, *Surviving,* p. 263.

106. BB, "Eichmann; The System; The Victims," *New Republic,* June 15, 1963, p. 33.

107. See, for example, BB, "The Ignored Lesson of Anne Frank," *Harper's,* Nov. 1960, pp. 45–50.

108. Manifest, S.S. *Gerolstein,* NA; *New York Times,* May 12, 1939.

109. Michael Barnes, writer and producer, *Bruno Bettelheim: A Sense of Surviving,* documentary film, British Broadcasting Corp., London, 1986.

CHAPTER FOUR: *Chicago and Rockford*

1. TBT.

2. Ibid.

3. Interview with Hedda Bolgar.

4. BB to A. M. Warren, May 16, 1939, BB visa file, NA.

5. Chronology of the Emergency Committee on Relief and Immigration of the American Psychoanalytic Association, 1938–48, p. 27.

6. Edith Buxbaum, unpublished memoir written not long before her death in 1982 and made available by her executor, Herbert J. Belch.

7. Theron Raines, unpublished manuscript, BBP.

8. Buxbaum, unpublished memoir.

9. Raines, unpublished manuscript, BBP.

10. Richard Kaplan, producer, *The Exiles,* transcript of interview for documentary film, A Richard Kaplan Production, Inc., New York, 1989.

11. Raines, unpublished manuscript, BBP.

12. Manifest of S.S. *Pennland,* NA.

13. TBT.

14. Ibid.

15. Ibid.

16. Peter Gay, *Freud: A Life for Our Times* (New York: W. W. Norton, 1988), pp. 137–38.

17. BB, *The Unspoken Message,* text of speech delivered at dedication of Pekow Hall of OS, Oct. 20, 1966 (Chicago: University of Chicago Foundation for Emotionally Disturbed Children).

18. Interview with Jill Schwab; Raines, unpublished manuscript, BBP.

19. TBT.

20. BB, *Surviving and Other Essays* (New York: Alfred A. Knopf, 1979), p. 296.

21. TBT.

22. Interview with Louise Friedberg Strouse; interview with Elizabeth Block Kuklick.

23. Interview with Louise Friedberg Strouse.

24. TBT.

25. Ibid.

26. Ibid.

27. Ibid.

28. Serge Klarsfeld, *Memorial to the Jews Transported from France: Documentation of the Deportation of the Victims of the Final Solution in France* (New York: Beate Klarsfeld Foundation, 1983), pp. 259–60, 266.

29. Ibid.

30. Ulrich Middeldorf to Mary Ashby Cheek, Aug. 26, 1941, Mary Ashby Cheek papers, Howard Colman Library, Rockford College, Rockford, Ill.

31. Ralph Tyler to Cheek, Aug. 29, 1941, Cheek papers.

32. Cheek to BB, Sept. 9 and 13, 1941, Cheek papers.

33. Telegram, BB to Cheek, Sept. 17, 1941, Cheek papers.

34. Cheek to Tyler, Jan. 21, 1942, Cheek papers.

35. Cheek to BB, June 16, 1942, Cheek papers.

36. *The Purple Parrot,* Oct. 10, 1941.

37. BB curriculum vitae, Cheek papers.

38. BB to Cheek, June 17, 1942, Cheek papers.

39. Tyler to Cheek, Aug. 29, 1941, Cheek papers.

40. Affidavit, July 10, 1945, in *Trial of the Major War Criminals Before the International Military Tribunal,* vol. 37 (Nuremberg, 1947–49), p. 818.

41. Communication to the minister of science and education in Berlin from the University of Vienna, July 3, 1938, registrar, University of Vienna.

42. BB to Cheek, Aug. 12, 1942, Cheek papers.

43. Interview with Marianne Ettlinger Cohen.

44. Interview with Natalie Menke Brown.

45. Ibid.

46. Interview with Mary Jane Wilcox Rachner.

47. Interview with Mildred Berry.

48. Interview with Natalie Menke Brown.

49. Aimee Isgrig, "Refugee Without Refuge," *Rockford Review,* vol. 33 (May 1944), p. 21.

50. Cheek to BB, May 4, 1944, Cheek papers.

51. Interview with Aimee Isgrig Horton.

52. Cheek to BB, May 4, 1944, Cheek papers.

53. Interview with Mildred Berry.

54. Interview with Betty Bruce Keegan.

CHAPTER FIVE: *Extreme Situations*

1. BB, *Surviving and Other Essays* (New York: Alfred A. Knopf, 1979), pp. 14–15.

2. Ibid., p. 16.

3. BB, "Individual and Mass Behavior in Extreme Situations," *Journal of Abnormal and Social Psychology,* vol. 38, no. 4 (Oct. 1943), pp. 417–52.

4. Ibid., p. 417.

5. Ibid., p. 420.

6. Ibid., p. 423.

7. Ibid., p. 451.

8. Ibid., pp. 418–19.

9. Ibid., p. 437.

10. Ibid., pp. 444–45.

11. Ibid., p. 445.

12. Ibid., p. 447.

13. Ibid., p. 448.

14. David A. Hackett, ed. and trans., *The Buchenwald Report* (Boulder, Colo.: Westview Press, 1995), p. 39.

15. BB, "Extreme Situations," pp. 448–50.

16. Ibid., p. 449.

17. Ibid.

18. Ibid., p. 452.

19. Ibid., p. 423.

20. Ibid.

21. Ernst Federn, *Witnessing Psychoanalysis: From Vienna Back to Vienna via Buchenwald and the USA* (London: Karnac Books, 1990), p. 5.

22. BB, "Extreme Situations," p. 451.

23. Ibid., p. 425.

24. Ibid., p. 433.

25. Ibid., p. 443.

26. Ibid., p. 434. Emphasis added.

27. BB, "Ten Eventful Years: Concentration Camps, German," *Encyclopaedia Britannica* (Chicago: Encyclopaedia Britannica, 1947), vol. 2, p. 6.

28. BB, "Extreme Situations," p. 435.

29. Ibid., p. 451.

30. BB, "The Concentration Camp as a Class State," *Modern Review*, vol. 1, no. 8 (Oct. 1947), p. 628.

31. Jan Levcik, "Buchenwald Before the War," *Politics,* June 1945, pp. 173–74.

32. BB, "Extreme Situations," p. 429n.

33. Paul Cummins, *Dachau Song: The Twentieth Century Odyssey of Herbert Zipper* (New York: Peter Lang, 1992), pp. 86–87; interview with Herbert Zipper.

34. BB, "Extreme Situations," p. 421.

35. BB, "Concentration Camp as Class State," p. 635.

36. James T. Farrell, "After Love, Insight," *New York Times Book Review,* May 29, 1955, p. 6.

37. *Politics,* Feb. 1944, p. 30; Macdonald to BB, Feb. 29, 1944, DM.

38. BB to Macdonald, April 10, 1944, DM.

39. BB to Macdonald, Aug. 11, 1944, DM.

40. Anthony Heilbut, *Exiled in Paradise: German Rufugee Artists and Intellectuals in America, from the 1930s to the Present* (New York: Viking Press, 1983), p. 91.

41. *Journal of the American Medical Association,* Feb. 5, 1944, pp. 363–64.

42. Gordon Allport to BB, June 15, 1945.

43. BB, review of *The Aesthetic Process* by Bertram Morris, *College Art Journal*, vol. 3 (May 1944), p. 166.

44. Interview with Jerald Brauer.

45. W. H. Auden, "In Memory of Sigmund Freud (d. Sept. 1939)," in *W. H. Auden Collected Poems,* ed. Edward Mendelson (New York: Random House, 1976), p. 217.

46. Peter Blos, remarks presented at Eighth International Congress of the International Association of Child Psychiatry and Allied Professions, Philadelphia, July 1974.

47. BB, *The Informed Heart: Autonomy in a Mass Age* (Glencoe, Ill.: Free Press, 1960), p. 19.

48. BB, *The Empty Fortress: Infantile Autism and the Birth of the Self* (New York: Free Press, 1967), p. 8.

49. "World Without 'I,' " *Newsweek,* March 27, 1967, p. 70.

50. BB, *Surviving,* p. 113.

51. BB, *A Good Enough Parent: A Book on Child-Rearing* (New York: Alfred A. Knopf, 1987), p. 4.

52. BB, *A Home for the Heart* (New York: Alfred A. Knopf, 1974), p. 12.

53. BB, *Good Enough Parent,* pp. 199–201.

54. Daniel Karlin, director, *Last Meeting with Bruno Bettelheim,* documentary film, La Sept Flach TV BBS Productions, Paris, 1990.

55. Crane recorded her marital history on an affidavit proving her American citizenship, July 17, 1939, NA.

56. BB, *Home for the Heart,* p. 214.

57. Michael Jenuwine, "A History of the Orthogenic School of the University of Chicago from 1912 to 1990," Dec. 1990, p. 6.

58. Ralph Tyler to E. T. Filbey and Robert Redfield, July 6, 1942, President's papers, Special Collections, Regenstein Library, UC.

59. Ruth Shayman to RP, Feb. 22, 1991.

60. Report on the Orthogenic School, Dec. 1941, President's papers, UC.

61. Interview with Helen Martinson.

62. Michael Jenuwine, "A History of the Orthogenic School," p. 35.

63. August Aichhorn, *Wayward Youth* (New York: Viking Press, 1965), p. 150.

64. Theron Raines, unpublished manuscript, BBP.

65. BB described the meeting in Hutchins's office to David James Fisher and Theron Raines, among others; Ralph Tyler recounted a similar version of the session, according to Rocco Motto, for many years director of the Reiss-Davis Child Study Center in Los Angeles.

66. Interview with Jill Schwab; Raines, unpublished manuscript, BBP.

67. Richard Kaplan, producer, *The Exiles,* transcript of interview for documentary film, A Richard Kaplan Production, Inc., New York, 1989.

CHAPTER SIX: *The Orthogenic School*

1. Michael Jenuwine, "A History of the Orthogenic School of the University of Chicago from 1912 to 1990," Dec. 1990, p. 29.

2. BB, *Love Is Not Enough: The Treatment of Emotionally Disturbed Children* (Glencoe, Ill.: Free Press, 1950), p. 16.

3. Jenuwine, "History of the Orthogenic School," p. 33.

4. BB, *Love Is Not Enough,* p. 16.

5. BB, *Truants from Life: The Rehabilitation of Emotionally Disturbed Children* (Glencoe, Ill.: Free Press, 1955), pp. 406–7; interview with Gayle Shulenberger Janowitz.

6. Interview with Josette Wingo Lowdon.

7. For a useful survey, see Joseph Noshpitz, "History of Milieu in Residential Treatment," in *Educating the Emotions: Bruno Bettelheim and Psychoanalytic Development,* ed. Nathan M. Szajnberg (New York: Plenum Press, 1992), pp. 91–120.

8. Interview with Gayle Shulenberger Janowitz.

9. Interview with Josette Wingo Lowdon.

10. Ibid.

11. BB and Benjamin Wright, "The Role of Residential Treatment for Children," *American Journal of Orthopsychiatry,* vol. 25 (Oct. 1955), p. 705.

12. Noshpitz, "History of Milieu," p. 110.

13. BB and Emmy Sylvester, "Milieu Therapy; Indications and Illustrations," *Psychoanalytic Review,* vol. 36 (Jan. 1949), p. 54.

14. BB, *Love Is Not Enough,* p. viii.

15. BB, *A Home for the Heart* (New York: Alfred A. Knopf, 1974), p. 10.

16. BB, *Surviving and Other Essays* (New York: Alfred A. Knopf, 1979), p. 36.

17. BB, *Home for the Heart,* p. 11.

18. BB, *The Informed Heart: Autonomy in a Mass Age* (Glencoe, Ill.: Free Press, 1960), p. 23.

19. BB, *Surviving,* p. 114.

20. BB, "Schizophrenia as a Reaction to Extreme Situations," *American Journal of Orthopsychiatry,* vol. 26, no. 3 (July 1956), p. 507.

21. Paul Celan, *Speech-Grille and Selected Poems,* trans. Joachim Neugroschel (New York: E. P. Dutton, 1971), pp. 28–29.

22. See, for example, Jerry Glenn, *Paul Celan* (Boston: Twayn Publishers, 1943), p. 69–70.

23. BB, *Surviving,* p. 111.

24. Ibid., p. 114.

25. BB, "Schizophrenia," p. 512.

26. BB, review of *Searchlights on Delinquency: New Psychoanalytic Studies,* ed. K. R. Eissler, *American Journal of Sociology,* July 1950, p. 104.

27. BB, "Schizophrenia," pp. 513–14.

28. Ibid., p. 517.

29. D. Patrick Zimmerman, "The Clinical Thought of Bruno Bettelheim: A Critical Historical Review," in *Milieu Therapy: Significant Issues and Innovative Applications,* ed. Jerome Goldsmith and Jacquelyn Sanders (New York: Haworth Press, 1993), p. 28.

30. BB to David Rapaport, Aug. 22, 1952, David Rapaport papers, LC.

31. Michael Barnes, writer and producer, *Bruno Bettelheim: A Way of Surviving,* documentary film, British Broadcasting Corp., London, 1986.

32. Interview with Leslie Aranow Cleaver.

33. BB, *Informed Heart,* p. 4.

34. Josette Wingo Lowdon, "My Life at the Orthogenic School," draft of remarks delivered at *Festschrift* for BB at UC, May 23–24, 1986, BBP.

35. Daniel Karlin, director, *Portrait de Bruno Bettelheim,* documentary film, O.R.T.F., Channel 1, Paris, 1974.

36. Interview with Mary Cahn Schwartz.

37. Bertram Cohler, remarks at Bettelheim Symposium, Division 39, American Psychological Association, Washington, D.C., April 16, 1994.

38. Interview with Robert Bergman.

39. BB, *Home for the Heart,* p. 403.

40. Ibid., p. 263.

41. Interview with Toni.

42. Interview with Karen Carlson Zelan.

43. JSS, eulogy for BB, Rockefeller Memorial Chapel, UC, May 4, 1990.

44. Ibid.

45. Ibid.

46. Linnea Brandwein Vacca to RP, Jan. 10, 1995.

47. BB, *Truants from Life,* pp. 405–6; interview with Gayle Shulenberger Janowitz.

48. Interview with Ugo Formigoni.

49. Diana Grossman Kahn, "A Safe Place to Learn: Educating the Emotions with Bruno Bettelheim at the Orthogenic School," draft of remarks prepared for BB's *Festschrift,* May 23–24, 1986, p. 14, BBP.

50. BB, "The Unspoken Message," text of speech delivered at dedication of Pekow Hall of OS, Oct. 20, 1966 (Chicago: University of Chicago Foundation for Emotionally Disturbed Children), p. 1.

51. BB, *Home for the Heart,* p. 93.

52. BB, *Love Is Not Enough,* p. 170.

53. BB, *Truants from Life,* p. 28.

54. BB, *Home for the Heart,* pp. 65–66.

55. Interview with Benjamin Wright.

56. BB, *Home for the Heart,* p. 192.

57. Interview with JSS.

58. BB, "Dialogue with Mothers," *Ladies' Home Journal,* Dec. 1971, p. 14.

59. "Some Facts About the Orthogenic School," Dec. 15, 1947, President's papers, UC.

60. Interview with Lou Harper.

61. Memo, F. Howell Wright to R. Wendell Harrison, Oct. 4, 1948, President's papers, UC.

62. Letter to Robert M. Hutchins, Oct. 10, 1945, BBP.

63. Memo, BB to Robert M. Hutchins, Oct. 30, 1945, BBP.

64. Memo, E. T. Filbey to E. C. Colwell, Oct. 19, 1948, President's papers, UC.

65. Chicago *Daily News,* Feb. 23, 1963.

66. Freud, *SE,* vol. 7, p. 20.

67. René Spitz, *The First Year of Life: A Psychoanalytic Study of Normal and Deviant Development of Object Relations* (New York: International Universities Press, 1965), p. 206.

68. Barbara Ehrenreich and Deirdre English, *For Her Own Good: 150 Years of Experts' Advice to Women* (New York: Anchor Books, 1978), p. 235.

69. Ibid.

70. Ibid., p. 237.

71. Cited in ibid., p. 236.

72. Cited in ibid., p. 237.

73. BB, "Memorandum on the Needs of the Orthogenic School," July 27, 1945, BBP.

74. Jenuwine, "History of the Orthogenic School," p. 36.

75. Minutes of the UC board of trustees, May 12, 1949.

76. BB, *Truants from Life,* p. 28.

77. Ibid., p. 27.

78. Chicago *Sun-Times,* Aug. 28, 1967.

79. BB to Farrell, Nov. 12, 1953, JTF.

80. Memo, BB to Ralph Tyler, Oct. 2, 1947; Ralph Tyler to Women's Auxiliary, Oct. 28, 1947, BBP.

CHAPTER SEVEN: *The Feast-Day Garment*

1. BB to ND, March 10, 1977.

2. Thomas Mann, *Reflections of a Nonpolitical Man,* tr. with an introduction by Walter D. Morris (New York: Frederick Ungar Publishing Co., 1983), pp. 298–99; original title, *Betrachtungen eines Unpolitischen* (Berlin: Fischer Verlag, 1918).

3. BB, *The Children of the Dream: Communal Child-Rearing and American Education* (New York: Free Press, 1969), p. xiii.

4. Interview with Benjamin Wright.

5. BB, *The Informed Heart: Autonomy in a Mass Age* (Glencoe, Ill.: Free Press, 1960), p. 33.

6. Macdonald to BB, n.d., DM.

7. Ibid.; BB to Macdonald, Jan. 7, 1948, DM.

8. BB, "Exodus," *Politics,* vol. 5 (Winter 1948), p. 16.

9. BB to Farrell, Aug. 22, 1945, JTF.

10. BB to Macdonald, June 15, 1944, DM.

11. BB to Macdonald, Aug. 11, 1944, DM.

12. BB to Macdonald, Oct. 23, 1944, DM.

13. BB to Macdonald, April 4, 1945, DM.

14. Interview with Bertram Cohler.

15. BB to Ernst Federn, Sept. 9, 1945.

16. BB to Ernst Federn, May 26, 1946, BBP.

17. BB with Morris Janowitz, *The Dynamics of Prejudice: A Psychological and Sociological Study of Veterans,* vol. 2, Studies in Prejudice series (New York: Harper & Brothers, 1950), pp. xvii–xviii.

18. Ibid., p. xviii.

19. Ibid., pp. 5–6.

20. D. Patrick Zimmerman, "The Clinical Thought of Bruno Bettelheim: A Criti-

cal Historical View," in *Milieu Therapy: Significant Issues and Innovative Applications,* ed. Jerome Goldsmith and Jacquelyn Sanders (New York: Haworth Press, 1993), p. 15.

21. BB with Janowitz, *Dynamics of Prejudice,* p. 163.
22. Ibid., p. 50.
23. Ibid., p. 39.
24. Ibid., p. 157.
25. Ibid.
26. Ibid., p. 2.
27. Ibid., p. 183.
28. Joseph Zubin, review of *Dynamics of Prejudice, Jewish Social Studies,* vol. 13, no. 3 (July 1951), p. 268.
29. BB with Janowitz, *Dynamics of Prejudice,* pp. 174–75.
30. BB, *Love Is Not Enough: The Treatment of Emotionally Disturbed Children* (Glencoe, Ill.: Free Press, 1950), pp. 3–4.
31. Ibid., p. 5.
32. BB, "Some Facts About the Orthogenic School," Dec. 15, 1947, President's papers, UC, p. 8.
33. BB, *Love Is Not Enough,* p. 102.
34. Ibid., p. 138.
35. Ibid., p. 333.
36. Ibid., p. 17.
37. Ibid., p. 15.
38. Ibid., p. 342.
39. Ibid., p. 358.
40. Ibid., p. 343.
41. Ibid., p. 374.
42. BB, *Truants from Life: The Rehabilitation of Emotionally Disturbed Children* (Glencoe, Ill.: Free Press, 1955), p. 1.
43. Ibid., p. 8.
44. Ibid., p. 390.
45. Ibid., p. 477.
46. Ibid., p. xvi.
47. Ibid., p. 46.
48. Ibid., p. 278.
49. Ibid., p. 390.
50. Ibid., p. 66.
51. Ibid., p. 170n.
52. Ibid., p. 290–91.
53. Ibid., p. 407.
54. Ibid., p. 267.
55. Ibid., p. 387.
56. Ibid., p. 386.
57. Ibid., p. 470.
58. Ibid., p. 467.
59. Ibid., p. 154.
60. Ibid., p. 270.
61. Milton Barron, review of *Truants from Life, Nation,* July 30, 1955, p. 99.
62. James T. Farrell, review of *Truants from Life, New York Times Book Review,* May 29, 1955, p. 6.
63. Theodore Shapiro, "A View from the Bridge," *Journal of American Psychoanalytic Association,* vol. 41, no. 4 (1993), p. 927.
64. BB to David Rapaport, Aug. 22, 1952, David Rapaport papers, LC.
65. BB, *Truants from Life,* p. 474.

66. BB to Macdonald, Jan. 11, 1950, DM.

67. Macdonald manuscript, DM.

68. BB, *Love Is Not Enough,* pp. 374–75n.

69. BB, *Truants from Life,* p. 13.

70. Ibid., pp. 14–15.

71. BB, *A Home for the Heart* (New York: Alfred A. Knopf, 1974), pp. 5, 12.

72. BB, *Truants from Life,* p. 477.

73. BB, *The Empty Fortress: Infantile Autism and the Birth of the Self* (New York: Free Press, 1967), p. 206.

74. BB, *Truants from Life,* p. 148.

75. Ibid., p. 149.

76. Ibid., p. 144.

77. Michael Barnes, writer and producer, *Bruno Bettelheim: A Way of Surviving,* documentary film, British Broadcasting Corp., London, 1986.

78. Zimmerman database.

79. BB, *Empty Fortress,* p. 63.

80. William Blau, letter, Chicago *Reader,* July 6, 1990.

81. David Dempsey, "Bruno Bettelheim Is Dr. No," *New York Times Magazine,* Jan. 11, 1970.

82. Alida Jatich, letter, *University of Chicago Magazine,* Oct. 1990, pp. 3–4.

83. Barbara Fish and Edward Ritvo, "Psychoses of Childhood," in *Basic Handbook of Child Psychiatry,* vol. 2, ed. Joseph Noshpitz (New York: Basic Books, 1979), p. 275.

84. Review of *Love Is Not Enough,* Chicago *Sun-Times,* June 6, 1950.

85. Donald W. Fiske, review of *Love Is Not Enough,* Chicago *Tribune,* July 16, 1950.

86. Gertrude Samuels, review of *Love Is Not Enough, New York Times Book Review,* Sept. 17, 1950, p. 16.

87. Review of *Love Is Not Enough,* San Francisco *Chronicle,* July 16, 1950.

88. David Riesman, review of *Love Is Not Enough, Nation,* June 24, 1950, p. 629.

89. BB, review of *The Lonely Crowd, University of Chicago Magazine,* March 1951, p. 10.

90. Norman V. Lourie, review of *Love Is Not Enough, Child Welfare,* May 1951, p. 17.

91. See, for instance, Anselm Strauss, *American Sociological Review,* vol. 15, no. 6 (Dec. 1950), p. 825.

92. Therese Benedek, review of *Love Is Not Enough, Marriage and Family Living,* vol. 12, no. 4 (Fall 1950), p. 153.

93. BB, *Love Is Not Enough,* p. 41. Emphasis added.

94. Virginia Axline, review of *Love Is Not Enough, Journal of Abnormal and Social Psychology* vol. 46, no. 3 (July 1951), p. 449.

95. Interview with Shelton Key.

CHAPTER EIGHT: *The Big Bad Wolf*

1. BB, *Dialogues with Mothers* (Glencoe, Ill.: Free Press, 1962), p. 169.

2. BB, *A Good Enough Parent: A Book on Child-Rearing* (New York: Alfred A. Knopf, 1987), p. 97.

3. BB, *A Home for the Heart* (New York: Alfred A. Knopf, 1974), p. 17.

4. *Time,* July 5, 1968, p. 49.

5. A transcript of BB's interview on *Good Morning America* is in the BBP. It was mailed to him by JSS on June 24, 1980. Her letter implies that he had appeared recently, but the transcript carries no date, and *Good Morning America* was unable to locate a record of the program.

6. David Dempsey, "Bruno Bettelheim Is Dr. No," *New York Times Magazine,* Jan. 11, 1970, p. 110.

7. Tom Wallace Lyons, *The Pelican and After: A Novel About Emotional Disturbance* (Richmond: Prescott, Durrell & Co., 1983), p. 27.

8. New Haven *Register,* Aug. 4, 1984.

9. Charles Pekow, "The Other Dr. Bettelheim," Washington *Post,* Aug. 26, 1990.

10. Chicago *Sun-Times,* Sept. 16, 1990.

11. *University of Chicago Magazine,* vol. 8, no. 1 (Oct. 1990), p. 3.

12. *All Things Considered,* National Public Radio, March 18, 1991.

13. Chicago *Reader,* June 8, 1990.

14. Ronald Angres, "Who, Really, Was Bruno Bettelheim?," *Commentary,* vol. 90, no. 4 (Oct. 1990), pp. 27–28.

15. *Newsweek,* Sept. 10, 1990, p. 59.

16. Interview with Betty Lou Pingree Rellahan.

17. Chicago *Sun-Times,* Sept. 16, 1990.

18. Fae Lohn Tyroler, Karen Carlson Zelan, et al., letter, Chicago *Sun-Times,* Oct. 3, 1990.

19. Washington *Post,* Oct. 6, 1990.

20. Alida Jatich, letter, Chicago *Reader,* April 6, 1990. This letter is signed "Name withheld," but Jatich later abandoned her anonymity; see her letter to *University of Chicago Magazine,* vol. 8, no. 1 (Oct. 1990), pp. 3–4.

21. Chicago *Sun-Times,* Sept. 16, 1990.

22. Interview with Arnold Granville.

23. Interview with Paul.

24. BB, *Freud's Vienna and Other Essays* (New York: Alfred A. Knopf, 1990), p. 123.

25. BB, *A Home for the Heart,* p. 161.

26. BB, *Surviving and Other Essays* (New York: Alfred A. Knopf, 1979), pp. 399–400.

27. Interview with Charles Pekow; interview with Patty Pickett McKnight.

28. Pekow, "The Other Dr. Bettelheim."

29. Angres, "Who, Really, Was Bruno Bettelheim?," p. 28.

30. BB, *Love Is Not Enough: The Treatment of Emotionally Disturbed Children* (Glencoe, Ill.: Free Press, 1950), p. 314.

31. Pekow, "The Other Dr. Bettelheim."

32. BB, *The Informed Heart: Autonomy in a Mass Age* (Glencoe, Ill.: Free Press, 1960), p. 131.

33. BB, *The Empty Fortress: Infantile Autism and the Birth of the Self* (New York: Free Press, 1967), pp. 410–11.

34. David Dempsey to RP, July 18, 1994.

35. See, for instance, Paul Roazen, "The Rise and Fall of Bruno Bettelheim," *Psychohistory Review,* vol. 20, no. 3 (Spring 1992), pp. 235–36.

36. BB, *Love Is Not Enough,* p. 35n.

37. Interview with Benjamin Wright.

38. Interview with George Pollock.

39. Alice Miller, *For Your Own Good: Hidden Cruelty in Child-Rearing and the Roots of Violence* (New York: Noonday Press, 1990), p. xvii.

40. BB to ND, Feb. 14, 1976.

41. JSS, *A Greenhouse for the Mind* (Chicago: University of Chicago Press, 1989), p. 50.

42. The Orthogenic School Manual, p. 77.

43. *All Things Considered,* March 18, 1991.

44. Interview with Nell Pekarsky.

45. Interview with Charles Feldstein.

CHAPTER NINE: *The Terror of Judd Hall*

1. Anthony Heilbut, *Exiled in Paradise: German Refugee Artists and Intellectuals in America, from the 1930s to the Present* (New York: Viking Press, 1983), p. 78.

2. David Riesman, "My Education in Soc 2," in *General Education in the Social Sciences: Centennial Reflections on the College of the University of Chicago*, ed. John MacAloon (Chicago: University of Chicago Press, 1992), pp. 189–90n.

3. BB, letter, *New York Times Magazine*, Feb. 8, 1970, pp. 21, 101.

4. JSS, "Private Reflections on a Public Presentation," *Psychologist Psychoanalyst*, vol. 10, no. 3 (Summer 1990), p. 17.

5. Interview with Marc Lubin.

6. Interview with Dorothy Johnson.

7. Interview with David Gutmann.

8. BB to ND, March 30, 1984.

9. Interview with Dorothy Johnson.

10. Robert Ginsburg, "Through the Lens of a Career," in *General Education in the Social Sciences*, ed. MacAloon, p. 150.

11. Interview with Dennis Duginske.

12. Interview with Jonathan Farber.

13. Interview with David Gutmann.

14. BB, *Dialogues with Mothers* (Glencoe, Ill.: Free Press, 1962), p. 8.

15. Ibid., pp. 94–95.

16. Ibid., p. 85.

17. Interview with Sue Duncan.

18. BB, *Dialogues with Mothers*, pp. 115, 123, 23, 127, 29.

19. Ibid., p. 157.

20. Ibid., pp. 157–58.

21. Ibid., p. 12.

22. Ibid., p. 58.

23. Chicago *Daily News*, July 25, 1946.

24. Chicago *Daily News*, April 19, 1951.

25. Chicago *Daily News*, April 20, 1956.

26. Chicago *Sun-Times*, March 25, 1963.

27. Robert Hauptman to RP, April 2, 1991.

28. Joy Calhoun, letter, Chicago *Reader*, April 20, 1990.

29. BB's FBI file, no. 62–58619, was obtained under Freedom of Information-Privacy Acts request no. 359852, April 30, 1992. The file is incomplete and heavily redacted.

30. Interview with NB.

31. FBI file.

32. BB to Farrell, Nov. 2, 1956, JTF.

33. Chicago *Sun-Times*, May 30, 1959.

34. UC *Maroon*, Feb. 20, 1963.

35. Francis Chase to Edward Levi, Dec. 18, 1962, Dept. of Education, UC.

36. UC *Maroon*, Feb. 20, 1963.

37. Sam King to Francis Chase, Feb. 2, 1963, Dept. of Education, UC.

38. Interview with Maria Piers; interview with Matthew Piers.

39. Interview with GW.

40. BB and Emmy Sylvester, "Physical Symptoms in Emotionally Disturbed Children," *Psychoanalytic Study of the Child*, vols. 3 and 4 (1949), pp. 353–68.

BB and Emmy Sylvester, "Delinquency and Morality," *Psychoanalytic Study of the Child*, vol. 5 (1950), pp. 329–42.

41. John Frosch to BB, Jan. 12, 1961, Max Gittelson papers, LC.

42. BB to John Frosch, Jan. 25, 1961, Max Gittelson papers, LC.

43. Interview with Benjamin Wright.

44. Interview with JSS.

45. BB to Francis Chase, April 27, 1964, Dept. of Education, UC.

46. Eric Schopler, "The Anatomy of a Negative Role Model," in *The Undaunted Psychologist: Adventures in Research,* eds. Gary Brannigan and Matthew Merrens (Philadelphia: Temple University Press, 1993), pp. 176–77.

47. BB, "How to Arm Our Children Against Anti-Semitism?," *Commentary,* Sept. 1951, p. 209.

48. BB, "Individual and Mass Behavior in Extreme Situations," *Journal of Abnormal and Social Psychology,* vol. 38, no.4 (Oct. 1943), p. 449.

49. Chicago *Sun-Times,* Feb. 7, 1963.

50. *Severn Darden at the Second City: The Sound of My Own Voice and Other Noises* (Mercury Records, OCM2202), recorded before a live audience at The Second City Cabaret, Chicago, Jan. 30, 1961.

51. See, in particular, *Truants from Life: The Rehabilitation of Emotionally Disturbed Children* (Glencoe, Ill.: Free Press, 1955); *The Informed Heart: Autonomy in a Mass Age* (Glencoe, Ill.: Free Press, 1960); *The Empty Fortress: Infantile Autism and the Birth of the Self* (New York: Free Press, 1967); and *The Children of the Dream: Communal Child-Rearing and American Education* (New York: Free Press, 1969).

52. BB to Erik Erikson, Nov. 26, 1956.

53. BB to ND, Jan. 20, 1976.

54. BB to ND, March 10, 1977. Erik Erikson's parents were Danish, his mother Jewish, his father Protestant; they separated before their son's birth, and when Erik was three years old, in 1905, his mother married Theodor Homburger, a Jewish pediatrician, in Karlsruhe, Germany. See *Current Biography Yearbook 1971,* ed. Charles Moritz (New York: W. H. Wilson, 1971), p. 118.

55. BB with Morris B. Janowitz, *Social Change and Prejudice* (Glencoe, Ill.: Free Press, 1964), p. 5.

56. BB to ND, Nov. 18, 1974; Jan. 28, 19[82].

57. BB, *Informed Heart,* p. 12.

58. BB with Alvin Rosenfeld, *The Art of the Obvious: Developing Insight for Psychotherapy and Everyday Life* (New York: Alfred A. Knopf, 1993), p. 225.

59. Interview with EB.

60. BB, *Informed Heart,* pp. 15–20.

61. BB, *Surviving and Other Essays* (New York: Alfred A. Knopf, 1979), p. 13.

62. BB, *Informed Heart,* p. 12.

63. Ibid.

CHAPTER TEN: *The Other Family*

1. Interview with NB.

2. BB to Farrell, Jan. n.d., 1954, JTF.

3. Interview with EB.

4. BB's medical records, Palo Alto (California) Medical Foundation.

5. Interview with NB.

6. I am indebted to Jane Kallir of Galerie St. Etienne, New York City, and Dr. Karin Frank v. Maur of the Staatsgalerie Stuttgart, Germany, for helping me understand the history and value of Egon Schiele's *Vorstadt I.*

7. Paul Hofmann, *The Viennese: Splendor, Twilight and Exile* (New York: Anchor Books, 1989), pp. 4–5.

8. BB, "Death—Life's Purpose?," *Chicago Review,* vol. 9, no. 2 (Summer 1955), p. 14.

9. Interview with EB.

10. BB to David Riesman, Nov. 3, 1960, BBP.

11. BB, "Fathers Shouldn't Try to Be Mothers," *Parents' Magazine,* Oct. 1956, p. 125.

12. *Ladies' Home Journal,* June 1967, p. 51.

13. BB, talk to the North Shore Health Resort, Lake Forest, Ill., Feb. 14, 1951, Menninger Archives, Topeka, Kansas.

14. Interview with Bertram Cohler.

15. Interview with Martha Friedberg.

16. See, for example, "Growing Up Female," *Harper's,* Oct. 1962, pp. 120–28.

17. BB to ND, Aug. 2, 1983; Aug. 24, 1974; March 11, 1982.

18. Interview with Richard Stern.

19. BB to Morris Janowitz, n.d. [c. 1960].

20. BB to Rapaport, May 23, 1958, Rapaport papers, LC.

21. BB to ND, Nov. 12, 1986.

22. Interview with Ugo Formigoni.

23. Interview with Jacob Getzels.

24. Interview with Martha Friedberg.

25. Interview with Leslie Aranow Cleaver.

26. Interview with GW.

27. Interview with Catherine Weinmann Isenstadt.

CHAPTER ELEVEN: *Autism*

1. BB, "Application for a Grant Permitting a Research Program in Therapy of Infantile Autism and Dynamics of Early Ego Development," Aug. 9, 1955, FF.

2. Uta Frith, "Asperger and His Syndrome," in *Autism and Asperger Syndrome,* ed. Uta Frith (Cambridge: Cambridge University Press, 1991), pp. 3–4.

3. Ibid., p. 2; see also *Diagnostic and Statistical Manual of Mental Disorders,* 4th ed. *(DSM-IV),* ed. Michael First (Washington, D.C.: American Psychiatric Association, 1994), pp. 66–71.

4. Leo Kanner, "Problems of Nosology and Psychodynamics of Early Infantile Autism," *American Journal of Orthopsychiatry,* vol. 19 (July 1949), p. 425.

5. Leo Kanner and Leon Eisenberg, "Notes on the Follow-Up Studies of Autistic Children," in *Psychopathology of Childhood,* ed. P. Hoch and J. Zubin (New York: Grune & Stratton, 1955), pp. 227–39.

6. Editha Sterba, "An Abnormal Child," *Psychoanalytic Quarterly,* vol. 5, no. 3 (July 1936), p. 375; vol. 5, no. 4 (Oct. 1936), p. 560.

7. Lawrence Kimpton to Joseph McDaniel, Jr., Oct. 7, 1955, FF.

8. Seymour Kety to Bernard Berelson, Nov. 28, 1955, FF.

9. Ibid.

10. Francis Chase to BB, July 5, 1956, Dept. of Education, UC.

11. Bernard Rimland, *Infantile Autism: The Syndrome and Its Implications for a Neural Theory of Behavior* (Englewood Cliffs, N.J.: Prentice Hall, 1964), p. 6.

12. *DSM-IV,* p. 68.

13. Zimmerman database.

14. BB to David Rapaport, June 24, 1958, David Rapaport papers, LC.

15. BB to Joseph McDaniel, July 17, 1958, FF.

16. Interview with Bertram Cohler.

17. BB, "Schizophrenic Art: A Case Study," *Scientific American,* vol. 186, no. 4 (April 1952), pp. 30–34.

18. BB to Joseph McDaniel, Jr., June 24, 1959, FF.

19. BB to Joseph McDaniel, Jr., July 7, 1960, FF.

20. BB, "Joey: A 'Mechanical Boy,' " *Scientific American,* vol. 200, no. 3 (March 1959), p. 117.

21. BB, *The Empty Fortress: Infantile Autism and the Birth of the Self* (New York: Free Press, 1967), p. 346.

22. BB, "Feral Children and Autistic Children," *American Journal of Sociology,* vol. 64 (March 1959), p. 455.

23. Ibid., p. 456.

24. Ibid., p. 458.

25. Ibid.

26. Interview with Dorothy Johnson; mother to Robert M. Hutchins, Oct. 10, 1945.

27. BB, "Feral Children," p. 457.

28. Ibid., p. 467.

29. *The Hidden World* appeared at 10 P.M. EST on CBS, Nov. 23, 1960.

30. BB screened *The Hidden World* at a dinner of the F.E.D.C. in Chicago, Jan. 18, 1961.

31. BB, *Empty Fortress,* p. 155n.

32. BB to Bernard Berelson, March 29, 1957, FF.

33. *New York Times,* May 8, 1960.

34. Robert Chandler to BB, Feb. 5, 1960, FF.

35. BB to Robert Chandler, Feb. 11, 1960, FF.

36. Interview with JSS.

37. BB to David Hunter, June 27, 1962, FF.

38. BB to William Nims, Jan. 21, 1964, FF.

39. BB, *Empty Fortress,* p. 8.

40. Ibid., p. 8.

41. Ibid., p. 68.

42. Ibid., p. 71.

43. Ibid., p. 71.

44. Ibid., p. 154.

45. Ibid., p. 343.

46. Ibid., pp. 17, 35, 78, 141, 147, 149, 150, 176n, 193, 202, 202n, 203, 221, 236, 395, 458.

47. Donna Williams, *Nobody Nowhere: The Extraordinary Autobiography of an Autistic* (New York: Times Books, 1992), pp. 101–2.

48. Charles Rycroft, "Lost Children," *New York Review of Books,* May 4, 1967, p. 16.

49. Donna Williams to RP, n.d., received March 22, 1993.

50. BB, *Empty Fortress,* p. 248.

51. Ibid., p. 273.

52. Ibid., p. 304.

53. Ibid., p. 163.

54. Ibid., p. 163.

55. Interview with Mary Cahn Schwartz.

56. Interview with Gayle Shulenberger Janowitz.

57. BB, *Empty Fortress,* p. 217n.

58. Zimmerman database.

59. BB, *Empty Fortress,* p. 442.

60. Ibid., p. 155.

61. Ibid., p. 413.

62. Interview with Judith Stacey.

63. Zimmerman database.

64. Ibid.

65. BB, *A Home for the Heart* (New York: Alfred A. Knopf, 1974), p. 177.

66. D. Patrick Zimmerman, "Bruno Bettelheim: The Mysterious Other, Historical Reflections on the Treatment of Childhood Psychosis," p. 19.

67. Kanner, foreword to Rimland, *Infantile Autism,* p. v.

68. Barbara Fish and Edward Ritvo, "Psychoses of Childhood," in *Basic Handbook of Child Psychiatry,* vol. 2, ed. Joseph Noshpitz (New York: Basic Books, 1979), p. 275.

69. Ronald Angres to Jeffrey Masson, n.d.

70. Jacques May, letter, *Scientific American,* vol. 200, no. 5 (May 1959), p. 12.

71. Peter Hobson, "On Psychoanalytic Approaches to Autism," *American Journal of Orthopsychiatry,* vol. 60, no. 3 (July 1990), p. 325.

72. Norris Haring and E. Lakin Phillips, *Educating Emotionally Disturbed Children* (New York: McGraw-Hill, 1962), p. 21.

73. BB, *Harvard Educational Review,* vol. 33, no. 3, Summer 1963, p. 329n.

74. C. Gary Merritt, review of *The Empty Fortress, American Journal of Orthopsychiatry,* vol. 38, no. 5 (Oct. 1968), p. 926–30.

75. BB, "Reply by Bruno Bettelheim," *American Journal of Orthopsychiatry,* vol. 38 no. 5 (Oct. 1968), p. 932. Emphasis added.

76. Chicago *Sun-Times,* Aug. 30, 1967.

77. Merritt, review of *Empty Fortress,,* p. 938.

78. "World Without 'I,' " *Newsweek,* March 27, 1967, p. 70.

79. "Chicago's 'Dr. Yes,' " *Time,* July 5, 1968, p. 49.

80. William Ryan, "The Holy Work of Bruno Bettelheim," *Commonweal,* May 26, 1967, p. 283.

81. Robert Coles, "A Hero of Our Time," *New Republic,* March 3, 1967, p. 23.

82. *Scientific American,* vol. 217, no. 5 (Nov. 1967), pp. 131–32.

83. Carol Kleiman, review of *The Empty Fortress,* Chicago *Tribune,* Jan. 22, 1967.

84. *New York Times,* March, 10, 1967; *New York Times Book Review,* Feb. 26, 1967, p. 45.

85. Peter Gay, review of *The Empty Fortress, New Yorker,* May 18, 1968, p. 160.

86. Ibid.

87. Ibid., p. 172.

88. Ibid.

89. Ibid., p. 173.

90. BB, "Where Self Begins," *New York Times Magazine,* Feb. 12, 1967, p. 65.

91. BB, *Empty Fortress,* pp. 7, 94.

92. Tape, *Studs Terkel Show,* WFMT-FM, Chicago, Jan. 24, 1984.

93. Carl H. Klaus et al., eds., *In Depth: Essayists for Our Time,* 2d ed. (New York: Harcourt Brace Jovanovich, 1993), p. 93.

94. Irving Cutler, *The Jews of Chicago: From Shtetl to Suburb* (Urbana, Ill.: University of Illinois Press, 1996), p. 162.

95. BB, *Empty Fortress,* p. 125.

96. Ibid., p. 239.

97. Ibid., p. 96.

98. Ibid., p. 159.

99. Ibid., p. 403.

100. Interview with Molly Finn.

101. *DSM-IV,* p. 69.

102. Fish and Ritvo, "Childhood Psychoses," p. 272.

103. Leon Eisenberg and Leo Kanner, "Early Infantile Autism—1943–1955," *American Journal of Orthopsychiatry,* vol. 26 (July 1956), p. 563.

104. Beata Rank, in *Emotional Problems of Early Childhood,* ed. G. Caplan (New York: Basic Books, 1955), pp. 491–501.

105. BB, "Joey: The 'Mechanical Boy,'" *Reader's Digest,* vol. 74, no. 446 (June 1959), pp. 45–48.

106. Clara Claiborne Park, *The Siege: The First Eight Years of an Autistic Child, with an Epilogue, Fifteen Years After* (Boston: Atlantic–Little, Brown, 1982), p. 131.

107. Interview with Clara Claiborne Park.

108. Bernard Rimland, "Psychogenesis Versus Biogenesis: The Issues and the Evidence," in *Changing Perspectives in Mental Illness* (New York: Holt Rinehart & Winston, 1969), p. 704.

109. Rimland, introduction to *Children with Autism: A Parents' Guide,* ed. Michael Powers (Rockville, Md.: Woodbine House, 1989), p. x.

110. Ibid., p. xiii.

111. Rimland, *Infantile Autism,* p. 62.

112. Ibid., p. 88.

113. Ibid., p. 217.

114. Ibid., p. v.

115. Ibid., p. vii.

116. Bernard Rimland to BB, March 22, 1965.

117. BB to Rimland, March 25, 1965.

118. Rimland to BB, April 5, 1966.

119. Rimland, *Infantile Autism,* p. 64.

120. BB to Rimland, April 9, 1966.

121. BB, *Empty Fortress,* p. 401.

122. Rimland, *Infantile Autism,* p. 29 ff.

123. BB, *Empty Fortress,* p. 418.

124. Eric Schopler et al., "Do Autistic Children Come from Upper Middle-Class Parents?" *Journal of Autism and Developmental Disorders,* vol. 9 (1979), pp. 139–52.

125. BB, *Empty Fortress,* p. 403.

126. Ibid., p. 401.

127. Ruth Sullivan, "There Can Be No Crops Without Plowing: 25 Years in the Field," proceedings, 1990 Annual Conference of the Autism Society of America, Buena Park, Calif., July 11–14, 1990, p. 173.

128. Eric Schopler, "Parents of Psychotic Children as Scapegoats," *Journal of Contemporary Psychotherapy,* vol. 4, no. 1 (Winter 1971), p. 20.

129. Interview with Susanna Morganthau; interview with Karen Carlson Zelan; interview with David James Fisher.

130. Interview with Ernst Federn.

131. I am grateful to Peter Neubauer for providing me with a tape of the Great Pioneers panel.

CHAPTER TWELVE: *The Kibbutzim*

1. "Contemporaries," interview with BB, *Modern Medicine,* Sept. 6, 1971, p. 27; see also Mary Harrington Hall, "The Psychology of Involvement," *Psychology Today,* vol. 2 (May 1969), p. 22.

2. David Rapaport, "The Study of Kibbutz Education and Its Bearing on the Theory of Development," *American Journal of Orthopsychiatry,* vol. 28, no. 3 (July 1958), pp. 587–97.

3. Interview with Nechama Levi-Edelman.

4. BB, "Nakhes fun Kinder," *Reconstructionist,* vol. 25, no. 4 (April 3, 1959), pp. 23–24.

5. Ibid., p. 22.

6. BB, "Does Communal Education Work? The Case of the Kibbutz," *Commentary,* vol. 33, no. 2 (Feb. 1962), p. 123.

7. BB, "Nakhes fun Kinder," p. 23.

8. BB, "Does Communal Education Work?," p. 123.

9. Ibid., p. 117n.

10. Ibid., p. 122.

11. Ibid., p. 125.

12. Transcripts of BB's interviews and meetings at Ramat Yohanan, BBP.

13. BB to Ruth Marquis, May 6, 1964, BBP.

14. Ibid.

15. Ramat Yohanan transcripts, BBP.

16. Interview with Nechama Levi-Edelman.

17. Interview with Nell Pekarsky.

18. BB to CF, Nov. 4, 1973.

19. BB to ND, Nov. 18, 1974.

20. BB, *The Children of the Dream: Communal Child-Rearing and American Education* (New York: Free Press, 1969), pp. 71, 324.

21. Ibid., p. 324.

22. Ibid., pp. 324–25.

23. Ibid., pp. 323–30.

24. Ibid., p. xi.

25. Ramat Yohanan transcripts, BBP.

26. BB, *Children of the Dream*, pp. 325–26.

27. Ibid., p. xiii.

28. Ibid., p. xi.

29. Ibid., p. 324.

30. Robert Mendelsohn, "The Dangerous Views of Bruno Bettelheim," *Congress Bi-Weekly: A Journal of Opinion and Jewish Affairs,* vol. 37, no. 3 (Feb. 20, 1970), p. 18.

31. BB, *Children of the Dream*, pp. 187–88.

32. Ibid., p. 7.

33. Ibid., p. 43.

34. Ibid., p. 52.

35. Ibid., p. 287.

36. Ibid., p. 294.

37. Ibid., p. 213.

38. Ibid., p. 261.

39. Ibid., pp. 289–90.

40. Benjamin Schlesinger, "Family Life in the Kibbutz of Israel," *International Journal of Comparative Sociology,* vol. 11, no. 4 (Dec. 1970), p. 261.

41. BB, *Children of the Dream*, p. 299.

42. Mordecai Kaffman, "Kibbutz Youth: Recent Past and Present," *Journal of Youth and Adolescence,* vol. 22, no. 6 (Dec. 1993), p. 575.

43. BB, *Children of the Dream*, p. 107.

44. Menachem Gerson, "The Family in the Kibbutz," *Journal of Child Psychology and Psychiatry,* vol. 15, no. 1 (Jan. 1974), p. 49.

45. Schlesinger, "Family Life in the Kibbutz," p. 256.

46. Chicago *Daily News,* April 18, 1969.

47. Ora Aviezer et al., " 'Children of the Dream' Revisited: 70 Years of Collective Early Child Care in Israeli Kibbutzim," *Psychological Bulletin,* vol. 116, no. 1 (July 1994), p. 101.

48. Ramat Yohanan transcripts, BBP.

49. BB, *Children of the Dream*, p. 4.

50. Ibid., p. 49.

51. *New York Times,* March 17, 1969.

52. *New York Times,* Nov. 5, 1969.

53. Sylvia Krown, "Preschool Programs for Disadvantaged Children," *Children,* vol. 15, no. 6 (Nov.–Dec. 1968), p. 239.

54. Mendelsohn reports Sarah Gluck's thoughts in "Dangerous Views of Bruno Bettelheim," p. 21.

55. BB, "A Scientific Approach to the Problem of Prejudice," speech at public-relations workshop, American Council on Race Relations, Chicago, Sept. 1946.

56. BB with Morris Janowitz, *The Dynamics of Prejudice, A Psychological and Sociological Study of Veterans* (New York: Harper & Brothers, 1950), p. 174; BB with Morris Janowitz, *Social Change and Prejudice* (Glencoe, Ill.: Free Press, 1964).

57. BB, "Sputnik and Segregation: Should the Gifted Be Educated Separately?," *Commentary,* vol. 26, no. 4 (Oct. 1958), p. 339.

58. BB, "How Much Can a Man Change?," *New York Review of Books,* vol. 3, no. 2 (Sept. 10, 1964), p. 4.

59. BB, *Dialogues with Mothers* (Glencoe, Ill.: Free Press, 1962), p. 58.

60. Interview with Itamar Yahalom.

61. Henry Near, "The Kibbutz Psychoanalysed," Jerusalem *Post,* June 16, 1969, p. 14.

62. Leon Eisenberg, "What to Learn from Kibbutz Kids," *Life,* April 4, 1969, p. R.

63. Menachem Gerson, "Bettelheim's 'Children of the Dream,' " *Israel Horizons,* vol. 17, no. 9 (Nov. 1969), pp. 22–23.

64. *New York Times,* March 17, 1969.

65. Chicago *Sun-Times,* March 23, 1969.

66. Chicago *Tribune,* April 27, 1969.

67. *New York Times,* March 24, 1969.

68. Paul Roazen, "The Children of the Dream," *New York Times Book Review,* April 6, 1969, p. 3.

69. Paul Roazen, "The Rise and Fall of Bruno Bettelheim," *Psychohistory Review,* vol. 20, no. 3 (Spring 1992), p. 235.

CHAPTER THIRTEEN: *Young Nazis Redux*

1. Chicago *Maroon,* Nov. 15, 1968.

2. For a chronology of events leading up to and following the sit-in, see Chicago *Maroon,* Feb. 14, 1969; the confrontation is also described in *One in Spirit: A Retrospective View of the University of Chicago on the Occasion of Its Centennial* (Chicago: University Publications Office, 1991), pp. 143–51.

3. Chicago *American,* Jan. 31, 1969.

4. Chicago *Daily News,* Jan. 31, 1969.

5. Tape of BB interview on WHPK-FM, Feb. 2, 1969.

6. Chicago *Maroon,* Feb. 6, 1969.

7. Interview with John Schnebly.

8. Interview with Michael Claffey.

9. Chicago *Sun-Times,* Feb. 1, 1969; Chicago *Daily News,* Jan. 31, 1969.

10. Interview with Bertram Cohler; interview with Peter Dembowski; interview with Gayle Shulenberger Janowitz.

11. Interview with Joan Deutsch Herczeg.

12. *Congressional Record,* 91st Cong., 1st sess., Mar. 27, 1969, p. 8047.

13. House Subcommittee on Education and Labor, *Campus Unrest,* 91st Cong., 1st sess., Mar. 20, 1969, pp. 258–86.

14. San Jose *Mercury-News,* March 21, 1969.

15. *New York Times,* March 21, 1969.

16. *New York Times,* March 23, 1969.

17. Washington *Post,* March 23, 1969.

18. Chicago *Tribune,* March 21, 1969.

19. Chicago *Tribune,* March 25, 1969.

20. Chicago *Tribune,* May 4, 1969.

21. *Playboy,* March 1971, p. 106.

22. BB, "Obsolete Youth," *Encounter,* Sept. 1969, p. 29.

23. BB, "Children Must Learn to Fear," *New York Times Magazine,* April 13, 1969, p. 135.

24. Ibid., pp. 143, 145.

25. BB, *Ladies' Home Journal,* July 1969, p. 25.

26. BB, *Ladies' Home Journal,* June 1968, p. 38; see also, BB, "Obsolete Youth," p. 42.

27. Ibid., p. 38.

28. Dempsey, "Bruno Bettelheim Is Dr. No," *New York Times Magazine,* Jan. 11, 1970, p. 107.

29. Chicago *Maroon,* Feb. 20, 1963.

30. BB, *The Informed Heart: Autonomy in a Mass Age* (Glencoe, Ill.: Free Press, 1960), p. 103.

31. Dempsey, "Bruno Bettelheim Is Dr. No," p. 22.

32. BB, *Ladies' Home Journal,* June 1968, p. 33; *Bartlett's* attributes the "right or wrong" slogan to two Americans: Stephen Decatur, a U.S. naval officer in the war of 1812, and John Jordan Crittenden, who served in the U.S. Senate before the Civil War. See John Bartlett, *Familiar Quotations,* 15th ed., ed. Emily Beck (Boston: Little, Brown, 1980), p. 445.

33. Transcript of dialogues-with-mothers session, Oct. 21, 1967, BBP.

34. BB, "Obsolete Youth," p. 41.

35. BB to Peter Viereck, June 30, 1977.

36. BB to ND, March 10, 1975.

37. BB to CF, June 22, 1975.

38. Ibid.

39. San Jose *Mercury-News,* July 27, 1974.

40. Chicago *Daily News,* March 22, 1962.

41. Interview with William Sugden; interview with Philip Goldbloom; interview with Charles Marks, Jr.

42. BB, "Discrimination and Science," *Commentary,* vol. 21, no. 4 (April 1956), pp. 384–85.

43. "Chicago's 'Dr. Yes,' " *Time,* July 5, 1968, p. 49.

44. David Dempsey to RP, Dec. 19, 1990.

45. Saul Bellow to RP, Jan. 25, 1990.

46. BB to Farrell, Jan. 27, 1970, JTF.

47. Chicago *Sun-Times,* April 8, 1970.

48. Chicago *Sun-Times,* Jan. 12, 1967.

49. Text of speech, BBP.

50. BB, *A Home for the Heart* (New York: Alfred A. Knopf, 1974), p. 97.

51. Linnea Brandwein Vacca to RP, Jan. 10, 1995.

52. BB, *A Home for the Heart,* p. 106.

53. Ibid., plate 1.

54. Ibid., p. 107.

55. Ibid., p. 111.

56. Ibid., p. 114.

57. Ibid., pp. 115–16.

58. Ibid., p. 112.

59. Penelope Mesic, "The Abuses of Enchantment," *Chicago,* Aug. 1991, p. 102.
60. Interview with Leslie Aranow Cleaver.
61. BB to DK, May 9, 1981.
62. BB to DK, Nov. 4, 1974.
63. Interview with JSS; interview with DK.
64. *Le Quotidien de Paris,* Oct. 11, 1974.
65. Interview with Emarina Radonowicz-Harttmann.
66. Interview with Alvin Rosenfeld.
67. Interview with Rory Childers.
68. Daniel Schorr, reporter, "A Boy Named Terry Egan," *CBS Reports,* Oct. 11, 1973.

CHAPTER FOURTEEN: *California and Fairy Tales*

1. BB to ND, Nov. 20, 1973.
2. San Jose *Mercury-News,* Dec. 5, 1973.
3. JSS to BB, June 7, 1987, BBP.
4. BB, *The Children of the Dream: Communal Child-Rearing and American Education* (New York: Free Press, 1969), p. xiii.
5. For an account of Ruth Marquis's disillusionment with BB, see Nina Sutton, *Bettelheim: A Life and a Legacy* (New York: Basic Books, 1996), p. 326.
6. Memo, Emanuel Geltman to Jeremiah Kaplan and George McCune, Dec. 10, 1963.
7. BB to Emanuel Geltman, Feb. 24, 1966.
8. Elizabeth Janeway, review of *A Home for the Heart, New York Times Book Review,* March 17, 1974, p. 27.
9. Elsa First, review of *A Home for the Heart, New York Review of Books,* vol. 21, no. 9 (May 30, 1974), p. 4.
10. *New York Times,* March 25, 1974.
11. BB to Joyce Jack, July 26, 1972.
12. Bertram Cohler, remarks at Bettelheim Symposium, Division 39, American Psychological Association, Washington, D.C., April 16, 1994.
13. Eric Schopler, "The Art and Science of Bruno Bettelheim," *Journal of Autism and Childhood Schizophrenia,* vol. 6, no. 2 (June 1976), p. 196.
14. Daniel Karlin screened *Un Autre Regard sur la Folie* for me in his Paris studio on May 25, 1992.
15. *Le Figaro,* Oct. 6, 1974.
16. *Le Figaro,* Oct. 9, 1974.
17. *Le Figaro,* Oct. 15, 1974.
18. Paul Guimard, in *L'Express,* Oct. 21–27, 1974.
19. *Le Quotidien de Paris,* Oct. 11, 1974.
20. *Télé 7 Jours,* Oct. 19–25, 1974.
21. *L'Humanité,* Oct. 14, 1974.
22. *Minute,* Oct. 16, 1974.
23. BB's medical records, Palo Alto (California) Medical Foundation.
24. BB to CF, Jan. 13, 1975.
25. BB to ND, Nov. 5, 1975.
26. BB's medical records.
27. BB to CF, Dec. 22, 1973.
28. Interview with Joyce Jack.
29. BB to CF, Jan. 13, 1975.
30. BB to CF, Dec. 22, 1973.

31. BB to Joyce Jack, Oct. 5, 1973.

32. BB to Joyce Jack, Jan. 31, 1974.

33. Robert Gottlieb to BB, June 19, 1975.

34. BB to Robert Gottlieb, June 26, 1975.

35. Julius Heuscher, *A Psychiatric Study of Fairy Tales: Their Origin, Meaning and Usefulness* (Springfield, Ill.: Charles C. Thomas, 1963).

36. My assessment of BB's use of Heuscher's material is based on my own reading of the two books and an independent examination of their texts by Andrew Cohen, a research assistant; see also Joan Blos, "The Emperor's Clothes," *Merrill-Palmer Quarterly*, vol. 24, no. 1 (Jan. 1978), pp. 67–75; Alan Dundes, "Bruno Bettelheim's Uses of Enchantment and Abuses of Scholarship," *Journal of the American Folklore Society*, vol. 104 (Winter 1991), pp. 74–83.

37. Martin Buber, *I and Thou: A New Translation with a Prologue "I and You" and Notes by Walter Kaufmann* (New York: Scribner, 1970).

38. Géza Róheim, "Myth and Folk-Tale," *American Imago*, vol. 2, no. 3 (Sept. 1941), pp. 266–79.

39. Otto Rank, *The Myth of the Birth of the Hero* (New York: Vintage Books, 1959), p. 72.

40. Alison Lurie, "The Haunted Wood," *Harper's*, June 1976, p. 94; see also Erich Fromm, *The Forgotten Language* (New York: Rinehart, 1951).

41. BB, *The Uses of Enchantment: The Meaning and Importance of Fairy Tales* (New York: Alfred A. Knopf, 1977), pp. 4–5.

42. Ibid., pp. 29–31.

43. Ibid., p. 219.

44. As quoted by Stefan Kanfer, "Narrow Couch," *Time*, May 3, 1976, p. 71.

45. Robert Darnton, *The Great Cat Massacre and Other Episodes in French Cultural History* (New York: Vintage Books, 1985), p. 13.

46. Jack Zipes, *Breaking the Magic Spell: Radical Theories of Folk and Fairy Tales* (New York: Routledge, 1992), p. 169.

47. This version of "Little Red Riding Hood" is recounted in Darnton, *Great Cat Massacre*, pp. 9–10.

48. BB, *Uses of Enchantment*, p. 177.

49. Ibid., p. 181.

50. Ibid., p. 8.

51. BB, *Ladies' Home Journal*, March 1969, p. 48.

52. Maurice Sendak, *Where the Wild Things Are* (New York: HarperCollins, 1988).

53. BB, *Ladies' Home Journal*, March 1969, p. 48.

54. Martin Lebowitz, review of *The Uses of Enchantment*, Chicago *Sun-Times*, June 6, 1976.

55. Blos, "The Emperor's Clothes," p. 74.

56. Dundes, "Abuses of Scholarship," pp. 74–83.

57. *Newsweek*, Feb. 18, 1991, p. 75.

58. *Los Angeles Times*, Feb. 7, 1991.

59. Harold Bloom, review of *The Uses of Enchantment*, *New York Review of Books*, vol. 23, no. 12 (July 15, 1976), p. 10.

60. John Updike, review of *The Uses of Enchantment*, *New York Times Book Review*, May 23, 1976, p. 1.

61. BB, *Uses of Enchantment*, p. 122.

62. Elizabeth Diefendorf, ed., *The New York Public Library Books of the Century* (New York: Oxford University Press, 1996).

63. National Book Award speech, April 13, 1977, BBP.

64. BB to ND, April 28, 1977.

65. BB to ND, April 16, 1976; June 14, 1976. BB reviewed Thomas Szasz's *The Facts of Life: An Essay in Feelings, Facts and Fantasy,* and R. D. Laing's *Heresies* for *The New York Times Book Review,* May 30, 1976, pp. 5, 12.

66. BB to ND, April 2, 1981.

67. Interview with Charles Feldstein; interview with JSS.

68. BB to DK, Nov. 4, 1974.

69. BB with Alvin Rosenfeld, *The Art of the Obvious: Developing Insight for Psychotherapy and Everyday Life* (New York: Alfred A. Knopf, 1993), p. 3.

70. Interview with Alvin Rosenfeld; see also BB with Rosenfeld, *Art of the Obvious,* pp. 3–23.

71. BB with Rosenfeld, *Art of the Obvious,* p. 10.

72. Ibid., p. 12.

73. Ibid., p. xi.

74. BB to ND, Feb. 14, 1976.

75. BB to ND, April 16, 1976.

76. BB to CF, Nov. 4, 1974.

77. BB to CF, Jan. 13, 1975.

CHAPTER FIFTEEN: *The Survivor and the Holocaust*

1. BB, "Freedom from Ghetto Thinking," *Midstream: A Quarterly Jewish Review,* vol. 8, no. 2 (Spring 1962), p. 19.

2. BB, "The Ignored Lesson of Anne Frank," *Harper's,* Nov. 1960, p. 46; see also BB, "Freedom from Ghetto Thinking," pp. 24–25, and BB, *The Informed Heart: Autonomy in a Mass Age* (Glencoe, Ill.: Free Press, 1960), p. 252ff.

3. Hans Zeisel to RP, Feb. 25, 1992.

4. BB, *Informed Heart,* p. 117.

5. This account of BB's appearance at Hillel House is based on interviews with Benjamin and Sophie Bloom, Marc Galanter, Judith Getzels, Benson Ginsburg, Gretel Lowinski, Nell Pekarsky, and Barbara Probst Solomon, all of whom were present, and also on Hans Zeisel to RP, Feb. 25, 1992. Because the archive of programs for Hillel House events is incomplete, I was unable to ascertain the exact date of the meeting; it probably took place on a Sunday afternoon not long after BB's ghetto-thinking article appeared in the Spring 1962 *Midstream.*

6. Raul Hilberg, *The Destruction of the European Jews* (Chicago: Quadrangle Books, 1961), vol. 3, p. 666.

7. Lucy S. Dawidowicz, *The Holocaust and the Historians* (Cambridge, Mass.: Harvard University Press, 1981), p. 178, n. 16. This work is central to any discussion of Holocaust historiography, especially pp. 125–41; see also, Isaiah Trunk, *Judenrat: The Jewish Councils in Eastern Europe Under the Nazi Occupation* (New York: Macmillan, 1972), and Philip Friedman, *Roads to Extinction* (New York: Jewish Publication Society of America, 1980).

8. Hannah Arendt, *Eichmann in Jerusalem: A Report on the Banality of Evil,* rev. ed. (New York: Viking, 1965), p. 125.

9. Ibid., pp. 11ff.

10. Hannah Arendt, letter to *Midstream,* vol. 8, no. 3 (Sept. 1962), p. 86.

11. BB, "Individual and Mass Behavior in Extreme Situations," *Journal of Abnormal and Social Psychology,* vol. 38, no. 4 (Oct. 1943), p. 451.

12. BB, "Behavior in Extreme Situations," *Politics,* Aug. 1944, pp. 199–209.

13. BB, "Ten Eventful Years: Concentration Camps, German," *Encyclopaedia Britannica* (Chicago: Encyclopaedia Britannica, 1947), vol. 2, pp. 1–12.

14. BB, "Individual and Mass Behavior in Extreme Situations," *Basic Values and Human Relationships,* Sept. 1947, pp. 65–72.

15. BB, "Individual and Mass Behavior in Extreme Situations," in *Readings in Social Psychology,* rev. ed., ed. Guy E. Swanson et al. (New York: Henry Holt, 1952), pp. 33–43.

16. BB, *Informed Heart,* p. 107.

17. Ibid., p. 109.

18. Ernst Federn, "The Terror as a System: The Concentration Camp: Buchenwald As It Was," *Psychiatric Quarterly Supplement,* vol. 22, pt. 2 (1948), p. 71.

19. BB, *Informed Heart,* p. 118n.

20. Federn, "Terror as a System," pp. 74–79. Among other works that focus on psychology in the camps that were available to BB when he was writing *The Informed Heart* and that he ignored are: P. Friedman, "Some Aspects of Concentration Camp Psychology," *American Journal of Psychiatry,* vol. 105, no. 8 (Feb. 1949), pp. 601–5, and J. Tas, "Psychical Disorders Among Inmates of Concentration Camps and Repatriates," *Psychiatric Quarterly,* vol. 25, no. 4 (Oct. 1951), pp. 679–90.

21. BB to Ernst Federn, July 21, 1946.

22. Edith Jacobson, "Observations on the Psychological Effect of Imprisonment on Female Political Prisoners," in *Searchlights on Delinquency: New Psychoanalytic Studies,* ed. Kurt Eissler (New York: International Universities Press, 1966 [1st ed., 1949]), p. 362.

23. Elie Cohen, *Human Behavior in the Concentration Camp,* trans. M. H. Braaksma (New York: Grosset & Dunlap, 1953), p. 277; originally published in Dutch as *Het duities concentratiekamp: Een medische en psychologische studie* (Amsterdam: H. J. Paris, 1952).

24. Viktor Frankl, *Man's Search for Meaning: Revised and Updated* (New York: Washington Square Press, 1985), p. 86.

25. Viktor Frankl, *From Death-Camp to Existentialism: A Psychiatrist's Path to a New Therapy,* trans. Ilse Lasch (Boston: Beacon Press, 1959).

26. Viktor Frankl, *Ein Psycholog erlebt das Konzentrationslager* (Vienna: Jugend & Volk, 1946). For a discussion of the two survivors' differing outlooks, see Stanley J. Schacter, "Bettelheim and Frankl: Contrasting Views of the Holocaust," *Reconstructionist,* vol. 26, no. 20 (Feb. 10, 1961), pp. 6–11.

27. BB, *Informed Heart,* p. 265. Bettelheim cited the original German edition of Eugen Kogon's book, *Der SS-Staat* (Munich: Karl Alber Verlag, 1946), p. 132; in English, *The Theory and Practice of Hell: The German Concentration Camps and the System Behind Them,* trans. Heinz Norden (New York: Berkley Publishing Corporation, 1980), p. 240.

28. BB, *Informed Heart,* p. 263.

29. Interviews with Donna Heizer, Daniel King, and Charles Marks, Jr.

30. BB, *Informed Heart,* pp. 248–49.

31. Jacob Robinson, *Psychoanalysis in a Vacuum: Bruno Bettelheim and the Holocaust* (New York: Yad Vashem-Yivo Documentary Projects, 1970), pp. 30–31.

32. Ibid., p. 20.

33. BB, *Informed Heart,* p. 254.

34. Ibid.

35. Ibid., p. 253.

36. BB, letter to the editor, *Midstream,* vol. 7, no. 2 (Spring 1961), p. 86.

37. Margo Jefferson to RP, Sept. 25, 1995.

38. David Barnouw and Gerrold van der Stroom, eds., *The Diary of Anne Frank: The Critical Edition,* prepared by the Netherlands State Institute for War Documentation, trans. Arnold J. Pomerans and B. M. Mooyaart-Doubleday (New York: Doubleday, 1989), p. 694; see also Frances Goodrich and Albert Hackett, *The Diary of Anne Frank* (New York: Random House, 1956), p. 168, and the 1959 film of the same name, directed by George Stevens.

39. BB, *Informed Heart,* p. 254.

40. Hannah Arendt, letter to the editor, *Midstream,* vol. 8, no. 3 (Sept. 1962), pp. 85–86.

41. For a portrait of Levin's fixation, see Lawrence Graver, *An Obsession with Anne Frank: Meyer Levin and the Diary* (Berkeley: University of California Press, 1995).

42. Robinson, *Psychoanalysis in a Vacuum*, p. 28; see also Leni Yahil, *The Holocaust: The Fate of European Jewry* (New York: Oxford University Press, 1990), p. 176.

43. Yahil, *Holocaust*, p. 440.

44. Barnouw and van der Stroom, *Diary of Anne Frank*, pp. 50–51.

45. BB, *Informed Heart*, p. 253.

46. Robinson, *Psychoanalysis in a Vacuum*, p. 27.

47. BB, *Informed Heart*, p. 258.

48. Ibid., p. 100.

49. Robert Lane, review of *The Informed Heart*, *American Political Science Review*, vol. 55, no. 2 (June 1961), p. 394.

50. BB, *Informed Heart*, p. 137.

51. Ibid., p. 147.

52. Ibid., p. 235.

53. Ibid., p. 295.

54. BB, "The Helpless and the Guilty," *Common Sense*, vol. 14, no. 6 (July 1945), p. 26.

55. BB, *Informed Heart*, p. 286.

56. BB, "Eichmann; the System; the Victims," *New Republic*, June 15, 1963, p. 25.

57. Ibid., p. 27.

58. BB, "Helpless and Guilty," p. 27.

59. BB to Ernst Federn, Jan. 11, 1946.

60. BB, "Returning to Dachau: The Living and the Dead," *Commentary*, vol. 21, no. 2 (Feb. 1956), p. 144.

61. Ibid., p. 145.

62. Ibid., pp. 146–47.

63. Ibid., p. 147.

64. Ibid., p. 148.

65. Ibid.

66. Ibid., p. 151.

67. Franz Alexander, "Mass-Man in Death Camp Society," *New York Times Book Review*, Oct. 8, 1961, p. 42.

68. Maurice Richardson, "The Lesson of Horror," *New Statesman*, March 17, 1961, p. 430.

69. Edited transcript of Studs Terkel interview with BB on WFMT-FM in Chicago, May 25, 1961, *WFMT Perspective*, March 1962, p. 23.

70. George Steiner, *Language and Silence: Essays on Language, Literature, and the Inhuman* (New York: Atheneum, 1967), p. 388.

71. Reginald Gibbons, "A Note in Memoriam: Terrence Des Pres," *TriQuarterly*, vol. 71 (Winter 1988), p. 230.

72. Alfred Kazin, review of *The Survivor*, *New York Times Book Review*, March 14, 1976, p. 1.

73. Terrence Des Pres, *The Survivor: An Anatomy of Life in the Death Camps* (New York: Oxford University Press, 1976), pp. 155–57.

74. Ibid., p. 57.

75. BB, *Informed Heart*, p. 37.

76. Paul Marcus and Alan Rosenberg, "Reevaluating Bruno Bettelheim's Work on the Nazi Concentration Camps: The Limits of His Psychoanalytic Approach," *Psychoanalytic Review*, vol. 81 (Fall 1994), p. 543.

77. Des Pres, *Survivor*, p. 103. BB wrote about the *Sonderkommando* revolt in *The Informed Heart*, pp. 263–64; he drew his information from Miklos Nyiszli, *Auschwitz: A*

Doctor's Eyewitness Account, trans. Tibere Kremer and Richard Seaver (New York: Frederick Fell, 1960), for which he had written the foreword. For another account of the Auschwitz uprising, see Yahil, *Holocaust,* pp. 485–86.

78. Des Pres, *Survivor,* pp. 161–62.

79. BB to ND, Feb. 14, 1976; for excerpts from *The Survivor,* see "Victory in the Concentration Camps," *Harper's,* Feb. 1976, pp. 47–54, and "Victims and Survivors," *Dissent,* vol. 23, no. 1 (Winter 1976), pp. 49–53.

80. BB to CF, March 13, 1976.

81. Jack Kroll, "Wertmüller's Inferno," *Newsweek,* Jan. 26, 1976, p. 78.

82. John Simon, "Wertmüller's 'Seven Beauties'—Call It a Masterpiece," *New York,* Feb. 2, 1976, p. 24.

83. Pauline Kael, "Seven Fatties," in Pauline Kael, *When the Lights Go Down* (New York: Holt, Rinehart and Winston, 1980), pp. 136–140.

84. BB, "Surviving," *New Yorker,* Aug. 2, 1976, pp. 31–35.

85. Ibid., p. 36.

86. Des Pres, *Survivor,* p. 192.

87. Ibid., p. 207.

88. BB, "Surviving," pp. 36, 38, 45, 47, 52, for example.

89. Ibid., p. 38.

90. Terrence Des Pres, "The Bettelheim Problem," *social research: An International Quarterly of the Social Sciences,* Winter 1979, p. 647.

91. BB, *Surviving and Other Essays* (New York: Alfred A. Knopf, 1979), p. 92. This essay, "The Holocaust—One Generation Later," is an edited version of BB's speech at the Holocaust conference in San Jose, California, over the weekend of Feb. 13–15, 1977. It is not substantially different from the speech as tape-recorded and furnished to me by the conference's cosponsor, the San Jose chapter of the National Conference of Christians and Jews.

92. BB, *Surviving.* For "genocide," see pp. 8, 24, 35, 258, 269, 274, 276; for "Holocaust," see pp. 10, 24, 33, 275, 280, 282.

93. Paul Robinson, "Apologist for the Superego," *New York Times Book Review,* April 29, 1979, p. 7.

94. Unsigned review of *Surviving, Kirkus Reviews,* March 1, 1979, p. 299.

95. Rosemary Dinnage, "No Surrender," *New York Review of Books,* vol. 26, no. 6 (April 19, 1979), p. 15.

CHAPTER SIXTEEN: *A Rage to Die*

1. BB to CF, Sept. 20, 1979.

2. For the descriptions of BB and TB's declining health in this chapter, I have depended primarily on BB's letters to ND and CF and on his records at the Palo Alto Medical Center, Palo Alto, California.

3. BB to ND, Dec. 13, 1981.

4. BB to CF, May 10, 1981.

5. BB to CF, June 22, 1975.

6. BB to CF, Dec. 10, 1982.

7. BB to Joyce Jack, March 10, 1980.

8. Providence *Evening Bulletin,* Nov. 14, 1979.

9. This account of BB's appearance in San Francisco is based on Jim Jacobs, "A Day with Bruno Bettelheim," *California Living* (Sunday magazine of San Francisco *Chronicle*), June 15, 1980, pp. 20–24.

10. Mordecai Kaffman, "Kibbutz Youth: Recent Past and Present," *Journal of Youth and Adolescence,* vol. 22, no. 6 (Dec. 1993), p. 588.

11. BB and Karen Zelan, *On Learning to Read: The Child's Fascination with Meaning* (New York: Alfred A. Knopf, 1982).

12. Robert Gottlieb to BB, Nov. 3, 1980.

13. Martin Kirby, review of *On Learning to Read*, Philadelphia *Inquirer*, Feb. 28, 1982.

14. John Turner, review of *On Learning to Read. American Spectator*, Sept. 1982, p. 34.

15. Dan Cryer, review of *On Learning to Read*, *Newsday*, Jan. 31, 1982.

16. Christopher Lehmann-Haupt, review of *On Learning to Read*, *New York Times*, Jan. 7, 1982.

17. BB and Zelan, *On Learning to Read*, p. 57.

18. Ibid., p. 110n.

19. Joan Beck, review of *On Learning to Read*, Chicago *Tribune*, Feb. 21, 1982.

20. BB and Zelan, *On Learning to Read*, p. 48n; see also BB, "Janet and Mark and the New Illiteracy," *Encounter*, Nov. 1974, pp. 15–23.

21. BB and Zelan, *On Learning to Read*, p. 305.

22. Jerome Bruner, "Reading for Signs of Life," *New York Review of Books*, April 1, 1982, p. 19.

23. BB and Zelan, *On Learning to Read*, p. 64.

24. Ibid., pp. vii–viii.

25. Ibid., p. 87.

26. Ibid., pp. 90–91.

27. BB, " 'Children Must Learn to Fear,' " *New York Times Magazine*, April 13, 1969, p. 136.

28. BB and Zelan, *On Learning to Read*, p. 79.

29. Gottlieb to BB, Nov. 3, 1980.

30. Emily M. Beck, ed., *Bartlett's Familiar Quotations*, 15th ed. (Boston: Little, Brown, 1980), p. 679.

31. BB, "Reflections: The Uses of Enchantment," *New Yorker*, Dec. 8, 1975, pp. 50–114.

32. Review of *On Learning to Read*, *New Yorker*, Jan. 25, 1982, p. 103.

33. BB, "Reflections: Freud and the Soul," *New Yorker*, March 1, 1982, pp. 52–93; BB, *Freud and Man's Soul* (New York: Alfred A. Knopf, 1983).

34. BB, *Freud and Man's Soul*, p. 72.

35. Ibid., p. 5.

36. Ibid.

37. Ibid., p. 53.

38. Ibid., p. vii.

39. L. Brandt, "Some Notes on English Freudian Terminology," *Journal of the American Psychoanalytic Association*, vol. 9 (1961), pp. 331–39; F. H. Brull, "A Reconsideration of Some Translations of Sigmund Freud," *Psychotherapy: Theory, Research and Practice*, vol. 12 (1975), pp. 273–79.

40. Darius Gray Ornston, Jr., ed., *Translating Freud* (New Haven: Yale University Press, 1992), p. 1.

41. BB, *Freud and Man's Soul*, p. viii.

42. As quoted in Ornston, *Translating Freud*, p. 1.

43. Darius Gray Ornston, Jr., "Freud and Man's Soul," in Ornston, *Translating Freud*, p. 70.

44. BB, *Freud and Man's Soul*, p. 32.

45. Ibid., p. 51.

46. Frank Kermode, "Freud Is Better in German," *New York Times Book Review*, Feb. 6, 1983, p. 25.

47. BB, "Scandal in the Family," *New York Review of Books*, June 30, 1983, pp. 39–

44. BB was discussing Aldo Carotenuto, *A Secret Symmetry: Sabina Spielrein Between Jung and Freud,* trans. Arno Pomerans et al. (New York: Pantheon, 1982).

48. BB to CF, Feb. 19, 1982.

49. BB to CF, Sept. 1, 1982.

50. BB to ND, July 51 [sic], 1975.

51. BB to CF, Oct. 4, 1983.

52. BB to CF, Nov. 10, 1984.

53. Bard College commencement program, Annandale-on-Hudson, N.Y., May 13, 1987.

54. Klaus von Bismarck to BB, Dec. 13, 1982.

55. Michael Barnes, writer and producer, *Bruno Bettelheim: A Sense of Surviving,* documentary film, British Broadcasting Corp., London, 1986.

56. BB's remarks at the 1987 symposium were published in German in *Vertriebene Vernunft II: Emigration und Exil Österreichischer Wissenschaft* (Vienna: Jugend and Volk, 1988), pp. 216–20.

57. BB to ND, June 7, 1986.

58. BB to ND, Feb. 8, 1985.

59. BB to ND, Sept. 11, 1986.

60. Interview with Sandy Lewis.

61. BB to CF, Dec. 14, 1986.

62. Interview with Joyce Jack; interview with Robert Gottlieb; BB to ND, Oct. 4, 1985.

63. BB, *A Good Enough Parent* (New York: Alfred A. Knopf, 1987).

64. Ibid., p. ix.

65. Ibid., p. 36.

66. Ibid., p. 4.

67. Barnes, *A Sense of Surviving.*

68. BB, "Janusz Korczak: A Tale for Our Time," in BB, *Freud's Vienna and Other Essays* (New York: Alfred A. Knopf, 1990), p. 206.

69. Ibid., p. 200.

70. Interview with Rudolf Ekstein.

71. Interview with Constance Katzenstein.

72. Interview with NB; interview with EB.

73. Los Angeles *Times,* April 3, 1990.

74. David James Fisher, "An Interview with Bruno Bettelheim," *Los Angeles Psychoanalytic Bulletin,* Winter 1990, p. 6.

75. Ibid., pp. 3–23.

76. Interview with NB.

77. BB to CF, March 6, 1988.

78. David James Fisher, "The Suicide of a Survivor: Some Intimate Perceptions of Bettelheim's Suicide," *Psychoanalytic Review,* vol. 79, no. 4 (Winter 1992), pp. 593–94.

79. Jan Schouten to BB, April 18, 1989. BBP.

80. Interview with NB.

81. BB, *Freud's Vienna,* p. 107.

82. BB to Alex Elson, Feb. 26, 1990.

83. BB, *Good Enough Parent,* p. 354.

84. A copy of BB's suicide note is on record at the Office of the Chief Medical Examiner, State of Maryland.

BIBLIOGRAPHY

BOOKS BY BRUNO BETTELHEIM

Love Is Not Enough: The Treatment of Emotionally Disturbed Children. Glencoe, Ill.: Free Press, 1950.

With Morris B. Janowitz. *The Dynamics of Prejudice: A Psychological and Sociological Study of Veterans.* New York: Harper & Brothers, 1950.

Symbolic Wounds: Puberty Rites and the Envious Male. Glencoe, Ill.: Free Press, 1954.

Truants from Life: The Rehabilitation of Emotionally Disturbed Children. Glencoe, Ill.: Free Press, 1955.

The Informed Heart: Autonomy in a Mass Age. Glencoe, Ill.: Free Press, 1960.

Paul and Mary: Two Cases from "Truants from Life." Garden City, N.Y.: Anchor Books, 1961.

Dialogues with Mothers. Glencoe, Ill.: Free Press, 1962.

With Morris B. Janowitz. *Social Change and Prejudice.* Glencoe, Ill.: Free Press, 1964.

The Empty Fortress: Infantile Autism and the Birth of the Self. New York: Free Press, 1967.

The Children of the Dream: Communal Child-Rearing and American Education. New York: Free Press, 1969.

A Home for the Heart. New York: Alfred A. Knopf, 1974.

The Uses of Enchantment: The Meaning and Importance of Fairy Tales. New York: Alfred A. Knopf, 1977.

Surviving and Other Essays. New York: Alfred A. Knopf, 1979.

Freud and Man's Soul. New York: Alfred A. Knopf, 1982.

With Karen Zelan. *On Learning to Read.* New York: Alfred A. Knopf, 1982.

A Good Enough Parent: A Book on Child-Rearing. New York: Alfred A. Knopf, 1987.

Freud's Vienna and Other Essays. New York: Alfred A. Knopf, 1990.

With Alvin Rosenfeld. *The Art of the Obvious: Developing Insight for Psychotherapy and Everyday Life.* New York: Alfred A. Knopf, 1993.

SELECTED ARTICLES BY BRUNO BETTELHEIM

"Individual and Mass Behavior in Extreme Situations." *Journal of Abnormal and Social Psychology,* vol. 38 (October 1943): 417–52.

"Returning to Dachau." *Commentary,* vol. 21 (February 1956): 144–51.

"Schizophrenia as a Reaction to Extreme Situations." *American Journal of Orthopsychiatry,* vol. 26 (July 1956): 507–18.

"Feral Children and Autistic Children." *American Journal of Sociology,* vol. 64 (March 1959): 455–67.

"Joey: A 'Mechanical Boy.' " *Scientific American,* vol. 200, no. 3 (March 1959): 116–27.

"The Ignored Lesson of Anne Frank." *Harper's,* vol. 221 (November 1960): 45–50.

"Does Communal Education Work? The Case of the Kibbutz." *Commentary,* vol. 33, no. 2 (February 1962): 117–25.

"Freedom from Ghetto Thinking." *Midstream,* vol. 8 (Spring 1962): 16–25.

"Growing Up Female." *Harper's,* vol. 225 (October 1962): 120–28.

"Eichmann; the System; the Victims." *New Republic,* vol. 148 (June 15, 1963): 23–33.

"Children Must Learn to Fear." *New York Times Magazine,* April 13, 1969, pp. 125, 135–36, 140–45.

"On Campus Rebellion." Chicago *Tribune Sunday Magazine,* May 4, 1969, pp. 78–81, 108–10.

"Portnoy Psychoanalyzed—Therapy Notes Found in the Files of Dr. O. Spielvogel, a New York Psychoanalyst." *Midstream,* vol. 15 (June–July 1969): 3–10.

"Obsolete Youth." *Encounter,* vol. 33 (September 1969): 29–42.

"The Roots of Radicalism." *Playboy* (March 1971): 106, 124, 206–8.

BOOKS

Aichhorn, August. *Wayward Youth.* New York: Viking Press, 1965.

Ainszstein, Reuben. *Jewish Resistance in Nazi Occupied Eastern Europe.* New York: Barnes & Noble Books, 1974.

Arendt, Hannah. *Eichmann in Jerusalem: A Report on the Banality of Evil.* New York: Viking Press, 1964.

Ashmore, Harry S. *Unseasonable Truths: The Life of Robert Maynard Hutchins.* Boston: Little, Brown, 1989.

Beller, Steven. *Vienna and the Jews, 1867–1938: A Cultural History.* Cambridge: Cambridge University Press, 1990.

Berben, P. *Dachau, 1933–1945: The Official History.* London: Norfolk Press, 1975.

Berkley, George E. *Vienna and Its Jews: The Tragedy of Success, 1880s–1990s.* Cambridge, Mass.: Abt Books, 1987.

Block, Jean F. *Hyde Park Houses: An Informal History, 1856–1910.* Chicago: University of Chicago Press, 1978.

Bok, Sissela. *Lying: Moral Choice in Public and Private Life.* New York: Vintage Books, 1989.

Cohen, Elie Aron. *Human Behavior in the Concentration Camps.* Translated by H. H. Braaksma. New York: Grosset & Dunlap, 1953.

Crews, Frederick. *The Memory Wars: Freud's Legacy in Dispute.* New York: A New York Review Book, 1995.

Cummins, Paul. *Dachau Song: The Twentieth Century Odyssey of Herbert Zipper.* New York: Peter Lang, 1992.

Darnton, Robert. *The Great Cat Massacre and Other Episodes in French Cultural History.* New York: Vintage Books, 1985.

Dawidowicz, Lucy S. *The Holocaust and the Historians.* Cambridge, Mass.: Harvard University Press, 1981.

Deckard, Barbara S. *The Women's Movement: Political, Socioeconomic and Psychological Issues.* 3d ed. New York: Harper & Row, 1983.

Des Pres, Terrence. *The Survivor: An Anatomy of Life in the Death Camps.* New York: Oxford University Press, 1976.

Distel, Barbara, and Ruth Jakusch, eds. *Concentration Camp Dachau, 1933–1945.* Brussels: Comité International de Dachau, 1978.

Donat, Alexander. *Jewish Resistance.* New York: Waldon Press, 1964.

Edel, Leon. *Writing Lives: Principia Biographica.* New York: W. W. Norton, 1984.

Edelheit, Abraham I., and Herschel E. Edelheit. *Bibliography on Holocaust Literature.* Boulder: Westview Press, 1986.

Ehrenreich, Barbara, and Deirdre English. *For Her Own Good: 150 Years of Experts' Advice to Women.* New York: Anchor Books, 1978.

Elkins, Stanley M. *Slavery: A Problem in American Institutional and Intellectual Life.* 3d ed., rev. Chicago: University of Chicago Press, 1976.

Federn, Ernst. *Witnessing Psychoanalysis: From Vienna Back to Vienna via Buchenwald and the USA.* London: Karnac Books, 1990.

Feig, Konnilyn G. *Hitler's Death Camps: The Sanity of Madness.* New York: Holmes & Meier, 1979.

Fermi, Laura. *Illustrious Immigrants: The Intellectual Migration from Europe, 1930–41.* 2d ed. Chicago: University of Chicago Press, 1971.

Fraenkel, Josef. *The Jews of Austria: Essays on Their Life, History and Destruction.* London: Vallentine, Mitchel & Co., 1967.

Frankl, Viktor E. *Man's Search for Meaning.* Rev. ed. New York: Washington Square Press, 1985.

Freud, Sigmund. *Standard Edition of the Complete Psychological Works of Sigmund Freud.* Edited and translated by James Strachey. 24 vols. London: Hogarth Press, 1953–1974.

Friedlander, Albert H., ed. *Out of the Whirlwind: A Reader of Holocaust Literature.* New York: Schocken Books, 1976.

Frith, Uta, ed. *Autism and Asperger Syndrome.* Cambridge: Cambridge University Press, 1991.

Gay, Peter. *Freud: A Life for Our Times.* New York: W. W. Norton, 1988.

Gilman, Sander L. *Jewish Self-Hatred: Anti-Semistism and the Hidden Language of the Jews.* Baltimore: Johns Hopkins University Press, 1986.

Goldsmith, Jerome M., and Jacquelyn Sanders, eds. *Milieu Therapy: Significant Issues and Innovative Applications.* New York: Haworth Press, 1993.

Gutman, Yisrael, ed. *Encyclopedia of the Holocaust.* 4 vols. New York: Macmillan, 1990.

Gutman, Yisrael and Avital Saf, eds. *The Nazi Concentration Camps: Structure and Aims, the Image of the Prisoner, the Jews in the Camps. Proceedings of the Fourth Yad Vashem International Historical Conference, January 1980.* Jerusalem: Yad Vashem, 1984.

Hackett, David A., ed. and trans. *The Buchenwald Report.* Boulder: Westview Press, 1995.

Hale, Nathan G., Jr. *The Rise and Crisis of Psychoanalysis in the United States: Freud and the Americans, 1917–1985.* New York: Oxford University Press, 1995.

Heilbut, Anthony. *Exiled in Paradise: German Refugee Artists and Intellectuals in America, from the 1930s to the Present.* New York: Viking Press, 1983.

Heilig, Bruno. *Men Crucified.* London: Eyre & Spottiswoode, 1941.

Heuscher, Julius E. *A Psychiatric Study of Fairy Tales: Their Origin, Meaning and Usefulness.* Springfield, Ill.: Charles C. Thomas, 1963.

Hilberg, Raul. *The Destruction of the European Jews.* Rev. ed. 3 vols. New York: Holmes & Meier, 1985.

Hofmann, Paul. *The Viennese: Splendor, Twilight and Exile.* New York: Anchor Books, 1989.

———. *The Spell of the Vienna Woods: Inspiration and Influence from Beethoven to Kafka.* New York: Henry Holt, 1994.

Hull, Cordell. *The Memoirs of Cordell Hull.* 2 vols. New York: Macmillan, 1948.

Hunt, Morton. *The Story of Psychology.* New York: Doubleday, 1993.

Jay, Martin. *The Dialectical Imagination: A History of the Frankfurt School and the Institute of Social Research, 1923–1950.* Boston: Little, Brown, 1973.

Kogon, Eugen. *The Theory and Practice of Hell: The German Concentration Camps and the System Behind Them.* Translated by Heinz Norden. New York: Farrar, Straus, 1950.

Kramer, Rita. *Maria Montessori: A Biography.* New York: G. P. Putnam's Sons, 1976.

Krausnick, Helmut, et al. *Anatomy of the SS State.* Translated by Richard Barry, Marian Jackson, and Dorothy Long. New York: Walker, 1968.

Levi, Primo. *Survival in Auschwitz: The Nazi Assault on Humanity.* Translated by Stuart Woolf. New York: Collier Books, 1961.

Lyons, Tom Wallace. *The Pelican and After: A Novel About Emotional Disturbance.* Richmond: Prescott, Durrell, 1983.

Masson, Jeffrey Moussaieff. *Against Therapy.* Monroe, Maine: Common Courage Press, 1990.

———. *Final Analysis: The Making and Unmaking of a Psychoanalyst.* New York: Addison-Wesley, Inc., 1990.

Medawar, Peter. *Pluto's Republic.* New York: Oxford University Press, 1982.

Miller, Alice. *For Your Own Good: Hidden Cruelty in Child-Rearing and the Roots of Violence.* New York: Noonday Press, 1990.

Miller, Sue. *Family Pictures.* New York: Harper & Row, 1990.

Mitchell, Stephen A., and Margaret J. Black. *Freud and Beyond: A History of Modern Psychoanalytic Thought.* New York: Basic Books, 1995.

Nolte, Ernst et al. *Forever in the Shadow of Hitler? Original Documents of the Historikerstreit, the Controversy Concerning the Singularity of the Holocaust.* Translated by James Knowlton and Truett Cates. New Jersey: Humanities Press, 1993.

Office of the United States Chief of Counsel For Persecution of Axis Criminality. *Nazi Conspiracy and Aggression.* Vol. 7. Washington, D.C.: United States Government Printing Office, 1946.

Ornston, Darius Gray, Jr. *Translating Freud.* New Haven: Yale University Press, 1992.

Park, Clara Claiborne. *The Siege: The First Eight Years of an Autistic Child, with an Epilogue, Fifteen Years After.* Boston: Atlantic–Little, Brown, 1982.

Proceedings: 1990 Annual Conference of the Autism Society of America. Autism Society of America, 1990.

Quétel, Claude. *History of Syphilis.* Translated by Judith Braddock and Brian Pike. Cambridge: Polity Press, 1990.

Read, Anthony, and David Fisher. *Kristallnacht: The Nazi Night of Terror.* New York: Times Books, 1989.

Riesman, David, Nathan Glazer, and Reuel Denney. *The Lonely Crowd: A Study of the Changing American Character.* New York: Doubleday Anchor Books, 1995.

Robinson, Paul. *Freud and His Critics.* Berkeley: University of California Press, 1993.

Sanders, Jacquelyn Seevak. *A Greenhouse for the Mind.* Chicago: University of Chicago Press, 1989.

Schorske, Carl. *Fin-de-Siècle Vienna.* New York: Vintage Books, 1981.

Shirer, William L. *Berlin Diary: The Journal of a Foreign Correspondent, 1934–41.* Boston: Little, Brown, 1941.

———. *The Rise and Fall of the Third Reich: A History of Nazi Germany.* New York: Touchstone, 1981.

Smith, Marcus J. *The Harrowing of Hell Dachau.* Albuquerque: University of New Mexico Press, 1972.

Staples, Brent. *Parallel Time: Growing Up in Black and White.* New York: Pantheon Books, 1994.

Sterba, Richard F. *Reminiscences of a Viennese Psychoanalyst.* Detroit: Wayne State University Press, 1982.

Sulloway, Frank J. *Freud, Biologist of the Mind: Beyond the Psychoanalytic Legend.* New York: Basic Books, 1979.

Sutton, Nina. *Bettelheim: A Life and a Legacy.* New York: Basic Books, 1996. Translated by David Sharp, in collaboration with the author.

Szajnberg, Nathan M., ed. *Educating the Emotions: Bruno Bettelheim and Psychoanalytic Development.* New York: Plenum Press, 1992.

Trial of the Major War Criminals Before the International Military Tribunal. Vol. 37. Nurem-
  berg, 1947–49.
Wreszin, Michael. *A Rebel in Defense of Tradition: The Life and Politics of Dwight Macdonald.*
  New York: Basic Books, 1994.
Wyman, David S. *The Abandonment of the Jews: America and the Holocaust, 1941–1945.*
  New York: Pantheon Books, 1984.
———. *Paper Walls: America and the Refugee Crisis, 1938–1941.* New York: Pantheon
  Books, 1985.
Yahil, Leni. *The Holocaust: The Fate of European Jewry, 1932–1945.* New York: Oxford
  University Press, 1990.
Zipes, Jack. *Breaking the Magic Spell: Radical Theories of Folk and Fairy Tales.* New York:
  Routledge, 1992.

SELECTED ARTICLES

Angres, Ronald. "Who, Really, Was Bruno Bettelheim?" *Commentary,* October 1990,
  pp. 26–30.
Bartrop, Paul R. "Bruno Bettelheim and the Extreme Situation: The Debate over
  Prisoner Behaviour in Nazi Concentration Camps (1943–76)." *Menorah: Australian
  Journal of Jewish Studies,* vol. 3, no. 2 (December 1989): 32–47.
Crews, Frederick. "The Freudian Way of Knowledge." *New Criterion,* June 1984, pp. 7–
  25.
Des Pres, Terrence. "The Bettelheim Problem." *Social Research,* Winter 1979, pp. 619–
  47.
Federn, Ernst. "The Terror as a System—The Concentration Camp: Buchenwald as It
  Was." *Psychiatric Quarterly Supplement,* vol. 22, pt. 2 (1948): 52–86.
Fisher, David James. "An Interview with Bruno Bettelheim." *Los Angeles Psychoanalytic
  Bulletin,* Fall 1990, pp. 3–23.
Luchterhand, Elmer. "Prisoner Behavior and Social System in the Nazi Concentration
  Camp." In *Mass Society in Crisis: Social Problems and Social Pathology,* eds. Bernard
  Rosenberg et al. 2d ed. New York: Macmillan, 1971. pp. 59–84.
Marcus, Paul, and Alan Rosenberg, eds. "Bruno Bettelheim's Contribution to Psycho-
  analysis." *Psychoanalytic Review,* special issue, vol. 81, no. 3 (Fall 1994).
Roazen, Paul. "The Rise and Fall of Bruno Bettelheim." *Psychohistory Review,* vol. 20,
  no. 3 (Spring 1992): 221–50.
Robinson, Jacob. "Psychoanalysis in a Vacuum: Bruno Bettelheim and the Holocaust."
  Yad Vashem–Yivo Documentary Projects, 1970, pp. 3–36.
Rosenman, Stanley. "The Psychoanalytic Writer on the Holocaust and Bettelheim."
  American Journal of Social Psychiatry, vol. 4 (Spring 1984): 62–71.
Zimmerman, D. Patrick. "The Clinical Thought of Bruno Bettelheim: A Critical His-
  torical Review." *Psychoanalysis and Contemporary Thought,* vol. 14, no. 4 (1991):
  685–721.

ACKNOWLEDGMENTS

Over the many months that I worked on this book, I was gratified again and again by the willingness of so many people to share their impressions of Bruno Bettelheim and his work, some of them sitting for several tape-recorded interviews. I have listed the names of these generous participants at the beginning of the endnotes, but that bare roster does not begin to reflect the debt I owe. In particular, this book could not have been written without the testimony of the former residents of the Sonia Shankman Orthogenic School, some of whom grappled with considerable anxiety before agreeing to be interviewed, and when they did talk often found it difficult to speak about a time when they had been struggling with painful emotional problems. For their information and insights I am enormously grateful, and apologize again for any unhappiness my intrusions may have caused. I also thank the school's many former staff members who described what it was like to work with the children and Bruno Bettelheim.

Almost without exception, the librarians and archivists I encountered on my searches responded as if they had been waiting all their professional lives for me to walk in and pester them about Bruno Bettelheim and related matters. I am particularly indebted to Richard Popp and his colleagues for guiding me through the Bruno Bettelheim Papers and other material in special collections at the University of Chicago's Regenstein Library. For helping me unearth the correspondence of Mary Ashby Cheek, I thank Joan Clark of the Howard Colman Library at Rockford College in Illinois. Nancy Shawcross in special collections at the Van Pelt–Dietrich Library of the University of Pennsylvania helped me with the papers of James T. Farrell, and William Massa, Jr., did likewise for the papers of Dwight Macdonald in the manuscript division of Sterling Library at Yale University. Others who labored diligently on my behalf include Dane Hartgrove and John Butler and their staffs at the National Archives in Washington, D.C., and at the National Record Center in Suitland, Maryland; Fred Bauman and his colleagues at the Library of Congress; Constance Menninger at the Menninger Clinic in Topeka, Kansas; Judith Madura at the Alumni Association of the University of Chicago; Frances Seeber at the Franklin D. Roosevelt Library in Hyde Park, New York; Pat Wise at the Center for Military History in Washington, D.C.; David Haigh at the Dwight D. Eisenhower Library in Abilene, Kansas; Friederike Zeitlhofer at the Austrian Cultural Institute in New York City; Aaron Kornblum, Robert Kesting, and Sarah Ogilvie at the United States Holocaust Memorial Museum in Washington, D.C.; the staffs of the Leo Baeck Institute and the Yivo Institute for Jewish Research in New York City; Bill Kelly at the Institute for Psychoanalysis in Chicago; Ruth Sullivan of the Autism Services Center in Huntington, West Virginia; Annette Muffs Botnick at the Jewish Theological Library in New York City; Katharine Branning at the Alliance Française in New York City; Lee Freehling at the Reiss-Davis Child Study Center in Los Angeles; George Makari at the history-of-psychiatry section of New York Hospital in New York City;

Patricia Bartkowski of the Walter Reuther Library at Wayne State University in Detroit; Heidi Heilemann and John Wilson at the Lane Medical Library at Stanford University; the archivists at the Ford Foundation, and the dedicated staff at that temple of knowledge, The New York Public Library. I especially thank Columbia University for granting an outsider library privileges, and salute Olha Della Cava and her colleagues at the Butler Library reference desk and at other libraries on campus for repeatedly and patiently pointing me in the right direction when I came searching for information, and for providing me with a quiet sanctuary only a few steps from my home.

In Vienna, Elke Mühlleitner furnished invaluable assistance in gathering and translating information about Bruno Bettelheim's forebears and his early years. Edith Blaschitz and Ellen Dennis also helped me in these searches. Archivists who aided me in that city include H. Weiss at the Israelitische Kultusgemeinde, Kurt Mühlberger at the University of Vienna, and Rudolf Jeřabek at the Österreich Staatsarchiv. I was also supported in Vienna by my friends Cynthia and Herbert Weininger. For providing key concentration-camp dates and records, I thank Harry Stein of Gedenkstätte Buchenwald, Barbara Distel of KZ-Gedenkstätte Dachau, and Judith Kleiman at Yad Vashem in Jerusalem. I was also supported in Israel by Jerry Barach and Zvi Lamm at Hebrew University, Ada Lekach at Ramat Yohanan, and my friends Jessie Meltsner and Brian Britt, whose interview with Nechama Levi-Edelman helped me focus my questions when I later talked with her about Bettelheim's visit to that kibbutz. In Amsterdam, David Barnouw, of the Dutch State Institute for War Documentation, and Jan Erik Dubbelman, at the Anne Frank House, helped clarify my thinking about Bettelheim's criticism of the Frank family.

Bruno Bettelheim almost always wrote in English after he arrived in the United States in 1939, but I was dependent on translators for important material by and about him in German from the years before that. I am particularly indebted to my good friend Werner Dickel for skillfully translating Bettelheim's concentration-camp letters, and to Wilhelm Werthern for doing the same for his University of Vienna dissertation. Others who came to my rescue, in French and Dutch as well as in German, were Christine Breede, George Fletcher, Peter Habicht, Maya Kastler, Deirdre Mahoney, Bill Spiegelberger, Jared Stark, and Claudia Swan.

Bettelheim purposely did not save many of his letters, but fortunately several of the recipients did. Some of these letters are in archives, and I have indicated where they repose in the endnotes. Others are in private hands. I thank Dean Rodeheaver for making available to me the lengthy correspondence his late wife, Nancy Datan, had with her former teacher, and Ljuba Frankenstein, who readily shared the exchanges Bettelheim had with her late husband, Carl Frankenstein, in the 1970s and 1980s. Among the others who generously let me see letters Bettelheim wrote to them are Rudolf Ekstein, Ernst Federn, Joyce Jack, Daniel Karlin, Fae Lohn Tyroler, and Linnea Brandwein Vacca.

Many others came to my assistance in innumerable ways. They include Sam Abt, Roger Alcaly, Aaron Antonovsky, Robert Ashenhurst, Benjamin Barber, Sharone Bergner, Kai Bird, Lynn Bloomberg, Judy Blume, Lila Brown, Michael Bush, Roane Carey, James Chace, Andrew Cohen, Henry Cohen, Mark Dessauce, Therese Dessauce, Gabrielle Edgcomb, Dennis Flynn, Robert Friedman, Sanford Gifford, Ramona Hartwig, Anthony Heilbut, Ernest Herman, Margo Jefferson, Julie Johnson, Margaret Keller, Felicia Kentridge, Sydney Kentridge, I. W. Klein, Jonathan Kleinbard, Marlisa Kopinski, Jan Kruger, Jürgen Kruger, Sharon Kruger, Charles Larmore, Daniel Leifer, Alan Levenstein, Katherine Lewis, Robert Lipgar, James Lombard, J. Anthony Lukas, Rita Mendelsohn, Gaby Mueller-Oelrichs, Stephen Nordlinger, Daniel Okrent, William Pattison, Burton Pike, Christopher Porterfield, Tina Press, Sergio and Penny Proserpi, Michael Remer, Lewis Rowland, Oliver Sacks, Melford Spiro, Richard Stillerman, Jean Strouse, Peter Swales, Baylis Thomas, Calvin Trillin, Freke Vuijst, Chris Welles, Laurens White, and Elizabeth Young-Bruehl. To those I have inadvertently overlooked, I apologize.

I never would have embarked on this book had my old friends Heli and Michael Meltsner not introduced me to Jennifer Josephy, who first encouraged me to explore writing about Bruno Bettelheim. Ted Solotaroff and Aaron Asher also gave this project a crucial push forward at the beginning. I thank Victor Navasky for keeping me on the staff of *The Nation* for so many months while I worked at an enterprise that left so little time for magazine writing and editing. To my friend and computer guru, George Cooper, many thanks for explaining the difference between bytes and bauds and patiently dealing with my barrage of Luddities. And for putting me up—and putting up with me—on my many visits to Hyde Park, I bow down to my good friends Irene and Marshall Patner, whose guest bedroom was as comfortable as their refrigerator was always well stocked.

Understanding the intimate relationships within a family may be the biographer's most difficult task. If I have succeeded at all in illuminating this private world, it is due largely to the cooperation of Eric and Naomi Bettelheim. In several interviews, they described what life in their home was like when they were growing up in Hyde Park and, in particular, what kind of parents Bruno and Trude Bettelheim were. I thank them both for lending their support to this book. I regret that their sister, Ruth Bettelheim, chose not to talk to me, but I respect her decision and hope that, despite the absence of what undoubtedly would have been a valuable contribution, I have managed to give a fair portrait of her family.

My agent, Peter Shepherd, supported this undertaking from the start, and I thank him for his friendship and wise counsel, even though he had the temerity to retire and go sailing in the middle of this project. Wendy Schmalz, his colleague at Harold Ober Associates, smoothly stepped to the helm and helped guide the book into safe harbor. Aaron Asher, George Cooper, Ken and Barbara Eisold, Leonard Groopman, Pauline Kael, Michael Meltsner, Clara and David Park, Eric Schopler and Baylis Thomas read all or portions of the manuscript and gave me helpful advice; Ed Davis read every page with an eye to the law, and I am grateful for his care. The manuscript was improved at Simon & Schuster under the watchful eyes of Elizabeth Stein, Isolde Sauer, and in particular Terry Zaroff-Evans, whose careful copy editing sharpened the writing on every page. For coordinating this team, for helping me better organize the manuscript, for displaying such patience when I missed deadlines, and, most of all, for believing in this book, I thank my editor, Alice Mayhew.

Three other remarkable women came with me on this journey.

Gina Weinmann sat for many hours helping me understand Bruno Bettelheim's Vienna years, and the relationship that grew out of those interviews in her welcoming garden apartment in San Francisco inspired me every step of the way. I feel lucky to have gained her friendship and will cherish it always, and not soon forget her cheerful dismissal of the *Symphonie Fantastique* as movie music.

The shining countenance and mind of my daughter, Amanda Pollak, has been a tonic since the day she was born, and watching her flower into womanhood as I struggled with these pages boosted my morale again and again. If she finds in this book a standard anywhere near the one she sets for herself as a documentary filmmaker, I will be satisfied.

Last and first, Diane Walsh. She is in every paragraph of this book—with her constant reassurance, her acute editorial eye, her gentle prodding, and, when the ultimate deadline loomed, her willingness to abandon her keyboard and the sublime notes of Schubert and Mozart for my keyboard and the mundane endnotes of scholarship. She organized this close work with the same dedication and discipline she employs to get a gnarly bar of Brahms into her wondrous hands. I kiss those hands, hug her again for her enveloping smile, her endless patience, and her sustaining love, and dedicate this book to her.

organized this close work with the same dedication and discipline she employs to get a gnarly bar of Brahms into her wondrous hands. I kiss those hands, hug her again for her enveloping smile, her endless patience, and her sustaining love, and dedicate this book to her.

INDEX

Gay, Peter, 271, 272–73, 277, 381, 392
Geist, Raymond, 84
geistige Entwicklung des Kindes, Die
(Bühler), 49–50
General Introduction to Psychoanalysis, A
(Freud), 38
Generation of Vipers (Wylie), 161
genocide, use of term, 382
German Jews:
Bettelheim's admiration of, 228, 309
Bettelheim's criticisms of, 80
Chicago community of, 103, 186
prewar emigration of, 63, 86
Germany, Nazi, 59, 61, 63, 98, 105
Austria invaded by, *see Anschluss*
psychology of, 120
rise of, 42
Germany, Weimar Republic of, 127
Gerolstein, S.S., 92–93, 116
Gerson, Menachem, 304
Gestapo, 53, 73, 84, 87, 90, 91, 123, 359,
363
see also SS concentration camp guards
ghetto thinking, 17, 229, 357, 358, 359,
361
GI Bill, 219
Gildermeester Emigration Aid Society,
86
Gill, Merton, 252
Gingrich, Newt, 302
Ginsburg, Benson E., 280, 360
Gluck, Sarah, 302
Goethe Institute, 399–400
Goethe Medal, 399
Goldbloom, Philip, 197, 204–5, 230,
231, 268
Goldsmith, Jerome, 322, 323
Goldstein, Frieda, 86, 87
Good Enough Parent, A (Bettelheim), 128,
403, 411
Good Morning America, 191
Goodrich, Frances, 367–68
Göring, Hermann, 68
Gottlieb, Robert, 334, 342, 343, 348,
390, 392, 399, 403
Granville, Arnold, 204, 325
Gray, Hanna, 354
Great Books project, 10, 102, 127
Greenfeld family, 274, 279
Greenwich, Conn., 59, 71, 83, 93
Grinker, Roy, 186
Grossman, Diana, 153
Grynszpan, Herschel, 80

Gutmann, David, 212, 215, 218–19
Gypsies, 63, 75

Habsburg Empire, 28, 101
Hackett, Albert, 367–68
"Hänsel and Gretel," 262–63, 345
Harper, Lou, 157
Harper, William Rainey, 127
Harper's, 358, 378, 383
Harrison, R. Wendell, 157
Harry (Orthogenic School resident), 137,
152, 161, 176, 178
Hartman, David, 191
Harvard Educational Review, 269
Harvard Law School, 104
Harvard Medical School, 160
Harvard University, 186, 231
Hatschek, Anni, 30, 32, 47
Hawthorne Cedar Knolls, 137, 189, 322
Haydon, Harold, 322
Hebrew, 295, 296
Hebrew University, 302, 328
Hedwig (maid), 34, 40, 47
Heilig, Bruno, 62, 65, 74, 79, 88–89, 116
Heimwehren (Home Defense Forces), 42
Helping Hands (Kollwitz), 244
Helstein, Nina, 187, 196–97
Henry, Jules, 254
Herczeg, Steve, 327
Heuscher, Julius, 343–46, 350, 351
Hidden World, The, 259–60, 276
hérédo, 26
Hilfsverein der Deutschen Juden, 86
Hilkevitch, Aaron, 201, 202
Hilberg, Raul, 360–61, 382
Hillel House, 227, 230, 294, 358, 360
Himmler, Heinrich, 75, 85
Histadrut, 291
"History as Projecting Meaning into the
Meaningless" (Lessing), 15
*History of Materialism and Critique of Its
Present Significance* (Lange), 15
Hitler, Adolf, 43, 55, 59, 63, 68, 89, 105,
127, 409
Anschluss and, 51, 52–53, 58
as self-declared chancellor, 42
in Vienna, 41–42, 52–53, 56
Hitler Youth, 138
see also Nazi youth, student antiwar
protesters compared with
Hoboken, N.J., 93
Hochschule für Welthandel, 29
Hofmann, Paul, 51